NATIONAL LAW ENFORCEMENT DIRECTORY

EASTERN USA

MARY GONZALES BRHEL
MARTIN C. BRHEL, JR.

A COPPER BIBLE BOOK

Dedication

This book is dedicated to the brave, steadfast men and women who keep America safe from domestic bad guys, just as our military does, with the foreign variety. Sadly, some make the final sacrifice. I have personally buried law enforcement brothers, who have paid the ultimate price, in the line of duty.

Some were murdered. Others lost their lives because motorists failed to put their brains in gear, before starting their vehicle's engine. Other still have schools named after them. Others have their names emblazoned on roadways. I'd rather each of them were anonymous, but still alive. However, such decisions are not left to the hands of mere mortals, like us, privileged to have such friendships.

Okay, where do I begin? My lovely wife, Mary, is co-author. She and I researched all the contact information in *NLED's* 860-some pages. I actually began writing this national directory in 2006. FYI, one project Mary temporarily shelved, in order to work on *NLED*, was her first cookbook.

Frankly, I don't like telephones. Probably the end result of being awakened, too many times in the middle of the night, by cops I was privileged to serve with, who were 10-8, but not necessarily Code 4. Any information I was unable to find, online, Mary obtained telephonically, literally speaking with countless people, to obtain E-mail and physical addresses, as well as names and titles of relevant people.

First and foremost, as noted hereinabove, our heartfelt thanks go to the courageous men and women who keep their communities safe from those who would otherwise harm innocent people. Without peace officers, *NLED* wouldn't exist. But, this isn't a perfect world. Ergo, we have *NLED*. Res ipsa loquitur.

It's uncommon to have your own name affixed, even posthumously, to a roadway or public building. If that happens because you sacrificed your own life to protect someone you don't even know, such recognition is pyrrhic, at best. I proudly served with several officers who met such fates. Let it suffice to say many tears, including my own, were shed at their respective gravesides. But, we will not dishonor their service, or their passing, by saying more here, other than may God bless each of them.

Hopefully all, whom my bride invited to hang with us, at our SoCal beach area abode, do not arrive the same weekend. If they do, the laws of physics will control. And, I may need to find a hotel. But, should that happen, each honored guest will be treated to mouth-watering, home-cooked meals, plenty of TLC, and a scenic tour of our own community by la reina de la casa.

Several friends I met years ago also deserve heartfelt kudos. Each is a retired cop. One time NYPD Officer Chuck Mackey provided me his old department's E-mail address. We weren't able to otherwise obtain it, without the equivalent of pulling teeth, even by PC Frank Reagan.

Retired Albemarle County, Virginia PD Dep. Chief/USMC *Gunny*, George Noteman provided needed contact info about his own former department. And, retired PA Attorney General Supervising Investigator Luther *Luke* Henry provided the following link, demystifying why his own state has so many townships and boroughs: www.lgc.state.pa.us/deskbook06/Basics01_Local_Government_Entities.pdf.

Retired Crystal Lakes, MO PD Chief Dennis Postel patiently put up with my daily grousing, as I laboriously plowed my way through this momentous labor of love. To each of you, thanks for honoring me, with your friendship, and for your contributions to this much needed tome.

I save Bill Kasal for last. Multi-talented man. *Magic man.* Way too humble for his many aptitudes. Simply incongruous. Among his many other achievements, Bill is the former Palm Springs PD Reserve Captain, proudly serving his community for 10 years. Fellow author, and blogger, Bill has done it all.

Radio DJ, host of his own TV show, *Desert Living & Entertainment*, creator of the striking covers for each and every **Copper Bible** book, formatter of everything into proper form, and my invaluable tutor. Without Bill, I would have no published books. He was even able to tame capacious *NLED*.

This is true, whether it's one of my Courtroom Survival tomes, a *Joshua Travers DA, Adventure Series* novel, a biography, or this directory. I'd be devoid of any manners, whatsoever, if I didn't salute Bill for his involvement. I can never thank Captain Kasal enough for his involvement in my writing life.

Sans, my **Copper Bible Book Company** Executive Editor, this book would lack its remarkable cover, proper formatting, not to mention Bill's predictable lessons on issues too numerous to mention herein. From the bottom of my heart, what can I say, other than *thank you, thank you, thank you*? The end.

Marty & Mary, aka M&M

NATIONAL LAW ENFORCEMENT DIRECTORY-Eastern USA

Table of Contents

ALABAMA

Autauga County

- Autauga County SO
- Sheriff James *Herbie* Johnson
  162 W. 4th St.
  Prattville, AL 36067
  (334) 365-3211
  acso@autaugasheriff.org
- Autaugaville PD
- Chief Kelvin Scott Bowers
  109 No. Taylor St.
  Autaugaville, AL 36003
  (334) 365-9335
  soubi1963@aol.com
- Prattville PD
- Chief Mark Thompson
  101 W. Main St.
  Prattville, AL 36067
  (334) 361-3671
  mark.thompson@prattvilleal.gov

Baldwin County

- Baldwin County SO
- Sheriff Huey *Hoss* Mack
  Courthouse Sq.
  Bay Minette, AL 36507
  (251) 937-0200
  hmack@baldwincounty.gov
- Bay Minette PD
- Chief Clarence Crook III
  300 No. Hoyle Ave.
  Bay Minette, AL 36507
  (251) 580-2559
  ccrook@ci.bay-minette.al.us
- Daphne PD
- Chief David Carpenter
  1502 US Hwy 98
  Daphne, AL 36526
  (251) 621-9100
  dcarpenter@daphne.org
- Fairhope PD
- Chief Joe Petties
  107 No. Section St.
  Fairhope, AL 36532
  (251) 928-2385
  Joe.Petties@cofairhope.com
- Foley PD
- Chief Brant Standridge
  200 E. Section Ave.
  Foley, AL 36535
  (251) 943-4431
  bstandridge@ci.foley.mn.us
- Gulf Shores PD
- Chief Edward J. Delmore
  220 Clubhouse Dr.
  Gulf Shores, AL 36542
  (251) 968-2431
  edelmore@gulfshoresal.gov
- Orange Beach PD
- Chief William *Billy* Wilkins
  PO Box 1039
  Orange Beach, AL 36561
  (251) 981-9777
  info@obpd.org
- Robertsdale PD
- Chief Brad Kendrick
  22647 Racine
  Robertsdale, AL 36567
  (251) 947-2222
  bradkendrick@robertsdale.org
- Spanish Fort PD
- Chief David Edgar
  7851 Spanish Fort Blvd
  Spanish Fort, AL 36577
  (251) 626-4884
  chiefedgar@cityofspanishfort.com

Barbour County

- Barbour County SO
- Sheriff LeRoy Upshaw
  113 Court Sq.
  Clayton, AL 36016
  (334) 775-3434
  info@barbourcountysheriff.com
- Clio PD
- Chief Richard Johnson
  3265 Louisville St.
  Clio, AL 36017
  (334) 397-4402
  chiefjohnsoncliopd@centurytel.net
- Eufaula PD
- Chief Kenneth Walker
  545 E. Barbour St.
  Eufaula, AL 36027
  (334) 687-1200
  eufaulapolice@zebra.net

Bibb County

- Bibb County SO
- Sheriff Keith Hannah
  121 Court Sq.
  Centreville, AL 35042
  (205) 926-4683
  khannahbibb700@yahoo.com
-

- Brent PD
- Chief Terry Nichols
  22 1st St.
  Brent, AL 35034
  (205) 926-4643
  brentpd@bellsouth.net
- Centreville PD
- Chief Michael R. Nichols
  486 Walnut St.
  Centreville, AL 35042
  (205) 926-5052
  centreville101@live.com
- West Blocton PD
- Chief Keith Whatley
  1139 Main St. PO Box 187
  West Blocton, AL 35184
  (205) 938-7842
  policedrugcop@aol.com

Blount County

- Blount County SO
- Sheriff Loyd Arlington
  225 Industrial Park Dr.
  Oneonta, AL 35121
  (205) 625-4127
  LArlington@blountsheriffal.com
- Blountsville PD
- Chief C. Ray Baxley
  10017 Lee St. W.
  Blountsville, AL 35031
  (205) 429-3479
  blountsvillepd@yahoo.com
- Oneonta PD
- Chief James Chapman
  111 Jack Fendley Dr.
  Oneonta, AL 35121
  (205) 625-4362
  jchapman@otelco.net

Bullock County

- Bullock County SO
- Sheriff Lynn Anderson
  217 No. Prairie St.
  Union Springs, AL 36089
  (334) 738-2670
  tips@bullochsheriff.com

Butler County

- Butler County SO
- Sheriff Harden
  700 Court Sq.
  Greenville, AL 36037
  (334) 382-6521
  sheriffharden@camelliacom.com
- Greenville PD
- Chief Lonzo Ingram
  PO Box 158
  Greenville, AL 36037
  (334) 382-7461
  chieflonzo@yahoo.com

Calhoun County

- Calhoun County SO
- Sheriff Larry Amerson
  400 W. 8th St.
  Anniston, AL 36201
  (256) 237-4731
  mwade@calcoso.org
- Anniston PD
- Chief Shane Denham
  1200 Gurnee Ave.
  Anniston, AL 36201
  (256) 238-1800
  apd@annistonal.gov
- Jacksonville PD
- Chief TL Thompson
  116 Ladiga St. SE
  Jacksonville, AL 36265
  (256) 435-6448
  jpdchief@cableone.net
- Oxford PD
- Chief Bill Partridge
  100 Choccolocco St.
  Oxford, AL 36203
  (256) 831-3121
  tmedinaopd@cableone.net
- Piedmont PD
- Chief Steven Tidwell
  116 W. Ladiga St.
  Piedmont, AL 36272
  (256) 447-9091
  steven.tidwell@piedmontcity.org
- Weaver PD
- Chief Wayne Bush
  500 Anniston St.
  Weaver, AL 36277
  (256) 820-0530
  police@weaver-alabama.org

Chambers County

- Chambers County SO
- Sheriff Sid Lockhart
  2 Lafayette St.
  Lafayette, AL 36862
  (334) 864-9862
  sheriff.lockhart@chamberscountyal.gov

- Lafayette PD
- Chief Kenneth Vines
  50 Alabama Ave. W.
  Lafayette, AL 36862
  (334) 864-2211
  kvines@cityoflafayetteal.com
- Lanett PD
- Chief Angie Spates
  401 No. Lanier Ave.
  Lanett, AL 36863
  (334) 644-2146
  aspates@cityoflanett.com

Cherokee County

- Cherokee County SO
- Sheriff Jeff Shaver
  100 Cedar Bluff Rd.
  Centre, AL 35960
  (256) 927-3629
  jshaver@cherokeecounty-al.gov
- Cedar Bluff PD
- Chief Steve Walden
  4920 Main St.
  Cedar Bluff, AL 35959
  (256) 779-6835
  chiefwalden@tds.net
- Centre PD
- Chief Kirk Blankenship
  100 Cedar Bluff Rd.
  Centre, AL 35960
  (256) 927-3661
  centreal@tds.net

Chilton County

- Chilton County SO
- Sheriff Kevin Davis
  500 2nd Ave. No.
  Clanton, AL 35045
  (205) 755-4698
  kevin.davis@chiltoncountyso.org
- Clanton PD
- Chief Brian Stilwell
  601 1st Ave.
  Clanton, AL 35045
  (205) 755-1194
  brian.stillwell@clantonpd.org
- Jemison PD
- Chief Shane Fulmer
  PO Box 609
  Jemison, AL 35085
  (205) 688-4491
  CityofJemison@gmail.com
- Thorsby PD
- Chief Rodney Barnett
  PO Box 608
  Thorsby, AL 35171
  (205) 646-3555
  thorsbypolicedept@centurytel.net

Choctaw County

- Choctaw County SO
- Sheriff Tom Abate
  117 So. Mulberry St.
  Butler, AL 36904
  (205) 459-2166
  Choctaw_so@tds.net
- Butler PD
- Chief Jimmy Huckeba
  114 Academy Ave. No.
  Butler, AL 36904
  (205) 459-3794
  jimmy.huckeba@alacop.gov
- Pennington PD
- Chief Kenneth Thomas
  PO Box 40
  Pennington, AL 36916
  (205) 654-2526
  tcherry@tds.net

Clarke County

- Grove Hill PD
- Chief Leo Frazier
  111 So. Church St.
  Grove Hill, AL 36451
  (251) 275-3153
  policechief@grovehilltownhall.com
- Jackson PD
- Chief Charles Burge
  350 Commerce St.
  Jackson, AL 36545
  (334) 246-4484
  chief@jacksonpd.com
- Thomasville PD
- Chief Mitchell Stuckey
  137 Adams Ave.
  Thomasville, AL 36784
  (334) 636-2174
  mstuckey@thomasvilleal.com

Clay County

- Clay County SO
- Sheriff Ray Latham
  41771 Hwy 77
  Ashland, AL 36251
  (256) 354-2176
  sheriff@clayso.net

- Ashland PD
- Chief Benny Davis
  2nd Ave. No.
  Ashland, AL 36251
  (256) 354-2122
  adprecords@centurytel.net

Cleburne County

- Cleburne County SO
- Sheriff Joe Jacks
  120 Vickery St.
  Heflin, AL 36264
  (256) 463-2277
  jjacks@cleburnecounty.us
- Heflin PD
- Chief AJ Benefield
  405 Ross St.
  Heflin, AL 36264
  (256) 463-2292
  cityhall@cityofheflin.org

Coffee County

- Coffee County SO
- Sheriff Dave Sutton
  4 County Complex
  New Brockton, AL 36351
  (334) 894-5535
  dsutton@coffeecountysheriff.net
- Elba PD
- Chief Freddie Hanchey
  200 Buford St.
  Elba, AL 36323
  (334) 897-2555
  elbapd@hotmail.com
- Enterprise PD
- Chief TD Jones
  501 So. Main St.
  Enterprise, AL 36330
  (334) 347-1211
  tdjones@entercomp.com
- Kinston PD
- Chief Russell Young
  856 Main St.
  Kinston, AL 36453
  (334) 565-3114
  kpd@oppcatv.com
- New Brockton PD
- Chief Dale Grimes
  202 So. John St.
  New Brockton, AL 36351
  (334) 894-5559
  nbpd@centurytel.net

Colbert County

- Colbert County SD
- Sheriff Ronnie May
  201 No. Main St.
  Tuscumbia, AL 35674
  (256) 383-0741
  wytwolf@hiway.net
- Cherokee PD
- Chief Thomas Marshall
  3752 Old Lee Hwy
  Cherokee, AL 35616
  (256) 359-4959
  t.marshall31.tm@gmail.com
- Leighton PD
- Chief Brandon Hood
  8900 Main St.
  Leighton, AL 35646
  (256) 446-0722
  bthood4@gmail.com
- Muscle Shoals PD
- Chief Robert Evans
  1000 Avalon Ave. PO Box 2624
  Muscle Shoals, AL 35662
  (256) 383-6746
  Jrevans@hiwaay.net
- Sheffield PD
- Chief Greg Ray
  600 No. Montgomery Ave.
  Sheffield, AL 35660
  (256) 383-1771
  gray@sheffieldpolice.org
- Tuscumbia PD
- Chief Tony Logan
  218 So. Dickson St.
  Tuscumbia, AL 35674
  (256) 383-3121
  Tuscumbiapd@usacops.com

Conecuh County

- Conecuh County SO
- Sheriff Edwin Booker
  Jackson St., Courthouse Sq.
  Evergreen, AL 36401
  (251) 578-1260
  ccsd7318@hotmail.com
- Evergreen PD
- Chief James Simpson
  210 E. Front St.
  Evergreen, AL 36401
  (251) 578-1111
  judychamblin@bellsouth.net

Coosa County

- Coosa County SO
- Sheriff Terry Wilson
  Coosa County Courthouse
  Rockford, AL 35136
  (256) 377-4922
  office@coosaso.com
- Goodwater PD
- Chief Gerald Wattstone
  Main St.
  Goodwater, AL 35072
  (256) 839-6321
  gpd@charter.net

Covington County

- Covington County SO
- Sheriff Dennis Meeks
  290 Hillcrest Dr.
  Andalusia, AL 36420
  (334) 428-2640
  dennismeeks@covingtonso.com
- Andalusia PD
- Chief Wilbur Williams
  102 Opp Ave.
  Andalusia, AL 36420
  (334) 222-1155
  wilbur.williams@andalusiapolice.com
- Florala PD
- Chief Sonny Bedsole
  1407 Wall St.
  Florala, AL 36442
  (334) 858-3244
  floralachief@fairpoint.net
- Opp PD
- Chief Mike McDonald
  Main St.
  Opp, AL 36467
  (334) 493-4511
  opp.pd@oppcatv.com

Crenshaw County

- Brantley PD
- Chief Titus Averett
  10 MLK
  Brantley, AL 36009
  (334) 527-3244
  bpolice@troycable.net
- Luverne PD
- Chief Paul Allen
  Forest Ave.
  Luverne, AL 36049
  (334) 335-3334
  lpd@fcbl.net

Cullman County

- Cullman County SO
- Sheriff Mike Rainey
  1910 Beech Ave. SE
  Cullman, AL 35055
  (256) 734-0342
  rcrawford@cullmansheriff.org
- Cullman PD
- Chief Kenny Culpepper
  204 2nd Ave. NE
  Cullman, AL 35055
  (256) 734-1434
  kculpepper@cullmanpd.com
- Hanceville PD
- Chief Bob Long
  203 Bangor Ave.
  Hanceville, AL 35077
  (256) 352-9811
  hanceville201@yahoo.com

Dale County

- Dale County SO
- Sheriff Wally Olson
  Court Sq. Reynolds St.
  Ozark, AL 36360
  (334) 774-2335
  wolson@daleso.com
- Daleville PD
- Chief Ronnie Williamson
  730 So. Daleville Ave.
  Daleville, AL 36322
  (334) 598-4442
  police@dalevilleal.com
- Napier Field PD
- Chief Rozeallan Allan Smith
  400 Headquarters St.
  Napier Field, AL 36303
  (334) 983-3548
  townofnapierfield@yahoo.com
- Ozark PD
- Chief Tony R. Spivey
  417 No. Union Ave.
  Ozark, AL 36361-1987
  (334) 445-6321
  chief@ozarkalabama.us

Dallas County

- Dallas County SO
- Sheriff Harris Huffman, Jr.
  105 Lauderdale St.
  Selma, AL 36702
  (334) 874-2530
  harris.huffman@dallascounty-al.org

- Selma PD
- Chief William T. Riley III
  1300 Alabama Ave.
  Selma, AL 36702
  (334) 874-2120
  wriley@selma-al.gov

DeKalb County

- DeKalb County SO
- Sheriff Jimmy Harris
  210 Grand Ave. So.
  Fort Payne, AL 35967
  (256) 845-8561
  jharris@dekalbcountysheriff.org
- Crossville PD
- Chief Chris West
  14521 Hwy 68
  Crossville, AL 35962
  (256) 528-7121
  cvilletownclerk@crossvillealabama.com
- Fort Payne PD
- Chief Randy Bynum
  200 Gault Ave. So., Ste. 1
  Fort Payne, A 35967
  (256) 845-1414
  112cidpolice@forpayne.org
- Rainsville PD
- Chief Charles Centers
  42 McCurdy Ave. So.
  Rainsville, AL 35986
  (256) 638-2157
  chiefcenters@farmerstel.com
- Sylvania PD
- Chief Brad Gregg
  AL Hwy 75
  Sylvania, AL 35988
  (256) 638-2604
  policechief@sylvaniaalabama.com

Elmore County

- Elmore County SO
- Sheriff Bill Franklin
  8955 US Hwy 231
  Wetumpka, AL 36092
  (334) 567-5546
  leilabrocknell@elmorre.com
- Millbrook PD
- Chief P.K. Johnson
  3841 Grandview Rd.
  Millbrook, AL 36054
  (334) 285-5603
  pkjohnson@cityofmillbrook-al.gov
- Tallassee PD
- Chief Jimmy Rodgers III
  214 Barnett Blvd
  Tallassee, AL 36078
  (334) 283-6586
  police@tallassee.al.us
- Wetumpka PD
- Chief Celia Dixon
  203 E. Charles Ave.
  Wetumpka, AL 36092
  (334) 567-8432
  wpd@elmore.rr.com

Escambia County

- Escambia County SO
- Sheriff Grover W. Smith
  316 Court St.
  Brewton, AL 36426
  (251) 867-0304
  gsmith@co.escambia.al.us
- Atmore PD
- Chief Jason Dean
  201 E. Louisville Ave.
  Atmore, AL 36504
  (251) 368-9141
  atmore_police@yahoo.com
- Brewton PD
- Chief Monte McGougin
  1010A Douglas Ave.
  Brewton, AL 36426
  (251) 867-3212
  valerie.boutwell@alacop.gov
- East Brewton PD
- Chief Forrest Ave
  Forrest Ave.
  East Brewton, AL 36427
  (251) 867-4864
  valerie.boutwell@alacop.gov
- Flomaton PD
- Chief Stony Daw
  22475 Hwy 31
  Flomaton, AL 36441
  (251) 296-5811
  sdaw@flomatonal.org

Etowah County

- Etowah County SO
- Sheriff Todd Entrekin
  827 Forrest Ave.
  Gadsden, AL 35901
  (256) 546-2825
  tentrekin@etowahcounty.org

- Altoona PD
- Chief Chris Snyder
  PO Box 100
  Altoona, AL 35952
  (205) 589-2311
  altoonaclerk@yahoo.com
- Gadsden PD
- Chief John Crane
  90 Broad St.
  Gadsden, AL 35901
  (256) 549-4500
  darnold@gadsdenpd.org
- Glencoe PD
- Chief Jonathon W. Horton
  201 W. Chastain Blvd
  Glencoe, AL 35905
  (256) 492-1424
  robertgriffith@cityofglencoe.net
- Rainbow City PD
- Chief Greg Carroll
  3700 Rainbow Dr.
  Rainbow City, AL 35906
  (256) 442-2511
  police@rbcalabama.com
- Southside PD
- Chief Chris Jones
  2255 Hwy 77
  Southside, AL 35901
  (256) 442-2255
  spdchief@cityofsouthside.com

Fayette County

- Fayette County SO
- Sheriff Rodney Ingle
  113 1st Ave. W.
  Fayette, AL 35555
  (205) 932-3205
  sheriffingle@fayetteso.com
- Berry PD
- Chief Gerald Dedaux
  30 School Ave.
  Berry, AL 35546
  (205) 689-4562
  townofberry@century.tel.net

Franklin County

- Phil Campbell PD
- Chief Merrell Potter
  PO Box 489
  Phil Campbell, AL 35581
  (205) 993-5313
  chiefpc@ymail.com
- Red Bay PD
- Chief Janna Jackson
  112 5th Ave. SE
  Red Bay, AL 35582
  (256) 356-4455
  redbaypd@bellsouth.com
- Russellville PD
- Chief Chris Hargett
  400 No. Jackson Ave.
  Russellville, AL 35653
  (256) 332-2230
  rpd400@charter.net

Geneva County

- Hartford PD
- Chief Ben Berry
  114 4th Ave.
  Hartford, AL 36344
  (334) 588-2222
  wec@wiregrass.coop
- Slocomb PD
- Chief Don White
  PO Box 1147
  Slocomb, AL 36375
  (334) 886-3333
  slocombcity@alaweb.com

Greene County

- Greene County SO
- Sheriff Jonathan Benison
  400 Morrow Ave.
  Eutaw, AL 35462
  (205) 372-3242
  gcsheriff@greenecoal.net
- Eutaw PD
- Chief Derrick Coleman
  116 Main St.
  Eutaw, AL 35462
  (205) 372-4334
  eutawpd@bellsouth.net

Hale County

- Hale County SO
- Sheriff Kenneth W. Ellis
  1001 Main St.
  Greensboro, AL 36744
  (334) 624-3081
  sheriffellis@mound.net

Henry County

- Henry County SO
- Sheriff William K. Maddox
  101 W. Court Sq., Ste. G
  Abbeville, AL 36310
  (334) 585-3131
  sheriff.maddox@henrycountyso.org

- Abbeville PD
- Chief Mike Jones
  101 E. Washington St.
  Abbeville, AL 36310
  (334) 585-2221
  mjones@cityofabbeville.org
- Headland PD
- Chief Mark D. Jones
  9 Park St.
  Headland, AL 36345
  (334) 693-2222
  chiefjoneshpd@comcast.net

Houston County

- Houston County SO
- Sheriff Andy Hughes
  144 No. Oates St.
  Dothan, AL 36302
  (334) 677-4882
  ahughes@houstoncosheriff.org
- Ashford PD
- Chief Jim Stanley
  519 No. Broadway PO Box 428
  Ashford, AL 36312
  (334) 899-5113
  ashfordpd@graceba.net
- Cottonwood PD
- Chief Jim Smith
  1414 Metcalf St. PO Box 447
  Cottonwood, AL 36320
  (334)691-2113
  cwoodpd@graceba.net
- Dothan PD
- Chief Gregory J. Benton
  210 No. Saint Andrews St.
  (334) 615-3000
  dpd@dothan.org

Jackson County

- Jackson County SO
- Sheriff Charles Philips
  102 E. Laurel St.
  Scottsboro, AL 35768
  (256) 574-2610
  chuckphilipsj1@yahoo.com
- Bridgeport PD
- Chief Joe Stovall
  State St.
  Bridgeport, AL 35740
  (256) 495-2140
  bpd@cityofbridgeportalabama.com
- Scottsboro PD
- Chief Ralph Dawe
  23123 John T. Reid Pkwy
  Scottsboro, AL 35768
  (256) 574-3333
  rdawespd@scottsboro.org

Jefferson County

- Jefferson County SO
- Sheriff Mike Hale
  2200 8th Ave. No.
  Birmingham, AL 35203
  (205) 325-5700
  sheriff@jeffcosheriff.org
- Adamsville PD
- Chief Robert Carter
  4911 Main St.
  Adamsville, AL 35005
  (205) 674-5671
  rcarter@cityofadamsville.org
- Bessemer PD
- Chief Nathaniel Rutledge, Jr.
  #23 No. 15th St.
  Bessemer, AL 35020
  (205) 425-2411
  policechief@bessemeral.org
- Birmingham PD
- Chief AC Roper
  710 20th St. No.
  Birmingham, AL 35203
  (205) 254-2000
  BPD@birminghamal.gov
- Gardendale PD
- Chief Mike Walker
  970 Main St.
  Gardendale, AL 35071
  (205) 631-8787
  police@gardendale.com
- Homewood PD
- Chief Jim Roberson
  1833 29th Ave. So.
  Homewood, AL 35209
  (205) 332-6235
  jim.roberson@homewoodal.org
- Hueytown PD
- Chief Chuck Hagler
  1318 Hueytown Rd.
  Hueytown, AL 35023
  (205) 491-3523
  policedepartment@hueytownal.org

- Irondale PD
- Chief Jerry McIntosh
  101 So. 20th St.
  Irondale, AL 35210
  (205) 956-5990
  thomas.johnson@alacop.gov
- Jefferson County Distr. 4
- Constable Gilbert F. Douglas III
  1868 Patton Chapel Rd.
  Birmingham, AL 35226
  (205) 222-7664
  KE4NRL@bellsouth.net
- Kimberly PD
- Chief James Belding
  9256 Stouts Rd.
  Kimberly, AL 35091
  (205) 647-5531
  swaidkimberlyclerk@hotmail.com
- Leeds PD
- Chief Byron Jackson
  1040 Park Dr.
  Leeds, AL 35094
  (205) 699-2581
  bjackson@leedsalabama.gov
- Mountain Brook PD
- Chief Ted Cook
  100 Tibbett St.
  Mountain Brook, AL 35213
  (205) 879-0486
  policedept@mtnbrook.org
- Trussville PD
- Chief Don C. Sivley
  PO Box 159
  Trussville, AL 35173
  (205) 655-2101
  dsivley@trussville.org
- Vestavia Hills PD
- Chief Dan Rary
  513 Montgomery Hwy
  Vestavia Hills, AL 35216
  (205) 823-1153
  admin.sgt.@ci.vestaviahills.al.us
- Warrior PD
- Chief Raymond Horn
  215 Main St.
  Warrior, AL 35180
  (205) 647-0521
  rhorn@cityofwarrior.com

Lamar County

- Lamar County SO
- Sheriff Terry Perkins
  330 1st St. NE
  Vernon, AL 35592
  (205) 695-7470
  daind82@yahoo.com
- Kennedy PD
- Chief Jake Fowler
  AL 96
  Kennedy, AL 35574
  (205) 695-7103
  kth1@frontiernet.net
- Millport PD
  Chief Charles White
  920 Black St.
  Millport, AL 35576
  (205) 662-4228
  chiefwhitempd@frontiernet.net
- Sulligent PD
- Chief Willis Stanford
  5795 Hwy 278
  Sulligent, AL 35586
  (205) 698-9111
  sullclerk@fayette.net
- Vernon PD
- Chief Ted Collins
  44425 Hwy 17
  Vernon, AL 35592
  (205) 695-7022
  cityofvernon@hotmail.com

Lauderdale County

- Lauderdale County SO
- Sheriff Ronnie Willis
  200 So. Court St.
  Florence, AL 35630
  (256) 760-5757
  cidchief@comcast.net
- Florence PD
- Chief Ron Tyler
  702 So. Seminary St.
  Florence, AL 35630
  (256) 760-6500
  chieftyler@florencepd.org
- Rogersville PD
- Chief Terry Holden
  36 Wheeler Dr.
  Rogersville, AL 35652
  (256) 247-0740
  rsingleton@florenceal.org

Lawrence County

- Lawrence County SO
- Sheriff Gene Mitchell
  242 Parker Rd.
  Moulton, AL 35650
  (256) 974-9291
  lawco.shelton@gmail.com
- North Courtland PD
- Chief Alex Taylor
  PO Box 93
  Courtland, AL 35618
  (256) 637-8452
  ncpd@bellsouth.net

Lee County

- Lee County SO
- Sheriff Jay Jones
  2311 Gateway Dr.
  Opelika, AL 36801
  (334) 749-5651
  lcso@leecountysheriff.org
- Auburn PD
- Chief Tommy Dawson
  161 No. Ross St.
  Auburn, AL 36830
  (334) 501-3100
  ccurentlen@auburnalabama.org
- Opelika PD
- Chief Ed Clark
  501 So. 10th St.
  Opelika, AL 36803
  (334) 705-5200
  eclark@ci.opelika.al.us

Limestone County

- Limestone County SO
- Sheriff Mike Blakely
  309 W. Green St.
  Athens, AL 35611
  (256) 232-0111
  rking@limestonesheriff.com
- Ardmore PD
- Chief David Whitt
  26704 Main St.
  Ardmore, AL 35739
  (256) 423-2146
  ardmorepolicedepartment@yahoo.com
- Athens PD
- Chief Floyd Johnson
  951 E. Hobbs St.
  Athens, AL 35611
  (256) 233-8700
  fjohnson@athensal.us

Lowndes County

- Lowndes County SO
- Sheriff: John Williams
  Washington St.
  Hayneville, AL 36040
  (334) 548-6151
  fscott7353@yahoo.com

Macon County

- Macon County SO
- Sheriff David Warren
  246 County Rd. 10
  Tuskegee, AL 36083
  (334) 727-2500
  mcsd4615@aol.com
- Tuskegee PD
- Chief Lester Patrick
  1106 Notasulga Hwy
  Tuskegee, AL 36083
  (334) 727-0200
  lcpatrick@charterinternet.com

Madison County

- Madison County SO
- Sheriff Blake Dorning
  100 Northside Sq.
  Huntsville, AL 35801
  (256) 532-3417
  sheriff@madisoncountyal.gov
- Huntsville PD
- Chief Lewis Morris
  815 Wheeler Ave.
  Huntsville, AL 35801
  (256) 427-7001
  lewis.morris@huntsvilleal.gov
- Madison PD
- Chief Larry Muncey
  100 Hughes Rd.
  Madison, AL 35758
  (256) 772-5689
  larry.muncey@madisonal.gov
- New Hope PD
- Chief Richard Foster
  5496 Main Dr.
  New Hope, AL 35760
  (256) 723-2616
  rhcityclerk@nehp.net
- Triana PD
- Chief Michael Walker
  640 6th St.
  Madison, AL 35756
  (256) 772-0152
  ttriana@bellsouth.net

Marengo County

- Marengo County SO
- Sheriff Richard E. *Ben* Bates
  101 Dunn St.
  Linden, AL 36748
  (334) 295-4208
  mcso@westal.net
- Demopolis PD
- Chief Tommie J. Reese
  301 E. Washington St.
  Demopolis, AL 36732
  (334) 289-3073
  tommie.reese@demopolisal.gov
- Linden PD
- Chief Jeff Laduron
  211 No. Main St.
  Linden, AL 36748
  (334) 295-8697
  linden36748@gmail.com
- Myrtlewood PD
- Chief William Vick
  210 No. Magnolia
  Myrtlewood, AL 36763
  (334) 295-4191
  myrtlewoodpd@bellsouth.net

Marion County

- Marion County SO
- Sheriff Kevin Williams
  280 Winchester
  Hamilton, AL 35570
  (205) 921-7433
  kwilliams@marionsoal.com
- Guin PD
- Chief G.B. Blaylock
  PO Box 249
  Guin, AL 35563
  (205) 468-3363
  guinpd@guinal.org
- Hamilton PD
- Chief Ronny Bickery
  427 James Crump Memorial Dr.
  Hamilton, AL 35570
  (205) 921-7424
  rbickery@hamiltoncityal.org
- Winfield PD
- Chief Scott Welch
  111 Bankhead Hwy
  Winfield, AL 35594
  (205) 487-4333
  constablec12@gmail.com

Marshall County

- Marshall County SO
- Sheriff Scott Walls
  423 Blount Ave.
  Guntersville, AL 35976
  (256) 582-2034
  soreceptionist@marshallco.org
- Albertville PD
- Chief Benny Womack
  201 So. Broad St.
  Albertville, AL 35950
  (256) 878-1212
  abercrombie407@charter.net
- Boaz PD
- Chief Terry Davis
  101 Line Ave.
  Boaz, AL 35957
  (256) 593-6812
  terry.davis@cityofboaz.org
- Guntersville PD
- Chief Jim Peterson
  341 Blount Ave.
  Guntersville, AL 35976
  (256) 571-7571
  jpeterson@guntersvillepd.org

Mobile County

- Mobile County SO
- Sheriff Sam Cochran
  510 So. Royal St. PO Box 113
  Mobile, AL 36601
  (251) 574-8633
  scochran@mobileso.com
- Chickasaw PD
- Chief Mike Reynolds
  8 Lange Dr.
  Chickasaw, AL 36611
  (251) 452-6470
  jerry.scarbourgh@chickasaw.net
- Citronelle PD
- Chief Shane Stringer
  19135 So. Mobile St.
  Citronelle, AL 36522
  (251) 866-5527
  Kendra.mason@alacop.gov
- Mobile County Office
- Constable Leo Bullock
  PO Box 6351
  Mobile, AL 36660
  (251) 479-8330
  leobullock22@gmail.com

- Mobile PD
- Chief Michael T. Williams
  2460 Government Blvd
  Mobile, AL 36606
  (251) 208-1701
  yokleyb@cityofmobile.org
- Mount Vernon PD
- Chief Steve Reed
  1565 Boyles Ave.
  Mount Vernon, AL 36560
  (251) 829-6631
  mtvernonpolicedepartment@yahoo.com
- Prichard PD
- Chief Jimmie Gardner
  216 E. Prichard Ave.
  Prichard, AL 36610
  (251) 452-2211
  j.gardner@thecityofprichard.org
- Saraland PD
- Chief JC West
  716 Hwy 43 So.
  Saraland, AL 36571
  (251) 675-5331
  jwest@saraland.org
- Satsuma PD
- Chief Mclean
  5668 2nd St.
  Satsuma, AL 36572
  (251) 675-0151
  spolice21@mchsi.com

Monroe County

- Monroe County SO
- Sheriff Thomas Tate
  Courthouse
  Monroeville, AL 36460
  (251) 575-2963
  maeholder04@gmail.com
- Excel PD
- Chief Paul Lindsey
  PO Box 225
  Excel, AL 36439
  (251) 765-2558
  townofexcel@conexuswireless.net
- Monroeville PD
- Chief Rudolph Munnerlyn
  57 So. Mt. Pleasant Ave.
  Monroeville, AL 36460
  (251) 575-3246
  Monropd1@frontiernet.net

Montgomery County

- Montgomery County SO
- Sheriff David DT Marshall
  115 So. Perry St.
  Montgomery, AL 36103
  (334) 832-4980
  DavidMarshall@mc-ala.org
- Montgomery County Prosecutor
- Ellen Brooks, District Attorney
  251 So. Lawrence St.
  Montgomery, AL 36104
  (334) 832-1632
  mcdaadmin@mc-ala.org
- Montgomery PD
- Chief Kevin J. Murphy
  320 No. Ripley St. PO Drawer 159
  Montgomery, AL 36101
  (334) 241-2810
  kmurphy@montgomeryal.gov

Morgan County

- Decatur PD
- Chief Ed Taylor
  PO Box 488
  Decatur, AL 35602
  (256) 353-2515
  edtaylor@decatur-al.gov
- Falkville PD
- Chief Chris Free
  PO Box 407
  Falkville, AL 35622
  (256) 784-5237
  chris@faulkville.org
- Priceville PD
- Chief Billy Peebles
  242 Marco Dr.
  Priceville, AL 35603
  (256) 355-5476
  PricevillePD@cji.net
- Trinity PD
- Chief Chris McLemore
  34 Preston Dr.
  Trinity, AL 35673
  (256) 353-2474
  townoftrinity@trinityal.gov

Perry County

- Perry County SO
- Sheriff James Hood
  202 Pickens St.
  Marion, AL 36756
  (334) 683-6534
  pcshood@yahoo.com

Pickens County

- Pickens County SO
- Sheriff David Abston
  188 Cemetery St.
  Carrollton, AL 35447
  (205) 367-2000
  pickensso@yahoo.com
- Gordo PD
- Chief Tire Hall
  Main St.
  Gordo, AL 35466
  (205) 364-7111
  tiredhall@yahoo.com
- Reform PD
- Chief Richard Black
  104 3rd Ave. SE PO Box 489
  Reform, AL 35481
  (205) 375-6363
  vickypetty2@yahoo.com

Pike County

- Pike County SO
- Sheriff Richard N. Henderson
  Church St. Courthouse
  Troy, AL 36081
  (334) 566-4347
  rhenderson@pikecosheriff.com
- Brundidge PD
- Chief Moses Davenport
  115 No. Main St.
  Brundidge, AL 36010
  (334) 735-3333
  citymanager@troycable.net
- Troy PD
- Chief James J. Ennis
  300 E. Elm St. PO Box 549
  Troy, AL 36081
  (334) 566-0500
  jennis@pd.troyal.gov

Randolph County

- Roanoke PD
- Chief Adam Melton
  138 So. Chesnut
  Roanoke, AL 36274
  (334) 863-2121
  amelton@roanokealabama.com
- Wadley PD
- Chief Chad Ogletree
  311 Main St.
  Wadley, AL 36276
  (256) 395-2261
  WadleyPD@communicomm.com

Russell County

- Russell County SO
- Sheriff Heath Taylor
  305 Prentiss Dr.
  Phenix City, AL 36868
  (334) 298-6535
  htaylor@rcso.org
- Phenix City PD
- Chief Raymond Smith
  1111 Broad St.
  Phenix City, AL 36867
  (334) 448-2800
  rsmith@phenixcityal.us

Saint Clair County

- Saint Clair County SO
- Sheriff Terry Surles
  6th Ave.
  Ashville, AL 35953
  (205) 594-2140
  sheriff@stclairco.com
- Moody PD
- Chief Thomas Hunt
  2900 Daniel Dr.
  Moody, AL 35004
  (205) 640-5121
  thunt@moodyalabama.gov
- Odenville PD
- Chief Adam Pardue
  183 Alabama St.
  Odenville, AL 35120
  (205) 629-3333
  melissagilbert.cityofodenville@yahoo.com
- Pell City PD
- Chief Gregory Dean Greg Turley
  1905 1st Ave. No.
  Pell City, AL 35125
  (205) 884-3334
  pellcitypolice@yahoo.com
- Ragland PD
- Chief James Brown
  146 Church
  Ragland, AL 35131
  (205) 472-2151
  chief@ragland.net
- Springville PD
- Chief Bill Lyle
  6327 US Hwy 11
  Springville, AL 35146
  (205) 467-6133
  springvillepd@windstream.net

Shelby County

- Shelby County SO
- Sheriff Chris Curry
  104 Depot St.
  Columbiana, AL 35051
  (205) 669-4181
  ccurry@shelbyso.com
- Calera PD
- Chief Sean Lemley
  10947 Hwy 25 PO Box 730
  Calera, AL 35040
  (205) 668-3505
  cpd201@aol.com
- Columbiana PD
- Chief Lamar Vick
  107 Mildred St.
  Columbiana, AL 35051
  (205) 669-5800
  lvick@columbianapolice.com
- Harpersville PD
- Chief David Latimer
  PO Box 370
  Harpersville, AL 35078
  (205) 672-2490
  mayor@townofharpersville.com
- Helena PD
- Chief Douglas W Jones
  816 Hwy 52 E. PO Box 262
  Helena, AL 35080
  (205) 663-6499
  helenapolice@aol.com
- Hoover PD
- Chief Nick Derzis
  100 Municipal Dr.
  Hoover, AL 35216
  (205) 444-7700
  carpentc@ci.hoover.al.us
- Pelham PD
- Chief Larry Palmer
  3162 Pelham Pkwy
  Pelham, AL 35124
  (205) 620-6550
  police@pelhamonline.com
- Vincent PD
- Chief James Srygley
  25 Florey St.
  Vincent, AL 35178
  (205) 672-2261
  townofvincent@aol.com
- Wilsonville PD
- Chief Nick Watt
  9905 No. Main St.
  Wilsonville, AL 35186
  (205) 669-6180
  nickwat@co.clackamas.or.us

Sumter County

- Sumter County SO
- Sheriff Tyrone Clark, Sr.
  118 Hospital Dr.
  Livingston, AL 35470
  (205) 652-7984
  sheriffclark@aol.com
- Livingston DPS
- Chief Ashley Welborn
  502 Lafayette St.
  Livingston, AL 35470
  (205) 652-9525
  awelborn@bellsouth.net

Talladega County

- Talladega County SO
- Sheriff Jerry Studdard
  400 No. Norton Ave.
  Talladega, AL 35160
  (256) 245-5121
  tcso@talladegacountyal.org
- Childersburg PD
- Chief Charles Chuck Brown
  118 6th Ave. SW
  Childersburg, AL 35044
  (256) 378-7593
  administration@childersburg.org
- Sylacauga PD
- Chief Kris M. Carden
  301 No. Broadway PO Box 2460
  Sylacauga, AL 35150
  (256) 401-2448
  kepperson@sylacaugaal.gov
- Talladega PD
- Chief Alan Watson
  PO Box 761
  Talladega, AL 35161
  (256) 362-4163
  talladegacouncil@yahoo.com

Tallapoosa County

- Tallapoosa County SO
- Sheriff Jimmy Abbett
  316 Industrial Park Dr.
  Dadeville, AL 36853
  (256) 825-4264
  sheriff@tallaco.com

- Alexander City PD
- Chief Charles Rafford
  1 Court Sq.
  Alexander City, AL 35011
  (256) 234-3421
  chief@alexandercityal.gov
- Dadeville PD
- Chief David E. Barbour
  192 So. Broadnax St.
  Dadeville, AL 36853
  (256)825-6212
  police@dadevillepd.org
- New Site PD
- Chief John McKelvey
  12791 Hwy 22 E.
  New Site, AL 36256
  (256) 234-2049
  townofnewsite1@charter.net

Tuscaloosa County

- Tuscaloosa County SO
- Sheriff Ted Sexton
  714½ Greensboro Ave.
  Tuscaloosa, AL 35401
  (205) 752-0616
  sheriff@tcsoal.org
- Lake View PD
- Chief Eddie Frederick
  21289 Phyllis Dr.
  Lakeview, AL 35111
  (205) 477-1289
  lvpdasstchief@bellsouth.net
- Northport PD
- Chief Kevin Vespia
  1910 Lurleen B. Wallace Blvd No.
  Northport, AL 35476
  (205) 339-6600
  KVespia@northportpd.com
- Tuscaloosa PD
- Chief Steven D. Anderson
  3801 Mill Creek Ave.
  Tuscaloosa, AL 35401
  (205) 349-2121
  tpd.adm@tuscaloosa.com

Walker County

- Walker County SO
- Sheriff John Mark Tirey
  2001 2nd Ave.
  Jasper, AL 35501
  (205) 302-6464
  jtirey@walkercosheriff.com
- Carbon Hill PD
- Chief Heath Allred
  170 NW 2nd Ave.
  Carbon Hill, AL 35549
  (205) 924-4411
  chiefpetiempd@hotmail.com
- Cordova PD
- Chief John Bentley
  74 Main St.
  Cordova, AL 35550
  (205) 483-7378
  cordovapdcr2@aol.com
- Dora PD
- Chief John Duchock
  1485 Sharon Blvd
  Dora, AL 35062
  (205) 648-3211
  dorapd401@aol.com
- Jasper PD
- Chief Connie Rowe
  1610 Alabama Ave.
  Jasper, AL 35501
  (205) 221-8109
  ccain@jasperpd.us
- Walker County, Beat 22
- Constable Hugh Plyar
  PO Box 245
  Parrish, AL 35580
  (205) 686-9725
  hjplylar@yahoo.com

Washington County

- Washington County SO
- Sheriff Richard Stringer
  PO Box 307
  Chatom, AL 36518
  (251) 847-2202
  stringer@millry.net
- Chatom PD
- Chief Brent L. Callihan
  101 Cochran Ave.
  Chatom, AL 36518
  (251) 847-2117
  chatom@millry.net

Wilcox County

- Wilcox County SO
- Sheriff Earnest Ivey Evans
  12 Water St.
  Camden, AL 36726
  (334) 682-9115
  Sheriffevans@frontier.com

Winston County

- Winston County SO
- Sheriff Rick Harris
  11 Blake Dr. PO Box 10
  Double Springs, AL 35553-0010
  (205) 489-8765
  sheriff@winstoncountysheriff.com
- Double Springs PD
- Chief Kim Miller
  Main St.
  Double Springs, AL 35553
  (205) 489-5115
  millerdspd@yahoo.com

State Agencies

- AL DPS Highway Patrol
- Dir. (*Col.*) Hugh B. McCall
  301 So. Ripley St.
  PO Box 1511
  Montgomery, AL 36102-1511
  (334) 242-4393
  debbie.taylor@dps.alabama.gov
- UAB PD
- Chief Anthony B. Purcell
  1117 14th St. So.
  Birmingham, AL 35205
  (205) 934-2297
  bpurcell@uab.edu
- Jacksonville State U. DPS
- Dir. Shawn Giddy
  700 Pelham Rd. No.
  Jacksonville, AL 36265
  (256) 782-5050
  upd@jsu.edu

CONNECTICUT

Fairfield County

- Bethel PD
- Chief Jeffrey Finch
  49 Plum Trees Rd.
  Bethel, CT 06801
  (203) 743-5500
  jfinch@bethelpd.com
- Bridgeport PD
- Chief Joseph L. Gaudett, Jr.
  300 Congress St.
  Bridgeport, CT 06604
  (203) 576-7611
  bptctpd@bridgeportct.gov
- Bridgeport Park PD
- Chief Joseph L. Gaudett, Jr.
  1 Barnum Dyke
  Bridgeport, CT 06604
  (203) 576-7233
  bptctpd@bridgeportct.gov
- Brookfield PD
- Chief Robin Montgomery
  63 Silvermine Rd.
  Brookfield, CT 06804
  (203) 740-4110
  rmontgomery@brookfieldct.gov
- Danbury PD
- Chief Alan D. Baker
  375 Main St.
  Danbury, CT 06810
  (203) 797-4603
  a.baker@danbury-ct.gov
- Darien PD
- Chief Duane J. Lovello
  25 Hecker Ave.
  Darien, CT 06820
  (203) 662-5300
  dlovello@darienct.gov
- Easton PD
- Chief James Candee
  700 Morehouse PO Box 7
  Easton, CT 06612
  (203) 268-4111
  main@eastonctpolice.com
- Greenwich PD
- Chief Jim Heavey
  11 Bruce Pl.
  Greenwich, CT 06830
  (203) 622-8002
  jheavey@greenwichct.org
- New Canaan PD
- Chief Edward Nadriczny
  174 So. Ave.
  New Canaan, CT 06840
  (203) 594-3500
  Edward.Nadriczny@newcanaanct.gov
- Newtown PD
- Chief Michael Kehoe
  3 Main St.
  Newtown, CT 06470
  (203) 270-4255
  michael.kehoe@newtown-ct.gov
- Norwalk PD
- Chief William R. Pennington
  297 West Ave.
  Norwalk, CT 06852
  (203) 854-3051
  policehqunit@norwalkct.org
- Ridgefield PD
- Chief John Roche
  76 E. Ridge Rd.
  Ridgefield, CT 06877
  (203) 438-6531
  police@ridgefieldct.org
- Shelton PD
- Chief Joel W. Hurliman
  85 Wheeler St.
  Shelton, CT 06484
  (203) 924-1544
  administration@sheltonpolice.net
- Stratford PD
- Chief Patrick Ridenhour
  900 Longbrook Ave.
  Stratford, CT 06614-5099
  (203) 385-4110
  webmaster@stratfordctpd.com
- Trumbull PD
- Chief Thomas H. Kiely
  158 Edison Rd.
  Trumbull, CT 06611
  (203) 261-3665
  police@trumbull-ct.gov
- Weston PD
- Chief John Troxell
  56 Norfield Rd.
  Weston, CT 06883
  (203) 222-2636
  jtroxell@westonpolice.com

- Westport PD
- Chief Dale E. Call
  50 Jesup Rd.
  Westport, CT 06880
  (203) 341-6000
  dcall@westportct.gov
- Wilton PD
- Chief Michael Lombardo
  240 Danbury Rd.
  Wilton, CT 06897
  (203) 834-6260
  michael.lombardo@wiltonct.org

Hartford County

- Avon PD
- Chief Michael Rinaldo
  60 W. Main St.
  Avon, CT 06001
  (860) 409-4200
  mrinaldo@town.avon.ct.us
- Berlin PD
- Chief Paul Fitzgerald
  240 Kensington Rd.
  Kensington, CT 06037
  (860) 828-7080
  policechief@town.berlin.ct.us
- Bloomfield PD
- Chief Paul B. Hammick
  785 Park Ave.
  Bloomfield, CT 06002
  (860) 242-6060
  p.hammick@bloomfieldpolice.org
- Bristol PD
- Chief Thomas Grimaldi
  131 No. Main St.
  Bristol, CT 06010
  (860) 584-3011
  tomgrimaldi@bristolct.gov
- Canton PD
- Chief Christopher G. Arciero
  45 River Rd.
  Collinsville, CT 06019
  (860) 693-0221
  carciero@cantonpd.org
- East Hartford PD
- Chief Mark J. Sirois
  31 School St.
  East Hartford, CT 06108
  (860) 528-4401
  msirois@easthartfordct.gov
- East Windsor PD
- Chief Edward J. DeMarco, Jr.
  25 School St.
  East Windsor, CT 06088
  (860) 292-8240
  demarcoe@eastwindsorpd.com
- Enfield PD
- Chief Carl Sferrazza
  293 Elm St.
  Enfield, CT 06082
  (860) 763-6400
  PoliceChief@enfield.org
- Farmington PD
- Chief Paul J. Melanson
  319 New Britain Ave.
  Unionville, CT 06085
  (860) 675-2400
  melansonp@farmington-ct.org
- Glastonbury PD
- Chief David A. Caron
  2108 Main St.
  Glastonbury, CT 06033
  (860) 633-8301
  david.caron@glastonbury-ct.gov
- Granby PD
- Chief Carl Rosensweig
  15 No. Granby Rd.
  Granby, CT 06035
  (860) 844-5335
  crosensweig@granby-ct.gov
- City of Hartford PD
- Chief James C. Rovella
  50 Jennings Rd.
  Hartford, CT 06120
  (860) 527-6300
  rovej001@hartford.gov
- New Britain PD
- Chief James Wardwell
  125 Columbus Blvd
  New Britain, CT 06051
  (860) 826-3000
  kperugini@newbritainct.gov
- Newington PD
- Chief Richard Mulhall
  131 Cedar St.
  Newington, CT 06111
  (860) 666-8445
  rmulhall@newingtonct.gov

- Plainville PD
- Chief Matthew Catania
  19 Neal Ct.
  Plainville, CT 06062
  (860) 747-1616
  catania@plainville-ct.gov
- Rocky Hill PD
- Chief Michael D. Custer
  699 Old Main St.
  Rocky Hill, CT 06067
  (860) 258-7640
  mcuster@rockyhillct.gov
- Simsbury PD
- Chief Peter N. Ingvertsen
  933 Hopmeadow St.
  Simsbury, CT 06070
  (860) 658-3101
  PIngvertsen@PD.Simsbury-ct.gov
- South Windsor PD
- Chief Matthew Reed
  151 Sand Hill Rd.
  South Windsor, CT 06074
  (860) 648-6214
  matthew.reed@southwindsor.org
- Southington PD
- Chief John. F. Daly
  69 Lazy Ln.
  Southington, CT 06489
  (860) 378-1600
  webmaster@southingtonpolice.org
- Suffield PD
- Chief Michael Manzi
  911 Mountain Rd.
  Suffield, CT 06078
  (860) 668-3870
  mmanzi@suffieldtownhall.com
- West Hartford PD
- Chief Tracey G. Gove
  103 Raymond Rd.
  West Hartford, CT 06107
  (860) 523-5203
  TGove@westhartford.org
- Wethersfield PD
- Chief James L. Cetran
  250 Silas Deane Hwy
  Wethersfield, CT 06109
  (860) 721-2900
  james.cetran@wethersfieldct.com
- Windsor PD
- Chief Kevin Searles
  340 Bloomfield Ave.
  Windsor, CT 06095
  (860) 688-5273
  police@townofwindsorct.com
- Windsor Locks PD
- Chief Eric Osanitsch
  4 Volunteer Dr.
  Windsor Locks, CT 06096
  (860) 627-1461
  eosanitsch@windsorlockspolice.com

Litchfield County

- New Milford PD
- Chief Shawn Boyne
  49 Poplar St.
  New Milford, CT 06776
  (860) 355-3133
  Sboyne@newmilfordpolice.org
- Watertown PD
- Chief John Gavallas
  195 French St.
  Watertown, CT 06795
  (860) 945-5200
  JGavallas@watertownctpd.org
- Winchester PD
- Chief Robert M. Scannell
  338 Main St.
  Winsted, CT 06098
  (860) 379-2721
  Wnchstr.pd@snet.net

Middlesex County

- Clinton PD
- Chief Todd Lawrie
  170 E. Main St.
  Clinton, CT 06413
  (860) 669-0451
  tlawrie@clintonct.org
- Cromwell PD
- Chief Anthony J. Salvatore
  5 West St.
  Cromwell, CT 06416
  (860) 635-2256
  chief.salvatore@cromwellpd.com
- East Hampton PD
- Chief Matthew Reimondo
  20 E. High St.
  East Hampton, CT 06424
  (860) 267-9922
  policechief@easthamptonct.org

- Middletown PD
- Chief William McKenna
  222 Main St.
  Middletown, CT 06457
  (860) 344-3201
  wmckenna@middletownctpolice.com
- Old Saybrook PD
- Chief Michael A. Spera
  225 Main St.
  Old Saybrook, CT 06475
  (860) 395-3140
  mspera@oldsaybrookpolice.com

New Haven County

- Ansonia PD
- Chief Kevin Hale
  2 Elm St.
  Ansonia, CT 06401
  (203) 735-1885
  jlester@ansoniact.org
- Branford PD
- Chief Kevin Halloran
  33 Laurel St.
  Branford, CT 06405
  (203) 481-4241
  branfordpolice@branfordpolice.com
- Cheshire PD
- Chief Neil Dryfe
  500 Highland Ave.
  Cheshire, CT 06410
  (203) 271-5500
  ndryfe@cheshirect.org
  Derby PD
  Chief Gerald D. Narowski
  125 Water St.
  Derby, CT 06418
  (203) 735-7811
  gerald.narowski@derbypd.org
- East Haven PD
- Chief Brent Larrabee
  471 No. High St.
  East Haven, CT 06512
  (203) 468-3820
  blarrabee@easthavenpolice.com
- Guilford PD
- Chief Thomas A. Terribile
  400 Church St.
  Guilford, CT 06437
  (203) 453-8061
  guilfordpolice@snet.net
- Hamden PD
- Chief Thomas J. Wydra
  2900 Dixwell Ave.
  Hamden, CT 06518
  (203) 230-4000
  wydra@hamden.com
- Madison Police Services
- Chief Jack Drumm
  # 9 Campus Dr.
  Madison, CT 06443
  (203) 245-2721
  infopd@madisonct.org
- Meriden PD
- Chief Jeffry W. Cossette
  50 W. Main St.
  Meriden, CT 06450
  (203) 238-1911
  jcossette@meridenct.gov
- Milford PD
- Chief Keith L. Mello
  430 Boston Post Rd.
  Milford, CT 06460
  (203) 878-6551
  police@ci.milford.ct.us
- Naugatuck PD
- Chief Christopher J. Edson
  211 Spring St
  Naugatuck, CT 06770
  (203) 729-5221
  bcammarata@naugatuckpd.org
- New Haven DPS
- Chief Dean M. Esserman
  1 Union Ave
  New Haven, CT 06519
  (203) 946-6333
  desserman@newhavenct.net
- North Branford PD
- Chief Matthew Canelli
  909 Foxon Rd.
  North Branford, CT 06471
  (203) 484-2703
  canelli@nbpolicect.org
- North Haven PD
- Chief Thomas J. McLoughlin
  18 Church St.
  North Haven, CT 06473
  (203) 239-5321
  policechief@town.north-haven.ct.us

- Orange PD
- Chief Robert Gagne
  314 Lambert Rd.
  Orange, CT 06477
  (203) 891-2136
  rgagne@orange-ct.gov
- Seymour PD
- Chief Michael Metzler
  11 Franklin St.
  Seymour, CT 06483
  (203) 888-3828
  metzler@seymourpolice.org
- Southbury PD
- Supt. (*Res. Trooper*) Michael O'Donnell
  421 Main St. So.
  Southbury, CT 06488
  (203) 264-5912
  southburycrimealert@gmail.com
- Wallingford PD
- Chief Douglas Dortenzio
  135 No. Main St.
  Wallingford, CT 06492
  (203) 294-2865
  bdighello@wallingfordpd.org
- Waterbury PD
- Chief Vernon Riddick
  255 E. Main St.
  Waterbury, CT 06702
  (203) 574-6907
  tkluntz@waterburypd.org
- Woodbridge PD
- Chief Eugene *Gene* Marcucci
  4 Meetinghouse Ln.
  Woodbridge, CT 06525
  (203) 387-2511
  emarcucci@woodbridgepd.com

<u>New London County</u>

- East Lyme PD
- Act. Chief (*Sgt.*) Wilfred Blanchette
  278 Main St.
  Niantic, CT 06357
  (860) 739-5900
  wblanchette@eastlymepolice.com
- City of Groton PD
- Chief Thomas Davoren
  295 Meridian St.
  Groton, CT 06340
  (860) 445-2451
  police@cityofgroton.com
- Groton PD
- Chief Michael J. Crowley
  68 Groton Long Point Rd.
  Groton, CT 06340
  (860) 445-9721
  info@groton-ct.gov
- Groton Long Point PD
- Chief Jack Drumm
  3 Atlantic Ave.
  Groton Long Point, CT 06340
  (860) 536-4921
  info@glppd.us
- Montville PD
- Act. Chief (*Lt.*) Leonard G. Bunnell, Sr.
  89 Fort Shantok Rd.
  Uncasville, CT 06382
  (860) 848-7510
  lbunnell@montvillepolice.org
- New London PD
- Chief Margaret Ackley
  5 Governor Winthrop Blvd
  New London, CT 06320
  (860) 447-5269
  mackley@ci.new-london.ct.us
- Norwich PD
- Chief Louis J. Fusaro, Sr.
  70 Thames St.
  Norwich, CT 06360
  (860) 886-5561
  lfusaro@cityofnorwich.org
- Stonington PD
- Chief J. Darren Stewart
  166 So. Broad St.
  Pawcatuck, CT 06379
  (860) 599-4411
  jstewart@stonington-ct.gov
- Waterford PD
- Chief Murray J. Pendleton
  41 Avery Ln.
  Waterford, CT 06385
  (860) 442-9451
  mpendleton@waterfordct.org

<u>Tolland County</u>

- Coventry PD
- Chief Mark Palmer
  1712 Main St.
  Coventry, CT 06238
  (860) 742-7331
  mpalmer@coventryct.org

- Vernon PD
- Chief James Kenny
  725 Hartford Turnpike
  Vernon, CT 06066
  (860) 872-9126
  jkenny@vernon-ct.gov

Windham County

- Plainfield PD
- Chief Michael G. Surprenant
  210 Norwich Rd.
  Plainfield, CT 06374
  (203) 564-0804
  M.Surprenant@plainfieldctpolice.com
- Putnam PD
- Chief Rick Hayes
  189 Church St.
  Putnam, CT 06260
  (860) 928-6565
  rick.hayes@putnampolice.com
- Willimantic PD
- Chief Lisa Maruzo-Bolduc
  22 Meadow St. PO Box 5
  Willimantic, CT 06226
  (860) 465-3135
  wmtc@pol.snet.net

State Agencies

- CT Div. of State
- Police Comm. (*Col.*) Danny R. Stebbins
  1111 Country Club Rd.
  Middletown, CT 06457
  (860) 685-8000
  danny.stebbins@ct.gov
- CT State Marshal
- Marshal Ralph J. Serafino, Jr.
  PO Box 373
  Stamford, CT 06904
  (203) 323-6127
  info@ct-state-marshal.com
- Western CT State U. PD
- Chief CG McLaughlin, Jr.
  181 White St.
  Danbury, Ct 06810
  (203) 837-9300
  mclaughlinn@wcsu.edu

DELAWARE

Kent County

- Clayton PD
- Chief Brian C. Hill
  314 W. Main St.
  Clayton, DE 19938
  (302) 653-8186
  Brian.Hill@cj.state.de.us
- Dover PD
- Chief James Hosfelt
  400 So. Queen St.
  Dover, DE 19901
  (302) 736-7100
  james.hosfelt@cj.state.de.us
- Felton PD
- Chief Levi D. Brown
  PO Box 329
  Felton, DE 19943
  (302) 284-8441
  levi.brown@CJ.state.de.us
- Harrington PD
- Chief Norman R. Barlow
  10 Mechanic St.
  Harrington, DE 19952
  (302) 398-4493
  norman.barlow@CJ.State.de.us
- Milford PD
- Chief E. Keith Hudson
  400 NE Front St.
  Milford, DE 19963
  (302) 422-8081
  keith.hudson@cj.state.de.us
- Smyrna PD
- Chief Wilbert Bordley
  325 W. Glenwood Ave.
  Smyrna, DE 19977
  (302) 653-9217
  wbordley@smyrna.delaware.gov
- Wyoming PD
- Chief Martin Willey
  1 No. Railroad Ave.
  Wyoming, DE 19934
  (302) 697-7960
  martin.willey@cj.state.de.us

New Castle County

- Delaware City PD
- Chief Al Kaczorowski
  407 Clinton St.
  Delaware City, DE 19706
  (302) 834-4573
  townhall@ci.delaware-city.de.us
- New Castle PD
- Lt. Adam Brams
  1 Municipal Blvd
  New Castle, DE 19720
  (302) 322-9800
  adam.brams@cj.state.de.us
- New Castle County PD
- Chief Elmer Setting
  87 Reads Way
  New Castle, DE 19720
  (302) 395-8010
  esetting@nccde.org
- Newark PD
- Chief Paul M. Tieman
  220 So. Main St.
  Newark, DE 19711
  (302) 366-7104
  paul.tiernan@cj.state.de.us
- Newport PD
- Chief Michael J. Capriglione
  226 No. James St.
  Newport, DE 19804
  (302) 995-1411
  michael.capriglione@cj.state.de.us
- Wilmington PD
- Chief Christine R. Dunning
  300 No. Walnut St.
  Wilmington, DE 19801
  (302) 576-3940
  lisa.hemphill@cj.state.de.us

Sussex County

- Sussex County SO
- Sheriff Jeffrey Christopher
  22215 So. Dupont PO Box 69
  Georgetown, DE 19947
  (302)855-7830
  jchristopher@sussexcountyde.gov
- Bethany Beach PD
- Chief Mike Redmon
  214 Garfield Pkwy
  Bethany Beach, DE 19930
  (302) 539-8102
  admin@townofbethanybeach.com
- Blades PD
- Chief Edwin Cooke
  20 W. 4th St.
  Blades, DE 19973
  (302) 629-7329
  edwin.cooke@cj.state.de.us

- Bridgeville PD
- Chief Robert Longo
  302 Market St.
  Bridgeville, DE 19933
  (302) 337-8302
  robin.dohn@cj.state.de.us
- Dagsboro PD
- Chief Floyd Toomey, Jr.
  33134 Main St. PO Box 420
  Dagsboro, DE 19939
  (302) 732-3777
  townclerk@townofdagsboro.com
- Delmar PD
- Chief Harold Sayer
  PO Box 11
  Delmar, DE 19940
  (302) 846-2320
  chief@delmarpolice.com
- Dewey Beach PD
- Chief Sam Mackert
  105 Rodney Ave.
  Dewey Beach, DE 19971
  Ph: (302) 227-1110
  Fax (302) 227-6580
  deweybeachpd@hotmail.com
- Fenwick Island PD
- Chief William H. Boyden
  800 Coastal Hwy
  Fenwick Island, DE 19944
  (302) 539-2000
  policeclerk@fenwickisland.org
- Georgetown PD
- Chief William Topping
  335 No. Race St.
  Georgetown, DE 19947
  (302) 856-6613
  William.topping@cj.state.de.us
- Laurel PD
- Chief Michael J. Wilson
  PO Box 622
  Laurel, DE 19956
  (302) 875-2244
  michael.wilson@cj.state.de.us
- Lewes PD
- Chief Jeffrey Horvath
  PO Box 227
  Lewes, DE 19958
  (302) 645-6264
  jeffrey.horvath@cj.state.de.us
- Milton PD
- Chief William E. Phillips
  101 Federal St.
  Milton, DE 19968
  (302) 684-8547
  William.philips@cj.state.de.us
- Ocean View PD
- Chief Kenneth McLaughlin
  6 Oakwood Ave.
  Ocean View, DE 19970
  (302) 539-1111
  Kenneth.mclaughlin@cj.state.de.us
- Rehoboth Beach PD
- Chief Keith W. Banks
  229 Rehoboth Ave.
  Rehoboth Beach, DE 19971
  (302) 227-2577
  keith.banks@cj.state.de.us
- Seaford PD
- Chief Gary Morris
  300 Virginia Ave
  Seaford, DE 19973
  (302) 629-6644
  info@seafordde.com
- Selbyville PD
- Chief W. Scott Collins
  68 W. Church St. PO Box 106
  Selbyville, DE 19975
  (302) 436-5085
  ward.collins@cj.state.de.us
- South Bethany PD
- Act. Chief (*Pfc*) Patrick Wiley
  402 Evergreen Rd.
  South Bethany, DE 19930
  (302) 539-3996, ext. 225
  Patrick.wiley@cj.state.de.us
- Woodland PD
- Chief Dan Bellini
  Woodland Rd.
  Seaford, DE 19973
  (302) 542-7168
  webmaster@cityofwoodland.org

State Agencies

- Delaware State Police
- Col. Nathaniel McQueen, Jr.
  1441 No. Dupont Hwy PO Box 403
  Dover, DE 19903-0430
  (302) 739-5900
  nathaniel.mcqueen@state.de.us

DISTRICT OF COLUMBIA

- Metro. PD
- Chief Cathy L. Lanier
  300 Indiana Ave. NW, Rm. 5059
  Washington, DC 20001
  (202) 727-4383
  mpd@dc.gov

Note: Other Washington, DC law enforcement agencies are not included herein, as *NLED* is limited to municipal, county, and state agencies.

FLORIDA

Alachua County

- Alachua County SO
- Sheriff Sadie Darnell
  PO Box 1210
  Gainesville, FL 32602
  (352) 367-4019
  sheriffdarnell@alachuasheriff.org
- Alachua PD
- Chief Joel Recourse, Jr.
  15000 NW 142 Terrace
  Alachua, FL 32615
  (386) 462-1396
  jdecoursey@cityofalachua.org
- Gainesville PD
- Chief Tony Jones
  721 NW 6th St.
  Gainesville, FL 32601
  (352) 334-2400
  gpdwebmaster@gainesvillepd.org
- High Springs PD
- Chief James *Steve* Holley
  110 NW 2nd Ave. PO Box 1008
  High Springs, FL 32643
  (386) 454-1415
  jsholley@highspringspd.com

Baker County

- Baker County SO
- Sheriff Joey B. Dobson
  1 Sheriff's Office Dr.
  MacClenny, FL 32063
  (904) 259-2231
  jdobson@bakerso.com

Bay County

- Bay County SO
- Sheriff Frank McKeithen
  3421 No. Hwy 77
  Panama City, FL 32405
  (850) 747-4700
  fmckeithen@bayso.org
- Cedar Grove PD
- Chief Richard Vanderstreet
  2728 E. 14th St.
  Cedar Grove, FL 32401
  (850) 763-1578
  chief@cedargrovepd.org
- Lynn Haven PD
- Chief David Messer
  1412 Pennsylvania Ave.
  Lynn Haven, FL 32444
  (850) 265-1112
  policedept@cityoflynnhaven.com
- Panama City PD
- Chief Scott Ervin
  1209 E. 15th St.
  Panama City, FL 32405
  (850) 872-3102
  servin@pcgov.org
- Panama City Beach PD
- Chief Drew R. Whitman
  17110 Firenzo St.
  Panama City Beach, FL 32413
  (850) 233-5000
  admin@beachpolice.org
- Springfield PD
- Chief Phillip Thorne
  3529 E. 3rd St.
  Springfield, FL 32401
  (850) 872-7545
  pthorne@springfield.fl.gov

Bradford County

- Bradford County SO
- Sheriff Gordon Smith
  945-B No. Temple PO Box 400
  Starke, FL 32091
  (904) 966-6380
  info@bradfordsheriff.org
- Starke PD
- Chief Jeff Johnson
  830 Edwards Rd.
  Starke, FL 32091
  (904) 964-5400
  starkepd@yahoo.com

Brevard County

- Brevard County SO
- Sheriff Wayne Ivey
  700 So. Park Ave., Bldg. J
  Titusville, FL 32780
  (321) 264-5201
  admin@bcso.us
- Cocoa PD
- Chief Mark Klayman
  1226 W. King St.
  Cocoa, FL 32922
  (321) 639-7620
  chief@cocoapolice.com
- Cocoa Beach PD
- Chief Arthur *Bud* Ayres
  20 So. Orlando Ave.
  Cocoa Beach, FL 32931
  (321) 868-3203
  police@cityofcocoabeach.com

- Indialantic PD
- Chief Troy W. Morris
  220 5th Ave.
  Indialantic, FL 32903
  (321) 723-7788
  tmorris@indialantic.com
- Indian Harbour Beach PD
- Chief Robert Sullivan
  40 Cheyenne Ct.
  Indian Harbour Beach, FL 32937
  (321) 773-3030
  bsullivan@indianharbour.org
- Melbourne PD
- Chief Steve Mimbs
  650 No. Apollo Blvd
  Melbourne, FL 32935
  (321) 409-2200
  Smimbs@melbourneflorida.org
- Melbourne Beach PD
- Chief Dan Duncan
  507 Ocean Ave.
  Melbourne Beach, FL 32951
  (321) 723-4343
  dand@melbournebeachfl.org
- Melbourne Village PD
- Chief Jack King
  555 Hammock Rd.
  Melbourne Village, FL 32904
  (321) 725-7224
  mvpdcontact@gmail.com
- Palm Bay PD
- Chief Doug Muldoon
  130 Malabar Rd. SE
  Palm Bay, FL 32907
  (321) 952-3456
  muldoond@palmbayflorida.org
- Rockledge PD
- Chief Lionel A. Cole
  123 Barton Blvd
  Rockledge, FL 32955
  (321) 690-3988
  lcote@cityofrockledge.org
- Satellite Beach PD
- Chief Jeff M. Pearson
  510 Cinnamon Dr.
  Satellite Beach, FL 32937
  (321) 773-4400
  jpearson@satellitebeach.org
- Titusville PD
- Chief John Lau
  1100 John Glenn Blvd
  Titusville, FL 32780
  (321) 264-7800
  john.lau@titusville.com
- West Melbourne PD
- Chief Richard T. Wiley
  2290 Minton Rd.
  West Melbourne, FL 32904
  (321) 723-9673
  rwiley@westmelbourne.org

Broward County

- Broward County SO
- Sheriff Scott J. Israel
  2601 W. Broward Blvd
  Fort Lauderdale, FL 33312
  (954) 831-8901
  ask_the_sheriff@sheriff.org
- Coconut Creek PD
- Sheriff Michael J. Mann
  4800 W. Copans Rd.
  Coconut Creek, FL 33063
  (954) 973-6700
  mmann@coconutcreek.net
- Coral Springs PD
- Chief Tony Pustizzi
  2801 Coral Springs Dr.
  Coral Springs, FL 33065
  (954) 346-1200
  APustizzi@coralsprings.org
- Fort Lauderdale PD
- Chief Franklin Adderley
  1300 W. Broward Blvd
  Fort Lauderdale, FL 33312
  (954) 828-5700
  internalaffairs@fortlauderdale.gov
- Hallandale Beach PD
- Chief Dwayne S. Flournoy
  400 So. Federal Hwy
  Hallandale Beach, FL 33009
  (954) 457-1400
  police_office@hallandalebeachfl.gov
- Hollywood PD
- Chief Vincent Affanato
  3250 Hollywood Blvd
  Hollywood, FL 33021
  (954) 967-4300
  vaffanato@hollywoodfl.org

- Lauderhill PD
- Chief Andrew Smalling
  6279 W. Oakland Park Blvd
  Lauderhill, FL 33313
  (954) 497-4700
  asmalling@lauderhill-fl.gov
- Lighthouse Point PD
- Chief Ross Licata
  3760 NE 22nd Ave.
  Lighthouse Point, FL 33064
  (954) 942-8080
  rlicata@lighthousepoint.com
- Margate PD
- Chief Dana E. Watson
  5790 Margate Blvd
  Margate, FL 33063
  (954) 972-7111
  mpd@margatefl.com
- Miramar PD
- Chief Keith F. Dunn
  3064 No. Commerce Pkwy
  Miramar, FL 33025
  (954) 602-4400
  kdunn@ci.miramar.fl.us
- Parkland PD
- Act. Chief (*Capt.*) Marvin Stoner
  6500 Parkside Dr.
  Parkland, FL 33067
  (954) 753-5050
  marvin_stoner@sheriff.org
- Pembroke Pines PD
- Chief Dan Giustino
  9500 Pines Blvd
  Pembroke Pines, FL 33024
  (954) 431-2200
  dgiustino@ppines.com
- Plantation PD
- Chief W. Howard Harrison
  451 NW 70th
  Plantation, FL 33317
  (954) 797-2139
  hharrison@psd.plantation.org
- Sunrise PD
- Chief John E. Brooks
  10440 W. Oakland Park Blvd
  Sunrise, FL 33351
  (954) 746-3600
  Police@sunrisefl.gov
- Wilton Manors PD
- Chief Paul O'Connell
  524 NE 21st Ct.
  Wilton Manors, FL 33305
  (954) 390-2162
  poconnell@wmpd.org

Calhoun County

- Calhoun County SO
- Sheriff Glenn H. Kimbrel
  20776 Central Ave. E.
  Blountstown, FL 32424
  (850) 674-5049
  gkimbrel@calhounsheriff.com
- Blountstown PD
- Chief Rodney W. Smith
  120 W. Central Ave.
  Blountstown, FL 32424
  (850) 674-5987
  smithrw@flcjn.net

Charlotte County

- Charlotte County SO
- Sheriff William G. *Bill* Prummell Jr.
  7474 Utilities Rd.
  Punta Gorda, FL 33982
  (941) 639-2101
  Bill.Prummell@ccso.org
- Punta Gorda PD
- Chief Albert A. Arenal
  1410 So. Tamiami Tr.
  Punta Gorda, FL 33950
  (941) 639-4111
  barenal@ci.punta-gorda.fl.us

Citrus County

- Citrus County SO
- Sheriff Jeffrey J. *Jeff* Dawsy
  1 Dr. Martin Luther King Jr. Ave.
  Inverness, FL 34450
  (352) 726-4488
  jdawsy@sheriffcitrus.org

Clay County

- Clay County SO
- Sheriff Rick Beseler
  901 No. Orange PO Box 548
  Green Cove Springs, FL 32043
  (904) 284-7575
  rbeseler@claysheriff.com

- Green Cove Springs PD
- Chief Robert A. Musco
  205 Spring St.
  Green Cove Springs, FL 32043
  (904) 529-2220
  Rmusco@gcspd.com
- Orange Park PD
- Chief Gary Goble
  331 Stowe Ave.
  Orange Park, FL 32073
  (904) 264-5555
  ggoble@orangeparkpolice.com

Collier County

- Collier County SO
- Sheriff Kevin J. Rambosk
  3301 Tamiami Tr. E., Bldg. J
  Naples, FL 34112
  Ph: (239) 252-0555
  sheriff@colliersheriff.net
- Naples Police & Employment Services
- Chief Thomas Weschler
  355 Riverside Cir.
  Naples, FL 34102
  (239) 213-4844
  tweschler@naplesgov.com

Columbia County

- Columbia County SO
- Sheriff Mark A. Hunter
  4917 E. US Hwy 90 PO Box 650
  Lake City, FL 32056
  (386) 752-9212
  mark.hunter@columbiasheriff.org
- Lake City PD
- Chief Argatha Gilmore
  201 No. 1st St.
  Lake City, FL 32055
  (386) 752-4344
  gilmorea@lcflapd.com

DeSoto County

- DeSoto County SO
- Sheriff William P. *Will* Wise
  208 E. Cypress St.
  Arcadia, FL 34266
  (863) 993-4700
  sheriffwise@desotosheriff.org
- Arcadia PD
- Marshall Charles Lee
  725 No. Brevard Ave.
  Arcadia, FL 34266
  (863) 993-4660
  arcadiapd725@gmail.com

Dixie County

- Dixie County SO
- Sheriff Dewey H. Hatcher
  214 NE 351 Hwy PO Box 470
  Cross City, FL 32628
  (352) 498-1220
  deweyhatcher@dixiecountysheriff.com
- Cross City PD
- Chief Wesley Jones PO Box 417
  Cross City, FL 32628
  (352) 498-3507
  joneswk@flcjn.net

Duval/Jacksonville County

- Duval/Jacksonville SO
- Sheriff John H. Rutherford
  501 E. Bay St., Rm. 303
  Jacksonville, FL 32202
  (904) 630-2120
  JSOzone1@jaxsheriff.org
- Atlantic Beach PD
- Chief Michael Classey
  850 Seminole Rd.
  Atlantic Beach, FL 32233
  (904) 247-5859
  mclassey@coab.us
- Jacksonville Beach PD
- Int. Chief Patrick K. Dooley
  101 Penman Rd. So.
  Jacksonville Beach, FL 32250
  (904) 247-6343
  rgreene@jaxbechfl.net
- Neptune Beach PD
- Chief David W. Sembach
  116 1st St.
  Neptune Beach, FL 32266
  (904) 270-2400
  dsembach@neptune-beach.com

Escambia County

- Escambia County SO
- Sheriff David Morgan
  1700 W. Leonard PO Box 18770
  Pensacola, FL 32501
  (850) 436-9630
  sheriff@escambiaso.com
- Pensacola PD
- Chief Chip W. Simmons
  711 No. Hayne St.
  Pensacola, FL 32501
  (850) 435-1900
  CSimmons@cityofpensacola.com

Flagler County

- Flagler County SO
- Sheriff Jim Manfre
  1001 Justice Ln.
  Bunnell, FL 32110
  (386) 437-4116
  jmanfre@flaglersheriff.com
- Bunnell PD
- Chief Jeff Hoffman
  200 So. Church St.
  Bunnell, FL 32110
  (386) 437-7508
  jhoffman@bunnellpd.us
- Flagler Beach PD
- Chief Dan Cody
  204 So. Flagler Ave.
  Flagler Beach, FL 32136
  (386) 517-2020
  dcody@fbpd.org

Franklin County

- Franklin County SO
- Sheriff Mike Mock
  270 State Rd. 65
  Eastpoint, FL 32328
  (850) 670-8519
  fcso@franklinsheriff.com
- Apalachicola PD
- Chief Bobby Varnes
  127 Ave. E
  Apalachicola, FL 32320
  (850) 653-9755
  Chief@apalachicolapolice.com
- Carrabelle PD
- Chief Joseph Ham
  1001 Gray Ave. PO Drawer 569
  Carrabelle, FL 32322
  (850) 697-3691
  ltham@carrabellepolice.com

Gadsden County

- Gadsden County SO
- Sheriff Morris A. Young
  339 E. Jefferson PO Box 1709
  Quincy, FL 32351 *(32353-1709)*
  (850) 627-9233
  gcso@tds.net
- Chattahoochee PD
- Chief Vann Pullen
  32 Jefferson St.
  Chattahoochee, FL 32324
  (850) 663-4383
  vannpullen@fairpoint.net
- Havana PD
- Chief Tracy Smith
  121 7th Ave. E.
  Havana, FL 32333
  (850) 539-2801
  tsmith4848@bellsouth.net
- Quincy PD
- Chief Walter A. McNeil
  121 E. Jefferson St.
  Quincy, FL 32351
  (850) 875-7340
  wmcneil@myquincy.net

Gilchrist County

- Gilchrist County SO
- Sheriff Robert D. *Bobby* Schultz III
  9239 So. US 129
  Trenton, FL 32693
  (352) 463-3181
  bschultz@gcso.us

Glades County

- Glades County SO
- Sheriff Stuart Whiddon
  1297 E. State Rd. 78
  Moore Haven, FL 33471
  (863) 946-1600
  sheriff1@gladessheriff.org

Gulf County

- Gulf County SO
- Sheriff Mike Harrison
  1000 Cecil G. Costin Sr. Blvd
  Port St. Joe, FL 32456
  (850) 227-1115
  sheriff@gulfsheriff.com
- Port Saint Joe PD
- Chief David Barnes
  410 Williams Ave.
  Port Saint Joe, FL 32456
  (850) 227-1414
  dbarnes@psj.fl.gov

Hamilton County

- Hamilton County SO
- Sheriff J. Harrell Reid
  207 NE 1st St. PO Drawer A
  Jasper, FL 32052
  (386) 792-2004
  reidjh@flcjn.net

- Jasper PD
- Chief Jeff McGuire
  205 1st St. SW
  Jasper, FL 32052
  (386) 792-1130
  jmcguire@windstream.net
- White Springs PD
- Chief Ken Brookins
  Wesson Ave.
  White Springs, FL 32096
  (386) 397-2222
  kbrookins@whitespringsfl.us

Hardee County

- Hardee County SO
- Sheriff Arnold Lanier
  900 E. Summit St.
  Wauchula, FL 33873
  (863) 773-0304
  alanier@hardeeso.com
- Bowling Green PD
- Chief John Sheel
  104 E. Main St.
  Bowling Green, FL 33834
  (863) 375-3549
  jscheel@bowlinggreenfl.org
- Wauchula PD
- Chief John M. Eason
  303 W. Main St.
  Wauchula, FL 33873
  (863) 773-3265
  jeason@wauchulapolice.com

Hendry County

- Hendry County SO
- Sheriff Stephen H. *Steve* Whidden
  101 So. Bridge St. PO Box 579
  La Belle, FL 33935
  (863) 674-5600
  pwegschid@hendrysheriff.org
- Clewiston PD
- Chief Don Gutshall
  205 W. Ventura Ave.
  Clewiston, FL 33440
  (863) 983-1474
  gutshalld@flcjn.net

Hernando County

- Hernando County SO
- Sheriff Al Nienhuis
  18900 Cortez Blvd PO Box 10070
  Brooksville, FL 34601
  (352) 754-6830
  sheriffnienhuis@hernandosheriff.org
- Brooksville PD
- Chief George B. Turner
  85 Veterans Ave.
  Brooksville, FL 34601
  (352) 754-6800
  GeorgeT@cityofbrooksville.us

Highlands County

- Highlands County SO
- Sheriff Susan Benton
  434 Fernleaf Ave.
  Sebring, FL 33870
  (863) 402-7200
  sheriff@highlandssheriff.org
- Avon Park PD
- Chief Michael J. Rowan
  1535 State Rd. 64 W, Ste. 101
  Avon Park, FL 33825
  (863) 453-6622
  publicsafety@avonparkpublicsafety.com
- Lake Placid PD
- Chief James Fansler
  8 No. Oak St.
  Lake Placid, FL 33852
  (863) 699-3757
  lppd.JF@gmail.com
- Sebring PD
- Chief Thomas M. Dettman
  307 No. Ridgewood Dr.
  Sebring, FL 33870
  (863) 471-5108
  thomasdetman@mysebring.com

Hillsborough County

- Hillsborough County SO
- Sheriff David A. Gee
  2008 E. 8th Ave. PO Box 3371
  Tampa, FL 33605
  (813) 247-8000
  wdstanek@hcso.tampa.fl.us
- Plant City PD
- Chief Bill McDaniel
  1 Police Pl. PO 4709
  Plant City, FL 33566
  (813) 757-9200
  police@plantcitygov.com
- Tampa PD
- Chief Jane Castor
  411 No. Franklin St.
  Tampa, FL 33602
  (813) 276-3200
  jane.castor@tampagov.net

- Temple Terrace PD
- Chief Kenneth R. Albano
  11250 No. 56th St.
  Temple Terrace, FL 33617
  (813) 989-7110
  kalbano@templeterrace.com

Holmes County

- Holmes County SO
- Sheriff Tim Brown
  211 No. Oklahoma St.
  Bonifay, FL 32425
  (850) 547-4421
  brownt@holmescosheriff.org
- Bonifay PD
- Chief Chris Wells
  809 So. Waukashua St.
  Bonifay, FL 32425
  (850) 547-3661
  chiefwells@bonifaypolice.com

Indian River County

- Indian River County SO
- Sheriff Deryl B. Loar
  4055 41st Ave.
  Vero Beach, FL 32960
  (772) 569-6700
  dloar@ircsheriff.org
- Fellsmere PD
- Chief Scott A. Melanson
  21 So. Cypress St.
  Fellsmere, FL 32948
  (772) 571-1360
  policechief@cityoffellsmere.org
- Indian River Shores DPS
- Dir. Robert H. Stabe, Jr.
  6001 No. Hwy A1A
  Indian River Shores, FL 32963
  (772) 231-2451
  admin@irspsd.org
- Sebastian PD
- Chief J. Michelle Morris
  1201 Main St.
  Sebastian, FL 32958
  (772) 589-5233
  spd@cityofsebastian.org
- Vero Beach PD
- Chief David E. Currey
  1055 20th St.
  Vero Beach, FL 32960
  (772) 978-4600
  dcurrey@vbpd.org

Jackson County

- Jackson County SO
- Sheriff Louis S. *Lou* Roberts III
  4012 Lafayette St. PO Box 919
  Marianna, FL 32446
  (850) 482-9624
  robertsls@flcjn.net
- Cottondale PD
- Chief William Watford
  PO Box 398
  Cottondale, FL 32431
  (850) 352-4361
  watfordw@flcjn.net
- Graceville PD
- Chief Timothy E. Horton
  5348 Cliff St.
  Graceville, FL 32440
  (850) 263-3944
  gracevillepd@flcjn.net
- Marianna PD
- Chief Hayes Baggett
  2890 Green St.
  Marianna, FL 32447
  (850) 526-3125
  baggetth@cityofmarianna.com
- Sneads PD
- Chief Burt McAlpin
  2033 3rd Ave. PO Box 126
  Sneads, FL 32460
  (850) 593-6403
  info@sneadsfl.com

Jefferson County

- Jefferson County SO
- Sheriff David C. Hobbs
  171 Industrial Park
  Monticello, FL 32344
  (850) 997-2523
  hobbsdc@flcjn.net
- Monticello PD
- Chief Fred Mosley
  195 So. Mulberry
  Monticello, FL 32345
  (850) 342-0150
  fmosley@mymonticello.net

Lafayette County

- Lafayette County SD
- Sheriff Brian N. Lamb
  231 NW Monroe PO Box 227
  Mayo, FL 32066
  (386) 294-1222
  lcso@windstream.net

Lake County

- Lake County SO
- Sheriff Gary S. Borders
  360 W. Ruby St.
  Tavares, FL 32778
  (352) 343-9500
  gary.borders@lcso.org
- Clermont PD
- Chief Charles Broadway
  865 W. Montrose St.
  Clermont, FL 34711
  (352) 394-5588
  CBroadway@clermontfl.org
- Eustis PD
- Chief Fred *A.M.* Cobb
  51 E. Norton Ave.
  Eustis, FL 32726
  (352) 483-5400
  eustispolice@ci.eustis.fl.us
- Fruitland Park PD
- Chief Terry Isaacs
  506 W. Berckman St.
  Fruitland Park, FL 34731
  (352) 360-6655
  tissaacs@fruitlandpark.org
- Groveland PD
- Chief Mark Palmer
  408 W. Orange St.
  Groveland, FL 34736
  (352) 429-4166
  Mark.Palmer@groveland-fl.gov
- Leesburg PD
- Chief William *Bill* Chrisman
  115 E. Magnolia St.
  Leesburg, FL 34748
  (352) 787-2121
  bill.chrisman@leesburgflorida.gov
- Mascotte PD
- Chief Rolando S. Banasco
  529 E. Myers Blvd
  Mascotte, FL 34753
  (352) 429-3393
  rolando.banasco@cityofmascotte.com
- Mount Dora PD
- Chief Randy Scoggins
  1300 No. Donnelly St.
  Mount Dora, FL 32757
  (352) 735-7170
  ScogginsR@ci.mount-dora.fl.us
- Tavares PD
- Chief Stoney Lubins
  201 E. Main St.
  Tavares, FL 32778
  (352) 742-6200
  slubins@tavares.org
- Umatilla PD
- Chief Douglas O. Foster
  251 No. Central Ave.
  Umatilla, FL 32784
  (352) 669-3561
  dfoster@umatillafl.org

Lee County

- Lee County SO
- Sheriff Mike Scott
  14750 Six Mile Cypress Pkwy
  Fort Myers, FL 33912
  (239) 477-1000
  mscott@sheriffleesl.org
- Cape Coral PD
- Chief Jay Murphy
  815 Nicholas Pkwy
  Cape Coral, FL 33990
  (239) 574-0699
  jmurphy@capecoral.net
- Fort Myers PD
- Chief Douglas E. Baker
  2210 Widman Way
  Fort Myers, FL 33901
  (239) 334-4155
  dbaker@fmpolice.com
- Sanibel PD
- Chief William E. Tomlinson
  800 Dunlop Rd.
  Sanibel, FL 33957
  (239) 472-3111
  b.tomlinson@mysanibel.com

Leon County

- Leon County SO
- Sheriff Larry Campbell
  2825 Municipal PO Box 727
  Tallahassee, FL 32304
  (850) 922-3300
  campbell@leoncountyfl.gov
- Tallahassee PD
- Chief Dennis Michael Jones
  234 E. 7th Ave.
  Tallahassee, FL 32303
  (850) 891-4341
  tpdpublicinfo@talgov.com

Levy County

- Levy County SO
- Sheriff Robert B. *Bobby* McCallum
  9150 NE 80th Ave. PO Drawer 1719
  Bronson, FL 32621
  (352) 486-5111
  online@levyso.com
- Cedar Key PD
- Chief Virgil Sandlin
  PO Box 339
  Cedar Key, FL 32625
  (352) 543-5180
  cedarkeypd@cedarkeyfl.us
- Chiefland PD
- Chief Robert Douglas
  14 E. Park Ave.
  Chiefland, FL 32626
  (352) 493-6777
  chieflandpd@gmail.com
- Inglis PD
- Chief Steve Dixon
  26 Hwy 40 W.
  Inglis, FL 34449
  (352) 447-0970
  inglispolicedepartment@bellsouth.net
- Williston PD
- Chief Dennis Strow
  5 SW 1st Ave.
  Williston, FL 32696
  (352) 528-4991
  dennis.strow@willistonpolice.org

Madison County

- Madison County SO
- Sheriff Benjamin J. Stewart
  2364 W. US 90
  Madison, FL 32340
  (850) 973-4151
  Sheriff@mcso-fl.org
- Greenville PD
- Chief Hassan Aden
  102 Church St.
  Greenville, FL 32331
  (850) 948-2241
  haden@greenvillenc.gov
- Madison PD
- Chief Gary Calhoun
  108 SW Rutledge St.
  Madison, FL 32340
  (850) 973-5077
  info@cityofmadisonfl.com

Manatee County

- Manatee County SO
- Sheriff W. Brad Steube
  600 301 Blvd W.
  Bradenton, FL 34205
  (941) 747-3011
  Dave.Bristow@manateesheriff.com
- Bradenton PD
- Chief Keith Davis
  100 10th St. W.
  Bradenton, FL 34205
  (941) 932-9300
  keith.davis@cityofbradenton.com
- Bradenton Beach PD
- Chief Sam J. Speciale
  403 Highland Ave.
  Bradenton Beach, FL 34217
  (941) 778-6311
  info@cityofbradentonbeach.com
- Holmes Beach PD
- Int. Chief Dale Stephenson
  5801 Marina Dr.
  Holmes Beach, FL 34217
  (941) 708-5804
  admin@holmesbeach.org
- Palmetto PD
- Chief Rick Wells
  1115 10th St. W.
  Palmetto, FL 34221
  (941) 723-4587
  chief@palmettopolice.com

Marion County

- Marion County SO
- Sheriff Chris Blair
  PO Box 1987
  Ocala, FL 34478
  (352) 732-8181
  cblair@marionso.com
- Belleview PD
- Chief Lee Strickland
  5350 SE 110th St.
  Belleview, FL 34420
  (352) 245-7044
  lstrickland@belleviewfl.org
- Dunnellon PD
- Chief Joanne M. Black
  12014 So. Williams St.
  Dunnellon, FL 34432
  (352) 465-8510
  jblack@dunnellonpd.org

- Ocala PD
- Chief Greg Graham
  402 So. Pine Ave.
  Ocala, FL 34471
  (352) 369-7000
  ggraham@ocalapd.org

Martin County

- Martin County SO
- Sheriff William D. Snyder
  800 SE Monterey Rd.
  Stuart, FL 34994
  (772) 220-7000
  roadpatrol@sheriff.martin.fl.us
- Sewall's Point PD
- Chief John J. Donadio
  1 So. Sewall's Point Rd.
  Sewall's Point, FL 34996
  (772) 781-3378
  jdonadio@sewallspoint.org
- Stuart PD
- Chief David Dyess
  830 Martin Luther King Jr. Blvd
  Stuart, FL 34994
  (772) 287-1122
  ddyess@ci.stuart.fl.us

Miami Dade County

- Aventura PD
- Chief Steve Steinberg
  19200 W. Country Club Dr.
  Aventura, FL 33180
  (305) 466-8989
  ssteinberg@aventurapolice.com
- Bal Harbour PD
- Chief Mike Daddario
  655 96th St.
  Bal Harbour, FL 33154
  (305) 866-5000
  mdaddario@balharborflorida.com
- Bay Harbor Islands PD
- Chief Sean Hemingway
  9665 Bay Harbor Terrace
  Bay Harbor Islands, FL 33154
  (305) 866-6242
  shemingway@bayharborislands.net
- Coral Gables PD
- Chief Dennis Weiner
  2801 Salzedo St.
  Coral Gables, FL 33134
  (305) 442-1600
  dweiner@coralgables.com
- Florida City PD
- Chief Pedro W. Taylor
  404 W. Palm Dr.
  Florida City, FL 33034
  (305) 247-8223
  ptaylor@floridacityfl.gov
- Hialeah PD
- Chief Sergio Velazquez
  5555 E. 8th Ave.
  Hialeah, FL 33013
  (305) 953-5300
  Sergio@hialeahfl.gov
- Hialeah Gardens PD
- Chief Van Toth
  10001 NW 87th Ave.
  Hialeah Gardens, FL 33016
  (305) 558-3333
  chief@cityofhialeahgardens.com
- Homestead PD
- Chief Alexander E. Rolle, Jr.
  4 So. Krome Ave.
  Homestead, FL 33030
  (305) 247-1535
  arolle@homesteadpolice.com
- Medley PD
- Chief Jeanette Said Jinete
  7777 NW 72nd Ave.
  Medley, FL 33166-2409
  (305) 883-2047
  jsaid@medleypd.com
- Miami PD
- Chief Manuel Orosa
  400 NW 2nd Ave.
  Miami, FL 33128
  (305) 579-6565
  mptc@miami-police.org
- Miami-Dade County PD
- Dir. J.D. Patterson
  9105 NW 25th St.
  Miami, FL 33172-1500
  (305) 471-3518
  trbinfo@mdpd.com
- Miami-Dade School PD
- Chief Gerald Kitchell
  6100 NW 2nd Ave.
  Miami, FL 33127
  (305) 757-7727
  gkitchell@dadeschool.net

- Miami Shores PD
- Chief Kevin Lystad
  9990 NE 2nd Ave.
  Miami Shores, FL 33138
  (305) 759-2468
  kevin.lystad@mspd.org
- North Miami PD
- Chief Marc Elias, Jr.
  700 NE 124th St.
  North Miami, FL 33161
  (305) 891-0294
  melias@northmiamipolice.com
- North Miami Beach PD
- Chief Larry Gomer
  16901 NE 19th Ave.
  North Miami Beach, FL 33162
  (305) 948-2995
  larry.gomer@nmbpd.org
- Opa Locka PD
- Chief Cheryl Cason
  2495 Ali Baba Ave.
  Opa Locka, FL 33054
  (305) 681-1033
  chiefsec@opalockafl.gov
- South Miami PD
- Chief Orlando Martinez de Castro
  6130 Sunset Dr.
  South Miami, FL 33143
  (305) 663-6336
  OMartinezdeCastro@southmiamifl.gov
- Sunny Isles Beach PD
- Chief Fred A. Maas
  18070 Collins Ave.
  Sunny Isles Beach, FL 33160
  (305) 947-4440
  fmas@sibfl.net
- Surfside PD
- Chief David Allen
  9293 Harding Ave.
  Surfside, FL 33154
  (305) 861-4862
  dallen@townofsurfsidefl.gov
- Sweetwater PD
- Chief Roberto Fulgueira
  500 SW 109 Ave.
  Sweetwater, FL 33174
  (305) 552-9900
  rfulgueira@cityofsweetwater.fl.gov

Monroe County

- Monroe County SO
- Sheriff Rick Ramsay
  5525 College Rd.
  Key West, FL 33040
  (305) 292-7000
  rramsay@keysso.net
- Key Colony Beach PD
- Chief Kris DiGiovanni
  600 W. Ocean Dr.
  Key Colony Beach, FL 33051
  (305) 743-5380
  chief@keycolonybeach.net
- Key West PD
- Chief Donald J. Lee, Jr.
  1604 No. Roosevelt Blvd
  Key West, FL 33040
  (305) 809-1000
  wm@keywestcity.com

Nassau County

- Nassau County SO
- Sheriff Bill Leeper
  76001 Bobby Moore Cir.
  Yulee, FL 32097
  (904) 225-0331
  bleepers@nassaucountysheriff.com
- Fernandina Beach PD
- Chief James T. Hurley
  1525 Lime St.
  Fernandina Beach, FL 32034
  (904) 277-7342
  jhurley@fbfl.org

Okaloosa County

- Okaloosa County SO
- Sheriff Larry R. Ashley
  1250 Eglin Pkwy
  Shalimar, FL 32579
  (850) 651-7400
  pio@sheriff-okaloosa.org
- Crestview PD
- Chief Tony Taylor
  201 Stillwell Blvd
  Crestview, FL 32536
  (850) 682-3544
  taylort@crestviewpd.org
- Fort Walton Beach PD
- Chief Ted Litschauer
  7 Hollywood Blvd
  Fort Walton Beach, FL 32548
  (850) 833-9533
  tlitschauer@fwb.org

- Niceville PD
- Chief David Popwell
  212 No. Partin Dr.
  Niceville, FL 32578
  (850) 729-4030
  pdadmin@niceville.org
- Valparaiso PD
- Chief Joseph Hart
  465 Valparaiso Pkwy
  Valparaiso, FL 32580
  (850) 729-5400
  dbruckemyers@valp.org

Okeechobee County

- Okeechobee County SO
- Sheriff Paul C. May
  504 NW 4th St. PO Drawer 1397
  Okeechobee, FL 34973
  (863) 763-3117
  pmay@okeesheriff.org
  Chief Dennis Davis
  55 SE 3rd Ave.
  Okeechobee, FL 34974
  (863) 763-5521
  ddavis@cityofokeechobee.com

Orange County

- Orange County SO
- Sheriff Jerry L. Demings
  2500 W. Colonial PO Box 1440
  Orlando, FL 32804
  (407) 254-7000
  jerry.demings@ocfl.net
- Apopka PD
- Chief Robert M. Manley
  112 E. 6th St.
  Apopka, FL 32703
  (407) 703-1771
  police@apopka.net
- Eatonville PD
- Chief Joseph Joe Jenkins
  11 People Ave.
  Eatonville, FL 32751
  (407) 623-1300
  jjenkinds@eatonvillepolice.com
- Edgewood PD
- Chief Peter Marcus
  5565 So. Orange Ave.
  Edgewood, FL 32809
  (407) 851-2820
  pmarcus@edgewood-fl.gov
- Maitland PD
- Chief Douglas M. Ball
  1776 Independence Ln.
  Maitland, FL 32751
  (407) 539-6261
  dball@itsmymaitland.com
- Oakland PD
- Chief Steven R. Thomas
  5399 No. Dixie Hwy, Ste 1
  Oakland, FL 34760
  Ph: (954) 202.3131
  Al_Hubrig@sheriff.org
- Ocoee PD
- Chief Charles J. *Charlie* Brown
  646 Ocoee Commerce Pkwy
  Ocoee, FL 34761
  (407) 905-3160
  PoliceDirector@ci.ocoee.fl.us
- Orlando PD
- Chief Paul Rooney
  100 So. Hughey PO Box 913
  Orlando, FL 32802-0913
  (407) 246-2470
  opd@cityoforlando.net
- Windermere PD
- Chief David Ogden
  620 Main St.
  Windermere, FL 34786
  (407) 876-3757
  dogden@town.windermere.fl.us
- Winter Garden PD
- Chief George Brennan
  251 W. Plant St.
  Winter Garden, FL 34787
  (407) 656-5959
  gbrennan@cwgdn.com
- Winter Park PD
- Chief Brett C. Railey
  500 No. Virginia Ave.
  Winter Park, FL 32789
  (407) 599-3272
  brailey@cityofwinterpark.org

Osceola County

- Osceola County SO
- Sheriff Bob Hansell
  2601 E. Irlo Bronson Hwy
  Kissimmee, FL 34744-4912
  (407) 348-1100
  dbat@osceola.org

- Kissimmee PD
- Chief Lee Massie
  8 No. Stewart Ave.
  Kissimmee, FL 34741
  (407) 847-0176
  lmassie@kissimmee.org
- St. Cloud PD
- Chief Pete Gauntlett
  4700 Neptune Rd.
  St Cloud, FL 34769
  (407) 891-6707
  pgauntlett@stcloud.org

Palm Beach County

- Palm Beach County SO
- Sheriff Ric L. Bradshaw
  3228 Gun Club PO Box 24681
  West Palm Beach, FL 33406
  (561) 688-3021
  BradshawR@pbso.org
- Atlantis PD
- Chief Robert G. Mangold
  260 Orange Tree Dr.
  Atlantis, FL 33462
  (561) 965-1700
  rmangold@atlantisfl.gov
- Boca Raton PD
- Chief Daniel C. Alexander
  100 NW Boca Raton Blvd
  Boca Raton, FL 33432
  (561) 338-1234
  DCAlexander@myboca.us
- Delray Beach PD
- Chief Anthony Strianese
  300 W. Atlantic Ave.
  Delray Beach, FL 33444
  (561) 243-7851
  PoliceChief@mydelraybeach.com
- Highland Beach PD
- Chief Craig Hartman
  3614 So. Ocean Blvd
  Highland Beach, FL 33487
  (561) 266-5800
  chartmann@ci.highland-beach.fl.us
- Juno Beach PD
- Chief Brian J. Smith
  340 Ocean Dr.
  Juno Beach, FL 33408
  (561) 656-0334
  bsmith@junobeachpd.com
- Jupiter PD
- Chief Frank J. Kitzerow
  210 Military Tr.
  Jupiter, Florida 33458
  (561) 746-6201
  frankk@jupiter.fl.us
- Lantana PD
- Chief Sean Scheller
  500 Greynolds Cir.
  Lantana, FL 33462
  (561) 540-5701
  sscheller@lantana.org
- North Palm Beach PD
- Chief Richard Jenkins
  560 US Hwy 1
  North Palm Beach, FL 33408
  (561) 882-1143
  police@village-npb.org
- Ocean Ridge PD
- Chief Christopher T. Yannuzzi
  6450 No. Ocean Blvd
  Ocean Ridge, FL 33435
  (561) 732-8331
  cyannuzzi@oceanridgeflorida.com
- Palm Beach PD
- Dir. Kirk W. Blouin
  345 So. County Rd.
  Palm Beach, FL 33480
  (561) 838-5454
  kblouin@palmbeachpolice.com
- Palm Beach Gardens PD
- Chief Stephen J. Stepp
  10500 No. Military Tr.
  Palm Beach Gardens, FL 33410
  (561) 799-4445
  sstepp@pbgfl.com
- Palm Beach Shores PD
- Chief Steven Kniffin
  247 Edwards Ln.
  Palm Beach Shores, FL 33404
  (561) 844-3456
  skniffin@pbspolice.org
- Riviera Beach PD
- Chief Clarence D. Williams III
  600 W. Blue Heron Blvd
  Riviera Beach, FL 33404
  (561) 845-4123
  cwilliams@rivierabch.com

- Tequesta PD
- Chief Pete *G.F.* Pitoccehelli
  357 Tequesta Dr.
  Tequesta, FL 33469
  (561) 575-6210
  gpitocchelli@tequesta.org
- West Palm Beach PD
- Chief Vincent Demasi
  600 Banyan Blvd
  West Palm Beach, FL 33401
  (561) 822-1900
  vdemasi@wpb.org

Pasco County

- Pasco County SO
- Sheriff Chris Nocco
  8700 Citizen Dr.
  New Port Richey, FL 34654
  (727) 847-5878
  cnocco@pascosheriff.org
- Dade City PD
- Chief Ray Velboom
  38042 Pasco Ave.
  Dade City, FL 33525
  (352) 521-1495
  chief@dadecityfl.com
- New Port Richey PD
- Chief James Steffens
  6739 Adams St.
  New Port Richey, FL 34652
  (727) 841-4550
  steffensj@cityofnewportrichey.org
- Port Richey PD
- Chief Dave Brown
  6333 Ridge Rd.
  Port Richey, FL 34668
  (727) 816-1900, ext. 215
  d.brown@cityofportrichey.com
- Zephyrhills PD
- Chief David Shears
  6118 8th St.
  Zephyrhills, FL 33542
  (813) 780-0050
  dshears@police.zephyrhills.fl.us

Pinellas County

- Pinellas County SO
- Sheriff Robert A. *Bob* Gualtieri
  10750 Ulmerton
  PO Box 2500
  Largo, FL 33779
  (727) 582-6200
  rgualtieri@pcsonet.com
- Belleair PD
- Chief Thomas Edwards
  901 Ponce De Leon Blvd
  Belleair, FL 34616
  (727) 588-3769, Ext 201
  tedwards@townofbelleair.net
- Clearwater PD
- Chief Anthony Holloway
  645 Pierce St.
  Clearwater, FL 33756
  (727) 562-4242
  police@myclearwater.com
- Gulfport PD
- Chief Robert Vincent
  2401 53rd St. So.
  Gulfport, FL 33707
  (727) 893-1049
  chief@gulfportpolice.com
- Indian Shores PD
- Chief E.D. Williams
  19305 Gulf Blvd
  Indian Shores, FL 33785
  (727) 595-5414
  ewilliams@myindianshores.com
- Kenneth City PD
- Chief Michael Rossi
  4600 58th St. No.
  Kenneth City, FL 33709
  (727) 498-8942
  rossim@kennethcityfl.org
- Largo PD
- Chief John L. Carroll
  201 Highland Ave.
  Largo, FL 33770
  (727) 587-6730
  policechief@largo.com
- Pinellas Park PD
- Chief Dorene Thomas
  7700 59th St.
  Pinellas Park, FL 33781
  (727) 541-0760
  Dthomas@pinellas-park.com
- St. Petersburg PD
- Chief Charles *Chuck* Harmon
  1300 1st Ave. No.
  St Petersburg, FL 33705
  (727) 893-7780
  charles.harmon@stpete.org

- Tarpon Springs PD
- Chief Robert P. Kochen
  444 So. Huey Ave.
  Tarpon Springs, FL 34689
  (727) 938-2849
  rkochen@tspd.us
- Treasure Island PD
- Chief Tim Casey
  180 108th Ave.
  Treasure Island, FL 33706
  (727) 547-4595
  tcasey@mytreasureisland.org

Polk County

- Polk County SO
- Sheriff Grady Judd
  1891 Jim Keene Blvd
  Bartow, FL 33830
  (863) 298-6200
  gjudd@polksheriff.org
- Auburndale PD
- Chief Chris Nelson
  2 Bobby Green Plaza
  Auburndale, FL 33823
  (863) 965-5555
  cnelson@auburndalefl.com
- Bartow PD
- Chief Joe Hall
  450 No. Broadway Ave.
  Bartow, Florida 33830
  (863) 534-5034
  Jhall.pd@cityofbartow.net
- Davenport PD
- Chief Larry Holden
  6 Bay West St. PO Box 125
  Davenport, FL 33836
  (863) 419-3307
  lholden@mydavenport.org
- Haines City PD
- Chief Richard H. Sloan
  35400 Hwy 27
  Haines City, FL 33844
  (863) 421-3636
  chiefsloan@hainescitypd.com
- Lake Alfred PD
- Chief Art Bodenheimer
  190 No. Seminole Ave.
  Lake Alfred, FL 33850
  (863) 291-5200
  ABodenheimer@mylakealfred.com
- Lake Hamilton PD
- Chief Edward Freeman
  100 Smith Ave.
  Lake Hamilton, FL 33851
  (863) 439-1561
  edwardfreeman@townoflakehamilton.com
- Lake Wales PD
- Chief Christopher Velasquez
  133 E. Tillman Ave.
  Lake Wales, FL 33853
  (863) 678-4223
  cvelasquez@cityoflakewales.com
- Lakeland PD
- Chief Lisa Womack
  219 No. Massachusetts Ave.
  Lakeland, FL 33801
  (863) 834-6907
  lisa.womack@lakelandgov.net
- Winter Haven PD
- Chief Gary Hester
  125 No. Lake Silver Dr.
  Winter Haven, FL 33881
  (863) 291-5874
  ghester@mywinterhaven.com

Putnam County

- Putnam County SO
- Sheriff Jeff Hardy
  130 Orie Griffin PO Drawer 1578
  Palatka, FL 32177
  jhardy@putnamsheriff.org
  (386) 329-0800
- Crescent City PD
- Chief Robert Johnson
  19 No. Summit St.
  Crescent City, FL 32112
  (386) 698-1211
  chief@crescentcitypd.org
- Palatka PD
- Chief Gary Getchell
  110 No. 11th St.
  Palatka, FL 32177
  (386) 329-0110
  ggetchell@palatka-fl.gov
- Welaka PD
- Chief Charlie Piwowarski
  400 4th Ave. PO Box 1098
  Welaka, FL 32193
  (386) 467-2303
  welakaPD@welaka-fl.gov

St. Johns County

- St Johns County SO
- Sheriff David B. Shoar
  4015 Lewis Speedway
  St Augustine, FL 32084
  (904) 824-8304
  dshoar@sjso.org
- St. Augustine PD
- Chief Loran Lueders
  PO Box 1950
  St Augustine, FL 32085
  (904) 825-1075
  llueders@sapd.ci.st-augustine.fl.us
- St. Augustine Beach PD
- Chief Loran K. Lueders
  2300 A1A So.
  St Augustine Beach, FL 32084
  (904) 471-3600
  llueders@sapd.ci.st-augustine.fl.us

St. Lucie County

- St. Lucie County SO
- Sheriff Ken J. Mascara
  4700 W. Midway Rd.
  Fort Pierce, FL 34981
  (772) 462-7300
  kmascara@stluciesheriff.com
- Fort Pierce PD
- Chief R. Sean Baldwin
  920 So. US 1
  Fort Pierce, FL 34950
  (772) 467-6800
  sbaldwin@fppd.org
- Port St. Lucie PD
- Chief John A. Bolduc
  121 SW Port St. Lucie Blvd
  Port St. Lucie, FL 34984
  (772) 871-5000
  pdrecords@pslpd.us

Santa Rosa County

- Santa Rosa County SO
- Sheriff O. Wendell Hall
  PO Box 7129
  Milton, FL 32570
  (850) 983-1100
  whall@srso.net
- Gulf Breeze PD
- Chief Robert Randle
  311 Fairpoint Dr.
  Gulf Breeze, FL 32561
  (850) 934-5121
  rrandle@gulfbreezefl.gov
- Milton PD
- Chief Gregory J. Brand
  609 Alabama St.
  Milton, FL 32572
  (850) 983-5420
  police@mymiltonflorida.com

Sarasota County

- Sarasota County SO
- Sheriff Tom Knight
  2071 Ringling PO Box 4115
  Sarasota, FL 34230-4115
  (941) 861-5800
  SRQsher@scgov.net
- Longboat Key PD
- Chief Peter A. Cumming
  5460 Gulf of Mexico Dr.
  Longboat Key, FL 34228
  (941) 316-1977, ext. 222
  pcumming@longboatkey.org
- North Port PD
- Chief Kevin Vespia
  4980 City Hall Blvd
  North Port, FL 34286
  (941) 429-7306
  KVespia@northportpd.com
- Sarasota PD
- Chief Bernadette A. DiPino
  2050 Ringling Blvd
  Sarasota, FL 34237
  (941) 954-7001
  Bernadette.DiPino@sarasotagov
- Venice PD
- Chief Tom McNulty
  1350 Ridgewood Ave.
  Venice, FL 34292
  (941) 486-2444, ext. 3240
  tmcnulty@venicegov.com

Seminole County

- Seminole County SO
- Sheriff Donald F. *Don* Eslinger
  100 Bush Blvd
  Sanford, FL 32773
  (407) 665-6600
  scso@seminolesheriff.org
- Altamonte Springs PD
- Chief Michael J. McCoy
  225 Newburyport Ave.
  Altamonte Springs, FL 32701
  (407) 571-8191
  MJMcCoy@altamonte.org

- Casselberry PD
- Chief William McNeil
  4195 So. US Hwy 17-92
  Casselberry, FL 32707
  (407) 262-7616, ext. 1064
  bmcneil@casselberry.org
- Lake Mary PD
- Chief Steve Bracknell
  165 E. Crystal Lake Ave.
  Lake Mary, FL 32746
  (407) 585-1301
  sbracknell@lakemaryfl.com
- Longwood PD
- Chief Troy K. Hickson
  235 W. Church Ave.
  Longwood, FL 32750
  (407) 260-3402
  Thickson@longwoodfl.org
- Oviedo PD
- Chief Jeffrey A. Chudnow
  300 Alexandria Blvd
  Oviedo, FL 32765
  (407) 977-6146
  jchudnow@cityofoviedo.net
- Sanford PD
- Int. Chief Richard W. Myers
  815 Historic Goldsboro Blvd
  Sanford, FL 32771
  (407) 688-5070
  Richard.Myers@sanfordfl.gov
- Winter Springs PD
- Chief Kevin P. Brunelle
  300 No. Moss Rd.
  Winter Springs, FL 32708
  (407) 327-7964
  kbrunelle@winterspringsfl.org

Sumter County

- Sumter County SO
- Sheriff William O. *Bill* Farmer, Jr.
  1010 No. Main St.
  Bushnell, FL 33513
  (352) 569-1600
  wfarmer@sumtercountysheriff.org
- Wildwood PD
- Chief E.W. Reeser
  100 E. Huey St.
  Wildwood, FL 34785
  (352) 330-1355
  wildwoodpd@sum.net

Suwannee County

- Suwannee County SO
- Sheriff Tony G. Cameron
  200 So. Ohio Ave., Ste. 105
  Live Oak, FL 32064
  (386) 362-2222
  Sheriff@suwanneesheriff.com
- Live Oak PD
- Chief Alton *Buddy* Williams
  844 Pinewood Way SW
  Live Oak, FL 32064
  (386) 362-7463
  williamsb@liveoakpd.org

Taylor County

- Taylor County SO
- Sheriff L.E. *Bummy* Williams
  108 No. Jefferson St., Ste. 103
  Perry, FL 32347
  (850) 584-4225
  bummy@tcso.org
- Perry PD
- Chief Vern Clark
  211 So. Washington
  Perry, FL 32347
  (850) 584-5121
  perrypd@flcjn.net

Union County

- Union County SO
- Sheriff Jerry Whitehead
  55 W. Main St.
  Lake Butler, FL 32054
  (386) 496-2501
  whiteheadj@unionsheriff.us

Volusia County

- Volusia County SO
- Sheriff Ben F. Johnson
  116 W. Indiana PO Box 569
  Deland, FL 32720
  (386) 736-5961
  BJohnson@vcso.us
- Daytona Beach PD
- Chief Michael Chitwood
  129 Valor Blvd, Rm. 3001
  Daytona Beach, FL 32114
  (386) 671-5102
  chitwoodm@dbpd.us

- DeLand PD
- Chief Bill Ridgway
  219 W. Howry
  DeLand, FL 32720
  (386) 626-7414
  ridgewayb@deland.org
- Edgewater PD
- Chief Dave Arcieri
  104 No. Riverside Dr.
  Edgewater, FL 32132
  (386) 424-2400, ext. 2102
  police@cityofedgewater.org
- Holly Hill PD
- Chief Mark D. Barker
  1065 Ridgewood Ave.
  Holly Hill, FL 32117
  (386) 248-9491
  mbarker@hollyhillfl.org
- Lake Helen PD
- Chief Mike Walker
  493 So. Lakeview Dr.
  Lake Helen, FL 32744
  (386) 228-2145
  mwalker@lakehelen.com
- New Smyrna Beach PD
- Chief Michael Brouillette
  246 Industrial Park Ave.
  New Smyrna Beach, FL 32168
  (386) 424-2220
  mbrouillette@cityofnsb.com
- Orange City PD
- Chief Peter C. Thomas
  207 No. Holly Ave.
  Orange City, FL 32763
  (386) 775-5474
  pthomas@ourorangecity.com
- Ormond Beach PD
- Chief Andy Osterkamp
  170 W. Granada Blvd
  Ormond Beach, FL 32174
  (386) 676-3500
  Andy.Osterkamp@ormondbeach.org
- Ponce Inlet PD
- Chief Frank G. Fabrizio
  4301 So. Peninsula Dr.
  Ponce Inlet, FL 32127
  (386) 236-2160
  ffabrizio@ponce-inlet.org
- Port Orange PD
- Chief Gerald M. Monahan, Jr.
  4545 Clyde Morris Blvd
  Port Orange, FL 32129
  (386) 506-5800
  gmonahan@port-orange.org
- South Daytona PD
- Act. Chief Ronald Wright
  1672 So. Ridgewood Ave.
  South Daytona, FL 32121
  (386) 322-3045
  rwright@southdaytona.org

Wakulla County

- Wakulla County SO
- Sheriff Charles W. *Charlie* Creel
  15 Oak St.
  Crawfordville, FL 32327
  (850) 745-7100
  ccreel@wcso.org

Walton County

- Walton County SO
- Sheriff Michael A. Adkinson, Jr.
  752 Triple G Rd.
  Defuniak Springs, FL 32433
  (850) 892-8186
  madkinson@waltonso.org
- Defuniak Springs PD
- City Marshal/Chief Mark Weeks
  355 US Hwy 90 E.
  Defuniak Springs, FL 32433
  (850) 892-8513
  weeksma@defuniakspringspolice.net

Washington County

- Washington County SO
- Sheriff Robert C. *Bobby* Haddock
  1293 Jackson Ave., Bldg. 400
  Chipley, FL 32428
  (850) 638-6111
  sheriff@wcso.us
- Chipley PD
- Chief Kevin Crews
  802 Hwy 90
  Chipley, FL 32428
  (850) 638-6310
  crewsk@flcjn.net

State Agencies

- FL Highway Patrol-HQ
- Dir. (*Col.*) David H. Brierton, Jr.
  2900 Apalachee Pkwy MS 44
  Tallahassee, FL 32399-0553
  (850) 617-2301
  DavidBrierton@flhsmv.gov

- FL International U. PD
- Chief Alexander D. Casas
  885 SW 109th Ave.
  Miami, FL 33199
  (305) 348-2623
  adcasas@fiu.edu
- FL State U. PD
- Chief David L. Perry
  830 W. Jefferson St.
  Tallahassee, FL 32306
  (850) 644-1234
  dlperry@admin.fsu.edu
- New College of FL PD
- Chief Michael Kessie
  501 College Dr.
  Sarasota, FL 34243
  (941) 487-4210
  mkessie@ncf.edu
- U. of Central FL PD
- Chief Richard Beary
  4000 Central Florida Blvd, Bldg. # 49
  Orlando, FL 32816
  (407) 823-5555
  policedept@mail.ucf.edu
- U. of North FL PD
- Chief John E. Dean
  4567 St. Johns Bluff Rd. So.
  Jacksonville, FL 32224
  (904) 620-1020
  jdean@unf.edu

GEORGIA

Appling County

- Appling County SO
- Sheriff Benny Deloach
  560 Barnes St, Ste. B
  Baxley, GA 31513
  (912) 367-8182
  ACSO@APPLINGCOUNTYSHERIFFSOFFICE.COM

Atkinson County

- Atkinson County SO
- Sheriff David Moore
  PO Box 157
  Pearson, GA 31642
  (912) 422-3611
  atcoso@atkinson-ga.org
- Willacoochee PD
- Dir. William Gillard
  Florida Rd.
  Willacoochee, GA 31650
  (912) 534-5151
  pd@willacoochee.com

Bacon County

- Bacon County SO
- Sheriff Richard R. Foskey
  307 So. Dixon St. PO Box 237
  Alma, GA 31510
  (912) 632-2658
  bcso@baconcountyso.com

Baker County

- Baker County SO
- Sheriff Dana Meade
  167 Baker Pl. PO Box 441
  Newton, GA 31770
  (912) 734-3002
  info@bakercountysheriffoffice.org
- Newton PD
- Chief Aubrey Suggs
  PO Box 238
  Newton, GA 39870
  (229)734-5331
  chiefsuggs1@yahoo.com

Baldwin County

- Baldwin County SO
- Sheriff Bill Massee
  119 Old Monticello Rd.
  Milledgeville, GA 31061
  (478) 445-4726
  bmassee@windstream.net
- Milledgeville PD
- Chief Dray Swicord
  125 W. McIntosh St.
  Milledgeville, GA 31061
  (478) 445-4893
  aswicord@milledgevillepd.com

Banks County

- Banks County SO
- Sheriff Billy C. Speed
  160 Windmill Farm Rd.
  Homer, GA 30547
  (706) 677-2248
  bcsorequests@live.com
- Baldwin PD
- Chief Daren *Bear* Osborn
  155 Willingham Ave.
  Baldwin, GA 30511
  (See also Habersham County)
  (706) 776-5256
  dosborn@cityofbaldwin.org

Barrow County

- Barrow County SO
- Sheriff Jud Smith
  30 No. Broad St.
  Winder, GA 30680
  (770) 307-3081
  jsmith@barrowsheriff.com
- Auburn PD
- Chief Paul Nadeau
  1369 4th Ave.
  PO Box 1059
  Auburn, GA 30011
  (770) 963-4002, ext. 213
  pnadeau@cityofauburn-ga.org
- Winder PD
- Chief Dennis Dorsey
  94 No. Broad St.
  Winder, GA 30680
  (678) 867-2156
  dennis.dorsey@cityofwinder.com

Bartow County

- Bartow County SO
- Sheriff Clark Millsap
  104 Zena Dr.
  Cartersville, GA 30120
  (770) 382-5050, ext. 96065
  sheriffmillsap@bartow.org

- Cartersville PD
- Chief Thomas N. Culpepper
  178 W. Main St.
  Cartersville, GA 30120
  (770) 382-2526
  cpd@cartersvillepolice.com
- Emerson PD
- Chief Stan Bradley
  700 Hwy 293
  Emerson, GA 30137
  (770) 386-6696
  sbradley@emersonpolice.com
- Euharlee PD
- Chief Terry J. Harget
  30 Burge's Mill Rd.
  Euharlee, GA 30145
  (770) 386-7339
  chiefharget@yahoo.com
- Kingston PD
- Chief Billy Pickett
  30 W. Main St.
  Kingston, GA 30145
  (770) 336-5507
  kngstnpd@bellsouth.net

Ben Hill County

- Ben Hill County SO
- Sheriff Bobby McLemore
  255 Appomattox Rd.
  Fitzgerald, GA 31750
  (229) 426-5161
  sheriffmclemore@mchsi.com
- Fitzgerald PD
- Chief Bill Smallwood
  255 Appomattox Rd.
  Fitzgerald, GA 31750
  (229) 426-5000
  police@fitzgeraldga.org

Berrien County

- Berrien County SO
- Sheriff Anthony Heath
  500 County Farm Rd.
  Nashville, GA 31639
  (229) 686-7071
  aheathsheriff@windstream.net
- Ray City PD
- Chief Ray Bamburg
  PO Box 128
  Ray City, GA 31645
  (229) 455-4921
  rbamburg@raycityga.gov

Bibb County

- Bibb County SO
- Sheriff David J. Davis
  668 Oglethorpe PO Box 930
  Macon, GA 31298
  (478) 746-9441
  ddavis@co.bibb.ga.us
- Macon PD
- Int. Chief Mike Caswell
  682 Cherry St. PO Box 247
  Macon, GA 31201
  (478) 751-7500
  mcaswell@mpd.macon.ga.us

Bleckley County

- Cochran PD
- Chief Key S. McGuire
  102 No. 2nd St.
  Cochran, GA 31014
  (912) 934-4282
  kmcguire@cochranpd.com

Brantley County

- Brantley County SD
- Sheriff Jack Whisenant
  95 John Wilson St. PO Box 251
  Nahunta, GA 31553
  (912) 462-6141
  info@brantleycountysheriffsoffice.com
- Hoboken PD
- Chief Jonathan McMillian
  PO Box 345
  Hoboken, GA 31542
  (912) 458-2575
  lhenderson1948@hotmail.com
- Nahunta PD
- Chief Gene Solana
  111 No. Main St. PO Box 156
  Nahunta, GA 31553
  (912) 462-5844
  nahuntapd@btconline.net

Brooks County

- Brooks County SO
- Sheriff Mike Dewey
  1 Screven St. PO Box 487
  Quitman, GA 31643
  (229) 263-7558
  sheriffdewey@brookssheriff.com
- Quitman PD
- Chief Wesley Ross
  100 No. Lee St.
  Quitman, GA 31643
  (229) 263-7556
  qpd_wross@quitmanwireless.net

Bryan County

- Bryan County SO
- Sheriff Clyde R. Smith
  95 Public Safety PO Box 960
  Pembroke, GA 31321
  (912) 653-3800
  debbieodom@bryan-county.org
- Pembroke PD
- Chief Mark Crowe
  59 W. Railroad St.
  Pembroke, GA 31321
  (912) 653-4409
  info@pembrokega.net
- Richmond Hill PD
- Chief Billy D. Reynolds
  PO Box 250
  Richmond Hill, GA 31324
  (912) 756-5645
  breynolds@richmondhill-ga.gov

Bulloch County

- Bulloch County SO
- Sheriff Lynn M. Anderson
  17257 US Hwy 301 No.
  Statesboro, GA 30458-7500
  (912) 764-8888
  tips@bullochsheriff.com
- Brooklet PD
- Chief Michael L. Buchan
  202 E. Lee St. PO Box 67
  Brooklet, GA 30415
  (912) 842-9911
  brookletpd104@hotmail.com
- Statesboro PD
- Dir. Wendell Turner
  22 W. Grady St.
  Statesboro, GA 30458
  (912) 764-9911
  statesboropd@statesboroga.gov

Burke County

- Burke County SO
- Sheriff Greg Coursey
  225 Hwy 24 So. PO Box 702
  Waynesboro, GA 30830
  (706) 554-2133
  burkesheriff1@bellsouth.net
- Waynesboro PD
- Chief Alfonzo Williams
  628 Myrick St.
  Waynesboro, GA 30830
  (706) 554- 8029
  awilliams@waynesboroga.com

Butts County

- Butts County SO
- Sheriff Gary Long
  835 Ernest Biles Dr.
  Jackson, GA 30233
  (770) 775-8216
  glong@buttscountysheriff.com
- Jackson PD
- Chief Mike Riley
  116 Byars St. PO Box 838
  Jackson, GA 30233
  (770) 775-7878
  jacksongapd@bellsouth.net

Calhoun County

- Calhoun County SO
- Sheriff Josh Hilton
  66 Court St. PO Box 211
  Morgan, GA 31766
  (229) 849-2555
  sheriffjhilton@windstream.net
- Arlington PD
- Chief Casey Taylor
  PO Box 126
  Arlington, GA 31713
  (229) 725-4211
  arlingtonpolicedept@yahoo.com

Camden County

- Camden County SO
- Sheriff Jim Proctor
  209 E. 4th St. PO Box 699
  Woodbine, GA 31569
  (912) 510-5100
  sheriff@co.camden.ga.us
- Kingsland PD
- Chief Darryl Griffis
  111 So. Seaboard St.
  Kingsland, GA 31548
  (912) 729-8254
  dgriffis@kingslandgeorgia.com
- St. Mary's PD
- Chief Tim Hatch
  563 Point Peter Rd.
  St. Mary's, GA 31558
  (912) 882-4488
  tim.hatch@stmarysga.gov

Candler County

- Candler County SO
- Sheriff Homer Bell
  E. Hiawatha PO Box 693
  Metter, GA 30439
  (912) 685-2568
  staff@candlersheriff.com
- Metter PD
- Chief Dennis Nelson
  10 W. Candler St.
  Metter, GA 30439
  (912) 685-5437
  dnelson@metterpd.com

Carroll County

- Carroll County SO
- Sheriff Terry Langley
  1000 Newnan Rd.
  Carrollton, GA 30116
  (770) 830-5888
  tlangley@carrollsheriff.com
- Bowdon PD
- Chief Mark Brock
  136 City Hall Ave.
  Bowdon, GA 30108
  (770) 258-3301
  mbrock@bowdonpolice.com
- Carrollton PD
- Chief Joel Richards
  115 W. Center St. PO Box 1949
  Carrollton, GA 30117
  (770) 834-4451
  jrichards@carrollton-ga.gov
- Mount Zion PD
- Int. Chief Bryan Simms
  4455 Mount Zion Rd.
  Mount Zion, GA 30150
  (770) 832-1622
  teresa@cityofmountzion.com
- Villa Rica PD
- Chief Michael P. Mansour
  101 Main St.
  Villa Rica, GA 30180
  (678) 785-1101
  mmansour@villarica.org

Catoosa County

- Catoosa County SO
- Sheriff Gary Sisk
  5842 Hwy 41 PO Box 909
  Ringgold, GA 30736
  (706) 935-2424
  gary.sisk@catoosa.com
- Fort Oglethorpe PD
- Chief Jeff Holcomb
  900 City Hall Dr.
  Fort Oglethorpe, GA 30742
  (706) 806-0536
  fopd@fortogov.com
- Ringgold PD
- Chief Dan Bilbrey
  150 Tennessee St.
  Ringgold, GA 30736
  (706) 935-3066
  ringgoldpd@catt.com

Charlton County

- Charlton County SO
- Sheriff Dobie Conner
  1548 3rd St.
  Folkston, GA 31537
  (912) 496-7321
  Sheriffconner@charltonsheriff.org
- Folkston PD
- Chief Wesley Green
  541 1st St.
  Folkston, GA 31537
  (912) 496-2563
  folkston1@windstream.net

Chatham County

- Chatham County SO
- Sheriff Al St. Lawrence
  1050 Carl Griffin PO Box 10026
  Savannah, GA 31405
  (912) 652-7632
  astlawrence@chathamcounty.org
- Bloomingdale PD
- Chief Roy L. Pike
  6 Adams Rd.
  Bloomingdale, GA 31302
  (912) 748-8302
  chief@bloomingdalepd.org
- Garden City PD
- Chief David L. Lyons
  100 Main St.
  Garden City, GA 31408
  (912) 966-7770
  dlyons@gardencity-ga.gov
- Port Wentworth PD
- Chief Matthew Libby
  305 So. Coastal Hwy
  Port Wentworth, GA 31407
  (912) 964-4360
  gjones@cityofportwentworth.com

- Savannah-Chatham PD
- Chief Willie Lovett
  201 Habersham St.
  Savannah, GA 31402
  (912) 651-6675
  wlovett@savannahga.gov
- Thunderbolt PD
- Int. Chief (*Capt.*) James Pierce
  415-F Bonaventure Rd.
  Thunderbolt, GA 31404
  (912) 354-3818
  watch.tbolt@gmail.com
- Tybee Island PD
- Chief: Robert Bryson
  PO Box 1340
  Tybee Island, GA 31328
  (912) 786-5635
  police@cityoftybee.org

Chattahoochee County

- Chattahoochee County SO
- Sheriff Glynn Cooper
  379 Broad St. PO Box 144
  Cusseta, GA 31805
  (706) 989-3644
  sheriff@ugoccc.us

Chattooga County

- Chattooga County SO
- Sheriff Mark Schrader
  35 W. Washington St.
  Summerville, GA 30747
  (706) 857-3411
  mschrader@chattoogasheriff.us
- Trion PD
- Chief Chad Spraggins
  1220 Pine St.
  Trion, GA 30753
  (706) 734- 3665
  lisa.richardson323@gmail.com

Cherokee County

- Cherokee County SO
- Sheriff Roger Garrison
  498 Chattin Dr.
  Canton, GA 30115
  (678) 493-4100
  rdgarrison@cherokeega.com
- Ball Ground PD
- Chief Dana E. Davis
  PO Box 285
  Ball Ground, GA 30107
  (770) 735-2123
  ddavis@cityofballground.com
- Canton PD
- Chief Robert Merchant
  221 E. Marietta St.
  Canton, GA 30114
  (770) 720-4883
  robert.merchant@canton-georgia.com
- Cherokee County Marshal
- Chief Marshal Chris Collett
  2782 Marietta Hwy, Ste. 100
  Canton, GA 30114
  (678) 493-6200
  ccollett@cherokeega.com
- Cherokee County School PD
- Chief Mark E. Kissel
  110 Academy St.
  Canton, GA 30114
  (770) 704-4346
  Mark.Kissel@cherokee.k12.ga.us

Clarke County

- Clarke County SO
- Sheriff Ira Edwards Jr.
  325 E. Washington St., Ste. 125
  Athens, GA 30601
  (706) 613-3250
  sheriff@athensclarkecounty.com
- Athens-Clarke County PD
- Chief Joseph H. Lumpkin Sr.
  3035 Lexington Rd.
  Athens, GA 30605
  (706) 613-3888, ext. 244
  Joseph.Lumpkin@athensclarkecounty.com

Clay County

- Clay County SO
- Sheriff Roger D. Shivers
  Washington St. PO Box 22
  Fort Gaines, GA 31751
  (229) 768-2505
  claycountysheriff@windstream.net

Clayton County

- Clayton County PD
- Chief Gregory Porter
  7911 No. McDonough St.
  Jonesboro, GA 30236
  (770) 477-3599
  greg.porter@co.clayton.ga.us
- Jonesboro PD
- Chief Franklin Allen
  170 So. Main St.
  Jonesboro, GA 30236
  (770) 478-7407
  fallen@jonesboroga.com

- Lake City PD
- Chief David Colwell
  5455 Jonesboro Rd.
  Lake City, GA 30260
  (404) 366-8035
  dcolwell@lakecityga.net
- Morrow PD
- Chief Christopher Leighty
  6311-A Murphy Dr.
  Morrow, GA 30260
  (770) 961-4006
  cleighty@cityofmorrow.com
- Riverdale PD
- Chief Samuel F. Patterson
  6690 Church St.
  Riverdale, GA 30274
  (770) 996-3382
  spatterson@riverdalega.gov
- State Farmers Market PD
- Chief Glenn Howard
  16 Forest Pkwy
  Forest Park, GA 30297
  (404) 675-6283
  glenn.howard@agr.georgia.gov

Clinch County

- Clinch County SO
- Sheriff Winston Peterson
  115 Court Sq.
  Homerville, GA 31634
  (912) 487-5316
  sissysuggs@yahoo.com
- Homerville PD
- Chief Mark Register
  20 So. College St. PO Box 535
  Homerville, GA 31634
  (912) 487-5305
  chief@cityofhomerville.com

Cobb County

- Acworth PD
- Chief Wayne Dennard
  4400 Acworth Industrial Blvd
  Acworth, GA 30101-5655
  (770) 974-1232
  wdennard@acworth.org
- Austell PD
- Chief Bob Starrett
  2721 Joe Jerkins Blvd
  Austell, GA 30106
  (770) 944-4331
  auspd@bellsouth.net
- Kennesaw PD
- Chief William Westenberger
  2539 J.O. Stephenson Ave.
  Kennesaw, GA 30144
  (770) 429-4535
  wwestenberger@kennesaw-ga.gov
- Marietta PD
- Chief Dan Flynn
  240 Lemon St.
  Marietta, GA 30060
  (770) 794-5300
  DFlynn@mariettaga.gov
- Powder Springs PD
- Chief William Charles Sewell
  1114 Richard D. Sailors Pkwy
  Powder Springs, GA 30073
  (770) 943-1616
  csewell@cityofpowdersprings.org
- Smyrna PD
- Chief David Lee
  2646 Atlanta Rd.
  Smyrna, GA 30080
  (678) 631-5099
  dlee@smyrnaga.gov

Coffee County

- Douglas PD
- Chief Gary Casteloes
  225 W. Bryan St.
  Douglas, GA 31533
  (912) 384-2222
  gcasteloes@cityofdouglas.com

Colquitt County

- Doerun PD
- Chief Shane Fulford
  226 W. Broad Ave.
  Doerun, GA 31744
  (229) 782-5441
  doerunpd@yahoo.com
- Moultrie PD
- Chief Frank Lang
  128 1st St. SW
  Moultrie, GA 31768
  (229) 985-3131
  frank.lang@moultriega.com

Columbia County

- Columbia County SO
- Sheriff Clay N. Whittle
  2273 County Camp
  Appling, GA 30802
  (706) 541-1043
  ccsoinfo@columbiacountyso.org

- Columbia County Office
- Chief Marshal Shaun A. Brooks
  640 Ronald Reagan
  Evans, GA 30809
  (706) 868-3319
  sbrooks@columbiacountyga.gov
- Grovetown DPS
- Dir. Gary Owens
  306 E. Robinson Ave.
  Grovetown, GA 30813
  (706) 863-1212
  publicsafety@cityofgrovetown.com

Cook County

- Cook County SO
- Sheriff Douglas Hanks
  1000 County Farm Rd.
  Adel, GA 31620
  (229) 896-7471
  n.bell@cookcogasheriff.com
- Adel PD
- Chief Chad Castleberry
  204 E. 3rd St.
  Adel, GA 31620
  (229) 896-3771
  ccastleberry@southlink.us

Coweta County

- Coweta County SO
- Sheriff Mike Yeager
  560 Greison Tr.
  Newnan, GA 30264
  (770) 253-1502
  CCSO@coweta.ga.us
- Newnan PD
- Chief Douglas L. *Buster* Meadows
  25 Jefferson St.
  Newnan, GA 30264
  (770) 254-2355, ext. 102
  rriggs@cityofnewnan.org

Crawford County

- Crawford County SO
- Sheriff Lewis S. Walker
  1009 Roberta PO Box 1009
  Knoxville, GA 31078
  (478) 836-3116
  lwalker@crawfordsheriff.net

Crisp County

- Crisp County SO
- Sheriff Donnie Haralson
  197 Hwy 300 So.
  Cordele, GA 31015
  (229) 276-2600
  dharalson@crispcounty.com
- Cordele PD
- Chief William Hooper
  501 No. 7th St.
  Cordele, GA 31015
  (229) 276-2921
  cordelepd@cityofcordele.com

Dade County

- Dade County SO
- Sheriff Ray Cross
  75 Case Ave. PO Box 920
  Trenton, GA 30752
  (706) 657-3233
  hdoyle@dadesheriff.com
- Trenton PD
- Chief Roger Castleberry
  12882 No. Main PO Box 518
  Trenton, GA 30752
  (706) 657-4167
  trentonpd@hotmail.com

Dawson County

- Dawson County SO
- Sheriff Billy Carlisle
  19 Tucker Ave.
  Dawsonville, GA 30534
  (706) 344-3535
  carlisle@dawsoncountysheriff.org

Decatur County

- Decatur County SO
- Sheriff Wiley Griffin
  912 Spring Creek Rd.
  Bainbridge, GA 31717
  (229) 248-3044
  wgriffin@decaturso.com

Dekalb County

- Dekalb County SO
- Sheriff Thomas E. Brown
  4415 Memorial Dr.
  Decatur, GA 30032
  (404) 298-8400
  tbrown@dekalbcountyga.gov

- Avondale Estates PD
- Chief Gary L. Broden
  21 No. Avondale Plaza
  Avondale Estates, GA 30002
  (404) 294-5410
  gbroden@avondaleestates.org
- Chamblee PD
- Chief R. Marc Johnson
  3518 Broad St.
  Chamblee, GA 30341
  (770) 986-5005
  chiefmj@chambleepd.com
- Clarkston PD
- Chief Christine Hudson
  3921 Church St.
  Clarkston, GA 30021
  (404) 292-9465
  chudson@clarkstonpd.com
- Decatur PD
- Chief Mike Booker
  420 W. Trinity Pl.
  Decatur, GA 30030
  (404) 373-6551
  Mike.Booker@decaturga.com
- Doraville PD
- Chief John King
  3750 Park Ave.
  Doraville, GA 30340
  (770) 455-1000
  info@doravillega.us
- Pine Lake PD
- Chief Sarai Y'hudah-Green
  459 Pine Dr.
  Pine Lake, GA 30072
  (404) 292-4250
  plcourt241@bellsouth.net
- Stone Mountain PD
- Chief Chancey H. Troutman
  922 Main St.
  Stone Mountain, GA 30083
  (770) 879-4980
  ctroutman@stonemountaincity.org

Dodge County

- Dodge County SO
- Sheriff Lynn Sheffield
  5401 Anson Ave.
  Eastman, GA 31023
  (478) 374-8131
  dodgecoso@yahoo.com

Dooly County

- Dooly County SO
- Sheriff Van Peavy, Jr.
  576 Pinehurst/Hawkinsville
  Vienna, GA 31092
  (229) 645-0920
  lmooney602@Doolycountysheriff.com

Dougherty County

- Dougherty County SO
- Sheriff Kevin Sproul
  225 Pine Ave.
  Albany, GA 31702
  (229) 431-3259
  ksproul@dougherty.ga.us
- Dougherty County PD
- Chief Donald M. Cheek
  2106 Habersham Rd.
  Albany, GA 31701
  (229) 430-6600
  dcp@dougherty.ga.us

Douglas County

- Douglas County SO
- Sheriff Phil D. Miller
  6856 Broad St.
  Douglasville, GA 30134
  (770) 949-5656
  pmiller@sheriff.douglas.ga.us
- Douglasville PD
- Chief Chris Womack
  2083 Fairburn Rd.
  Douglasville, GA 30134
  (678) 293-1813
  womackc@douglasvillega.gov

Early County

- Early County SO
- Sheriff William C. Price
  111 Court Sq. PO Box 939
  Blakely, GA 31723
  (229) 723-3577
  w.price@earlycountysheriff.com

Echols County

- Echols County SO
- Sheriff Randy Courson
  PO Box 189
  Statenville, GA 31648
  (229) 559-5603
  april.maine7@gmail.com

Effingham County

- Effingham County SO
- Sheriff Jimmy McDuffie
  130 1st St. PO Box 1015
  Springfield, GA 31329
  (912) 754-3449
  jmcduffie@effinghamcounty.org
- Rincon PD
- Chief Phillip Scholl
  107 W. 17th
  Rincon, GA 31326
  (912) 826-5200
  pscholl@cityofrincon.com
- Springfield PD
- Chief Paul Winn
  130 So. Laurel St.
  Springfield, GA 31329
  (912) 754-3061
  springfieldpd@cityofspringfield.com

Elbert County

- Elbert County SO
- Sheriff Melvin T. Andrews
  47 Forest Ave.
  Elberton, GA 30635
  (706) 283-2421
  ecso@elbertco.net
- Elberton PD
- Chief Mark Welsh
  209 Elbert S-t.
  Elberton, GA 30635
  (706) 283-1211
  mwelsh@cityofelberton.net

Emanuel County

- Swainsboro PD
- Chief Randy Ellison
  212 No. Main St.
  Swainsboro, GA 30401
  (478) 237-8967
  police@cityofswainsboro.org
- Twin City PD
- Chief Johnny Lane
  2790 Hwy 80 E. PO Box 980
  Twin City, GA 30471
  (478) 763-2695
  chieftcpd@pineland.net

Evans County

- Claxton PD
- Chief Edward Oglesbee
  204 W. Railroad St.
  Claxton, GA 30417
  (912) 739-2121
  cpd401@att.net

Fannin County

- Fannin County SO
- Sheriff Dane Kirby
  645 W. 1st St.
  Blue Ridge, GA 30513
  (706) 632-2044
  dkirby@fannincountyga.org
- McCaysville PD
- Chief W.L. Panter
  163 Blue Ridge PO Box 6
  McCaysville, GA 30555
  (706) 492-4636
  mcaysvillepd@etcmail.com

Fayette County

- Fayette County SO
- Sheriff Barry H. Babb
  155 Johnson Ave.
  Fayetteville, GA 30214
  (770) 461-6353
  bbabb@fayettecountyga.gov
- Fayetteville PD
- Chief Steven D. Heaton
  760 Jimmy Mayfield Blvd
  Fayetteville, GA 30215
  (770) 461-4441
  sheaton@fayetteville-ga.gov
- Peachtree City PD
- Chief H.C. *Skip* Clark II
  350 So. Hwy 74
  Peachtree City, GA 30269
  (770) 487-8866
  policepublicinfo@peachtree-city.org

Floyd County

- Floyd County SO
- Sheriff Tim Burkhalter
  3 Government Plaza
  Rome, GA 30162
  (706) 314-0710
  floydsheriff@comcast.net

- Rome PD
- Chief Elaine Snow
  #5 Government Plaza, Ste 300
  Rome, GA 30161
  (706) 238-5111
  snow@romepolice.com

Forsyth County

- Forsyth County SO
- Sheriff Duane Piper
  202 Veterans Memorial Blvd
  Cumming, GA 30040
  (770) 781-3077
  dkpiper@forsythco.com
- Cumming PD
- Chief Casey Tatum
  301 Veteran's Memorial Blvd
  Cumming, GA 30040
  (770) 781-2000
  police@cummingpd.net

Franklin County

- Franklin County SO
- Sheriff Stevie D. Thomas
  1 James Little St. PO Box 310
  Carnesville, GA 30521
  (706) 384-2525
  614@franklincosheriff.net
- Canon PD
- Chief John Thomas
  5071 Hwy 17 PO Box 159
  Canon, GA 30520
  (706) 245-8155
  cityofcanon@bellsouth.net
- Lavonia PD
- Chief Bruce Carlisle
  851 Grogan St. PO Box 564
  Lavonia, GA 30553
  (706) 356-4848
  Carlisle@lavoniapd.com
- Royston PD
- Chief Donnie Bolemon
  634 Franklin Springs St.
  Royston, GA 30662
  (706) 245-7232
  policechief@cityofroyston.com

Fulton County

- Fulton County SD
- Sheriff Theodore Jackson
  185 Central Ave SW, 9th Fl.
  Atlanta, GA 30303
  (404) 612-5100
  info@fultonsheriff.net
- Atlanta PD
- Chief George N. Turner
  226 Peachtree St. SW
  Atlanta, GA 30303
  (404) 546-7290
  gturner@atlanta.gov
- College Park PD
- Chief Ron Fears
  3717 College St.
  College Park, GA 30337
  (404) 766-3618
  rfears@collegeparkga.com
- East Point PD
- Chief Woodrow Blue
  2727 East Point St.
  East Point, GA 30344
  (404) 765-1101
  wblue@eastpointcity.org
- Fairburn PD
- Chief J.A. McCarthy
  191 W. Broad St.
  Fairburn, GA 30213
  (770) 964-1441
  chiefmccarthy@fairburn.com
- Fulton County PD
- Chief Cassandra A. Jones
  5440 Fulton Industrial Blvd SW
  Atlanta, GA 30303
  (404) 613-5711
  cjones@fultonpolice.org
- Hapeville PD
- Chief Richard Glasovek
  700 Doug Davis Dr.
  Hapeville, GA 30354
  (404) 768-7171
  rglavosek@hapeville.org
- Palmetto PD
- Chief B.L. Fronebarger
  401 Carlton Rd.
  PO Box 190
  Palmetto, GA 30268
  (770) 463-9068
  bfronebarger@palmettopolice.org
- Roswell PD
- Chief Rusty Grant
  39 Hill St.
  Roswell, GA 30075
  (770) 640-4100
  rgrant@roswellgov.com

- Union City PD
- Chief Charles Odom
  5060 Union St.
  Union City, GA 30291
  (770) 964-1333
  contactuc@unioncityga.org

Gilmer County

- Gilmer County SO
- Sheriff Stacy L. Nicholson
  1 Broad St., Ste #103
  Ellijay, GA 30540
  (706) 635-4162
  snicholson@gilmersheriff.com
- East Ellijay PD
- Chief Edward D. Lacey III
  197 No. Main St. PO Box 599
  East Ellijay, GA 30539
  (706) 635-7430, ext. 101
  edlacey@ellijay.com

Glascock County

- Glascock County SO
- Sheriff Dean Couch
  74 E. Main St. PO Box 7
  Gibson, GA 30810
  (706) 598-2881
  glso@bellsouth.net

Glynn County

- Glynn County SO
- Sheriff E. Neal Jump
  1812 Newcastle PO Box 793
  Brunswick, GA 31520
  (912) 554-7600
  sheriff@glynncounty-ga.gov
- Brunswick PD
- Chief Tobe C. Green
  206 Mansfield St.
  Brunswick, GA 31520
  (912) 267-5559
  info@brunswickpolice.org
- Glynn County PD
- Chief Matt Doering
  157 Public Safety Blvd
  Brunswick, GA 31525
  (912) 554-7800
  gcpdchief@glynncounty-ga.gov

Gordon County

- Gordon County SO
- Sheriff Mitch Ralston
  2700 US 41 NW
  Calhoun, GA 30701
  (706) 629-1244
  mralston@gordoncounty.org
- Calhoun PD
- Chief Garry Moss
  200 No. Wall St.
  Calhoun, GA 30701
  (706) 629-1234
  sjolley@calnet-ga.net

Grady County

- Grady County SO
- Sheriff Harry C. Young
  250 No. Broad PO Box 690
  Cairo, GA 39828
  (229) 377-5200
  sheriff@gradycountyga.gov
- Cairo PD
- Chief Keith P. Sandefur
  4 So. Broad St.
  Cairo, GA 39828
  (229) 378-3096
  ksandefur@cairopd.com

Greene County

- Greene County SO
- Sheriff Chris Houston
  1201 Kevin Roberts Way
  Greensboro, GA 30642
  (706) 453-3351, ext. 331
  chouston@greeneso.org
- Greensboro PD
- Chief Ossie Mapp
  212 No. Main St.
  Greensboro, GA 30642
  (706) 453-7555
  chiefom@greensboroga.gov
- Union Point PD
- Chief Gregory Perkins, Sr.
  107 Scott St.
  Union Point, GA 30669
  (706) 486-4102
  gperkins@unionpointga.org

Gwinnett County

- Gwinnett County SO
- Sheriff R.L. *Butch* Conway
  2900 University Pkwy
  Lawrenceville, GA 30043
  (770) 822-3140
  Butch.Conway@gwinnettcounty.com
- Duluth PD
- Chief R.D. Belcher
  3276 Buford Hwy
  Duluth, GA 30096
  (770) 476-4151
  chief@duluth.com
- Gwinnett County PD
- Chief Charles M. Walters
  770 Hi Hope Rd.
  Lawrenceville, GA 30043
  (770) 513-5000
  Charles.Walters@gwinnettcounty.com
- Lawrenceville PD
- Chief L. *Randy* Johnson
  300 Jackson St. PO Box 2200
  Lawrenceville, GA 30045
  (770) 963-2443
  police@lawrencevillega.org
- Lilburn PD
- Chief Bruce Hedley
  76 Main St.
  Lilburn, GA 30247
  (770) 921-2211
  bhedley@cityoflilburn.com
- Loganville PD
- Chief Mike McHugh
  605 Tom Brewer Rd.
  Loganville, GA 30052
  (770) 466-8087
  mchu601@bellsouth.net
- Norcross PD
- Chief Warren Summers
  65 Lawrenceville St.
  Norcross, GA 30071
  (770) 448-2111
  Warren.Summers@norcrosspd.com
- Snellville PD
- Chief Roy Whitehead
  2315 Wisteria Dr.
  Snellville, GA 30039
  (770) 985-3555
  rwhitehead@snellville.org
- Suwanee PD
- Chief Mike Jones
  373 Buford Hwy
  Suwanee, GA 30024
  (770) 945-8995
  mjones@suwanee.com

Habersham County

- Habersham County SO
- Sheriff Joey Terrell
  1000 Detention Dr.
  Clarkesville, GA 30523
  (706) 754-6666
  jterrell@habershamga.com
- Baldwin PD
- Chief Daren *Bear* Osborn
  155 Willingham Ave.
  Baldwin, GA 30511
  (See also Banks County)
  (706) 776-5256
  dosborn@cityofbaldwin.org
- Clarkesville PD
- Chief Brad Barrett
  210 E. Water St. PO Box 21
  Clarkesville, GA 30523
  (706) 754-5390
  bbarrett@clarkesvillega.com
- Cornelia PD
- Chief Rick Darby
  181 Larkin St. PO Box 785
  Cornelia, GA 30531
  (706) 778-4314
  chiefrdarby@alltel.net

Hall County

- Hall County SO
- Sheriff Gerald Couch
  610 Main St. SW
  Gainesville, GA 30501
  (770) 531-6900
  sheriff@hallcounty.org
- Gainesville PD
- Chief Brian P. Kelly
  701 Queen City Pkwy SW
  Gainesville, GA 30501
  (770) 534-5252
  police@gainesville.org
- Oakwood PD
- Chief Randall K. *Randy* Moon
  4009 Railroad St.
  Oakwood, GA 30566
  (770) 534-2364, ext. 22
  rmoon@CityOfOakwood.net

Hancock County

- Hancock County SO
- Sheriff Tomlyn *Terrell* Primus
  67 Spring St.
  Sparta, GA 31087
  (706) 444-6471
  sheriffprimas@aol.com
- Sparta PD
- Chief Ronnie Evans
  12688 Broad St.
  Sparta, GA 31087
  (706) 444-5777
  spartapd@bellsouth.net

Haralson County

- Haralson County SO
- Sheriff Eddie Mixon
  224 Holly St. PO Box 309
  Buchanan, GA 30113
  (770) 646-2011
  admin@sheriffhcga.com
- Bremen PD
- Chief Keith Pesnell
  516-A Tallapoosa St.
  Bremen, GA 30110
  (770) 537-4441
  kpesnell@bremenga.gov
- Buchanan PD
- Chief Tracy Lambert
  PO Box 6
  Buchanan, GA 30113
  (770) 646-5246
  tlambert@buchananga.com
- Tallapoosa PD
- Chief Scott Worthy
  15 E. Alabama St.
  Tallapoosa, GA 30176
  (770) 574-7211
  sworthy@tallapoosaga.gov

Harris County

- Harris County SO
- Sheriff Mike Jolley
  9825 Hwy 116 PO Box 286
  Hamilton, GA 31811
  (706) 628-4211
  d.frantum@harriscountysheriff.org
- Shiloh PD
- Chief Ron Arndt
  PO Box 25
  Shiloh, GA 31826
  (706) 846-3814
  cityofshiloh@ymail.com
- Waverly Hall PD
- Chief Archie Hand
  9108 GA Hwy 85 PO Box 357
  Waverly Hall, GA 31831
  (706) 582-2345
  whpd31@aol.com
- West Point PD
- Chief Jeffery *J.K.* Cato
  730 1st Ave.
  (See also Troup County)
  West Point, GA 31833
  (706) 645-3525
  jcato@cityofwestpointga.com

Hart County

- Hart County SO
- Sheriff Mike Cleveland
  890 Vickery St. PO Box 886
  Hartwell, GA 30643
  (706) 376-3114
  sheriff@hartcom.net

Heard County

- Heard County SO
- Sheriff Ross Henry
  11820 Hwy 100 PO Box 339
  Franklin, GA 30217
  (706) 675-3329
  rhenry@heardcountyga.com
- Franklin PD
- Chief Kevin Hannah
  118 Davis St.
  Franklin, GA 30217
  (706) 675-6624
  chiefhannah@franklingapolice.com

Henry County

- Henry County SO
- Sheriff Keith McBrayer
  120 Henry Pkwy
  McDonough, GA 30253
  (770) 288-7105
  sheriffsoffice@co.henry.ga.us
- Hampton PD
- Chief Rad Porter
  20 E. Main St. So.
  Hampton, GA 30228
  (770) 946-4513
  rporter@cityofhampton-ga.gov

- Henry County PD
- Chief Keith Nichols
  108 So. Zack Hinton Pkwy
  McDonough, GA 30253
  (770) 288-8200
  knichols@co.henry.ga.us

Houston County

- Houston County SD
- Sheriff Cullen Talton
  202 Carl Vinson Pkwy
  Warner Robins, GA 31088
  (478) 542-2125
  rwright@houstoncountyga.org
- Centerville PD
- Chief Sidney B. Andrews, Jr.
  500 No. Houston Lake Blvd
  Centerville, GA 31028
  (478) 953-4222
  chief@centervillepd.org
- Perry PD
- Chief George A. Potter
  1207 Washington PO Box 2030
  Perry, GA 31069
  (478) 988-2804
  chief.potter@perry-ga.gov
- Warner Robins PD
- Chief Brett Evans
  202 No. Davis Dr. PMB 718
  Warner Robins, GA 31099
  (478) 929-1170
  info@wrpolice.org

Irwin County

- Ocilla PD
- Chief Billy J. Hancock
  400 So. Irwin Ave.
  Ocilla, GA 31774
  (912) 468-7494
  ocillapd@alltel.net

Jackson County

- Jackson County SO
- Sheriff Janis G. Mangum
  555 General Jackson Dr.
  Jefferson, GA 30549
  (706) 367-8718
  jmangum@jacksoncountygov.com
- Braselton PD
- Chief Terry Esco
  4982 Hwy 53
  Braselton, GA 30517
  (706) 658-2852
  police@braselton.net
- Jefferson PD
- Chief Joseph *Joe* Wirthman
  140 Mahaffey St.
  Jefferson, GA 30549
  (706) 367-5231
  jwirthman@cityofjeffersonga.com
- Pendergrass PD
- Chief Bob Russell
  11 Smith Bridges PO Box 95
  Pendergrass, GA 30567
  (706) 693-2386
  cityhall@cityofpendergrass.com

Jasper County

- Jasper County SO
- Sheriff Donnie Pope
  1551 Hwy 212 W. PO Box 311
  Monticello, GA 31064
  (706) 468-4912
  jkirksey@jaspercosheriff.com
- Monticello PD
- Chief Bobby Norris
  222 Funderburg PO Box 269
  Monticello, GA 31064
  (706) 468-6911
  ycarter42@bellsouth.net

Jeff Davis County

- Jeff Davis County SO
- Sheriff Preston W. Bohannon
  100 Jeff Davis St. PO Box 237
  Hazelhurst, GA 31539
  (912) 375-6600
  jdso1@yahoo.com
- Hazelhurst PD
- Chief Stephen C. Land
  106 So. Williams St.
  Hazelhurst, GA 31539
  (912) 375-6688
  sland@hazelhurstpolice.com

Jefferson County

- Louisville PD
- Chief Jimmy Miller
  1011 Peachtree PO Box 527
  Louisville, GA 30434
  (478) 625-8897
  lpd101@bellsouth.net
- Wadley PD
- Chief Wesley Lewis
  22 No. Main St.
  Wadley, GA 30477
  (478) 252-5214
  wadleydept@bellsouth.net

- Wrens PD
- Chief Garry McCord
  401 Broad St. NE
  Wrens, GA 30833
  (706) 547-3232
  mccordwrens@hotmail.com

Jenkins County

- Jenkins County SO
- Sheriff Robert Oglesby
  112 So. Masonic Ave.
  Millen, GA 30442
  (478) 982-4211
  acrosson@csrardc.org
- Millen Police & Fire Services
- Chief Dwayne Herrington
  919 College Ave.
  Millen, GA 30442
  (478) 982-2750
  dherrington@csrardc.org

Lamar County

- Lamar County SO
- Sheriff Brad White
  121 Roberta Dr.
  Barnesville, GA 30204
  (770) 358-5159
  bwhite@lamarcountysheriff.com
- Barnesville PD
- Chief Charles *Chuck* Keadle
  100 Mill St.
  Barnesville, GA 30204
  (770) 358-1234
  chuck.keadle@cityofbarnesville.com

Lanier County

- Lanier County SO
- Sheriff Nick Norton
  63 W. Church St.
  Lakeland, GA 31635
  (229) 482-3545
  sheriffnorton@lanierso.com

Laurens County

- Laurens County SO
- Sheriff W.A. *Bill* Harrell
  511 Southern Pines Rd.
  Dublin, GA 31021
  (478) 272-1522
  lcsheriffwbmas@live.com
- Dublin PD
- Chief Wayne Cain
  346 So. Jefferson St.
  Dublin, GA 31021
  (478) 277-5023
  cainw@dlcga.com

Lee County

- Lee County SD
- Sheriff Reggie Rachals
  119 Pinewood PO Box 610
  Leesburg, GA 31763
  (229) 759-6012
  rrachals@lee.ga.us
- Leesburg PD
- Chief Charles Moore
  107 Walnut Ave No. PO Box 890
  Leesburg, GA 31763
  (229) 759-6464
  chrlmoo@aol.com

Liberty County

- Liberty County SO
- Sheriff Steve C. Sikes
  201 So. Main St., Ste. 1300
  Hinesville, GA 31313
  (912) 876-2131
  sheriff@libertycountyga.com
- Hinesville PD
- Chief George Stagmeier
  123 W. ML King Jr. Dr.
  Hinesville, GA 31313
  (912) 368-8211
  crprev@cityofhinesville.org

Lincoln County

- Lincoln County SO
- Sheriff Bruce Beggs
  145 School St. PO Box 970
  Lincolnton, GA 30817
  (706) 359-4118
  sheriff@lincolncountyga.com
- Lincolnton PD
- Chief Jim Justice
  148 Ward St.
  Lincolnton, GA 30817
  (706) 359-4121
  JJustice@cityoflincolnton.com

Long County

- Long County SO
- Sheriff Craig Nobles
  6 E. Academy St. PO Box 368
  Ludowici, GA 31316
  (912) 545-2118
  craignobles@longcountyso.org
- Ludowici PD
- Chief Richard Robertson
  214 So. McDonald PO Box 800
  Ludowici, GA 31316
  (912) 545-2222
  email@ludowicipd.com

Lowndes County

- Lowndes County SO
- Sheriff Chris Prine
  PO Box 667
  Valdosta, GA 31603
  (229) 671-2900
  cprine@lowndescounty.com
- Hahira PD
- Chief Terry Davis
  102 So. Church St.
  Hahira, GA 31632
  (229) 245-5270
  hpd@hahira.ga.us
- Valdosta PD
- Chief Brian K. Childress
  500 No. Toombs St.
  Valdosta, GA 31603
  (229) 242-2606
  bchildress@valdostacity.com

Lumpkin County

- Lumpkin County SO
- Sheriff Stacy Jarrard
  385 E. Main St.
  Dahlonega, GA 30533
  (706) 864-0414
  stacy.jarrard@lumpkincounty.gov

Macon County

- Macon County SO
- Sheriff Charles M. Cannon
  117 Crescent St. PO Box 345
  Oglethorpe, GA 31068
  (478) 472-6447
  mcso1@windstream.net
- Montezuma PD
- Chief Eric Finch
  408 So. Dooly St.
  Montezuma, GA 31063
  (478) 472-6260
  efinch1054@aol.com

Madison County

- Madison County SO
- Sheriff Kip C. Thomas
  1436 Hwy 98 W. PO Box 65
  Danielsville, GA 30633
  (706) 795-6202
  sheriff@madisonco.us
- Comer PD
- Chief Dennis Bell
  Hwy 72 E.
  Comer, GA 30629
  (706) 783-4552
  chiefdbell@gmail.com

Marion County

- Marion County SO
- Sheriff Derrell Neal
  Hwy 41 No. PO Box 32
  Buena Vista, GA 31803
  (229) 649-3841
  marionsheriff@windstream.net

McDuffie County

- McDuffie County SO
- Sheriff Logan Marshall
  751 Public Safety PO Box 360
  Thomson, GA 30824
  (706) 595-2040
  rwilliamson@thomson-mcduffie.net
- Thomson PD
- Chief John Seay
  W. Hall St.
  Thomson, GA 30824
  (706) 595-2166
  john.seay@thomson-mcduffie.net

McIntosh County

- Darien PD
- Chief Donnie Howard
  206 North Way PO Box 452
  Darien, GA 31305
  (912) 437-6644
  darienpd101@darientel.net

Meriwether County

- Meriwether County SO
- Sheriff Chuck Smith
  17400 Roosevelt PO Box 476
  Greenville, GA 30222
  (706) 672-4489
  info@meriwethercountysheriff.org

- Greenville PD
- Chief Wayne Frazier
  202 No. Depot St.
  Greenville, GA 30222
  (706) 672-4211
  frzrlwyn@yahoo.com
- Manchester PD
- Chief Gray Couch
  120 2nd St. PO Box 366
  Manchester, GA 31816
  (706) 846-3155
  rgcouch@alltel.net
- Woodbury PD
- Chief Reed A. Merinuk
  200 No. Broad St.
  Woodbury, GA 30293
  (706) 845-0065
  rmerinuk@woodburypd.com

Miller County

- Colquitt PD
- Chief Scott Worsley
  154 West St.
  Colquitt, GA 31737
  (229) 758-1008
  chief.scott@cityofcolquitt.com

Mitchell County

- Mitchell County SO
- Sheriff W.E. Bozeman
  4815 Hwy 37 PO Box 28
  Camilla, GA 31730
  (229) 336-2030
  webozeman@mitchellso.com
- Camilla PD
- Chief Ray Folsom
  80 W. Broad St.
  Camilla, GA 31730
  (229) 336- 2201
  answers@cns-internet.com
- Pelham PD
- Chief Nealie McCormick
  159 Mathewson Ave.
  Pelham, GA 31779
  (229) 294-6000
  pelhampd@gmail.com

Monroe County

- Monroe County SO
- Sheriff John Cary Bittick
  145 L. Cary Bittick PO Box 276
  Forsyth, GA 31029
  (478) 994-7048
  info@monroecosheriffga.us
- Forsyth PD
- Chief Keith Corley
  200 So. Kimbell St.
  Forsyth, GA 31029
  (478) 994-6022
  kcorley@cityofforsyth.com

Montgomery County

- Mount Vernon PD
- Chief Calvin Burns
  435 So. Railroad PO Box 237
  Mount Vernon, GA 30445
  (912) 583-2323
  info@gmanet.com

Morgan County

- Morgan County SO
- Sheriff Robert S. Markley
  1380 Monticello Rd.
  Madison, GA 30650
  (706) 342-1507
  rmarkley@morganga.org
- Madison PD
- Chief William *Bill* Ashburn
  118 No. Main St.
  Madison, GA 30650
  (706) 342-1275
  BAshburn@madisonga.com

Murray County

- Murray County SD
- Sheriff Gary Langford
  810½ G.I. Maddox Pkwy
  Chatsworth, GA 30705
  (706) 695-4592
  mcso@windstream.net
- Chatsworth PD
- Chief Terry P. Martin
  501 No. 3rd Ave. PO Box 516
  Chatsworth, GA 30705
  (706) 695-9667
  chatsworthpd@windstream.net
- Eton PD
- Chief Brent Hooper
  3475 Hwy 411 No.
  Eton, GA 30724
  (706) 695-2652
  chiefhooper@windstream.net

Muscogee County

- Muscogee County SO
- Sheriff John T. Darr
  100 10th St., 4th Fl. PO Box 1338
  Columbus, GA 31902
  (706) 653-4225
  muscosheriff@columbusga.org
- Columbus PD
- Chief Ricky Boren
  510 10th St. PO Box 1866
  Columbus, GA 31902
  (706) 653-3100
  columbuspolice@columbusga.org

Newton County

- Newton County SO
- Sheriff Ezell Brown
  15151 Alcovy-Jersey Rd.
  Covington, GA 30014
  (678) 625-1400
  ebrown@newtonsheriffga.org
- Covington PD
- Chief Stacey L. Cotton
  1143 Oak St. SE
  Covington, GA 30014
  (770) 786-4425
  stacey.cotton@covingtonpolice.com
- Oxford PD
- Chief Dave Harvey
  810 Whatcoat St.
  Oxford, GA 30054
  (770) 788-1390
  dharvey@oxfordgeorgia.org
- Porterdale PD
- Chief Geoff Jacobs
  2602 Main St. PO Box 667
  Porterdale, GA 30070
  (770) 786-2226
  policechief@cityofporterdale.com

Oconee County

- Oconee County SO
- Sheriff Scott R. Berry
  1140 Experiment Station
  Watkinsville, GA 30677
  (706) 769-3945
  sberry@oconeesheriff.org

Oglethorpe County

- Oglethorpe County SO
- Sheriff Mike Smith
  115 Buddy Faust PO Box 17
  Crawford, GA 30630
  (706) 743-8101
  sheriffmikesmith@windstream.net

Paulding County

- Paulding County SO
- Sheriff Gary Gulledge
  247 Industrial Way No.
  Dallas, GA 30132
  (770) 443-3010
  ggulledge@paulding.gov

Peach County

- Peach County SO
- Sheriff Terry W. Deese
  1007 Spruce St. Ext.
  Fort Valley, GA 31030
  (478) 825-826
  Sheriff-deese@peachcounty.net
- Byron PD
- Chief Wesley H. Cannon
  401 Main St.
  Byron, GA 31008
  (478) 956-2880
  wcannon@byronga.com
- Fort Valley PD
- Dir. Lawrence Z. Spurgeon
  200 W. Church PO Box 956
  Fort Valley, GA 31030
  (478) 825-3383
  info@fortvalleypolice.com

Pickens County

- Pickens County SO
- Sheriff Donnie Craig
  2985 Camp Rd
  Jasper, GA 30143
  (706) 253-8900
  dcraig@pickensgasheriff.com
- Jasper PD
- Chief Greg Lovell
  200 Burnt Mountain Rd.
  Jasper, GA 30143
  (706) 253-9110
  glovell@jasper-ga.us
- Nelson PD
- Chief Heath Mitchell
  1985 Kennesaw Ave.
  Nelson, GA 30151
  (See Cherokee County)
  (770) 735-2211
  heath.mitchell@nelsonpolice.com

Pierce County

- Pierce County SO
- Sheriff Ramsey Bennett
  300 Industrial Blvd
  Blackshear, GA 31516
  (912) 449-2011
  rbennett@piercecountyga.org
- Blackshear PD
- Chief Chris Wright
  219 Nichols St.
  Blackshear, GA 31516
  (912) 449-7011
  bpd_clerks@yahoo.com

Pike County

- Pike County SD
- Sheriff Jimmy Thomas
  89 Jackson St. PO Box 236
  Zebulon, GA 30295
  (770) 567-8431
  sheriff_pikeco@bellsouth.net
- Zebulon PD
- Chief Chuck Ledbetter
  7818 Hwy 19 So. PO Box 385
  Zebulon, GA 30295
  (770) 567-8441
  gcledbetter@yahoo.com

Polk County

- Polk County SO
- Sheriff Johnny Moats
  1676 Rockmart Hwy
  Cedartown, GA 30125
  (770) 749-2900
  polkso@bellsouth.net
- Aragon PD
- Chief Wayne Sanders
  2814 E. Rome Hwy
  Aragon, GA 30104
  (770) 684-6563, ext. 103
  aragon-info@cityofaragon.com
- Cedartown PD
- Chief Henry King
  118 No. Philpot PO Box 389
  Cedartown, GA 30125
  (770) 748-4123
  hking@cedartowngeorgia.gov
- Polk County PD
- Chief Kenny Dodd
  73 Clines Ingrams Jackson Rd.
  Cedartown, GA 30125
  (770) 748-7331
  chiefdodd@polkga.org
- Rockmart PD
- Chief Keith Sorrells
  PO Box 231
  Rockmart, GA 30153
  (770) 684-6558
  ksorrells@rockmart-ga.gov

Pulaski County

- Pulaski County SO
- Sheriff William C. *Billy* Cape
  350 Commerce PO Box 330
  Hawkinsville, GA 31036
  (478) 783-1521
  sheriff@pulaskisheriff.org

Putnam County

- Putnam County SO
- Sheriff Howard R. Sills
  111 Ridley Dr. PO Box 3637
  Eatonton, GA 31024
  (706) 485-8557
  sheriffsills@putnamcountysheriff.org
- Eatonton PD
- Chief Kent Lawrence
  214 W. Marion St.
  Eatonton, GA 31024
  (706) 485-3551
  klawrence@eatontonga.us

Quitman County

- Quitman County SO
- Sheriff Billy Joe Foster
  121 Main St. PO Box 338
  Georgetown, GA 31754
  (229) 334-3726
  bfoster@quitmansheriff.com

Rabun County

- Rabun County SO
- Sheriff Frank W. Andrews
  25 Courthouse Sq., Ste. 301
  Clayton, GA 30525
  (706) 782-3612
  rcso@rabunsheriff.org
- Dillard PD
- Chief Shane Watts
  892 Franklin St.
  Dillard, GA 30537
  (706) 746-5891
  dillardChiefofpolice@windstream.net

- Sky Valley PD
- Chief Scott Dills
  23 Sky Valley Way #93
  Sky Valley, GA 30537
  (706) 746-5584
  skyvalleypatrol@yahoo.com

Randolph County

- Randolph County SO
- Sheriff Gary Yochum, Sr.
  156 Peachtree St. PO Box 506
  Cuthbert, GA 31740
  (912) 732-2525
  sheriff@randolphgasheriff.org

Richmond County

- Richmond County SO
- Sheriff Richard Roundtree
  Law Enforcement Center
  401 Walton Way
  Augusta, GA 30901
  (706) 821-1000
  sgay@augustaga.gov
- Hephzibah PD
- Chief Dwayne Flowers
  2530 Hwy 88 PO Box 30815
  (706) 592-4423
  chief.flowers@gmail.com
- Richmond County Office
- Marshal Steve Smith
  530 Greene St., Rm. 704
  Augusta, GA 30911
  (706) 821-2368
  ssmith@augustaga.gov

Rockdale County

- Rockdale County SO
- Sheriff Eric Levett
  911 Chambers Dr.
  Conyers, GA 30207
  (770) 278-8000
  eric.levett@rockdalecounty.org
- Conyers PD
- Chief Gene Wilson
  1194 Scott St SE
  Conyers, GA 30012
  (770) 483-6600
  police@conyersga.com

Schley County

- Schley County SO
- Sheriff Shane Tondee
  101 No. Pecan St. PO Box 809
  Ellaville, GA 31806
  (229) 937-2101
  scso@windstream.net
- Ellaville PD
- Chief Robby Lightner
  101 No. Pecan St.
  Ellaville, GA 31806
  (229) 937-2104
  rlightnercoe@windstream.net

Screven County

- Screven County SO
- Sheriff Mike Kile
  202 Rocky Ford Rd.
  Sylvania, GA 30467
  (912) 564-2013
  screvensos2@yahoo.com

Seminole County

- Seminole County SO
- Sheriff Heath Elliott
  208 Court St.
  Donalsonville, GA 39845
  (229) 524-5115
  helliott@seminoleso.com
- Donalsonville PD
- Chief Jimmy Holt
  204 So. Woolfork Ave.
  Donalsonville, GA 39845
  (229) 524-2175
  jholt@cityofdonalsonvillega.com

Spalding County

- Spalding County SO
- Sheriff Wendell Beam
  401 Justice Blvd
  Griffin, GA 30223
  (770) 467-4282
  info@spaldingcounty.com
- Griffin PD
- Chief C. Franklin Strickland
  868 W. Poplar St.
  Griffin, GA 30224
  (770) 229-6450
  fstrickland@cityofgriffin.com

Stephens County

- Stephens County SO
- Sheriff Randy Shirley
  70 No. Alexander St., Ste. 205
  Toccoa, GA 30577
  (706) 886-2525
  rshirley@stephenssheriff.com

- Toccoa PD
- Chief Tim Jarrell
  203 No. Alexander St.
  Toccoa, GA 30577
  (706) 886-8655
  tjarrell@toccoapolicedepartment.com

Stewart County

- Stewart County SO
- Sheriff Larry Jones
  Broad St. PO Box 817
  Lumpkin, GA 31815
  (229) 838-4393
  mail@stewartcounty.net
- Lumpkin PD
- Chief Javier Garcia
  110 No. Martin Luther King, Jr. Dr.
  Lumpkin, GA 31815-0278
  (229) 838-6101
  jgarcia@lumpkinpd.com
- Richland PD
- Chief Robbie Wells
  110 Wall St.
  Richland, GA 31825
  (229) 887-3530
  info@cityofrichlandga.com

Sumter County

- Sumter County SO
- Sheriff Pete Smith
  352 McMath Mill PO Box 726
  Americus, GA 31709
  (229) 924-4094
  psmith@sumtercountyga.us

Taliaferro County

- Taliaferro County SO
- Sheriff Marc Richards
  758 Warrenton Rd. SE
  Crawfordville, GA 30631
  (706) 456-2345
  sheriff@tcsoga.com

Tattnall County

- Tattnall County SO
- Sheriff Quinton Rush
  PO Box 545
  Reidsville, GA 30453
  (912) 557-6777
  tcsheriff@windstream.net

- Collins PD
- Chief Stephen Eubanks
  300 Main St. PO Box 96
  Collins, GA 30421
  (912) 693-2581
  collinspolice@altell.net

Taylor County

- Taylor County SO
- Sheriff Jeff Watson
  101 No. Ivy PO Box 606
  Butler, GA 31006
  (478) 862-5444
  taylorcoso@pstel.net
- Butler PD
- Chief Jimmy Towns
  104 Cedar St.
  Butler, GA 31006
  (912) 862-9333
  jtowns@cityofbutlerga.com
- Reynolds PD
- Chief Lonnie Holder
  3 E. William Wainwright St.
  Reynolds, GA 31076
  (912) 847-3435
  lonnieholder@reynoldsga.com

Telfair County

- Telfair County SO
- Sheriff Chris Steverson
  19 E. Oak St., Ste. B
  McRae, GA 31055
  (229) 868-6621
  steverson@telfairco.org
- Milan PD
- Chief Allan Hammock
  5 SE Railroad St.
  Milan, GA 31060
  (229) 362-4271
  cityofmilan@windstream.net

Terrell County

- Terrell County SO
- Sheriff John W. Bowens
  3108 Albany Hwy PO Box 463
  Dawson, GA 39842
  (229) 995-4488
  sheriff@terrellsheriff.org
- Dawson PD
- Chief Charlie C. Whitehead, Jr.
  432 Crawford St.
  Dawson, GA 39842
  (229) 995-4414
  info@dawsongapd.com

Thomas County

- Thomas County SO
- Sheriff R. Carlton Powell
  921 Smith Ave. PO Box 588
  Thomasville, GA 31792
  (229) 225-3300
  thoscoso@rose.net
- Boston PD
- Chief Ferrell Howell
  120 So. Main St.
  Boston, GA 31626
  (229) 498-8024
  city@bostonga.com
  Thomasville PD
  Chief Ellis C. Jackson
  921 Smith Ave.
  Thomasville, GA 31792
  (229) 227-3249
  ellis@thomasville.org

Tift County

- Tift County SO
- Sheriff Gene Scarbrough
  500 Morgan Dr. PO Box 46
  Tifton, GA 31794
  (229) 388-6020
  gene.scarbrough@tiftcounty.org
- Omega PD
- Chief Eric Windmoller
  5518 Alabama Ave.
  Omega, GA 31775
  (229) 528-4911
  omegacityhall@mchsi.com
- Tifton PD
- Chief Buddy Dowdy
  527 Commerce Way
  Tifton, GA 31794
  (229) 382-3132
  bdowdy@tifton.net

Toombs County

- Toombs County SO
- Sheriff Alvie Lee *Junior* Kight
  357 NW Broad St., Ste. #1
  Lyons, GA 30436
  (912) 526-6778
  sheriffkight@yahoo.com
  Lyons PD
  Chief Wesley Walker
  257 No. State St.
  Lyons, GA 30436
  (912) 526-3638
  wwalker@lyonspolice.com
- Vidalia PD
- Chief J. Frank Waits
  302 1st St. E.
  Vidalia, GA 30474
  (912) 537-4123
  contact@vidaliaga.com

Towns County

- Towns County SO
- Sheriff Chris Clinton
  48 River St., Ste F
  Hiawassee, GA 30546
  (706) 896-4444
  chrisclinton@windstream.net
- Young Harris College PD
- Chief Ken Henderson
  #1 College St. PO Box 116
  Young Harris, GA 30582
  (706) 379-4569
  kenh@yhc.edu

Treutlen County

- Treutlen County SO
- Sheriff Tommy Corbin
  110 3rd St. PO Box 316
  Soperton, GA 30457
  (912) 529-3222
  sheriff@soperton-treutlen.org
- Soperton PD
- Chief Luke Kicklighter
  7921 Metter Rd. PO Box 229
  Soperton, GA 30457
  (912) 529-4221
  sotnpd@planttel.net

Troup County

- Troup County SO
- Sheriff James Woodruff
  130 Sam Walker Dr.
  Lagrange, GA 30240
  (706) 883-1616
  jtwoodruff@troupco.org
- Hogansville PD
- Chief Moses Ector
  117 Lincoln St.
  Hogansville, GA 30230
  (706) 637-6648
  mector@hogansvillepd.com
- LaGrange PD
- Chief Louis M. Dekmar
  100 Haralson St.
  LaGrange, GA 30240
  (706) 883-2603
  officeofchiefofpolice@lagrange-ga.org

- West Point PD
- Chief Jeffery *J.K.* Cato
  730 1st Ave.
  West Point, GA 31833
  (See also Harris County)
  (706) 645-3525
  jcato@cityofwestpointga.com

Turner County

- Turner County SO
- Sheriff Andy Hester
  1301 Industrial Dr.
  Ashburn, GA 31714
  (229) 567-2401
  ahester@turnercountyso.com
- Ashburn PD
- Chief Joe Saxon
  121 E. Madison Ave.
  Ashburn, GA 31714
  (229) 567-2323
  ashburnpolice@mchsi.com
- Sycamore PD
- Chief Mike Hancock
  2529 US Hwy 41 So.
  Sycamore, GA 31790
  (229) 567-8978
  jhbrown62@windstream.net

Union County

- Union County SO
- Sheriff Mack Mason
  378 Beasley St.
  Blairsville, GA 30512
  (706) 439-6066
  sheriffmason@unioncountysoga.org

Upson County

- Upson County SO
- Sheriff Dan Kilgore
  235 Aviation Dr.
  Thomaston, GA 30286
  (706) 647-7900
  dkilgore@upsoncountysheriff.com
- Thomaston PD
- Chief Bobby Ellington
  1100 Barnesville St.
  Thomaston, GA 30286
  (706) 647-5455
  bellington@cityofthomaston.com

Walker County

- Walker County SO
- Sheriff Steve Wilson
  105 So. Duke St. PO Box 767
  Lafayette, GA 30728
  (706) 638-1909
  swilson@walkerso.com
- Lafayette PD
- Chief Bengie Clift
  208 No. Main
  Lafayette, GA 30728
  (706) 639-1540
  bclift@cityoflafayettega.org
- Lookout Mountain PD
- Chief Todd Gann
  1214 Lula Lake Rd.
  Lookout Mountain, GA 30750
  (706) 820-1051
  toddgann@comcast.net

Walton County

- Walton County SO
- Sheriff Joe Chapman
  1425 So. Madison Ave.
  Monroe, GA 30655
  (770) 267-6557
  jchapman@co.walton.ga.us
- Loganville PD
- Chief Mike McHugh
  4385 Pecan St. PO Box 39
  Loganville, GA 30052
  (770) 466.1165
  mchu601@bellsouth.net
- Monroe PD
- Chief Keith Glass
  227 So. Broad St.
  Monroe, GA 30655
  (770) 267-7576
  kglass@monroega.gov

Ware County

- Ware County SO
- Sheriff Randy F. Royal
  3487 Harris Rd.
  Waycross, GA 31503
  (912) 287-4326
  rroyal@warecounty.com
- Ware County PD
- Chief Dennis Hagood
  201 State St., Ste. 300
  Waycross, GA 31501
  (912) 207-4379
  dhagood@warecounty.com

- Waycross PD
- Chief Anthony H. *Tony* Tanner
  512 Oak St.
  Waycross, GA 31501
  (912) 287-2921
  ttanner@waycrossga.com

Warren County

- Warren County SO
- Sheriff Joe Peebles
  169 No. Hwy 80
  PO Box 626
  Warrenton, GA 30828
  (706) 465-3340
  wcso@warrencountyga.org

Washington County

- Washington County SO
- Sheriff Thomas H. Smith
  1735 Kaolin Rd. PO Drawer 30
  Sandersville, GA 31082
  (478) 552-4795
  wcso2@mylink.net

Wayne County

- Wayne County SO
- Sheriff John G. Carter
  266 E. Walnut St.
  Jesup, GA 31545
  (912) 427-5970
  sheriff@jesup.net

Webster County

- Webster County SO
- Sheriff Randy Dely
  175 Montgomery St.
  Preston, GA 31824
  (229) 828-7712
  sheriff@webstercosheriff.org

Wheeler County

- Wheeler County SO
- Sheriff Maurice Johnson, Jr.
  21 W. Forest Ave. PO Box 126
  Alamo, GA 30411
  (912) 568-7107
  wsheriff@windstream.net

White County

- White County SO
- Sheriff Neal Walden
  1210 Hulsey Rd.
  Cleveland, GA 30528
  (706) 865-6370
  nwalden@whitecounty.net
- Cleveland PD
- Chief John Foster
  85 So. Main St.
  Cleveland, GA 30528
  (706) 865-2111
  chieffoster@cityofcleavlandga.org

Whitfield County

- Whitfield County SO
- Sheriff Scott Chitwood
  805 Professional PO Box 652
  Dalton, GA 30720
  (706) 272-1260
  wcso@whitfieldcountyga.com
- Cohutta PD
- Chief Raymond Grossman
  5102 Red Clay PO Box 290
  Cohutta, GA 30710
  (706) 694-3330
  cohuttapolice@gmail.com
- Hamilton Med. Center PD
- Dir. Jerry Tatum
  1200 Memorial PO Box 1168
  Dalton, GA 30720
  (706) 272-6082
  JTatum@hhcs.org
- Varnell PD
- Chief Lyle Grant
  103 E. Main St.
  Varnell, GA 30756
  (706) 694-3141
  lgrant@cityofvarnell.com

Wilcox County

- Abbeville PD
- Chief John Hendley
  215 So. Depot St.
  Abbeville, GA 31001
  (229) 467-3200
  abbevillega@windstream.net
- Rochelle PD
- Chief Grover Barfield
  410 Stephens St. PO Box 156
  Rochelle, GA 31079
  (229) 365-2246
  rochelle1889city@yahoo.com

Wilkes County

- Washington PD
- Chief Mike L. Davis
  118 Spring St.
  Washington, GA 30673
  (706) 678-3244
  washpd@washingtonwilkes.org

Wilkinson County

- Gordon PD
- Chief Mike Hall
  105 Railroad St. SW
  Gordon, GA 31031
  (478) 628-2323
  Gordon_pd@yahoo.com
- Ivey PD
- Chief John C Richards, Sr.
  148-A Hwy 243
  Ivey, GA 31031
  (478) 628-2479
  iveypd@windstream.net

Worth County

- Worth County SO
- Sheriff Jeff Hobby
  201 No. Main St., Rm. 14
  Sylvester, GA 31791
  (229) 776-8211
  felicia@worthcosheriff.com
- Sylvester PD
- Chief Robert *Wayne* Jennings
  102 So. Isabella St.
  Sylvester, GA 31791
  (229) 776-8501
  wjennings@cityofsylvester.com

State Agencies

- GA State Patrol-HQ
- Comm. (*Col.*) Mark W. McDonough
  959 E. Confederate Ave., SE
  Atlanta, GA 30316
  (404) 624-7477
  adhodge@gps.net
- GA State U. PD
- Chief Connie Sampson
  15 Edgewood PO Box 3965
  Atlanta, GA 30303
  (404) 651-2100
  police@gsu.edu

ILLINOIS

Adams County

- Adams County SO
- Sheriff Brent A. Fischer
  521 Vermont St.
  Quincy, IL 62301
  (217) 277-2206
  bfischer@co.adams.il.us
- Camp Point PD
- Chief Randy Mathewson
  PO Box 355
  Camp Point, IL 62320
  (217) 593-6622
  village@adams.net
- Quincy PD
- Chief Robert Copley
  110 So. 8th St.
  Quincy, IL 62301
  (217) 228-4470
  qpd@quincyil.gov

Alexander County

- Alexander County SO
- Sheriff Timothy Brown
  2000 Washington Ave.
  Cairo, IL 62914
  (618) 734-2141
  alexandercntysd@yahoo.com

Bond County

- Bond County SO
- Sheriff Jeffrey Brown
  403 So. 2nd St.
  Greenville, IL 62246
  (618) 664-2151
  jeffbrownbcsd@sbcglobal.net
- Greenville PD
- Chief Lou Lorton
  404 So. 3rd St.
  Greenville, IL 62246
  (618) 664-2131
  llorton@greenvilleillinois.com

Boone County

- Boone County SO
- Sheriff Duane Wirth
  615 No. Main St.
  Belvidere, IL 61008
  (815) 544-9322, ext. 5060
  Admin@BooneCountySheriff.com
- Belvidere PD
- Chief Jan Noble
  615 No. Main St.
  Belvidere, IL 61008
  (815) 544-9626
  noble@belviderepolice.com

Brown County

- Brown County SO
- Sheriff Karl Groesch
  200 E. Court St., Rm. #1
  Mt. Sterling, IL 62353
  (217) 773-2011
  karlgroesch@gmail.com
- Mount Sterling PD
- Chief Bill Wilson
  145 W. Main St.
  Mount Sterling, IL 62353
  (217) 773-3961
  mspd@casscomm.com

Bureau County

- Bureau County SO
- Sheriff John E. Thompson
  700 So. Main St.
  Princeton, IL 61356
  (815) 875-3344
  sheriff@bureaucountysheriff.org
- Ladd PD
- Chief Bill Gaefcke
  121 No. Main St.
  Ladd, IL 61329
  (815) 894-2351
  laddpolice@comcast.net
- Princeton PD
- Chief Thomas F. Root
  605 Elm Pl.
  Princeton, IL 61356
  (815) 872-2351
  troot@princeton-il.com
- Spring Valley PD
- Chief Kevin Sangston
  215 No. Greenwood St.
  Spring Valley, IL 61362
  (815) 663-2351
  springvalleypolice@comcast.net
- Walnut PD
- Chief Thomas A. Ptasnik
  114 Jackson St.
  Walnut, IL 61376
  (815) 379-9000
  walnutpd@gmail.com

Calhoun County

- Calhoun County SO
- Sheriff William Heffington
  County Rd. PO Box 635
  Hardin, IL 62047
  (618) 576-9041
  sheriff@calhouncountyil.com

Carroll County

- Carroll County SO
- Sheriff Jeffrey Doran
  301 No. Main St.
  Mt Carroll, IL 61053
  (815) 244-9171
  jeff_doran_cop@yahoo.com
- Chadwick PD
- Chief Ryan G. Lambert
  10 W. 2nd St.
  Chadwick, IL 61014
  (815) 684-5264
  ChadwickPd@frontiernet.net
- Savanna PD
- Chief Michael Moon
  333 Chicago Ave.
  Savanna, IL 61074
  (815) 273-2246
  citypolice@mchsi.com
- Thomson PD
- Chief Elizabeth R. Evans-Balk
  2100 Market St.
  Thomson, IL 61285
  (815) 259-3905
  chiefofpolice@thomsonil.com

Cass County

- Cass County SO
- Sheriff Bob Fair
  101 Front St.
  Virginia, IL 62691
  (217) 452-7718
  casssheriff@casscomm.com
- Beardstown PD
- Chief Tom Schlueter
  418 E. Main PO Box 467
  Beardstown, IL 62618
  (217) 323-3131
  bpd@casscomm.com

Champaign County

- Champaign County SO
- Sheriff Dan Walsh
  204 E. Main St.
  Urbana, IL 61801
  (217) 384-3818
  dwalsh@co.champaign.il.us
- Champaign PD
- Chief Anthony Cobb
  82 E. University Ave.
  Champaign, IL 61820
  (217) 403-6907
  Anthony.Cobb@ci.champaign.il.us
- Mahomet PD
- Chief Mike Metzler
  303 E. Oak St.
  Mahomet, IL 61853
  (217) 586-5533
  mahometpolice@police.mahomet-il.gov
- Parkland College PD
- Chief Von D. Young
  2400 W. Bradley Ave.
  Champaign, IL 61821-1899
  (217) 351-2369, ext. 109
  vyoung@parkland.edu
- Urbana PD
- Chief Patrick Connolly
  308 So. Vine St.
  Urbana, IL 61801
  (217) 384-2324
  connolpj@urbanaillinois.us

Christian County

- Christian County SO
- Sheriff Bruce Kettelkamp
  301 W. Franklin
  Taylorville, IL 62568
  (217) 824-4961
  bkettelkamp@christiancountysheriff.com
- Edinburg PD
- Chief Rolando Castaneda
  1702 So. Closner Blvd
  Edinburg, IL 62531
  (956) 383-7411
  sochoa@cityofedinburg.com

Clark County

- Clark County SD
- Sheriff Jerry Parsley
  207 No. 5th St.
  Marshall, IL 62441
  (217) 826-6393
  jparsley@marshall.k12.il.us
- Casey PD
- Chief Mark T. Jenkins
  108 E. Main St.
  Casey, IL 62420
  (217) 932-2800
  cpdchief@mchsi.com

- Martinsville PD
- Chief Herman A. Davidson
  19 W. Cumberland St.
  Martinsville, IL 62442
  (217) 382-4023
  martinsvillecity@fairpoint.net

Clay County

- Clay County SO
- Sheriff James Sulsberger
  300 Broadway PO Box 267
  Louisville, IL 62858
  (618) 665-3316
  claycoso1@wabash.net
- Flora PD
- Chief John Nicholson
  123 No. Locust St.
  Flora, IL 62839
  (618) 662-9111
  florapd1@florail.us

Clinton County

- Clinton County SD
- Sheriff Mike Kreke
  810 Franklin
  Carlyle, IL 62231
  (618) 594-4555
  mike.kreke@clintonco.illinois.gov
- Beckemeyer PD
- Chief Kenneth McElroy
  191 E. 1st St. PO Box 278
  Beckemeyer, IL 62219
  (618) 227-4884
  villageofbec@ezeeweb.com
- Breese PD
- Chief Robert Fix
  500 No. 1st St.
  Breese, IL 62230
  (618) 526-7226
  breesepolice@yahoo.com
- Carlyle PD
- Chief Mark Pingsterhaus
  850 Franklin St.
  Carlyle, IL 62231
  (618) 594-2488
  admin@playandstaycarlyle.com
- New Baden PD
- Chief Mike Riley
  100 E. Hanover St.
  New Baden, IL 62265
  (618) 588-7741
  pdchief@newbadenil.com

- Trenton PD
- Chief Mike Jones
  25 W. Indiana St.
  Trenton, IL 62293
  (618) 224-9226
  mjones@trenton-il.com

Coles County

- Coles County SO
- Sheriff Darrell Cox
  701 7th St.
  Charleston, IL 61920
  (217) 348-0585
  dcox@co.coles.il.us
- Mattoon PD
- Chief Jeff Branson
  1710 Wabash Ave.
  Mattoon, IL 61938
  (217) 235-5451
  mpdadmin@matoonillnois.org

Cook County

- Cook County SO
- Sheriff Thomas J. Dart
  50 W. Washington
  Chicago, IL 60602
  (312) 603-6444
  sheriff.dart@cookcountyil.gov
- Alsip PD
- Chief Christopher *Chris* Radz
  4500 W. 123rd St.
  Alsip, IL 60803
  (708) 385-6902, ext. 254
  cradz@villageofalsip.org
- Barrington PD
- Chief Jerry Libit
  400 No. NW Hwy
  Barrington, IL 60010
  (See also Lake County)
  (847) 304-3300
  jlibit@barrington-il.gov
- Berkeley PD
- Chief Dale Gustafson
  5819 Electric Ave.
  Berkeley, IL 60163
  (708) 234-2627
  dgustafson@berkeley.il.us
- Bridgeview PD
- Chief Russell Harvey
  7500 So. Oketo Ave.
  Bridgeview, IL 60455
  (708) 458-2131
  rharvey@villageofbridgeview.com

- Broadview PD
- Chief Luis C. Tigera
  2350 So. 25th Ave.
  Broadview, IL 60153
  (708) 345-65504
  pwilliams@broadview-il.gov
- Buffalo Grove PD
- Chief Steve S. Balinski
  46 Raupp Blvd
  Buffalo Grove, IL 60089
  (See also Lake County)
  (847) 459-2560
  police@vbg.org
- Burbank PD
- Chief Bruce Radowicz
  5650 W. 75th Pl.
  Burbank, IL 60459
  (708) 924-7300
  BRadowicz@Burbankil.gov
- Burnham PD
- Chief Peter Belos
  14450 Manistee Ave.
  Burnham, IL 60633
  (708) 891-2122
  pbelos@villageofburnhamil.com
- Burr Ridge PD
- Chief John W. Madden
  7700 County Line Rd.
  Burr Ridge, IL 60527
  (See also DuPage County)
  (630) 323-8181
  jmadden@burr-ridge.gov
- Calumet City PD
- Chief Edward L. Gilmore
  1200 Pulaski Rd.
  Calumet City, IL 60409
  (708) 868-2500
  egilmore@calumetcity.org
- Calumet Park PD
- Chief Mark M. Davis
  12409 So. Throop St.
  Calumet Park, IL 60827
  (708) 385-6862
  chiefdavis6947@aol.com
- Chicago PD
- Supt. Garry F. McCarthy
  3510 So. Michigan Ave.
  Chicago, IL 60653
  (312) 746-6000
  CLEARPATH@chicagopolice.org
- Chicago PD 11th District
- Comm. Eric T. Washington
  3151 W. Harrison St.
  Chicago, IL 60612
  (312) 746-8386
  CAPS.011District@chicagopolice.org
- Chicago Heights PD
- Chief Charles A. Guiliani, Jr.
  1601 Halsted St.
  Chicago Heights, IL 60411
  (708) 756-6400
  cguiliani@chicagoheights.net
- Chicago Ridge PD
- Chief Robert D. Pyznarski
  10425 So. Ridgeland Ave.
  Chicago Ridge, IL 60415
  (708) 425-7831
  rpyznarski@chicagoridge.org
- Countryside PD
- Int. Chief Scott Novak
  5550 East Ave.
  Countryside, IL 60525
  (708) 352-2171
  police@countrysidepolice.org
- Crestwood PD
- Chief Theresa Neubauer
  13840 So. Cicero Ave.
  Crestwood, IL 60445
  (708) 371-4800
  crestwoodpolice@gmail.com
- Elk Grove Village PD
- Chief Stephen F. Schmidt
  901 Wellington Ave.
  Elk Grove Village, IL 60007
  (847) 357-4100
  sschmidt@elkgrove.org
- Elmwood Park PD
- Chief Frank Fagiano
  11 Conti Pkwy
  Elmwood Park, IL 60635
  (708) 452-3924
  ffagiano@elmwoodpark.org
- Evanston PD
- Chief Richard Eddington
  1454 Elmwood Ave.
  Evanston, IL 60201
  (847) 866-5000
  police@cityofevanston.org

- Evergreen Park PD
- Chief Michael D. Saunders
  9420 So. Kedzie Ave.
  Evergreen Park, IL 60642
  (708) 422-2142
  epinf@hotmail.com
- Forest Park PD
- Chief Jim Ryan
  517 Des Plaines Ave.
  Forest Park, IL 60130
  (708) 615-6299
  jryan@forestpark.net
- Glencoe DPS
- Chief Alan Kebby
  675 Village Ct.
  Glencoe, IL 60022
  (847) 835-4112
  akebby@villageofglencoe.org
- Glenview PD
- Chief William Fitzpatrick
  2500 E. Lake Ave.
  Glenview, IL 60025
  (847) 729-5000
  wfitzpatrick@glenview.il.us
- Harvey PD
- Act. Chief Denard Eaves
  15301 So. Dixie Hwy
  Harvey, IL 60426
  (708) 331-3030
  deaves@harveypolice.org
- Harwood Heights PD
- Chief Mario Ricchio
  7300 W. Wilson
  Harwood Heights, IL 60656
  (708) 867-4353
  ricchiom@harwoodheights.org
- Hickory Hills PD
- Chief Alan Vodicka
  8652 W. 95th St.
  Hickory Hills, IL 60457
  (708) 598-4900
  avodicka@hickoryhillspd.us
- Hillside PD
- Chief Joseph M. Lukaszek
  425 Hillside Ave.
  Hillside, IL 60162
  (708) 449-6133
  dbrown@hillside-il.org
- Hodgkins PD
- Chief Ernest E. Millsap
  6015 Lenzi Ave.
  Hodgkins, IL 60525
  (708) 352-4623
  emillsap@hodgkinspd.org
- Hoffman Estates PD
- Chief Michael Hish
  411 W. Higgins Rd.
  Hoffman Estates, IL 60169
  (847) 781-2800
  michael.hish@hoffmanestates.org
- Inverness PD
- Chief Robert *Bob* Haas, Jr.
  1415 Baldwin Rd.
  Inverness, IL 60067
  (847) 358-7766
  police@villageofjustice.org
- Kenilworth PD
- Supt. John V. Petersen
  419 Richmond Rd.
  Kenilworth, IL 60043
  (847) 251-2141
  jpetersen@kenilworthpd.org
- La Grange PD
- Chief Michael Holub
  304 W. Burlington Ave.
  La Grange, IL 60525
  (708) 579-2333
  mholub@villageoflagrange.com
- Lemont PD
- Chief Kevin W. Shaughnessy
  14600 127th St.
  Lemont, IL 60439
  (630) 257-2229
  kshaughnessy@lemont.il.us
- Lincolnwood PD
- Chief Robert LaMantia
  6900 No. Lincoln Ave.
  Lincolnwood, IL 60646
  (847) 673-2167
  pdal@lwd.org
- Lyons PD
- Chief Harley Schinker
  4200 Lawndale Ave.
  Lyons, IL 60534
  (708) 447-1225
  webmail@villageoflyons-il.net

- Markham PD
- Chief Mack Sanders
  16313 So. Kedzie Pkwy
  Markham, IL 60426
  (708) 331-2171
  msanders@cityofmarkham.net
- Midlothian PD
- Chief David Burk
  14801 So. Pulaski Rd.
  Midlothian, IL 60445
  (708) 385-2534
  pchief@villageofmidlothian.net
- Moraine Valley Coll. PD
- Chief Patrick O'Connor
  10900 So. 88th Ave.
  Palos Hills, IL 60465
  (708) 974-5555
  oconnorp@morainevalley.edu
- Morton Grove PD
- Chief Mark Erickson
  6101 Capulina Ave.
  Morton Grove, IL 60053
  (847) 470-5208
  vmg@mortongroveil.org
- Mount Prospect PD
- Chief Mike Semkiu
  112 E. NW Hwy
  Mount Prospect, IL 60056
  (847) 870-5656
  policedepartment@mountprospect.org
- Niles PD
- Chief Dean H. Strzelecki
  7000 W. Touhy Ave.
  Niles, IL 60714
  (847) 588-6500
  Police@vniles.com
- Norridge PD
- Chief James J. Jobe
  4020 No. Olcott Ave.
  Norridge, IL 60634
  (708) 453-47704
  jjobe@norridgepd.com
- North Riverside PD
- Chief Anthony Garvey
  2359 So. Desplaines Ave.
  North Riverside, IL 60546
  (708) 447-9191
  AGarvey@northriverside-il.org
- Northbrook PD
- Chief Charles J. Wernick
  1401 Landwehr Rd.
  Northbrook, IL 60062
  (847) 664-4410
  charles.wernick@northbrook.il.us
- Northlake PD
- Chief Dennis Koletsos
  55 E. North Ave.
  Northlake, IL 60164
  (708) 531-5755
  dkoletsos@northlakecity.com
- Oak Forest PD
- Chief Greg Anderson
  15440 So. Central Ave.
  Oak Forest, IL 60452
  (708) 687-1376, ext. 1200
  ganderson@oak-forest.org
- Oak Park PD
- Chief Rick C. Tanksley
  1 Village Hall Plaza
  Oak Park, IL 60302
  (708) 358-2700
  Police@oak-park.us
- Olympia Fields PD
- Chief John A. Krull
  20040 Governor's Hwy
  Olympia Fields, IL 60461
  (708) 503-8100
  volfields1@olympia-fields.com
- Orland Hills PD
- Chief Thomas Scully
  16033 So. 94th Ave.
  Orland Hills, IL 60477-4623
  (708) 349-4434
  tscully@orlandhillspolice.org
- Orland Park PD
- Chief Timothy McCarthy
  14600 Ravinia Ave.
  Orland Park, IL 60462
  (708) 349-4111
  tjmccarthy@orland-park.il.us
- Palatine PD
- Chief John Koziol
  595 No. Hicks Rd.
  Palatine, IL 60067
  (847) 359-9000
  jkoziol@palatine.il.us

- Palos Heights PD
- Chief Larry Yott
  7607 W. College Dr.
  Palos Heights, IL 60463
  (708) 448-5060
  lyott@palosheightspd.org
- Palos Park PD
- Chief Joe Miller
  8999 W. 123rd St.
  Palos Park, IL 60464
  (708) 671-3770
  jmiller@palospark.org
- Park Ridge PD
- Chief Frank J. Kaminski
  200 So. Vine Ave.
  Park Ridge, IL 60068
  (847) 318-5252
  info@parkridgepolice.org
- Posen PD
- Chief Doug Hogland
  2440 W. Walter Zimny Dr.
  Posen, IL 60469
  (708) 385-0277
  dhoglund@villageofposen.org
- Prospect Heights PD
- Chief Jamie Dunne
  14 E. Camp McDonald Rd.
  Prospect Heights, IL 60070
  (847) 398-5511, ext. 116
  jdunne@prospect-heights.org
- Richton Park PD
- Chief Elvia P. Williams-Yancey
  4455 W. Sauk Tr.
  Richton Park, IL 60471
  (708) 481-8956
  eyancey@richtonpark.org
- River Grove PD
- Chief Rodger Loni
  2621 No. Thatcher Ave.
  River Grove, IL 60171
  (708) 453-2121, ext. 322
  chief@vorg.us
- Riverdale PD
- Chief William McHenry
  725 W. 138th St.
  Riverdale, IL 60827
  (708) 841-2203
  wmchenry@villageofriverdale.org
- Riverside PD
- Chief Tom Weitzel
  31 Riverside Rd.
  Riverside, IL 60546
  (708) 447-2127
  tweitzel@riverside.il.us
- Robbins PD
- Chief Jerome Guinn
  3323 W. 137th St.
  Robbins, IL 60472
  (708) 385-4121
  jguinn@robbins-il.com
- Rolling Meadows PD
- Chief Tom Calcagno
  3600 Kirchoff Rd.
  Rolling Meadows, IL 60008
  (847) 255-2416
  Calcagno@cityofrm.org
- Schaumburg PD
- Int. Chief Kenneth Bouche
  1000 W. Schaumburg Rd.
  Schaumburg, IL 60194
  (847) 348.7006
  kbouche@ci.schaumburg.il.us
- Schiller Park PD
- Chief Daniel Schulze
  9526 W. Irving Park Rd.
  Schiller Park, IL 60176
  (847) 678-4794
  dschulze@villageofschillerpark.com
- South Holland PD
- Chief George Baker
  16220 Wausau Ave.
  South Holland, IL 60473
  (708) 331-3131
  gbaker@southholland.org
- Steger PD
- Chief Richard L. Stultz
  35 W. 34th St.
  Steger, IL 60475
  (708) 754-8121
  stultz@stegerpolice.org
- Stickney PD
- Chief Joseph Kretch
  6533 W. Pershing Rd.
  Stickney, IL 60402
  (708) 788-2131
  joseph.kretch@stickneypolice.com

- Stone Park PD
- Chief Giuseppe *Joe* Capece
  1629 No. Mannheim Rd.
  Stone Park, IL 0165
  Ph: (708) 450-3215
  chiefcapece@stoneparkpd.com
- Streamwood PD
- Chief James T. Keegan
  401 E. Irving Park Rd.
  Streamwood, IL 60107
  (630) 736-3700
  police@streamwood.org
- Thornton PD
- Chief Douglas Beckman
  700 Park Ave.
  Thornton, IL 60476
  (708) 877-4440
  dbeckman@thornton60476.com
- Tinley Park PD
- Chief Steve Neubauer
  7850 W. 183rd St.
  Tinley Park, IL 60477
  (708) 444-5300
  sneubauer@tinleypark.org
- Westchester PD
- Chief April Padalik
  10300 W. Roosevelt Rd.
  Westchester, IL 60154
  (708) 345-0060
  apadalik@westchesterpolice.com
- Western Springs PD
- Chief Pamela K. Church
  740 Hillgrove Ave.
  Western Springs, IL 60558
  (708) 246-1800, ext. 153
  pchurch@wsprings.com
- Wheeling PD
- Chief William Benson
  1 Community Blvd
  Wheeling, IL 60090
  (847) 459-2634
  wbenson@wheelingil.gov
- Winnetka PD
- Chief Patrick Kreis
  410 Green Bay Rd.
  Winnetka, IL 60093
  (847) 501-6034
  pkreis@winnetka.org
- Woodridge PD
- Chief Ken Boehm
  1 Plaza Dr.
  Woodridge, IL 60517
  (See also DuPage County)
  (630) 719-4728
  kboehm@vil.woodridge.il.us
- Worth PD
- Chief Martin Knolmayer
  7112 W. 111th St.
  Worth, IL 60482
  (708) 448-3979
  mknolmayer@villageofworth.com

Crawford County

- Crawford County SO
- Sheriff Todd Liston
  203 So. Jefferson PO Box 591
  Robinson, IL 62454
  (618) 546-1515
  sheriff@crawfordcountycentral.com
- Oblong PD
- Chief Chad E. Pusey
  202 So. Range St.
  Oblong, IL 62449
  (618) 592-4715
  police@villageofoblong.com
- Robinson PD
- Chief Bill Ackman
  300 So. Lincoln St.
  Robinson, IL 62454
  (618) 544-2217
  chief@cityofrobinson.com

Cumberland County

- Cumberland County SO
- Sheriff Stephen Ozier
  166 Courthouse PO Box 56
  Toledo, IL 62468
  (217) 849-2571
  cumbcosheriff@live.com
- Greenup PD
- Chief James Cline
  115 E. Cumberland Ave.
  Greenup, IL 62428
  (217) 923-5555
  pdgreenup@villageofgreenup.com

DeKalb County

- DeKalb County SO
- Sheriff Roger A. Scott
  150 No. Main St.
  Sycamore, IL 60178
  (815) 895-5829
  rscott@dekalbcounty.org

- Cortland PD
- Chief Dennis Medema
  300 W. Lincoln Hwy, Ste. 1
  Cortland, IL 60112
  (815) 756-2558
  cortlandpd@cortlandil.org
- Dekalb PD
- Chief Gene Lowery
  200 So. 4th St.
  Dekalb, IL 60115
  (815) 748-8400
  dekalb.police@cityofdekalb.com
- Genoa PD
- Chief Ty Lynch
  1131/2 No. Genoa St.
  (Mailing: 333 E. 1st St.)
  Genoa, IL 60135
  (815) 784-6633
  tlynch@genoapd.com
- Hinckley PD
- Chief Gregg Waikus
  700 James St.
  Hinckley, IL 60520
  (815) 286-3836
  policechief@hinckleyil.com
- Kirkland PD
- Chief Stanley L. Smith
  511 W. Main St.
  Box 550
  Kirkland, IL 60146
  (815) 522-3315
  slsoink@yahoo.com
- Malta PD
- Chief Glenn B. Gustafson
  115 So. 3rd St.
  Malta, IL 60150
  (815) 825-2200
  villageofmalta@aol.com
- Sandwich PD
- Chief William King
  308 E. College St.
  Sandwich, IL 60548
  (815) 786~7261
  sandwichpd@sandwichilpolice.org
- Somonauk PD
- Chief Richard A. Smith
  140 W. DeKalb St. Box 218
  Somonauk, IL 60552
  (See also LaSalle County)
  (815) 498-2351
  somonaukpolice@hotmail.com
- Sycamore PD
- Chief Donald M. Thomas
  535 DeKalb Ave.
  Sycamore, IL 60178
  (815) 895-34354
  manderson@sycamorepd.com

Dewitt County

- Dewitt County SO
- Sheriff Jered Shofner
  101 W. Washington St.
  Clinton, IL 61727
  (217) 935-9507
  sheriffshofner@dewittcountyill.com
- Clinton PD
- Chief Michael J. Reidy
  118 W. Washington St.
  Clinton, IL 61727
  (217) 935~9441
  mreidy@clintonillinois.com

Douglas County

- Douglas County SO
- Sheriff Charlie McGrew
  401 So. Center St.
  Tuscola, IL 61953
  (217) 253-2913
  sheriff@douglascountyil.com
- Tuscola PD
- Chief Craig Hastings
  214 No. Parke St.
  Tuscola, IL 61953
  (217) 253-2351
  tuscolapolice@hotmail.com
- Villa Grove PD
- Chief Dennis Gire
  116 No. Main St.
  Villa Grove, IL 61956
  (217) 832-2521
  villagrovepolice@yahoo.com

DuPage County

- DuPage County SO
- Sheriff John E. Zaruba
  501 No. County Farm Rd.
  Wheaton, IL 60187
  (630) 407-2000
  sheriff@dupagesheriff.org
- Addison PD
- Dir. Timothy *Bill* Hayden
  3 Friendship Plaza
  Addison, IL 60101
  (630) 543-3080, ext. 7901
  THayden@addison-il.org

- Aurora PD
- Chief Gregory S. Thomas
  1200 E. Indian Trail Rd.
  Aurora, IL 60506
  (630) 256-5001
  thomasg@apd.aurora.il.us
- Bensenville PD
- Chief Frank J. Kosman
  100 No. Church Rd.
  Bensenville, IL 60106
  (630) 350-3455
  FKosman@bensenville.il.us
- Burr Ridge PD
- Chief John W. Madden
  7660 So. County Line Rd. # 1
  Burr Ridge, IL 60527
  (See also Cook County)
  (630) 323-8181
  BRVillage@burr-ridge.gov
- Carol Stream PD
- Chief Kevin Orr
  500 No. Gary Ave.
  Carol Stream, ILK 60188
  (630) 668-2167
  Police@carolstream.org
- Clarendon Hills PD
- Chief Ted Jenkins
  448 Park Ave.
  Clarendon Hills, IL 60514
  (630) 286-5465
  tjenkins@clarendonhills.us
- Darien PD
- Chief Ernest Brown
  1710 Plainfield Rd.
  Darien, IL 60561
  (630) 353-8351
  ebrown@darienil.gov
- Downers Grove PD
- Chief Robert Porter
  825 Burlington Ave.
  Downers Grove, IL 60515
  (630) 434-5625
  rporter@downers.us
- Elmhurst PD
- Chief Michael R. Ruth
  125 E. 1st St.
  Elmhurst, IL 60126
  (630) 530-3050
  policeinfo@elmhurst.org
- Glen Ellyn PD
- Chief Philip Norton
  535 Duane St., 1st Fl.
  Glen Ellyn, IL 60137
  (630) 469-1187
  pnorton@glenellyninfo.org
- Glendale Heights PD
- Chief Michael Marron
  300 Civic Center Plaza
  Glendale Heights, IL 60139
  (630) 260-6000
  mmarron@glendaleheights.org
- Itasca PD
- Chief Scott Heher
  540 W. Irving Park Rd.
  Itasca, IL 60143
  (630) 773-1004
  police@itasca.com
- Lombard PD
- Chief Ray Byrne
  235 E. Wilson Ave.
  Lombard, IL 60148
  (630) 873-4400
  police@villageoflombard.org
- Naperville PD
- Chief Robert *Bob* Marshall
  1350 Aurora Ave.
  Naperville, IL 60540
  (See also Will County)
  (630) 420-6666
  marshallr@naperville.il.us
- Oak Brook PD
- Chief James Kruger
  1200 Oak Brook Rd.
  Oak Brook, IL 60521
  (630) 368-8710
  jkruger@oak-brook.org
- Oakbrook Terrace PD
- Chief Wayne Holakovsky
  17 W. 275 Butterfield Rd.
  Oakbrook Terrace, IL 60181
  (630) 941-8320
  wholakovsky@oakbrookterrace.net
- Roselle PD
- Chief Steve Herron
  103 So. Prospect St.
  Roselle, IL 60172
  (630) 980-2025
  rosellepd@roselle.il.us

- Warrenville PD
- Chief Raymond Turano
  3S245 Warren Ave.
  Warrenville, Il 60555
  (630) 393-2131
  rturano@warrenville.il.us
- West Chicago PD
- Chief Laz Perez
  325 Spencer St.
  West Chicago, IL 60185
  (See also Kane County)
  (630) 293-2222
  lperez@westchicago.org
- Wheaton PD
- Chief Mark Field
  900 W. Liberty Dr.
  Wheaton, IL 60187
  (630) 260-2161
  mfield@wheaton.il.us
- Willowbrook PD
- Chief Mark Shelton
  7760 Quincy St.
  Willowbrook, IL 60521
  (630) 325-2808
  mshelton@willowbrook.il.us
- Winfield PD
- Chief Stacy Reever
  27 W. 465 Jewell Rd.
  Winfield, IL 60190
  (630) 933-7160
  sreever@villageofwinfield.com
- Wood Dale PD
- Chief Greg Vesta
  404 No. Wood Dale Rd.
  Wood Dale, IL 60191
  (630) 766-2060
  gvesta@wooddale.com
- Woodridge PD
- Chief Ken Boehm
  1 Plaza Dr.
  Woodridge, IL 60517
  (See also Cook County)
  (630) 719-4728
  kboehm@vil.woodridge.il.us

Edgar County

- Edgar County SO
- Sheriff Edward B. Motley
  228 No. Central
  Paris, IL 61944
  (217) 465-4166
  ecsheriff@edgarcounty-il.gov

Effingham County

- Effingham County SO
- Sheriff John H. Monnet
  101 No. 4th, Ste 101
  Effingham, IL 62401
  (217) 342-8463
  sheriff@co.effingham.il.us
- Altamont PD
- Chief Alan Heiens
  202 No. 2nd St.
  Altamont, IL 62411
  (618) 483-5212
  aheiens@altamontil.net
- Effingham Water Auth. PD
- Chief Gene Arnold
  9352 E. Park Ln.
  Effingham, IL 62401
  (217) 868-2787
  genearnold@mchsi.com

Fayette County

- Fayette County SO
- Sheriff Aaron Lay
  221 So. 7th St., Rm. 500
  Vandalia, IL 62471
  (618) 283-2141
  fayettecountysheriff@gmail.com
- Vandalia PD
- Chief Larry Eason
  2219 So. 5th St.
  Vandalia, IL 62471
  (618) 283-2131
  pdchief@vandaliaillinois.com

Ford County

- Ford County SO
- Sheriff Mark Doran
  235 No. American
  Paxton, IL 60957
  (217) 379-2324
  mdoran@fcsheriff.com
- Gibson City PD
- Chief Steven Cushman
  109 E. 8th St.
  Gibson City, IL 60936
  (217) 784-8666
  gcpd@gcpd.net

Franklin County

- Franklin County SO
- Sheriff Donald R. Jones
  403 E. Main St.
  Benton, IL 62812
  (618) 438-8211
  djones@sherifffranklincounty.com
- Sesser PD
- Chief J. Robert Barrett
  302 W. Franklin Ave.
  Sesser, IL 62884
  (618) 625-2341
  sesserpolice@speednet.com
- West Frankfort PD
- Chief Shawn Talluto
  201 E. Nolen St.
  West Frankfort, IL 62896
  (618) 937-3502
  wfpd@midwest.net

Fulton County

- Fulton County SO
- Sheriff Jeff Standard
  268 W. Washington Ave.
  Lewistown, IL 61542
  (309) 547-2277
  JStandard.FCSO@fultonco.org
- Canton PD
- Chief Rick Nichols
  2 No. Main St.
  Canton, IL 61520
  (309) 647-5131
  rnichols@cantoncityhall.org
- Lewistown PD
- Chief John Werland
  119 So. Adams
  Lewistown, IL 61542
  (309) 547-2226
  lewistownpolice@comcast.net

Gallatin County

- Gallatin County SO
- Sheriff Shannon Bradley
  Lincoln Blvd PO Box 340
  Shawneetown, IL 62984
  (618) 269-3137
  gcsheriff90@live.com

Greene County

- Greene County SO
- Sheriff Rob McMillen
  403 7th St.
  Carrollton, IL 62016
  (217) 942-6901
  gcsocc@gcctv.com
- White Hall PD
- Chief Jack W. Wallis
  116 E. Sherman St.
  White Hall, IL 62092
  (217) 374-2135
  rmcmillen@whitehallcitygov.com

Grundy County

- Grundy County SO
- Sheriff Kevin Callahan
  111 E. Washington St.
  Morris, IL 60450
  (815) 942-6645
  kcallahan@grundycountysheriff.com
- Coal City PD
- Chief Tom Best
  545 So. Broadway
  Coal City, IL 60416
  (815) 634-2341
  tbest@coalcity-il.com
- Minooka PD
- Chief Justin Meyer
  121 E. McEvilly Rd.
  Minooka, IL 60447
  (See also Kendall & Will counties)
  (815) 467-2151
  justin.meyer@minooka.com

Hamilton County

- Hamilton County SO
- Sheriff Greg Brenner
  100 So. Jackson St.
  McLeansboro, IL 62859
  (618) 643-2511
  hcsd841@yahoo.com
- McLeansboro PD
- Chief Robert Crow
  102 W. Main St.
  McLeansboro, IL 62859
  (618) 643-3621
  mctown@gmail.com

Hancock County

- Hancock County SO
- Sheriff Scott Bentzinger
  98 Buchanan St.
  Carthage, IL 62321
  (217) 357-2115
  scotthc2@mchsi.com
- Hamilton PD
- Chief Robb Bell
  1010 Broadway St.
  Hamilton, IL 62341
  (217) 847-3347
  rjbell.hamiltonpd@live.com

Hardin County

- Hardin County SO
- Sheriff Jerry Fricker
  1 Courthouse Hill PO Box 246
  Elizabethtown, IL 62931
  (618) 287-2271
  hardincountycops@yahoo.com

Henderson County

- Henderson County SO
- Sheriff Steven Haynes PO Box 228
  Oquawka, IL 61469
  (309) 867-4291
  hendsheriff@9thjudicial.org

Henry County

- Henry County SD
- Sheriff James Padilla
  311 W. Center St.
  Cambridge, IL 61238-1251
  (309) 937-3911
  henrycountysheriff@henrycty.com
- Annawan PD
- Chief Marty Burroughs
  200 No. Meadow Ln., Ste. 3
  Annawan, IL 61234
  (309) 935-6250
  annawanpd@annawanillinois.org
- Geneseo PD
- Chief Thomas Piotrowski
  119 So. Oakwood Ave.
  Geneseo, IL 61254
  (309) 944-5141
  gpd@cityofgeneseo.com
- Kewanee PD
- Chief James F. Dison
  401 E. 3rd St.
  Kewanee, IL 61443
  (309) 853-1911
  jdison@cityofkewanee.net

Iroquois County

- Iroquois County SD
- Sheriff Derek Hagen
  550 So. 10th St.
  Watseka, IL 60970
  (815) 432-6992
  dhagen@co.iroquois.il.us
- Chebanse PD
- Chief Tim Kent
  275 So. Oak St.
  PO Box 311
  Chebanse, IL 60922
  (See also Kankakee County)
  (815) 697-2214
  clerk@chebanseillinois.org
- Gilman PD
- Chief Fred Voigt
  215 No. Central St. PO Box 215
  Gilman, IL 60938
  (815) 432-4918
  cityofgilman_04@sbcglobal.net
- Milford PD
- Chief Thomas O'Laughlin
  PO Box 137
  Milford, IL 60953
  (815) 889-4085
  milfordpolice@wigi.us
- Watseka PD
- Chief Roger Lebeck
  201 Brianna Dr. PO Box 318
  Watseka, IL 60970
  (815) 432-2433
  watsekapdw1@yahoo.com

Jackson County

- Jackson County SO
- Sheriff Robert Burns
  1001 Mulberry St.
  Murphysboro, IL 62966
  (618) 687-3822
  jcsoburns@yahoo.com
- Carbondale PD
- Chief Jody O'Guinn
  501 So. Washington
  Carbondale, IL 62902
  (618) 457-3200
  police@ci.carbondale.il.us
- DeSoto PD
- Chief Ben Doan
  210 W. Lincoln St. PO Box 467
  DeSoto, IL 62924
  (618) 867-2315
  desotopd@frontier.com

- Murphysboro PD
- Chief Jeffrey J. Bock
  202 No. 11th St.
  Murphysboro, IL 62966
  (618) 684-5244
  policechief@murphysboro-il.gov

Jasper County

- Jasper County SO
- Sheriff Ed Francis
  106 E. Morgan
  Newton, IL 62448
  (618) 783-8477
  jcso@psbnewton.com
- Newton PD
- Chief Mike Swick
  108 No. Van Buren St.
  Newton, IL 62448
  (618) 783-8478
  npd1280@yahoo.com

Jefferson County

- Jefferson County SO
- Sheriff Roger Mulch
  911 Casey Ave.
  Mt Vernon, IL 62864
  (618) 244-8004
  rmulch@jeffil.us
- Bonnie PD
- Chief Travis Allen
  270 So. Railroad PO Box 117
  Bonnie, IL 62816
  (618) 231-6894
  travisallen232@gmail.com
- Mount Vernon PD
- Chief Chris Mendenall
  211 No. 10th St.
  Mount Vernon, IL 62864
  (618) 242-2727
  police@mvn.net

Jersey County

- Jersey County SO
- Sheriff Mark Kallal
  114 No. Washington St.
  Jerseyville, IL 62052
  (618) 498-6881
  mkallal@jerseycounty-il.us
- Jerseyville PD
- Chief Brad Blackorby
  200 So. Jefferson
  Jerseyville, IL 62052
  (618) 498-2131
  jerseyvillepd@jerseyville-il.us

Jo Daviess County

- Jo Daviess County SO
- Sheriff Kevin Turner
  330 No. Bench St.
  Galena, IL 61036
  (815) 777-2141
  kturner@jodaviess.org
- East Dubuque PD
- Chief Steven M O'Connell
  193 Sinsinawa Ave.
  East Dubuque, IL 61025
  (815) 747-3913
  soconnell@cityofeastdubuque.com
- Stockton PD
- Chief Robert Beeter
  155 W. Front St.
  Stockton, IL 61085
  (815) 947-2512
  rbeeter@villageofstockton.com

Johnson County

- Johnson County SO
- Sheriff Elry Faulkner
  113½ No. 5th St. PO Box 546
  Vienna, IL 62995
  (618) 658-8264
  jcsojc31@live.com

Kane County

- Kane County SO
- Sheriff Pat Perez
  37W755 Rt. 38, Ste. A
  St. Charles, IL 60175
  (630) 208-2000
  perezpatrick@co.kane.il.us
- Village of Algonquin PD
- Chief Russell Laine
  2200 Harnish Dr.
  Algonquin, IL 60102
  (See also McHenry County)
  (847) 658-4531
  rlaine@algonquin.org
- Batavia PD
- Chief Gary J. Schira
  100 No. Island Ave.
  Batavia, IL 60510
  (630) 454-2500
  gschira@cityofbatavia.net
- Carpentersville PD
- Chief Al Popp
  1200 LW. Besinger Dr.
  Carpentersville, IL 60110
  (847) 551-3481
  apopp@vil.carpentersville.il.us

- East Dundee PD
- Chief Terry Mee
  120 Barrington Ave.
  East Dundee, IL 60118
  (847) 428-4034
  tmee@eastdundee.net
- Elgin PD
- Chief Jeffrey Swoboda
  151 Douglas Ave.
  Elgin, IL 60120
  (847) 289-2760
  swoboda_j@cityofelgin.org
- Geneva PD
- Chief Steve Mexin
  20 Police Plaza
  Geneva, IL 60134
  (630) 232-4736
  smexin@geneva.il.us
- Hampshire PD
- Chief Brian Thompson
  215 Industrial Dr.
  Hampshire, IL 60140
  (847) 683-2240
  bthompson@hampshireill.org
- Montgomery PD
- Chief Daniel Meyers
  10 Civic Center Ave.
  Montgomery, IL 60538
  (See also Kendall County)
  (630) 897-8707
  police@ci.montgomery.il.us
- North Aurora PD
- Chief David Summer
  200 So. Lincolnway
  North Aurora, IL 60542
  (630) 897-8705
  dsummer@vil.north-aurora.il.us
- Sleepy Hollow PD
- Chief James R. Linane
  1 Thorobred Ln.
  Sleepy Hollow, IL 60118
  (847) 426-4425
  jlinane@sleepyhollowil.org
- St. Charles PD
- Chief James E. Lamkin
  2 State Ave.
  St Charles, IL 60174
  (630) 377-4435
  jlamkin@stcharlesil.gov
- Sugar Grove PD
- Chief Brad Sauer
  10 Municipal Dr.
  Sugar Grove, IL 60554
  (630) 466-4526
  policechief@sugar-grove.il.us
- Waubonsee PD
- Chief Thomas Roman
  Rt. 47 & Waubonsee Dr.
  Sugar Grove, IL 60554
  (630) 466-2552
  troman@waubonsee.edu
- West Chicago PD
- Chief Laz Perez
  325 Spencer St.
  West Chicago, IL 60185
  (See also DuPage County)
  (630) 293-2222
  lperez@westchicago.org
- West Dundee PD
- Chief Andrew Wieteska
  555 So. 8th St.
  West Dundee, IL 60118
  (847) 551-3810
  awieteska@wdundee.org

Kankakee County

- Kankakee County SO
- Sheriff Tim Bukowski
  3000 So. Justice Way
  Kankakee, IL 60901
  (815) 802-7100
  tbukowski@k3county.net
- Bourbonnais PD
- Chief Jim Phelps
  700 Main St. NW
  Bourbonnais, IL 60914
  (815) 937-3577
  police@villageofbourbonnais.com
- Bradley PD
- Chief Steven E. Coy
  147 So. Michigan Ave.
  Bradley, IL 60915
  (815) 932-4040
  secoy@thevillageofbradley.com
- Chebanse PD
- Chief Tim Kent
  275 So. Oak St. PO Box 311
  Chebanse, IL 60922
  (See also Iroquois County)
  (815) 697-2214
  clerk@chebanseillinois.org

- Herscher PD
- Chief Rick Gilbert
  272 E. 2nd St.
  Herscher, IL 60941
  (815) 426-2131
  Herschervillage@netscape.net
- Kankakee PD
- Chief Larry Regnier
  385 E. Oak
  Kankakee, IL 60901
  (815) 933-0401
  lregnier@citykankakee-il.gov
- Manteno PD
- Chief Bernie Thompson
  269 No. Main St.
  Manteno, IL 60950
  (815) 929-4801
  mpd@villageofmanteno.com
- Momence PD
- Chief Timothy J. Swanson
  123 W. River St.
  Momence, IL 60954
  (815) 472-2021
  police@cityofmomence.com

Kendall County

- Kendall County SO
- Sheriff Richard Randall
  1102 Cornell Ln.
  Yorkville, IL 60560
  (630) 553-7500, ext. 1111
  rrandall@co.kendall.il.us
- Minooka PD
- Chief Justin Meyer
  121 E. McEvilly Rd.
  Minooka, IL 60447
  (See also Grundy & Will counties)
  (815) 467-2151
  justin.meyer@minooka.com
- Montgomery PD
- Chief Daniel Meyers
  10 Civic Center Ave.
  Montgomery, IL 60538
  (See also Kane County)
  (630) 897-8707
  police@ci.montgomery.il.us
- Oswego PD
- Chief Dwight A. Baird
  3525 Rt. 34
  Oswego, IL 60543
  (630) 551-7300
  admin@oswegopoliceil.org
- Plano PD
- Chief Steven Eaves
  9 E. North St.
  Plano, IL 60545
  (630) 552-7232
  chiefseaves1@yahoo.com
- Yorkville PD
- Chief Richard T. Hart
  804 Game Farm Rd.
  Yorkville, IL 60560
  (630) 553-4340
  rhart@yorkville.il.us

Knox County

- Knox County SO
- Sheriff David Clague
  152 So. Kellogg St.
  Galesburg, IL 61401
  (309) 345-3733
  sheriff@ci.galeburg.il.us
- Galesburg PD
- Chief David Christensen
  150 So. Broad St.
  Galesburg, IL 61401
  (309) 343-9151
  chief@ci.galesburg.il.us

Lake County

- Lake County SO
- Sheriff Mark Curran
  25 So. Martin Luther King Jr. Ave.
  Waukegan, IL 60085
  (847) 377-4050
  mcurran@co.lake.il.us
- Antioch PD
- Chief Craig Somerville
  433 Orchard St.
  Antioch, IL 60002
  (847) 395-8585, ext. 3
  csomerville@antiochpd.com
- Bannockburn PD
- Chief Ronald Price
  2275 Telegraph Rd.
  Bannockburn, IL 60015
  (847) 945-8490
  rprice@bannockburn.org
- Barrington PD
- Chief Jerry Libit
  400 No. NW Hwy
  Barrington, IL 60010
  (See also Cook County)
  (847) 304-3300
  jlibit@barrington-il.gov

- Buffalo Grove PD
- Chief Steve S. Balinski
  46 Raupp Blvd
  Buffalo Grove, IL 60089
  (See also Cook County)
  (847) 459-2560
  police@vbg.org
- Fox Lake PD
- Chief Michael F. Behan
  301 So. Rt. 59
  Fox Lake, IL 60020
  (847) 587-3100
  behanm@foxlake.org
- Gurnee PD
- Chief Kevin Woodside
  100 No. O'Plaine Rd.
  Gurnee, IL 60031
  (847) 599-7050
  jayp@police.gurnee.il.us
- Hawthorn Woods PD
- Chief Jennifer Paulus
  2 Lagoon Rd.
  Hawthorn Woods, IL 60047
  (847) 438-9050
  jpaulus@hwpd.com
- Highland Park PD
- Chief Paul Shafer
  1677 Old Deerfield Rd.
  Highland Park, IL 60035
  (847) 432-7730
  pshafer@cityhpil.com
- Highwood PD
- Chief Dave Wentz
  17 Highwood Ave.
  Highwood, IL 60040
  (847) 432-2151
  dwentz@highwoodpolice.org
- Kildeer PD
- Chief John Filantres
  21911 Quentin Rd.
  Kildeer, IL 60047
  (847) 438-6644
  jfilantres@kildeerpolice.com
- Lake Bluff PD
- Chief William Gallagher
  45 E. Center Ave.
  Lake Bluff, IL 60044
  (847) 234-2153
  wgallagher@lakebluff.org
- Lake Forest PD
- Chief James Held
  255 W. Deerpath Rd.
  Lake Forest, IL 60045
  (847) 810-3802
  heldj@cityoflakeforest.com
- Lakemoor PD
- Chief David Godlewski
  27901 Concrete Dr.
  Lakemoor, IL 60051
  (815) 385-4111
  (See also McHenry County)
  police@lakemoor.net
- Lindenhurst PD
- Chief Kevin Klahs
  2300 E. Grand Ave.
  Lindenhurst, IL 60046
  (847) 356-5400
  mail@lindenhurstil.org
- Mundelein PD
- Chief Eric Guenther
  221 No. Lake St.
  Mundelein, IL 60060
  (847) 968-4600
  mpd@mundelein.org
- Round Lake PD
- Chief Michael Gillette
  741 W. Town Line Rd.
  Round Lake, IL 60073
  (847) 546-8112
  mgillette@eroundlake.com
- Round Lake Heights PD
- Chief John R. Roehlk
  619 W. Pontiac Ct.
  Round Lake Heights, IL 60073-1305
  (847) 546-9704
  chiefrlhpd@comcast.net
- Round Lake Park PD
- Chief George Filenko
  215 E. Main St.
  Round Lake Park, IL 60073
  (847) 546-7275
  rlp570@roundlakepark.us
- Tower Lakes PD
- Chief Samuel P. Sinacore
  400 No. Rt. 59
  Tower Lakes, IL 60010
  (847) 526-0444
  tlpolicechief@comcast.net

- Winthrop Harbor PD
- Chief Joel H. Brumlik
  830 Sheridan Rd.
  Winthrop Harbor, IL 60096
  (847) 872-2131
  chiefbrumlik@whpd.org
- Zion PD
- Chief Wayne Brooks
  2101 Salem Blvd
  Zion, IL 60099
  (847) 872-8000
  wayneb@zion.il.us

LaSalle County

- LaSalle County SO
- Sheriff Tom Templeton
  707 Etna Rd.
  Ottawa, IL 61350
  (815) 434-2161
  tjtempleton@lasallecounty.org
- LaSalle PD
- Chief Rob Uranich
  745 2nd St.
  La Salle, IL 61301
  (815) 223-2131
  chief@lasalle-il.gov
- Leland PD
- Chief Dennis C. Clifford
  175 No. Main St. PO Box 55
  Leland, IL 60531
  (815) 495-2351
  dclifford@lelandpolice.com
- Marseilles PD
- Chief James Hovious
  209 Lincoln St.
  Marseilles, IL 61341
  (815) 795-2131
  marspd@mtco.com
- Mendota PD
- Chief Thomas L. Smith
  607 8th Ave.
  Mendota, IL 61342
  (815) 539-9331
  mendotapd@comcast.net
- Oglesby PD
- Chief James Knoblauch
  128 W. Walnut St.
  Oglesby, IL 61348
  (815) 883-8404
  oglesbypd@comcast.net
- Ottawa PD
- Chief Brian L. Zeilmann
  301 W. Lafayette St.
  Ottawa, IL 61350
  (815) 433-2131
  chief@cityofottawa.org
- Peru PD
- Chief Douglas P. Bernabei
  1503 4th St.
  Peru, IL 61354
  (815) 223-2151
  chiefbernabei@perupolice.org
- Seneca PD
- Chief John Covington
  303 Cash St.
  Seneca, IL 61360
  (815) 357-1616
  jcovington@senecapd.com
- Somonauk PD
- Chief Richard A. Smith
  140 W. DeKalb St. Box 218
  Somonauk, IL 60552
  (See also DeKalb County)
  (815) 498-2351
  somonaukpolice@hotmail.com
- Streator PD
- Chief Kurt Pastirik
  204 So. Bloomington St.
  Streator, IL 61364
  (815) 672-3111
  cop@ci.streator.il.us

Lawrence County

- Lawrence County SO
- Sheriff Russell Adams
  1306 Lexington St.
  Lawrenceville, IL 62439
  (618) 943-8094
  russ62466@yahoo.com
- Bridgeport PD
- Chief Scott Murry
  235 Washington St.
  Bridgeport, IL 62417
  (618) 945-2351
  Bridgeport_city@frontier.com

Lee County

- Lee County SO
- Sheriff John Varga
  306 So. Hennepin
  Dixon, IL 61021
  (815) 284-5217
  sheriff@countyoflee.org

- Amboy PD
- Chief Paul Smith
  227 E. Main St.
  Amboy, IL 61310
  (815) 857-3400
  amboypd@comcast.net
- Dixon PD
- Chief Danny D. Langloss, Jr.
  220 So. Hennepin Ave.
  Dixon, IL 61021
  (815) 288-4411
  ddlangloss@dixonpd.com

Livingston County

- Livingston County SO
- Sheriff Martin Meredith
  844 W. Lincoln St.
  Pontiac, IL 61764
  (815) 844-2774
  livingstonsheriff@mcshi.com
- Dwight PD
- Chief Tim Henson
  209 So. Prairie Ave.
  Dwight, IL 60420
  (815) 584-3132
  police@dwightillinois.com
- Fairbury PD
- Chief Michael P. Frickey
  201 W. Locust St.
  Fairbury, IL 61739
  (815) 692-3351
  fairburypolice@route24.net

Logan County

- Logan County SO
- Sheriff Steve Nichols
  601 Broadway, Rm. 23
  Lincoln, IL 62656
  (217) 732-2156
  snichols@co.logan.il.us
- Lincoln PD
- Chief Kenneth Greenslate
  911 Pekin St.
  Lincoln, IL 62656
  (217) 732-2151
  kgreenslate@lincolnpolice.us
- San Jose PD
- Chief Aaron Hodgson
  301 So. 2nd St. PO Box 351
  San Jose, IL 62682
  (309) 247-1234
  sanjoseil.police@yahoo.com

Macon County

- Macon County SO
- Sheriff Thomas Schneider
  333 So. Franklin St.
  Decatur, IL 62523
  (217) 424-13211332
  tschneider@sheriff-macon-il.us
- Decatur PD
- Chief Todd Walker
  333 So. Franklin St.
  Decatur, IL 62523
  (217) 424-2711
  twalker@decaturil.gov
- Mount Zion PD
- Chief Doug Dunn
  410 W. Main St.
  Mount Zion, IL 62549
  (217) 864-4012
  j_miller@mtzion.com

Macoupin County

- Macoupin County SO
- Sheriff Don Albrecht
  215 So. East St., Ste. 1
  Carlinville, IL 62626
  (217) 854-3135
  daalbrecht@frontiernet.net
- Carlinville PD
- Chief David Haley
  570 No. Broad St.
  Carlinville, IL 62626
  (217) 854-3221
  info@carlinvillepolice.com
- Staunton PD
- Chief Robert Mertz
  105 So. Wood St.
  Staunton, IL 62088
  (618) 635-3333
  info@stauntonil.com

Madison County

- Madison County SD
- Sheriff Robert J. Hertz
  405 Randle St.
  Edwardsville, IL 62025
  (618) 692-6087
  sbhertz@co.madison.il.us
- Collinsville PD
- Chief Eric Van Hook
  200 W. Clay
  Collinsville, IL 62234
  (618) 344-2131, ext. 5100
  ehook@collinsvilleil.org

- East Alton PD
- Chief Dwynn D. Isringhausen
  211 No. Shamrock
  East Alton, IL 62024
  (618) 259-6212
  eapolice@eapolice.org
- Edwardsville PD
- Dir. Jay Keeven
  400 No. Main St.
  Edwardsville, IL 62025
  (618) 692-7521
  jkeeven@cityofedwardsville.com
- Glen Carbon PD
- Chief John Lakin
  151 No. Main St. PO Box 550
  Glen Carbon, IL 62034
  (618) 288-7226
  jlakin@glen-carbon.il.us
- Highland PD
- Chief Terry Bell
  820 Mulberry St.
  Highland, IL 62249
  (618) 654-2131
  tbell@highlandil.gov
- Madison PD
- Chief Steven Shelby
  615 Madison Ave.
  Madison, IL 62060
  (618) 876-4300
  SShelby@cityofmadisonil.com
- Maryville PD
- Chief Richard Schardan
  2500 No. Center
  Maryville, IL 62062
  (618) 344-8899
  chief.schardan@maryville-il.us
- Roxana PD
- Chief Dennis J. Smith
  400 So. Central Ave.
  Roxana, IL 62084
  (618) 254-1945
  jsmith@roxana-il.org
- South Roxana PD
- Chief Dennis L Carpenter
  211 Sinclair Ave.
  South Roxana, IL 62087
  (618) 254-7469
  chiefcarpenter@charter.net
- Troy PD
- Chief Robert A. Rizzi, Jr.
  116 E. Market St.
  Troy, IL 62294
  (618) 667-6731
  rrizzi@troypolice.us
- Wood River PD
- Chief Otis Steward
  111 Wood River Ave.
  Wood River, IL 62095
  (618) 251-3113
  osteward@woodriverpolice.com
- Worden PD
- Chief Chad Grammer
  115 W. Wall
  PO Box 355
  Worden, IL 62097
  (618) 459-2240
  sgt.grammer@villageofworden.us

Marion County

- Marion County SO
- Sheriff Jerry DeVore
  204 No. Washington St.
  Salem, IL 62881
  (618) 548-2141
  marioncountysheriff@gmail.com
- Centralia PD
- Chief Larry Evans
  222 So. Poplar St.
  Centralia, IL 62801
  (618) 533-7603
  levans333@yahoo.com
- Salem PD
- Chief Ron Campo
  201 So. Rotan St.
  Salem, IL 62881
  (618) 548-2232
  rcampo@salemilpolice.org

Marshall County

- Marshall County SO
- Sheriff Rob Russell
  520 6th St.
  Lacon, IL 61540
  (309) 246-2115
  mcsd062@yahoo.com
- Henry PD
- Chief William Calbow
  218 Railroad Ave.
  Henry, IL 61537
  (309) 364-3933
  hpd61537@live.com

Mason County

- Mason County SD
- Sheriff Wayne Youell
  102 W. Market St.
  Havana, IL 62644
  (309) 543-2231
  mcso@grics.net
- Easton PD
- Chief Bill Barnes
  104 So. 1st
  Easton, IL 62633
  (309) 543-2231
  legend@grics.net
- Manito PD
- Chief Scott Montgomery
  109 No. Broadway PO Box 735
  Manito, IL 61546
  (309) 968-6010
  manitopd@casscomm.com
- San Jose PD
- Chief Aaron Hodgson
  311 So. 2nd St. PO Box 351
  San Jose, IL 62682
  (309) 247-1234
  sanjoseil.police@yahoo.com

Massac County

- Massac County SO
- Sheriff Ted Holder
  519 Market St.
  Metropolis, IL 62960
  (618) 524-2912
  tholdermcso@comcast.net
- Metropolis City PD
- Chief Harry Masse
  1020 Broadway St.
  Metropolis, IL 62960
  (618) 524-2310
  metropdchief@comcast.net

McDonough County

- McDonough County SO
- Sheriff Rick VanBrooker
  110 So. McArthur St.
  Macomb, IL 61455
  (309) 833-2323
  rvanbrooker@sheriff.mcdonough.il.us
- Bushnell PD
- Chief Joe Fosdyck
  138 E. Hail St.
  Bushnell, IL 61422
  (309) 772- 9052
  jfosdyck@bushnellpolice.mcdonough.il.us

McHenry County

- McHenry County SD
- Sheriff Keith Nygren
  2200 No. Seminary Ave.
  Woodstock, IL 60098
  (815) 334-4715
  sheriff@co.mchenry.il.us
- Village of Algonquin PD
- Chief Russell Laine
  2200 Harnish Dr.
  Algonquin, IL 60102
  (See also Kane County)
  (847) 658-4531
  rlaine@algonquin.org
- Cary PD
- Chief Steven R. Casstevens
  654 Village Hall Dr.
  Cary, IL 60013
  (847) 639-2341
  scasstevens@caryillinois.com
- Crystal Lake PD
- Chief James R. Black
  121 W. Woodstock St.
  Crystal Lake, IL 60014
  (815) 356-3633
  jblack@crystallake.org
- Crystal Lake Park Dist. PD
- Chief Ronald L. Lyons
  One E. Crystal Lake Ave.
  Crystal Lake, IL 60014
  (815) 459-0680, ext. 221
  Chief@clpd.org
- Fox River Grove PD
- Chief Ron Lukasik
  305 Illinois St.
  Fox River Grove, IL 60021
  (847) 639-2411, ext. 112
  r.lukasik@foxrivergrove.org
- Harvard PD
- Chief Dan Kazy-Garey
  201 W. Front St.
  Harvard, IL 60033
  (815) 943-4431
  kazy-garey@cityofharvard.org
- Huntley PD
- Chief John Perkins
  10911 Main St.
  Huntley, IL 60142
  (847) 515-5311
  jperkins@huntley.il.us

- Johnsburg PD
- Chief Keith Von Allmen
  3611 Chapel Hill Rd.
  Johnsburg, IL 60050
  (815) 385-6024
  kvonallmen@johnsburg.org
- Lakemoor PD
- Chief David Godlewski
  234 W. Rand Rd.
  Lakemoor, IL 60051
  (815) 385-4111
  (See also Lake County)
  police@lakemoor.net
- Marengo PD
- Chief Joseph Hallman
  142 E. Prairie St.
  Marengo, IL 60152
  (815) 568-7231
  police@cityofmarengo.com
- McHenry PD
- Chief John M. Jones
  333 So. Green St.
  McHenry, IL 60050
  (815) 363-2200
  jjones@ci.mchenry.il.us
- Woodstock PD
- Chief Robert W. Lowen
  656 Lake Ave.
  Woodstock, IL 60098
  (815) 338-2131
  policedept@woodstockil.gov

McLean County

- McLean County SO
- Sheriff Mike Emery
  104 W. Front St. PO Box 2400
  Bloomington, IL 61702-2400
  (309) 888-5034
  mike.emery@mcleancountyil.gov
- Bloomington PD
- Chief Randall D. McKinley
  305 So. East St.
  Bloomington, IL 61701
  (309) 820-8888
  police@cityblm.org
- Chenoa PD
- Chief Travis Cornwall
  201 Green St. PO Box 167
  Chenoa, IL 61726
  (815) 945-7111
  police@chenoail.org
- Heyworth PD
- Chief Chris Lane
  108 So. Buchanan PO Box 439
  Heyworth, IL 61745
  (309) 473-2481
  policechief@heyworth-il.gov
- Hudson PD
- Chief Dale Sparks
  217 Shiner St. PO Box 221
  Hudson, IL 61748
  (309) 726-1001
  chiefsparks@hudsonil.org
- LeRoy PD
- Chief Gordon J. Beck
  111 E. Center St.
  LeRoy, IL 61752
  (Mail only: 207 So. East St.)
  (309) 962-3310
  leroypd@leroy.org
- Lexington PD
- Chief Dave Schneider
  329 W. Main St.
  Lexington, IL 61753
  (309) 365- 3871
  policelexingtonil@hotmail.com
- Normal PD
- Chief Rick Bleichner
  100 E. Phoenix Ave.
  Normal, IL 61761
  (309) 454-9526
  rbleichner@normal.org

Menard County

- Menard County SO
- Sheriff Chuck Jones
  315 So. 6th St. PO Box 476
  Petersburg, IL 62675
  (217) 632-2273
  cjones@co.menard.il.us
- Petersburg PD
- Chief Dave Coulter
  122 So. 6th St. PO Box 139
  Petersburg, IL 62675
  (217) 632-2251
  petersburgpd@casscomm.com

Mercer County

- Mercer County SO
- Sheriff Tom Thompson
  906 SW 3rd St.
  Aledo, IL 61231
  (309) 582-5194
  tthomps3@leo.gov

- Viola PD
- Chief Tom Mulder
  1305 17th Ave. PO Box 278
  Viola, IL 61486
  (309) 596-4111
  policechief@villageofviola.org

Monroe County

- Monroe County SO
- Sheriff Daniel Kelley
  225 E. 3rd St.
  Waterloo, IL 62298
  (618) 939-8651
  sheriff@htc.net
- Waterloo PD
- Chief Jim Trantham
  301 So. Main St.
  Waterloo, IL 62298
  (618) 939-3377
  jtrantham@waterloo.il.us

Montgomery County

- Montgomery County SO
- Sheriff Jim Vazzi
  140 No. Main St.
  Hillsboro, IL 62049
  (217) 532-9511
  mcdeputy@montgomery.k12.il.us
- Harvel PD
- Chief Tim Fortkamp
  201 So. Main St.
  Harvel, IL 62538
  (217) 229-3422
  harvelpolicedepartment@hotmail.com
- Litchfield PD
- Chief BJ Wilkinson
  120 E. Ryder St.
  Litchfield, IL 62056
  (217) 324-5991
  BWilkinson@cityoflitchfieldil.com

Morgan County

- Morgan County SO
- Sheriff Randy Duvendack
  300 W. Court St.
  Jacksonville, IL 62650
  (217) 245-4143
  rduvendack@net-axess.com
- Jacksonville PD
- Chief Anthony Grootens
  200 W. Douglas Ave.
  Jacksonville, IL 62650
  (217) 479-4630
  jpdchief@jacksonvilleil.com
- Meredosia PD
- Chief Mike A Beard
  315 Main St.
  Meredosia, IL 62665
  (217) 584-1128
  mpd@bluffsnet.com
- South Jacksonville PD
- Chief Richard A. Evans
  301 Dewey Dr.
  South Jacksonville, IL 62650
  (217) 245-9222
  sjpd@southjacksonville.org

Moultrie County

- Moultrie County SO
- Sheriff Jeff Thomas
  1505 W. Hagerman Rd.
  Sullivan, IL 61951
  (217) 728-4386
  jthomas@moultriesheriff.com
- Lovington PD
- Chief Jim Minor
  145 So. County St.
  Lovington, IL 61937
  (217) 873-9922
  lov_police@lovington-il.gov
- Sullivan PD
- Chief John Love
  307 So. Van Buren St.
  Sullivan, IL 61951
  (217) 728-4351
  JohnL@sullivanil.us

Ogle County

- Ogle County SO
- Sheriff Michael Harn
  103 Jefferson St.
  Oregon, IL 61061
  (815) 732-6666
  oglesheriff@oglecounty.org
- Byron PD
- Chief Todd R. Murray
  120 No. Union St.
  Byron, IL 61010
  (815) 234-5072
  TMurray@byronil.net
- Hillcrest PD
- Chief Danny White
  204 Hillcrest Ave.
  Hillcrest, IL 61068
  (815) 562-2081
  police@hillcrestil.us

- Mount Morris PD
- Chief Jason White
  105 W. Lincoln St.
  Mount Morris, IL 61054
  (815) 734-4106
  mmpolice@essex1.com
- Oregon PD
- Chief Darin J. DeHaan
  115 No. 3rd St.
  Oregon, IL 61061
  (815) 732-2162
  dehaan140@comcast.net
- Rochelle PD
- Chief Eric Higby
  416 No. 6th St.
  Rochelle, IL 61068
  (815) 562-2131
  ehigby@rochelleil.us

Peoria County

- Peoria County SO
- Sheriff Michael McCoy
  301 No. Maxwell Rd.
  Peoria, IL 61604
  (309) 697-7858
  mmccoy@peoriacounty.org
- Bartonville PD
- Chief Brian Fengel
  5918 So. Adams St.
  Bartonville, IL 61607
  (309) 697-2323
  chieffengel@comcast.net
- Peoria PD
- Chief Steven M. Settingsgaard
  600 SW Adams St.
  Peoria, IL 61602
  (309) 673-4521
  ssettingsgaard@ci.peoria.il.us
- Peoria Heights PD
- Chief Dustin Sutton
  4901 Prospect Rd.
  Peoria Heights, IL 61616
  (309) 688-3461
  dsutton@heightspd.com

Perry County

- Perry County SO
- Sheriff Keith Kellerman
  12 E. Water St.
  Pinckneyville, IL 62274
  (618) 357-5212
  pcso@verizon.net
- Pinckneyville PD
- Chief John Griffin
  104 So. Walnut St.
  Pinckneyville, IL 62274
  (618) 357-8231
  police@ci.pinckneyville.il.us

Piatt County

- Piatt County SO
- Sheriff David Hunt
  1216 Raymond Rd.
  Monticello, IL 61856
  (217) 762-7822
  hunt.d@mchsi.com
- Monticello PD
- Chief Michael Galloway
  301 No. Hamilton
  Monticello, IL 61856
  (217) 762-9307
  mgalloway@monticellopolice.net

Pike County

- Pike County SO
- Sheriff Paul Petty
  204 E. Adams St.
  Pittsfield, IL 62363
  (217) 285-5011
  sheriffpetty@pikecountysd.org
- Pittsfield PD
- Chief Dennis Jennings
  215 No. Monroe St.
  Pittsfield, IL 62363
  (217) 285-5011
  chief@pittsfieldpolice.org
- Pleasant Hill PD
- Chief Zack Orr
  104 W. Quincy St. PO Box 187
  Pleasant Hill, IL 62366
  (217) 734-2113
  zorr@pikecountysd.org

Pope County

- Pope County SD
- Sheriff Jerry Suits
  216 E. Decatur St. PO Box 807
  Golconda, IL 62938
  (618) 683-4321
  jernkate@hughes.net
- Golconda PD
- Chief Larry W Fisher
  216 E. Decatur St. PO Box 1
  Golconda, IL 62938
  (618) 683-4321
  whec64@yahoo.com

Pulaski County

- Pulaski County SD
- Sheriff Randy Kern
  500 Illinois Ave., Rm. # A
  Mound City, IL 62963
  (618) 748-9374
  pcs771@yahoo.com

Putnam County

- Putnam County SO
- Sheriff Kevin Doyle
  120 No. 4th St.
  Hennepin, IL 61327
  (815) 925-7084
  kevin.doyle@leo.gov
- Granville PD
- Chief Kevin Moore
  316 So. McCoy PO Box 580
  Granville, IL 61326
  (815) 339-2514
  granville.policedept@mchsi.com

Randolph County

- Randolph County SO
- Sheriff Mike Hoelscher
  200 W. Buena Vista
  Chester, IL 62233
  (618) 826-5484
  MikeHoelscher@randolphcso.com
- Red Bud PD
- Chief Dan Brotz
  200 E. Market St.
  Red Bud, IL 62278
  (618) 282-6118
  dan@cityofredbud.org
- Sparta PD
- Chief Thomas Ashley
  112 W. Jackson St.
  Sparta, IL 62286
  (618) 443-4331
  Spdtc2000@yahoo.com
- Steeleville PD
- Chief Lyndon Thies
  107 W. Broadway
  Steeleville, IL 62288
  (618) 965-3134
  svpd@steeleville.org

Richland County

- Richland County SO
- Sheriff Andrew Hires
  211 W. Market
  Olney, IL 62450
  (618) 395-7481
  richlandso@frontier.com

Rock Island County

- Rock Island County SO
- Sheriff Jeff Boyd
  1317-3rd Ave.
  Rock Island, IL 61201
  (309) 794-1230
  jeffb@geonline.com
- Andalusia PD
- Chief Wilbur Williams
  102 Opp Ave. PO Box 429
  Andalusia, IL 61232
  (334) 222-1155
  wilbur.williams@andalusiapolice.com
- Coal Valley PD
- Chief Mark Poulos
  900 1st St. PO Box 121
  Coal Valley, IL 61240-0121
  (309) 799-5416
  CoalValleyPD@coalvalleyillinois.org
- East Moline PD
- Chief Victor Moreno
  915 16th Ave.
  East Moline, IL 61244
  (309) 752-1556
  vm3064@eastmoline.com
- Hampton PD
- Chief Robert W. Fuller
  901 4th St. PO Box 227
  Hampton, IL 61256
  (309) 496-9123
  hamptonpd@mchsi.com
- Milan PD
- Chief Shawn C. Johnson
  321 W. 2nd Ave.
  Milan, IL 61264
  (309) 787-8520
  shawnjohnson@milan.il.us
- Moline PD
- Chief Kim Hankins
  1640 6th Ave.
  Moline, IL 61265
  (309) 797-0401
  swilliams@moline.il.us

- Rock Island PD
- Chief Jeffrey R. VenHuizen
  316 16th St.
  Rock Island, IL 61201
  (309) 732-2677
  policemail@rigov.org
- Silvis PD
- Chief Bill Brasche
  1040-1st Ave.
  Silvis, IL 61282
  (309) 792-1841
  bbrasche@silvispd.org

Saint Clair County

- Saint Clair County SO
- Sheriff Rick Watson
  700 No. 5th St.
  Belleville, IL 62220
  (618) 277-3505, ext. 5722
  sheriff@norcom2000.com
- Caseyville PD
- Chief JD Roth
  10 W. Morris St.
  Caseyville, IL 62232
  (618) 344-2151
  jdroth@caseyville.org
- East St Louis PD
- Chief Michael Floore
  301 River Park Dr.
  East St Louis, IL 62201
  (618) 482-6724
  mfloore@eslpd.com
- Fairview Heights PD
- Chief Nick Gailius
  10027 Bunkum Rd.
  Fairview Heights, IL 62208
  (618) 489-2150
  gailius@fairviewpd.org
- Freeburg PD
- Chief Mel Woodruff
  14 Southgate Center
  Freeburg, IL 62243
  (618) 539-3132
  fpd1@freeburg.com
- Lebanon PD
- Chief Dale Warke
  403 W. St. Louis
  Lebanon, IL 62254
  (618) 537-6131
  Chief@LebanonPD.com
- Mascoutah PD
- Chief Bruce W. Fleshren
  3 W. Main St.
  Mascoutah, IL 62258
  (618) 566-2976, ext. 110
  mpd@mascoutah.com
- Millstadt PD
- Chief Edward T. *Ed* Wilkerson
  108 W. White St.
  Millstadt, IL 62260
  (618) 476-7250
  chief@millstadtpolice.org
- New Athens PD
- Act. Chief (*Lt.*) Tim Buehler
  905 Spotsylvania
  New Athens, IL 62264
  (618) 475-2133
  tim.villagena@htc.net
- O'Fallon PD
- Chief John Betten
  285 No. Seven Hills Rd.
  O'Fallon, IL 62269
  (618) 624-4545
  jbetten@ofallon.org
- Shiloh PD
- Chief Jim Stover
  3498 Lebanon Ave.
  Shiloh, IL 62269
  (618) 632-9047
  shilohpd@shilohil.org
- Swansea PD
- Chief Michael J. Arnold
  1400 No. Illinois St.
  Swansea, IL 62226
  (618) 233-8114
  marnold@swanseail.org

Saline County

- Saline County SO
- Sheriff Keith Brown
  1 No. Main
  Harrisburg, IL 62946
  (618) 252-8661
  sheriff@clearwave.com
- Carrier Mills PD
- Chief Chuck Rubright
  PO Box 7
  Carrier Mills, IL 62917
  (618) 994-4411
  millspolice@hotmail.com

Sangamon County

- Sangamon County SO
- Sheriff Neil Williamson
  1 Sheriffs Plaza
  Springfield, IL 62701
  (217) 753-6855
  nw2473@co.sangamon.il.us
- Auburn PD
- Chief Bruce Centko
  324 W. Jefferson St.
  Auburn, IL 62615
  (217) 438-3351
  Bruce.Centko@auburnillinois.us
- Chatham PD
- Chief John Holm
  117 E. Mulberry St.
  Chatham, IL 62629
  (217) 483-2456
  VernF@ChathamIL.net
- Divernon PD
- Chief Jamie Lomelino
  50 E. Brown
  Divernon, IL 62530
  (217) 628-3355
  divvlg@comcast.net
- New Berlin PD
- Chief Terry Nydegger
  301 E. Illinois
  New Berlin, IL 62670
  (217) 488-6102
  police@newberlin.il.us
- Pawnee PD
- Chief Jan Bowsher
  617 7th St. PO Box 560
  Pawnee, IL 62558
  (217) 625-2341
  pawneepd@comcast.net
- Riverton PD
- Chief Dave Smith
  1200 E. Riverton Rd.
  Riverton, IL 62561-8200
  (217) 629-9800
  RivertonPD@gmail.com
- Rochester PD
- Chief William Marass
  1 Community Dr.
  Rochester, IL 62563
  (217) 498-8424
  police@rochesteril.org
- Sherman PD
- Chief Eric Smith
  2629 E. Andrew Rd.
  Sherman, IL 62684
  (217) 496-3256
  esmith@shermanil.org
- Springfield PD
- Chief Robert Williams
  800 E. Monroe St. #345
  Springfield, IL 62701
  (217) 788-8325
  bob.davidsmeyer@cwlp.com

Schuyler County

- Schuyler County SO
- Sheriff Don Schieferdecker
  216 W. Lafayette St.
  Rushville, IL 62681
  (217) 322-4366
  schylercoso@casscomm.com
- Rushville PD
- Chief Bill White
  220 W. Washington St.
  Rushville, IL 62681
  (217) 322-3833
  cityinfo@rushville-illinois.com

Scott County

- Scott County SO
- Sheriff David King
  101 E. Market St.
  Winchester, IL 62694
  (217) 742-3141
  scsd@irtc.net

Shelby County

- Shelby County SO
- Sheriff Michael Miller
  151 No. Morgan St.
  Shelbyville, IL 62565
  (217) 774-3941
  sheriff_miller@consolidated.net
- Windsor PD
- Chief Sean McQueen
  1016 Maine St.
  Windsor, IL 61957
  (217) 459-2282
  wpd805@yahoo.com

Stark County

- Stark County SO
- Sheriff Jim Dison
  130 W. Jefferson
  Toulon, IL 61483
  (309) 286-2541
  sheriff@starkco.illinois.gov

Stephenson County

- Stephenson County SO
- Sheriff David Snyders
  15 No. Galena
  Freeport, IL 61032
  (815) 235-8290
  dasnyders98@yahoo.com
- Lena PD
- Chief Jessie Keplinger
  117 E. Main St.
  Lena, IL 61048
  (920) 829-5950
  lenapd@villageoflena.net

Tazewell County

- Tazewell County SD
- Sheriff Robert Huston
  101 So. Capitol St.
  Pekin, IL 61554-4108
  (309) 478-5607
  rhuston@tazewell.com
- Creve Coeur PD
- Chief Peter A. Fisher
  105 No. Thorncrest Ave.
  Creve Coeur, IL 61610
  (309) 699-9511
  info@crevecoeurpd.com
- Delavan PD
- Chief Colin Suprunowski
  219 Locust St.
  Delavan, IL 61734
  (309) 244-7721
  department@delavanpolice.com
- East Peoria PD
- Chief Dick Ganschow
  201 W. Washington St.
  East Peoria, IL 60611
  (309) 698-4700
  dickganschow@cityofeastpeoria.com
- Fondulac Park District PD
- Chief Michael Johnson
  3701 No. Main St.
  East Peoria, IL 61611
  (309) 698-4700
  police@fondulacpark.com
- Green Valley PD
- Chief Donald Bridges
  109 E. Main St.
  Green Valley, IL 61534
  (309) 352-2111
  gvpd@mchsi.com
- Minier-Armington PD
- Chief Daryl Weseloh
  110 W. Central
  Minier, IL 61759
  (800) 322-0166
  minierpd@mchsi.com
- Morton PD
- Chief Craig Hilliard
  375 W. Birchwood St.
  Morton, IL 61550
  (309) 266-6666
  hilliard@morton-il.gov
- Pekin PD
- Chief Greg Nelson
  111 So. Capitol St.
  Pekin, IL 61554
  (309) 346-3132
  gnelson@ci.pekin.il.us
- Tremont PD
- Chief Michael Dodwell
  211 So. Sampson St.
  Tremont, IL 61568
  (309) 925- 5102
  tremontpd@comcast.net
- Washington PD
- Chief James W. *Jim* Kuchenbecker
  115 W. Jefferson St.
  Washington, IL 61571
  (309) 444-2313
  jkuchenbecker@ci.washington.il.us

Union County

- Union County SD
- Sheriff David Livesay
  307 W. Market St.
  Jonesboro, IL 62952
  (618) 833-5500
  ucso091@mail.com
- Anna PD
- Chief Dale Foster
  201 E. Vienna St.
  Anna, IL 62906
  (618) 833-8571
  cityhall@cityofanna.org

Vermilion County

- Vermilion County SD
- Sheriff Pat Hartshorn
  2 E. South St.
  Danville, IL 61832
  (217) 442-4080
  phartshorn@vermilionsheriff.org
- Danville PD
- Chief Larry Thomason
  2 E. South St.
  Danville, IL 61832
  (217) 431-2234
  lthomason@danvillepd.org
- Hoopeston PD
- Chief Mark S. Drollinger
  301 W. Main St.
  Hoopeston, IL 60942
  (217) 283-5196
  chief@hoopestonpolice.org
- Rossville PD
- Chief Bill Shannon
  120 E. Attica St.
  Rossville, IL 60963
  (217) 283-5196
  clerk@villageofrossville.org

Wabash County

- Wabash County SD
- Sheriff Joe Keeling
  120 E. 4th St.
  Mount Carmel, IL 62863
  (618) 262-4186
  wabashcountysheriff@gmail.com
- Mt Carmel PD
- Chief Jeff Besing
  110 E. 4th St.
  Mount Carmel, IL 62863
  (618) 262-4114
  jlockhard@wabash911.net

Warren County

- Warren County SO
- Sheriff Martin Edwards
  121 No. A St.
  Monmouth, IL 61462
  (309) 734-8505
  sheriff_warren@9thjudicial.org

Washington County

- Washington County SO
- Sheriff Charlie Parker
  245 No. Kaskaskia St.
  Nashville, IL 62263
  (618) 327-8273
  clp396wc@hotmail.com

Wayne County

- Wayne County SO
- Sheriff Mike Everett
  305 E. Court St.
  Fairfield, IL 62837
  (618) 842-6631
  sheriffeverett@gmail.com
- Fairfield PD
- Chief William Winter
  1002 Leininger Rd.
  Fairfield, IL 62837
  (618) 842-2151
  winter@fairfieldpd.org

White County

- White County SO
- Sheriff Doug Maier
  108 No. Main Cross St.
  Carmi, IL 62821
  (618) 382-5321
  sheriff@whitecounty-il.gov
- Carmi PD
- Chief Randy Hamblin
  108 No. Main Cross St.
  Carmi, IL 62821
  (618) 382-4633
  police@carmipd.com

Whiteside County

- Whiteside County SO
- Sheriff Kelly Wilhelmi
  400 No. Cherry St.
  Morrison, IL 61270
  (815) 772-4044
  kwilhelmi@whiteside.org
- Morrison PD
- Chief Brian R. Melton
  200 W. Main St.
  Morrison, IL 61270
  (815) 772-7650
  bmelton@morrisonil.org

- Rock Falls PD
- Chief Michael Kuelper
  1013 7th Ave.
  Rock Falls, IL 61071
  (815) 622-1140
  rfpolice@rockfalls61071.com
- Sterling PD
- Chief Ron Potthoff
  212-3rd Ave.
  Sterling, IL 61081
  (815) 632-6600
  rpotthoff@sterling-il.gov

Will County

- Will County SD
- Sheriff Paul Kaupas
  14 W. Jefferson St.
  Joliet, IL 60432
  (815) 727-8798
  pkaupas@willcosheriff.org
- Beecher PD
- Chief Jeffrey L. Weissgerber
  724 Penfield St. PO Box 1114
  Beecher, IL 60401
  (708) 946-2341
  policechief@villageofbeecher.org
- Bolingbrook PD
- Chief Kevin McCarthy
  375 W. Briarcliff Rd.
  Bolingbrook, IL 60440
  (630) 226-8600
  police@bolingbrook.com
- Braidwood PD
- Act. Chief Richard Girot
  141 W. Main St.
  Braidwood, IL 60408
  (815) 458-2341
  rgirot@braidwood.us
- Channahon PD
- Chief Jeff Wold
  24555 So. Navajo Dr.
  Channahon, IL 60410
  (815) 467-5152
  jwold@channahon.org
- Crete PD
- Chief James M. Paoletti
  1370 Benton St.
  Crete, IL 60417
  (708) 672-0912
  jpaoletti@villageofcrete.org
- Frankfort PD
- Chief John Burica
  20602 Lincoln Way Ln.
  Frankfort, IL 60423
  (815) 469-9435
  jburica@frankfortpolice.net
- Joliet PD
- Chief Michael P. Trafton
  150 W. Washington St.
  Joliet, IL 60432
  (815) 724-3201
  chiefsoffice@jolietcity.org
- Joliet Jr. College PD
- Chief Pete Comanda
  1215 Houbolt Rd.
  Joliet, IL 60431
  (815) 280-6606
  pcomanda@jjc.edu
- Minooka PD
- Chief Justin Meyer
  121 E. McEvilly Rd.
  Minooka, IL 60447
  (See also Grundy & Kendall counties)
  (815) 467-2151
  justin.meyer@minooka.com
- Mokena PD
- Chief Randy Rajewski
  10907 Front
  Mokena, IL 60448
  (708) 479-3912
  admin@mokenapd.com
- Naperville PD
- Chief Robert *Bob* Marshall
  1350 Aurora Ave.
  Naperville, IL 60540
  (See also DuPage County)
  (630) 420-6666
  marshallr@naperville.il.us
- New Lenox PD
- Chief Bob Sterba
  701 W. Haven Ave.
  New Lenox, IL 60451
  (815) 462-6100
  newlenoxpd@newlenox.net
- Park Forest PD
- Dep. Chief Clifford Butz
  200 Lakewood Blvd
  Park Forest, IL 60466
  (708) 748-4700
  cbutz@vopf.com

- Peotone PD
- Chief Bill Mort
  208 E. Main St.
  Peotone, IL 60468
  (708) 258-3003
  wmort@villageofpeotone.com
- Plainfield PD
- Chief John Konopek
  14300 So. Coil Plus Dr.
  Plainfield, IL 60544
  (815) 436-2341
  jkonopek@plainfieldpd.com
- Shorewood PD
- Chief Aaron Klima
  903 W. Jefferson St.
  Shorewood, IL 60435
  (815) 725-4636
  aklima@vil.shorewood.il.us
- Steger PD
- Chief Richard L. Stultz
  35 W. 34th St.
  Steger, IL 60475
  (708) 754-8121
  stultz@stegerpolice.org
- Tinley Park PD
- Chief Steve Neubauer
  7850 W. 183rd St.
  Tinley Park, IL 60477
  (708) 444-5300
  sneubauer@tinleypark.org
- University Park PD
- Int. Chief Darryl Stroud
  698 Burnham Dr.
  University Park, IL 60466
  (708) 534-0913
  dstroud@university-park-il.com
- Woodridge PD
- Chief Ken Boehm
  1 Plaza Dr.
  Woodridge, IL 60517
  (630) 719-4728
  kboehm@vil.woodridge.il.us

Williamson County

- Williamson County SO
- Sheriff Bennie Vick
  200 W. Jefferson St.
  Marion, IL 62959
  (618) 997-6541
  bvick@wcsheriff.com
- Carterville PD
- Chief Monty S. Jeralds
  121 W. Illinois Ave.
  Carterville, IL 62918
  (618) 985-4853
  sergentcville@msn.com
- Energy PD
- Chief Shawn Ladd
  210 No. Pershing
  Energy, IL 62933
  (618) 942-5833
  sml9401@hotmail.com
- Herrin PD
- Chief Stewart W. Ridings
  321 No. 14th St.
  Herrin, IL 62948
  (618) 942-4132
  HerrinPoliceDepartment@gmail.com

Winnebago County

- Winnebago County SO
- Sheriff Richard Meyers
  420 W. State St.
  Rockford, IL 61101
  (815) 319-6005
  meyersr@sheriff.co.winnebago.il.us
- Cherry Valley PD
- Chief Todd Houde
  212 E. State St.
  Cherry Valley, IL 61016
  (815) 332-3432
  thoude@cherryvalley.org
- Loves Park PD
- Chief James R. Puckett
  540 Loves Park Dr.
  Loves Park, IL 61111
  (815) 654-5015
  policeinfo@loves-park.il.us
- Pecatonica PD
- Chief Robert Smith
  405 Main St.
  PO Box 82
  Pecatonica, IL 61063
  (815) 239-2373
  pecatonica-police@frontier.com
- Rockford Park District PD
- Chief Theo Glover
  401 So. Main St.
  Rockford, IL 61101
  (815) 966-2900
  rpdmail@rockfordparkdistrict.org

- Rockton PD
- Chief Stephen Dickson
  110 E. Main St.
  Rockton, IL 61072
  (815) 624-8881
  webmaster@rocktonpolice.org
- Roscoe PD
- Chief Jamie Evans
  10595 Main St.
  Roscoe, IL 61073
  (815) 623-7338
  jevans7892@roscoepolice.com
- South Beloit PD
- Chief Dean Stiegemeier
  519 Blackhawk Blvd
  South Beloit, IL 61080
  (815) 389-3491
  d.stiegemeier@southbeloit.org
- Winnebago PD
- Chief Todd Stockburger
  108 W. Main St.
  Winnebago, IL 61088
  (815) 335-2020
  chief@bagopolice.com

Woodford County

- Woodford County SD
- Sheriff James Pierceall
  111 E. Court St.
  Eureka, IL 61530
  (309) 467-2375
  wcsheriff@mchsi.com
- El Paso PD
- Chief Jeffrey L. Price
  540 E. Main St.
  El Paso, IL 61738
  (309) 527-5340
  Price101@fairpoint.net

State Agencies

- IL State Police
- Dir. Hiram Grau
  801 So. 7th St., Ste. 1000-S
  Springfield, IL 62703
  (217) 782-7263
  Hiram_Grau@isp.state.il.us
- Benedictine U. PD
- Chief Michael Salatino
  5700 College Rd.
  Lisle, IL 60532
  (630) 829-6122, ext. 6667
  publicsafety@ben.edu
- Governor's State U. PD
- Int. Chief James R. McGee
  1 University Pkwy, Rm. C1375
  University Park, IL 60466
  (708) 534-4900
  jmcgee@govst.edu

INDIANA

Adams County

- Adams County SO
- Sheriff Shane L. Rekeweg
  313 So. 1st St. PO Box 608
  Decatur, IN 46733
  (260) 724-5345
  srekeweg@co.adams.in.us
- Berne PD
- Chief Tim Taylor
  1160 W. Main St.
  Berne, IN 46711
  (260) 589-2169
  nlindsey@bernepd.org

Allen County

- Allen County SO
- Sheriff Kenneth C. *Ken* Fries
  715 So. Calhoun St., Rm. 101
  Fort Wayne, IN 46802
  (260) 449-7535
  steve.stone@co.allen.in.us
- Fort Wayne PD
- Chief Rusty York
  1 E. Main
  Fort Wayne, IN 46803
  (260) 427-1230
  russell.york@cityoffortwayne.org
- New Haven PD
- Chief Stephan Poiry
  815 Lincoln Hwy E. PO Box 570
  New Haven, IN 46774
  (260) 748-7080
  nhpd@newhavenin.org

Benton County

- Bi-State Drug Task Force
- Chief George Frantz
  (See also Fountain, Jasper, Newton & Warren counties)
  PO Box 56
  Williamsport, IN 47993
  (765) 426-2328
  bistatedrugs@go.com
- Fowler PD
- Chief Michael Brand
  311 E. 5th St.
  Fowler, IN 47944
  (765) 834-3254
  fowlerpd@ci.fowler.ca.us

Blackford County

- Blackford County SO
- Sheriff John A. Lancaster
  64 No. 500 E
  Hartford City, IN 47348
  (765) 348-0930
  jlancaster@blackfordcounty.com
- Hartford City PD
- Chief Bill Meyer
  700 No. Walnut St.
  Hartford City, IN 47348
  (765) 348-4819
  hcpd@hartfordcity.net

Boone County

- Lebanon PD
- Chief Sam Myers
  201 E. Main St.
  Lebanon, IN 46052
  (765) 482-8836
  police@cityoflebanon.org
- Zionsville PD
- Chief Robert Knox
  1075 Parkway Dr.
  Zionsville, IN 46077
  (317) 873-5967
  police@zionsvillepd.com

Brown County

- Brown County SO
- Sheriff Rick D. Followell
  55 State Rd. 46 E. PO Box 95
  Nashville, IN 47448
  (812) 988-6655
  sheriff@browncounty-in.us

Carroll County

- Carroll County SO
- Sheriff Tony L. Burns
  310 W. Main St.
  Delphi, IN 46923
  (765) 564-2413
  jailer@cacoshrs.com
- Delphi PD
- Chief John M. Chapman
  201 So. Union St.
  Delphi, IN 46923
  (765) 564-2345
  101@cityofdelphi.org

Cass County

- Cass County SO
- Sheriff Randolph L. *Randy* Pryor
  200 Court Park
  Logansport, IN 46947
  (574) 753-7800
  leeann.morales@co.cass.in.us
- Logansport PD
- Chief Michael L. Clark
  601 E. Broadway
  Logansport, IN 46947
  (574) 753- 2551
  mclark@logansportpolice.com

Clark County

- Charlestown PD
- Chief (*Col.*) Keith McDonald
  701 Main St.
  Charlestown, IN 47111
  (812) 256-6345, ext. 102
  chiefmcdonald@ctownpd.com
- Clarksville PD
- Chief Mark Palmer
  1970 Broadway
  Clarksville, IN 47129
  (812) 288-7151
  m.palmer@clarksvillepolice.com
- Sellersburg PD
- Chief Russ Whelan
  101 So. New Albany St.
  Sellersburg, IN 47172
  (812) 246-4491
  russ.whelan@sellersburgpd.org

Clinton County

- Clinton County SO
- Sheriff Jeffrey L. *Jeff* Ward
  301 E. Walnut
  Frankfort, IN 46041
  (765) 659-6393
  jmink@clintonco.com
- Colfax PD
- Marshal Duane Lewellen
  210 W. Main St.
  Colfax, IN 46035
  (765) 324-2777
  colfaxpd@tctc.com

Daviess County

- Washington PD
- Chief Mike Healy
  101 NE 3rd St.
  Washington, IN 47501
  (812) 254-4410
  mhealy@washingtonin.us

Dearborn County

- Dearborn County SO
- Sheriff Michael R. Kreinhop
  301 W. High St.
  Lawrenceburg, IN 47025
  (812) 537-8700
  mkreinhop@dearborncounty.in.gov
- Aurora PD
- Chief Bryan H. Fields
  233 Main St.
  Aurora, IN 47001
  (812) 926-1101
  bfields@aurora.in.us
- Lawrenceburg PD
- Chief Gene Hunefeld
  249 Walnut St.
  Lawrenceburg, IN 47025
  (812) 537-2284
  ghunefeld@lawrenceburgpolice.com
- St Leon PD
- Chief William D. Wendt
  7582 Church Ln.
  St Leon, IN 47012
  (812) 576-5366
  SLPD15@aol.com

Decatur County

- Decatur County SD
- Sheriff Gregory D. Allen
  315 So. Ireland St.
  Greensburg, IN 47240
  (812) 663-8125
  gdallen@decanturcounty.in.gov
- St. Paul PD
- Marshal Josh Kuntz
  108 Webster St.
  St. Paul, IN 47272
  (765) 525-7695
  chrisvierling@yahoo.com
- Westport PD
- Marshal Joe Talkington
  203 E. Mulberry PO Box 579
  Westport, IN 47283
  (812) 591-2651
  J.Talkington@westportpolice.com

DeKalb County

- DeKalb County SO
- Sheriff Donald J. *Don* Lauer
  215 E. 8th St.
  Auburn, IN 46706
  (260) 925-3365
  dlauer@co.dekalb.in.us

- Ashley PD
- Town Marshal Scott Barnhart
  500 So. Gonser PO Box 70
  Ashley, IN 46705
  (260) 587-9388
  marshal461@ashley.in.gov
- Auburn PD
- Chief Martin D. McCoy
  210 So. Cedar St. PO Box 506
  Auburn, IN 46706
  (260) 920-3200
  police@ci.auburn.in.us
- Butler PD
- Chief Jim Nichols
  120 W. Main St.
  Butler, IN 46721
  (260) 868-2171
  bpdchief@butler.in.us
- Garrett PD
- Chief Keith Hefner
  200 No. Cowen St.
  Garrett, IN 46738
  (260) 357-5151, ext. 3160
  chiefhefner@garrettindiana.us

Delaware County

- Delaware County SD
- Sheriff Michael S. Scroggins
  100 W. Washington St.
  Muncie, IN 47305
  (765) 747-7885
  mscroggins@co.delaware.in.us
- Daleville PD
- Chief James King
  8019 So. Walnut
  Daleville, IN 47334
  (765) 378-6343
  jdkingsr@comcast.net
- Eaton PD
- Chief Jon Snodgrass
  211 W. Harris St.
  Eaton, IN 47338
  (765) 396-3297
  epd9404@yahoo.com
- Muncie PD
- Chief Steve Stewart
  300 No. High St.
  Muncie, IN 47305
  (765) 747-4822
  chief@munciepolice.org
- Yorktown PD
- Town Marshal Richard T. *Todd* St. John
  9730 W. Smith St.
  Yorktown, IN 47396
  (765) 759-7760
  rstjohn@yorktownindiana.org

Dubois County

- Dubois County SO
- Sheriff Donald R. *Donny* Lampert
  255 Brucke Strasse Rd.
  Jasper, IN 47547
  (812) 482-3522
  donnylampert@duboiscounty.org
- Ferdinand PD
- Chief Ted Bieker
  243 W. 10th St.
  Ferdinand, IN 47532
  (812) 367-1806
  twbeiker@ferdinandindiana.org

Elkhart County

- Elkhart County SD
- Sheriff Bradley D. *Brad* Rogers
  26861 County Rd. 26
  Elkhart, IN 46516
  (574) 891-2100
  brogers@elkhartcountysheriff.com
- Bristol PD
- Marshal Mike Swallow
  301 E. Vistula St. PO Box 325
  Bristol, IN 46507
  (574) 848-4464
  bristolpd@bristolpolice.org
- Elkhart PD
- Chief Dale Pflibsen
  175 Waterfall Dr.
  Elkhart, IN 46516
  (574) 295-7070
  dale.pflibsen@elkhartpolice.org
- Goshen PD
- Chief Wade Branson
  111 E. Jefferson St., Ste. 5
  Goshen, IN 46526
  (574) 533-8661
  police@goshencity.com
- Nappanee PD
- Chief Julie Dijkstra
  301 W. Lincoln St.
  Nappanee, IN 46550
  (574) 773-4111
  jdijkstra@nappaneepolice.com

- Wakarusa PD
- Town Marshal Bob Cunningham
  102 So. Spring St.
  Wakarusa, IN 46573
  (574) 862-4200
  wakarusapd@wakarusapolice.com

Fayette County

- Fayette County SD
- Sheriff William E. *Billy* Wayson
  123 W. 4th St.
  Connersville, IN 47331
  (765) 825-1110
  faycoinsd@hotmail.com
- Connersville PD
- Chief David Counceller
  500 No. Central Ave.
  Connersville, IN 47331
  (765) 825-2111
  deputychiefperkins@gmail.com

Floyd County

- Floyd County SO
- Sheriff Darrell W. Mills
  311 Hauss Sq.
  New Albany, IN 47150
  (812) 948-5400
  dmills@fcsdin.net
- Georgetown PD
- Chief Dennis Kunkel
  1636 Henriott Rd. PO Box 455
  Georgetown, IN 47122
  (812) 951-2508
  dennis.kunkel@georgetown.in.gov
- New Albany PD
- Chief Sherri Knight
  311 Hauss Sq., Rm. 131
  New Albany, IN 47150
  (812) 944-6411
  sknight@cityofnewalbany.com

Fountain County

- Fountain County SO
- Sheriff William D. *Bill* Sanders, Jr.
  216 Union St.
  Covington, IN 47932
  (765) 793-3545
  billsanders1956@yahoo.com
- Bi-State Drug Task Force
- Chief George Frantz
  (See also Benton, Jasper, Newton & Warren counties)
  PO Box 56
  Williamsport, IN 47993
  (765) 426-2328
  bistatedrugs@go.com
- Covington PD
- Chief Larry Weber
  1329 2nd St. PO Box 248
  Covington, IN 47932
  (765) 793-3311
  covingtonpd@sbcglobal.net
- Veedersburg PD
- Marshal Neil E Beck
  100 So. Main St.
  Veedersburg, IN 47987
  (765) 294-2345
  veedersburgpd@sbcglobal.net

Franklin County

- Franklin County SO
- Sheriff Kenneth A. Murphy
  371 Main St.
  Brookville, IN 47012
  (765) 647-4138
  sheriff@franklincounty.in.gov
- Brookville PD
- Chief Phil Wietholter
  634 Main St.
  Brookville, IN 47012
  (765) 647-4178
  philw4@etczone.com

Fulton County

- Rochester PD
- Chief Jodi Miller
  312 Main St.
  Rochester, IN 46975
  (574) 223-3313
  Chiefpolice@Rochester.IN.US

Gibson County

- Fort Branch PD
- Town Marshal Rick Sides
  210 W. Locust PO Box 40
  Fort Branch, IN 47648
  (812) 753-3824
  fbpd@insightbb.com

- Princeton PD
- Chief WW George
  310 W. State St.
  Princeton, IN 47670
  (812) 385-3437
  p.police@insight.com

Grant County

- Grant County SO
- Sheriff Darrell L. Himelick
  214 E. 4th St
  Marion, IN 46953
  (765) 662-9836
  sheriff@grantcounty.net
- Converse PD
- Town Marshal Roger Bowland
  210 No. Jefferson PO Box 473
  Converse, IN 46919
  (765)395-9000
  Conversepd@sbcglobal.net
- Gas City PD
- Chief Kirk McCollum
  211 E. Main St.
  Gas City, IN 46933
  (765) 674-2278
  gcpolice@indy.rr.com
- Marion PD
- Chief David Gilbert
  301 So. Branson St.
  Marion, IN 46952
  (765) 668-4412
  ccook@marionindiana.us
- Sweetser PD
- Town Marshal Chris Tarlton
  113 No. Main St.
  Sweetser, IN 46987
  (765) 383-7222
  sweetsermarshal@yahoo.com

Greene County

- Bloomfield PD
- Town Marshal Kenneth R. Tharp
  12 E. Main St.
  Bloomfield, IN 47424
  (812) 384-4114
  marshal@bloomfieldpd.com
- Jasonville PD
- Chief Rick A. Van Horn
  145 So. Lawton St.
  Jasonville, IN 47438
  (812) 665-2694
  rickvh@jasonvillepd.com
- Linton PD
- Chief Troy R. Jerrell
  49 NW A St.
  Linton, IN 47441
  (812) 847-4411
  jerrell@lintonpolice.com
- Worthington PD
- Town Marshall Don Richardson
  225 So. Commercial St.
  Worthington, IN 47471
  (812) 875-2424
  worthingtonpd@yahoo.com

Hamilton County

- Hamilton County SO
- Sheriff Mark J. Bowen
  18100 Cumberland Rd.
  Noblesville, IN 46060
  (317) 773-1872
  mark.bowen@hamiltoncounty.in.gov
- Atlanta PD
- Town Marshal Jai M. Cook
  105 E. Main St.
  PO Box 133
  Atlanta, IN 46031
  (765) 292-2355
  atlantapolice@comcast.net
- Fishers PD
- Chief George Kehl
  4 Municipal Dr.
  Fishers, IN 46038
  (317) 595-3300
  kehlg@fishers.in.us
- Noblesville PD
- Chief Kevin Jowitt
  135 So. 9th St.
  Noblesville, IN 46060
  (317) 776-6340
  npd@noblesville.in.us
- Westfield PD
- Chief Joel D. Rush
  17535 Dartown Rd.
  Westfield, IN 46074
  (317) 804-3200
  jrush@westfield.in.gov

Hancock County

- Hancock County SD
- Sheriff Michael G. *Mike* Shepherd
  123 E. Main St.
  Greenfield, IN 46140
  (317) 477-1144
  mshepherd@hancockcoingov.org

- Fortville PD
- Town Marshal William *Bill* Knauer
  714 E. Broadway St.
  Fortville, IN 46040
  (317) 485-4044, ext. 112
  bknauer@fortvilleindiana.org
- Greenfield PD
- Chief John Jester
  116 So. State St.
  Greenfield, IN 46140
  (317) 477-4410
  police@greenfieldin.org
- McCordsville PD
- Chief Harold Rogers, Jr.
  6280 W. 800 No.
  McCordsville, IN 46055
  (317) 335-2812
  hrodgers@mccordsville.org
- Wilkinson PD
- Town Marshal Dennis Hoppes
  215 No. Main St. PO Box 6
  Wilkinson, IN 46186
  (765)781-2605
  wilkinsonpd@wilkinsonin.org

Harrison County

- Harrison County SO
- Sheriff Rodney V. Seelye
  1445 Gardner Ln. NW, Ste. 1000
  Corydon, IN 47112
  (812) 738-2195
  sheriff@hcsdin.net
- Corydon PD
- Town Marshal James Kendall
  113 No. Oak St.
  Corydon, IN 47112
  (812) 738-3959
  policedepartment@corydon-in.gov

Hendricks County

- Hendricks County SO
- Sheriff David D. Galloway
  925 E. Main St.
  Danville, IN 46122
  (317) 745-6269
  swagner@co.hendricks.in.us
- Avon PD
- Chief Jack Miller
  6550 E. US Hwy 36
  Avon, IN 46123
  (317) 272-4485
  jmiller@avongov.org
- Brownsburg PD
- Chief Michael Dove
  31 No. Green St.
  Brownsburg, IN 46112
  (317) 858-6012
  mdove@brownsburgpolice.org
- Danville PD
- Chief Keith Gill
  147 W. Main St.
  Danville, IN 46122
  (317) 745-5446
  kgill@danvilleindiana.org
- Lizton PD
- Town Marshal Eric Mohr
  PO Box 61
  Lizton, IN 46149
  (317) 994-6000
  police@townoflizton.com
- Pittsboro PD
- Chief Christi L. Patterson
  80 No. Meridian PO Box 185
  Pittsboro, IN 46167
  (317) 892-3329
  cpatterson@pittsboropolice.org
- Plainfield PD
- Chief Jeff Mitny
  1075 W. Main St.
  Plainfield, IN 46168
  (317) 838-3565
  jeff.mitny@plainfieldpd.org
- Stilesville PD
- Chief Brady McManama
  8353 No. Hendricks St.
  Stilesville, IN 46180
  (317) 539-2237
  Brady.McNamama@stilesvillepd.org

Henry County

- Henry County SO
- Sheriff Bruce R. *Butch* Baker
  127 No. 12th St.
  New Castle, IN 47362
  (765) 529-5201
  bbaker@emgsvcs.net
- Middletown PD
- Town Marshal Robert *Tony* Robbins
  653 Locust St.
  Middletown, IN 47356
  (765) 354-2281
  lavonna@mail.com

- New Castle PD
- Chief Bradley *Brad* Catron
  227 No. Main St.
  New Castle, IN 47362
  (765) 528-6810
  bradley-catron@cityofnewcastle.net

Howard County

- Howard County SO
- Sheriff Steven R. Rogers
  1800 W. Markland
  Kokomo, IN 46901
  (765) 457-1105
  hcsd@co.howard.in.us
- Greentown PD
- Town Marshal Jeff Bennett
  112 No. Meridian St.
  Greentown, IN 46936
  (765) 628-3434
  jbennett@greentownpolice.us
- Kokomo PD
- Chief Robert Baker
  100 So. Union St.
  Kokomo, IN 46901
  (765) 456-7100
  police@cityofkokomo.org
- Russiaville PD
- Town Marshal Roger L. Waddell
  205 E. Kinsey Dr.
  Russiaville, IN 46979
  (765) 883-5739
  roger@russiavillepd.com

Huntington County

- Huntington County SO
- Sheriff Terry J. Stoffel
  332 E. State St.
  Huntington, IN 46750
  (260) 356-2520
  sheriff@huntington.in.us
- Huntington PD
- Chief Everett *E.J.* Carroll
  300 Cherry St.
  Huntington, IN 46750
  (260) 356-7110
  ej.carroll@huntington.in.us
- Huntington U. PD
- Dir. Barry Cochran
  2023 College Ave.
  Huntington, IN 46750
  (260) 224-1412
  bcochran@huntington.edu

Jackson County

- Jackson County SO
- Sheriff Michael E. *Mike* Carothers
  150 E. State Rd. 250
  Brownstown, IN 47220
  (812) 358-2141
  mecarothers@gmail.com
- Seymour PD
- Chief Bill Abbott
  220 No. Chestnut St.
  Seymour, IN 47274
  (812) 522-5131
  wva3470@yahoo.com

Jasper County

- Jasper County SO
- Sheriff Terry J. Risner
  2171 No. McKinley Ave.
  Rensselaer, IN 47978
  (219) 866-4950
  sheriff@netnitco.net
- Bi-State Drug Task Force
- Chief George Frantz
  (See also Benton, Fountain, Newton & Warren counties)
  PO Box 56
  Williamsport, IN 47993
  (765) 426-2328
  bistatedrugs@go.com
- De Motte PD
- Chief Tom Jarrette
  112 Carnation St. SE
  De Motte, IN 46310
  (219) 987-3344
  dmpolice@comcast.net
- Rensselaer PD
- Chief Jeffrey S. Phillips
  122 So. Van Rensselaer
  Rensselaer, IN 47978
  (219) 866-7602
  jphillips@cityofrensselaerin.com

Jay County

- Portland PD
- Chief Robert E. Sours
  319 No. Meridian St.
  Portland, IN 47371
  (260) 726-9490
  rs701@thecityofportland.net

Jefferson County

- Jefferson County SO
- Sheriff John I. Wallace
  317 So. Walnut St.
  Madison, IN 47250
  (812) 265-2648
  john.wallace@jeffersoncounty.in.gov
- Madison PD
- Chief Dan Thurston
  101 W. Main St.
  Madison, IN 47250
  (812) 265-3347
  dthurston@madisonpd.com

Jennings County

- Jennings County SO
- Sheriff Stephan D. *Steve* Hoppock
  925 So. State St. PO Box 367
  North Vernon, IN 47282
  (812) 346-8642
  shoppock@jenningssheriff.org
- North Vernon PD
- Chief James Webster
  101 Madison Ave.
  North Vernon, IN 47265
  (812) 346-2345
  jwebster@nvpd.org

Johnson County

- Johnson County SO
- Sheriff Douglas F. *Doug* Cox
  1091 Hospital Rd.
  Franklin, IN 46131
  (317) 736-9155
  dcox@co.johnson.in.us
- Bargersville PD
- Chief Judd N. Green
  15 No. Baldwin PO Box 336
  Bargersville, IN 46106
  (317) 422-1222
  police@townofbargersville.org
- Edinburgh PD
- Chief David *Dave* Mann
  107 So. Holland PO Box 65
  Edinburgh, IN 46124
  (812) 526-2636
  dmann@edinburghpolice.org
- Franklin PD
- Chief Tim O'Sullivan
  2801 No. Morton St.
  Franklin, IN 46131
  (317) 736-3670
  tosullivan@franklin.in.gov
- Greenwood PD
- Chief John Laut
  186 Surina Way
  Greenwood, IN 46142
  (317) 887-5210
  police@greenwood.in.gov
- Prince's Lakes Marshal's Office
- Town Marshal Greg Southers
  14 E. Lakeview Dr.
  Nineveh, IN 46164
  (317) 933-3517
  gsouthers@princeslakes.in.gov

Knox County

- Knox County SO
- Sheriff Michael P. *Mike* Morris
  2375 So. Old Decker Rd.
  Vincennes, IN 47591
  (812) 882-7660
  mike4203@senergymetro.net
- Vincennes PD
- Chief Dusty Luking
  501 Busseron St.
  Vincennes, IN 47591
  (812) 882-1630
  dluking@vincennespd.wvc.net

Kosciusko County

- Kosciusko County SO
- Sheriff William R. Goshert
  221 W. Main
  Warsaw, IN 46580
  (574) 267-5667
  rgoshert@kcgov.com
- Syracuse PD
- Chief Tony Ciriello
  310 No. Huntington St.
  Syracuse, IN 46567
  (574) 457-5333
  spd@kconline.com
- Warsaw PD
- Chief Scott D. Whitaker
  2191 E. Ft. Wayne PO Box 1297
  Warsaw, IN 46580
  (574) 372-9515
  swhitaker@warsaw.in.gov
- Winona Lake PD
- Chief Paul Schmitt
  1310 Park Ave.
  Winona Lake, IN 46590
  (574)267-8622
  wlpd@kconline.com

LaGrange County

- LaGrange County SD
- Sheriff Terry A. Martin
  0875 So. SR 9
  LaGrange, IN 46761
  (260) 463-7491
  tmartin@lagrangecounty.org
- Lagrange PD
- Town Marshal Richard Snyder
  1201 No. Townline Rd.
  Lagrange, IN 46761-1157
  (260) 463-7031
  lag.police@mchsi.com
- Shipshewana PD
- Town Marshal Tom M. Fitch II
  345 No. Morton PO Box 486
  Shipshewana, IN 46565
  (260) 768-4310
  police@shipshewana.org
- Wolcottville PD
- Town Marshal Ryan Kauffman
  104 Race St.
  Wolcottville, IN 46795
  (260) 854-2930
  townofwolcottville@embarqmail.com

Lake County

- Lake County SD
- Sheriff John Buncich
  2293 No. Main St.
  Crown Point, IN 46307
  (219) 755-3400
  info@lakecountysheriff.com
- Cedar Lake PD
- Int. Chief Gerald H. *Jerry* Smith
  7408 Constitution Ave.
  Cedar Lake, IN 46303
  (219) 374-5416
  jerry.smith@cedarlakein.org
- Dyer PD
- Chief David W. Hein
  2150 Hart St.
  Dyer, IN 46311
  (219) 865-1163
  police@townofdyer.com
- East Chicago PD
- Chief Mark J. Becker
  2301 E. Columbus Dr.
  East Chicago, IN 46312
  (219) 391-8331
  mbecker@eastchicago.com
- Gary PD
- Chief Wade Ingram
  555 Polk St.
  Gary, IN 46407
  (219) 881-1201
  wingram@ci.gary.in.us
- Hammond PD
- Chief Brian Miller
  509 Douglas St.
  Hammond, IN 46320
  (219) 853-6310
  police@hammondpolice.com
- Highland PD
- Chief Peter Hojnicki
  3333 Ridge Rd.
  Highland, IN 46322
  (219) 838-3184
  phojnicki@highland.in.gov
- Lake Station PD
- Chief Kevin Garber
  1969 Central Ave.
  Lake Station, IN 46405
  (219) 962-1186
  kgarber@lakestation-in.gov
- Lowell PD
- Int. Chief Eric Matson
  1333 E. Commercial Ave.
  Lowell, Indiana 46356
  (219) 696-0411
  ematson@696cops.com
- Munster PD
- Chief Steve Scheckel
  1001 Ridge Rd.
  Munster, IN 46321
  (219) 836-6655
  sscheckel@munster.org
- Schererville PD
- Chief David A. Dowling
  25 E. Joliet St.
  Schererville, IN 46375
  (219) 322-500
  ddowling@schererville.org
- Schneider PD
- Town Marshal Robert Marine
  23800 Parrish PO Box 207
  Schneider, IN 46376-0207
  (219) 552-9497
  spdspdone@yahoo.com

- Whiting PD
- Chief Stephen E. Miller
  1914 Schrage Ave.
  Whiting, IN 46394
  (219) 659-2131
  smiller@whitingindiana.com

La Porte County

- La Porte County SO
- Sheriff Michael F. Mollenhauer
  809 State St., Ste. 202A
  La Porte, IN 46350
  (219) 326-7700
  mmollenhauer@lcso.in.gov
- LaPorte PD
- Chief Adam Klimczak
  1206 Michigan Ave.
  LaPorte, IN 46350
  (219) 362-9446
  aklimcc@lpcitypd.com
- Long Beach PD
- Chief Marshal Robert *Bob* Sulkowski
  2400 Oriole Tr.
  Long Beach, IN 46360
  (219) 874-4243
  tolbpd@comcast.net
- Michigan City PD
- Chief Mark Swistek
  102 W. 2nd St.
  Michigan City, IN 46360
  (219) 874-3221
  mswistek@emichigancity.com
- Westville PD
- Chief Marshal Jim Gunning
  106 Ridge St. PO Box 221
  Westville, IN 46391
  (219) 785-4177
  westvillepolice@csinet.net

Lawrence County

- Lawrence County SO
- Sheriff Samuel J. Craig
  1420 I St.
  Bedford, IN 47421
  (812) 275-3316
  scraig@lawrencecounty.in.gov

Madison County

- Alexandria PD
- Chief Brian Burnett
  201 E. Washington St.
  Alexandria, IN 46001
  (765) 724-3222
  alexpolicechief@comcast.net
- Anderson PD
- Chief Larry Crenshaw
  1040 Main St.
  Anderson, IN 46016-1746
  (765) 648- 6710
  lcrenshaw@cityofanderson.com
- Edgewood PD
- Town Marshal Andrew S. Ellingwood
  3405 Nichol Ave.
  Anderson, IN 46011
  (765) 642-3200
  edgewoodpolice@townofedgewoodin.us
- Elwood PD
- Chief Samuel E. *Sam* Hanna
  1505 So. B St.
  Elwood, IN 46036
  (765) 552-3376
  shanna@cityofelwood.com
- Frankton PD
- Chief David W. *Dave* Huffman
  105 Church St. PO Box 614
  Frankton, IN 46044
  (765) 754-8833
  dave.huffman@franktonpolice.com
- Lapel PD
- Chief Dennis Molina
  720 Ford St.
  Lapel, IN 46051
  (765) 534-4600
  police@lapelindiana.org
- Orestes PD
- Town Marshal Craig Bousman
  2 So. Superior St.
  Orestes, IN 46063
  (765)754-7187
  orestespd@cji.net

Marion County

- Marion County SD
- Sheriff John R. Layton
  40 So. Alabama St.
  Indianapolis, IN 46204
  (317) 327-1700
  mcsdweb@indy.gov
- Beech Grove PD
- Chief Mark Swartz
  340 E. Churchman Ave.
  Beech Grove, IN 46107
  (317) 782-4934
  Mark.Swartz@beechgrove.com

- Cumberland PD
- Chief Michael P. Crooke
  11501 E. Washington St.
  Cumberland, IN 46229
  (317) 894-3525
  cumberlandpd@cupd.org
- Southport PD
- Chief Randy Ellison
  6901 Derbyshire Rd.
  Southport, IN 46227-5133
  (317) 787-7595
  policechief@southport.in.gov
- Speedway PD
- Chief James Campbell
  1410 No. Lynhurst Dr.
  Speedway, Indiana 46224
  (317) 246-4300
  jcampbell@speedwaypolice.net

Marshall County

- Argos PD
- Chief Rodney Rudd
  125 W. Walnut St.
  Argos, IN 46501
  (574) 892-5122
  rrudd@townofargos.com
- Bourbon PD
- Chief Bill Martin
  224 No. Main St.
  Bourbon, IN 46504
  (574) 342-3105
  wmartin@bourbon-in.gov
- Bremen PD
- Chief Matt Hassel
  123 So. Center St.
  Bremen, IN 46506
  (574) 546-3456
  bremenpolicedept@mchsi.com
- Culver PD
- Chief Wayne A. Bean
  200 E. Washington St.
  Culver, IN 46511
  (574) 842-2525
  clerk@townofculver.org
- Plymouth PD
- Chief David M. Bacon
  215 W. Washington St.
  Plymouth, IN 46563
  (574) 936-2126
  dbaconppd@plymouthin.com

Martin County

- Loogootee PD
- Chief Kelly Rayhill
  401 JFK Ave.
  Loogootee, IN 47553
  (812) 295-2246
  police@loogootee.com

Miami County

- Miami County SD
- Sheriff Timothy G. Miller
  1104 W. 200 N
  Peru, IN 46970
  (765) 472-1322
  kbrown@miamicountyin.gov
- Peru PD
- Chief Jonie Kennedy
  35 So. Broadway
  Peru, IN 46970
  (765) 473-2150
  jkennedy@perupd.org

Monroe County

- Monroe County SO
- Sheriff James L. Kennedy
  301 No. College Ave., Rm. 203
  Bloomington, IN 47404
  (812) 349-2780
  sheriffsoffice@co.monroe.in.us
- Bloomington PD
- Chief Michael Diekhoff
  220 E. 3rd St.
  Bloomington, IN 47401
  (812) 339-4477
  police@bloomington.in.gov
- Ellettsville PD
- Town Marshal Anthony *Tony* Bowlen
  1406 W. Temperance St.
  Ellettsville, IN 47429
  (812) 876-2270
  abowlen@ellettsvillepolice.com

Montgomery County

- Montgomery County SO
- Sheriff Mark A. Casteel
  600 Memorial Dr.
  Crawfordsville, IN 47933
  (765) 362-3740
  mark.casteel@montgomeryco.net

- Crawfordsville PD
- Chief Mike Norman
  311 No. Green St.
  Crawfordsville, IN 47933
  (765) 362-3762
  mnorman@crawfordsvillepolice.com

Morgan County

- Martinsville PD
- Chief Darrell Davis
  59 So. JeffersonPO Box 1415
  Martinsville, IN 46151
  (765) 342-6614
  chief@martinsville.in.gov
- Mooresville PD
- Chief Timothy C. Viles
  104 W. Main St.
  Mooresville, IN 46158
  (317) 831-3434
  MooresvillePD@Comcast.net

Newton County

- Newton County SD
- Sheriff Donald E. *Don* Hartman, Sr.
  304 E. Seymour St.
  Kentland, IN 47951
  (219) 474-3331
  dhartman@newton-sheriff.com
- Bi-State Drug Task Force
- Chief George Frantz
  (See also Benton, Fountain, Jasper & Warren counties)
  PO Box 56
  Williamsport, IN 47993
  (765) 426-2328
  bistatedrugs@go.com

Noble County

- Albion PD
- Town Marshal Tom Lock
  211 E. Park Dr. PO Box 27
  Albion, IN 46701
  (260) 636-7157
  albionpd@frontier.com
- Kendallville PD
- Chief Rob Wiley
  234 So. Main St.
  Kendallville, IN 46755
  (260) 347-0654
  police@kendallville-in.org
- Ligonier PD
- Chief Bryan K. Shearer
  301 Cavin St.
  Ligonier, IN 46767
  (260) 894-4111
  police@ligonier-in.org

Ohio County

- Rising Sun PD
- Chief David Hewitt
  300 So. Poplar St.
  Rising Sun, IN 47040
  (812) 438-3737
  mail@risingsunpolice.net

Orange County

- French Lick PD
- Chief Thomas J. McCracken
  8671 W. Main St. PO Box 10
  French Lick, IN 47432
  (812) 865-2222
  flpd936@bluemarble.net

Owen County

- Owen County SO
- Sheriff Chester H. Richardson III
  291 Vandalia Ave.
  Spencer, IN 47460
  (812) 829-4874
  sheriff@ccrtc.com
- Spencer PD
- Town Marshal Richard *Rich* Foutch
  90 No. West St.
  Spencer, IN 47460
  (812) 829-3932
  rich.foutch@spencer.in.gov

Perry County

- Perry County SO
- Sheriff Lee B. Chestnut
  119 So. 7th
  Cannelton, IN 47520
  (812) 547-2441
  pcsd@psci.net
- Cannelton PD
- Chief Lee A. Hall
  210 So. 8th St., Ste. 4
  Cannelton, IN 47520
  (812) 547-2111
  chief.hall@canneltonpolice.com

Pike County

- Petersburg PD
- Chief Chuck Baumgart
  702 E. Main St.
  Petersburg, IN 47567
  (812) 354-8716
  chiefbaugart@gmail.com

Porter County

- Porter County SO
- Sheriff David E. Lain
  2755 State Rd. 49
  Valparaiso, IN 46383
  (219) 477-3000
  sheriff@portercountysheriff.com
- Burns Harbor PD
- Chief Mike Heckman
  1240 No. Boo Rd.
  Burns Harbor, IN 46304
  (219) 787-9411
  mheckman638@aol.com
- Chesterton PD
- Chief David Cincoski
  790 Broadway
  Chesterton, IN 46304
  (219) 926-1136
  dcincoski@chestertonin.org
- Hebron PD
- Chief Steven *Steve* Sibbrell
  104 E. Sigler St.
  Hebron, IN 46341
  (219) 996-2747
  steve.sibbrell@visithebron.org
- Portage PD
- Chief Troy Williams
  2693 Irving St.
  Portage, IN 46368
  (219) 762-3122
  twilliams@portage-in.com
- Porter PD
- Chief James Spanier
  50 Francis St.
  Porter, IN 46304
  (219) 926-7611
  jspanier@townofporter.com
- Valparaiso PD
- Chief Michael Brickner
  355 So. Washington St.
  Valparaiso, IN 46383
  (219) 462-2135
  mbrickner@valpopd.com

Posey County

- Posey County SO
- Sheriff Gregory R. Oeth
  1201 O'Donnell Rd.
  Mt Vernon, IN 47620
  (812) 838-1321
  sheriff@poseycountygov.org
- Mount Vernon PD
- Chief Grant Beloat
  526 Main St.
  Mount Vernon, IN 47620
  (812) 838-8705
  sjwillis@insightbb.com
- Poseyville PD
- Town Marshal Doug Saltzman
  77 No. St. Francis Ave.
  Poseyville, IN 47633
  (812) 874-2211
  jcm211@hotmail.com

Pulaski County

- Pulaski County SO
- Sheriff Michael L. Gayer
  110 E. Meridian St.
  Winamac, IN 46996
  (574) 946-3341
  mgayer@pulaskisheriff.net

Putnam County

- Putnam County SO
- Sheriff Steve Fenwick
  13 Keightly Rd.
  Greencastle, IN 46135
  (765) 653-3211
  sbfenwick@yahoo.com

Randolph County

- Union City PD
- Chief Cobie Wells
  219 So. Howard St.
  Union City, IN 47390
  (765) 964-5353
  729@unioncityinpolice.com
- Winchester PD
- Chief Michael A. *Mike* Burk
  113 E. Washington St.
  Winchester, IN 47394
  (765) 584- 1056
  Mike.Burk@winchester-in.gov

Ripley County

- Ripley County SO
- Sheriff Thomas J. Grills
  210 No. Monroe PO Box 686
  Versailles, IN 47042
  (812) 689-5555
  sheriff@ripleycounty.com
- Batesville PD
- Chief Stan Holt
  104 E. Catherine St.
  Batesville, IN 47006
  (812) 934-3131
  sholt@batesvillepolice.org
- Milan PD
- Town Marshal Gary Skaggs
  Lakeside Dr.
  Milan, IN 47031
  (812) 654-2211
  gary.skaggs@milan-in-gov.net

Rush County

- Rush County SO
- Sheriff Jeffery D. *Jeff* Sherwood
  131 E. 1st St.
  Rushville, IN 46173
  (765) 932-2931
  sheriff@rushcountyin.gov
- Rushville PD
- Chief Craig Tucker
  270 W. 15th St.
  Rushville, IN 46173
  (765) 932-3907
  ctucker@cityofrushville.in.gov

Saint Joseph County

- Saint Joseph County SO
- Sheriff Michael D. Grzegorek
  401 W. Sample St.
  South Bend, IN 46601
  (574) 245-6540
  bmiller@co.st-joseph.in.us
- Mishawaka PD
- Chief Kenneth Witkowski, Jr.
  200 No. Church St.
  Mishawaka, IN 46544
  (574) 258- 1678
  kwitkowski@mishawaka.in.gov
- New Carlisle PD
- Chief Jeff Roseboom
  124 E. Michigan St.
  New Carlisle, IN 46552
  (574) 654-3544
  jroseboom@townofnewcarlisle.com
- North Liberty PD
- Chief Michael R. Sawdon
  PO Box 516
  North Liberty, IN 46554
  (574) 656-4411
  nlpolice@kconline.com
- South Bend PD
- Chief Ron Teachman
  701 W. Sample St.
  South Bend, IN 46601
  (574) 235-9201
  ptrent@southbendin.gov
- Walkerton PD
- Chief Gary Layer
  402 Michigan St.
  Walkerton, IN 46574
  (574) 586-3511
  police@walkerton.org

Scott County

- Scott County SD
- Sheriff J. Daniel McClain
  111 So. 1st St.
  Scottsburg, IN 47170
  (812) 752-8400
  info@scottcountysheriff.org

Shelby County

- Shelby County SO
- Sheriff Michael D. Bowlby
  107 W. Taylor St.
  Shelbyville, IN 46176
  (317) 392-6345
  mbowlby@county.shelby.in.us
- Shelbyville PD
- Chief Keith England
  105 W. Taylor St.
  Shelbyville, IN 46176
  (317) 392-5106
  kengland@cityofshelbyvillein.com

Spencer County

- Spencer County SO
- Sheriff Kermitt L. Lindsey
  120 No. 2nd St.
  Rockport, IN 47635
  (812) 649-2286
  sheriff@spencercounty.in.gov
- Shelbyville PD
- Chief Keith England
  105 W. Taylor St.
  Shelbyville, IN 46176
  (317) 392-5106
  kengland@cityofshelbyvillein.com

Starke County

- Starke County SO
- Sheriff Oscar O. Cowen, Jr.
  108 No. Pearl St.
  Knox, IN 46534
  (574) 772-3771
  sheriff@co.starke.in.us
- Knox PD
- Chief Clint Norem
  101 W. Washington St.
  Knox, IN 46534
  (574) 772-4122
  knoxpolice@cityofknox.net
- North Judson PD
- Chief Douglas J Vessely
  206 Keller Ave.
  North Judson, IN 46366
  (574) 772-5914
  njpd@mchsi.com

Steuben County

- Steuben County SO
- Sheriff Tim R. Troyer
  206 E. Gale St.
  Angola, IN 46703-1900
  (260) 668-1000
  sheriff@co.steuben.in.us
- Angola PD
- Chief Stuart Hamblen
  202 W. Gilmore St.
  Angola, IN 46703
  (260) 665-2121
  police@angolain.org
- Ashley PD
- Town Marshal Scott Barnhart
  500 So. Gonser PO Box 70
  Ashley, IN 46705
  (260) 587-9388
  marshal461@ashley.in.gov
- Fremont PD
- Town Marshal Joe Patterson
  205 No. Tolford
  Fremont, IN 46737
  (260) 495-9848
  fremontpolice1@townoffremont.org

Sullivan County

- Sullivan County SO
- Sheriff Bryan L. Kinnett
  24 So. State
  Sullivan, IN 47882
  (812) 268-4044
  scsd@joink.com
- Sullivan City PD
- Chief Jesse Morin
  32 No. Court St.
  Sullivan, IN 47882
  (812) 268-6077
  jesse.morin@cityofsullivan.org

Switzerland County

- Switzerland County SO
- Sheriff Roy A. Leap
  305 Liberty St.
  Vevay, IN 47043
  (812) 427-3636
  rleap@scso-in.org
- Vevay PD
- Chief James Richards
  210 Ferry St PO Box 52
  Vevay, IN 47043
  (812) 427-3737
  jrichards@vevaypolice.org

Tippecanoe County

- Tippecanoe County SO
- Sheriff Tracy A. Brown
  2640 Duncan Rd.
  Lafayette, IN 47904
  (765) 423-9388
  tabrown@tippecanoelaw.com
- Lafayette PD
- Chief Patrick J. Flannelly
  20 No. 6th St.
  Lafayette, IN 47901
  (765) 807-1200
  pjflannelly@lafayette.in.gov
- West Lafayette PD
- Chief Jason Dombkowski
  711 W. Navajo Dr.
  West Lafayette, IN 47906
  (765) 775-5200
  jldombkowski@westlafayettepd.us

Union County

- Union County SO
- Sheriff Eric Cantrell
  106 E. Union St.
  Liberty, IN 47353
  (765) 458-5194
  unioncosheriff@frontier.com
- Liberty PD
- Chief Barry Bryant
  1 So. Fairground St.
  Liberty, IN 47353
  (765) 458-5721
  libertypd@verizon.net

Vanderburgh County

- Vanderburgh County SO
- Sheriff Eric R. Williams
  3500 No. Harlan Ave.
  Evansville, IN 47711
  (812) 421-6200
  postcommand@vanderburghsheriff.com
- Evansville PD
- Chief Billy Bolin
  15 NW MLK Blvd
  Evansville, IN 47708
  (812) 436-7896
  info@evansvillepolice.com

Vermillion County

- Vermillion County SD
- Sheriff Robert J. Spence
  1888 So. State Rd. 63
  Newport, IN 47966
  (765) 492-3737
  sheriffspence@vcsheriff.com

Vigo County

- Vigo County SD
- Sheriff Gregory T. Ewing
  201 Cherry St.
  Terre Haute, IN 47807
  (812) 462-3226
  clark.cottom@vigocounty.In.Gov
- Terre Haute PD
- Chief John Plasse
  17 Harding Ave.
  Terre Haute, IN 47807
  (812) 238-1661, ext. 2289
  Police@TerreHaute.IN.Gov

Wabash County

- Wabash County SO
- Sheriff Robert E. Land
  79 W. Main St.
  Wabash, IN 46992
  (260) 563-8891
  sheriffland@wcsd.us
- North Manchester PD
- Town Marshal Jeffrey L. *Jeff* Perry
  709 W. Main St.
  North Manchester, IN 46962
  (260) 982-8555
  nmpd@mchsi.com
- Wabash PD
- Chief Charles Smith
  1340 Manchester Ave.
  Wabash, IN 46992
  (260) 563-1111
  info@wabashpd.us

Warren County

- Bi-State Drug Task Force
- Chief George Frantz
  (See also Benton, Fountain, Jasper & Newton counties)
  PO Box 56
  Williamsport, IN 47993
  (765) 426-2328
  bistatedrugs@go.com

Warrick County

- Warrick County SO
- Sheriff Brett W. Kruse
  100 State Rd. 62 W.
  Boonville, IN 47601
  (812) 897-6180
  bkruse@warrickcountysheriff.com
- Boonville PD
- Chief Daryl Saltzman
  121 E. Locust St.
  Boonville, IN 47601
  (812) 897-6550
  dstaltzman@boonvillepolice.com
- Chandler PD
- Chief Marlin Weisheit
  417 E. Jefferson St.
  Chandler, IN 47610
  (812) 925-6898
  kwarren@townofchandler.org
- Elberfeld Town Office
- Marshal Kim Miley
  175 W. Sycamore St.
  Elberfeld, IN 47613
  (812) 983-4365
  ElberfeldPolice@hotmail.com
- Newburgh PD
- Chief Brett Sprinkle
  527 State St.
  Newburgh, IN 47630
  (812) 853-1723
  bsprinkle@newburghpd.org

Washington County

- Salem PD
- Chief Troy Merry
  #38 Public Sq.
  Salem, IN 47167
  (812) 883-5100
  salempolice@cityofsalem.com

Wayne County

- Wayne County SO
- Sheriff Jeff F. Cappa
  200 E. Main St.
  Richmond, IN 47374
  (765) 973-9393
  sheriff@co.wayne.in.us
- Hagerstown PD
- Chief Keith Folkner
  49 E. College St.
  Hagerstown, IN 47346
  (765) 489-4711
  folknerk9@yahoo.com
- Richmond PD
- Chief Kris J. Wolski
  50 No. 5th St.
  Richmond, IN 47374
  (765) 983-7247
  kwolski@richmondindiana.gov

Wells County

- Wells County SO
- Sheriff Monte L. Fisher
  1615 W. Western Ave.
  Bluffton, IN 46714
  (260) 824-3426
  admin@wellscountysheriff.com
- Bluffton PD
- Chief Tammy Schaeffer
  200 E. Market St.
  Bluffton, IN 46714
  (260) 824-3320
  police@ci.bluffton.in.us

White County

- White County SO
- Sheriff Patrick E. Shafer
  915 W. Hanawalt PO Box 703
  Monticello, IN 47960
  (574) 583-2251
  pshafer@wcsheriff-in.us
- Monticello PD
- Chief Randy Soliday
  229 No. Main St.
  Monticello, IN 47960
  (574) 583-2256
  police@monticelloin.gov

Whitley County

- Whitley County SO
- Sheriff Mark E. Hodges
  101 W. Market St.
  Columbia City, IN 46725
  (260) 244-6410
  mjones@whitleysd.com
- Columbia City PD
- Chief Tim Longenbaugh
  112 So. Chauncey St.
  Columbia City, IN 46725
  (260) 248-5121
  tlongenbaugh@columbiacity.net

State Agencies

- IN State Police-HQ
- Supt. Doug Carter
  100 No. Senate Ave., 3rd Fl.
  Indianapolis, IN 46204-2259
  (317) 899-8293, ext. 6
  DBursten@isp.in.gov

KENTUCKY

Adair County

- Adair County SO
- Sheriff Ralph Curry
  500 Public Sq.
  Columbia, KY 42728
  (270) 384-2776
  adaircosheriff@duocounty.com
- District 1
- Constable William *Bill* Troutwine
  225 Estell Asbury Rd.
  Columbia, KY 42728
  (270) 385-9597
  williamanddonna@windstream.net
- District 3
- Constable Robert Loy
  1666 Hwy 768 E.
  Columbia, KY 42728
  (270) 378-6001
  robo@duo-county.com
- District 6
- Constable (*Col.*) Jason Rector
  89 Timber Ln.
  Columbia, KY 42728
  (270) 384-9187
  jasontrector@gmail.com
- District 7
- Constable Joe Collins Jr.
  2471 Campbellsville Rd.
  Columbia, KY 42728
  (270) 384-5047
  adairoil@hotmail.com

Allen County

- Allen County SO
- Sheriff Jeff Cooke
  194 Wood St.
  Scottsville, KY 42164
  (270) 237-3210
  sheriffjcooke@nctc.com
- Scottsville PD
- Chief Jeff Pearson
  194 W. Wood St.
  Scottsville, KY 42164
  (270) 237-3611
  chiefjeff.pearson@gmail.com

Anderson County

- Anderson County SO
- Sheriff Troy L. Young
  208 So. Main St.
  Lawrenceburg, KY 40342
  (502) 839-4021
  deckman@adelphia.net
- District 1
- Constable Joseph Marshall
  208 Bluebird Ct.
  Lawrenceburg, KY 40342
  (502) 859-9979
  pastormarshall57@yahoo.com
- District 4
- Constable Jerry Shouse
  1050 Hickory Hill Dr.
  Lawrenceburg, KY 40342
  (502) 839-4041
  constable@kybs.net
- District 6
- Constable Finley Willis, Jr.
  1324 Drydock Rd.
  Lawrenceburg, KY 40342
  (502) 839-6796
  fwjr@earthlink.net
- Lawrenceburg PD
- Chief Chris Atkins
  201 E. Woodford
  Lawrenceburg, KY 40342
  (502) 839-5125
  catkins@lawrenceburgky.org

Ballard County

- Ballard County SO
- Sheriff Todd Cooper
  437 Ohio St.
  Wickliffe, KY 42087
  (270) 335-3561
  sheriff@brtc.net
- District 2
- Constable Jeremy A. Renfrow
  4664 Oscar Rd.
  Barlow, KY 42024
  (270) 224-2928
  jarenfrow@gmail.com
- District 4
- Constable Mark J. Sanders
  2543 Oscar Rd.
  Barlow, KY 42024
  (270) 334-3560
  msanders@brtc.net
- District 5
- Constable Lawrence Otey
  461 Shepherd Ln.
  Wickliffe, KY 42087
  (270) 335-5145
  otey2001@gmail.com

- La Center PD
- Chief Herbert Hendrickson, Jr.
  333 Broadway
  La Center, KY 42056
  (270) 665-5340
  lacityhall@brtc.net

Barren County

- Barren County SO
- Sheriff Chris Eaton
  117-1B No.
  Glasgow, KY 42141
  (270) 651-2771
  chris_eaton@glasgow-ky.com
- District 2
- Constable James D. Glass
  535 Bradshaw Rd.
  Austin, KY 42123
  (270) 646-3487
  glass@scrtc.com
- District 3
- Constable Mark Oliver
  364 Barbour Rd.
  Glasgow, KY 42141
  (270) 590-1995
  markoliver@yahoo.com
- District 6
- Constable George Hutchens
  303 No. Hunstman PO Box 191
  Cave City, KY 42127
  (270)773-3201
  jollybear@scrtc.com
- Cave City PD
- Chief Jeff Wright
  103 Duke St.
  Cave City, KY 42127
  (270) 773-2441
  cityhall@caveland.net
- Glasgow PD
- Chief Guy J. Turcotte
  201 So. Broadway St.
  Glasgow, KY 42141
  (270) 651-5151
  gpdgturcotte@glasgow-ky.com

Bath County

- Bath County SO
- Sheriff John Snedega
  17 W. Main St. PO Box 95
  Owingsville, KY 40360
  (606) 674-2931
  bathso@yahoo.com
- District 1
- Constable Wes Tincher
  PO Box 352
  Sharpsburg, KY 40374
  (606) 247-2201
  wes40374@gmail.com
- Owingsville PD
- Chief Todd W. Tout
  19 Goodpaster Ave. PO Box 386
  Owingsville, KY 40360
  (606) 674-2341
  owingsvillepd@windstream.net

Bell County

- Bell County SO
- Sheriff Bruce Bennett
  PO Box 336
  Pineville, KY 40977
  (606) 337-3102
  bcsd@wwdaptel.com
- District 3
- Constable Jeff Bowling
  190 Bowling Rd.
  Middlesboro, KY 40965
  (606) 269-9313
  jabowling@setel.com
- District 4
- Constable Kevin M. Gordon
  PO Box 2526
  Middlesboro, KY 40965
  (606) 269-4717
  kevingordon@hotmail.com

Boone County

- Boone County SO
- Sheriff Michael A. Helmig
  3000 Conrad Ln.
  Burlington, KY 41005-0198
  (859) 334-2175
  bcs@boonecountyky.org
- District 2
- Constable Ken Baumgartner
  14107 Vest Ln.
  Verona, KY 41092
  (859) 485-4061
  kenb@albaumgartner.com
- District 3
- Constable Joe Kalil
  649 Devonshire Cir.
  Florence, KY 41042
  jkalil1@insightbb.com

- Cincinnati/No. KY Airport PD
- Chief Kevin Murphy
  PO Box 752000
  Cincinnati, OH 45275-2000
  (859) 767-3123
  info@cvgairport.com
- Florence PD
- Chief John McDermond
  8100 Ewing Blvd
  Florence, KY 41042-7588
  (859) 647-5420
  John.mcdermond@florence-ky.gov

Bourbon County

- District 1
- Constable Norman Clark
  425 Hume Dr.
  Paris, KY 43062
  (859) 987-5328
  clarknr@aol.com
- District 4
- Constable Daryl Kelly
  PO Box 504
  Millersburg, KY 40348
  (859) 749-8074
  dkelly855@yahoo.com
- Millersburg PD
- Chief Kevin Booth
  101 E. 5th St.
  Millersburg, KY 40348
  (859) 484-3427
  police@millersburgky.gov
- Paris PD
- Chief Kevin Sutton
  525 High, 3rd Fl.
  Paris, KY 40361
  (859) 987-2100
  ksutton@parispolice.org

Boyd County

- Boyd County SO
- Sheriff Terry Keelin
  PO Box 536
  Catlettsburg, KY 41129
  (606) 739-5135
  sheriff@boydcountysheriff.com
- District 1
- Constable Timothy B. Woods
  1016 Cedar Point Cir.
  Catlettsburg, KY 41129
  (606) 928-0332
  bcems820@yahoo.com
- District 2
- Constable Tim A. Duley
  3119 So. 29th St.
  Ashland, KY 41102
  (606) 325-1950
  timduley@windstream.net
- Ashland PD
- Chief Robert W. Ratliff
  1700 Greenup PO Box 1864
  Ashland, KY 41105
  (606) 327-2020
  chiefratliff@Ashlandkypd.com
- Catlettsburg PD
- Chief John Justice
  2600 Broadway St.
  Catlettsburg, KY 41129
  (606) 739-5126
  CatlettsburgPolice@Alltel.net

Boyle County

- District 3
- Constable James Murphy
  217 Fox Run Tr.
  Danville, KY 40422
  (859) 326-2346
  james.murphy@danville.kyschools.us
- District 4
- Constable James M. Gies
  623 Apache Tr.
  Danville, KY 40422
  (859) 583-3498
  tacmedic0112@yahoo.com
- District 5
- Constable Tim Dextere
  537 Barbee Way
  Danville, KY 40422
  (859) 236-8830
  tim@dexteragency.com
- Danville PD
- Chief Tony Gray
  145 W. Main St. PO Box 670
  Danville, KY 40423
  (859) 238-1224
  tgray@danvilleky.org

Bracken County

- Bracken County SO
- Sheriff Howard Niemeier
  Locust St.
  Brooksville, KY 41004
  (606) 735-3233
  bcso@maysvilleky.net

- District 1
- Constable William *Bill* Ruf
  1559 Western Hills Rd.
  Foster, KY 41043
  (859) 240-7362
  billruf@windstream.net
- District 6
- Constable Kenny Carl
  PO Box 37
  Brooksville, KY 41004
  (606) 782-2493
  kennyc1975@yahoo.com

Breathitt County

- Jackson PD
- Chief John Marshall
  333 Broadway
  Jackson, KY 41339
  (606) 666-2424
  jacksonpd@setel.com

Breckinridge County

- Breckinridge County SO
- Sheriff Todd Pate
  Breckinridge County Courthouse
  Hardinsburg, KY 40143
  (270) 756-2361
  info@breckinridgecountysheriff.net
- Cloverport PD
- Chief Jeff Hendrick
  212 W. Main St.
  Cloverport, KY 40111
  (270) 788-3751
  cloverportpd@bbtel.com
- Irvington PD
- Chief Ernest Fox
  216 No. 1st St. PO Box 374
  Irvington, KY 40146
  (270) 547-3835
  fox@irvingtonpd.com

Bullitt County

- Bullitt County SO
- Sheriff Dave Greenwell
  300 So. Buckman PO Box 205
  Shepherdsville, KY 40165
  (502) 543-2514
  dgreenwell@bcky.org
- Hillview PD
- Chief (*Col.*) Glenn Caple
  283 Crestwood Ln.
  Louisville, KY 40229
  (502) 955-6808
  GCaple@HillviewPolice.com
- Pioneer Village PD
- Chief DJ Reynolds
  4700 Summit Dr.
  Louisville, KY 40229
  (502) 957-3800
  cityclerk@cityofpioneervillage.org
- Shepherdsville PD
- Chief (*Col.*) Douglas E. Puckett
  200 Frank E. Simon Ave.
  Shepherdsville, KY 40165
  (502) 921-1000
  dpuckett@shepspolice.com

Butler County

- Butler County SO
- Sheriff Scottie Ward
  110 No. Main St. PO Box 100
  Morgantown, KY 42261
  (502) 526-3676
  sward@butlercoky.com
- Morgantown PD
- Chief Charles Swiney
  117 No. Main St. PO Box 397
  Morgantown, KY 42261
  (502) 526-3662
  charles.swiney@morgantownpolice.org

Caldwell County

- Caldwell County SO
- Sheriff Stan Hudson
  100 E. Market St., 2nd Fl.
  Princeton, KY 42445
  (270) 365-2088
  ccso47@caldwellcourthouse.com
- District 2
- Constable James K. Poindexter
  PO Box 934
  Princeton, KY 42445
  kevin_poindexter@yahoo.com
- District 4
- Constable Steven *Steve* Tays
  1931 Caldwell Chapel Rd.
  Princeton, KY 42445
  (270) 365-3041
  steve@gunknifecountry.com

Calloway County

- Calloway County SD
- Sheriff William *Bill* Marcum
  701 Olive St.
  Murray, KY 42071
  (270) 753-3151
  tvickerson@callkyso.com

- District 1
- Constable Randy Lee
  1982 Palestine Church Rd.
  Dexter, KY 42036
  (270) 474-8810
  kathy.lee@murraystate.edu
- District 3
- Constable Tim Stone
  1718 Oakhill Dr.
  Murray, KY 42071
  (270) 767-2654
  tjrmc@bellsouth.net
- Murray PD
- Chief Jeff Liles
  407 Poplar St.
  Murray, KY 42071
  (270) 753-1621
  generalinfo@murrayky.gov

Campbell County

- District 3
- Constable James Peluso
  51 Summer Hill Ave.
  Newport, KY 41071
  (859) 491-9247
  jim.peluso@fuse.net
- Alexandria PD
- Chief Mike Ward
  8326 W. Main St.
  Alexandria, KY 41001
  (859) 635-4126
  mward@alexandriaky.org
- Bellevue PD
- Chief (*Col.*) Wayne Turner
  616 Poplar St.
  Bellevue, KY 41073
  (859) 261-1122
  wayne.turner@bellevueky.org
- Campbell County Det. Center
- Jailer Earl L. Ping
  601 Central Ave.
  Newport, KY 41071
  (859) 431-4611
  csteele@campbellcountyky.org
- Dayton PD
- Chief Scott O'Brien
  514 6th Ave.
  Dayton, KY 41074
  (859) 261-1471
  sobrien@daytonky.com
- Fort Thomas PD
- Chief Michael G. *Mike* Daly
  130 No. Fort Thomas Ave.
  Fort Thomas, KY 41075
  (859) 441-6562
  mdaly@ftthomas.org
- Highland Heights PD
- Chief Robert Thomas
  176 Johns Hill Rd.
  Highland Heights, KY 41076
  (859) 441-8956
  chiefthomas@hhky.com
- Newport PD
- Chief Thomas Collins
  998 Monmouth
  Newport, KY 41071
  (859) 292-3625
  npd@police.newportky.gov

Carlisle County

- Carlisle County SO
- Sheriff Steve Perry
  PO Box 487
  Bardwell, KY 42023
  (270) 628-3377
  sheriff@ccfcky.com
- District 3
- Constable Kelly R. Laird
  1300 State Rt. 1371
  South Bardwell, KY 42023
  (270) 705-1362
  burls136@yahoo.com

Carroll County

- Carroll County SO
- Sheriff Jamie Kinman
  440 Main St.
  Carrollton, KY 41008
  (502) 732-7010
  kinmands@yahoo.com
- Carrollton PD
- Chief Michael Willhoite
  750 Clay St.
  Carrollton, KY 41008
  (502) 732-6621
  mwillhoite@carrolltonky.net

Carter County

- Carter County SO
- Sheriff Casey Brammell
  300 W. Main St., Rm. 224
  Grayson, KY 41143
  (606) 474-5616
  cartercojudgeexeuctive@hotmail.com

- District 5
- Constable Phillip Blevins
  PO Box 491
  Olive Hill, KY 41164
  (606) 286-2622
  skybeaver70@hotmail.com
- Grayson PD
- Chief Ed Ginter
  302 E. Main St.
  Grayson, KY 41143
  (606) 474-4308
  e.ginter@graysonpolicedepartment.org
- Olive Hill PD
- Chief Bobby Hall
  225 Roger Patton PO Box 1660
  Olive Hill, KY 41164
  (606) 286-2551
  olivehillpolice@yahoo.com

Casey County

- Casey County SO
- Sheriff Jerry Coffman
  625 Campbellsville PO Box 100
  Liberty, KY 42539
  (606) 787-6821
  caseycoso@yahoo.com

Christian County

- Christian County SO
- Sheriff Livy Leavell, Jr.
  216 W. 7th St.
  Hopkinsville, KY 42240
  (270) 887-4143
  judge@christiancountyky.gov
- District 4
- Constable Tommy Gary
  209 Pyle Ln.
  Hopkinsville, KY 42240
  (270) 886-6485
  garyfamily@bellsouth.net
- District 5
- Constable Mark Graham
  3500 Bahama Dr.
  Hopkinsville, KY 42240
  (270) 885-3749
  markgraham1@bellsouth.net
- District 7
- Constable Richard Leavell III
  330 Jonaquin Dr.
  Hopkinsville, KY 42240
  (270) 885-1885
  leavellfarms@yahoo.com
- Pembroke PD
- Chief Mark Goforth
  222 So. Main St.
  Pembroke, KY 42266
  (270) 475-4343
  pembrokepd@mchsi.com

Clark County

- Clark County SO
- Sheriff Berl Perdue, Jr.
  17 Cleveland St.
  Winchester, KY 40391
  (859) 744-4390
  bperdue@clarkcokysheriff.com
- District 2
- Constable Danny R. Hunt
  161 Calmes Blvd
  Winchester, KY 40391
  (859) 338-0984
  dhunt1947@gmail.com
- Winchester PD
- Chief Kevin Palmer
  16 So. Maple St.
  Winchester, KY 40391
  (859) 745-7403
  kpalmer@winchesterky.com

Clay County

- Manchester PD
- Chief Chris Fulz
  PO Box 279
  Manchester, KY 40962
  (606) 598-8411
  policechieffulz@cityofmanchesterky.org

Clinton County

- Clinton County SO
- Sheriff Rick Riddle
  Courthouse
  Albany, KY 42602
  (606) 387-5111
  clintoncosheriff@hotmail.com
- District 1
- Constable James Adkins
  PO Box 832
  Albany, KY 42602
  (606) 306-4712
  j.adkins53@yahoo.com

Crittenden County

- Crittenden County SO
- Sheriff Wayne Agent
  107 So. Main St.
  Marion, KY 42064
  (270) 965-3400
  ccso@apex.net

- Marion PD
- Chief Ray O'Neal
  108 E. Bellville St.
  Marion, KY 42064
  (270) 965-3500
  roneal@marionky.gov

Cumberland County

- Cumberland County SO
- Sheriff James Pruitt
  600 Courthouse PO Box 838
  Burkeville, KY 42717
  (502) 864-4321
  cumberlandsheriff@windstream.net

Daviess County

- Daviess County SD
- Sheriff Keith Cain
  212 St. Ann
  Owensboro, KY 42303
  (270) 685-8444
  keithrcain@mindspring.com
- Owensboro PD
- Chief Art Ealum, Jr.
  222 E. 9th St.
  Owensboro, KY 42303
  (270) 687-8888
  ealumae@owensboro.org

Edmonson County

- Edmonson County SO
- Sheriff Wil Cannon
  PO Box 100
  Brownsville, KY 42210
  (270) 597-2157
  Edmonson.kysheriff@gmail.com

Elliott County

- Elliott County SO
- Sheriff Ronnie Stephens
  PO Box 729
  Sandy Hook, KY 41171
  (606) 738-5422
  ecsrs@mrtc.com
- District 4
- Constable Billy R. Henderson
  209 Henderson Ridge #1 Cemetery Rd.
  Olive Hill, KY 41166
  (606) 738-4853
  b.henderson@srggi.com

Estill County

- Estill County SO
- Sheriff Gary Lynn Freeman
  130 Main St., Rm. 107
  Irvine, KY 40336
  (606) 723-2323
  ecsheriff@irvineonline.net
- District 1
- Constable Danny Conrad
  350 Geneva Ave.
  Irvine, KY 40336
  (606) 723-0101
  constable.conrad@irvineonline.net

Fayette County

- Fayette County SO
- Sheriff Kathy Witt
  150 No. Limestone, Ste. 265
  Lexington, KY 40507
  (859) 252-1771
  sheriffkathywitt@fayettesheriff.com
- District 2
- Constable Jim McKenzie
  3495 Greentree Rd.
  Lexington, KY 40517
  (859) 539-0006
  jim.mckenzie@insightbb.com
- District 3
- Constable Steve Hamlin
  3261 Mount Foraker Dr.
  Lexington, KY 40515
  (859) 803-4448
  s.hamlin@fayetteconstable.com
- KY Horse Park PD
- Act. Chief (*Capt.*) Lisa Rakes
  4089 Ironworks Pike
  Lexington, KY 40517
  (859) 259-4250
  police@kyhorsepark.com
- Lexington PD
- Chief Ronnie J. Bastin
  150 E. Main St.
  Lexington, KY 40507
  (859) 258-3600
  policechief@lexingtonky.gov

Fleming County

- Fleming County SO
- Sheriff Scotty Royse
  115 W. Main St.
  Flemingsburg, KY 41041
  (606) 845-4701
  sheriff@flemingcountyky.org

- District 1
- Constable Danny Belcher
  1206 Planck Rd.
  Flemingsburg, KY 41041
  (606) 845-0435
  tfogreasy@windstream.net
- Flemingsburg PD
- Chief Randy Sergent
  116 So. Main Cross St.
  Flemingsburg, KY 41041
  (606) 845-2321
  flemingsburg103@hotmail.com

Franklin County

- Franklin County SO
- Sheriff Pat Melton
  PO Box 5260
  Frankfort, KY 40601
  (502) 875-8740
  pat.melton@franklincountyky.com
- District 2
- Constable Tom Banta
  205 Palmer Dr.
  Frankfort, KY 40601
  (502) 695-9014
  tsb@fcwpb.net
- District 6
- Constable Richard Sandifer
  3766 Mt. Zion Rd.
  Frankfort, KY 40601
  (502) 223-3601
  rds4715@yahoo.com
- Frankfort PD
- Chief Mark Wilhoite
  300 W. 2nd St.
  Frankfort, KY 40602
  (502) 875-8523
  mwilhoite@frankfort.ky.gov

Fulton County

- Fulton County SO
- Sheriff Robert *Bobby* Hopper
  2216 Myron Cory PO Box 7
  Hickman, KY 42050
  (270) 236-2545
  office@fultoncountysheriff.net
- Fulton PD
- Chief Terry G. Powell
  340 Browder St.
  Fulton, KY 42041
  (270) 472-3465
  fpdchief@newwavecomm.net

Gallatin County

- Gallatin County SO
- Sheriff Josh Neale
  106 No. Main St. PO Box 1025
  Warsaw, KY 41095
  (859) 567-5751
  k.mcfarland@live.com
- Warsaw PD
- Chief Donnie Gould
  303 E. Main
  Warsaw, KY 41095
  (859) 567-5900
  police@cityofwarsawky.org

Garrard County

- Garrard County SD
- Sheriff Ronald Wardrip
  #15 Public Sq., Ste. 4
  Lancaster, KY 40444
  (859) 792-3591
  rgwsher@windstream.net
- District 2
- Constable Daniel Napier
  102 Miles Dr.
  Lancaster, KY 40444
  (859) 329-3516
  danielnpr@yahoo.com
- District 3
- Constable John Dixon
  91 Duncan Way
  Lancaster, KY 40444
  (859) 548-5305
  johndixon@windstream.net

Grant County

- District 1
- Constable Patrick Stanley
  123 Ridgelea Dr.
  Williamstown, KY 41097
  (859) 824-1872
  kyarms@fuse.net
- District 3
- Constable John Childers
  292 Fairway Dr.
  Dry Ridge, KY 41035
  (859) 620-5773
  john.childers@myemail.indwes.edu

Graves County

- Graves County SO
- Sheriff John Davis
  101 E. South St. #3
  Mayfield, KY 42066
  (270) 247-4501
  gravessheriff@wk.net

- District 2
- Constable Randy Wyatt
  1578 Bellemeade
  Mayfield, KY 42066
  (270) 247-4084
  thewyatt54@newwavecomm.net
- Mayfield PD
- Chief Bryan Morrison
  211 E. Broadway St.
  Mayfield, KY 42066
  (270) 247-1621
  bmorrison@cityofmayfield.org

Grayson County

- Grayson County SO
- Sheriff Rick Clemons
  44 Public Sq.
  Leitchfield, KY 42754
  (270) 259-3024
  gcsoclemons@yahoo.com
- District 1
- Constable James Anderson
  PO Box 13
  Clarkson, KY 42726
  (270) 242-6681
  jefukn@windstream.net
- District 3
- Constable Mike Lindsey
  330 Taylor Cemetery Rd.
  Leitchfield, KY 42754
  (270) 879-4341
  malind7050@yahoo.com

Green County

- Green County SO
- Sheriff Robby Beard
  203 W. Court St.
  Greensburg, KY 42743
  (270) 932-5641
  greencountyso@windstream.net
- Greensburg PD
- Chief Wayne Hedgespeth
  110 W. Court St.
  Greensburg, KY 42743
  (270) 932-4202
  policechief@greensburgonline.com

Greenup County

- Greenup County SO
- Sheriff Keith Cooper
  PO Box 318
  Greenup, KY 41144
  (606) 473-9833
  gcsoso1@yahoo.com
- Bellefonte PD
- Chief Mark Ballard
  705 Bellefonte Princess Rd.
  Ashland, KY 41101
  (606) 325-0608
  bellefontepd@yahoo.com
- Worthington PD
- Chief George *Mike* Hartman
  PO Box 366
  Worthington, KY 41183
  (606) 836- 6821
  cow1926@hotmail.com

Hancock County

- Hancock County SO
- Sheriff Ralph D. Bozarth
  225 Main Cross St.
  Hawesville, KY 42348
  (270) 927-6247
  dale_bozarth@yahoo.com

Hardin County

- Hardin County SD
- Sheriff Charlie Williams
  100 Public Sq., Ste. 101
  Elizabethtown, KY 42701
  (270) 765-5133
  info.hcso@hcky.org
- District 1
- Constable Dennis M. Blair
  1828 Preston St.
  Radcliff, KY 40160
  (270) 352-4404
  d.m.blair@insightbb.com
- District 4
- Constable Randall *Randy* Morris
  272 Mt. Zion Rd.
  Elizabethtown, KY 42701
  (270) 737-1086
  randyrm@comcast.net
- District 6
- Constable Sylvester Bennett
  3147 Middle Creek Rd.
  Elizabethtown, KY 42701
  (270) 769-2109
  bennettsly@live.com
- District 8
- Constable Frank. W. Donehoo
  316 Greenbriar St.
  Vine Grove, KY 40175
  (270) 272-6359
  hcc1508@aol.com

- Elizabethtown PD
- Chief Tracy A. Schiller
  300 So. Mulberry St.
  Elizabethtown, KY 42701
  (270) 765-4125
  tracy.schiller@elizabethtownky.gov
- Radcliff PD
- Chief (*Col.*) Jeffrey A. Cross
  220 Freedoms Way
  Radcliff, KY 40160
  (270) 351-7070, ext. 900
  jcross@radcliff.org
- Vine Grove PD
- Chief Kenneth L. Mattingly
  300 W. Main St.
  Vine Grove, KY 40175
  (270) 877-2252
  policechief@vinegrove.org
- West Point PD
- Chief Vernon *Butch* Curl
  509 Elm St.
  West Point, KY 40177
  (502) 922-4135, ext. 13
  butch@westpointky.org

Harlan County

- District 3
- Constable Jason S. Blanton
  PO Box 386
  Grays Knob, KY 40829
  (606) 273-0589
  dist3constable@hotmail.com
- Evarts PD
- Chief Lupe Blas
  PO Box 208
  Evarts, KY 40828
  (606) 837-8183
  cityofevarts@windstream.net

Harrison County

- Harrison County SO
- Sheriff Bruce Hampton
  113 W. Pike St.
  Cynthiana, KY 41031
  (859) 234-7135
  donniefuller@setel.com
- District 4
- Constable Donald R. Fuller
  51 Simmons Ct.
  Cynthiana, KY 41031
  donniefuller@setel.com
- District 5
- Constable Jeffery Hunter
  302 W. Mill St.
  Cynthiana, KY 41031
  (859) 298-1651
  tforceprotection@yahoo.com
- District 6
- Constable Dwight *Keith* Clifford
  1478 KY Hwy 1842 E.
  Cynthiana, KY 41031
  (859) 588-9305
  kclifford@hughes.net
- Cynthiana PD
- Chief Ray Johnson
  420 E. Pleasant PO Box 431
  Cynthiana, KY 41031
  (859) 234-7157
  cynpd@setel.com

Hart County

- Hart County SO
- Sheriff Boston Hensley
  116 E. Union PO Box 206
  Munfordville, KY 42765
  (270) 524-2341
  hcsd@scrtc.com
- Horse Cave PD
- Chief Alan Shirley
  PO Box 7
  Horse Cave, KY 42749
  (270) 786-4357
  horsecavechief@hotmail.com

Henderson County

- Henderson County SO
- Sheriff Ed Brady
  20 No. Main St., Ste. 112
  Henderson, KY 42420
  (270) 826-2713
  frankgropp@hendersonky.us
- District 3
- Constable Larry Taylor
  2858 Diamond Island Rd.
  Corydon, KY 42406
  (270) 533-6372
  larrytaylor84@bellsouth.net
- Henderson PD
- Chief John C. Reed, Jr.
  1990 Barret Ct.
  Henderson, KY 42420
  (270) 831-1295, ext. 201
  jcreed@cityofhendersonky.org

Henry County

- Henry County SO
- Sheriff Danny Cravens
  30 No. Main St., Ste. C
  New Castle, KY 40050
  (502) 845-2909
  henrycosheriff@insightbb.com
- District 4
- Constable Brandon Cobb
  332 No. Main St. PO Box 69
  New Castle, KY 40050
  (502) 845-0205
  brandon.cobb@jefferson.kyschools.us

Hickman County

- Hickman County SO
- Sheriff Mark Green
  110 E. Clay St.
  Clinton, KY 42031
  (502) 653-2241
  hcso2006@hotmail.com

Hopkins County

- Hopkins County SO
- Sheriff Frank Latham
  56 No. Main St.
  Madisonville, KY 42431
  (270) 821-5661
  sheriff@hopkinscountysheriff.com
- District 3
- Constable George Pointer
  557 E. Center St.
  Madisonville, KY 42431
  constablepointer43@hotmail.com
- District 4
- Constable Janet A. Vaughn
  3510 Stagecoach Rd.
  Hanson, KY 42413
  (270) 322-8964
  janadavau@newwavecomm.net
- Dawson Springs PD
- Chief William Bill Crider
  200 W. Arcadia PO Box 345
  Dawson Springs, KY 42408
  (502) 797-2277
  william.crider@dawsonspringsky.com
- Earlington PD
- Chief Chris Proctor
  103 W. Main St.
  Earlington, KY 42410
  (270) 383-5364
  chris.proctor@earlingtongovcity.com
- Madisonville PD
- Chief Wade Williams
  99 E. Center St.
  Madisonville, KY 42431
  (270) 821-1720
  mpd@madisonvillepd.com
- Mortons Gap PD
- Chief Todd Bennett
  102 So. Main PO Box 367
  Mortons Gap, KY 42440
  (270) 258-5362
  mgpd@bellsouth.net

Jackson County

- Jackson County SO
- Sheriff Tim Fee
  PO Box 426
  McKee, KY 40447
  (606) 287-7121
  jcso@prtcnet.org

Jefferson County

- Jefferson County SO
- Sheriff (*Col.*) John Aubrey
  531 Court Pl., Ste. 604
  Louisville, KY 40202
  (502) 574-5400
  jaubrey@jcsoky.org
- Anchorage PD
- Chief (*Col.*) Christopher L. *Chris* Winders
  11506 Park Rd.
  Anchorage, KY 40223
  (502) 245-4334
  chiefofanchorage@insightbb.com
- Audubon Park PD
- Chief (*Col.*) Jeffrey L. Cox
  3340 Robin Rd.
  Audubon Park, KY 40213
  (502) 574-5471
  clerk@audubonparkky.org
- Indian Hills PD
- Chief (*Col.*) Kelly Spratt
  3738 River Rd.
  Indian Hills, KY 40207
  (502) 893-1375
  police@ihpd.org
- Jeffersontown PD
- Chief Rick Sanders
  10410 Taylorsville Rd.
  Jeffersontown, KY 40299
  (502) 267-0503
  hhogue@jtownkypd.org

- Prospect PD
- Chief Jeff Sherrard
  9200 US 42
  Prospect, KY 40059
  (502) 228-1121
  chief@prospectky.com
- Shively PD
- Chief (*Col.*) Kevin Higdon
  1800 Park Rd
  Shively, KY 40216
  (502) 448-6181
  chiefhigdon@shivelypolice.org

Jessamine County

- Jessamine County SO
- Sheriff Kevin Corman
  101 So. 2nd St.
  Nicholasville, KY 40356
  (859) 885-4139
  kcorman@jessamine.org
- District 1
- Constable Chauncey Tudor
  109 Keeneway Dr.
  Nicholasville, KY 40390
  (859) 887-5050
  chauncey727@windstream.net
- District 3
- Constable James Lewis
  288 Murphy Ln.
  Nicholasville, KY 40356
  (859) 509-1812
  jessaminecoconstabledist3@yahoo.com
- District 4
- Constable Bobby Wombles, Jr.
  217 Whispering Brook Dr.
  Nicholasville, KY 40356
  (859) 421-1358
  bobby@womblescharters.com
- District 5
- Constable Bobby Sams
  125 Glenbrook Ct.
  Nicholasville, KY 40356
  (859) 885-6574
  kathysams1@aol.com
- Nicholasville PD
- Chief Barry Waldrop
  510 No. Main St.
  Nicholasville, KY 40356
  (859) 885-9467
  barry_waldrop@nicholasville.org
- Wilmore PD
- Chief Bill Craig
  335 E. Main St.
  Wilmore, KY 40390
  (859) 858-3535
  wilmorepolice2@juno.com

Kenton County

- Kenton County SO
- Sheriff Charles L. *Chuck* Korzenborn
  303 Court St. PO Box 632
  Covington, KY 41012
  (859) 392-1800
  chuck.korzenborn@kentoncounty.org
- District 2
- Constable Timothy W. Saylor
  4600 Winston Ave., Apt #7
  Taylor Mill, KY 41015
  (859) 815-0624
  tsaylorconstable@aol.com
- Covington PD
- Chief (*Col.*) Michael *Spike* Jones
  1929 Madison Ave.
  Covington, KY 41014
  (859) 292-2220
  spikejones@covingtonky.gov
- Erlanger PD
- Chief(*Col.*) Marc Fields
  505 Commonwealth Ave.
  Erlanger, KY 41018
  (859) 727-2424
  marc.fields@erlangerpd.com
- Kenton County PD
- Chief Brian Capps
  11777 Madison Pike
  Independence, KY 41051
  (859) 392-1940
  brian.capps@kentoncounty.org
- Park Hills PD
- Chief Cody Stanley
  1106 Amsterdam Rd.
  Park Hills, KY 41011
  (859) 431-6172
  cityofparkhills@insightbb.com
- Taylor Mill PD
- Chief Steve Knauf
  5227 Taylor Mill Rd.
  Taylor Mill, KY 41015
  (859) 581-1192
  info@taylormillky.gov

- Villa Hills PD
- Chief Daniel P. Goodenough
  719 Rogers Rd.
  Villa Hills, KY 41017
  (859) 341-3535
  information@villahillsky.org

Knott County

- Knott County SO
- Sheriff Dale Richardson
  54 Main St. W.
  Hindman, KY 41822
  (606) 785-5354
  kcso500@yahoo.com
- Pippa Passes PD
- Chief David Gooslin
  100 Purpose Rd.
  Pippa Passes, KY 41844
  (606) 368-2121
  chiefgooslin@pvscable.com

Knox County

- Knox County SO
- Sheriff John D. Pickard
  234 Court Sq., Ste. 108
  Barbourville, KY 40906
  (606) 546-3181
  libby@kcsoky.us

LaRue County

- LaRue County SD
- Sheriff Bobby Shoffner
  207 W. High St.
  Hodgenville, KY 42748
  (270) 358-3120
  sheriff@laruecounty.org
- Hodgenville PD
- Act. Chief (*Lt.*) Steve Johnson
  109 W. High St.
  Hodgenville, KY 42748
  (270) 358-3013
  steve133@windstream.net

Laurel County

- London PD
- Chief Stewart Walker
  503 So. Main
  London, KY 40741
  (606) 878-7004
  sgtsmith@londonpd.com

Lawrence County

- Lawrence County SO
- Sheriff Garrett Roberts
  122 So. Main Cross St.
  Louisa, KY 41230
  (606) 638-4368
  sheriffroberts@lawrencecokysheriff.com
- District 2
- Constable James Wilkinson
  103 So. Boone St.
  Louisa, KY 41230
  (606) 638-9051
  jrw7146@att.net
- Louisa PD
- Chief Greg A. Fugitt
  215 No. Main Cross St.
  Louisa, KY 41230
  (606) 638-4058
  gfugitt@louisapd.org

Lee County

- District 1
- Constable Jonathan R. Shuler
  PO Box 461
  Beattyville, KY 41311
  (606) 464-0522
  shuler16827@hotmail.com

Leslie County

- Leslie County SO
- Sheriff Paul Howard
  22010 Main St. PO Box 912
  Hyden, KY 41749
  (606) 672-2200
  lesliecountyso2007@yahoo.com

Letcher County

- Letcher County SO
- Sheriff Danny Webb
  6 Broadway St.
  Whitesburg, KY 41858
  (606) 633-2293
  sheriffwebb@letcherso.com
- District 5
- Constable Roger Hall
  36 Straight Row
  Jenkins, KY 41537
  (606) 832-4431
  kykop155@yahoo.com

- City of Jenkins PD
- Chief Roland Crast
  PO Box 568
  Jenkins, KY 41537
  (606) 832-4411
  mayors@microtec.com
- Whitesburg PD
- Chief Robert Tyrone Fields
  215 E. Main St.
  Whitesburg, KY 41858
  (606) 633-2737
  police@cityofwhitesburg.com

Lewis County

- Lewis County SD
- Sheriff William D. Lewis
  514 2nd St.
  Vanceburg, KY 41179
  (606) 796-2912
  information@lewiscountysheriff.org
- Vanceburg PD
- Chief Joe Billman
  189 2nd St.
  Vanceburg, KY 41179
  (606) 796-2111
  vpdbillman@ekns.net

Lincoln County

- Lincoln County SO
- Sheriff Curt Folger
  102 No. 2nd St.
  Stanford, KY 40484
  (606) 365-2696
  cfolger@lincolnky.com
- District 1
- Constable Freddie Fox
  437 Redwood Dr.
  Stanford, KY 40484
  (606) 365-2274
  constable58@msn.com

Logan County

- District 6
- Constable Mike Weldon
  2156 Halls Store Rd.
  Russelville, KY 42276
  (270) 726-2939
  fuelman681@gmail.com
- Auburn PD
- Chief Ron Mills
  106 Spring St.
  Auburn, KY 42206
  (270) 542-4149
  mail@auburnkyusa.com

Lyon County

- Lyon County SO
- Sheriff Kent Murphy
  PO Box 126
  Eddyville, KY 42038
  (270) 388-2311
  kmurphysheriff@hotmail.com
- District 3
- Constable Bob Bennett
  52 Poplar Ck. Blvd
  Kuttawa, KY 42055
  (270) 388-2464
  bennett861028@bellsouth.net
- Eddyville PD
- Chief Shane Allison
  419 Dogwood Ave.
  Eddyville, KY 42038
  (270) 388-2287
  103@eddyvilleky.com

Madison County

- Madison County SO
- Int. Sheriff Mike Coyle
  135 W. Irvine St., Ste. B01
  Richmond, KY 40475
  (859) 623-1511
  sheriff@madisoncountyky.us
- Berea PD
- Chief David Gregory
  212 Chestnut St.
  Berea, KY 40403
  (859) 986-8456, ext. 2
  dgregory@bereaky.gov
- Richmond PD
- Chief Larry R. Brock
  1721 Lexington Rd.
  Richmond, KY 40475
  (859) 623-1162
  chief@richmond.ky.us

Marion County

- Marion County SO
- Sheriff Jimmy Clements
  223 No. Spalding Ave., Ste. 101
  Lebanon, KY 40033
  (270) 692-3051
  mcso223@windstream.net
- Lebanon PD
- Chief Wally Brady
  124 W. Mulberry PO Box 840
  Lebanon, KY 40033
  (270) 692-2121
  wbrady@lebanonky.org

Marshall County

- Marshall County SD
- Sheriff R. Kevin Byars
  52 Judicial Dr.
  Benton, KY 42025
  (270) 527-3112
  kevin.byars@ky.gov
- District 3
- Constable Danny L. Cope
  530 Sharpe School Rd.
  Calvert City, KY 42029
  (270) 337-7636
  dannycope51@gmail.com
- Benton PD
- Chief Tracy Watwood
  1009 Main St.
  Benton, KY 42025
  (270) 527-3126
  policeinfo@cityofbenton.org
- Calvert City PD
- Chief David Elliot
  861 E. 5th Ave.
  Calvert City, KY 42029
  (270) 395-4545
  calvertcity@calvertcity.com

Martin County

- Martin County SO
- Sheriff Garmon D. Preece
  32 E. Main St.
  Inez, KY 41224
  (606) 298-2828
  martinco_s@yahoo.com

Mason County

- Mason County SO
- Sheriff Patrick Boggs
  120 W. 3rd St.
  Maysville, KY 41056
  (606) 564-3309
  patrick.boggs@masoncountysheriffky.com
- Maysville PD
- Chief Ron Rice
  212 Government St.
  Maysville, KY 41056
  (606) 564-9411
  rrice@maysvilleky.net

McCracken County

- McCracken County SO
- Sheriff Jon Hayden
  301 So. 6th St.
  Paducah, KY 42003
  (270) 444-4719, ext. 2515
  jhayden@co.mccracken.ky.us
- District 1
- Constable Mark Hayden
  835 Said Rd.
  Paducah, KY 42003
  (270) 331-3921
  markhayden07@hotmail.com
- District 3
- Constable Scott Wathen
  4845 Stanley Dr.
  Paducah, KY 42001
  (270) 443-6887
  hsswathen@att.net
- Paducah PD
- Chief James Berry
  1400 Broadway
  Paducah, KY 42002
  (270) 444-8590
  jberry@paducahky.gov

McCreary County

- McCreary County SO
- Sheriff Gus H. Skinner, Jr.
  36 Court St. PO Box 627
  Whitley City, KY 42653
  (606) 376-2322
  mcso@mccrearysheriff.com

McLean County

- McLean County SO
- Sheriff Frank S. Cox
  210 Main St. PO Box 292
  Calhoun, KY 42327
  (270) 273-3276
  mcleancoso@cji.net
- District SE
- Constable Johnny Vandiver
  656 Vandiver Rd.
  Island, KY 42350
  (270) 486-3433
  jvandive@live.com

Meade County

- Meade County SO
- Sheriff William *Butch* Kerrick
  516 Hillcrest Dr., Ste. 14
  Brandenburg, KY 40108
  (502) 422-4937
  msheriff@bbtel.com
- District 1
- Constable Christopher William
  725 So. Main St.
  Muldraugh, KY 40122
  (502) 298-0688
  army42001@aol.com
- District 2
- Constable Bob Colasanti
  145 Sassafras Ct.
  Brandenburg, KY 40108
  (270) 422-5660
  bobbyc@bbtel.com
- District 4
- Constable Jason Fore
  204 Fireside Dr.
  Brandenburg, KY 40108
  (270) 422-3689
  jfore@att.blackberry.net
- District 5
- Constable James Perguson
  745 Smith Rd.
  Elkron, KY 40117
  (270) 828-3487
  james.perguson@gmail.com
- Brandenburg PD
- Chief Scotty Singleton
  737 High St.
  Brandenburg, KY 40108
  (270) 422-4981
  singleton@brandenburgpolice.com

Menifee County

- Menifee County SO
- Sheriff Rodney Coffey
  PO Box 142
  Frenchburg, KY 40322
  (606) 768-3875
  menifeeso@cji.net
- District 2
- Constable Denzil Back
  15 Old Milestone Rd.
  Wellington, KY 40387
  (606) 768-4969
  denb@mrtc.com

Mercer County

- Mercer County SO
- Sheriff Ernie Kelty
  207 W. Lexington PO Box 126
  Harrodsburg, KY 40330
  (859) 734-4221
  office@mercercosheriff.com
- Burgin PD
- Chief James Caldwell
  115 So. Maple St.
  Burgin, KY 40310
  (859) 748-5220
  mmrussell@bellsouth.net
- Harrodsburg PD
- Chief Billy Whitenack
  411 No. Greenville St.
  Harrodsburg, KY 40330
  (859) 734-3311
  hburgpd@harrodsburgpd.org

Metcalfe County

- District 2
- Constable Coy Neal
  125 H. Poynter Rd.
  Knob Lick, KY 42154
  (270) 565-4444
  annburton04@yahoo.com

Monroe County

- Monroe County SO
- Sheriff Jerry Gee
  200 No. Main St., Ste. E
  Tompkinsville, KY 42167
  (270) 487-6622
  gee@monroecountykysheriff.com
- Tompkinsville PD
- Chief Dale Ford
  201 E. 2nd St.
  Tompkinsville, KY 42167
  (270) 487-6191
  tvillepd@scrtc.com

Montgomery County

- District 4
- Constable Larry Harris
  950 Hwy 213
  Jeffersonville, KY 40337
  (859) 498-9424
  10harris49@yahoo.com

Morgan County

- West Liberty PD
- Chief Kelse Hensley
  561 Main St.
  West Liberty, KY 41472
  (606) 743-4385
  information@westlibertypd.com

Muhlenberg County

- Muhlenberg County SO
- Sheriff Charles E. Perry
  100 Main St. PO Box 227
  Greenville, KY 42345
  (270) 338-3345
  Co.sheriff@muhlon.com
- District 4
- Constable Darrin Albro
  2353 Sharon Depoy Rd.
  Greenville, KY 42345
  (270) 338-3266
  darrin.albro@muhlenberg.kyschools.us
- District 5
- Constable Jim *JJ* Johnson
  4098 State Rt. 81
  Central City, KY 42330
  (270) 608-0136
  jjjohnson44@bellsouth.net
- Central City PD
- Chief (*Col.*) Brent Roberson
  214 No. 1st St.
  Central City, KY 42330
  (270) 754-2464
  ccpd@centralcitypd.org
- Greenville PD
- Chief Darren S. Harvey
  200 Court St. PO Box 289
  Greenville, KY 42345
  (270) 338-3133
  gpd@greenvillekypd.com

Nelson County

- Nelson County SO
- Sheriff Stephen Campbell
  210 Nelson County Plaza
  Bardstown, KY 40004
  (502) 348-1870
  stephen.campbell@nelsoncountysheriff.com
- Bardstown PD
- Chief Rick McCubbin
  220 No. 5th St.
  Bardstown, KY 40004
  (502) 348-6811, ext. 2401
  marksbur@bardstowncable.net
- Bloomfield PD
- Chief William K. Downs, Jr.
  PO Box 206
  Bloomfield, KY 40008
  (502) 252-8222
  bpd01@bardstowncable.net

Ohio County

- Ohio County SO
- Sheriff David Thompson
  301 So. Main St. PO Box 186
  Hartford, Kentucky 42347
  (270) 298-4444
  david.thompson@ohiocountyky.gov
- District 2
- Constable Greg S. Embry
  154 Old Liberty Church Rd.
  Beaver Dam, KY 42320
  (270) 274-7150
  oldlibertychurch@yahoo.com
- District 4
- Constable Helen Dever
  152 Dever Dr.
  Narrows, KY 42347
  (270) 276-3413
  helendever@yahoo.com
- District 5
- Constable Kenneth House
  386 River Rd.
  Cromwell, KY 42333
  (270) 775-5811
  kmadmax@hotmail.com
- Beaver Dam PD
- Chief Mike Allen
  PO Box 408
  Beaver Dam, KY 42320
  (270) 274-7106
  bdcity@bellsouth.net

Oldham County

- Oldham County SD
- Sheriff Steve Sparrow
  100 W. Jefferson St.
  Lagrange, KY 40031
  (502) 222-9501
  info@oldhamcountysheriff.com
- La Grange PD
- Chief Kevin Collett
  410 W. Jefferson St.
  La Grange, KY 40031
  (502) 225-0444
  chief@lagrangepolice.com

- Oldham County PD
- Chief (*Col.*) Greg Smith
  1855 No. Hwy 393
  LaGrange, KY 40031
  (502) 222-1300
  gsmith@oldhamcountypolice.com

Owen County

- Owen County SO
- Sheriff Zemer Hammond
  102 No. Madison PO Box 496
  Owenton, KY 40359
  (502) 484-3363
  crwright51@yahoo.com
- District 2
- Constable Don Slaughter
  290 Davis Lake Rd.
  Owenton, KY 40359
  (502) 484-3379
  djs0972@att.net
- District 3
- Constable Bob Risch
  1580 Hwy 330
  Owenton, KY 40359
  (502) 484-8098
  constable_young@yahoo.com

Pendleton County

- Pendleton County SO
- Sheriff William *Craig* Peoples
  202 Chapel St.
  Falmouth, KY 41040
  (859) 654-4511
  craigpeop.pendsheriff@fuse.net
- District 1
- Constable Gregory A. Littleton
  236 Serenity Tr.
  Demossville, KY 41033
  (859) 472-1956
  lilton56@fuse.net
- District 2
- Constable Kenny Stapleton
  1160 Fisher Rd.
  Foster, KY 41043
  (859) 496-0001
  kwpc2constable@yahoo.com
- District 3
- Constable Louis McCord
  360 Kennedy Ridge Rd.
  Falmouth, KY 41040
  (859) 654-1361
  mccordlouis@yahoo.com
- Falmouth PD
- Chief Mark Posey
  212 Main St.
  Falmouth, KY 41040
  (859) 654-5555
  mposey100@fuse.net

Perry County

- Hazard PD
- Chief Minor Allen
  800 High St.
  Hazard, KY 41701
  (606) 436-2222
  hazardweb@hazardpd.org

Pike County

- Pike County SO
- Sheriff Charles *Fuzzy* Keesee
  PO Box 839
  Pikeville, KY 41502
  (606) 432-6260
  dino@mikrotc.com
- Elkhorn City PD
- Chief Todd Mattingly
  PO Box 681
  Elkhorn City, KY 41522
  (606) 754-4030
  elkhorncityhall@bellsouth.net
- Pikeville City PD
- Chief Phillip D. Reed
  101 Division St.
  Pikeville, KY 41501
  (606) 437-6236
  preed@pikevillecity.com

Powell County

- Stanton PD
- Chief Kevin Neal
  98 Court St. PO Box 970
  Stanton, KY 40380
  (606) 663-1459
  Jameswatson130@bellsouth.net

Pulaski County

- Pulaski County SD
- Sheriff Todd Wood
  100 No. Main St. PO Box 752
  Somerset, KY 42502
  (606) 678-514
  todd.wood@pulaskisheriff.com
- District 2
- Constable Shane D. Haste
  636 Old Salts Rd.
  Somerset, KY 42503
  (606) 423-4142
  sdh1999@newwave.com

- District 3
- Constable Gene Palmer
  1017 Woodland Dr.
  Somerset, KY 42501
  (606) 219-0671
  sfberet@newwavecomm.net
- Somerset PD
- Chief Doug Nelson
  400 E. Mt. Vernon
  PO Box 107
  Somerset, KY 42502 *(42501)*
  (606) 678-5176
  william.hunt@sumersetpd.com

Robertson County

- Robertson County SO
- Sheriff Billy Allison
  26 Court St. PO Box 76
  Mt Olivet, KY 41064
  (606) 724-5615
  brallison@alltel.net

Rockcastle County

- Rockcastle County SO
- Sheriff Mike Peters
  205 E. Main St. Box 2
  Mt Vernon, KY 40456
  (606) 256-2032
  rocksheriffdept@alltel.net
- District 4
- Constable Richard Dean
  4376 No. Wilderness Rd.
  Mount Vernon, KY 40456
  (606) 256-9020
  richarddean@yahoo.com
- Mount Vernon PD
- Chief Brian Carter
  PO Box 1465
  Mount Vernon, KY 40456
  (606) 256-3441
  mayor@mtvernonky.org

Rowan County

- Rowan County SD
- Sheriff Jack Carter
  600 W. Main St.
  Morehead, KY 40351
  (606) 784-5446
  j.carter@rowancountysheriff.net
- District 4
- Constable Larry J. Stevens
  7565 US 60 E.
  Morehead, KY 40351
  (606) 784-6334
  v.stevens@moreheadstate.edu

Russell County

- District 5
- Constable Michael Bray
  PO Box 1433
  Russell Springs, KY 42642
  (270) 866-9306
  toejoespawn@yahoo.com
- Russell Springs PD
- Chief Joseph Irvin
  72 High St.
  Russell Springs, KY 42642
  (502) 866-3636
  rspd@duo-county.com

Scott County

- Scott County SO
- Sheriff Tony Hampton
  119 No. Hamilton St.
  Georgetown, KY 40324
  (502) 863-7855
  Info@scott.kysheriff.org
- District 2
- Constable Terry *Wayne* Slone
  148 Mulberry St.
  Stamping Ground, KY 40379
  (502) 906-4022
  crash1369@myway.com
- District 6
- Constable Bobby Townsend
  126 So. Water St.
  Georgetown, KY 40324
  (502) 863-6029
  kylawman606@aol.com

Shelby County

- Shelby County SO
- Sheriff Mike Armstrong
  501 Main St., Ste. 8
  Shelbyville, KY 40065
  (502) 633-4324
  mike.armstrong@shelbycoky.com
- District 4
- Constable Donnie Bruner
  503 Emma Wade Rd.
  Bagdad, KY 40003
  (502) 747-0380
  donniebruner@bellsouth.net

- Shelbyville PD
- Chief Robert A. Schutte
  303 Main St.
  Shelbyville, KY 40065
  (502) 633-2326
  info@shelbyvillekypd.com

Simpson County

- Simpson County SO
- Sheriff Chris Cline
  203 E. Kentucky PO Box 434
  Franklin, KY 42134
  (270) 586-7425
  nlaw@simpsoncounty.us
- Franklin PD
- Chief Anthony *Todd* Holder
  100 So. Court St. Mailbox 29
  Franklin, KY 42134
  (270) 586-7167
  THOLDER@FRANKLINPOLICE.NET

Spencer County

- Spencer County SO
- Sheriff Buddy Stump
  18 E. Main St. PO Box 475
  Taylorsville, KY 40071
  (502) 477-3200
  buddystump@spencercountyky.gov
- District 1
- Constable James Ashley
  3330 Elk Creek Rd.
  Taylorsville, KY 40071
  (502) 477-2580
  spencercountyconstable@gmail.com
- Taylorsville PD
- Chief Toby Lewis
  70 Taylorsville Rd. PO Box 279
  Taylorsville, KY 40071
  (502) 477-3231
  tlewis@taylorsvillepd.org

Taylor County

- Taylor County SO
- Sheriff Allen Newton
  203 No. Court St., Ste. 6
  Campbellsville, KY 42718
  (270) 465-4351
  sheriff@taylorcounty.us
- District 5
- Constable Wayne Parsons
  313 Candace St.
  Campbellsville, KY 42718
  (270) 789-0800
  parson1534@comcast.net
- District 6
- Constable Rick Reynolds
  349 Chestnut Grove Rd.
  Campbellsville, KY 42718
  (270) 849-7633
  rlrcons@yahoo.com
- Campbellsville PD
- Chief Tim Hazlette
  100 Terri St.
  Campbellsville, KY 42718
  (270) 465-4122
  info@campbellsville.us

Todd County

- Todd County SO
- Sheriff Joey Johnson
  101 Washington PO Box 557
  Elkton, KY 42220
  (502) 265-9966, ext. 2
  joeyjohnsontoddso@yahoo.com
- District 5
- Constable Chad Johnson
  PO Box 582
  Guthrie, KY 42234
  (270) 483-1992
  constable_cjohnson@att.net
- Elkton PD
- Chief Bruce Marklin
  73 Public Sq. PO Box 578
  Elkton, KY 42220
  (502) 265-9879
  bmarklin@elktonky.com

Trigg County

- Trigg County SO
- Sheriff Ray Burnam
  PO Box 1690
  Cadiz, KY 42211
  (270) 522-6014
  triggsheriff@mediacombb.net
- District 6
- Constable Dennis Whitten
  303 Livingston Way
  Cadiz, KY 42211
  (270) 522-1850
  dwhitten@bellsouth.net
- Cadiz PD
- Chief Chad Grace
  11 Marion St. Box 1667
  Cadiz, KY 42211
  (270) 522-8369
  cadizpd@bellsouth.net

Trimble County

- Trimble County SO
- Sheriff Tim Coons
  Hwy 42 E. PO Box 30
  Bedford, KY 40006
  (502) 255-7138
  tcso@iglou.com
- District 3
- Constable Craig Lacefield
  528 Northridge Dr.
  Bedford, KY 40006
  (502) 255-7875
  tcc3@insightbb.com

Warren County

- Warren County SO
- Sheriff Jerry *Peanuts* Gaines
  429 E. 10th St. PO 807
  Bowling Green, KY 42101
  (270) 842-1633
  sheriff@wcsoky.net
- District 1
- Constable C.E. *Gene* Willett
  1341 Western St.
  Bowling Green, KY 42104
  (270) 779-8705
  gcwillett@msn.com
- District 2
- Constable Brandon Bradshaw
  305 Butler Way
  Bowling Green, KY 42101
  (270) 282-1520
  mrbrandonbradshaw@gmail.com
- District 4
- Constable Rick Bruce
  930 Bethel Ln.
  Bowling Green, KY 42103
  (270) 791-6795
  rickbruce2000@hotmail.com
- District 6
- Constable Pat Dawkins
  1042 Memphis Junction Rd.
  Bowling Green, KY 42101
  (270) 781-7846
  dawkins1@bellsouth.net
- Smith's Grove PD
- Chief Tom Suoy
  146 So. Main St.
  Smiths Grove, KY 42171
  (270) 563-4014
  chiefsuoy@smithsgrove.org

Washington County

- Washington County SO
- Sheriff Tommy Bartley
  PO Box 127
  Springfield, KY 40069
  (859) 336-5400
  information@wcsoky.com
- Springfield PD
- Chief Jim Smith
  127 W. Main St.
  Springfield, KY 40069
  (859) 336-5450
  springfieldkypd@gmail.com

Wayne County

- Wayne County SO
- Sheriff Charles L. Boston
  55 No. Main St., Ste. #2
  Monticello, KY 42633
  (606) 348-5416
  wcsheriff@windstream.net
- District 2
- Constable Jamie Piercy
  PO Box 10
  Alpha, KY 42603
  (606) 307-5017
  d2constablejpiercy@yahoo.com

Webster County

- Sebree PD
- Chief Randy Durbin
  36 So. Spring St.
  Sebree, KY 42455
  (270) 835-7501
  cosebree1@bellsouth.net

Whitley County

- Whitley County SO
- Sheriff Colan Harrell
  201 Main, Ste. 4 PO Box 118
  Williamsburg, KY 40769
  (606) 549-6006
  wcso@2geton.net
- District 4
- Constable Andy Moses
  PO Box 990
  Corbin, KY 40702
  (606) 528-5700
  constableandymoses@att.net

- Williamsburg PD
- Chief Wayne Bird
  116 No. 2nd St.
  Williamsburg, KY 40769
  (606) 549-6087
  Wayne.Bird@williamsburgpd.com

Woodford County

- Woodford County SO
- Sheriff Wayne *Tiny* Wright
  103 So. Main St.
  Versailles, KY 40383
  (859) 873-3119
  wwright@woodfordcountyky.org
- District 6
- Constable Robert Goh
  6521 Delaney Ferry Ext.
  Versailles, KY 40383
  (859) 312-7100
  rgoh224@gmail.com
- District 7
- Constable Stephen Van Miller
  6521 Delaney Ferry Ext.
  Versailles, KY 40383
  (859) 312-7100
  srx171@aol.com

State Agencies

- KY State Police-HQ
- Comm. Rodney Brewer
  919 Versailles Rd.
  Frankfort, KY 40601
  502) 782-1800
  ksppubaff@ky.gov
- Western KY U. PD
- Chief Robert Deane
  1906 College Heights Blvd #11050
  Bowling Green, KY 42101-1050
  (270) 745-2548
  robert.deane@wku.edu

MAINE

Androscoggin County

- Androscoggin County SO
- Sheriff Guy P. Desjardins
  2 Turner St.
  Auburn, ME 04210
  (207) 784-7361
  GDesjardins@androscoggincountymaine.gov
- Auburn PD
- Chief Phillip L. Crowell, Jr.
  1 Minot Ave.
  Auburn, ME 04210
  (207) 333.6650, ext. 2052
  pcrowell@auburnmaine.gov
- Lewiston PD
- Chief Michael Bussiere
  171 Park St.
  Lewiston, ME 04240
  (207) 513-3137
  mbussiere@lewistonmaine.gov
- Livermore Falls PD
- Chief Ernest N. Steward, Jr.
  2 Main St.
  Livermore Falls, ME 04254
  (207) 897-3424
  thomas.gould@lfme.org
- Mechanic Falls PD
- Chief Jeffrey Goss
  108 Lewiston St.
  Mechanic Falls, ME 04256
  (207) 345-9021
  mcfallschief@roadrunner.com
- Sabattus PD
- Chief Anthony Ward
  190 Middle Rd. PO Box 190
  Sabattus, ME 04280
  (207) 375-6952
  award@sabattus.org

Aroostook County

- Aroostook County SO
- Sheriff James P. Madore
  25 School St., Ste. 216
  Houlton, ME 04730
  (207) 532-3471
  sheriff@aroostook.me.us
- Caribou PD
- Chief Michael W. Gahagan
  25 High St.
  Caribou, ME 04736
  (207) 493-3301
  policechief@cariboumaine.org
- Fort Kent PD
- Chief Kenneth Michaud
  111 W. Main St.
  Fort Kent, ME 04743
  (207) 834-5678
  police@fortkent.org
- Houlton PD
- Chief Butch Asselin
  95 Military St.
  Houlton, ME 04730
  (207) 532-2287
  police.chief@houlton-maine.com
- Madawaska PD
- Chief Carroll Theriault
  428 Main St.
  Madawaska, ME 04756
  (207) 728-6356
  madawaskapolice@yahoo.com
- Presque Isle PD
- Chief Matthew Irwin
  43 North St., Ste. 2
  Presque Isle, ME 04769
  (207) 764- 4476
  mirwin@presqueisleme.us
- Washburn PD
- Chief Roy Guidry Jr.
  1285 Main PO Box 505
  Washburn, ME 04786
  (207) 455-4043
  police@washburnmaine.org

Cumberland County

- Cumberland County SO
- Sheriff Kevin Joyce
  36 County Way
  Portland, ME 04102
  (207) 774-1444
  joyce@cumberlandcounty.org
- Bridgton PD
- Chief Kevin L. Schofield
  8 Iredale St.
  Bridgton, ME 04009-1272
  (207) 647-8814
  kschofield@bridgtonmaine.org
- Brunswick PD
- Chief Richard J. Rizzo
  28 Federal St.
  Brunswick, ME 04011
  (207) 725-6634
  rrizzo@brunswickpd.org

- Cape Elizabeth PD
- Chief Neil Williams
  325 Ocean House Rd.
  Cape Elizabeth, ME 04107
  (207) 767-3323
  neil.williams@capeelizabeth.org
- Falmouth PD
- Chief Edward J. Tolan
  2 Marshal Dr.
  Falmouth, ME 04105
  (207) 781-2300
  police@town.falmouth.me.us
- Gorham PD
- Chief Ronald Shepard
  270 Main St.
  Gorham, ME 04038
  (207) 839-5581
  RShepard@gorham.me.us
- Portland PD
- Chief Michael Sauschuck
  109 Middle St.
  Portland, ME 04101
  (207) 874-8300
  mjs@portlandmaine.gov
- Scarborough PD
- Chief Robert Moulton
  246 Rt. 1
  Scarborough, ME 04074
  (207) 883-6361
  rmoult@ci.scarborough.me.us
- South Portland PD
- Chief Edward Googins
  30 Anthoine St.
  South Portland, ME 04106
  (207) 799-5511, ext. 7230
  egoogins@southportland.org
- Yarmouth PD
- Chief Michael E. Morrill
  200 Main St.
  Yarmouth, ME 04096
  (207) 846-3333
  mmorrill@yarmouth.me.us

Franklin County

- Franklin County SO
- Sheriff Scott Nichols
  123 County Way Box 3160
  Farmington, ME 04938
  (207) 778-2680
  scottnichols@franklincountyso.net
- Carrabassett Valley PD
- Chief Mark Lopez
  9000 Main St. Village W.
  Carrabassett Valley, ME 04947
  (207) 237-3200
  mlopez@sugarloaf.com
- Farmington PD
- Chief Jack D. Peck, Jr.
  153 Farmington Falls Rd.
  Farmington, ME 04938
  (207) 778-6311
  farmpd@farmington-maine.org
- Jay PD
- Chief Larry White, Sr.
  340 Main St.
  Jay, ME 04239
  (207) 897-6766
  jpdchief@jay-maine.org
- Rangeley PD
- Chief Phillip Weymouth
  Robbins Ave. PO Box 1112
  Rangeley, ME 04970
  (207) 864-3579
  policechief@rangeleyme.org
- Wilton PD
- Chief Heidi Wilcox
  874 Main St.
  Wilton, ME 04294
  (207) 645-4222
  chief_wilcox@wpdme.com

Hancock County

- Hancock County SD
- Sheriff William F. Clark
  50 State St., Ste. 10
  Ellsworth, ME 04605
  (207) 667-7575
  topdog@hancockcountyso.org
- Bar Harbor PD
- Chief Nathan W. Young
  37 Firefly Ln.
  Bar Harbor, ME 04609
  (207) 288-3391
  nyoung@barharbormaine.gov
- Bucksport PD
- Chief Sean P. Geagan
  PO Box C-1
  Bucksport, ME 04416
  (207) 469-7951
  sgeagan@bucksportmaine.gov

- Gouldsboro PD
- Chief Glenn Grant
  PO Box 68
  Prospect Harbor, ME 04669
  (207) 963-5589
  glennkgrant@yahoo.com
- Southwest Harbor PD
- Chief David Chapais
  26 Village Green PO Box 1048
  Southwest Harbor, ME 04679
  (207) 244-7911
  dchapais@swhpolice.com

Kennebec County

- Kennebec County SO
- Sheriff Randall A. Liberty
  125 State St.
  Augusta, Maine 04330
  (207) 623-3614
  raliberty@kennebecso.com
- Augusta PD
- Chief Robert C. *Bob* Gregoire
  33 Union St.
  Augusta, ME 04330
  (207) 626-2380
  bob.gregoire@augustamaine.gov
- Gardiner PD
- Chief James M. Toman
  6 Church St.
  Gardiner, ME 04345
  (207) 582-5150
  police@gardinermaine.com
- Hallowell PD
- Chief Eric L. Nason
  1 Winthrop St.
  Hallowell, ME 04347
  (207) 622-9710
  ericnason@hallowellmaine.org
- Oakland PD
- Chief Michael *Mike* Tracy
  7 Fairfield St. PO Box 187
  Oakland, ME 04963
  (207) 465-2202
  mtracy@oakland-me.gov
- Waterville PD
- Chief Joseph Massey
  1 Common St.
  Waterville, ME 04901
  (207) 680-4700
  jmassey@waterville-me.gov
- Winslow PD
- Chief Jeffrey Fenlason
  114 Benton Ave.
  Winslow, ME 04901
  (207) 872-5215
  jfenlason@winslow-me.gov
- Winthrop PD
- Chief Joseph E. *Joe* Young, Sr.
  15 Town Hall Ln.
  Winthrop, ME 04364
  (207) 377-7227
  jyoung@winthropmaine.org

Knox County

- Knox County SO
- Sheriff Donna Dennison
  327 Park St.
  Rockland, ME 04841
  (207) 594-0429
  ddennison@kcso.org
- Camden PD
- Chief Randy M. Gagne
  31 Washington St.
  Camden, ME 04843
  (207) 236-7953
  rgagne@camdenmaine.gov
- Rockland PD
- Chief Bruce Boucher
  One Police Plaza
  Rockland, ME 04841
  (207) 594-0316
  bboucher@ci.rockland.me.us
- Rockport PD
- Chief Mark G. Kelley
  85 Main St.
  Rockport, ME 04856
  (207) 236-2027
  policechief@town.rockport.me.us
- Thomaston PD
- Chief Kevin A. Haj
  178 Main St.
  Thomaston, ME 04861
  (207) 354-2511
  khaj@midcoast.com

Lincoln County

- Lincoln County SO
- Sheriff Todd Brackett
  42 Bath Rd. PO Box 611
  Wiscasset, ME 04578
  (207) 882-7332
  tbrackett@co.lincoln.me.us

- Wiscasset PD
- Chief Troy Cline
  Municipal Bldg., US Rt. 1
  Wiscasset, ME 04578
  (207) 882-8202
  chief@wiscassetpd.org

Oxford County

- Oxford County SO
- Sheriff Wayne J. Gallant
  26 Western Ave. PO Box 179
  South Paris, ME 04281
  (207) 743-9554, ext. 111
  wjgallant@megalink.net
- Dixfield PD
- Chief Richard A. Pickett
  142 Wilton Rd PO Box 808
  Dixfield, ME 04224-0808
  (207) 562-4517
  magnum@megalink.net
- Fryeburg PD
- Chief Philip Weymouth
  2 Lovewells Pond Rd.
  Fryeburg, ME 04037
  (207) 935-3323
  fryeburgpd@fairpoint.net
- Mexico PD
- Chief John Madigan, Jr.
  32 Main St.
  Mexico, ME 04257
  (207) 364-7971
  jmadigan@mexicomaine.net
- Norway PD
- Chief Robert Federico
  26 Danforth St.
  Norway, ME 04268
  (207) 743-5303
  norwaypd@megalink.net
- Oxford PD
- Chief Jonathan *Jon* Tibbetts
  701 Main St.
  Oxford, ME 04270
  (207) 539-4414
  oxfordpd@megalink.net
- Paris PD
- Chief David Verrier
  35 Market Sq.
  South Paris, ME 04281
  (207) 743-7448
  PoliceChief@parismaine.org
- Rumford PD
- Chief Stacy Carter
  150 River St.
  Rumford, ME 04276
  (207) 364-4551
  chiefrpd@megalink.net

Penobscot County

- Penobscot County SO
- Sheriff Glenn C. Ross
  85 Hammond St.
  Bangor, ME 04401
  (207) 947-4585
  sheriff@penobscot-sheriff.net
- Bangor PD
- Chief Mark Hathaway
  240 Main St.
  Bangor, ME 04401
  (207) 947-7382
  jim.hassard@bangormaine.gov
- Brewer PD
- Chief Perry Antone, Sr.
  151 Parkway So.
  Brewer, ME 04412
  (207) 989-7001
  pantone@brewermaine.gov
- East Millinocket PD
- Chief Cameron McDunnah
  125 Main St.
  East Millinocket, ME 04430
  (207) 746-9951
  ericaingalls@myfairpoint.net
- Hampden PD
- Dir. Joseph L. Rogers
  106 Western Ave.
  Hampden, ME 04444
  (207) 862-4000
  jlrogers@hampdenmaine.gov
- Holden PD
- Chief Gene Worcester
  570 Main Rd.
  Holden, ME 04429
  (207) 843-5442
  gene@holdenmaine.com
- Lincoln PD
- Chief William Lawrence
  1 Adams St.
  Lincoln, ME 04457
  (207) 794-2221
  policechief@lincolnmaine.org

- Newport PD
- Chief Leonard MacDaid
  27 Water St.
  Newport, ME 04953
  (207) 368-3263
  info@newportmaine.net
- Old Town PD
- Chief Donald O'Halloran
  150 Brunswick St.
  Old Town, ME 04468
  (207) 827-3984
  dohalloran@oldtownpd.org
- Veazie PD
- Chief Mark Leonard
  1084 Main St.
  Veazie, ME 04401
  (207) 947-2358
  mleonard@veaziepd.net

Piscataquis County

- Piscataquis County SO
- Sheriff John J. Goggin
  52 Court St.
  Dover Foxcroft, ME 04426
  (207) 564-3304
  piscso@verizon.net
- Dover-Foxcroft PD
- Chief Dennis A. Dyer
  34 E. Main St.
  Dover-Foxcroft, ME 04426
  (207) 564-8021
  doverpd@doverfoxcroftpolice.com
- Milo PD
- Chief Damien Pickel
  Town Hall
  Milo, ME 04463
  (207) 943-2522
  dpickel@milopolice.com

Sagadahoc County

- Sagadahoc County SO
- Sheriff Joel A. Merry
  752 High St. PO Box 246
  Bath, ME 04530
  (207) 443-8201
  jmerry@sagsheriff.com
- Bath PD
- Chief Michael W. Field
  250 Water St.
  Bath, ME 04530
  (207) 443-8339
  mfield@cityofbath.com
- Richmond PD
- Chief Scott MacMaster
  26 Gardiner St., Ste. 102
  Richmond, ME 04357
  (207) 737-8518
  policeinfo@richmondmaine.com
- Topsham PD
- Chief Christopher Lewis
  100 Main St.
  Topsham, ME 04086
  (207) 725-4337
  clewis@topshammaine.com

Somerset County

- Somerset County SO
- Sheriff Barry A. Delong
  131 E. Madison Rd.
  Skowhegan, ME 04976
  (207) 474-9591
  barry.delong@somersetcounty-me.org
- Fairfield PD
- Int. Chief Joseph Massey
  One Police Plaza PO Box 149
  Fairfield, ME 04937
  (207) 453-9321
  info@fairfieldme.com
- Madison PD
- Chief Barry P. Moores
  26 Weston Ave PO Box 190
  Madison, ME 04950
  (207) 696-5373
  madisonpd@myfairpoint.net
- Pittsfield PD
- Chief Steven Emery
  16 Park St.
  Pittsfield, ME 04967
  (207) 487-3101
  policechief@pittsfield.org
- Skowhegan PD
- Chief Michael Emmons
  225 Water St.
  Skowhegan, ME 04976
  (207) 474-6908
  skowpd@skowhegan.org

Waldo County

- Waldo County SO
- Sheriff Scott Story
  45 Congress St.
  Belfast, ME 04915
  (207) 338- 6786
  sheriff@waldocountyme.gov

- Belfast PD
- Chief Michael J. McFadden
  112 Church St.
  Belfast, ME 04915
  (207) 338-2420
  chief@belfastmepd.org
- Searsport PD
- Chief Richard H. LaHaye, Jr.
  Searsport Public Safety Bldg
  Searsport, ME 04974
  (207) 548-2304

Washington County

- Washington County SO
- Sheriff Donnie Smith
  83 Court St.
  Machias, ME 04654
  (207) 255-4422
  sheriff@wcsheriffsoffice.com
- Calais PD
- Chief David Randall
  North St. PO Box 413
  Calais, ME 04619
  (207) 454-2753
  policechief@calaismaine.org

York County

- York County SD
- Sheriff Maurice Ouellette
  1 Layman Way
  Alfred, ME 04002
  (207) 324-1113
  ycso@co.york.me.us
- Berwick PD
- Chief Timothy Towne
  20 Wilson St. PO Box 644
  Berwick, ME 03901
  (207) 698-1136
  berwickpolice@berwickpolice.org
- Biddeford PD
- Chief Roger P. Beaupre
  39 Alfred St.
  Biddeford, ME 04005
  (207) 282-5127
  chief@bpd.net
- Eliot PD
- Chief Theodor G. Short
  27 Dixon Rd.
  Eliot, ME 03903
  (207) 439-1179
  chiefshort@eliotpd.com
- Kennebunk PD
- Chief Robert F. MacKenzie
  4 Summer St.
  Kennebunk, ME 04043
  (207) 604-1339
  RMackenzie@kennebunkmaine.us
- Kennebunkport PD
- Chief Craig Sanford
  101 Main St. PO Box 2720
  Kennebunkport, ME 04046
  (207) 967-2454
  csanford@kennebunkportme.gov
- Kittery PD
- Int. Chief Theodor G. Short
  200 Rogers Rd.
  Kittery, ME 03904
  (207) 439-1638
  tshort@kitterypolice.com
- North Berwick PD
- Chief Stephen Peasley
  21 Main St. PO Box 422
  North Berwick, ME 03906
  (207) 676-9860
  nbpd1@maine.rr.com
- Ogunquit PD
- Chief Patricia Arnaudin
  20 Cottage St.
  Ogunquit, ME 03907
  (207) 646-9361
  opd1@maine.rr.com
- Old Orchard Beach PD
- Chief Dana M. Kelley
  16 E. Emerson Cummings Blvd
  Old Orchard Beach, ME 04064
  (207) 934-4911
  dkelley@oobmaine.com
- Saco PD
- Chief Bradley S. *Brad* Paul
  20 Storer St.
  Saco, ME 04072
  (207) 284-4535
  bpaul@sacomaine.org
- South Berwick PD
- Chief Dana Lajoie
  180 Main St.
  South Berwick, ME 03908
  (207) 384-2254
  dlajoie@sbmaine.us

- Wells PD
- Chief Jo-Ann Putnam
  1563 Post Rd.   PO Box 949
  Wells, ME 04090
  (207) 646-9354
  jputnam@wellstown.org
- York PD
- Chief Douglas P. Bracy
  36 Main St.
  York, ME 03909
  (207) 363-1031
  dbracy@yorkpolice.org

State Agencies

- ME State Police-HQ
- Chief (*Col.*) Robert A. Williams
  42 State House Station
  45 Commerce Dr.
  Augusta, Maine 04333-0042
  (207) 624-7200
  robert.a.williams@maine.gov

MARYLAND

Allegany County

- Allegany County SO
- Sheriff Craig Robertson
  708 Furnace St. Ext.
  Cumberland, MD 21502
  (301) 777-1585
  crobertson@allconet.org
- Cumberland PD
- Chief Charles H. Hinnant
  20 Bedford St.
  Cumberland, MD 21502
  (301) 777-1600
  chinnant@allconet.org
- Frostburg PD
- Chief Royce C. Douty
  37 Broadway
  Frostburg, MD 21532
  (301) 689-3000
  fpd@allconet.org
- Lonaconing PD
- Chief Royce Douty
  7 Jackson St.
  Lonaconing, MD 21539
  (301) 463-3113
  awilt@allconet.org

Anne Arundel County

- Anne Arundel County SO
- Sheriff Ronald S. *Ron* Bateman
  7 Church Cir. PO Box 507
  Annapolis, MD 21404
  (410) 222-1571
  shport00@aacounty.org
- Annapolis PD
- Chief Michael A. Pristoop
  199 Taylor Ave.
  Annapolis, MD 21401
  (410) 268-9000
  police@annapolis.gov
- Anne Arundel County PD
- Chief Pamela Davis
  8495 Veterans Hwy
  Millersville, MD 21108
  (410) 222-8050
  PD_NorthernDistrict@aacounty.org
- Crofton PD
- Chief Earl D. Fox
  1576 Crofton Pkwy
  Crofton, MD 21114
  (410) 721-2301
  efox@fop70.org

Baltimore County

- Baltimore County SO
- Sheriff R. Jay Fisher
  401 Bosley Ave.
  Baltimore, MD 21204
  (410) 887-4070
  rjfisher@baltimorecountymd.gov
- Baltimore County PD
- Chief James W. Johnson
  700 E. Joppa Rd.
  Towson, MD 21286
  (410) 887-2214
  bcpd@baltimorecountymd.gov

Calvert County

- Calvert County SO
- Sheriff Mike Evans
  175 Main St.
  Prince Frederick, MD 20678
  (410) 535-2800
  evansem@co.cal.md.us

Caroline County

- Caroline County SO
- Sheriff Randy Bounds
  101 Gay St.
  Denton, MD 21629
  (410) 479-2515
  rbounds@carolinemd.org
- Denton PD
- Chief Rodney R. Cox
  100 No. 3rd St.
  Denton, MD 21629
  (410) 479-1414
  rcox@dentonmdpolice.com
- Federalsburg PD
- Chief Donald R. Nagel
  204 So. Main St.
  Federalsburg, MD 21632
  (410) 754-8966
  dnagel@federalsburg.org
- Greensboro PD
- Chief Jeff Jackson
  104 E. Sunset PO Box 451
  Greensboro, MD 21639
  (410) 482-6771
  jjackson@greensboromd.com
- Ridgely PD
- Chief Gary Manos
  105 W. Bell
  Ridgely, MD 21660
  (410) 634-2151
  gmanos@ridgelymd.org

Carroll County

- Carroll County SO
- Sheriff Kenneth Tregoning
  100 No. Court St.
  Westminster, MD 21157
  (410) 386-2900
  ktregoning@ccg.carr.org
- Hampstead PD
- Chief R. Kenneth Meekins
  1112 Main St.
  Hampstead, MD 21074
  (410) 239-8954
  Hampstead@carr.org
- Manchester PD
- Act. Chief (*Sgt.*) Stephen Goetz
  3215 Long Ln. PO Box 830
  Manchester, MD 21102
  (410) 239-6900
  manchestermd@comcast.net
- Sykesville PD
- Chief John R. Williams, Jr.
  7547 Main St.
  Sykesville, MD 21784
  (410) 795-0757
  jwilliams@sykesville.net
- Taneytown PD
- Chief W.E. Tyler
  120 E. Baltimore St.
  Taneytown, MD 21787
  (410) 751-1150
  WTyler@taneytown.org
- Westminster PD
- Chief Jeffrey Spaulding
  36 Locust St.
  Westminster, MD 21158
  (410) 848-4646
  wpd@westgov.com

Cecil County

- Cecil County SO
- Sheriff Barry A. Janney, Sr.
  500 Landing Ln.
  Elkton, MD 21921
  (410) 996-5500
  sheriff.ccso@dell.net
- Elkton PD
- Chief William E. Ryan, Sr.
  100 Railroad Ave.
  Elkton, MD 21921
  (410) 398-4200
  WRyan@ElktonPD.org
- North East PD
- Chief Darrell W. Hamilton
  106 So. Main St. PO Box 528
  North East, MD 21901
  (410) 287-5801
  info@northeastmd.org
- Rising Sun PD
- Chief F.D. *Chip* Peterson, Jr.
  1 E. Main St. PO Box 456
  Rising Sun, MD 21911
  (410) 658-4101
  chiefpeterson@risingsunmd.org

Charles County

- Charles County SO
- Sheriff Rex W. Coffey
  6855 Crain Hwy PO Box 189
  La Plata, MD 20646
  (301) 932-2222
  info@ccso.us

Dorchester County

- Dorchester County SO
- Sheriff James W. Phillips, Jr.
  829 Fieldcrest Rd.
  Cambridge, MD 21613
  (410) 228-4160
  Sheriff@shorenet.net
- Cambridge PD
- Chief Kenneth W. Malik
  8 Washington St.
  Cambridge, MD 21613
  (410) 228-3333
  cpdc1@cambridgepd.org
- Hurlock PD
- Chief Les Hutton
  200 Nealson St. PO Box 740
  Hurlock, MD 21643
  (410) 943-4020
  lhutton@townofhurlock.org

Frederick County

- Frederick County SO
- Sheriff Charles A. *Chuck* Jenkins
  110 Airport Dr. E.
  Frederick, MD 21701
  (301) 600-1532
  cjenkins@frederickcountymd.gov
- Brunswick PD
- Chief Milt Frech
  20 E. A St.
  Brunswick, MD 21716
  (301) 600-2071
  MFrech@FrederickCountyMD.gov

- Frederick PD
- Chief (*Col.*) Thomas Ledwell
  100 W. Patrick St.
  Frederick, MD 21701
  (301) 600-1216
  tledwell@frederickmdpolice.org
- Thurmont PD
- Chief Gregory L. Eyler
  800 E. Main St. PO Box 17
  Thurmont, MD 21788
  (301) 271-7315, ext. 103
  thurmontpolice@FrederickCountyMD.gov

Garrett County

- Garrett County SO
- Sheriff Robert E. Corley
  311 E. Alder St.
  Oakland, MD 21550
  (301) 334-1911
  gcso@garrettcounty.org
- Oakland PD
- Chief Randy Wright
  15 So. 3rd St.
  Oakland, MD 21550
  (301) 334-2691
  townofoak@gmail.com

Harford County

- Harford County SO
- Sheriff Jesse Bane
  45 So. Main St.
  Bel Air, MD 21014
  (410) 838-6600
  banej@hartfordsheriff.org
- Aberdeen PD
- Chief Henry Trabert
  60 No. Parke St.
  Aberdeen, MD 21001
  (410) 272-1600
  htrabert@aberdeen-md.org
- Bel Air PD
- Chief Leo F. Matrangola
  39 Hickory Ave.
  Bel Air, MD 21014
  (410) 638-4500
  lmatrangola@belairmd.org
- Havre De Grace PD
- Chief Teresa Walter
  715 Pennington Ave.
  Havre De Grace, MD 21078
  (410) 939-2121
  twalter@havredegracemd.com

Howard County

- Howard County SO
- Sheriff James F. Fitzgerald
  8360 Court Ave.
  Ellicott City, MD 21043
  (410) 313-4202
  HCSO@howardcountymd.gov
- Howard County PD
- Chief William McMahon
  3410 Courthouse Dr.
  Ellicott City, MD 21043
  (410) 313-3200
  policeliaison@howardcountymd.gov

Kent County

- Kent County SO
- Sheriff John F. Price IV
  104 Vickers Dr., Unit B
  Chestertown, MD 21620
  (410) 778-2279
  sheriff@kentgov.org
- Chestertown PD
- Chief G. Adrian Baker
  333 So. Cross St.
  Chestertown, MD 21620
  (410) 778-1800
  office@chestertown.com
- Rock Hall PD
- Chief Steven Moore
  5585 Main St. PO Box 367
  Rock Hall, MD 21661
  (410) 639-7222
  RockHallPD@rockhallmd.com

Montgomery County

- Montgomery County SO
- Sheriff Darren M. Popkin
  50 Maryland Ave.
  Rockville, MD 20850
  (240) 777-7007
  darren.popkin@montgomerycounty.gov
- Chevy Chase PD
- Chief John Fitzgerald
  5906 Connecticut Ave.
  Chevy Chase, MD 20815
  (301) 654-7302
  john.m.fitzgerald@montgomerycountymd.gov
- Gaithersburg PD
- Chief Mark P. Sroka
  14 Fulks Corner Ave.
  Gaithersburg, MD 20877
  (301) 258-6400
  police@gaithersburgmd.gov

- Takoma Park PD
- Chief Ronald Ricucci
  7500 Maple Ave.
  Takoma Park, MD 20912
  (301) 270-1100
  RonaldR@takomagov.org

Prince George's County

- Prince George's County SO
- Sheriff Melvin C. High
  5303 Chrysler Way
  Largo, MD 20774
  (301) 780-8610
  sheriffinfo@co.pg.md.us
- Bladensburg PD
- Act. Chief Charles L. Owens
  4910 Tilden Rd.
  Bladensburg, MD 20710
  (301) 864-6080
  chief@bladensburg.net
- Capitol Heights PD
- Chief Anthony Ayers
  401 Capitol Heights Blvd
  Capitol Heights, MD 20743
  (301) 333-4000
  alayers@capitolheightsmd.com
- Cheverly PD
- Chief Buddy Robshaw
  6401 Forest Rd.
  Cheverly, MD 20785
  (301) 341-1055
  Policechief@cheverly-md.gov
- Cottage City PD
- Chief Robert W. Patton
  3820 40th Ave.
  Cottage City, MD 20722
  (301) 927-9225
  chief@cottagecitypolice.org
- District Heights PD
- Chief Michael March
  2002 Marbury Dr.
  District Heights, MD 20747
  (301) 336-1400
  marchm@districtheights.org
- Forest Heights PD
- Chief Stewart Russell
  5508 Arapahoe Dr.
  Forest Heights, MD 20745
  (301) 839-4040
  srussell@forestheightsmd.gov
- Greenbelt PD
- Chief James Craze
  550 Crescent Rd.
  Greenbelt, MD 20770
  (301) 474-7200
  jcraze@greenbeltmd.gov
- Hyattsville PD
- Chief Douglas K. Holland
  4310 Gallatin St.
  Hyattsville, MD 20781
  (301) 985-5060
  dholland@hyattsville.org
- Landover Hills PD
- Chief (*Col.*) Henry Norris
  6904 Taylor St.
  Landover Hills, MD 20784
  (301) 773-6400
  lndvrhlls@aol.com
- Laurel PD
- Chief Rich McLaughlin
  811 5th St.
  Laurel, MD 20707
  (301) 498-0092
  lpd@laurel.md.us
- Mount Rainier PD
- Chief Michael E. Scott
  3409 Rhode Island Ave.
  Mount Rainier, MD 20712
  (301) 985-6580
  mscott@mountrainierpd.org
- New Carrollton City PD
- Chief David Rice
  6016 Princess Garden Pkwy
  New Carrollton, MD 20784
  (301) 459-0142
  drice@newcarrolltonpd.com
- Prince George's County PD
- Chief Mark A. Magaw
  7600 Barlowe Rd.
  Palmer Park, MD 20785
  (301) 352-1200
  Police_CustServ@co.pg.md.us
- Riverdale Park PD
- Chief David C. Morris
  5004 Queensbury Rd.
  Riverdale, MD 20737
  (301) 927-4343
  town@riverdaleparkmd.gov

Queen Anne's County

- Queen Anne's County SO
- Sheriff R. Gary Hofmann III
  505 Railroad Ave.
  Centreville, MD 21617
  (410) 758-0770, ext. 1213
  sheriff@qac.org
- Centreville PD
- Chief Charlie Rhodes
  420 No. Commerce St.
  Centreville, MD 21617-1019
  (410) 758-8437
  mfinck@qac.org

St. Mary's County

- St. Mary's County SO
- Sheriff Timothy K. *Tim* Cameron
  23150 Leonard Hall Dr.
  Leonardtown, MD 20650
  (301) 475-4200, ext. 1900
  sheriff@co.saint-marys.md.us

Somerset County

- Somerset County SO
- Sheriff Robert N. Jones
  30426A Sam Barnes Rd.
  Westover, MD 21871
  (410) 651-9225
  scso@intercom.net
- Crisfield PD
- Chief Michael Tabor
  319A W. Main St.
  Crisfield, MD 21817
  (410) 968-1323
  chief@crisfieldpd.com
- Princess Anne PD
- Chief Scott Keller
  11780 Beckford Ave.
  Princess Anne, MD 21853
  (410) 651-1822
  keller@princessannepolice.com

Talbot County

- Talbot County SO
- Sheriff Dallas Pope
  115 W. Dover St.
  Easton, MD 21601
  (410) 822-1020
  sheriff@talbotcountymd.gov
- Easton PD
- Chief David Spencer
  106 W. Dover St.
  Easton, MD 21601
  (410) 822-1111
  police@town-eastonmd.com
- Saint Michaels PD
- Chief Anthony Smith
  109 Talbot St.
  Saint Michaels, MD 21663
  (410) 745-9500
  asmith@townofstmichaels.org

Washington County

- Washington County SO
- Sheriff Douglas W. Mullendore
  500 Western Maryland Pkwy
  Hagerstown, MD 21740
  (240) 313-2103
  dmullendore@washco-md.net
- Hagerstown PD
- Chief Mark Holtzman
  50 No. Burhans Blvd
  Hagerstown, MD 21740
  (301) 790-3700
  info@hagerstownpd.org
- Hancock PD
- Chief Timothy J. Buskirk
  126 W. Main St.
  Hancock, MD 21750
  (301) 678-5633
  chief@townofhancock.org
- Smithsburg PD
- Chief George L. Knight, Jr.
  21 W. Water St. PO Box 282
  Smithsburg, MD 21783
  (301) 824-3500
  smithsburgpd@myactv.net

Wicomico County

- Wicomico County SO
- Sheriff Michael A. *Mike* Lewis
  401 Naylor Mill Rd.
  Salisbury, MD 21803
  (410) 548-4891
  rwierfberg@wicomicocounty.org
- Delmar PD
- Chief Harold Saylor
  400 So. Pennsylvania
  Delmar, MD 21875
  (410) 896-3132
  chief@delmarpolice.com

- Fruitland PD
- Chief Michael Phillips
  208 So. Division St.
  Fruitland, MD 21826
  (410) 548-2804
  mphillips@fruitlandpolice.com
- Salisbury PD
- Chief Barbara Duncan
  699 W. Salisbury Pkwy
  Salisbury, MD 21803
  (410) 548-3165
  SPD@salisburypd.com

Worcester County

- Worcester County SO
- Sheriff Reggie T. Mason, Sr.
  1 W. Market St., Rm. 1001
  Snow Hill, MD 21863
  (410) 632-1111
  askthesheriff@co.worcester.md.us
- Berlin PD
- Chief Arnold Downing
  10 William St.
  Berlin, MD 21811
  (410) 641-1334
  adowning@berlinmdpd.org
- Ocean City PD
- Chief Gregory Guiton
  6501 Coastal Hwy
  Ocean City, MD 21842
  (410) 723-6610
  policechief@oceancitymd.gov
- Pocomoke City PD
- Chief Kelvin D. Sewell
  1500 Market St.
  Pocomoke City, MD 21851
  (410) 957-1601
  pcpd@verizon.net
- Snow Hill PD
- Chief Kirk Daugherty
  427 W. Market St.
  Snow Hill, MD 21863
  (410) 632-2444
  daugherty@snowhillmd.com

State Agencies

- MD State Police-HQ
- Supt. (*Col.*) Marcus L. Brown
  1201 Reisterstown Rd.
  Pikesville, MD 21208-3899
  (410) 653-4219
  mspsuperintendent@maryland.gov
- MD Nat'l Capital Park PD
- Chief Antonio DeVaul
  Montgomery County Div.
  12751 Layhill Rd.
  Silver Spring, MD 20906
  (301) 929-2731
  Antonio.DeVaul@mncppc-mc.org
- MD Nat'l Capital Park PD
- Chief Larry Brownlee
  Prince George's County Div.
  6700 Riverdale Rd.
  Riverdale, MD 20737
  (301) 429-5658
  Larry.Brownlee@pgparks.com
- MD Trans. Authority PD
- Chief Michael Kundrat
  4330 Broening Hwy
  Baltimore, MD 21222
  (410) 537-7777
  Counties: Anne Arundel, Baltimore, Cecil, Charles, Harford, Howard, Queen Anne's
  mdtapolice@mdta.maryland.gov
- Morgan State U. PD
- Int. Chief Lance Hatcher
  1700 E. Coldspring Ln.
  Baltimore, MD 21251
  (443) 885-3100
  msupolice@morgan.edu

MASSACHUSETTS

Barnstable County

- Barnstable County SO
- Sheriff James M. *Jim* Cummings
  6000 Sheriff's Pl.
  Barnstable, MA 02630
  (508) 563-4302
  jcummings@bsheriff.net
- Barnstable PD
- Chief Paul MacDonald
  1200 Phinneys Ln.
  Hyannis, MA 02601
  (508) 775-0387
  email@town.barnstable.ma.us
- Bourne PD
- Chief Dennis Woodside
  175 Main St.
  Buzzards Bay, MA 02532
  (508) 759-4420, ext. 201
  dwoodside@townofbourne.com
- Brewster PD
- Chief Richard J. Koch Jr.
  631 Harwich Rd.
  Brewster, MA 02631
  (508) 896-7011, ext. 201
  rkoch@town.brewster.ma.us
- Chatham PD
- Chief Mark R. Pawlina
  249 George Ryder Rd.
  Chatham, MA 02633
  (508) 945-1213
  mpawlina@chatham-ma.gov
- Dennis PD
- Chief Mike Whalen
  90 Bob Crowell Rd.
  South Dennis, MA 02660
  (508) 394-1314
  mwhalen@town.dennis.ma.us
- Eastham PD
- Chief Edward Kulhawik
  2550 State Hwy
  North Eastham, MA 02651
  (508) 255-0551
  ekulhawik@eastham-ma.gov
- Falmouth PD
- Chief Edward Dunne
  750 Main St.
  Falmouth, MA 02540
  (508) 457-2527
  breid@falmouthpolice.us
- Harwich PD
- Chief William Mason
  183 Sisson Rd.
  Harwich, MA 02645
  (508) 430-7541, ext. 5204
  wmason@harwichpolice.com
- Mashpee PD
- Chief Rodney Collins
  19 Frank Hicks Dr.
  Mashpee, MA 02649
  (508) 539-1480
  rcollins@mashpeepd.com
- Orleans PD
- Chief Scott MacDonald
  90 So. Orleans Rd.
  Orleans, MA 02653
  (508) 255-0117
  smacdonald@orleanspd.com
- Provincetown PD
- Chief Jeff Jaran
  26 Shankpainter Rd.
  Provincetown, MA 02657
  (508) 487-1212
  jjaran@provincetown-ma.gov
- Sandwich PD
- Chief Peter N. Wack
  117 Rt. 6A
  Sandwich, MA 02563
  (508) 888-1212
  sandwichpd@townofsandwich.net
- Truro PD
- Chief Kyle Takakjian
  344 Rt. 6 PO Box 995
  Truro, MA 02666
  (508) 487-8730
  takakjian@truropolice.org
- Wellfleet PD
- Chief Ronald L. Fisette
  36 Gross Hill Rd.
  Wellfleet, MA 02667
  (508) 349-3702
  Ronald.Fisette@wellfleet-ma.gov

Berkshire County

- Berkshire County SO
- Sheriff Thomas Bowler
  467 Cheshire Rd.
  Pittsfield, MA 01201
  (413) 443-0008
  thomas.bowler@sdb.state.ma.us

- Adams PD
- Chief Donald A. Poirot
  4 School St.
  Adams, MA 01220
  (413) 743-1212
  dpoirot@town.adams.ma.us
- Cheshire PD
- Chief Timothy *Tim* Garner
  90 Church St. PO Box 536
  Cheshire, MA 01225
  (413) 743-1501
  chehchies1@roadrunner.com
- Dalton PD
- Chief Jeffrey E. Coe
  462 Main St.
  Dalton, MA 01226
  (413) 684-0300
  jcoedpd@nycap.rr.com
- Great Barrington PD
- Chief William Walsh
  20 Castle St.
  Great Barrington, MA 01230
  (413) 528-0306
  wwalsh@townofgb.org
- Lee PD
- Chief Joseph Buffis
  32 Main St.
  Lee, MA 01238
  (413) 243-5530
  jbuffis@town.lee.ma.us
- Lenox PD
- Chief Stephen E. O'Brien
  6 Walker St.
  Lenox, MA 01240
  (413) 637-2346
  LenoxChief@townoflenox.com
- Monterey PD
- Chief Gareth Backhaus
  435 Main Rd. PO Box 942
  Monterey, MA 01245
  (413) 528-1443, ext. 225
  mpdchief1@verizon.net
- Pittsfield PD
- Act. Chief Michael Wynn
  39 Allen St.
  Pittsfield, MA 01201
  (413) 448-9702
  mwynn@pittsfieldch.com
- Sheffield PD
- Act. Chief Eric R. Munson III
  10 So. Main St. PO Box 186
  Sheffield, MA 01257
  (413) 229-8522
  emunson@sheffieldpd.com
- Stockbridge PD
- Chief Richard B. Wilcox
  50 Main St. PO Box 417
  Stockbridge, MA 01262
  (413) 298-4179
  rwilcox@townofstockbridge.com
- Williamstown PD
- Chief Kyle J. Johnson
  31 North St.
  Williamstown, MA 01267
  (413) 458-5733
  kjohnson@williamstown.net

Bristol County

- Bristol County SO
- Sheriff Thomas M. Hodgson
  400 Faunce Corner Rd.
  Dartmouth, MA 02747
  (508) 995-7835
  sheriff@bcso-ma.org
- Acushnet PD
- Chief Michael G. Alves
  130 Main St.
  Acushnet, MA 02743
  (508) 998-0240
  MAlves@Acushnetpd.com
- Dartmouth PD
- Chief Timothy M. Lee
  249 Russells Mills Rd.
  Dartmouth, MA 02748
  (508) 910-1700
  tlee@dartmouthpd.org
- Dighton PD
- Chief Robert MacDonald
  1551 Somerset Ave.
  Dighton, MA 02715
  (508) 669-6711
  dpdkbowerque@comcast.com
- Easton PD
- Chief Allen R. Krajcik
  46 Lothrop St.
  North Easton, MA 02356
  (508) 230-3322
  akrajcik@easton.ma.us

- Fairhaven PD
- Chief Michael Myers
  1 Bryant Ln.
  Fairhaven, MA 02719
  (508) 997-7421
  chief@fairhavenpolice.org
- Fall River PD
- Chief Daniel S. Racine
  685 Pleasant St.
  Fall River, MA 02721
  (508) 676-8511
  dracine@frpd.org
- New Bedford PD
- Chief David A. Provencher
  871 Rockdale Ave.
  New Bedford, MA 02740
  (508) 991-6300, ext. 9
  chiefnbpd@newbedfordpd.com
- North Attleboro PD
- Chief John Reilly
  102 So. Washington St.
  North Attleboro, MA 02760
  (508) 695-1212
  jreilly@nattleboro.com
- Norton PD
- Chief Brian Clark
  82 E. Main St.
  Norton, MA 02766
  (508) 285-3337
  clark@nortonpolice.com
- Raynham PD
- Chief James Donovan
  53 Orchard St.
  Raynham, MA 02767
  (508) 824-2717
  jdonovan@raynhampd.com
- Rehoboth PD
- Act. Chief (*Lt.*) James J. Trombetta
  334 Anawan St.
  Rehoboth, MA 02769
  (508) 252-3722
  Jtrombetta@rehobothpd.org
- Seekonk PD
- Chief Craig Mace
  500 Taunton Ave.
  Seekonk, MA 02771
  (508) 336-8123
  macc@seekonkpd.com
- Somerset PD
- Chief (*Col.*) Joseph C. Ferreira
  465 County St.
  Somerset, MA 02726
  (508) 679-2138
  j_ferreira@somersetpd.org
- Swansea PD
- Chief George Arruda
  1700 G.A.R. Hwy
  Swansea, MA 02777
  (508) 674-8464
  george.arruda@swanseapolice.com
- Taunton PD
- Chief Edward James Walsh
  23 Summer St.
  Taunton, MA 02780
  (508) 824-7522
  chief@tauntonpd.com
- Westport PD
- Chief Keith A. Pelletier
  818 Main Rd.
  Westport, MA 02790
  (508) 636-1122
  ltpholden@aol.com

Dukes County

- Dukes County SO
- Sheriff Michael A. McCormack
  149 Main St.
  Edgartown, MA 02539
  (508) 627-5173
  mamccormack@dcsoma.org
- Aquinnah PD
- Chief Randhi P. Belain
  67 State Rd.
  Aquinnah, MA 02535
  (508) 645-2313
  RBelain@aquinnahpolice.us
- Chilmark PD
- Chief Brian Cioffi
  15 State Rd. PO Box 340
  Chilmark, MA 02535
  (508) 645-3310
  bcioffi@vineyard.net
- Edgartown PD
- Chief Antone J. Bettancourt
  72 Pease's Point Way So.
  Edgartown, MA 02539
  (508) 627-4343
  edgartownpd@comcast.net

- Tisbury PD
- Chief Daniel T. Hanavan
  32 Water St.
  PO Box 426
  Tisbury, MA 02568
  (508) 696-4240
  tisburypolice@hotmail.com
- West Tisbury PD
- Chief Daniel R. Rossi
  681 Edgartown PO Box 520
  West Tisbury, MA 02575
  (508) 693-0020
  drossi@wt-pd.com

Essex County

- Essex County SD
- Sheriff Frank G. Cousins, Jr.
  20 Manning Ave.
  PO Box 807
  Middleton, MA 01949
  (978) 750-1900, ext. 3370
  sheriff@eccf.com
- Amesbury PD
- Chief Mark Gagnon
  19 School St.
  Amesbury, MA 01913
  (978) 388-1212
  markg@amesburyma.gov
- Andover PD
- Chief Brian J. Pattullo
  32 No. Main St.
  Andover, MA 01810
  (978) 475-0411, ext. 1005
  omen@andoverps.net
- Beverly PD
- Chief Mark A. Ray
  191 Cabot St.
  Beverly, MA 01915
  (978) 921-6039
  mray@beverlyma.gov
- Boxford PD
- Chief Michael J. Murphy
  285 Ipswich Rd.
  Boxford, Massachusetts 01921
  (978) 887-8135
  mmurphy@town.boxford.ma.us
- Danvers PD
- Chief Neil F. Ouellette
  120 Ash St.
  Danvers, MA 01923
  (978) 774-1213
  police@mail.danvers-ma.org
- Essex PD
- Chief Peter Silva
  24 Martin St.
  Essex, MA 01929
  (978) 768-6628
  psilva@essexma.org
- Gloucester PD
- Chief Leonard Campanello
  197 Main St.
  Gloucester, MA 01930
  (978) 283-1212
  lcampanello@gloucester-ma.gov
- Groveland PD
- Chief Robert Kirmelewicz
  181 Main St.
  Groveland, MA 01834
  (978) 521-1212
  chief@grovelandpolice.com
- Hamilton PD
- Chief Russell Stevens
  265 Bay Rd.
  Hamilton, MA 01982
  (978) 468-1212
  police@hamiltonma.gov
- Haverhill PD
- Chief Alan R. DeNaro
  40 Bailey Blvd
  Haverhill, MA 01831
  (978) 373-1212
  ADeNaro@haverhillpolice.com
- Ipswich PD
- Chief Paul Nikas
  15 Elm St.
  Ipswich, MA 01938
  (978) 356-4343
  p2nikas@ipswichpolice.org
- Lawrence PD
- Chief John J. Romero
  90 Lowell St.
  Lawrence, MA 01840
  (978) 794-5900
  jromero@lawpd.com
- Lynn PD
- Chief Kevin F. Coppinger
  300 Washington St.
  Lynn, MA 01901
  (781) 595-2000
  kcoppinger@lynnpolice.org

- Lynnfield PD
- Chief David J. Breen
  55 Summer St.
  Lynnfield, MA 01940
  (781) 334-3132
  LynnfieldPolice@town.lynnfield.ma.us
- Manchester by the Sea PD
- Chief Glenn F. McKiel
  10 Central St.
  Manchester, MA 01944
  (978) 526-1212
  policeinfo@manchester.ma.us
- Marblehead PD
- Chief Robert O. Picariello
  11 Gerry St.
  Marblehead, MA 01945
  (781) 631-1212
  help@marblehead.org
- Merrimac PD
- Chief Eric M. Shears
  16 E. Main St.
  Merrimac, MA 01860
  (978) 346-8321
  police@townofmerrimac.com
- Methuen PD
- Chief Joseph Solomon
  90 Hampshire St.
  Methuen, MA 01844
  (978) 983-8698
  jcormier@ci.methuen.ma.us
- Middleton PD
- Chief James A. DiGianvitorio
  65 No. Main St.
  Middleton, MA 01949
  (978) 774-4424
  chief@middletonpolice.com
- Nahant PD
- Chief Robert C. Dwyer
  198 Nahant Rd.
  Nahant, MA 01908-1298
  (781) 581-1212
  rdwyer@nahantpolice.org
- Newbury PD
- Chief Michael A. Reilly
  25 High Rd.
  Newbury, MA 01951
  (978) 462-4440, ext. 120
  m.reilly@newburypolice.com
- Newburyport PD
- City Marshal/Chief Thomas H. Howard
  4 Green St.
  Newburyport, MA 01950
  (978) 462-4411
  thoward@newburyportpolice.com
- North Andover PD
- Chief Paul Gallagher
  1475 Osgood St.
  North Andover, MA 01845
  (978) 683-3168
  pgallagher@napd.us
- Peabody PD
- Chief Robert L. Champagne
  6 Allens Ln.
  Peabody, MA 01960
  (978) 538-6306
  chief@peabodypolice.org
- Rockport PD
- Chief John T. McCarthy
  37 Broadway PO Box 156
  Rockport, MA 01966
  (978) 546-1212
  chief@rockportpd.org
- Rowley PD
- Chief Robert R. Barker
  477 Haverhill St.
  PO Box 365
  Rowley, MA 01969
  (978) 948-7644
  chief@rowleypolice.com
- Salem PD
- Chief Paul F. Tucker
  95 Margin St.
  Salem, MA 01970
  (978) 744-0171
  admin@salempd.net
- Salisbury PD
- Chief Thomas W. Fowler
  24 Railroad Ave.
  Salisbury, MA 01952
  (978) 465-3121
  Admin@Salisburypolice.com
- Saugus PD
- Chief Domenic J. DiMella
  27 Hamilton St.
  Saugus, MA 01906
  (781) 941-1140
  DDimella@sauguspd.com

- Swampscott PD
- Chief Ron Madigan
  86 Burrill St.
  Swampscott, MA 01907
  (781) 595-1111
  RMadigan@swampscottpolice.com
- Topsfield PD
- Chief Evan *E.J.* Haglund
  210 Boston St.
  Topsfield, MA 01983
  (978) 887-6533
  topsfield101@gmail.com
- Wenham PD
- Chief Thomas Perkins
  1 Friend Ct. PO Box 536
  Wenham, MA 01984
  (978) 468-4000
  police@wenhamma.gov
- West Newbury PD
- Chief Lisa A. Holmes
  401 Main St.
  West Newbury, MA 01985
  (978) 363-1213
  police@westnewburysafety.org

Franklin County

- Franklin County SO
- Sheriff Christopher J. Donelan
  160 Elm St.
  Greenfield, MA 01301
  (413) 774-4014
  chris.donelan@fcs.state.ma.us
- Ashfield PD
- Chief Patrick Droney
  412 Main St. PO Box 355
  Ashfield, MA 01330
  (413) 625-8200
  chief@ashfield.org
- Buckland PD
- Chief James T. Hicks
  69½ Conway St.
  Shelburne Falls, MA 01370
  (413) 625-8200
  twnclerk@crocker.com
- Deerfield PD
- Chief John Paciorek, Jr.
  8 Conway St.
  Deerfield, MA 01373
  (413) 665-2606
  jpaciorek@police.deerfield.ma.us
- Erving PD
- Chief Christopher M. Blair
  71 French King Hwy
  Erving, Massachusetts 01344
  (413)423-3310
  ervingpd@comcast.net
- Greenfield PD
- Chief Joseph L. Burge
  321 High St.
  Greenfield, MA 01301
  (413) 773-5411, ext. 1306
  burgej@greenfieldpd.org
- Leverett PD
- Chief Gary Billings
  95 Montague Rd. PO Box 300
  Leverett, MA 01054
  (413) 548-4994
  police@leverett.ma.us
- Montague PD
- Chief Charles Dodge III
  180 Turnpike Rd.
  Turners Falls, MA 01376
  (413) 863-8911
  cdodge@montague.net
- Northfield PD
- Act. Chief Robert Leighton
  69 Main St.
  Northfield, MA 01360
  (413) 498-5118
  Police@TownNfld.com
- Sunderland PD
- Chief Jeffrey Gilbert
  105 River Rd.
  Sunderland, MA 01375
  (413) 665-7036
  sunderlandpolice@townofsunderland.us
- Whately PD
- Chief James A. Sevigne, Jr.
  77 Christian Ln.PO Box 251
  Whately, MA 01093
  (413) 665-0430
  whatelypdjs@comcast.net

Hampden County

- Hampden County SO
- Sheriff Michael J. Ashe
  627 Randall Rd.
  Ludlow, MA 01056
  (413) 547-8000
  michael.ashe@sdh.state.ma.us

- Chester PD
- Chief Dan Ilnicky
  15 Middlefield Rd.
  Chester, MA 01011
  (413) 354-7822
  chesterpd@comcast.net
- Chicopee PD
- Chief Thomas Charette
  110 Church St.
  Chicopee, MA 01020
  (413) 592-6341
  tcharette@chicopeepolice.com
- East Longmeadow PD
- Chief Douglas Mellis
  160 Somers Rd.
  East Longmeadow, MA 01028
  (413) 525-5440
  dmellis@eastlongmeadow.org
- Hampden PD
- Chief Jeff Farnsworth
  625 Main St.
  Hampden, MA 01103
  (413) 566-8011
  admin@hampdenpolice.org
- Holland PD
- Chief Bryan C. Haughey
  27 Sturbridge Rd.
  Holland, MA 01521
  (413) 245-0117
  bhaughey@town.holland.ma.us
- Holyoke College PD
- Chief Ralph J. Gould
  303 Homestead Ave.
  Holyoke, MA 01040-1099
  (413) 552-2400
  hccpd@hcc.mass.edu
- Holyoke PD
- Chief James M. Neiswanger
  138 Appleton St.
  Holyoke, MA 01040
  (413) 536-6431
  chiefofpolice@holyokepd.org
- Longmeadow PD
- Chief Robert F. Siano
  34 Williams St.
  Longmeadow, MA 01106
  (413) 567-3311
  bouano@longmeadowpolice.org
- Ludlow PD
- Chief James J. McGowan
  612 Chapin St.
  Ludlow, MA 01056
  (413) 583-8305
  ludlowpolice@ludlowpolice.com
- Monson PD
- Chief Stephen Kozloski
  110 Main St. PO Box 273
  Monson, MA 01057
  (413) 267-4128
  skozloski@monson-ma.gov
- Palmer PD
- Chief Robert P. Frydryk
  4417 Main St.
  Palmer, MA 01069
  (413) 283-8792
  chief@palmerpolice.org
- Springfield PD
- Comm. William J. Fitchet
  130 Pearl St.
  Springfield, MA 01101
  (413) 787-6313
  spd@springfieldpolice.net
- Wales PD
- Chief Dawn Charette
  3 Hollow Rd.
  Wales, MA 01081
  (413) 245-6030
  police@townofwales.net
- West Springfield PD
- Chief Ronald Campurciani
  26 Central St., Ste. 22
  West Springfield, MA 01089
  (413) 263-3210
  campurcianir@westspringfieldpolice.org
- Westfield PD
- Chief John A. Camerota
  15 Washington St.
  Westfield, MA 01085
  (413) 562-2133
  j.camerota@cityofwestfield.org
- Wilbraham PD
- Chief Roger W. Tucker
  16 Main St.
  Wilbraham, MA 01095
  (413) 596-3837
  wpdchief@wilbraham-ma.gov

Hampshire County

- Hampshire County SO
- Sheriff Robert J. Garvey
  205 Rock Hill Rd.
  Northampton, MA 01061
  (413) 584-5911
  robert.garvey@hsd.state.ma.us
- Amherst PD
- Chief Scott Livingstone
  111 Main St.
  Amherst, MA 01004
  (413) 256-4011
  police@amherstma.gov
- Belchertown PD
- Chief Francis Fox, Jr.
  70 State St.
  Belchertown, MA 01007
  (413) 323-6685
  ffox@belchertown.org
- Cummington PD
- Chief Dennis Forgea
  8 Fairgrounds Rd.
  PO Box 98
  Cummington, MA 01026
  (413) 634-0056
  chief@cummingtonpolice.com
- Easthampton PD
- Chief Bruce McMahon
  32 Payson Ave.
  Easthampton, MA 01027
  (413) 527-1212
  bmcmahon@easthampton.org
- Granby PD
- Chief Alan Wishart
  259A E. State St.
  Granby, MA 01033
  (413) 467-9222
  awishart@granbypd.org
- Hadley PD
- Chief Dennis J. Hukowicz
  15 East St.
  Hadley, MA 01035
  (413) 584-0883
  police@hadleyma.org
- Hatfield PD
- Chief Thomas J. Osley
  59 Main St.
  Hatfield, MA 01038
  (413) 247-0323
  hpd@hatfieldpolice.com
- Northampton PD
- Chief Russell P. Sienkiewicz
  29 Center St.
  Northampton, MA 01060
  (413) 587-1100
  rsienkiewicz@northamptonma.gov
- Pelham PD
- Chief Gary Thomann
  2 So. Valley Rd.
  Pelham, MA 01002
  (413) 253-0484
  pelhampolicema@yahoo.com
- South Hadley PD
- Chief David J. LaBrie
  41 Bridge St.
  South Hadley, MA 01075
  (413) 538-8231
  LabrieD@southhadleypolice.org
- Southampton PD
- Chief David G. Silvernail
  8 East St. PO Box 239
  Southampton, MA 01073
  (413) 527-1120
  Chiefsilvernail@southamptonpolice.com
- Ware PD
- Chief Dennis M. Healey
  22 North St.
  Ware, MA 01082
  (413) 967-3571
  warepolice@aim.com
- Williamsburg PD
- Chief Denise Wickland
  16 So. Main St. PO Box 172
  Haydenville, MA 01039
  (413) 268-7237
  wicklandd@williamsburgpd.org

Middlesex County

- Acton PD
- Chief Francis J. Widmayer III
  371 Main St. PO Box 2212
  Acton, MA 01720
  (978) 264-9638
  police@acton-ma.gov
- Arlington PD
- Chief Frederick Ryan
  112 Mystic St.
  Arlington, MA 02474
  (781) 316-3901
  fryan@town.arlington.ma.us

- Ashby PD
- Chief Edward Drew
  893 Main St.
  PO Box 280
  Ashby, MA 01431
  (978) 386-5652
  chief@ashbypolice.org
- Ashland PD
- Chief Stephen Doherty
  137 Main St.
  Ashland, MA 01721
  (508) 881-1212, ext. 11
  sdoherty@ashlandpd.org
- Ayer PD
- Chief William A. Murray
  54 Park St.
  Ayer, MA 01432
  (978) 772-8200
  pdchief@ayer.ma.us
- Bedford PD
- Chief Robert Bongiorno
  2 Mudge Way
  Bedford, MA 01730
  (781) 275-1212
  rbongiorno@police.bedfordma.gov
- Belmont PD
- Chief Richard J. McLaughlin
  460 Concord Ave.
  Belmont, MA 02478
  (617) 993-2500
  chief@belmontpd.org
- Boston College PD
- Chief John M. King
  140 Commonwealth Ave.
  Chestnut Hill, MA 02467
  (617) 552-4445
  john.king.2@bc.edu
- Boxborough PD
- Chief Warren B. Ryder
  520 Massachusetts Ave.
  Boxborough, MA 01719
  (978) 263-2628
  ryder@boxboroughpolice.com
- Burlington PD
- Chief Michael Kent
  45 Center St.
  Burlington, MA 01803
  (781) 505-4920
  mkent@bpd.org
- Cambridge PD
- Comm. Robert C. Haas
  125 6th St.
  Cambridge, MA 02139
  (617) 349-3300
  commissioner@cambridgepolice.org
- Concord PD
- Chief Barry R. Neal
  219 Walden St. PO Box 519
  Concord, MA 01742
  (978) 318-3400
  BNeal@concordma.gov
- Dracut PD
- Chief Kevin M. Richardson
  110 Loon Hill Rd.
  Dracut, MA 01826
  (978) 957-2123, ext. 100
  info@dracutpolice.com
- Framingham PD
- Chief Steven Carl
  1 William Welch Way
  Framingham, MA 01702
  (508) 532-5926
  cwd@framinghamma.gov
- Groton PD
- Chief Donald Palma
  99 Pleasant St.
  Groton, MA 01450
  (978) 448-5555
  dpalma@townofgroton.org
- Harvard U. PD
- Chief Francis D. *Bud* Riley
  1033 Massachusetts Ave., 6th Fl.
  Cambridge, MA 02138
  (617) 495-1215
  francis_riley@harvard.edu
- Holliston PD
- Chief John J. Moore
  550 Washington St.
  Holliston, MA 01746
  (508) 429-1212, ext. 115
  moorej@hollistonpolice.com
- Hopkinton PD
- Chief Richard A. Flannery
  74 Main St.
  Hopkinton, MA 01748
  (508) 497-3401
  Rflannery@hopkintonpd.org

- Hudson PD
- Chief David A. Stephens
  62 Packard St.
  Hudson, MA 01749
  (978) 562-7122
  dstephens@townofhudson.org
- Lexington PD
- Chief Mark J. Corr
  1575 Massachusetts Ave.
  Lexington, MA 02420
  (781) 862-1212
  PoliceInfo@lexingtonma.gov
- Littleton PD
- Chief John M. Kelly
  500 Great Rd.
  Littleton, MA 01460
  (978) 540-2300
  PCvitkovich@littletonpd.com
- Lowell PD
- Supt. Debra Friedl
  50 Arcand Dr.
  Lowell, MA 01852
  (978) 937-3200
  dfriedl@lowellma.gov
- Malden PD
- Chief Kevin Molis
  200 Pleasant St.
  Malden, MA 02148
  (781) 388-0609
  kmolis@maldenpd.com
- Maynard PD
- Chief Mark W. Dubois
  197 Main St.
  Maynard, MA 01754
  (978) 897-1012
  Mdubois@maynardpolice.com
- Melrose PD
- Chief Michael L. Lyle
  56 W. Foster St.
  Melrose, MA 02176
  (781) 665-1212
  mlyle@cityofmelrose.org
- Natick PD
- Chief James G. Hicks
  20 E. Central St.
  Natick, MA 01760
  (508) 647-9500
  hicks@natickpolice.com
- Newton PD
- Chief Howard Mintz
  1321 Washington St.
  West Newton, MA 02465
  (617) 796-2101
  hmintz@newtonma.gov
- North Reading PD
- Chief Michael P. Murphy
  152 Park St.
  North Reading, MA 01864
  (978) 357-5052
  mmurphy@nrpd.org
- Pepperell PD
- Chief David Scott
  59 Main St. PO Box 295
  Pepperell, MA 01463
  (978) 433-2424
  dscott@town.pepperell.ma.us
- Reading PD
- Chief James W. Cormier
  15 Union St.
  Reading, MA 01867
  (781) 944-1212
  jcormier@ci.reading.ma.us
- Sherborn PD
- Chief Richard R. Thompson III
  17 Washington St.
  Sherborn, MA 01770
  (508) 653-2424
  Rthompson@sherbornpolice.org
- Shirley PD
- Chief J. Gregory Massak
  11 Keady Way
  Shirley, MA 01464
  (978) 425-2642
  gmassak@shirley-mapd.org
- Somerville PD
- Chief Thomas Pasquarello
  220 Washington St.
  Somerville, MA 02143
  (617) 625-1600
  chief@police.somerville.ma.us
- Stoneham PD
- Chief James T. McIntyre
  47 Central St.
  Stoneham, MA 02180
  (781) 438-1215
  jmcintyre@police.stoneham.ma.us

- Stow PD
- Chief William Bosworth
  305 Great Rd.
  Stow, MA 01775
  (978) 897-4545
  stowpolice@stow-ma.gov
- Sudbury PD
- Chief Richard Glavin
  415 Boston Post Rd.
  Sudbury, MA 01776
  (978) 443-1042
  police@sudbury.ma.us
- Tewksbury PD
- Chief Timothy Sheehan
  918 Main St.
  Tewksbury, MA 01876
  (978) 851-7373, ext. 214
  tsheehan@tewksbury-ma.gov
- Townsend PD
- Chief Erving M. Marshall, Jr.
  70 Brookline Rd.
  Townsend, MA 01469
  (978) 597-6214
  emarshall@townsend.ma.us
- Tyngsboro PD
- Chief William F. Mulligan
  20 Westford Rd.
  Tyngsboro, MA 01879
  (978) 649-7504
  rhowe@tyngsboroma.gov
- Wakefield PD
- Chief Rick Smith
  1 Union St.
  Wakefield, MA 01880
  (781) 246-6323
  l.donaldson@wakefieldpd.org
- Watertown PD
- Chief Edward P. Deveau
  552 Main St.
  Watertown, MA 02472
  (617) 972-6500
  edeveau@police.watertown-ma.gov
- Wayland PD
- Chief Robert Irving
  38 Cochituate Rd.
  Wayland, MA 01778
  (508) 358-4721
  Chief@waylandpolice.com
- Westford PD
- Chief Thomas McEnaney
  53 Main St.
  Westford, MA 01886
  (978) 692-2161
  tmcenaney@westfordma.gov
- Weston PD
- Chief Steven F. Shaw
  180 Boston Post Rd.
  Weston, MA 02193
  (781) 786-6201
  shaw.s@westonmass.org
- Wilmington PD
- Chief Michael R. Begonis
  1 Adelaide St.
  Wilmington, MA 01887
  (978) 658-5071
  info@wpd.org
- Winchester PD
- Chief Ken Albertelli
  30 Mt. Vernon St.
  Winchester, MA 01890
  (781) 729-5429
  police@winchesterpd.org
- Woburn PD
- Chief Robert J. Ferullo, Jr.
  25 Harrison Ave.
  Woburn, MA 01801
  (781) 932-4510, ext. 818
  police@woburnpd.com

Nantucket County

- Nantucket County SO
- Sheriff James A. Perelman
  16 Broad St., 2nd Fl.
  Nantucket, MA 02554
  (508) 228-7263
  perelman@islandsheriff.com
- Nantucket PD
- Chief William Pittman
  4 Fairgrounds Rd.
  Nantucket, MA 02554
  (508) 228-1212
  wpittman@nantucketpolice.com

Norfolk County

- Norfolk County SO
- Sheriff Michael Bellotti
  200 West St. PO Box 149
  Dedham, MA 02026
  (781) 329-3300
  mbellotti@norfolksheriffma.org

- Bellingham PD
- Chief Gerard Daigle
  8 Mechanic St.
  Bellingham, MA 02019
  (508) 966-1515
  gdaigle@bellinghamma.org
- Braintree PD
- Chief Russell W. Jenkins
  282 Union St.
  Braintree, MA 02184
  (781) 794-8629
  rjenkins@braintreema.gov
- Brookline PD
- Chief Daniel C. O'Leary
  350 Washington St.
  Brookline, MA 02445-6851
  (617) 730-2249
  kflanagan@brooklinema.gov
- Canton PD
- Chief Kenneth N. Berkowitz
  1492 Washington St.
  Canton, MA 02021
  (781) 821-5090
  kberkowitz@town.canton.ma.us
- Cohasset PD
- Act. Chief William Quigley
  62 Elm St.
  Cohasset, MA 02025
  (781) 383-1212
  info@cohassetpolice.com
- Dedham PD
- Chief Michael D'Entremont
  600 High St.
  Dedham, MA 02026
  (781) 751-9324
  dpd201@comcast.net
- Dover PD
- Chief Peter A. McGowan
  3 Walpole St. PO Box 192
  Dover, MA 02030
  (508) 785-1130
  pamcgowan@dovermapd.com
- Franklin PD
- Chief Stephan H. Semerjian
  911 Panther Way
  Franklin, MA 02038
  (508) 528-1212
  ssemerjian@franklinpolice.com
- Holbrook PD
- Chief William D. Marble, Jr.
  300 So. Franklin St.
  Holbrook, MA 02343
  (781) 767-1212
  Chief@holbrookpolice.com
- Medfield PD
- Chief Robert E. Meaney, Jr.
  110 North St.
  Medfield, MA 02052
  (508) 359-2315
  medchief@medfield.net
- Medway PD
- Chief Allen M. Tingley
  315 Village St.
  Medway, MA. 02053
  (508) 533-3212
  tingley@medwaypolice.com
- Millis PD
- Chief Keith Edison
  885 Main St.
  Millis, MA 02054
  (508) 376-5112
  info@millispolice.com
- Milton PD
- Chief Richard G. Wells, Jr.
  40 Highland St.
  Milton, MA 02186
  (617) 698-3800
  rwells@mpdmilton.org
- Norfolk PD
- Chief Charles H. *Chuck* Stone, Jr.
  117 Main St. PO Box 3
  Norfolk, MA 02056
  (508) 528-3206
  stone@virtualnorfolk.org
- Norwood PD
- Chief William G. Brooks III
  137 Nahatan St.
  Norwood, MA 02062
  (781) 440-5100
  wbroooks@norwoodma.gov
- Plainville PD
- Int. Chief James Alfred
  157 South St.
  Plainville, MA 02762
  (508) 695-7115
  jalfred@plainville.ma.us

- Quincy PD
- Chief Paul Keenan
  1 Sea St.
  Quincy, MA 02169
  (617) 479-1212
  qpdinfo@quincyma.gov
- Randolph PD
- Chief William Pace
  41 So. Main St.
  Randolph, MA 02368
  (781) 963-1212
  williampace@randolphmapolice.com
- Stoughton PD
- Chief Paul J. Shastany
  26 Rose St.
  Stoughton, MA 02072
  (781) 344-2424
  CPOffice@stoughton-ma.gov
- Wellesley PD
- Chief Terrence M. *Terry* Cunningham
  485 Washington St.
  Wellesley, MA 02482
  (781) 235-0062
  chieftmc@wellesleyma.gov
- Westwood PD
- Int. Chief Jeffrey Roy
  590 High St.
  Westwood, MA 02090
  (781) 320-1000
  Jroy@westwoodpd.org
- Wrentham PD
- Chief James E. Anderson
  89 South St.
  Wrentham, MA 02093
  (508) 384-2121
  anderson@police.wrentham.ma.us

Plymouth County

- Plymouth County SD
- Sheriff Joseph D. McDonald, Jr.
  24 Long Pond Rd.
  Plymouth, MA 02360
  (508) 830-6200
  jmcdonald@pcsdma.org
- Abington PD
- Chief David G. Majenski
  215 Central St.
  Abington, MA 02351
  (781) 878-3232
  majic@abingtonpolice.org
- Carver PD
- Chief Michael Miksch
  112B Main St.
  Carver, MA 02330
  (508) 866-2000, ext. 110
  mmiksch@carverpolice.org
- Duxbury PD
- Chief Matthew Clancy
  155 Mayflower St.
  Duxbury, MA 02332
  (781) 934-5656, ext. 1142
  mclancy@duxburypolice.org
- East Bridgewater PD
- Chief John E. Cowan
  153 Central St. PO Box 475
  East Bridgewater, MA 02333
  (508) 378-7223
  jcowan@ebmass.com
- Halifax PD
- Chief Michael Manoogian
  540 Plymouth St.
  Halifax, MA 02338
  (781) 294-8713
  Chief@police.halifax.ma.us
- Hanover PD
- Chief Walter Sweeney
  129 Rockland St.
  Hanover, MA 02339
  (781) 826-3231, ext. 106
  Wsweeney@hanoverpolice.org
- Hanson PD
- Chief Arthur Parker
  775 Main St.
  Hanson, MA 02341
  (781) 293-4625
  nking@hansonpolice.org
- Hingham PD
- Chief Michael Peraino
  212 Central St.
  Hingham, MA 02043
  (781) 749-1212
  perainom@hingham-ma.com
- Hull PD
- Chief Richard K. Billings
  1 School St.
  Hull, MA 02045
  (781) 925-1212
  Info@hullpolice.org

- Kingston PD
- Chief Maurice J. Splaine
  244 Main St.
  Kingston, MA 02364
  (781) 585-0523
  www.msplaine@kpdmass.org
- Lakeville PD
- Chief Frank B. Alvilhiera
  296 Bedford St.
  Lakeville, MA 02347
  (508) 947-4422
  chief@lakevillepd.org
- Marion PD
- Chief Lincoln W. Miller
  550 Mill St. PO Box 636
  Marion, MA 02738
  (508) 748-1212
  chiefmiller@marionpolice.org
- Marshfield PD
- Chief Phillip A. Tavares
  1639 Ocean St.
  Marshfield, MA 02050
  (781) 834-6655, ext. 113
  Mmcdonough@marshfieldpolice.org
- Middleborough PD
- Chief Bruce Gates
  99 No. Main St.
  Middleboro, MA 02346
  (508) 946-2451
  PoliceWeb@middleborough.com
- Norwell PD
- Chief Theodore Ross
  40 River St.
  Norwell, MA 02061
  (781) 659-7979
  tross@norwellpolice.com
- Pembroke PD
- Chief Richard D. Wall
  80 Center St.
  Pembroke, MA 02359
  (781) 293-6363
  rwall@pembrokepolice.org
- Plymouth PD
- Chief Michael E. Botieri
  20 Long Pond Rd.
  Plymouth, MA 02360
  (508) 830-4220
  chiefbotieri@plymouthpolice.com
- Plympton PD
- Chief Patrick S. Dillon
  5 Palmer Rd. PO Box 125
  Plympton, MA 02367
  (781) 585-3339
  pdillon@plymptonpd.org
- Rockland PD
- Chief John R. Llewellyn
  490 Market St.
  Rockland, MA 02370
  (781) 871-3890, ext. 100
  chief@rocklandpolice.com
- Scituate PD
- Chief Brian E. Stewart
  600 Chief Justice Cushing Way
  Scituate, MA 02066
  (781) 545-1212
  bstewart@scituatepolice.org
- Wareham PD
- Chief Richard M. Stanley
  2515 Cranberry Hwy
  Wareham, MA 02571
  (508) 295-1212
  rstanley@warehampolice.com
- West Bridgewater PD
- Chief Donald H. Clark
  99 W. Center St.
  West Bridgewater, MA 02379
  (508) 586-2525
  dclark@wbpd.com
- Whitman PD
- Chief Scott Benton
  20 Essex St.
  Whitman, MA 02382
  (781) 447-1212
  sbenton@whitman-ma.gov

Suffolk County

- Suffolk County SD
- Sheriff Andrea J. Cabral
  20 Bradston St.
  Boston, MA 02118
  (617) 704-6507
  acabral@scsdma.org
- Boston PD
- Comm. Edward Davis
  One Schroeder Plaza
  Boston, MA 02120-2014
  (617) 343-4200
  Mediarelations.bpd@cityofboston.gov

- Chelsea PD
- Chief Brian A. Kyes
  19 Park St.
  Chelsea, MA 02150
  (617) 466-4855
  bkyes@chelseama.gov
- Revere PD
- Chief Joseph Cafarelli
  400 Revere Beach Pkwy
  Revere, MA 02151
  (781) 284-1212
  jcafarelli@reverepolice.org
- Winthrop PD
- Chief Terence M. Delehanty
  3 Metcalf Sq.
  Winthrop, MA 02152
  (617) 846-1212
  tdelehanty@town.winthrop.ma.us

Worcester County

- Worcester County SO
- Sheriff Lewis G. Evangelidis
  5 Paul X. Tivnan Dr.
  West Boylston, MA 01583
  (508) 854-1800
  levangelidis@sdw.state.ma.us
- Ashburnham PD
- Chief Loring Barrett, Jr.
  99 Central St.
  Ashburnham, MA 01430
  (978) 827-4413
  lbarrett@ashburnhampd.com
- Auburn PD
- Chief Andrew J. Sluckis, Jr.
  Auburn, MA 01501
  (508) 832-7777
  Andrew.Sluckis@AuburnMassPolice.org
- Berlin PD
- Int. Chief (*Sgt.*) John Geit
  23 Linden St.
  Berlin, MA 01503
  (978) 838-7355
  Police@TownOfBerlin.com
- Blackstone PD
- Chief Ross A. Atstupenas
  15 St. Paul
  Blackstone, MA 01504
  (508) 883-1212
  ratstupenas@blackstonepolice.org
- Bolton PD
- Chief Vincent C. Alfano
  697 Main St.
  Bolton, MA 01740
  (978) 779-2276
  info@bolton-ma.gov
- Boylston PD
- Chief Anthony G. Sahagian
  215 Main St.
  Boylston, MA 01505
  (508) 869- 2113
  cbissonnette@police.boylston-ma.gov
- Douglas PD
- Chief Patrick T. Foley
  29 Depot St. PO Box 244
  Douglas, MA 01516
  (508) 476-3333
  pfoley@douglasma.org
- East Brookfield PD
- Chief William J. Cournoyer
  122 Connie Mack PO Box 32
  East Brookfield, MA 01515
  (508) 867-6130
  www.ebpd@charterinternet.com
- Fitchburg PD
- Chief Robert A. DeMoura
  20 Elm St.
  Fitchburg, MA 01420
  (978) 345-9648
  rdemoura@fitchburgpolice.com
- Gardner PD
- Chief Neil Erickson
  31 City Hall Ave.
  Gardner, MA 01440
  (978) 632-3575
  nerickson@gardner-ma.gov
- Grafton PD
- Chief Normand A. Crepeau
  26 Providence Rd.
  Grafton, MA 01519
  (508) 839-2858
  chief@graftonpolice.com
- Holden PD
- Chief George R. Sherrill
  1370 Main St.
  Holden, MA 01520
  (508) 210-5600
  gsherrill@holdenma.gov

- Hubbardston PD
- Chief Dennis G. Perron
  7 Main St.
  Hubbardston, MA 01452
  (978) 928-1405
  Chiefperron@hubpd.net
- Lancaster PD
- Chief Kevin D. Lamb
  1055 Main St. PO Box 96
  Lancaster, MA 01523
  (978) 365-6308
  kdlamb@lancasterma.net
- Leicester PD
- Chief James Hurley
  90 So. Main St.
  Leicester, MA 01524
  (508) 892-7010
  hurleyj@leicesterpd.org
- Mendon PD
- Chief Ernest Horn
  22 Main St.
  Mendon, MA 01756
  (508) 478-2797
  ehorn@mendonpublicsafety.com
- Milford PD
- Chief Thomas J. O'Loughlin
  250 Main St.
  Milford, MA 01757
  (508) 473-1113
  chief@milfordpolice.org
- Millbury PD
- Chief Kenny A. Howell
  127 Elm St.
  Millbury, MA 01527
  (508) 865-3521
  khowell@millburypolice.com
- Millville PD
- Chief Ronald Landry
  10 Central St.
  Millville, MA 01529
  (508) 883-3117
  millvillepd@gmail.com
- North Brookfield PD
- Chief Aram Thomasian, Jr.
  4 Summer St.
  North Brookfield, MA 01535
  (508) 867-0206
  nbpd@nbpolice.net
- Northborough PD
- Chief Mark K. Leahy
  211 Main St.
  Northborough, MA 01532
  (508) 393-1515
  police@town.northborough.ma.us
- Oakham PD
- Chief Fred Gehring
  178 Barre Rd. PO Box 32
  Oakham, MA 01068
  (508) 882-3347
  policechief@oakham-ma.gov
- Oxford PD
- Chief Michael Hassett
  503 Main St.
  Oxford, MA 01540
  (508) 987-0156
  mhassett@town.oxford.ma.us
- Paxton PD
- Chief Robert Desrosiers
  10 West St.
  Paxton, MA 01612
  (508) 755-1104
  policechief@townofpaxton.net
- Rutland PD
- Chief Donald Haapakoski
  242 Main St.
  PO Box 242
  Rutland, MA 01543
  (508) 886-4033
  policechief@townofrutland.org
- Shrewsbury PD
- Chief James Hester, Jr.
  106 Maple Ave.
  Shrewsbury, MA 01545
  (508) 841-8577
  jhester@pd.ci.shrewsbury.ma.us
- Southborough PD
- Chief Jane Moran
  19 Main St.
  Southborough, MA 01772
  (508) 485-2121
  jmoran@southboroughma.com
- Spencer PD
- Chief David Darrin
  9 W. Main St.
  Spencer, MA 01562
  (508) 885-6333
  ddarrin@spencerma.gov

- Sterling PD
- Chief Gary M. Chamberland
  135 Leominster Rd.
  Sterling, MA 01564
  (508) 422-7331
  CHIEF@STERLINGPD.COM
- Sturbridge PD
- Chief Theo J. Ford III
  346 Main St.
  Sturbridge, MA 01566
  (508) 347-2525
  tford@town.sturbridge.ma.us
- Sutton PD
- Chief Dennis J. Towle
  4 Uxbridge Rd.
  Sutton, MA 01590
  (508) 865-8747
  d.towle@town.sutton.ma.us
- Templeton PD
- Chief David H. Whitaker
  33 South Rd.
  Templeton, MA 01468
  (978) 939-5638
  selectman@templeton1.org
- Upton PD
- Chief Michael J. Bradley, Jr.
  30 School St.
  Upton, MA 01568
  (508) 529-3200
  michael.bradley@uptonpolice.org
- Uxbridge PD
- Int. Chief Peter B. Emerick
  275 Douglas St.
  Uxbridge, MA 01569
  (508) 278-7755
  pemerick@uxbridge-ma.gov
- Warren PD
- Chief Bruce D. Spiewakowski
  1 Milton O. Fountain Way
  Warren, MA 01083
  (413) 436-9595
  warrenchief1@verizon.net
- West Boylston PD
- Chief Dennis Minnich
  39 Worcester St.
  West Boylston, MA 01583
  (508) 835-3233
  chiefminnich@wboylstonpolice.com
- West Brookfield PD
- Chief C. Thomas O'Donnell
  2 E. Main St.
  PO Box 671
  West Brookfield, MA 01585
  (508) 867-1405
  CTOdonnell@wbrookfield.com
- Westborough PD
- Chief Al Gordon
  45 W. Main St. PO Box 1123
  Westborough, MA 01581
  (508) 366-3060
  agordon@town.westborough.ma.us
- Westminster PD
- Chief Salvatore Albert
  7 South St.
  Westminster, MA 01473
  (978) 874-2900
  salbert@westminster-ma.gov
- Winchendon PD
- Chief Scott M. Livingston
  15 Pleasant St., Dept. 16
  Winchendon, MA 01475
  (978) 297-1212
  chiefwpd@comcast.net
- Worcester PD
- Chief Gary J. Gemme
  9-11 Lincoln Sq.
  Worcester, MA 01608
  (508) 799-8606
  wpd@worcesterma.gov

State Agencies

- MA State Police-HQ
- Supt. (*Col.*) Timothy P. Alben
  One Ashburton Pl., Rm. 1301
  Boston, MA 02108
  (617) 727-3200
  DPSInfo@state.ma.us

MICHIGAN

Alcona County

- Alcona County SO
- Sheriff Douglas Atchison
  214 W. Main St.
  Harrisville, MI 48740
  (989) 724-6271
  Atchison@alcona-county.net

Alger County

- Alger County SO
- Sheriff Robert Hughes
  101 E. Varnum
  Munising, MI 49862
  (906) 387-4444
  tbrock@algerso.com
- Munising PD
- Chief John Nelson
  301 E. Superior St.
  Munising, MI 49862
  (906) 387-2275
  chief@cityofmunising.org

Allegan County

- Allegan County SO
- Sheriff Blaine Koops
  112 Walnut St.
  Allegan, MI 49010
  (269) 673-0510
  SHERIFF@allegancounty.org
- Allegan PD
- Chief Rick Hoyer
  170 Water St.
  Allegan, MI 49010
  (269) 673-2115
  rhoyer@cityofallegan.org
- Douglas PD
- Chief Ken Giles
  47 Center St.
  Douglas, MI 49406
  (269) 857-4339
  douglas@ci.douglas.mi.us
- Wayland PD
- Chief Steven Harper
  160 W. Superior St.
  Wayland, MI 49348
  (269) 792-9366
  waylandpolice@cityofwayland.org

Alpena County

- Alpena PD
- Int. Chief Joel Jett
  501 W. Chisholm St.
  Alpena, MI 49707
  (989) 354-1800
  joelj@alpena.mi.us

Antrim County

- Antrim County SO
- Sheriff Daniel Bean
  110 Grove St. PO Box 568
  Bellaire, MI 49615
  (231) 533-8627
  beand@antrimcounty.org
- Bellaire PD
- Chief Brad Rowe
  202 No. Bridge St.
  PO Box 557
  Bellaire, MI 49615
  (231) 533- 8213
  vlgbellaire@bellairemichigan.com
- Elk Rapids PD
- Chief Tom Emerson
  321 Bridge St.
  Elk Rapids, MI 49629
  (231) 264-6592
  vllgclerk@elkrapids.org

Arenac County

- Arenac County SO
- Sheriff James Mosciski
  126 No. Grove
  Standish, MI 48658
  (989) 846-3002
  jmosciski@arenaccountygov.com

Baraga County

- Baraga County SO
- Sheriff Robert Teddy
  16 No. 3rd St.
  L'Anse, MI 49946
  (906) 524-6183
  bctra@up.net
- Baraga PD
- Chief Harry Miron
  440 No. Superior Ave.
  Baraga, MI 49908
  (906) 353-7181
  vobmgr@up.net

- Keweenaw Bay Tribal PD
- Comm. Dale Dakota
  16429 Beartown Rd.
  Baraga, MI 49908
  (906) 353-6626
  dale@kbic-nsn.gov

Barry County

- Barry County SO
- Sheriff Dar Leaf
  1212 W. State St.
  Hastings, MI 49058
  (269) 948-4805
  DLeaf@barrycounty.org
- Hastings PD
- Chief Jerry Sarver
  201 E. State St.
  Hastings, MI 49058
  (269) 945-5744
  jsarver@hastingsmi.org
- Nashville PD
- Chief Jerry Schray
  PO Box 327
  Nashville, MI 49073
  (517) 852-9866
  nashvillepdmi@sbcglobal.net
- Prairieville Twp PD
- Chief William Thompson
  10115 So. Norris Rd.
  Delton, MI 49046
  (269) 623-2691
  wbthompson@mei.net

Bay County

- Bay County SO
- Sheriff John E. Miller
  503 3rd St.
  Bay City, MI 48708
  (989) 895-4050
  millerj@baycounty.net
- Bay City PD
- Chief Michael J. Cecchini
  501 3rd St.
  Bay City, MI 48708
  (989) 892-8571
  mcecchini@baycitymi.org
- Essexville DPS
- Dir. Daniel J. Hages
  1107 Woodside Ave.
  Essexville, MI 48732
  (989) 892-2541
  dirpublicsafety@essexville.org
- Hampton PD
- Chief Gerald Runde
  745 W. Center Rd.
  Essexville, MI 48732
  (989) 892-0571
  grunde@hamptonpd.net

Benzie County

- Benzie County SO
- Sheriff Ted Schendel
  505 So. Michigan PO Box 116
  Beulah, MI 49617
  (231) 882-4484
  tschendel@benzieco.net

Berrien County

- Berrien County SO
- Sheriff L. Paul Bailey
  919 Port St.
  St Joseph, MI 49085
  (269) 983-7141
  Pbailey@berriencounty.org
- Berrien Springs-Oronoko PD
- Chief Milton A. Agay
  4411 E. Snow Rd. PO Box 97
  Berrien Springs, MI 49103
  (269) 471-2813
  agayma@bsopd.org
- Buchanan PD
- Chief Bill Marx
  107 W. Front St.
  Buchanan, MI 49107
  (269) 695-5120
  wmarx@buchananpolice.net
- Coloma Twp PD
- Chief Randel Pompey
  4919 Paw Paw Lake Rd.
  Coloma, MI 49038
  (269) 468-8291, ext. 17
  admin@colomatownship.org
- Grand Beach PD
- Chief Dan Schroeder
  48200 Perkins Blvd
  Grand Beach, MI 49117
  (269) 469-5000
  chief@grandbeach.org
- New Buffalo PD
- Chief Larry Pitchford
  224 W. Buffalo St.
  New Buffalo, MI 49117
  (269) 469-1593
  policechief@nbcpolice.com

- Niles PD
- Chief James Millin
  1600 Silverbrook Ave.
  Niles, MI 49120
  (269) 683-3282
  jmillin@nilesmi.org
- St. Joseph DPS
- Dir. Mark Clapp
  700 Broad St.
  St Joseph, MI 49085
  (269) 985-0300
  clapp@sjcity.com
- Three Oaks PD
- Chief Frank Nekvasil
  14 E. Maple St.
  Three Oaks, MI 49128
  (269) 756-9585
  nekvasil_1@hotmail.com
- Watervliet PD
- Chief Don Divis
  158 W. Pleasant St.
  Watervliet, MI 49098
  (269) 463-5112
  divis@watervliet.org

Branch County

- Branch County SO
- Sheriff C. John Pollack
  580 Marshall Rd.
  Coldwater, MI 49036
  (517) 278-2325
  sheriffbc@countyofbranch.com
- Bronson PD
- Chief Stephen P. Johnson
  124 So. Matteson St.
  Bronson, MI 49028
  (517) 369-9083
  s.johnson@bronson-mi.com
- Coldwater DPS
- Dir. Mark Bartell
  57 Division St.
  Coldwater, MI 49036
  (517) 278-4525
  mbartell@coldwater.org
- Quincy PD
- Chief Scot Olney
  47 Cole St.
  Quincy, MI 49082
  (517) 639- 9065, ext. 19
  policechief@quincy-mi.org
- Union City PD
- Chief Tom Case
  123 Hammond St.
  Union City, MI 49094
  (517) 741-7922
  unioncityplc@dmcibb.net

Calhoun County

- Calhoun County SO
- Sheriff Matthew M. *Matt* Saxton
  161 E. Michigan Ave.
  Battle Creek, MI 49014
  (269) 969-6450
  msaxton@calhouncountymi.gov
- Battle Creek PD
- Chief Jackie Hampton
  20 No. Division St.
  Battle Creek, MI 49014
  Ph: (269) 966-3375
  Fax: (269) 966-3636
  jdhampton@battlecreekmi.gov
- Homer PD
- Chief Steve Fisher
  130 E. Main St. PO Box 155
  Homer, MI 49245
  (517) 568-4312
  homerpolice@homermich.org
- Marshall PD
- Chief James Schwartz
  323 W. Michigan Ave.
  Marshall, MI 49068
  (269) 781-2596
  JSchwartz@cityofmarshall.com
- Springfield DPS
- Dir. Scott Furgason
  601 Ave. A
  Springfield, MI 49015
  (269) 965-7795
  sfurgason@springfieldmich.com

Cass County

- Dowagiac DPS
- Dir. Thomas Atkinson
  241 So. Front St.
  Dowagiac, MI 49047
  (269) 782-3210
  PublicSafetyDirector@dowagiac.org
- Marcellus PD
- Chief Thomas Jacobs
  177 E. Main St.
  Marcellus, MI 49067
  (269) 646-3166
  marcellusmichigan.org@gmail.com

- Pokagaon Tribal PD
- Chief Chris VanCompernolle
  58155 M-51 So.PO Box 180
  Dowagiac, MI 49047
  (269) 782-2232
  Chris.Vancompernolle@pokagonband-nsn.gov

Charlevoix County

- Charlevoix County SO
- Sheriff Don Schneider
  1000 Grant St.
  Charlevoix, MI 49720
  (231) 547-4461
  schneiderd@charlevoixcounty.org
- Charlevoix PD
- Chief Gerard Doan
  210 State St.
  Charlevoix, MI 49720
  (231) 547-3258
  gdoan@cityofcharlevoix.org
- East Jordan PD
- Chief Dale Boehm, Jr.
  201 Main St. PO Box 499
  East Jordan, MI 49727
  (231) 536-2273, ext. 21
  dboehm@eastjordancity.org

Cheboygan County

- Cheboygan County SO
- Sheriff Dale Clarmont
  870 So. Main St. PO Box 70
  Cheboygan, MI 49721
  (231) 627-3155
  sheriff@cheboygancounty.net
- Cheboygan DPS
- Dir. Kurt R. Jones
  403 No. Huron St. PO Box 39
  Cheboygan, MI 49721, ext. 125
  (231) 627-4321
  k.r.jones@cheboygan.org
- Mackinaw City PD
- Chief Patrick C. Wyman
  102 So. Huron
  Mackinaw City, MI 49701
  (231) 436-7861
  pwyman@mackinawcity.org

Chippewa County

- Chippewa County SO
- Sheriff Robert Savoie
  331 Court St.
  Sault Ste. Marie, MI 49783
  (906) 635-6355
  mbitnar@chippewacountymi.gov
- Sault Ste Marie PD
- Chief John Riley
  401 Hursley St.
  Sault Ste Marie, MI 49783
  (906) 632-3344
  jriley@sault.com

Clare County

- Clare County SO
- Sheriff John Wilson
  255 W. Main St. PO Box 407
  Harrison, MI 48625
  (989) 539-7166
  wilsonj@clareco.net
- Clare PD
- Chief Brian Gregory
  207 W. 5th St.
  Clare, MI 48617
  (989) 386-2121
  bgregory@cityofclare.org

Clinton County

- Clinton County SO
- Sheriff Wayne Kangas
  1347 E. Townsend Rd.
  St Johns, MI 48879
  (989) 224-5200
  sheriff@clinton-county.org
- Bath Twp PD
- Chief Scott D. Rose
  14480 Webster Rd.
  Bath, MI 48808
  (517) 641-6271
  police@bathtownship.us
- DeWitt Twp PD
- Chief Brian Russell
  1401 W. Herbison Rd.
  DeWitt, MI 48820
  (517) 669-6578
  police@dewitttwp.org
- St. Johns DPS
- Dir. Mike Madden
  109 E. State St.
  St Johns, MI 48879
  (989) 224-6721
  mmadden@ci.saint-johns.mi.us

Crawford County

- Crawford County SO
- Sheriff Kirk A. Wakefield
  200 W. Michigan Ave.
  Grayling, MI 49738
  (989) 348-4616
  sheriff@crawfordsheriff.org

- Grayling PD
- Chief Doug Baum
  103 So. James St.
  Grayling, MI 49738
  (989) 348-4601
  dbaum@cityofgrayling.org

Delta County

- Delta County SO
- Sheriff Gary Ballweg
  111 No. 3rd St.
  Escanaba, MI 49829
  (906) 786-3633
  gballweg@deltacountymi.org

Dickinson County

- Iron Mountain PD
- Chief Pete Flaminio
  111 E. Fleshiem St.
  Iron Mountain, MI 49801
  (906) 774-1234
  impd@cityofironmountain.com
- Norway PD
- Chief James E. Shafer II
  915 Main St.
  Norway, MI 49870
  (906) 563-5801
  policechief@norwaymi.com

Eaton County

- Eaton County SO
- Sheriff Tom Reich
  1025 Independence Blvd
  Charlotte, Michigan 48813
  (517) 543-3512
  makingIThappen@eatonccounty.org
- Bellevue PD
- Chief Greg Crawford
  201 No. Main St.
  Bellevue, MI 49021
  (269) 763-9429
  bellevuemi@bellevuemi.net
- Charlotte PD
- Chief William *Bill* Callahan
  111 E. Lawrence Ave.
  Charlotte, MI 48813
  (517) 543-1552
  bcallahan@charlottemi.org
- Eaton Rapids PD
- Chief Joe Fitzgerald
  101 Line St.
  Eaton Rapids, MI 48827
  (517) 663-8118
  joefitzgerald@cityofeatonrapids.com
- Olivet PD
- Chief Paul Weiss
  117 So. Main St. PO Box 367
  Olivet, MI 49076
  (616) 749-9961
  pweiss@cityofolivet.org

Emmet County

- Harbor Springs PD
- Chief Daniel Branson
  170 Zoll St.
  Harbor Springs, MI 49740
  (231) 526-6211
  dbranson@harborspringspolice.com

Genesee County

- Genesee County SO
- Sheriff Robert J. Pickell
  1002 So. Saginaw St.
  Flint, MI 48502
  (810) 257-3407
  rpickell@co.genesee.mi.us
- Burton PD
- Chief Tom Osterholzer
  4090 Manor Dr.
  Burton, MI 48519
  (810) 742-2542
  t.osterholzer@ci.burton.mi.us
- Clio PD
- Chief James A. McLellan
  505 W. Vienna St.
  Clio, MI 48420
  (810) 686-5010, ext. 212
  cliopd@comcast.net
- Davison PD
- Chief Bill Brandon
  200 E. Flint St.
  Davison, MI 48423
  (810) 653-4196
  bbrandon@cityofdavison.org
- Fenton PD
- Chief Rick Aro
  311 So. Leroy St.
  Fenton, MI 48430
  (810) 629-5311
  aror@fentonpolice.org
- Flint PD
- Chief Alvern Lock
  210 E. 5th St.
  Flint, MI 48502
  (810) 237-6868
  alock@cityofflint.com

- Flushing PD
- Chief Mark R. Hoornstra
  725 E. Main St.
  Flushing, MI 48433
  (810) 659-3119
  mhoornstra@flushingcity.com
- Grand Blanc PD
- Chief Steven P. Solomon
  203 E. Grand Blanc Rd.
  Grand Blanc, MI 48439
  (810) 694-1111
  gbpdchief@cityofgrandblanc.com
- Linden PD
- Chief Scott Sutter
  132 E. Broad St.
  Linden, MI 48451
  (810) 735-5454
  police@lindenmi.us
- Mount Morris PD
- Chief Keith Becker
  11649 No. Saginaw
  Mount Morris, MI 48458
  (810) 686-4402
  vfishell@cityofmtmorris.org

Gladwin County

- Gladwin PD
- Chief Charles Jones
  1000 W. Cedar Ave.
  Gladwin, MI 48624
  (989) 426-7879
  police@gladwin.org

Gogebic County

- Gogebic County SO
- Sheriff Pete Matonich
  100 W. Iron St.
  Bessemer, MI 49911
  (906) 667-0203
  pmatonich@gogebic.org
- Ironwood Public Safety Dept.
- Dir. Andrew DiGiorgio
  123 W. McLeod Ave.
  Ironwood, MI 49938
  (906) 932-1234
  Clemens@cityofironwood.org

Grand Traverse County

- Grand Traverse County SO
- Sheriff Thomas Bensley
  851 Woodmere Ave.
  Traverse City, MI 49684
  (231) 995-5001
  info@gtsheriff.org

Gratiot County

- Gratiot County SO
- Sheriff Doug Wright
  226 E. Center St.
  Ithaca, MI 48847
  (989) 875-5214
  dwright@gratiotmi.com
- Alma PD
- Dir. David Walsh
  525 E. Superior PO Box 278
  Alma, MI 48801
  (989) 463-8317, ext. 228
  dwalsh@ci.alma.mi.us
- St. Louis PD
- Chief Patrick Herblet
  108 W. Saginaw St.
  St Louis, MI 48880
  (989) 681-5285
  pherblet@stlouismi.com

Hillsdale County

- Hillsdale County SO
- Sheriff Stan Burchardt
  165 W. Fayette St.
  Hillsdale, MI 49242
  (517) 437-7317
  t.parker@co.hillsdale.mi.us
- Hillsdale PD
- Dir. Christopher Gutowski
  97 No. Broad St.
  Hillsdale, MI 49242
  (517) 437-6460
  cggutowski@ci.hillsdale.mi.us
- Litchfield PD
- Chief John Michelin
  221 Jonesville St.
  Litchfield, MI 49252
  (517) 542-3700
  police@cityoflitchfield.org
- Reading City PD
- Act. Chief (*Ofcr.-in-Charge*) Eric Stolberg
  109 So. Main St. PO Box 323
  Reading, MI 49274
  (517) 283-3133
  police@reading.mi.us

Houghton County

- Houghton County SO
- Sheriff Brian J. McLean
  403 E. Houghton Ave.
  Houghton, MI 49931
  (906) 482-0055
  bmclean@ccisd.k12.mi.us

- Hancock PD
- Chief Michael Beaudoin
  399 Quincy St.
  Hancock, MI 49930
  (906) 482-3102
  mwbeaudoin@hancockpd.com
- Houghton PD
- Chief John Donnelly
  616 Shelden Ave.
  Houghton, MI 49931
  (906) 487-5912
  policedepartment@cityofhoughton.com
- Lake Linden PD
- Chief Tonya Stefonich
  401 Calumet St.
  Lake Linden, MI 49945
  (906) 296-9911
  vll@lakelinden.net

Huron County

- Huron County SO
- Sheriff Kelly J. Hanson
  120 So. Heisterman
  Bad Axe, MI 48413
  (517) 269-9910
  SHERIFFDEPT@co.huron.mi.us
- Bad Axe PD
- Chief David W. Rothe
  100 So. Hanselman St.
  Bad Axe, MI 48413
  (989) 269-9242
  davidrothe@cityofbadaxe.com
- Caseville PD
- Chief Jamie Learman
  6767 Main St.
  Caseville, MI 48725
  (989) 856-3304
  cpd@caseville-gov.com
- Elkton PD
- Chief Scott Jobes
  57 No. Main PO Box 516
  Elkton, MI 48731
  (989) 375-4450
  elktonclerk@comcast.net
- Harbor Beach PD
- Chief Todd Bucholtz
  766 State St.
  Harbor Beach, MI 48441
  (989) 479-3353
  hbpd@harborbeachmi.org
- Pigeon PD
- Chief Eric Wissner
  29 So. Main St.
  Pigeon, MI 48755
  (989) 453-3001
  ewissner@advi.net
- Port Austin PD
- Chief Dale Hartsell
  17 W. State PO Box 336
  Port Austin, MI 48467
  (989) 738-5180
  trapson@airadvantage.net
- Ubly PD
- Chief Matthew J. Kuhl
  2272 Bingham St.
  Ubly, MI 48475
  (989) 658-2433
  ublypolice@ublymi.com

Ingham County

- Ingham County SO
- Sheriff Gene Wriggelsworth
  630 No. Cedar St.
  Mason, MI 48854
  (517) 676-2431
  so_wriggelsworth@ingham.org
- East Lansing PD
- Chief Juli Liebler
  409 Park Ln.
  East Lansing, MI 48823
  (517) 319-6865
  jlieble@cityofeastlansing.com
- Lansing PD
- Chief Michael Yankowski
  120 W. Michigan Ave.
  Lansing, MI 48933
  (517) 483-4800
  michael.yankowski@lansingmi.gov
- Leslie PD
- Chief Robert Delamarter
  151 Commercial
  Leslie, MI 49251
  (517) 589-9700
  delamarterr@cityofleslie.org
- Mason PD
- Chief John Stressman
  201 W. Ash St.
  Mason, MI 48854
  (517) 676-2458
  info@mason.mi.us

- Williamston PD
- Chief Bob Young
  1500 W. Grand River Rd.
  Williamston, MI 48895
  (517) 655-4222
  bob.young@williamston-mi.us

Ionia County

- Ionia County SO
- Sheriff Dale Miller
  133 E. Adams St.
  Lonia, MI 48846
  (616) 527-5737
  dmiller@ioniacounty.org
- Lake Odessa PD
- Chief Mark L. Bender
  839 4th Ave.
  Lake Odessa, MI 48849
  (616) 374-8845
  manager@lakeodessa.org
- Portland PD
- Chief Robert *Bob* Bauer
  773 E. Grand River Ave.
  Portland, MI 48875
  (517) 647-2934
  policechief@portland-michigan.org

Iosco County

- Iosco County SO
- Sheriff Allan L. MacGregor
  428 Lake St. PO Box 59
  Tawas City, MI 48764
  (989) 362-6164
  amacgregor@ioscocounty.org
- East Tawas PD
- Chief Mark Ferguson
  810 W. Westover St.
  East Tawas, MI 48730
  (989) 362-7718
  tawaspolice@tawaspd.us

Iron County

- Crystal Falls PD
- Chief Robert Sherwin
  401 Superior Ave.
  Crystal Falls, MI 49920
  (906) 875-3012
  CFCLERK@UP.NET

Isabella County

- Isabella County SO
- Sheriff Leo Mioduszewski
  207 Court St.
  Mt Pleasant, MI 48858
  (989) 772-5911
  sheriffleo@isabellacounty.org
- Shepherd PD
- Chief Michael Main
  251 W. Wright Ave.
  Shepherd, MI 48883
  (989) 828-5045
  mmain@villageofshepherd.org

Jackson County

- Jackson County SO
- Sheriff Steve Rand
  212 W. Wesley Ave.
  Jackson, MI 49201
  (517) 768-7900
  srand@co.jackson.mi.us
- Colombia Twp PD
- Chief David Elwell
  8500 Jefferson Rd.
  Brooklyn, MI 49230
  (517) 592-3122
  delwell@twp.columbia.mi.us
- Spring Arbor Twp PD
- Chief Russell R. Ratkiewicz
  107 Teft Rd. PO Box 250
  Spring Arbor, MI 49283
  (517) 750-2913, ext. 1
  russ@springarbor.org
- Springport Twp PD
- Chief Dave Luce
  137 E. Main St. PO Box 186
  Springport Twp, MI 49284
  (517) 857-2233
  spt-twp@springcom.com

Kalamazoo County

- Kalamazoo County SO
- Sheriff Richard C. Fuller
  1500 Lamont Ave.
  Kalamazoo, MI 49001
  (269) 385-6173
  rcfull@kalcounty.com
- Galesburg PD
- Chief Richard E. Mau
  200 E. Michigan Ave.
  Galesburg, MI 49053
  (269) 665-4200
  galesburgpd@gmail.com
- Schoolcraft PD
- Chief Bryan Campbell
  154 W. Eliza PO Box 8
  Schoolcraft, MI 49087
  (269) 679-5600
  bcampbell@villageofschoolcraft.com

- Vicksburg PD
- Chief Eric West
  126 No. Kalamazoo St.
  Vicksburg, MI 49097
  (269) 649-1144
  ewest@vicksburgmi.org

Kalkaska County

- Kalkaska County SO
- Sheriff David A. *Dave* Israel
  605 No. Birch St. PO Box 1119
  Kalkaska, MI 49646
  (231) 258-8686
  contact@kalso.org

Kent County

- Cedar Springs PD
- Chief Roger Parent
  66 So. Main St. PO Box 310
  Cedar Springs, MI 49319
  (616) 696-1311
  rparent@cedarspringspd.com
- Grand Rapids PD
- Chief Kevin Belk
  1 Monroe Center NW
  Grand Rapids, MI 49503
  (616) 456-3364
  kbelk@grcity.us
- Grandville PD
- Chief Vernon L. Snyder
  3181 Wilson Ave. SW
  Grandville, MI 49418
  (616) 538-6110
  police@cityofgrandville.com
- Lowell PD
- Chief Barry Getzen
  111 No. Monroe
  Lowell, MI 49331
  (616) 897-7123
  bgetzen@ci.lowell.mi.us
- Rockford PD
- Chief David Jones
  7 So. Monroe St.
  Rockford, MI 49341
  (616) 866-9557
  djones@rockford.mi.us
- Sand Lake PD
- Int. Chief David Price
  2 E. Maple St.
  PO Box 139
  Sand Lake, MI 49343
  (616) 636-8854
  slpd@usacops.com
- Sparta PD
- Chief Andrew Milanowski
  260 W. Division St.
  Sparta, MI 49345
  (616) 887-8716
  policechief@spartami.org
- Walker PD
- Dir. Catherine Garcia-Lindstrom
  4343 Remembrance Rd. NW
  Walker, MI 49544
  (616) 791-6800
  walkerpd@ci.walker.mi.us

Keweenaw County

- Keweenaw County SO
- Sheriff Ronald Lahti
  5105 4th St.
  Eagle River, MI 49950
  (906) 337-0528
  Ksheriff@pasty.net

Lake County

- Lake County SO
- Sheriff Robert Hilts
  1153 No. Michigan Ave.
  Baldwin, MI 49304
  (231) 745-2712
  rhilts@co.lake.mi.us

Lapeer County

- Almont PD
- Chief Pat Nael
  817 No. Main St.
  Almont, MI 48003
  (810) 798- 8655
  pnael@almontvillage.org
- Imlay City PD
- Chief John Stano
  395 E. 3rd St.
  Imlay City, MI 48444
  (313) 724-2345
  icpd@imlaycity.org
- Lapeer PD
- Chief Todd Alexander
  2300 W. Genesee St.
  Lapeer, MI 48446
  (810) 664-0833
  Talexander@ci.lapeer.mi.us

Leelanau County

- Leelanau County SO
- Sheriff Mike Borkovich
  8525 E. Government Dr.
  Suttons Bay, MI 49682
  (231) 256-8800
  mborkovich@co.leelanau.mi.us
- Suttons Bay PD
- Chief Del Moore
  321 St. Joseph, Ste's. C&D
  Suttons Bay, MI 49682
  (231) 271-3051
  sbpd911@suttonsbayvillage.org

Lenawee County

- Lenawee County SO
- Sheriff Jack Welsh
  405 No. Winter St.
  Adrian, MI 49221
  (517) 263-0524
  jack.welsh@lenawee.mi.us
- Adrian PD
- Chief Vince Emrick
  155 E. Maumee St.
  Adrian, MI 49221
  (517) 264-4808
  vemrick@adrianmi.gov
- Blissfield PD
- Chief Jane M. Kelley
  408 E. Adrian St. PO Box 129
  Blissfield, MI 49228
  (517) 486-4340
  chief@blissfieldmichigan.gov
- Hudson PD
- Chief Charles Weir
  121 No. Church St.
  Hudson, MI 49247
  (517) 448-8129
  hudsonpolice@hotmail.com
- Morenci PD
- Chief Larry Joe Weeks
  118 Orchard St.
  Morenci, MI 49256
  (517) 458-7104
  dvarga@cass.net

Livingston County

- Livingston County SO
- Sheriff Robert *Bob* Bezotte
  150 So. Highlander Way
  Howell, MI 48843
  (517) 546-2440
  bbezotte@co.livingston.mi.us
- Brighton PD
- Chief Thomas Wightman
  440 So. 3rd St.
  Brighton, Michigan 48116
  (810) 227-2700
  bpd@brightoncitypolice.org
- Fowlerville PD
- Chief Thomas A. Couling
  213 So. Grand Ave.
  Fowlerville, MI 48836
  (517) 223-8711
  tcouling@fowlerville.org
- Howell PD
- Chief George Basar
  611 E. Grand River Ave.
  Howell, MI 48843
  (517) 546-1330
  Police@cityofhowell.org
- Pinckney PD
- Chief Jeffrey Newton
  220 So. Howell St.
  Pinckney, MI 48169
  (734) 878-3700
  police@villageofpinckney.org
- Unadilla Twp PD
- Chief William Cook
  126 Webb St. PO Box 264
  Gregory, MI 48137
  (734) 498-2325, ext. 223
  wcook@unadillapolice.org

Luce County

- Luce County SO
- Sheriff Kevin Erickson
  411 W. Harrie St.
  Newberry, MI 49868
  (906) 293-8431
  kerickson@lighthouse.net

Mackinac County

- Mackinac County SO
- Sheriff Scott A. Strait
  100 No. Marley
  St. Ignace, MI 49781
  (906) 643-1911
  ahlbornt@mackinacsheriff.us
- Mackinac Island PD
- Chief James Marks
  7374 Market St. PO Box 188
  Mackinac Island, MI 49757
  (906) 847-3300
  mipdchief@cityofmi.org

- St. Ignace PD
- Chief Mark A. Wilk
  396 No. State St.
  St Ignace, MI 49781
  (906) 643-6077
  stignacepd@lighthouse.net

Macomb County

- Macomb County SO
- Sheriff Anthony Wickersham
  43565 Elizabeth Rd.
  Mt Clemens, MI 48043
  (586) 469-5151
  Sheriff@MacombSheriff.com
- Chesterfield Twp PD
- Chief Bruce J. Smith
  46525 Continental Dr.
  Chesterfield, MI 48047
  (586) 949-4118
  contact@chesterfieldpolice.org
- New Baltimore PD
- Chief Timothy P. Wiley
  37885 Green St.
  New Baltimore, MI 48047
  (586) 725-2181, ext. 1206
  twiley@cityofnewbaltimore.org
- Richmond PD
- Chief David A. Teske
  36725 Division Rd.
  Richmond, MI 48062
  (586) 727-4000
  richmondchief@comcast.net
- Romeo PD
- Chief Gregory Paduch
  121 W. St. Clair
  Romeo, MI 48065
  (586) 752-3587
  villageofromeo@yahoo.com
- Roseville PD
- Chief James Berlin
  29753 Gratiot Ave.
  Roseville, MI 48066
  (586) 447-4499
  police@roseville-mi.gov
- Shelby Twp PD
- Chief Roland Woelkers
  52530 Van Dyke Ave.
  Shelby Twp, MI 48316
  (586) 731-2121
  info@shelbytwp.org
- St. Clair Shores PD
- Chief Michael Walleman
  27665 Jefferson St.
  St Clair Shores, MI 48081
  (586) 445-5300
  crimewatch@scsmi.net
- Utica PD
- Chief David Faber
  7550 Auburn Rd.
  Utica, MI 48317
  (586) 731-2345
  dfaber@uticapd.org
- Warren PD
- Comm. Jere Green
  29900 Civic Center Blvd
  Warren, MI 48093
  (586) 574-4700
  police@warrenpd.org

Manistee County

- Little River Band-Ottawa Indians DPS
- Chief Michael Martin
  3031 Domres Rd.
  Manistee, MI 49660
  (231) 398-3413
  mmartin@lrboi.com
- Manistee PD
- Dir. Dave Bachman
  70 Maple St. PO Box 358
  Manistee, MI 49660
  (231) 723-2533
  dbachman@manisteemi.gov

Marquette County

- Marquette County SO
- Sheriff Mike Lovelace
  236 W. Baraga Ave.
  Marquette, MI 49855
  (906) 225-8435
  mlovelace@mqtcty.org
- Ishpeming PD
- Chief Dan Willey
  100 E. Division St.
  Ishpeming, MI 49849
  (906) 486-4416
  policechief@ishpemingcity.org
- Marquette PD
- Chief L. Michael Angeli
  300 W. Baraga Ave.
  Marquette, MI 49855
  (906) 228-0400
  police@mqtcty.org

- Negaunee PD
- Chief Jay Frusti
  100 Silver St.
  Negaunee, MI 49866
  (906) 475-4154, ext. 20
  jfrusti@cityofnegaunee.com

Mason County

- Ludington PD
- Chief Mark A. Barnett
  408 So. Harrison St.
  Ludington, MI 49431
  (231) 843-3425
  lbronson@ci.ludington.mi.us
- Scottville PD
- Chief Mark Barnett
  105 No. Main
  Scottville, MI 49454
  (231) 757-4729
  police@cityofscottville.org

Mecosta County

- Mecosta County SO
- Sheriff Todd M. Purcell
  225 So. Stewart
  Big Rapids, MI 49307
  (231) 592-0150
  tpurcell@co.mecosta.mi.us
- Big Rapids DPS
- Dep. Dir. Warren Hansen
  435 No. Michigan Ave.
  Big Rapids, MI 49307
  (231) 527-0005
  police@ci.big-rapids.mi.us

Menominee County

- Menominee County SO
- Sheriff Kenny Marks
  831 10th Ave.
  Menominee, MI 49858
  (906) 863-4441
  kmarks@menomineeco.com

Midland County

- Midland County SO
- Sheriff Scott Stephenson
  2727 Rodd St.
  Midland, MI 48640
  (989) 839-4627
  sstephenson@co.midland.mi.us
- Midland PD
- Chief Clifford Block
  2727 Rodd St.
  Midland, MI 48640
  (989) 631-5716
  citypolice@midland-mi.org

Missaukee County

- Missaukee County SO
- Sheriff James D. Bosscher
  110 Pine St. PO Box 800
  Lake City, MI 49651
  (231) 839-4338
  sheriff@missaukee.org

Monroe County

- Monroe County SO
- Sheriff Dale Malone
  100 E. 2nd St.
  Monroe, MI 48161
  (734) 240-7401
  tellthesheriff@monroemi.org
- Carleton PD
- Chief Henry Hank Runyan
  1143 Monroe St. PO Box 516
  Carleton, MI 48117
  (734) 654-6717
  hank_runyan@carletonpolice.us
- Erie Twp PD
- Chief Tony Konopka
  2065 E. Erie Rd. PO Box 187
  Erie, MI 48133
  (734) 848-4082
  jupchurch@erietownship.com
- Milan PD
- Chief Gerard Scherlinck
  35 Neckel Ct.
  Milan, MI 48160
  (See also Washtenaw County)
  (734) 439-1551
  info@ci.milan.mi.us
- Monroe DPS
- Dir. Thomas C. Moore
  120 E. 1st St.
  Monroe, MI 48161
  (734) 243-7500
  Records@monroepolice.org

Montcalm County

- Montcalm County SO
- Sheriff William Barnwell
  659 No. State
  Stanton, MI 48888
  (989) 831-7590
  bbarnwell@co.montcalm.mi.us
- Carson City PD
- Chief Bruce Partridge
  123 E. Main St.
  Carson City, MI 48811
  (989) 584-6448
  police@carsoncitymi.com

- Howard City PD
- Chief Steven DeWitt
  125 Shaw St. PO Box 510
  Howard City, MI 49329
  (231) 937-4311, ext. 3
  police@howardcity.org

Montmorency County

- Montmorency County SO
- Sheriff Donald *Don* Edwards
  11045 M-32 W.
  Atlanta, MI 49709
  (989) 785-4238
  edwardsd@montmorencysheriff.com

Muskegon County

- Montague PD
- Chief Robert J. Rought
  8778 Ferry St.
  Montague, MI 49437
  (231) 893-0810
  rrought900@gmail.com
- Muskegon Heights PD
- Chief Lynne Gill
  2715 Baker St.
  Muskegon Heights, MI 49444
  (231) 733-8900
  dpaige@cityofmuskegonheights.org
- North Muskegon PD
- Chief Thomas Korabik
  1114 Ruddiman Dr.
  North Muskegon, MI 49445
  (231) 744-4313
  www.NMuskegonPD@aol.com
- Norton Shores PD
- Chief Daniel Shaw
  4814 Henry St. # 1
  Norton Shores, MI 49441
  (231) 733-2691
  daniel.shaw@mcd911.net
- Roosevelt Park PD
- Chief David Boone
  900 Oakridge Rd.
  Muskegon, MI 49441
  (231) 755-3721, ext. 111
  cityof.rooseveltpark@verizon.net
- Whitehall PD
- Chief Roger D. Squiers
  405 E. Colby St.
  Whitehall, MI 49461
  (231) 894-4048
  roger.squiers@mcd911.net

Newaygo County

- Newaygo County SO
- Sheriff Michael S. Mercer
  1035 E. James St. PO Box 845
  White Cloud, MI 49349
  (231) 689-7303
  msm@co.newaygo.mi.us
- Fremont PD
- Chief Randall Wright
  101 E. Main St.
  Fremont, MI 49412
  (231) 924-2100, ext. 401
  rwright@cityoffremont.net
- Grant PD
- Chief Dan VanBelzen
  280 So. Maple St. PO Box 435
  Grant, MI 49327
  (231) 834-7212
  grantpdchief@sbcglobal.net
- White Cloud PD
- Chief Bob Mendham
  12 No. Charles St.
  White Cloud, MI 49349
  (231) 689-1696
  bobm@cityofwhitecloud.org

Oakland County

- Oakland County SO
- Sheriff Michael Bouchard
  1200 No. Telegraph Rd., Bldg 38E
  Pontiac, MI 48341
  (248) 858-5000
  ocso@oakgov.com
- Birmingham PD
- Chief Donald A. Studt
  151 Martin St. PO Box 301
  Birmingham, MI 48012
  (248) 530-1863
  dstudt@behamgov.org
- Bloomfield Twp PD
- Chief Kirt Bowden
  4200 Telegraph PO Box 489
  Bloomfield Hills, MI 48302
  (248) 433-7750
  kbowden@bloomfieldtwp.org
- Clawson PD
- Chief Harry C. Anderson
  425 No. Main St.
  Clawson, MI 48017
  (248) 435-5000
  Handerson@cityofclawson.com

- Farmington Hills PD
- Chief Chuck Nebus
  31655 W. 11 Mile Rd.
  Farmington Hills, MI 48336
  (248) 871-2702
  cnebus@fhgov.com
- Ferndale PD
- Chief Timothy D. Collins
  310 E. 9 Mile Rd.
  Ferndale, MI 48220
  (248) 546-2388
  sjennings@ferndalepolice.org
- Huntington Woods DPS
- Dir. Steve Fairman
  12755 W. 11 Mile Rd.
  Huntington Woods, MI 48070
  (248) 541-1180
  sfairman@ci.huntington-woods.mi.us
- Lake Orion PD
- Chief Jerry Narsh
  37 E. Flint St.
  Lake Orion, MI 48362
  (248) 693-8321
  rossmanh@lakeorion.org
- Lathrup Village PD
- Chief William Armstrong
  27400 Southfield Rd.
  Lathrup Village, MI 48076
  (248) 557-3600
  policechief@lathrupvillage.org
- Madison Heights PD
- Chief Anthony Roberts
  280 W. 13 Mile Rd.
  Madison Heights, MI 48071
  (248) 585-2100
  anthonyroberts@madison-heights.org
- Milford PD
- Chief Thomas C. Lindberg
  1100 Atlantic St.
  Milford, MI 48381
  (248) 684-1815
  ldemko@milfordpolice.com
- Novi PD
- Chief David Molloy
  45125 W. 10 Mile Rd.
  Novi, MI 48375
  (248) 347-0504
  dmolloy@cityofnovi.org
- Orchard Lake PD
- Chief Joe George
  3955 Orchard Lake Rd.
  Orchard Lake, MI 48323
  (248) 682-2400
  PoliceChief@CityofOrchardLake.com
- Oxford PD
- Chief Michael Neymanowski
  22 W. Burdick St.
  Oxford, MI 48371
  (248) 628-2581
  Info@oxfordvillagepolice.org
- Pleasant Ridge PD
- Chief Karl Swieczkowski
  23925 Woodward Ave.
  Pleasant Ridge, MI 48069
  (248) 541-2900
  cityclerk@cityofpleasantridge.org
- Rochester PD
- Chief Steven J. Schettenhelm
  400 6th St.
  Rochester, MI 48307
  (248) 651-9621
  sschettenhelm@rochestermi.org
- South Lyon PD
- Chief Lloyd T. Collins
  219 Whipple
  South Lyon, MI 48178
  (248) 437-1773
  chief@southlyonpolice.com
- Sylvan Lake PD
- Chief Mark Silver
  1820 Inverness St.
  Sylvan Lake, MI 48320
  (248) 682-2104
  Chief@sylvanlake.org
- Troy PD
- Chief Gary G. Mayer
  500 W. Big Beaver Rd.
  Troy, MI 48084
  (248) 524-3443
  mayergg@troymi.gov
- Waterford PD
- Chief Daniel T. McCaw
  5150 Civic Center Dr.
  Waterford, MI 48329
  (248) 674-0351
  wdolehan@twp.waterford.mi.us

- Wixom PD
- Dir. Clarence Goodlein
  49045 Pontiac Tr.
  Wixom, MI 48393
  (248) 624-6114
  Poladmin@wixomgov.org

Oceana County

- Hart PD
- Chief Daniel Leimback
  407 So. State St.
  Hart, MI 49420
  (231) 873-2488
  dleimback@ci.hart.mi.us
- Pentwater PD
- Chief Mike Schuitema
  326 So. Hancock
  Pentwater, MI 49449
  (231) 869-4630
  clerk@pentwatervillage.org

Ogemaw County

- Ogemaw County SO
- Sheriff Howie Hanft
  806 W. Wright St.
  West Branch, MI 48661
  (989) 345-3786
  dcasselman@ogsh.org
- Rose City PD
- Chief Max Garnett
  310 No. Williams
  Rose City, MI 48654
  (989) 685-3051
  cityhall@rosecitymi.net
- West Branch PD
- Chief Rodger Williams
  113 No. 1st St.
  West Branch, MI 48661
  (989) 345-2627
  williamsr@westbranch.com

Ontonagon County

- Ontonagon County SO
- Sheriff Dale Rantala
  620 Conglomerate St.
  Ontonagon, MI 49953
  (906) 884-4901
  drantala@ontonagoncounty.org

Osceola County

- Osceola County SO
- Sheriff James Crawford
  325 W. Upton Ave.
  Reed City, MI 49677
  (231) 832-2288
  oscsheriff@chartermi.net
- Evart PD
- Chief Kendra Backing
  200 So. Main St.
  Evart, MI 49631
  (231) 734-5911
  evartpd@sbcglobal.net
- Marion PD
- Chief Harry R. Daugherty
  120 E. Main
  Marion, MI 49665
  (231) 743-6801
  admin@marionpolice.co

Oscoda County

- Oscoda County SO
- Sheriff Kevin R. Grace
  301 So. Morenci PO Box 129
  Mio, MI 48647
  (989) 826-3214
  sheriff@oscodacountymi.com

Otsego County

- Otsego County SO
- Sheriff Matthew *Matt* Nowicki
  124 So. Court St.
  Gaylord, MI 49735
  (989) 732-3555
  usheriff69@otsegocountymi.gov
- Gaylord PD
- Chief Brett McVannel
  305 E. Main St.
  Gaylord, MI 49735
  (989) 732-1777
  CurtisB@cityofgaylord.org

Ottawa County

Ottawa County SO
- Sheriff Gary A. Rosema
  12220 Fillmore St.
  West Olive, MI 49460
  (616) 738-4000
  lhoeksema@miottawa.org

- Grand Haven DPS
- Dir. Jeffery Hawke
  525 Washington St.
  Grand Haven, MI 49417
  (616) 842-3460
  jhawke@grandhaven.org
- Spring Lake-Ferrysburg PD
- Chief Roger DeYoung
  17290 Roosevelt PO Box 38
  Ferrysburg, MI 49409
  (800) 249-0911
  info@ferrysburg.org
- Zeeland PD
- Chief William Olney
  29 W. Main St.
  Zeeland, MI 49464
  (616) 772-9125
  bolney@ci.zeeland.mi.us

Presque Isle County

- Presque Isle County SO
- Sheriff Robert W. Paschke
  267 No. 2nd St.
  Rogers City, MI 49779
  (989) 734-2156
  rpaschke@i2k.net
- Onaway PD
- Chief James Gibson
  3570 No. Veterans Dr.
  Onaway, MI 49765
  (989) 733-7755
  onawaych@src-milp.com
- Rogers City PD
- Chief Matthew D. Quaine
  193 E. Michigan Ave.
  Rogers City, MI 49779
  (989) 734-2330
  mquaine@rogerscity.com

Roscommon County

- Roscommon County SO
- Sheriff Randall Stevenson
  111 So. 2nd St. PO Box 206
  Roscommon, MI 48653
  (989) 275-5101
  roscosheriff@voyager.net

Saginaw County

- Saginaw County SO
- Sheriff William L. *Bill* Federspiel
  618 Cass St.
  Saginaw, MI 48602
  (989) 790-5456
  wfederspiel@saginawcounty.com
- Bridgeport PD
- Chief *(currently vacant)*
  6206 Dixie Hwy
  Bridgeport, MI 48722
  (989) 777-2800
  information@bridgeportmi.org
- Frankenmuth PD
- Chief Donald C. Mawer
  240 W. Genesee St.
  Frankenmuth, MI 48734
  (989) 652-8371
  dmawer@frankenmuthcity.com

Saint Clair County

- Saint Clair County SO
- Sheriff Tim Donnellon
  1170 Michigan Rd.
  Port Huron, MI 48060
  (810) 987-1712
  rmuxlow@stclaircounty.org
- Marine City PD
- Chief Don Tillery
  375 So. Parker
  Marine City, MI 48039
  (810) 765-4040
  mcinfo@marinecity-mi.org
- Marysville PD
- Chief Timothy *Tim* Buelow
  1355 Delaware Ave.
  Marysville, MI 48040
  (810) 364-6300
  tbuelow@cityofmarysvillemi.com
- Memphis PD
- Chief Jessica Beels
  80688 Union St.
  Memphis, MI 48041
  (810) 392-2144
  chiefbeels@yahoo.com
- Port Huron PD
- Chief Michael Reaves
  100 McMorran Blvd
  Port Huron, MI 48060
  (810) 984-9710
  reavesm@porthuron.org
- St. Clair PD
- Chief Rick Jefferson
  547 No. Carney Dr.
  St. Clair, MI 48079
  (810) 329-5710
  rjefferson@cityofstclair.com

- Yale PD
- Chief Michael Redman
  111 W. Mechanic St.
  Yale, MI 48097
  (810) 387-4201
  mredman@yalemi.us

Saint Joseph County

- Saint Joseph County SO
- Sheriff Bradley D. Balk
  650 E. Main PO Box 339
  Centreville, MI 49032
  (269) 467-9045
  balkb@stjosephcountymi.org
- Colon PD
- Chief Mark Brinkert
  127 E. State St.
  Colon, MI 49040
  (269) 432-3182
  chief.brinkert@colonpolice.com
- Constantine PD
- Chief James L. Bedell
  270 E. Water St.
  Constantine, MI 49042
  (269) 435-4355
  jbedell@constantinemi.com
- Sturgis PD
- Dir. David *Dave* Northrop
  122 No. Nottawa St.
  Sturgis, MI 49091
  (269) 659.7273
  dnorthrop@sturgismi.gov
- Three Rivers PD
- Chief Thomas J. Bringman
  333 W. Michigan Ave.
  Three Rivers, MI 49093
  (269) 278-1235, ext. 130
  tbringman@threeriversmi.org
- White Pigeon PD
- Chief Lynn *Dutch* Baker
  103 So. Kalamazoo St.
  White Pigeon, MI 49099
  (269) 483-7109
  whitepigeonpolice@comcast.net

Sanilac County

- Brown City PD
- Chief Ron Smith
  4205 Main St.
  Brown City, MI 48416
  (810) 346-2325
  brnctypd@greatlakes.net
- Croswell PD
- Chief Dave Hall
  100 No. Howard Ave.
  Croswell, MI 48422
  (810) 679-2200
  dhallcpd@sbcglobal.net
- Deckerville PD
- Chief Tim Torp
  3680 Range Line Rd.
  Deckerville, MI 48427
  (810) 376-6651
  dville@airadv.net
- Marlette PD
- Chief Brian P. McGinnis
  6436 Morris St.
  Marlette, MI 48453
  (517) 635-7448
  scargill@cityofmarlette.com
- Port Sanilac DPS
- Dir. Nathan L. Smith
  56 No. Ridge St. PO Box 502
  Port Sanilac, MI 48469
  (810) 622-9131
  portsanilacpoiice@airadv.net
- Sandusky PD
- Chief Brett Lester
  26 W. Speaker St.
  Sandusky, MI 48471
  (810) 648-4016
  blester@misandusky.com

Schoolcraft County

- Schoolcraft County SO
- Sheriff John Norrington
  300 Main St.
  Manistique, MI 49854
  (906) 341-2122
  sheriff@schoolcraftcounty.us

Shiawassee County

- Shiawassee County SO
- Sheriff George R. Braidwood II
  201 E. McArthur
  Corunna, MI 48817
  (989) 743-3411
  gbraidwood@shiawassee.net
- Corunna PD
- Chief Kim Williams
  402 No. Shiawassee St.
  Corunna, MI 48817
  (517) 743-6170
  kwilliams@corunna-mi.gov

- Durand PD
- Chief Tim Sampey
  215 W. Clinton St.
  Durand, MI 48429
  (517) 288-3113
  mailto:tsampey@durandmi.com
- Morrice PD
- Chief Mike Sheldon
  401 Main St. PO Box 247
  Morrice, MI 48857
  (517) 625-3430
  morricepolice@mi.us
- Perry PD
- Chief Kyle Bawks
  109 E. 2nd St.
  Perry, MI 48872
  (517) 625-3535, ext. 238
  policechief@perry.mi.us
- Vernon PD
- Chief Paul Hubble
  120 E. Main
  Vernon, MI 48476
  (517) 288-2300
  eglass@villageofvernon.org

Tuscola County

- Tuscola County SO
- Sheriff Leland Teschendorf
  420 Court St.
  Caro, MI 48723
  (989) 673-8161
  sheriff@tuscolacounty.org
- Cass City PD
- Chief Craig Haynes
  6737 Church St.
  Cass City, MI 48726
  (989) 872-2911
  ccpolicechief@casscity.org
- Mayville PD
- Chief David Forystek
  5950 Fox St.
  Mayville, MI 48744
  (989) 843-5301, ext. 303
  dforystek@villageofmayville.org
- Reese PD
- Chief Mike Hadd
  2073 Gates St. PO Box 369
  Reese, MI 48757
  (989) 868-4582
  clerk@villageofreese.us
- Vassar PD
- Chief Ben Guile
  287 E. Huron Ave.
  Vassar, MI 48768
  (989) 823-8531
  bguile@cityofvassar.org

Van Buren County

- Van Buren County SO
- Sheriff Dale Gribler
  205 So. Kalamazoo
  Paw Paw, MI 49079
  (269) 657-2006, ext. 3990
  griblerd@vbco.org
- Bangor PD
- Chief Gary Baker
  257 W. Monroe St.
  Bangor, MI 49013
  (269) 427-5418
  bangorpd@btc-bci.com
- Decatur PD
- Chief David McLeese
  114 No. Phelps St.
  Decatur, MI 49045
  (269) 423-2171
  decpd01@locallink.net
- Hartford PD
- Chief Ramon Beltran
  19 W. Main St.
  Hartford, MI 49057
  (269) 621-3225
  beltranr@cityofhartfordmi.org
- Mattawan PD
- Chief Donald L. VerHage
  24221 Front Ave.
  Mattawan, MI 49071
  (269) 668-3661
  offices@mattawanmi.com
- Paw Paw PD
- Chief Eric Marshall
  114 Harry L. Bush PO Box 179
  Paw Paw, MI 49079
  (269) 657-5501
  e.marshall@pawpaw.net
- South Haven PD
- Chief Tom Martin
  90 Blue Star Hwy
  South Haven, MI 49090
  (269) 637-5151
  tmartin@south-haven.com

Washtenaw County

- Washtenaw County SO
- Sheriff Jerry L. Clayton
  2201 Hogback Rd.
  Ann Arbor, MI 48105
  (734) 971-8400
  wyattk@ewashtenaw.org
- Ann Arbor PD
- Chief John Seto
  301 E. Huron
  Ann Arbor, MI 48104
  (734) 994-2911
  policedept@a2gov.org
- Chelsea PD
- Chief Ed Toth
  104 E. Middle St.
  Chelsea, MI 48118
  (734) 475-1771, ext. 101
  etoth@chelseapd.org
- Milan PD
- Chief Gerard Scherlinck
  35 Neckel Ct.
  Milan, MI 48160
  (See also Monroe County)
  (734) 439-1551
  info@ci.milan.mi.us
- Northfield Twp PD
- Chief Carl Watkins
  8350 Main St.
  Whitmore Lake, MI 48189
  (734) 449-9911
  northfield-police@twp.northfield.mi.us
- Pittsfield Twp PD
- Act. Chief (*Lt.*) Sean McCormick
  6227 W. Michigan Ave.
  Ann Arbor, MI 48108
  (734) 822-4911
  mccormicks@pittsfield-mi.gov
- Saline PD
- Chief Larry Hrinik
  100 No. Harris
  Saline, MI 48176
  (734) 429-7911, ext. 2102
  lhrinik@cityofsaline.org
- Ypsilanti PD
- Chief Amy F. Walker
  505 W. Michigan Ave.
  Ypsilanti, MI 48197
  (734) 483-8590
  awalker@cityofypsilanti.com

Wayne County

- Wayne County SO
- Sheriff Benny N. Napoleon, J.D.
  4747 Woodward
  Detroit, MI 48226
  (313) 224-2233
  info@sheriffconnect.com
- Belleville PD
- Chief Gene Taylor
  6 Main St.
  Belleville, MI 48111
  (734) 699-2710
  dda@belleville.mi.us
- Brownstown Twp PD
- Chief James Sclater
  21313 Telegraph Rd.
  Brownstown Township, MI 48183
  (734) 675-1300
  jsclater@wdl.net
- Canton DPS
- Dir. Todd L. Mutchler
  1150 So. Canton Center Rd.
  Canton, MI 48188
  (734) 394-5400
  publicsafetyadmin@canton-mi.org
- Dearborn Heights PD   Chief Lee Gavin
  25637 Michigan Ave.
  Dearborn Heights, MI 48127
  (313) 277-6770
  dhpd@ci.dearborn-heights.mi.us
- Detroit PD
- Chief Warren C. Evans
  1300 Beaubien St.
  Detroit, MI 48226
  (313) 596-1800
  chiefofpolice@dpdhq.ci.detroit.mi.us
- Flat Rock PD
- Chief Neal A. Rossow
  25500 Gibraltar Rd.
  Flat Rock, MI 48134
  (734) 782-2496
  chief@flatrockmi.org
- Garden City PD
- Chief Robert Muery
  6000 Middlebelt
  Garden City, MI 48135
  (734) 793-1730
  mueryr@gardencitymi.org

- Grosse Pointe Farms DPS
- Chief Daniel V. Jensen
  90 Kerby Rd.
  Grosse Pointe Farms, MI 48236
  (313) 885-2100, ext. 1203
  djensen@gpfdps.org
- Harper Woods PD
- Chief James R. Burke
  19617 Harper Ave.
  Harper Woods, MI 48225
  (313) 343-2530
  burkej@harperwoodspolice.org
- Lincoln Park PD
- Chief Brian Hawk
  1427 Cleophus
  Lincoln Park, MI 48146
  (313) 381-1800
  bhawk@citylp.com
- Livonia PD
- Chief Curtis Caid
  15050 Farmington Rd.
  Livonia, MI 48154
  (734) 466-2470
  training@lpdmail.com
- Melvindale PD
- Chief Chad Hayse
  3100 Oakwood Blvd
  Melvindale, MI 48122
  (313) 429-1070, ext. 3
  policechief@melvindale.org
- Plymouth PD
- Chief Al Cox
  201 So. Main St.
  Plymouth, MI 48170
  (734) 453-1234, ext. 219
  acox@ci.plymouth.mi.us
- Rockwood PD
- Chief Stephen P. Rowe
  32409 Fort Rd.
  Rockwood, MI 48173
  (734) 379-5323
  PDChief@RockwoodMI.org
- Trenton PD
- Chief James Nardone
  2872 W. Jefferson Ave.
  Trenton, MI 48183
  (734) 676-3737
  jnardone@trenton-mi.com
- Westland PD
- Chief Jeff Jedrusik
  36701 Ford Rd.
  Westland, MI 48185
  (734) 722-9600
  policechief@wlpd.net
- Woodhaven PD
- Chief Michael Graham
  21869 West Rd.
  Woodhaven, MI 48183
  (734) 675-4906
  pdchief@woodhavenmi.ecswebdesign.net

Wexford County

- Wexford County SO
- Sheriff Gary A. Finstrom
  820 So. Carmel St.
  Cadillac, MI 49601
  (231) 779-9211
  sheriff@wexfordcounty.org
- Cadillac PD
- Chief Matt Wohlfeill
  200 No. Lake St.
  Cadillac, MI 49601
  (231) 775-3491
  mwohlfeill@cadillac-mi.net
- Manton PD
- Chief Mike Long
  402 No. Michigan Ave.
  Manton, MI 49663
  (231) 824-6464
  info@mantonmichigan.org

State Agencies

- MI State Police-HQ
- Dir. (*Col.*) Kriste Kibbey Etue
  333 So. Grand
  PO Box 30634
  Lansing, MI 48909-0634
  (517) 241-0403
  kuzmerzk@michigan.gov
- East Grand Rapids DPS
- Act. Chief (*Capt.*) Brian Williams
  770 Lakeside Dr. SE
  East Grand Rapids, MI 49506
  (616) 949-7010
  bwilliam@eastgr.org

MISSISSIPPI

Adams County

- Adams County SD
- Sheriff Chuck Mayfield
  306 State St.
  Natchez, MS 39120
  (601) 442-2752
  sheriffmayfield@adamscosheriff.org
- Adams County Office
- Constable Randy Freeman
  2833 So. Harber PO Box 702
  Washington, MS 39190
  (601) 442-2459
  adams14_99@yahoo.com
- Natchez PD
- Chief Danny White
  233 D'evereaux Dr.
  Natchez, MS 39120
  (601) 445-5565
  dwhite@natchez.ms.us

Alcorn County

- Alcorn County SO
- Sheriff Charles Rinehart
  2837 So. Harper Rd.
  Corinth, MS 38834
  (662) 286-5521
  alcornso@comcast.net

Amite County

- Amite County SD
- Sheriff Tim Wroten
  243 So. Broad St. PO Box 208
  Liberty, MS 39645
  (601) 657-8057
  amiteso@yahoo.com

Attala County

- Attala County SO
- Sheriff William Lee
  112 W. Adams St.
  Kosciusko, MS 39090
  (662) 289-5556
  boardofsupervisors@attalacounty.net
- Kosciusko PD
- Chief R.J. Adams
  209 W. Adams St.
  Kosciusko, MS 39090
  (662) 289-3131
  ofc_k@bellsouth.net

Benton County

- Ashland PD
- Chief Barry Hobson
  15870 Boundary Dr.
  Ashland, MS 38603
  (662) 224-6282
  ashland@dixie-net.com

Bolivar County

- Bolivar County SO
- Sheriff Kelvin Williams
  Court St. PO Box 539
  Cleveland, MS 38732
  (601) 843-5378
  kwilliams@co.bolivar.ms.us
- Cleveland PD
- Chief Charles *Buster* Bingham
  301 So. Sharpe PO Box 1439
  Cleveland, MS 38732
  (601) 843-3611
  buster.bingham@cityofclevelandms.com
- Mound Bayou PD
- Chief Tony Warren
  106 Green St. W.
  Mound Bayou, MS 38762
  (601) 741-2191
  tony.warren@police.cityofmoundbayou.org

Calhoun County

- Calhoun County SO
- Sheriff Greg Pollan
  178 So. Murphree PO Box 158
  Pittsboro, MS 38951
  (662) 412-3149
  bsimpson@calhouncoms.com

Choctaw County

- Choctaw County SO
- Sheriff Cloyd Halford
  122 Jailhouse Rd.
  Ackerman, MS 39735
  (662) 285-6129
  sheriff@choctawcountyms.com

Claiborne County

- Claiborne County SO
- Sheriff Marvin Lucas
  410 Main St. PO Box 427
  Port Gibson, MS 39150
  (601) 437-5161
  info@claibornecountysheriff.org

Clarke County

- Clarke County SD
- Sheriff Todd Kemp
  444 W. Donald St.
  Quitman, MS 39355
  (601) 776-5252
  Todd.Kemp@clarkecountysheriff.com

Clay County

- Clay County SO
- Sheriff Laddie Huffman
  330 W. Broad St. PO Box 142
  West Point, MS 39773
  (662) 494-2896
  lhuffman@claycountyms.com
- West Point PD
- Chief Tim Brinkley
  310 E. Westbrook St.
  West Point, MS 39773
  (662) 494-1244
  tbrinkley@wpnet.org

Coahoma County

- Coahoma County SO
- Sheriff Charles Jones
  63 Sunflower Ave. PO Box 1182
  Clarksdale, MS 38614
  (662) 624-3081
  info@coahomacountysheriff.com
- Clarksdale PD
- Chief William *Whit* Read
  121 Sunflower PO Box 940
  Clarksdale, MS 38614
  (662) 621-8154
  police@cityofclarksdale.org

Copiah County

- Copiah County SO
- Sheriff Harold L. Jones
  20030 Hwy 51 PO Box 547
  Hazlehurst MS 39083
  (601) 892-2023
  star1cso@copiahcountyms.gov

Covington County

- Covington County SO
- Sheriff Stan Smith
  203 1st St. PO Box 545
  Collins, MS 39428
  (601) 765-8281
  ssmith@covingtoncountyms.gov

De Soto County

- Hernando PD
- Chief Mike Riley
  475 W. Commerce St.
  Hernando, MS 38632
  (662) 429-9096
  mriley@cityofhernando.org
- Horn Lake PD
- Chief Darryl Whaley
  3101 Goodman Rd.
  Horn Lake, MS 38637
  (662) 342-3525
  dwhaley@hornlakepolice.com
- Olive Branch PD
- Chief Don Gammage
  9245 Pigeon Roost Rd.
  Olive Branch, MS 38654
  (662) 892-9405
  dgammage@obms.us
- Southaven PD
- Chief Tom Long
  8791 Northwest Dr.
  Southaven, MS 38671
  (662) 393-8652
  tlong@southaven.org

Forrest County

- Forrest County SO
- Sheriff Billy McGee
  316 Forrest St. PO Box 747
  Hattiesburg, MS 39403
  (601) 544-7800
  bmcgee@co.forrest.ms.us
- Hattiesburg PD
- Chief Frazier Bolton
  1 Government Plaza
  Hattiesburg, MS 39401
  (601) 545-4900
  info@hattiesburgms.com
- Petal PD
- Chief Leonard Fuller
  127 W. 8th Ave.
  Petal, MS 39465
  (601) 544-5331
  lfuller@cityofpetal.com

George County

- George County SO
- Sheriff Dean Howell
  355 Cox St., Ste. B
  Lucedale, MS 39452
  (601) 947-4811
  info@georgecountymssheriff.com

Greene County

- Greene County SD
- Sheriff Stanley McLeod
  300 Lafayette St. PO Box 367
  Leakesville, MS 39451
  (601) 394-2341
  sheriff@greenecountyms.gov

Grenada County

- Grenada County SD
- Sheriff Jesse Alton Strider, Jr.
  35 Doak St.
  Grenada, MS 38901
  (662) 227-2877
  granadaso1@cableone.net
- Grenada PD
- Chief James R. Carver
  15 No. Main St.
  Grenada, MS 38901
  (662) 227-3455
  Grenadadetectives@yahoo.com

Hancock County

- Bay Saint Louis PD
- Chief Michael De Nardo
  310 Old Spanish Tr.
  Bay Saint Louis, MS 39520
  (601) 466-5476
  b2denardo@bellsouth.net
- Waveland PD
- Chief Kenny Hurt
  628 Hwy 90 W.
  Waveland, MS 39576
  (228) 467-3669
  khurt@wavelandpolice.com

Harrison County

- Harrison County SD
- Sheriff Melvin Brisolara
  10451 Larkin Smith PO Box 1480
  Gulfport, MS 39501
  (228) 896-0606
  sheriff.brisolara@harrisoncountysheriff.com
- Biloxi PD
- Chief John Miller
  170 Porter Ave.
  Biloxi, MS 39530
  (228) 435-6100
  jmiller@biloxi.ms.us
- Gulfport PD
- Chief Leonard Papania
  2220 15th St.
  Gulfport, MS 39502
  (228) 868-5900
  chiefofpolicesecretary@gulfport-ms.gov
- Long Beach PD
- Chief Wayne McDowell
  202 Alexander Rd.
  Long Beach, MS 39560
  (228) 865-1985
  chief@cityoflongbeachms.com
- Pass Christian PD
- Chief John Dubuisson
  525 Espy Ave. PO Box 368
  Pass Christian, MS 39571
  (228) 452-3301
  cityclerk@ci.pass-christian.ms.us

Hinds County

- Hinds County SO
- Sheriff Tyrone Lewis
  407 E. Pascagoula PO Box 1452
  Jackson, MS 39215
  (601) 974-2901
  tlewis@co.hinds.ms.us
- Clinton PD
- Chief Michael Warren
  305 Monroe St.
  Clinton, MS 39056
  (601) 924-5252
  warren108@clintonpd.org
- Edwards PD
- Chief Louis Johnson
  100 Utica St. PO Box 215
  Edwards, MS 39066
  (601) 852-4213
  townofedwards@aol.com
- Raymond PD
- Chief Jason Crotwell
  PO Box 10
  Raymond, MS 39154
  (601) 857-8041
  raymondpdms@yahoo.com

Humphreys County

- Humphreys County SD
- Sheriff J.D. *Bubba* Roseman
  106 Castleman St.
  Belzoni, MS 39038
  (662) 247-2551
  info@humphreyscountysheriff.org

- Belzoni PD
- Chief Mickey Foxworth
  314 No. Hayden St.
  Belzoni, MS 39038
  (662) 247-2181
  mayor@belzoni.com

Jackson County

- Jackson County SO
- Sheriff Michael *Mike* Byrd
  3104 Magnolia St. PO Box 998
  Pascagoula, MS 39568
  (228) 769-3024
  Mike_Byrd@co.jackson.ms.us
- Moss Point PD
- Chief Keith Davis
  4329 McInnis St.
  Moss Point, MS 39563
  (228) 475-1711
  keith.davis@cityofmosspoint.org
- Ocean Springs PD
- Chief Lionel Cothern
  3810 Bienville Blvd
  Ocean Springs, MS 39564
  (228) 875-2211
  lcothern@oceansprings-ms.gov
- Pascagoula PD
- Chief Kenny Johnson
  PO Box 1385
  Pascagoula, MS 39568
  (228) 938-6671
  kennyj@cityofpascagoula.com

Jasper County

- Jasper County SO
- Sheriff Chris Sargent
  8th Ave. PO Box 464
  Bay Springs, MS 39422
  (601) 764-2588
  jcedd@hotmail.com
- Bay Springs PD
- Chief Raymond Delk
  39 So. 6th St. PO Box 307
  Bay Springs, MS 39422
  (601) 764-3122
  karen@featherdesign.com

Jefferson County

- Jefferson County SO
- Sheriff Peter E. Walker
  1483 Main St. PO Box 218
  Fayette, MS 39069
  (601) 786-8475
  Jeffcorr@bellsouth.net

Jefferson Davis County

- Bassfield PD
- Chief Larry Joe Thompson
  PO Box 100
  Bassfield, MS 39421
  (601) 943-6300
  mayorsoffice@bassfieldms.com
- Prentiss PD
- Chief Jerry Q. Magee
  PO Box 1344
  Prentiss, MS 39474
  (601) 792-5198
  info@townofprentiss.com

Jones County

- Jones County SO
- Sheriff Alex Hodge
  419 Yates Ave. PO Box 185
  Laurel, MS 39441
  (601) 425-3147
  info@jonesso.com

Kemper County

- Kemper County SO
- Sheriff James Moore
  330 Stennis Industrial Park Rd.
  DeKalb, MS 39328
  (601) 743-4880, ext. 100
  info@kempercountysheriff.com
- Scooba PD
- Chief James Moore
  888 Kemper St PO Box 68
  Scooba, MS 39358
  (662) 476-8451
  Scoobacityof@bellsouth.nett

Lafayette County

- Lafayette County SO
- Sheriff F.D. *Buddy* East
  711 Jackson Ave.
  Oxford, MS 38655
  (662) 234-6421
  tprestage@lafayettecoms.com
- Oxford PD
- Chief Joey East
  715 Molly Barr Rd.
  Oxford, MS 38655
  (662) 232-2400
  jeast@oxfordpolice.net

Lamar County

- Lamar County SD
- Sheriff Danny Rigel
  205 Main St., Ste. B
  Purvis, MS 39475
  (601) 794-1005
  drigel@lamarcounty.com
- Lumberton PD
- Chief Adrian Fortenberry
  102 E. Main Ave. PO Box 211
  Lumberton, MS 39455
  (601) 796-7001
  lumbertonpolice@yahoo.com

Lauderdale County

- Lauderdale County SO
- Sheriff William D. *Billy* Sollie
  2001 5th St.
  Meridian, MS 39301
  (601) 482-9806
  sheriff@lauderdalecounty.org
- Meridian PD
- Act. Chief James Sharpe
  2415 6th St.
  Meridian, MS 39301
  (601) 485-1842
  police@meridianms.org

Lawrence County

- Monticello PD
- Chief David Stanley
  PO Box 100
  Monticello, MS 39654
  (601) 587-7732
  dhnichols@bellsouth.net

Leake County

- Lena PD
- Chief James Johnson
  PO Box 108
  Lena, MS 39094
  (601) 654-3332
  lenapolicedept@bellsouth.net

Lee County

- Guntown PD
- Chief Michael Hall
  1589 Main St.
  Guntown, MS 38849
  (662) 348-2208
  Info@guntownms.com
- Nettleton PD
- Chief Jackie Wimberley
  225 Main St.
  Nettleton, MS 38858
  (See also Monroe County)
  (662) 963-1185
  NPD1@dixie-net.com
- Saltillo PD
- Chief Steve Brooks
  PO Box 1426
  Saltillo, MS 38866
  (662) 869-5454
  police@saltilloms.com
- Sherman PD
- Chief Joel Spellins
  26 W. Lamar St.
  Sherman, MS 38869
  (662) 841-0079
  (See also Pontotoc & Union counties)
  shermanpolice@comcast.net
- Tupelo PD
- Chief Tony Carleton
  220 Front St. No.
  Tupelo, MS 38801
  (662) 841-6402
  tony.carleton@tupeloms.gov

Leflore County

- Greenwood PD
- Chief Henry Purnell
  406 Main St.
  Greenwood, MS 38930
  (662) 453-3311
  hpurnell@cityofgreenwood.org

Lincoln County

- Lincoln County SO
- Sheriff Steve Rushing
  215 Justice St. PO Box 587
  Brookhaven, MS 39601
  (601) 833-5231
  webmaster@43so.net
- Brookhaven PD
- Chief Arlustra *Pap* Henderson
  421 No. 3rd St.
  Brookhaven, MS 39601
  (601) 833-2424
  brookhaveninfo@brookhavenms.com

Lowndes County

- Columbus PD
- Chief Selvain McQueen
  115 6th St. No.
  Columbus, MS 39701
  (662) 244-3528
  smcqueen@columbusms.org

Madison County

- Canton PD
- Chief Vicki McNeil
  200 Park Dr.
  Canton, MS 39046
  (601) 859-2121
  mayortruly@yahoo.com
- Madison PD
- Chief M.E. *Gene* Waldrop
  2001 Main St. PO Box 2489
  Madison, MS 39110
  (601) 856-6111
  gwaldrop@madisonthecity.com
- Ridgeland PD
- Chief Jimmy Houston
  PO Box 875
  Ridgeland, MS 39158
  (601) 853-2014
  jimmy.houston@ridgelandms.org

Marion County

- Marion County SO
- Sheriff Berkley Hall
  219 Broad St.
  Columbia, MS 39429
  (601) 736-5051
  bhall@marioncountyms.com

Marshall County

- Byhalia PD
- Chief Gary Looney
  161 Hwy 309 So. PO Box 412
  Byhalia, MS 38611
  (662) 838-6000
  byhaliachieflooney@hotmail.com
- Holly Springs PD
- Chief Robert Pearson
  819 West St.
  Holly Springs, MS 38635
  (662) 252-2121
  Hollyspringspd@cji.net

Monroe County

- Monroe County SO
- Sheriff Cecil Cantrell
  So. Chestnut St. PO Box 683
  Aberdeen, MS 39730
  (662) 369-2468
  ccantrell@monroecoms.com
- Aberdeen PD
- Chief Henry Randle
  125 W. Commerce St.
  Aberdeen, MS 39730
  (662) 369-6454
  jbenson@ci.aberdeen.ms.us
- Amory PD
- Chief Ronnie Bowen
  200 So. Front St.
  Amory, MS 38821
  (662) 256-2676
  policechief@cityofamoryms.com
- Nettleton PD
- Chief Jackie Wimberley
  225 Main St.
  Nettleton, MS 38858
  (See also Lee County)
  (662) 963-1185
  NPD1@dixie-net.com
- Smithville PD
- Chief Darwin Hathcock
  63443 Hwy 25 No.
  Smithville, MS 38870
  (662) 651-4444
  tospd1@traceroad.net

Montgomery County

- Montgomery County SO
- Sheriff Jerry *Bubba* Nix, Jr.
  614 Summit PO Box 306
  Winona, MS 38967
  (662) 283-4612
  mcsd@uckwood.net

Neshoba County

- Neshoba County SD
- Sheriff Tommy G. Waddell
  401 Beacon St., Ste. 108
  Philadelphia, MS 39350
  (601) 656-7659
  sheriff@neshobacounty.net
- Philadelphia PD
- Chief Richard L. Sistrunk
  523 Main St.
  Philadelphia, MS 39350
  (601) 656-2131
  rsistrunk@philadelphiams.us

Noxubee County

- Macon PD
- Chief Petey Freshour
  105 W. Pulaski St. PO Box 29
  Macon, MS 39341
  (662) 726-5838
  pfreshour@cityofmacon.org

Oktibbeha County

- Oktibbeha County SO
- Sheriff Steve Gladney
  111 Dr. Douglas L. Connor Dr.
  Starkville, MS 39759
  (662) 323-2421
  general@sheriff.oktibbeha.ms.us
- Starkville PD
- Chief David Lindley
  101 Lampkin St.
  Starkville, MS 39759
  (662) 323-4134
  policechief@cityofstarkville.org

Panola County

- Panola County SO
- Sheriff Dennis L. Darby
  200 Broadway St. PO Box 273
  Batesville, MS 38606
  (662) 563-6230
  robbie@panola.com
- Batesville PD
- Chief William A. *Tony* Jones
  106 College St.
  Batesville, MS 38606
  (662) 563-5653
  batespd@panola.com

Pearl River County

- Pearl River County SO
- Sheriff David Allison
  200 Julia St.
  Poplarville, MS 39470
  (601) 403-2300
  comments@pearlrivercounty.net
- Picayune PD
- Chief Bryan Dawsey
  328 So. Main St.
  Picayune, MS 39466
  (601) 798-7411
  policechief@picayune.ms.us

Pike County

- Pike County SD
- Sheriff Mark Shepherd
  2109 Jessie Hall Memorial Rd.
  Magnolia, MS 39652
  (601) 783- 2327
  marks@co.pike.ms.us
- Magnolia PD
- Chief Ray Reynolds
  180 So. Cherry St.
  Magnolia, MS 39652
  (601) 783-5211
  cityofmagnoliams@bellsouth.net
- McComb PD
- Chief Gregory Martin
  501 Beech St.
  McComb, MS 39648
  (601) 684-6991
  wrawlings@mccomb-ms.gov
- Summit PD
- Chief Kenny Cotton
  706 Railroad Ave.
  Summit, MS 39666
  (601) 276-9511
  Kenny.cotton@us.army.mil

Pontotoc County

- Pontotoc County SO
- Sheriff Leo Mask
  490 Hwy 6th W. PO Box 240
  Pontotoc, MS 38863
  (662) 489-3915
  lmask@pontotoccoms.com
- Sherman PD
- Chief Joel Spellins
  26 W. Lamar St.
  Sherman, MS 38869
  (662) 841-0079
  (See also Lee & Union counties)
  shermanpolice@comcast.net

Prentiss County

- Prentiss County SD
- Sheriff Randy Tolar
  1901BE. Chambers Blvd
  Booneville, MS 38829
  (662) 728-6232
  info@prentisscountymssheriff.com

Quitman County

- Quitman County SD
- Sheriff Oliver Parker, Jr.
  233 Chestnut St. PO Box 365
  Marks, MS 38646
  (662) 326-3131
  oliverparker.qcone@yahoo.com

Rankin County

- Brandon PD
- Chief Ken McBroom
  1455 W. Government St.
  Brandon, MS 39042
  (601) 825-7225
  abean@ci.brandon.ms.us
- Florence PD
- Chief Richard Thomas
  203 College St. PO Box 187
  Florence, MS 39073
  (601) 845-8765
  police2@windstream.net
- Flowood PD
- Chief Johnny DeWitt
  2101 Airport Rd., Ste. B
  Flowood, MS 39208
  (601) 420-3368
  jdewitt@flowoodpd.com

Scott County

- Forest PD
- Chief Will Jones
  850 Park Rd.
  Forest, MS 39074
  (601) 469-4141
  forestpd@bellsouth.net

Sharkey County

- Sharkey County SO
- Sheriff Lindsey David Adams, Jr.
  120 Locust St.
  Rolling Fork, MS 39159
  (662) 873-4321
  sheriff@sharkeycountyms.gov
- Rolling Fork PD
- Chief Robert Taylor
  130 Walnut St.
  Rolling Fork, MS 39159
  (662) 873-2212
  chieftaylor@att.net

Simpson County

- Simpson County SD
- Sheriff Kenneth Lewis
  111 Pine Ave.
  Mendenhall, MS 39114
  (601) 847-2921
  info@simpsoncountysheriff.com
- Magee PD
- Chief Randy Crawford
  124 1st St. NE
  Magee, MS 39111
  (601) 849-2366
  rcrawford@mageepolice.com
- Mendenhall PD
- Chief Alexander *Candy* McCullum
  172 W. Maud Ave. PO Box 487
  Mendenhall, MS 39114
  (601) 847-2641
  info@ci.mendenhall.ms.us

Smith County

- Smith County SO
- Sheriff Charlie Crumpton
  200 Courthouse PO Box 307
  Raleigh, MS 39153
  (601) 782-4531
  astrausser@co.smith.ms.us

Stone County

- Stone County SD
- Sheriff Mike Farmer
  1420 Industrial Park Rd.
  Wiggins, MS 39577
  (601) 928-3191, ext. 13
  sheriffmfarmer@stonecountyms.gov
- Wiggins PD
- Chief Matt Barnett
  303 1st St.
  Wiggins, MS 39577
  (601) 928-5444
  POLICECHIEF@CITYOFWIGGINS.COM

Sunflower County

- Sunflower County SD
- Sheriff James Haywood
  1300 Allen Rd.
  Indianola, MS 38751
  (662) 887-2121
  x1811agentusdoj@aol.com
- Ruleville PD
- Chief Ernie L Scarber
  200 No. Chester Ave.
  Ruleville, MS 38771
  (662) 756-2793
  erniescarber@hotmail.com

Tate County

- Tate County SD
- Sheriff Brad Lance
  1 Justice Dr.
  Senatobia, MS 38668
  (662) 562-4434
  info@tatecountysheriff.com
- Senatobia PD
- Chief Steve Holts
  131 No. Front
  Senatobia, MS 38668
  (662) 562-5643
  sholts@cityofsenatobia.com

Tippah County

- Tippah County SD
- Sheriff Karl Gaillard
  205 W. Spring St.
  Ripley, MS 38663
  (662) 837-9336
  lesliemeeks@hotmail.com
- Ripley PD
- Chief Scott White
  604 So. Main
  Ripley, MS 38663
  (662) 837-2210
  ripleypd@dixie-net.com
- Walnut PD
- Chief Scott Jones
  621 Main St. PO Box 540
  Walnut, MS 38683
  (662) 223-4405
  walnutpolicedept@yahoo.com

Tishomingo County

- Tishomingo County SO
- Sheriff Glen Whitlock
  1208 Bettydale Dr.
  Iuka, MS 38852
  (662) 423-7000
  info@tishomingocountysheriff.com
- Belmont PD
- Chief Donald Reno
  Main St. PO Box 489
  Belmont, MS 38827
  (662) 454-3381
  www.hokismoki@yahoo.com
- Iuka PD
- Chief Randy Stringer
  118 So. Pearl St.
  Iuka, MS 38852
  (662) 423-6340
  iuka@bbimail.net

Tunica County

- Tunica County SD
- Sheriff K.C. Hamp
  5126 Old Moon Landing
  Tunica, Mississippi 38676
  (662) 363-1411
  info@tunicamssheriff.com

Union County

- New Albany PD
- Chief David Grisham
  110 E. Bankhead PO Box 54
  New Albany, MS 38652
  (662) 534-2222
  napolice@onecallinc.com
- Sherman PD
- Chief Joel Spellins
  26 W. Lamar St.
  Sherman, MS 38869
  (662) 841-0079
  (See also Lee & Pontotoc counties)
  shermanpolice@comcast.net

Walthall County

- Walthall County SO
- Sheriff Duane Dillon
  807 Magnolia Ave.
  Tylertown, MS 39667
  (601) 876-3481
  sheriffoffice@co.walthall.ms.us

Warren County

- DA's Office-9th District
- DA Gil Martin
  1009 Cherry St. PO Box 648
  Vicksburg, MS 39180
  (601) 636-5754
  da@msda9.com
- Vicksburg PD
- Chief Walter Armstrong
  810 Veto St.
  PO Box 150
  Vicksburg, MS 39180
  (601) 636-2511
  police@vicksburg.org

Washington County

- Washington County SO
- Sheriff Milton M. Gaston Sr.
  903 W. Alexander PO Box 786
  Greenville, MS 38701
  (662) 334-4523
  info@co.washington.ms.us

- Greenville PD
- Chief Freddie Cannon
  216 Main St.
  Greenville, MS 38701
  (662) 378-1531
  fcannon@greenvillems.org

Wayne County

- Wayne County SD
- Sheriff Darryl Woodson
  613 Court St.
  Waynesboro, MS 39367
  (601) 735-3801
  waynecounty6@yahoo.com
- Waynesboro PD
- Int. Chief James C. *Jimmy* Bunch
  714 Wayne St.
  Waynesboro, MS 39367
  (601) 735-3192
  waynesboropolice@cmaaccess.com

Wilkinson County

- Woodville PD
- Chief Calvin Gaines
  131 Courthouse PO Box 966
  Woodville, MS 39669
  (601) 888-4411
  woodvillepd@hotmail.com

Winston County

- Louisville PD
- Chief L. M. Claiborne, Jr.
  202 So. Church Ave.
  Louisville, MS 39339
  (662) 773-3511
  lclaiborne@winstoncounty.com

Yalobusha County

- Water Valley PD
- Chief M.W. King
  PO Box 231
  Water Valley, MS 38965
  (662) 473-2933
  wvpd@bellsouth.net

Yazoo County

- Yazoo City PD
- Chief Eric Snow
  305 Mike Espy Dr.
  Yazoo City, MS 39194
  (662) 746-1131, ext. 120
  snowwmannypd@yahoo.com

State Agencies

- MI HP-HQ
- Chief (*Col.*) Donnell Berry
  1900 E. Woodrow Wilson
  Jackson, MS 39216
  (601) 987-1212
  charper@dps.ms.gov
- MS Dept. of School Safety
- Dir. Robert Laird
  359 No. West St.
  Jackson, MS 39205
  (601) 359-1335
  rlaird@mde.k12.ms.us
- MS State U. PD
- Chief Georgia Lindley
  PO Box BJ
  Mississippi State, MS 39762
  (662) 325-1810
  georgia@saffairs.msstate.edu

NEW HAMPSHIRE

Belknap County

- Belknap County SO
- Sheriff Craig Wiggin
  42 County Dr.
  Laconia, NH 03246
  (603) 527-5454
  cwiggin@belknapcounty.org
- Alton PD
- Chief Ryan L. Heath
  15 Depot St.
  PO Box 240
  Alton, NH 03809
  (603) 875-3752
  police@alton.nh.gov
- Belmont PD
- Chief Mark Lewandoski
  15 Fuller St. PO Box 320
  Belmont, NH 03220
  (603) 267-8350
  PoliceChief@belmontnh.org
- Gilford PD
- Chief Kevin G. Keenan
  47 Cherry Valley Rd.
  Gilford, NH 03249
  (603) 527-4737
  k.keenan@gilfordpd.org
- Gilmanton PD
- Chief Joseph Collins
  297 NH Rt. 140 PO Box 190
  Gilmanton, NH 03837
  (603) 267-7401
  jcollins@gilmantonnh.org
- Laconia PD
- Chief Christopher A. *Chris* Adams
  126 New Salem St.
  Laconia, NH 03246
  (603) 524-5257, ext. 324
  CAdams@laconiapd.org
- Meredith PD
- Chief Kevin A. Morrow
  400 Daniel Webster PO Box 1366
  Meredith, NH 03253
  (603) 279-4561
  ktrue@meredithnh.org
- Sanbornton PD
- Chief Stephen Hankard
  565 Sanborn Rd.
  Sanbornton, NH 03269
  (603) 286-4323
  shankard@sanborntonpolice.org

Carroll County

- Bartlett PD
- Chief Timothy L. Connifey
  56 Town Hall Rd. Box 49
  Intervale, NH 03845
  (603) 356-5868
  townofbartlett@firstbridge.net
- Conway PD
- Chief Edward Wagner
  35 E. Conway Rd. PO Box 538
  Center Conway, NH 03813
  (603) 356-5715
  police@conwaypd.com
- Jackson PD
- Chief Karl Meyers
  54 Main St. Box 187
  Jackson, NH 03846
  (603) 383-9292
  jpd@jackson-nh.org
- Wakefield PD
- Chief Kenneth G. Fifield
  2017 Wakefield Rd.
  Sanbornville, NH 03872
  (603) 522-3232
  townadmin@wakefieldnh.com
- Wolfeboro PD
- Chief Stuart Chase
  251 So. Main St. PO Box 1689
  Wolfeboro, NH 03894
  (603) 569-1444
  schase@wolfeboropolice.org

Cheshire County

- Alstead PD
- Chief Marcello D'Allesandro
  15 Mechanic St. PO Box 60
  Alstead, NH 03602-0137
  (603) 835-6277
  TownofAlstead@comcast.net
- Dublin PD
- Chief James Letourneau
  1122 Main St. PO Box 283
  Dublin, NH 03444
  (603) 563-8411
  dublinpd81@townofdublin.org
- Jaffrey PD
- Chief William Oswalt
  26 Main St.
  Jaffrey, NH 03452
  (603) 532-7865
  oswaltw@townofjaffrey.com

- Keene PD
- Chief Kenneth J. Meola
  400 Marlboro St.
  Keene, NH 03431
  (603) 357-9815
  mayor@ci.keene.nh.us
- Marlborough PD
- Chief Christopher J. Lyons
  236 E. Main St.
  Marlborough, NH 03455
  (603) 876-3311
  cjlyons@marlboroughnh.org
- Surry PD
- Chief Gerald Clark
  1 Village Rd.
  Surry, NH 03431
  (603) 355-2000
  selectmen@townofsurry.org
- Troy PD
- Chief Howard M. Sheats, Jr.
  PO Box 597
  Troy, NH 03465
  (603) 242-7992
  troypolice@myfairpoint.net
- Winchester PD
- Chief Gary A. Phillips
  6 Parker
  Winchester, NH 03470
  (603) 239-4814
  gaphillips@winchester.nh.gov

Coos County

- Coos County SO
- Sheriff Gerald P. Marcou, Jr.
  55 School St., Ste. 102
  Lancaster, NH 03584
  (603) 788-5598
  gerald.marcou@cooscountynh.us
- Colebrook PD
- Chief Stephen Cass
  17 Bridge St.
  Colebrook, NH 03576
  (603) 237-4487
  colebrookpd@myfairpoint.net
- Gorham PD
- Chief P.J. Cyr
  20 Park St.
  Gorham, NH 03581
  (603) 466-3336
  pcyr@gorhamnh.org
- Lancaster PD
- Chief William H. Colborn
  11 Mechanic St.
  Lancaster, NH 03584
  (603) 788-4402
  police@lancasternh.org

Grafton County

- Grafton County SO
- Sheriff Douglas R. Dutile
  3785 Dartmouth College Hwy
  North Haverhill, NH 03774
  (603) 787-6911
  ddutile@co.grafton.nh.us
- Ashland PD
- Chief Anthony Randall
  20 Highland St. PO Box 885
  Ashland, NH 03217
  (603) 968- 4000
  trandall@ashland.nh.gov
- Benton PD
- Chief Stefan Cimikowski
  221 Coventry Rd.
  Benton, NH 03785-6112
  (603) 787-6911
  BentonNHPolice@nhecwb.com
- Bristol PD
- Chief Michael Lewis
  230 Lake St. PO Box 543
  Bristol, NH 03222
  (603) 744-6320
  bpd@townofbristolnh.org
- Canaan PD
- Chief Samuel Frank
  52 Rt. 118 PO Box 38
  Canaan, NH 03741
  (603) 523-7400
  sfrank@canaanpolice.com
- Enfield PD
- Chief Richard Crate Jr.
  19 Main St. PO Box 365
  Enfield, NH 03748
  (603) 632-7501
  rcrate@enfield.nh.us
- Groton PD
- Chief Joseph Pivirotto
  632 No. Groton Rd.
  Groton, NH 03241
  (603) 744-3703
  police@grotonnh.org

- Hanover PD
- Chief Nicholas J. Giaccone, Jr.
  46 Lyme Rd.
  Hanover, NH 03755
  (603) 643-2222
  policechief@hanovernh.org
- Lebanon PD
- Int. Chief Gary J. Smith
  36 Poverty Ln.
  Lebanon, NH 03766
  (603) 448-1212
  gary.smith@lebcity.com
- Lincoln PD
- Chief Theodore P. Smith
  148 Main St. PO Box 488
  Lincoln, NH 03251
  (603) 745- 2238
  tpsmith@roadrunner.com
- Lisbon PD
- Chief T. Joseph Tavernier
  46 School St. PO Box 222
  Lisbon, NH 03585
  (603) 838-6712
  lisbonpd@roadrunner.com
- Littleton PD
- Chief Paul J. Smith
  2 Kittridge Ln.
  Littleton, NH 03561
  (603) 444-7711
  info@littletonpd.org
- North Haverhill PD
- Chief Byron Charles
  2975 Dartmouth College Hwy
  North Haverhill, NH 03774
  (603) 787-2222
  hpd@haverhill-nh.com
- Orford PD
- Chief Christopher Kilmer
  2529 Rte. 25A
  Orford, NH 03777
  (603) 353-4252
  townclerk@orfordnh.us
- Plymouth PD
- Chief Stephen Lefebvre
  334 Main St.
  Plymouth, NH 03264
  (603) 536-1804, ext. 103
  slefebvre@plymouth.edu

Hillsborough County

- Hillsborough County SO
- Sheriff James A. Hardy
  329 Mast Rd.
  Goffstown, NH 03101
  (603) 247-8000
  hcso@hcso.tampa.fl.us
- Amherst PD
- Chief Mark O. Reams
  175 Amherst St. PO Box 703
  Amherst, NH 03031
  (603) 673-4900
  ndemers@amherstnh.gov
- Antrim PD
- Chief Scott Lester
  66 Main St. PO Box 517
  Antrim, NH 03440
  (603) 588-6613
  antrimatc@tds.net
- Bedford PD
- Chief John J. Bryfonski
  55 Constitution Dr.
  Bedford, NH 03110
  (603) 472-5113
  jbryfonski@bedfordnh.org
- Goffstown PD
- Chief Patrick Sullivan
  326 Mast Rd.
  Goffstown, NH 03045
  (603) 497-4858
  cball@goffstownnh.gov
- Hillsboro PD
- Chief David Roarick
  22 Municipal Dr. PO Box 1489
  Hillsboro, NH 03244
  (603) 464-5512
  debbie@hillsboroughnh.net
- Hollis PD
- Chief James Sartell
  9 Silver Lake Rd.
  Hollis, NH 03049
  (603) 465-7637
  police@hollisnh.org
- Hudson PD
- Chief Jason Lavoie
  1 Constitution Dr.
  Hudson, NH 03051
  (603) 886-6011
  jlavoie@hudsonnh.gov

- Litchfield PD
- Chief Joseph E. O'Brion, Jr.
  2 Liberty Way
  Litchfield, NH 03052
  (603) 424-4047
  chief@litchfieldpd.com
- Manchester PD
- Chief David J. Mara
  405 Valley St.
  Manchester, NH 03101
  (603) 668-8711
  dmara@manchesternh.gov
- Merrimack PD
- Chief Mark E. Doyle
  31 Baboosic Lake Rd.
  Merrimack, NH 03054
  (603) 424-3774
  policedept@merrimacknh.gov
- Milford PD
- Chief Michael *Mike* Viola
  19 Garden St.
  Milford, NH 03055
  (603) 249-0630
  mviola@milford.nh.gov
- Nashua PD
- Chief Steven Marshall
  0 Panther Dr. PO Box 785
  Nashua, NH 03061-0785
  (603) 594-3500
  NashuaMayor@NashuaNH.gov
- Pelham PD
- Chief Joseph A. Roark
  14 Village Green
  Pelham, NH 03076
  (603) 635-2411
  jroark@pelhampolice.com
- Peterborough PD
- Chief Scott Guinard
  73 Grove St.
  Peterborough, NH 03458
  (603) 924-8050
  police@townofpeterborough.us
- Temple-Greenville PD
- Chief James McTague
  38 Main St. PO Box 478
  Temple, NH 03084
  (603) 878-3474
  TempleBOS@comcast.net
- Wilton PD
- Chief Brent D. Hautanen
  7 Burns Hill Rd. PO Box 183
  Wilton, NH 03086
  (603) 654-9452
  tips@wiltonnhpd.com

Merrimack County

- Merrimack County SO
- Sheriff Scott Hilliard
  333 Daniel Webster Hwy
  Boscawen, NH 03303
  (603) 796-6600
  shilliard@mcso.net
- Concord PD
- Chief John F. Duval
  35 Green St.
  Concord, NH 03301
  (603) 225-8600
  jduval@concordpolice.com
- Franklin PD
- Chief David B. Goldstein
  5 Hancock Terrace
  Franklin, NH 03235
  (603) 934-2535
  dgoldstein@franklinnh.org
- Henniker PD
- Chief Ryan Murdough
  340 Western Ave.
  Henniker, NH 03242
  (603) 428-3213
  hennikerpd@conknet.com
- Hooksett PD
- Chief Peter Bartlett
  15 Legends Dr.
  Hooksett, NH 03106
  (603) 624-1560
  pbartlett@hooksettpolice.org
- Loudon PD
- Chief Robert N. Fiske
  8 Cooper St. PO Box 7059
  Loudon, NH 03307
  (603) 798-5521
  chieffiske@loudonpolice.com
- Pembroke PD
- Chief Dwayne Gilman
  247 Pembroke St.
  Pembroke, NH 03275
  (603) 485-9173, ext. 2204
  dgilman@pembroke-nh.com

- Pittsfield PD
- Chief Robert Wharem
  59 Main St. PO Box 98
  Pittsfield, NH 03263
  (603) 435-7535, ext. 11
  pittsfieldpd@metrocast.net
- Warner PD
- Chief William Chandler
  180 W. Main St PO Box 268
  Warner, NH 03278
  (603) 456-3433
  tbuskey@warner.nh.us

Rockingham County

- Rockingham County SO
- Sheriff Michael Downing
  101 North Rd.
  Brentwood, NH 03833
  (603) 679-2241
  mdowning@rockso.org
- Auburn PD
- Chief Edward Picard
  PO Box 339
  Auburn, NH 03032
  (603) 483-2134
  Chiefpicard@comcast.net
- Brentwood PD
- Chief Wayne Robinson
  1 Dalton Rd.
  Brentwood, NH 03833
  (603) 642-6400
  police@brentwood.town-center.org
- Deerfield PD
- Chief Michael Greeley
  8 Raymond Rd. PO Box 357
  Deerfield, NH 03037
  (603) 463-7258
  dfldpdchief@townofdeerfieldnh.com
- Derry PD
- Chief Edward B. Garone
  1 Municipal Dr.
  Derry, NH 03038
  (603) 432-6111
  egarone@derrynhpolice.com
- Epping PD
- Chief Michael Wallace
  37 Pleasant St.
  Epping, NH 03042
  (603) 679-5122
  m.wallace@eppingpd.com
- Exeter PD
- Chief Richard Kane
  20 Court St.
  Exeter, NH 03833
  (603) 772-1212
  rkane@town.exeter.nh.us
- Hampstead PD
- Chief Joseph A. Beaudoin, Jr.
  16 Emerson Ave. PO Box 540
  Hampstead, NH 03841
  (603) 329-5700
  j_beaudoin281@hotmail.com
- Londonderry PD
- Chief William R. Hart
  268A Mammoth Rd.
  Londonderry, NH 03053
  (603) 432-1118
  whart@londonderrynh.org
- New Castle PD
- Chief Donald A. White, Jr.
  49 Main St. PO Box 367
  New Castle, NH 03854
  (603) 436-3800
  chief.white@police.newcastlenh.org
- New Hampton PD
- Chief Merritt D. Salmon
  24 Intervale Dr.
  Hampton, NH 03256
  (603) 744-5423
  msalmon@new-hampton.nh.us
- Newmarket PD
- Chief Kevin P. Cyr
  70 Exeter St.
  Newmarket, NH 03857
  (603) 659-6636
  lsims@newmovarketnh.gov
- North Hampton PD
- Chief Brian P. Page
  233 Atlantic Ave. PO Box 575
  North Hampton, NH 03862
  (603) 964-8621
  bpage@northhampton-nh.gov
- Plaistow PD
- Chief Stephen C. Savage
  27 Elm St.
  Plaistow, NH 03865
  (603) 382-1200
  policedepartment@plaistow.com

- Portsmouth PD
- Chief Stephen DuBois
  3 Junkins Ave.
  Portsmouth, NH 03801
  (603) 427-1500
  info@pd.cityofportsmouth.com
- Raymond PD
- Chief David T. Salois
  1 Scribner Rd.
  Raymond, NH 03077
  (603) 895-4747
  dsalois@raymondnh.gov
- Rye PD
- Chief Kevin Walsh
  555 Washington Rd.
  Rye, NH 03870
  (603) 964-7450
  kwalsh@town.rye.nh.us
- Salem PD
- Chief Paul T. Donovan
  9 Veterans Memorial Pkwy
  Salem, NH 03079
  (603) 893-1911
  pdonovan@salempd.com
- Seabrook PD
- Chief Lee Bitomske
  7 Liberty Ln.
  Seabrook, NH 03874
  (603) 474-5200
  headquarters@seabrookpd.com
- South Hampton PD
- Chief Robert Donovan, Sr.
  128 Main Ave. PO Box 220
  East Kingston, NH 03827
  (603) 394-0105, ext. 109
  info@sohamptonpd.com
- Windham PD
- Chief Gerald Lewis
  4 Fellows Rd.
  Windham, NH 03087
  (603) 434-5577
  glewis@windhampd.com

Strafford County

- Dover PD
- Chief Anthony F. Colarusso, Jr.
  46 Locust St.
  Dover, NH 03820
  (603) 742-4646
  a.colarusso@dover.nh.gov
- Durham PD
- Chief David Kurz
  86 Dover Rd.
  Durham, NH 03824
  (603) 868-2324
  police@ci.durham.nh.us
- Farmington PD
- Chief Kevin Willey
  531 Main St.
  Farmington, NH 03835
  (603) 755-2731
  kwilley@farmingtonpd.com
- Lee PD
- Chief Chester Murch
  20 George Bennett Rd.
  Lee, NH 03824
  (603) 659-5866
  cmurch@leenhpolice.org
- Milton PD
- Chief Mark McGowan
  7 Townhouse Rd.
  Milton, NH 03851
  (603) 652-4514
  mmcgowan@miltonnhpd.com
- Rochester PD
- Chief Michael Allen
  23 Wakefield St.
  Rochester, NH 03867
  (603) 330-7127
  christopher.cost@rochesternh.net
- Rollinsford PD
- Chief Robert Ducharme
  667 Main St.
  Rollinsford, NH 03869
  (603) 742-8549, ext. 303
  rducharme@rollinsfordpolice.org
- Somersworth PD
- Chief Dean Crombie
  12 Lilac Ln.
  Somersworth, NH 03878
  (603) 692-3131
  dcrombie@somersworth.com

Sullivan County

- Sullivan County SO
- Sheriff Michael L. Prozzo, Jr.
  14 Main St. PO Box 27
  Newport, NH 03773
  (603) 863-4200
  sheriff@sullivancountynh.gov

- Charlestown PD
- Chief Edward Smith
  2 Claremont Rd. PO Box 1465
  Charlestown, NH 03603
  (603) 826-5747
  chief@charlestownpd.com
- Claremont PD
- Chief Alexander Scott
  58 Opera House Sq.
  Claremont, NH 03743
  (603) 542-9538
  ascott@claremontnh.com
- Newport PD
- Chief James C. Burroughs
  59 Main St.
  Newport, NH 03773
  (603) 863-3240
  policechief@newportnh.net
- Washington PD
- Chief Steven I. Marshall
  5 Halfmoon Pond Rd.
  Washington, NH 03280
  Ph: (603) 495-3294
  smarshall@washingtonnh.org

State Agencies

- NH Dept. of Safety
- Comm. John J. Barthelmes
  33 Hazen Dr.
  Concord, NH 03305
  Ph: (603) 223-3889
  john.barthelmes@dos.nh.gov

NEW JERSEY

Atlantic County

- Atlantic County SO
- Sheriff Frank X. Balles
  5903 Main St.
  Mays Landing, NJ 08330
  (609) 625-2276
  balles_frank@aclink.org
- Absecon PD
- Chief David K. Risley
  500 No. Mill Rd.
  Absecon, NJ 08201
  (609) 641-0667
  info@absecon-newjersey.org
- Atlantic City PD
- Chief Ernest Jubilee
  2715 Atlantic Ave.
  Atlantic City, NJ 08401
  (609) 347-5780
  webmaster@cityofatlanticcity.org
- Egg Harbor City PD
- Chief John McColgan
  500 London Ave.
  Egg Harbor City, NJ 08215
  (609) 965-2901
  megs@eggharborcity.org
- Hamilton Twp PD
- Chief Stacy Tappeiner
  6101 13th St.
  Mays Landing, NJ 08330
  (609) 625-2211
  HTPD.Chief@townshipofhamilton.com
- Linwood PD
- Chief Robert James
  400 Poplar Ave.
  Linwood, NJ 08221
  (609) 926-7978
  rjames@linwoodpolicedepartment.org
- Longport PD
- Chief Vince Pacentrilli
  2305 Atlantic Ave.
  Longport, NJ 08403
  (609) 822-2141
  hewitt_william@longportpd.org
- Mullica Twp PD
- Chief John Thompson
  4528 White Horse PO Box 317
  Elwood, NJ 08217
  (609) 561-7600, ext. 127
  pregister@mullicatownship.org
- Somers Point PD
- Chief Michael F. Boyd
  1 W. New Jersey Ave.
  Somers Point, NJ 08244
  (609) 927-6161
  Mboyd@somerspointpd.org
- Ventnor City PD
- Chief Michael S. Miller
  6201 Atlantic Ave.
  Ventnor City, NJ 08406
  (609) 822-2101
  vcpd@police.ventnorcity.org

Bergen County

- Alpine PD
- Act. Chief Christopher Belcolle
  100 Church St.
  Alpine, NJ 07620
  (201) 784-2910
  cbelcolle@alpinenj.org
- Bergenfield PD
- Chief Michael T. Carr
  198 No. Washington Ave.
  Bergenfield, NJ 07621
  (201) 387-4000
  mcarr@bergenfieldnjpd.org
- Bogota PD
- Chief John C. Burke
  375 Larch Ave.
  Bogota, NJ 07603
  (201) 487-2400
  jburke@bogotapolice.org
- Carlstadt PD
- Chief Thomas Nielsen
  500 Madison St.
  Carlstadt, NJ 07072
  (201) 438-4300
  tnielsen@carlstadtpolice.org
- Closter PD
- Chief Dennis Kaine
  295 Old Closter Dock Rd.
  Closter, NJ 07624
  (201) 768-5000
  boroadmin@closterboro.com
- Cresskill PD
- Chief Edward Wrixon
  67 Union Ave.
  Cresskill, NJ 07626
  (201) 568-1400
  EWrixon@cresskillpd.org

- Demarest PD
- Chief James Powderley III
  118 Serpentine Rd.
  Demarest, NJ 07627
  (201) 768-0167, ext. 18
  chief@demarestpd.org
- Dumont PD
- Chief Joseph L. Faulborn, Jr.
  50 Washington Ave.
  Dumont, NJ 07628
  (201) 387-5000
  chiefvenezio@dumontpolice.org
- East Rutherford PD
- Chief Larry Minda
  312 Grove St.
  East Rutherford, NJ 07073
  (201) 438-0167
  Police@erpd.org
- Edgewater PD
- Chief William Skidmore
  916 River Rd.
  Edgewater, NJ 07020
  (201) 943-2200, ext. 2112
  skidmore@edgewaternj.org
- Elmwood Park PD
- Chief Thomas Johnson
  182 Market St.
  Elmwood Park, NJ 07407
  (201) 796-0700
  kkazmark@elmwoodparknj.us
- Englewood PD
- Chief Arthur O'Keefe
  75 So. Van Brunt St.
  Englewood, NJ 07631
  (201) 568-2711
  aokeefe@cityofenglewood.org
- Englewood Cliffs PD
- Chief Michael Cioffi
  10 Kahn Terrace
  Englewood Cliffs, NJ 07632
  (201) 569-8300
  mcioffi@ecpolice.org
- Fairview PD
- Chief Frank Del Vecchio
  59 Anderson Ave.
  Fairview, NJ 07022
  (201) 943-2100
  info@fairviewpd.com
- Fort Lee PD
- Chief Keith M. Bendul
  1327 16th St.
  Fort Lee, NJ 07024-1949
  (201) 592-3700
  mayor@fortleenj.org
- Glen Rock PD
- Chief Frederick P. Stahman
  1 Harding Plaza
  Glen Rock, NJ 07452
  (201) 652-3800
  fstahman@glenrockpolice.com
- Hackensack PD
- Dir. Mike Mordaga
  225 State St.
  Hackensack, NJ 07601
  (201) 646-7777
  director@hackensackpd.org
- Ho-Ho-Kus PD
- Chief John Wannamaker
  55 Sycamore Ave.
  Ho-Ho-Kus, NJ 07423
  (201) 652-1700
  HHKPDWebsite@aol.com
- Little Ferry PD
- Chief Ralph C. Verdi
  215-217 Liberty St.
  Little Ferry, NJ 07643
  (201) 641-2770
  policedepartment@littleferrypd.org
- Lodi PD
- Chief Vincent J. Caruso
  1 Memorial Dr.
  Lodi, NJ 07644
  (973) 473-7600, ext. 117
  vcaruso@lodipd.org
- Mahwah PD
- Chief James N. Batelli
  221 Franklin Turnpike
  Mahwah, NJ 07430
  (201) 529-1000, ext. 200
  chief@mahwahpd.org
- Maywood PD
- Chief David T. Pegg
  15 Park Ave.
  Maywood, NJ 07607
  (201) 845-8800
  dpegg@maywoodpd.org

- Midland Park PD
- Act. Chief Michael Marra
  280 Godwin Ave.
  Midland Park, NJ 07432
  (201) 444-2300
  chief@mpnj.com
- Montvale PD
- Chief Jeremy Abrams
  12 Mercedes Dr.
  Montvale, NJ 07645
  (201) 391-4600, ext. 501
  montvalepd@montvale.org
- New Milford PD
- Chief Frank Papapietro
  930 River Rd.
  New Milford, NJ 07646
  (201) 261-1400
  fpapapietro@newmilfordboro.com
- Northvale PD
- Chief Vincent St. Angelo
  116 Paris Ave.
  Northvale, NJ 07647
  (201) 768-5900
  policechief@boroughofnorthvale.com
- Norwood PD
- Chief Jeffrey Krapels
  453 Broadway
  Norwood, NJ 07648
  (201) 768-0850
  lmcmackin@norwoodboro.org
- Oakland PD
- Chief Edward Kasper
  295 Ramapo Valley Rd.
  Oakland, NJ 07436
  (201) 337-6171
  oaklndpd@optonline.net
- Old Tappan PD
- Chief Thomas Shine
  21 Russell Ave.
  Old Tappan, NJ 07675
  (201) 664-1221
  policechief@oldtappan.net
- Oradell PD
- Chief Frank P. Florio
  355 Kinderkamack Rd.
  Oradell, NJ 07649
  (201) 261-0200
  fflorio@oradellpolice.org
- Paramus PD
- Chief Christopher Brock
  1 Carlough Dr.
  Paramus, NJ 07652
  (201) 262-3400, ext. 540
  chief@paramuspolice.org
- Park Ridge PD
- Chief Joseph J. Madden
  33 Park Ave.
  Park Ridge, NJ 07656
  (201) 391-5400
  Chief@parkridgepolice.com
- Ridgefield PD
- Chief Thomas J. Gallagher
  604 Broad Ave.
  Ridgefield, NJ 07657
  (201) 941-6207
  info@ridgefieldpolice.com
- Ridgewood PD
- Chief John Ward
  131 No. Maple Ave.
  Ridgewood, NJ 07450
  (201) 652-3900
  jward@ridgewoodnj.net
- River Edge PD
- Chief Tom Cariddi
  705 Kinderkamack Rd.
  River Edge, NJ 07661
  (201) 262-1233
  Police@RiverEdgePolice.org
- Saddle Brook PD
- Chief Robert J. Kugler
  63 Market St.
  Saddle Brook, NJ 07663
  (201) 843-7000
  chief@saddlebrookpd.com
- Saddle River PD
- Chief Timothy McWilliams
  83 E. Allendale Rd.
  Saddle River, NJ 07458
  (201) 327-5300
  tmcwilliams@saddleriverpd.com
- South Hackensack PD
- Chief Michael D. Frew
  227 Phillips Ave.
  South Hackensack, NJ 07606
  (201) 440-0042
  policechief@southhackensacknj.org

- Tenafly PD
- Chief Robert Chamberlain
  100 Riveredge Rd.
  Tenafly, NJ 07670
  (201) 568-5100
  rchamberlain@tenafly.net
- Upper Saddle River PD
- Chief Patrick A. Rotella
  368 W. Saddle River Rd.
  Upper Saddle River, NJ 07458
  (201) 327-2700
  police@usrpd.net
- Westwood PD
- Chief Frank Regino
  101 Washington Ave.
  Westwood, NJ 07675
  (201) 664-7000
  fregino@westwoodnj.gov
- Wyckoff PD
- Chief Benjamin C. Fox
  340 Franklin Ave.
  Wyckoff, NJ 07481
  (201) 891-2121
  wyckoffwebteam@wyckoff-nj.com

Burlington County

- Bordentown PD
- Chief Matthew J. Simmons III
  324 Farnsworth Ave.
  Bordentown, NJ 08505
  (609) 298-0103
  chiefsimmons@cityofbordentown.com
- Burlington PD
- Chief Anthony J. Wallace
  435 Veterans Dr.
  Burlington, NJ 08016
  (609) 386-0200, ext. 205
  awallace@burlingtonnj.us
- Chesterfield Twp PD
- Chief Kyle Wilson
  300 Bordentown-Chesterfield Rd.
  Trenton, NJ 08620
  (609) 291-0912
  chesterfieldpolice@comcast.net
- Cinnaminson Twp PD
- Dir. Michael King
  900 Manor Rd.
  Cinnaminson, NJ 08077
  (856) 829-6667
  info@cinnaminsonnj.org
- Delanco Twp PD
- Chief Jesse DeSanto
  515 Burlington Ave.
  Delanco Twp, NJ 08075
  (856) 461-0357, ext. 287
  jdesanto@delancotownship.com
- Eastampton Twp PD
- Chief Chris Muraglia
  725 Smithville Rd.
  Eastampton, NJ 08060
  (609) 261-1717
  cmuraglia@eastamptonpolicenj.us
- Evesham Twp PD
- Chief Michael Barth
  984 Tuckerton Rd.
  Marlton, NJ 08053
  (856) 983-1117
  facebook@eveshampd.org
- Lumberton Twp PD
- Chief Tony DiLoreto
  35 Municipal Dr.
  Lumberton, NJ 08048
  (609) 267-1111
  tdiloreto@lumbertontwp.com
- Mansfield Twp PD
- Chief Ronald Mulhall
  190-A Atlantic PO Box 177
  Columbus, NJ 08022
  (609) 723-8300
  mulhall@mansfieldpd.org
- Maple Shade Twp PD
- Chief Gary Gubbei
  200 Stiles Ave.
  Maple Shade, NJ 08052
  (856) 234-8300
  glavenia@mapleshade.com
- Medford Lakes PD
- Chief Stephen A. Carbone
  1 Cabin Circle Dr.
  Medford Lakes, NJ 08055
  (609) 654-2156
  scarbone@medfordlakespolice.org
- Moorestown Twp PD
- Dir. Harry E. Johnson
  1245 No. Church St., Ste 2
  Moorestown, NJ 08057
  (856) 914-3034
  hjohnson@moorestownpd.com

- Mt. Holly Twp PD
- Dir. Steven E. Martin
  23 Washington St.
  Mt. Holly, NJ 08060
  (609) 845-1150
  smartin@mountholly.info
- North Hanover Twp PD
- Chief Mark Keubler
  41 Schoolhouse Rd.
  North Hanover, NJ 08562
  (609) 758-2522, ext. 217
  mkeubler@northhanovertwp.com
- Palmyra PD
- Chief Scott Pearlman
  20 W. Broad St.
  Palmyra, NJ 08065
  (856) 829-0198
  police@boroughofpalmyra.com
- Pemberton Borough PD
- Chief Ed Hunter
  50 Egbert St.
  Pemberton, NJ 08068
  (609) 894-2632
  dist19@co.burlington.nj.us
- Pemberton Twp PD
- Chief David H. Jantas
  500 Pemberton Browns Mills Rd.
  Pemberton, NJ 08068
  (609) 894-3308
  djantas@pembertonpolice.com
- Riverside PD
- Chief Paul Tursi
  237 So. Pavilion Ave.
  Riverside, NJ 08075
  (856) 461-8820
  lorimhatch@gmail.com
- Riverton PD
- Chief John B. Shaw
  501 5th St.
  Riverton, NJ 08077
  (856) 829-1212
  jshaw@riverton-police.com
- Springfield Twp PD
- Chief John Cook
  100 Mountain Ave.
  Springfield, NJ 07081-1729
  (973) 376- 0400
  John.Cook@springfield-nj.us

Camden County

- Camden County SO
- Sheriff Charles H. Billingham
  520 Market St. PO Box 769
  Camden, NJ 08102
  (856) 225-5470
  sheriff@camdencounty.com
- Audubon PD
- Chief Thomas J. Tassi
  606 W. Nicholson Rd.
  Audubon, NJ 08106
  (856) 547-1171
  info@audubopd.com
- Barrington PD
- Chief Joe Eisenhardt
  227 Trenton Ave.
  Barrington, NJ 08007
  (856) 547-0028
  jeisenhardt@barringtonboro.com
- Brooklawn PD
- Chief Francis McKinney
  301 Christiana St.
  Brooklawn, NJ 08030
  (856) 456-0750, ext. 110
  chief@brooklawnpolice.com
- Collingswood PD
- Chief Richard J. Sarlo
  735 No. Atlantic Ave.
  Collingswood, NJ 08108
  (856) 854- 1901, ext. 224
  rsarlo@collingswood.com
- Gibbsboro PD
- Chief Joseph Mingori
  5 Foster Ave.
  Gibbsboro, NJ 08026
  (856) 783-0900
  gibbypd@comcast.net
- Gloucester City PD
- Chief George Berglund
  313 Monmouth St.
  Gloucester City, NJ 08030
  (856) 456-0408
  gberglund@gloucesterpolice.com
- Gloucester Twp PD
- Chief W. Harry Earle
  1261 Chews Landing Clementon Rd.
  Blackwood, NJ 08012
  (856) 228-4011
  police@gtpolice.com

- Haddon Heights PD
- Chief Richard Kinkler
  625 Station Ave.
  Haddon Heights, NJ 08035
  (856) 547-0613
  rkinkler@haddonhts.com
- Haddon Twp PD
- Chief Mark Cavallo
  135 Haddon Ave.
  Westmont, NJ 08108
  (856) 854-1176
  wschwartz@haddontwppolice.com
- Haddonfield PD
- Chief John Banning
  242 Kings Hwy E.
  Haddonfield, NJ 08033
  (856) 429-4700, ext. 250
  dbennett@haddonfield-nj.gov
- Laurel Springs PD
- Chief Carmen Rabottino
  723 W. Atlantic Ave.
  Laurel Springs, NJ 08021
  (856) 783-2887
  police@laurelsprings-nj.com
- Lawnside PD
- Sgt. William Plenty
  4 Douglas Ave.
  Lawnside, NJ 08045
  (856) 573-6205
  plenty2101@yahoo.com
- Magnolia PD
- Chief John Evans
  438 W. Evesham Ave.
  Magnolia, NJ 08049
  (856) 784-1884
  jkeenan@magnolia-nj.org
- Merchantville PD
- Chief Wayne Bauer
  1 W. Maple Ave.
  Merchantville, NJ 08109
  (856) 662-0507
  policechief@merchantvillenj.gov
- Mt. Ephraim PD
- Chief Brian Beppel
  121 So. Black Horse Pike
  Mt. Ephraim, NJ 08059
  (856) 931-2225
  bbeppel@mountephraimpd.com
- Pine Hill PD
- Chief Christopher J. Winters
  48 W. 6th Ave.
  Pine Hill, NJ 08021
  (856) 783-1549
  cwinters@pinehillpd.com
- Somerdale PD
- Chief Anthony Campbell
  105 Kennedy Blvd
  Somerdale, NJ 08083
  (856) 428-6324
  somerdalepolice@somerdale-nj.com
- Waterford Twp PD
- Chief John W. Knoll
  2131 Auburn Ave.
  Atco, NJ 08004
  (856) 767-2134, ext. 200
  police@wtpd.org
- Winslow Twp PD
- Act. Chief Robert Stimelski
  125 So. Rt. 73
  Hammonton, NJ 08037
  (609) 567-0700, ext. 1997
  rstimelski@winslowpd.com

Cape May County

- Cape May County SO
- Sheriff Gary G. Schaffer
  501 Cape May
  Cape May, NJ 08210
  (609) 465-1233
  sheriff@cmcsheriff.net
- Avalon PD
- Chief William McCormick
  3000 Dune Dr.
  Avalon, NJ 08202
  (609) 967-3411
  wmccormick@avalonboro.org
- Lower Twp PD
- Chief Brian Marker
  405 Breakwater Rd.
  Erma, NJ 08204
  (609) 886-1619, ext. 114
  Marker@lowertownshippolice.com
- Sea Isle City PD
- Chief Thomas J. D'Intino
  245 46th St.
  Sea Isle City, NJ 08243
  (609) 263-4311
  tdintino@police.seaislecitynj.us

- Stone Harbor PD
- Chief Paul Reynolds
  9508 2nd Ave.
  Stone Harbor, NJ 08247
  (609) 368-1455
  shpd@police.stone-harbor.nj.us
- Wildwood PD
- Chief Steven Long
  4400 New Jersey Ave.
  Wildwood, NJ 08260
  (609) 522-0222
  contact@wildwoodpd.com
- Wildwood Crest PD
- Chief Thomas DePaul
  6101 Pacific Ave.
  Wildwood Crest, NJ 08260
  (609) 522-2456
  tdepaul@wildwoodcrestpolice.org

Cumberland County

- Millville PD
- Chief Thomas Haas
  18 So. High St.
  Millville, NJ 08332
  (856) 825-3111
  millpd@millvillepd.com
- Vineland PD
- Chief Timothy Codispoti
  111 No. 6th St.
  Vineland, NJ 08360
  (856) 691-4111
  vpd@vinelandcity.org

Essex County

- Essex County SO
- Sheriff Armando B. Fontoura
  50 W. Market St.
  Newark, NJ 07102
  (973) 621-4105
  crimestoppers@essexsheriff.com
- Belleville PD
- Chief Joseph P. Rotonda
  152 Washington Ave.
  Belleville, NJ 07109
  (973) 450-3334
  jrotonda@bellevillenj.org
- Bloomfield Twp PD
- Chief Christopher Goul
  1 Municipal Plaza
  Bloomfield, NJ 07003
  (973) 680-4149
  policechief@bloomfieldnjpd.com
- East Orange PD
- Chief William Robinson
  15 So. Munn Ave.
  East Orange, NJ 07017
  (973) 266-5000
  wrobinson@njeopd.com
- Essex County Coll. PD
- Chief Anthony Cromartie
  303 University Ave.
  Newark, NJ 07102
  (973) 877-1873
  police@essex.edu
- Essex Fells PD
- Chief Vincent Kulik
  255 Roseland Ave.
  Essex Fells, NJ 07021
  (973) 226-3000
  vkulik@essexfellspd.org
- Fairfield PD
- Chief Charles G. Voelker, Jr
  230 Fairfield Rd.
  Fairfield, NJ 07004
  (973) 227-1400
  cvoelker@fairfieldnj.org
- Millburn Twp PD
- Chief Gregory G. Weber
  435 Essex St.
  Millburn, NJ 07041
  (973) 564-7001
  policedept@millburntwp.org
- North Caldwell PD
- Chief Mark A. Deuer
  136 Gould Ave.
  North Caldwell, NJ 07006
  (973) 226-0800
  ncpolice@northcaldwell.net
- Orange Twp PD
- Act. Dir. Hakim Sims
  29 Park St.
  Orange Twp, NJ 07050
  (973) 266-4111, ext. 5003
  william@ci.orange.nj.us
- Verona PD
- Chief Douglas J. Huber
  600 Bloomfield Ave.
  Verona, NJ 07044
  (973) 857-4814
  info@veronapolice.org

- West Orange PD
- Chief James P. Abbott
  60 Main St.
  West Orange, NJ 07052
  (973) 325-4030
  policechief@westorange.org

Gloucester County

- Gloucester County SO
- Sheriff Carmel M. Morina
  2 So. Broad St. PO Box 337
  Woodbury, NJ 08096
  (856) 384-6900
  cmorina@co.gloucester.nj.us
- Deptford Twp PD
- Chief Daniel Murphy
  1011 Cooper St.
  Deptford, NJ 08096
  (856) 845-6440
  dmurphy@deptford-nj.org
- Greenwich Twp PD
- Chief Joseph M. Giordano, Jr.
  421 W. Broad St.
  Gibbstown, NJ 08026
  (856) 423-1900
  jgiordano@greenwichpd.com
- Mantua Twp PD
- Chief: Rodney J. Sawyer
  405 Main St.
  Mantua, NJ 08051
  (856) 468-1920
  mantuapd@mantuatownship.com
- Pitman PD
- Chief Robert T. Zimmerman
  110 So. Broadway
  Pitman, NJ 08071
  (856) 589-3501
  chief@pitman.org
- South Harrison Twp PD
- Chief Nicholas Priore
  664 Harrisonville Rd.
  Harrisonville, NJ 08039
  (856) 769-8149
  npriore@southharrison-nj.org
- Washington Twp PD
- Chief Rafael Munoz
  1 McClure Dr.
  Sewell, NJ 08080
  (856) 589-6664
  chiefrmuniz@pd.twp.washington.nj.us
- West Deptford Twp PD
- Chief Craig Mangano
  400 Crown Point Rd.
  Thorofare, NJ 08086
  (856) 845-4004, ext. 157
  manganoc06@westdeptford.com
- Woodbury PD
- Chief Reed A. Merinuk
  200 No. Broad St.
  Woodbury, NJ 08096
  (856) 845-0065
  rmerinuk@woodburypd.com
- Woodbury Heights PD
- Chief George Lindsay
  500 Elm Ave. PO Box 44
  Woodbury Heights, NJ 08097
  (856) 848-6707
  glindsay@whpdnj.com
- Woolwich Twp PD
- Chief Russell H. Marino
  120 Village Green Dr.
  Woolwich Twp, NJ 08085
  (856) 467-1667, ext. 1125
  rmarino@woolwichtwp.org

Hudson County

- Hudson County SO
- Sheriff Frank Schillari
  595 Newark Ave.
  Jersey City, NJ 07306
  (201) 369-4330
  fschillari@hcnj.us
- Hoboken PD
- Dir. Jon Tooke
  One Police Plaza
  Hoboken, NJ 07030
  (201) 420-2245
  jtooke@hobokennj.org
- Kearny PD
- Chief John Dowie
  237 Laurel Ave.
  Kearny, NJ 07032
  (201) 998-1410
  jdowie@kearnynjpd.org
- North Bergen PD
- Chief Robert J. Dowd
  4233 Kennedy Blvd
  North Bergen, NJ 07047
  (201) 392-2100
  info@northbergenpd.com

- Secaucus PD
- Chief Dennis Corcoran
  1203 Paterson Plank Rd.
  Secaucus, NJ 07094
  (201) 330-2060
  dcorcoran@secaucus.net

Hunterdon County

- Hunterdon County SO
- Sheriff Frederick W. *Fred* Brown
  8 Court St. PO Box 2900
  Flemington, NJ 08822
  (908) 788-1166
  fbrown@co.hunterdon.nj.us
- Califon PD
- Chief Michael Bailey
  1 E. Springtown Rd.
  Long Valley, NJ 07830
  (908) 876-3232
  leidsvaag@califonboro.net
- Clinton Twp PD
- Dir. Robert Manney
  1370 Rt. 31 No.
  Annandale, NJ 08801
  (908) 735-6000, ext. 249
  rmanney@ctpd.org
- Flemington PD
- Chief George A. Becker
  100 Main St.
  Flemington, NJ 08822
  (908) 782-3434, ext. 225
  gbecker@flemingtonpd.org
- Frenchtown PD
- Chief Al Kurylka
  2nd St. PO Box 68
  Frenchtown, NJ 08825
  (908) 996-4820
  frenchtownpolice@yahoo.com
- Holland Twp PD
- Chief John D. Harris, Jr.
  61 Church Rd.
  Milford, NJ 08848
  (908) 995-2804
  tips@hollandpolice.org
- Lebanon Twp PD
- Chief Chris J. Mattson
  530 W. Hill Rd.
  Glen Gardner, NJ 08826
  (908) 638-8516
  lebanontwppolice@comcast.net
- Raritan Twp PD
- Chief Glenn S. Tabasko
  2 Municipal Dr.
  Flemington, NJ 08822
  (908) 782-8889, ext. 3317
  gtabasko@comcast.net
- Readington Twp PD
- Chief Sebastian Donaruma
  507 Rt. 523
  Whitehouse Station, NJ 08889
  (908) 534-4031, ext. 222
  Chiefofpolice@readingtonpolice.org
- Tewksbury Twp PD
- Chief Thomas Holmes
  167 Old Turnpike Rd.
  Califon, NJ 07830
  (908) 439-3477
  jmduhamel@tewksburytwp.net

Mercer County

- East Windsor Twp PD
- Chief James Monahan
  80 One Mile Rd.
  East Windsor, NJ 08520
  (609) 448-5678, ext. 237
  monahan@ewpd.com
- Ewing Twp PD
- Chief John P. Stemler III
  Jake Garzio Dr.
  Trenton, NJ 08628
  (609) 882-1313, ext. 7537
  policeadmin@ewingnj.org
- Hamilton Twp PD
- Chief James W. Collins
  1270 White Horse Ave.
  Hamilton, NJ 08619
  (609) 581-4044
  mayor@hamiltonnj.com
- Hopewell Twp PD
- Chief George C. Meyer
  201 Washington Crossing Pennington Rd.
  Titusville, NJ 08560
  (609) 737-3100
  gmeyer@hopewelltwp.org
- Lawrence Twp PD
- Chief Daniel A. Posluszny
  2207 Lawrenceville
  PO Box 6006
  Lawrenceville, NJ 08648
  (609) 896-1111
  lawrencepolice@lawrencetwp.com

- Pennington PD
- Dir. William Meytrott
  30 No. Main St.
  Pennington, NJ 08534
  (609) 737-2020
  sfriedman@penningtonboro.org
- Princeton Twp PD
- Chief David Dudeck
  1 Valley Rd.
  Princeton, NJ 08542
  (609) 921-2100
  ddudeck@princetonnj.gov
- West Windsor Twp PD
- Chief Joseph M. Pica, Jr.
  20 Municipal Dr.
  West Windsor, NJ 08520
  (609) 799-1222
  pica@westwindsorpolice.com

Middlesex County

- Middlesex County SO
- Sheriff Mildred S. Scott
  701 Livingston Ave.
  New Brunswick, NJ 08901
  (732) 745-3381
  sheriff@co.middlesex.nj.us
- Carteret PD
- Chief John Pieczyski
  230 Roosevelt Ave.
  Carteret, NJ 07008
  (732) 541-4181
  pieczyskij@carteret.net
- Cranbury PD
- Chief Rickey A. Varga
  1 Logan Dr.
  Cranbury, NJ 08512
  (609) 395-0031
  dmarabello@cranbury-nj.com
- Dunellen PD
- Chief Jeffrey Nelson
  355 North Ave.
  Dunellen, NJ 08812
  (732) 968-3000
  JNELSON@DUNELLENPD.COM
- Edison PD
- Chief Thomas Bryan
  100 Municipal Blvd
  Edison, NJ 08817
  (732) 248-7367
  tbryan@edisonpd.org
- Helmetta PD
- Chief Gregory Bennett
  51 Main St.
  Spotswood, NJ 08884-1233
  (732) 521-0386, ext. 121
  g.bennett@helmettaboro.com
- Highland Park PD
- Chief Stephen Rizco
  222 So. 5th Ave.
  Highland Park, NJ 08904
  (732) 572-3800
  srizco@hpboro.com
- Jamesburg PD
- Chief Martin Horvath
  131 Perrineville Rd.
  Jamesburg, NJ 08831
  (732) 521-0011, ext. 205
  mhorvath@jamesburgborough.org
- North Brunswick PD
- Dir. Ken McCormick
  710 Hermann Rd.
  North Brunswick, NJ 08902
  (732) 247-0922, ext. 400
  kmccor@northbrunswicknj.gov
- Old Bridge Twp PD
- Chief William A. Volkert
  1 Old Bridge Plaza
  Old Bridge Twp, NJ 08857
  (732) 721-5600, ext. 3412
  police@oldbridge.com
- Plainsboro PD
- Chief Guy Armour
  641 Plainsboro Rd.
  Plainsboro, NJ 08536
  (609) 799-2333, ext. 1607
  dmercier@plainsboropolice.com
- South Amboy PD
- Chief Darren Lavigne
  140 No. Broadway
  South Amboy, NJ 08879
  (732) 329-4000
  lavigned@southamboynj.gov
- South Brunswick Twp PD
- Chief Raymond J. Hayducka
  1 Police Plaza
  Monmouth Junction, NJ 08852
  (732) 329-4000, ext. 7461
  rhayduck@sbtnj.net

- South Plainfield PD
- Chief James Parker
  2480 Plainfield Ave.
  South Plainfield, NJ 07080
  (908) 755-0700
  jparker@southplainfieldnj.com
- South River PD
- Chief Mark Tinitigan
  61 Main St.
  South River, NJ 08882
  (732) 254-1150, ext. 108
  poconnor@southrivernj.org

Monmouth County

- Aberdeen Twp PD
- Chief John T. Powers
  1 Aberdeen Sq.
  Matawan, NJ 07747
  (732) 566-2054
  john.powers@aberdeennj.org
- Allenhurst PD
- Chief Robert C. Richter
  125 Corlies Ave.
  Allenhurst, NJ 07711
  (732) 531-2255
  chiefrichter@allenhurstnj.org
- Avon By The Sea PD
- Chief Terence Mahon
  301 Main St.
  Avon By The Sea, NJ 07717
  (732) 502-4500
  tmahon@avonpd.org
- Belmar PD
- Chief Thomas Palmisano
  601 Main St.
  Belmar, NJ 07719
  (732) 681-1700
  tpalmisano@belmarpd.com
- Brielle PD
- Chief Michael W. Palmer
  601 Union Ln.
  Brielle, NJ 08730
  (732) 528-5050
  townhall@brielleboro.com
- Colts Neck Twp PD
- Chief Kevin A. Sauter
  124 Cedar Dr.
  Colts Neck Twp, NJ 07722
  (732) 780-7323
  coltsnecknj@gmail.com
- Eatontown PD
- Chief Michael D. Goldfarb
  47 Broad St.
  Eatontown, NJ 07724
  (732) 542-0100
  chief@eatontownnj.com
- Englishtown Borough PD
- Lt. Peter S. Cooke, Jr.
  15 Main St.
  Englishtown Borough, NJ 07726
  (732) 446-7001, ext. 30
  pcooke@englishtownnj.com
- Fair Haven PD
- Chief Darryl G. Breckenridge, Sr.
  35 Fisk St.
  Fair Haven, NJ 07704
  (732) 747-0991
  dbreckenridge@fhboro.net
- Freehold Borough PD
- Chief Glenn Roberts
  36-38 Jackson St.
  Freehold, NJ 07728
  (732) 462-1233
  freeholdboropd@aol.com
- Freehold Twp PD
- Chief Ernest Schriefer
  1 Municipal Plaza
  Freehold, NJ 07728
  (732) 462-7908
  ftpd@twp.freehold.nj.us
- Holmdel Twp PD
- Chief John Mioduszewski
  4 Crawfords Corner Rd.
  Holmdel Twp, NJ 07733
  (732) 946-4400
  jmiod@holmdelpolice.org
- Howell Twp PD
- Chief Ronald T. Carter
  300 Old Tavern Rd.
  Howell Twp, NJ 07731
  (732) 938-4575, ext. 2813
  akudrick@howellpolice.org
- Interlaken PD
- Chief Stephen R. Carasia
  100 Grassmere Ave.
  Asbury Park, NJ 07712
  (732) 531-3688
  dmcdonald@interlakenboro.com

- Keyport PD
- Chief George Casaletto
  70 W. Front St.
  Keyport, NJ 07735
  (732) 264-0706
  mayoraumack@keyportonline.com
- Lake Como Borough PD
- Chief Fred Hope
  1740 Main St. PO Box 569
  Lake Como, NJ 07719
  (732) 681-3081
  fhope@boro.lake-como.nj.us
- Little Silver PD
- Chief Daniel Shaffery
  480 Prospect Ave.
  Little Silver, NJ 07739
  (732) 747-5900
  bobneff80@gmail.com
- Manalapan Twp PD
- Chief Christopher Marsala
  120 Rt. 522
  Manalapan, NJ 07726
  (732) 446-4300
  jmorrell@manalapanpolice.org
- Manasquan PD
- Chief Elliott Correia
  201 E. Main St.
  Manasquan, NJ 08736
  (732) 223-0544
  jdeiorio@manasquan-nj.com
- Matawan Borough PD
- Chief James M. Alston
  150 Main St.
  Matawan, NJ 07747
  (732) 290-2030
  administration@matawanpolice.org
- Monmouth Beach PD
- Chief Drew Winans
  14 Willow Ave.
  Monmouth Beach, NJ 07750
  (732) 229-1313
  mbpd07750@comcast.net
- Neptune City PD
- Dir. Edward D. Kirschenbaum, Sr.
  106 W. Sylvania Ave.
  Neptune City, NJ 07753
  (732) 775-1615
  Ekirschenbaum@neptunecitypolice.org
- Neptune Twp PD
- Chief Robert H. Adams
  25 Neptune Blvd
  Neptune, NJ 07753
  (732) 988-8000, ext. 402
  radams@neptunetownship.org
- Oceanport PD
- Chief Harold W. Sutton
  222 Monmouth Blvd
  Oceanport, NJ 07757
  (732) 222-6301
  policedepartment@oceanportboro.com
- Red Bank PD
- Chief Stephen G. McCarthy
  90 Monmouth St.
  Red Bank, NJ 07701
  (732) 530-2710
  pborghi@redbanknj.org
- Rumson PD
- Chief Scott A. Paterson
  80 E. River Rd.
  Rumson, NJ 07760
  (732) 842-3300
  info@rumsonnj.gov
- Sea Bright PD
- Chief John Sorrentino
  1099 E. Ocean Ave.
  Sea Bright, NJ 07760
  (732) 842-0010
  mayordinalong@gmail.com
- Sea Girt Borough PD
- Chief Robert P. Conway
  319 Baltimore PO Box 22
  Sea Girt, NJ 08750
  (732) 449-7300
  rconway@seagirtpd.net
- Shrewsbury PD
- Chief Louis G. Ferraro
  419 Sycamore PO Box 221
  Shrewsbury, NJ 07702
  (732) 741-2500
  lferraro@shrewsburyboro.com
- Spring Lake PD
- Chief Edward M. Kerr, Jr.
  311 Washington Ave.
  Spring Lake, NJ 07762
  (732) 449-1234, ext. 165
  ekerr@springlakeboro.org

- Spring Lake Heights PD
- Chief David Petriken
  555 Brighton Ave.
  Spring Lake, NJ 07762
  (732) 449-6161
  dpetriken@springlakehts.com
- Tinton Falls PD
- Chief John A. Scrivanic
  556 Tinton Ave.
  Tinton Falls, NJ 07724
  (732) 542-4422, ext. 275
  boroughcouncil@tintonfalls.com
- Union Beach PD
- Chief Scott Woolley
  650 Poole Ave.
  Union Beach, NJ 07735
  (732) 264-0313
  pauljsmithjr@optonline.net
- Wall Twp PD
- Chief Robert Brice
  2700 Allaire Rd.
  Wall Twp, NJ 07719
  (732) 449-4500
  jbertrand@townshipofwall.com
- West Long Branch PD
- Chief Lawrence L. Mihlon
  95 Poplar Ave.
  West Long Branch, NJ 07764
  (732) 229-5000
  lmihlon@westlongbranch.org

Morris County

- Morris County SO
- Sheriff Edward V. Rochford
  PO Box 900
  Morristown, NJ 07963
  (973) 285-6600
  erochford@co.morris.nj.us
- Boonton PD
- Chief David J. Mayhood
  100 Washington St.
  Boonton, NJ 07005
  (973) 402-9371
  sjones45@boontonpolice.org
- Boonton Twp PD
- Chief Paul C. Fortunato
  155 Powerville Rd.
  Boonton, NJ 07005
  (973) 402-4000
  pfortunato@btpolice.org
- Chatham Borough PD
- Chief Philip J. Crosson, Jr.
  54 Fairmount Ave.
  Chatham Borough, NJ 07928
  (973) 635-8000
  police@chathamborough.org
- Chatham Twp PD
- Chief Steven E. Hennelly
  401 Southern Blvd
  Chatham, NJ 07928
  (973) 377-0100
  shennelly@ctpd.net
- Chester Borough PD
- Chief Andre Kedrowitsch
  50 North Rd.
  Chester Borough, NJ 07930
  (908) 879-5626
  akedrowitsch@chesterborough.org
- Chester Twp PD
- Chief Wayne A. Martini
  1 Parker Rd.
  Chester Twp, NJ 07930
  (908) 879-5514
  mayorbill@chestertownship.org
- Denville PD
- Chief Christopher Wagner
  1 St. Mary's Pl.
  Denville, NJ 07834
  (973) 627-4900, ext. 330
  cwagner@denvillepolice.org
- Dover PD
- Chief Harold P. Valentine
  37 No. Sussex St.
  Dover, NJ 07801
  (973) 366-0302
  jdodd@dover.nj.us
- Drew U. DPS
- Chief Robert C. Lucid
  36 Madison Ave.
  Madison, NJ 07940
  (973) 408-3378
  rlucid@drew.edu
- East Hanover Twp PD
- Chief Stanley J. Hansen
  2 DeForest Ave.
  East Hanover Twp, NJ 07936
  (973) 887-0432
  shansen@ehpolice.com

- Florham Park PD
- Chief Patrick P. Montuore
  111 Ridgedale Ave.
  Florham Park, NJ 07932
  (973) 377-2200
  dammirato@florhamparkboro.net
- Hanover Twp PD
- Chief Stephen W. Gallagher
  1000 Rt. #10 PO Box 250
  Whippany, NJ 07981
  (973) 428-2512
  info@hanovertownship.com
- Jefferson Twp PD
- Chief Kevin M. Craig
  1033 Weldon Rd.
  Lake Hopatcong, NJ 07849
  (973) 208-6151
  kcraig@jeffersonpolice.com
- Kinnelon Borough PD
- Chief John G. Finkle
  130 Kinnelon Rd.
  Kinnelon, NJ 07405
  (973) 838-5400
  Chief@kinnelonboro.org
- Lincoln Park PD
- Chief Mark West
  34 Chapel Hill Rd.
  Lincoln Park, NJ 07035
  (973) 694-6100, ext. 2512
  MayorRunfeldt@bolp.org
- Longhill Twp PD
- Chief Dan Hedden
  264 Mercer St.
  Stirling, NJ 07980
  (908) 647-1800, ext. 228
  dhedden@longhillpolice.us
- Mendham Borough PD
- Chief Pasquale G. Libertino
  3 Cold Hill Rd. So.
  Mendham Borough, NJ 07945
  (973) 543-2545, ext. 11
  chieflibertino@mendhamnj.org
- Mendham Twp PD
- Chief Steven Crawford
  3 Cherry Ln.
  Brookside, NJ 07926
  (973) 543-2581
  scrawford@mendhamtownship.org
- Morris Plains PD
- Chief Scott Thompson
  531 Speedwell Ave.
  Morris Plains, NJ 07950
  (973) 538-2284, ext. 105
  sthompson@morrisplainsboro.org
- Morris Twp PD
- Chief John K. McGuinness
  49 Woodland Ave.
  Morris Twp, NJ 07960
  (973) 326-7470
  jmcguinness@mtpd1422.com
- Morristown Humane L.E.
- Chief Peter Demnitz
  200 South St.
  Morristown, NJ 07963-0914
  (973) 292-6731
  info@morristownhle.org
- Morristown PD
- Chief Peter Demnitz
  200 South St.
  Morristown, NJ 07963
  (973) 292-6655
  p-demnitz@morristownpolice.org
- Mountain Lakes PD
- Chief Shawn Bennett
  400 Blvd
  Mountain Lakes, NJ 07046
  (973) 334-1413
  borohall@mtnlakes.org
- Mt. Olive Twp PD
- Chief Mark Spitzer
  204 Flanders Drakestown Rd.
  Budd Lake, NJ 07828
  (973) 691-0900, ext. 7450
  mspitzer@mopd.org
- Pequannock Twp PD
- Chief Brian C. Spring
  530 Newark-Pompton Turnpike
  Pompton Plains, NJ 07444
  (973) 835-1700, ext. 142
  bspring@peqtwp.org
- Randolph PD
- Chief Robert Mason
  502 Millbrook Ave.
  Randolph, NJ 07869
  (973) 989-7014
  RMason@RandolphNJ.org

- Riverdale PD
- Chief Kevin Smith
  91 Newark-Pompton Turnpike
  Riverdale, NJ 07457
  (973) 835-0034
  gkeil@riverdalepd.org
- Rockaway Borough PD
- Chief Douglas Scheer
  33 Maple Ave.
  Rockaway Borough, NJ 07866
  (973) 627-1314
  boroughclerk@rockawayborough.org

Ocean County

- Ocean County SO
- Sheriff William T. Sommeling
  120 Hooper Ave.
  Toms River, NJ 08754
  (732) 929-2044
  wsommeling@co.ocean.nj.us
- Barnegat Twp PD
- Chief Arthur P. Drexler
  900 W. Bay Ave.
  Barnegat, NJ 08005
  (609) 698-5000
  chief@barnegat.net
- Beachwood PD
- Chief Robert Tapp
  1600 Pinewald Rd.
  Beachwood, NJ 08722
  (732) 341-1249
  beachwoodpolice@beachwoodusa.com
- Berkeley Twp PD
- Chief Karin DiMichele
  631 Pinewald-Keswick Rd.
  Bayville, NJ 08721
  (732) 341-1132
  dimichele@btpdnj.org
- Brick Twp PD
- Chief Nils *Rick* Bergquist
  401 Chambers Bridge Rd.
  Brick, NJ 08723
  (732) 262-1100
  mayor@twp.brick.nj.us
- Harvey Cedars PD
- Chief Thomas Preiser
  7606 Long Beach Blvd
  Harvey Cedars, NJ 08008
  (609) 494-6509
  police@harveycedars.org
- Island Heights PD
- Act. Chief (*Lt.*) Kevin C. Arnold
  1 E. End Ave. PO Box 177
  Island Heights, NJ 08732
  (732) 270-3000
  CouncilMemberSilver@islandheightsboro.com
- Jackson Twp PD
- Chief Matthew Kunz
  102 Jackson Dr.
  Jackson, NJ 08527
  (732) 928-1111
  mkunz@jacksontwpnj.net
- Lacey Twp PD
- Chief David A. Paprota, Ed.D.
  808 W. Lacey Rd.
  Forked River, NJ 08731
  (609) 693-6636
  laceypolice@laceytownship.org
- Lakehurst PD
- Chief Eric S. Higgins
  5 Union Ave.
  Lakehurst, NJ 08733
  (732) 657-7811
  ehiggins@lakehurstpolice.org
- Little Egg Harbor PD
- Chief Richard J. Buzby Jr.
  665 Radio Rd.
  Little Egg Harbor, NJ 08087
  (609) 296-3666
  rbuzby@lehpolice.com
- Mantoloking PD
- Chief Mark A. Wright
  202 Downer Ave. PO Box 247
  Mantoloking, NJ 08738
  (732) 295-1401
  policeservices@mantoloking.org
- Ocean Gate PD
- Chief Reece J. Fisher
  801 Ocean Gate Ave.
  Ocean Gate, NJ 08740
  (732) 269-6931, ext. 24
  ocinfo@co.ocean.nj.us
- Plumsted Twp PD
- Chief Matthew Petrecca
  2 Cedar St.
  New Egypt, NJ 08533
  (609) 758-3738
  PTPD@VERIZON.NET

- Point Pleasant Beach PD
- Chief Kevin R. O'Hara
  416 New Jersey Ave.
  Point Pleasant Beach, NJ 08742
  (732) 892-0500
  policeinfo@pointbeach.org
- Seaside Heights PD
- Chief Thomas Boyd
  116 Sherman Ave.
  Seaside Heights, NJ 08751
  (732) 793-1800
  Administrator@seaside-heightsnj.org
- South Toms River PD
- Chief Andrew Izatt
  144 Mill St.
  South Toms River, NJ 08757
  (732) 349-0313
  webmaster@strpd.com
- Stafford Twp PD
- Chief Joseph Giberson
  260 E. Bay Ave.
  Manahawkin, NJ 08050
  (609) 242-9675
  JGiberson@staffordpolice.org
- Surf City PD
- Chief William Z. Collins
  813 Long Beach Blvd
  Surf City, NJ 08008
  (609) 494-8121
  surfcitypolice@comcast.net
- Tuckerton PD
- Chief Michael Caputo
  445 So. Green St.
  Tuckerton, NJ 08087
  (609) 296-9416
  tuckertonpd@shorenetworks.com

Passaic County

- Passaic County SD
- Sheriff Richard H. Berdnik
  77 Hamilton St.
  Paterson, NJ 07509
  (973) 881-4200
  bmaer@pcsheriff.org
- Bloomingdale PD
- Chief Joseph Borell
  101 Hamburg Turnpike
  Bloomingdale, NJ 07403
  (973) 838-0158
  jdunleavy@bloomingdalenj.net
- Hawthorne PD
- Chief Richard McAuliffe
  445 Lafayette Ave.
  Hawthorne, NJ 07506
  (973) 427-1800
  rmcauliffe@hawthornepdnj.org
- Little Falls PD
- Chief John Dmuchowski
  35 Stevens Ave.
  Little Falls, NJ 07424
  (973) 256-0200
  chief@littlefallspd.org
- North Haledon PD
- Chief Robert Bracco
  103 Overlook Ave.
  North Haledon, NJ 07508
  (973) 423-1111
  relatab@northhaledon.com
- Passaic PD
- Chief Richard Diaz
  330 Passaic St.
  Passaic, NJ 07055
  (973) 365-3958
  info-police@cityofpassaicnj.gov
- Pompton Lakes PD
- Chief Moises Agosto
  25 Lenox Ave.
  Pompton Lakes, NJ 07442
  (973) 835-0400, ext. 246
  magosto@pomptonlakespolice.org
- Prospect Park PD
- Chief Charbel Atie
  106 Brown Ave.
  Prospect Park, NJ 07508
  (973) 790-7900
  cheifatie@prospectpark.net
- Ringwood Borough PD
- Chief Bernie Lombardo
  60 Margaret King Ave.
  Ringwood Borough, NJ 07456
  (973) 962-7017
  mayor@ringwoodnj.net
- Totowa PD
- Chief Robert Coyle
  537 Totowa Rd.
  Totowa, NJ 07512
  (973) 790-3700
  RCoyle@totowapd.org

- West Milford Twp PD
- Chief Timothy Storbeck
  1480 Union Valley Rd.
  West Milford Twp, NJ 07480
  (973) 728-2817
  PoliceChief@WestMilford.org

Salem County

- Salem County SO
- Sheriff Charles M. *Chuck* Miller
  94 Market St.
  Salem, NJ 08079
  (856) 935-7510
  helpdesk@salemcountynj.gov
- Elmer PD
- Chief Patrick Bryan, Jr.
  120 So. Main St.
  Elmer, NJ 08318
  (856) 358-3355
  lubElmer@comcast.net
- Pennsville PD
- Chief Bruce Maahs
  90 No. Broadway
  Pennsville, NJ 08070
  (856) 678-3089, ext. 581
  pvpdchief@pvtwp.com

Somerset County

- Somerset County SO
- Sheriff Frank J. Provenzano
  20 Grove St.
  Somerville, NJ 08876
  (908) 231-7140
  tindle@co.somerset.nj.us
- Bernards Twp PD
- Chief Brian Bobowicz
  One Collyer Ln.
  Basking Ridge, NJ 07920
  (908) 766-1122
  bbobowicz@bernardspd.org
- Bernardsville PD
- Chief Kevin J. Valentine
  166 Minebrook PO Box 158
  Bernardsville, NJ 07924
  (908) 766-0037, ext. 134
  police@bernardsvillepd.org
- Bridgewater Twp PD
- Chief Richard J. Borden
  100 Commons Way
  Bridgewater, NJ 08807
  (908).722-4111
  rborden@bridgewaterpd.com
- Hillsborough Twp PD
- Chief Paul A. Kaminsky
  379 So. Branch Rd.
  Hillsborough Twp, NJ 08844
  (908) 369-4323
  chiefkaminsky@hillsboroughpolice.org
- Manville PD
- Chief Mark A. Peltack
  2 No. Main St.
  Manville, NJ 08835
  (908) 725-1900
  contactus@manvillepd.org
- Montgomery Twp PD
- Dir. Robert E. Palmer
  2261 Van Horne Rd., Rt. 206 No.
  Belle Mead, NJ 08502
  (908) 359-2311
  rpalmer@police.montgomery.nj.us
- Somerville PD
- Chief Dennis Fanning
  24 So. Bridge St.
  Somerville, NJ 08876
  (908) 725-0331
  info@somervillepd.org
- South Bound Brook PD
- Chief William King
  12 Main St.
  South Bound Brook, NJ 08880
  (732) 356-0087
  Pkaminsky@southboundbrook.com
- Warren Twp PD
- Chief Russell W. Leffert
  44 Mountain Blvd
  Warren, NJ 07059
  (908) 753-1146
  rleffert@warrenpolice.com
- Watchung PD
- Chief Timothy Wenzel
  840 Somerset St.
  Watchung, NJ 07069
  (908) 756-3663
  TWenzel@WatchungPD.com

Sussex County

- Sussex County SO
- Sheriff Michael F. *Mike* Strada
  39 High St.
  Newton, NJ 07860
  (973) 579-08504
  hmanser@sussexcountysheriff.com

- Byram Twp PD
- Chief Raymond F. Rafferty
  10 Mansfield Dr.
  Stanhope, NJ 07874
  (973) 347-4008
  rrafferty@byrampd.org
- Franklin Borough PD
- Chief Eugene McInerney
  15 Corkhill Rd.
  Franklin Borough, NJ 07416
  (973) 827-7700, ext. 4
  emcinerney@franklinpd.org
- Hardystone Twp PD
- Chief Bret Alemy
  149 B Wheatsworth Rd.
  Hamburg, NJ 07419
  (973) 823-7022
  police@hardyston.com
- Hopatcong PD
- Chief Robert *Bob* Brennan
  111 River Styx Rd.
  Hopatcong, NJ 07843
  (973) 398-5000
  bbrennan@hopatcongpolice.org
- Newton PD
- Chief Michael S. Richards
  39 Trinity St.
  Newton, NJ 07860
  (973) 383-2525
  MRichards@newtonpolice.org
- Sparta Twp PD
- Chief Ernest Reigstad
  65 Main St.
  Sparta Twp, NJ 07871
  (973) 729-6121
  mary.coe@spartanj.org
- Stanhope Borough PD
- Chief Steven Pittigher
  77 Main St.
  Stanhope, NJ 07874
  (973) 347-4533
  bmcneilly@stanhopenj.gov

Union County

- Union County SO
- Sheriff Ralph Froehlich
  2 Broad St.
  Elizabeth, NJ 07207
  (908) 527-4450
  rfroehlich@ucnj.org
- Cranford PD
- Chief Eric G. Mason
  8 Springfield Ave.
  Cranford, NJ 07016
  (908) 272-2222
  police@cranfordnj.org
- Garwood PD
- Chief Bruce D. Underhill
  403 South Ave.
  Garwood, NJ 07027
  (908) 789-1666
  garwood@garwood.org
- Hillside PD
- Chief Louis Panarese
  140 Liberty Ave.
  Hillside, NJ 07205
  (973) 926-5800
  info@hillsidepolice.org
- Linden Auxiliary PD
- Chief Hugo Baeza
  301 No. Wood Ave.
  Linden, NJ 07036
  (908) 474-8500
  lapdnj@lindenauxiliarypolice.org
- Linden PD
- Chief James M. Schulhafer
  301 No. Wood Ave.
  Linden, NJ 07036
  (908) 474-8500
  rbanks@linden-nj.org
- Mountainside PD
- Chief James J. Debbie, Jr.
  1385 US Hwy 22 E.
  Mountainside, NJ 07092
  (908) 232-8100
  jdebbie@mountainside-nj.com
- Roselle PD
- Chief Gerard Orlando
  210 Chestnut St.
  Roselle, NJ 07203
  (908) 245-2000
  gorlando@rosellepd.com
- Roselle Park PD
- Chief Paul Morrison
  110 E. Westfield Ave.
  Roselle Park, NJ 07204
  (908) 245-2300
  pmorrison@rosellepark.net

- Scotch Plains PD
- Chief Brian T. Mahoney
  430 Park Ave.
  Scotch Plains, NJ 07076
  (908) 322-7100
  dluce@scotchplainsnj.com
- Springfield PD
- Chief John Cook
  100 Mountain Ave.
  Springfield, NJ 07081
  (973) 376-0400
  John.Cook@springfield-nj.us
- Summit PD
- Chief Robert Weck
  512 Springfield Ave.
  Summit, NJ 07901
  (908) 273-0051
  rweck@cityofsummit.org
- Union County PD
- Chief Daniel Vaniska
  300 North Ave. E. PO Box 2673
  Westfield, NJ 07090
  (908) 654-9800
  ucpd@ucnj.org
- Westfield PD
- Chief David Wayman
  425 E. Broad St.
  Westfield, NJ 07090
  (908) 789-4000
  police@wpdnj.org

Warren County

- Warren County SO
- Sheriff David P. Gallant
  413 2nd St.
  Belvidere, NJ 07823
  (908) 475-6309
  dgallant@co.warren.nj.us
- Belvidere PD
- Chief Robert R Yeisley
  691 Water St.
  Belvidere, NJ 07823
  (908) 475-2429
  clerk@belvidere-nj.us
- Hackettstown PD
- Chief James A. Macaulay
  215 Stiger St.
  Hackettstown, NJ 07840
  (908) 852-3302
  hpd29@hackettstownpd.net
- Lopatcong Twp PD
- Chief Scott Marinelli
  232 So. 3rd St.
  Phillipsburg, NJ 08865
  (201) 859-3355
  marinellis@lopatcongtwp.com
- Phillipsburg PD
- Chief James Faulborn
  675 Corliss Ave.
  Phillipsburg, NJ 08865
  (908) 454-1121
  police@pburg.org

State Agencies

- NJ State Police
- Supt. (*Col.*) Joseph R. *Rick* Fuentes
  PO Box 7068
  West Trenton, NJ 08628
  609-882-2000
  lppwiltp@gw.njsp.org
- Palisades Inter. Pkwy PD
- Chief John J. Parr
  PO Box 155
  Alpine, NJ 07620
  (201) 768-6001
  mail@njpalisades.org

NEW YORK

Albany County

- Albany County SO
- Sheriff Craig Apple
  16 Eagle St.
  Albany, NY 12207
  (518) 487-5440
  contactsheriff@albanycounty.com
- Albany PD
- Chief James Tuffey
  165 Henry Johnson Blvd
  Albany, NY 12210
  (518) 438-4000
  police@albany-ny.org
- Bethlehem PD
- Chief Lou Corsi
  447 Delaware Ave.
  Delmar, NY 12054
  (518) 439-9973
  rnagengast@townofbethlehem.org
- Coeymans PD
- Chief Gregory Darlington
  18 Russell Ave.
  Ravena, NY 12143
  (518) 756-2059
  chiefofpolice@coeymans.org
- Cohoes PD
- Chief William Heslin, Sr.
  97 Mohawk St.
  Cohoes, NY 12047
  (518) 237-5333
  police-chief@ci.cohoes.ny.us
- Colonie PD
- Chief Steven H. Heider
  312 Wolf Rd.
  Latham, NY 12110
  (518) 783-2744
  colonie@colonie.org
- Guilderland PD
- Chief Carol Lawlor
  5209 Western Turnpike
  Guilderland, NY 12084
  (518) 356-1501
  lawlorc@guilderlandpd.org
- Menands PD
- Chief Michael O'Brien
  250 Broadway
  Menands, NY 12204
  (518) 463-1681
  communications@menandspolice.com
- Watervliet PD
- Chief Ronald Boisvert
  2 15th St.
  Watervliet, NY 12189
  (518) 270-3819
  rboisvert@watervliet.com

Allegany County

- Allegany County SO
- Sheriff Rick L. Whitney
  4884 State Rt. 19
  Belmont, NY 14813
  (585) 268-9200
  WhitneyRl@alleganyco.com
- Alfred PD
- Chief Timothy J. O'Grady
  7 W. University St.
  Alfred, NY 14802
  (607) 587-8878
  alfredvillageclerk@gmail.com
- Cuba PD
- Chief Dustin T. Burch
  5 Bull St.
  Cuba, NY 14727
  (585) 968-1666
  DBurch.CubaPD@Yahoo.com

Bronx County

- Bronx County SO
- Sheriff Edgar A. Domenech
  Also Sheriff for Kings, NY, Queens & Richmond counties
  3030 3rd Ave.
  Bronx, NY 10455
  (718) 993-3880
  fucitoj@finance.nyc.gov

Broome County

- Broome County SO
- Sheriff David E. Harder
  155 Lt. Van Winkle Dr.
  Binghamton, NY 13905
  (607) 778-1911
  bcsheriff@co.broome.ny.us
- Endicott PD
- Chief Michael R. Cox
  1101 Park St.
  Endicott, NY 13760
  (607) 785-3341
  mrcox@endicottpd.org

- Johnson City PD
- Chief Joseph Zikuski
  31 Ave. C
  Johnson City, NY 13790
  (607) 798-9561
  jzikuski@vil.johnson-city.ny.us
- Vestal PD
- Chief John A. Butler
  605 Vestal Pkwy W.
  Vestal, NY 13850
  (607) 754-2386, ext. 341
  jbutler@vestalny.com

Cattaraugus County

- Allegany PD
- Chief Dominic G. Papasergi
  106 E. Main St. PO Box 25
  Allegany, NY 14706
  (716) 373-0873
  dpapasergi@allegany.org
- Olean PD
- Chief Terry Schnell
  Time Sq. Municipal Bldg
  Olean, NY 14760
  (716) 376-5675
  tschnell@cityofolean.org
- Salamanca PD
- Chief Gary Wind
  225 Wildwood Ave.
  Salamanca, NY 14779
  (716) 945-2330
  police@salmun.com

Cayugo County

- Cayugo County SO
- Sheriff David S. Gould
  7445 County House
  Auburn, NY 13021
  (315) 253-4337
  dgould@cayugacounty.us

Chautauqua County

- Chautauqua County SO
- Sheriff Joseph A. Gerace
  15 E. Chautauqua Box 128
  Mayville, NY 14757
  (716) 753-4900
  jg@sheriff.us

Chemung County

- Chemung County SO
- Sheriff Christopher J. Moss
  203 William St.
  Elmira, NY 14901
  (607) 737-2987
  sheriff@co.chemung.ny.us
- Elmira PD
- Chief Michael *Robby* Robertson
  317 E. Church St.
  Elmira, NY 14901
  (607) 737-5630
  mrobertson@cityofelmira.net

Chenango County

- Chenango County SO
- Sheriff Ernest Cutting
  279 County Rd. 46
  Norwich, NY 13815
  (607) 334-2000
  ernestc@co.chenango.ny.us
- Greene PD
- Act. Chief (*Ofcr.-in-Charge*) Don Brown
  29 No. Chenango St.
  Greene, NY 13778
  (607) 656-8501
  greenepolice@yahoo.com
- Norwich PD
- Chief Joseph G. Angelino
  18 E. Main St.
  Norwich, NY 13815
  (607) 334-2424
  info@norwichpd.org

Clinton County

- Clinton County SD
- Sheriff David N. Favro
  25 McCarthy Dr.
  Plattsburgh, NY 12901
  (518) 565-4330
  sheriff@co.clinton.ny.us
- Plattsburgh PD
- Chief Desmond Racicot
  45 Pine St.
  Plattsburgh, NY 12901
  (518) 563-3411
  branchm@plattsburghpd.com
- Rouses Point PD
- Chief Michael P. Bingel
  139 Lake St.
  Rouses Point, NY 12979
  (518) 297-5502, ext. 317
  Police@rousespointny.com

Columbia County

- Chatham PD
- Chief Kevin J. Boehme
  77 Main St.
  Chatham, NY 12037
  (518) 392-3451
  police@villageofchatham.com

Cortland County

- Cortland County SO
- Sheriff Lee A. Price
  54 Greenbush St.
  Cortland, NY 13045
  (607) 753-3311
  lprice@cortland-co.org
- Cortland PD
- Chief F. Michael Catalano
  25 Court St.
  Cortland, NY 13045
  (607) 753-3001
  police@cortland.org

Delaware County

- Delaware County SO
- Sheriff Thomas E. Mills
  280 Phoebe Ln., Ste. 1
  Delhi, NY 13753
  (607) 746-2336
  shrf@co.delaware.ny.us

Dutchess County

- Dutchess County SO
- Sheriff Adrian H. *Butch* Anderson
  150 No. Hamilton St.
  Poughkeepsie, NY 12601
  (845) 486-3800
  sheriff@dutchessny.gov
- Beacon PD
- Chief Douglas Solomon
  8 Ferry St.
  Beacon, NY 12508
  (845) 831-4111
  dsolomon@beaconpd.com
- Hyde Park PD
- Chief Eric Paolilli
  3 Cardinal Rd.
  Hyde Park, NY 12538
  (845) 229-9340
  police@hydeparkny.us
- Poughkeepsie PD
- Chief Ronald J. Knapp
  62 Civic Center PO Box 863
  Poughkeepsie, NY 12602
  (845) 451-4132
  police@cityofpoughkeepsie.com
- Rhinebeck PD
- Sgt. (*Ofcr.-in-Charge*) Peter Dunn
  76 E. Market St.
  Rhinebeck, NY 12572
  (845) 876-8181
  pdunn@rhinebeckpd.com

Erie County

- Erie County SO
- Sheriff Timothy B. Howard
  10 Delaware Ave.
  Buffalo, NY 14202
  (716) 858-7608
  sheriff@erie.gov
- Akron PD
- Chief Richard Lauricella
  21 Main St.
  Akron, NY 14001
  (716) 542-4481
  lauricella@akronvillage.us
- Amherst PD
- Chief John C. Askey
  500 John James Audubon Pkwy
  Amherst, NY 14228
  (716) 689-1311
  lkistner@amherst.ny.us
- Brant PD
- Chief Donald D. Hepkins
  1272 Brant-No. Collins Rd.
  Brant, NY 14027
  (716) 549-4040
  police@brantny.com
- Buffalo PD
- Chief Mitchell P. Weinzetl
  215 1st Ave. NE
  Buffalo, NY 14202
  (763) 682-5976
  mitch.weinzetl@ci.buffalo.mn.us
- Depew PD
- Chief Stan Carwile
  85 Manitou St.
  Depew, NY 14043
  (716) 683-1123
  info@villageofdepew.org
- East Aurora PD
- Chief Ronald R. Krowka
  571 Main St.
  East Aurora, NY 14052
  (716) 652-1313
  ron.krowka@east-aurora.ny.us
- Eden PD
- Chief Michael J. Felschow
  2795 E. Church St.
  Eden, NY 14057
  (716) 992-9211
  mlou15@aol.com

- Evans PD
- Chief Ernest P. Masullo
  8787 Erie Rd.
  Angola, NY 14006
  (716) 549-3600
  chief@evanspoliceny.com
- Kenmore PD
- Chief Peter Breitnauer
  2395 Elmwood Ave.
  Kenmore, NY 14217
  (716) 875-1234
  chiefpjb@kenmorepolice.org
- Lackawanna PD
- Dir. Dana J. Britton
  714 Ridge Rd.
  Lackawanna, NY 14218
  (716) 827-6499
  publicsaftey@lackny.com
- Orchard Park PD
- Chief Mark Pacholec
  4295 So. Buffalo St.
  Orchard Park, NY 14127
  (716) 662-6444
  oppolice@orchardparkny.org
- Tonawanda PD
- Chief John F. Ivancic
  200 Niagara St.
  Tonawanda, NY 14150
  (716) 692-2121
  wstrassburg@tonawandacitypd.com
- West Seneca PD
- Int. Chief Daniel M. Denz
  1250 Union Rd.
  West Seneca, NY 14224
  (716) 674-2280
  info@wspolice.com

Essex County

- Essex County SO
- Sheriff Richard Cutting
  7802 Stowersville PO Box 68
  Lewis, NY 12950
  518 873-6902
  rcutting@co.essex.ny.us
- Lake Placid PD
- Chief William Moore
  2693 Main St., Ste. 104
  Lake Placid, NY 12946
  (518) 523-3306
  moore@lakeplacidpd.com

Franklin County

- Franklin County SO
- Sheriff Kevin Mulverhill
  45 Bare Hill Rd.
  Malone, NY 12953
  (518) 483-3304
  kmulverhill@co.franklin.ny.us
- Malone PD
- Chief Chris Premo
  14 Elm St.
  Malone, NY 12953
  (518) 483-4570
  vmalone@westelcom.com
- Tupper Lake PD
- Chief Eric T. Proulx
  53 Park St.
  Tupper Lake, NY 12986
  (518) 359-3776
  proulx@tupperlakepd.com

Fulton County

- Fulton County SO
- Sheriff Thomas E. Lorey
  2712 State Hwy 29
  Johnstown, NY 12095
  (518) 736-2100
  fcso@co.fulton.ny.us
- Gloversville PD
- Chief Donald VanDeusen
  3 Frontage Rd.
  Gloversville, NY 12078
  (518) 773-4505
  daytonking@cityofgloversville.com
- Johnstown PD
- Chief Mark Gifford
  33-41 E. Main St.
  Johnstown, NY 12095
  (518) 736-4021
  jpd@cityofjohnstown.ny.gov

Genesee County

- Genesee County SO
- Sheriff Gary T. Maha
  165 Park Rd.
  Batavia, NY 14020
  (585) 345-3000
  sheriff@co.genesee.ny.us
- Batavia PD
- Chief Shawn Heubusch
  10 W. Main St.
  Batavia, NY 14020
  (585) 345-6444
  sheubusch@batavianewyork.com

Greene County

- Greene County SO
- Sheriff Gregory R. Seeley
  80 Bridge St.
  Catskill, NY 12414
  (518) 943-3300
  sheriff@discovergreene.com
- Cairo PD
- Act. Chief (*Sgt.*) Richard *Rick* Busch
  512 Main St. PO Box 728
  Cairo, NY 12413
  (518) 622-2324
  cairopolice@townofcairo.com
- Catskill PD
- Chief David Darling
  422 Main St.
  Catskill, NY 12414
  (518) 943-2244
  cmosley@villageofcatskill.net
- Hunter PD
- Chief Jennifer J. Thorp-Reich
  Town Hall PO Box 70
  Tannersville, NY 12485
  (518) 589-7200
  townofhunterpd@hvc.rr.com

Hamilton County

- Hamilton County SO
- Sheriff Karl G. Abrams
  So. Shore Rd.
  Lake Pleasant, NY 12108
  (518) 548-3113
  sheriff@hamiltoncountyny.gov
- Inlet PD
- Chief Andrew D. Kalil
  160 Rt. 28 Box 707
  Inlet, NY 13360
  (315) 357-5091
  police@inletny.com

Herkimer County

- Herkimer County SO
- Sheriff Christopher P. Farber
  320 No. Main
  Herkimer, NY 13367
  (315) 867-1167
  herkimercounty@herkimercounty.org
- Frankfort PD
- Chief Ronald Petrie
  110 Railroad St., Ste. 7
  Frankfort, NY 13340
  (315) 895-7566
  rpetrie@villageoffrankfortny.org
- Herkimer PD
- Chief Joseph Malone
  118 Green St.
  Herkimer, NY 13350
  (315) 866-4330
  office@village.herkimer.ny.us
- Little Falls PD
- Chief Michael Masi
  659 E. Main St.
  Little Falls, NY 13365
  (315) 823-1122
  JServidone@cityoflittlefalls.net
- Mohawk PD
- Chief Joseph Malone
  28 Columbia St.
  Mohawk, NY 13407
  (315) 866-3492
  MohawkPD@mohawk-ny.org
- Webb PD
- Chief John D. Russell
  Main St.
  Old Forge, NY 13420
  (315) 369-6515
  towclerk@oldforgeny.com

Jefferson County

- Adams PD
- Chief James Thomas
  2 No. Main St.
  Adams, NY 13605
  (315) 232-2912, ext. 3
  loricva@frontiernet.net
- Clayton PD
- Chief Kevin Patenaude
  425 Mary St. PO Box 250
  Clayton, NY 13624
  (315) 686-5592
  vclaytonpd@yahoo.com
- Watertown PD
- Chief Gary Comins
  751 Watertown Dr.
  Watertown, NY 13601
  (315) 782-2233
  wpd@watertown-ny.gov
- West Carthage PD
- Chief Reginald Huber
  West Carthage, NY 13619
  (315) 493-4821
  wcarthagepd@westelcom.com

Kings County

- Kings County SO
- Sheriff Edgar A. Domenech
  Also Sheriff for Bronx, NY, Queens & Richmond counties
  210 Joralemon St., Rm. 909
  Brooklyn, NY 11201
  (718) 802-3545
  fucitoj@finance.nyc.gov

Lewis County

- Lewis County SO
- Sheriff Michael Carpinelli
  5252 Outer Stowe St.
  Lowville, NY 13367
  (315) 376-3511
  LCSD@lewiscountyny.org

Livingston County

- Livingston County SO
- Sheriff John M. York
  4 Court St.
  Geneseo, NY 14454
  (585) 243-7100
  lcso@co.livingston.ny.us
- Geneseo PD
- Chief Eric Osganian
  119 Main St.
  Geneseo, NY 14454
  (585) 243-2420
  Police@GeneseoNY.org
- Mount Morris PD
- Chief Ken Mignemi
  117 Main St.
  Mount Morris, NY 14510
  (585) 658-2155
  kmignemi@mmpolice.org
- Nunda PD
- Chief Jeffrey Wilcox
  1 Mill St.
  Nunda, NY 14517
  (585) 468-2515
  jwilcox@nundapolice.org

Madison County

- Madison County SO
- Sheriff Allen Riley
  No. Court St. PO Box 16
  Wampsville, NY 13163
  (315) 366-2318
  allen.riley@madisoncounty.ny.gov
- Cazenovia PD
- Chief Michael A. Hayes
  90 Albany St.
  Cazenovia, NY 13035
  (315) 655-3276
  cazpolice@windstream.net
- Hamilton PD
- Chief Rick Gifford
  3 Broad St.
  Hamilton, NY 13346
  (315) 824-3311
  seang@hamilton-ny.gov
- Oneida PD
- Chief David Meeker
  108 No. Main St.
  Oneida, NY 13421
  (315) 363-9111
  dmeeker@oneidacity.com

Monroe County

- Monroe County SO
- Sheriff Patrick M. O'Flynn
  130 So. Plymouth Ave.
  Rochester, NY 14614
  (585) 753-4178
  johnhelfer@monroecounty.gov
- Brighton PD
- Chief Mark T. Henderson
  2300 Elmwood Ave.
  Rochester, NY 14618
  (585) 784-5150
  mark.henderson@townofbrighton.org
- Brockport PD
- Chief Daniel P. Varrenti
  1 Clinton St.
  Brockport, NY 14420
  (585) 637-1011
  chief@brockportpolice.org
- East Rochester PD
- Chief Steven J. Clancy
  254 W. Ivy St.
  East Rochester, NY 14445
  (585) 586-4399
  sclancy@eastrochester.org
- Greece PD
- Chief Todd K. Baxter
  400 Island Cottage Rd.
  Rochester, NY 14612
  (585) 865-9200
  tbaxter@greeceny.gov

- Irondequoit PD
- Chief Richard J. Boyan
  1300 Titus Ave.
  Rochester, NY 14617
  (585) 336-6000, ext. 2306
  police@irondequoit.org
- Monroe County M.E.
- Caroline R. Dignan, M.D.
  740 E. Henrietta Rd.
  Rochester, NY 14623
  (585) 753-5905
  medicalexaminer@monroecounty.gov
- Ogden PD
- Chief Douglas Nordquist
  269 Ogden Center Rd.
  Spencerport, NY 14559
  (585) 617-6100
  info@ogdenny.com
- Rochester PD
- Chief James M. Sheppard
  185 Exchange Blvd
  Rochester, NY 14614-2184
  (585) 428-7033
  shepparj@cityofrochester.gov
- Webster PD
- Chief Gerald L. Pickering
  1000 Ridge Rd.
  Webster, NY 14580
  (585) 872-1216, ext. 240
  police@ci.webster.ny.us

Montgomery County

- Amsterdam PD
- Chief Gregg Culick
  1 Guy Park Ave.
  Amsterdam, NY 12010
  (518) 842-1100
  infopd@amsterdampd.com
- Canajoharie PD
- Chief Bryan MacFadden
  75 Erie Blvd
  Canajoharie, NY 13317
  (518) 673-3111
  canajohariepolice@albany.twcbc.com
- St. Johnsville PD
- Chief Diana Callen
  14 Washington St.
  St. Johnsville, NY 13452
  (518) 568-2141
  desk@sjnypd.org

Nassau County

- Nassau County SD
- Sheriff Michael Sposato
  100 Carman Ave.
  East Meadow, NY 11554
  (516) 572-4100
  gabor@nassaucountyny.gov
- Centre Island PD
- Chief Michael A. Capobianco
  100 Centre Island Rd.
  Oyster Bay, NY 11771
  (516) 922-6466
  cipd@optonline.net
- Floral Park PD
- Comm. Stephen G. McAllister
  1 Floral Blvd
  Floral Park, NY 11002
  (516) 326-6400
  comments@fpvillage.org
- Freeport PD
- Chief Miguel Bermudez
  40 No. Ocean Ave.
  Freeport, NY 11520
  (516) 377-2411
  info@freeportpolice.org
- Garden City PD
- Comm. Kenneth Jackson
  349 Stewart Ave.
  Garden City, NY 11530
  (516) 465-4110
  kjackson@gardencityny.net
- Glen Cove PD
- Chief William Whitton
  1 Bridge St.
  Glen Cove, NY 11542
  (516) 676-1000
  rsuozzi@cityofglencoveny.org
- Hempstead PD
- Chief Michael McGowan
  99 Nichols Ct.
  Hempstead, NY 11550
  (516) 483-6263
  mayorsoffice@villageofhempsteadny.gov
- Kensington PD
- Act. Chief (*Lt.*) Michael Conlon
  1-A Beverly Rd.
  Great Neck, NY 11021
  (516) 482-0480
  villageclerk@villageofkensingtonny.gov

- Lake Success PD
- Chief William Lang
  318 Lakeville Rd.
  Lake Success, NY 11020
  (516) 482-4600
  Mayor@villageoflakesuccess.com
- Long Beach PD
- Comm. Michael Tangney
  1 W. Chester St.
  Long Beach, NY 11561
  (516) 431-1800
  info@longbeachny.gov
- Lynbrook PD
- Chief Joseph Neve
  1 Columbus Dr.
  Lynbrook, NY 11563
  (516) 599-3300
  lynbrookpolice@lynbrookvillage.com
- Malverne PD
- Chief John C Aresta
  1 Britton Cir.
  Malverne, NY 11565
  (516) 599-3141
  info@malvernevillage.org
- Old Brookville PD
- Chief Richard H. Smith
  5701 Northern Blvd
  Old Brookville, NY 11545
  (516) 626-1300
  oldbrookville@optonline.net
- Port Washington PD
- Chief William J. Kilfoil
  500 Port Washington Blvd
  Port Washington, NY 11050
  (516) 883-0500
  questions@portwashingtonpd.com
- Sands Point PD
- Chief Mark Mandel
  26 Tibbits Ln.
  Sands Point, NY 11050
  (516) 883-3100
  mmandel@police.sandspoint.org

New York County

- New York County SO
- Sheriff Edgar A. Domenech
  Also Sheriff for Bronx, Kings, Queens & Richmond counties
  66 John St., 13th Fl.
  New York, NY 10038
  (212) 487 9734
  fucitoj@finance.nyc.gov
- NYPD
- Comm. William J. Bratton
  One Police Plaza, 14th Fl.
  New York, NY 10038
  (646) 610-5000
  william.bratton@NYPD.org

Niagara County

- Niagara County SO
- Sheriff James R. Voutour
  5526 Niagara St. PO Box 496
  Lockport, NY 14095
  (716) 438-3370
  ncsd@niagaracounty.com
- Barker PD
- Chief Ross Annable
  8708 Main
  Barker, NY 14012
  (716) 795-3207
  barkerpolice@roadrunner.com
- Lewiston PD
- Chief Christopher Salada
  4059 Creek Rd.
  Lewiston, NY 14092
  (716) 754-8477
  csalada@lewpd.com
- Middleport PD
- Chief John J. Swick
  22 Main St. PO Box 186
  Middleport, NY 14105
  (716) 735-3373
  MiddleportPD@villageofmiddleport.org
- North Tonawanda PD
- Chief William R. Hall
  216 Payne Ave.
  North Tonawanda, NY 14120
  (716) 692-4111
  robertort@northtonawanda.org
- Niagara PD
- Chief H. James Suitor
  7105 Lockport Rd.
  Niagara Falls, NY 14305
  (716) 215-1480
  jsuitor@niagara-police.com
- Youngstown PD
- Chief Christopher Salada
  240 Lockport St. PO Box 168
  Youngstown, NY 14174
  (716) 745-3623
  police@youngstownnewyork.us

Oneida County

- Oneida County SO
- Sheriff Robert M. Maciol
  6065 Judd Rd.
  Oriskany, NY 13424
  (315) 765-2200
  webmaster@ocgov.net
- Boonville PD
- Chief James Galler
  13149 St., Rt. 12
  Boonville, NY 13309
  (315) 943-2050
  vboon@frontiernet.net
- Kirkland PD
- Chief Daniel J. English
  2 New St. PO Box B
  Clark Mills, NY 13321
  (315) 853-2924
  chiefenglish@kirklandpolice.com
- New Hartford PD
- Chief Michael S. Inserra
  32 Kellogg Rd.
  New Hartford, NY 13413
  (315) 724-7111
  msi108@town.new-hartford.ny.us
- New York Mills PD
- Chief Jim Van Schaick
  118 No. Main Ave.
  New York Mills, NY 13417
  (315) 385-2600
  nympd@lakesplus.com
- Oriskany PD
- Chief Richard Zabek
  708 Utica St. PO Box 904
  Oriskany, NY 13424
  (315) 736-2049
  oriskanypd@roadrunner.com
- Rome PD
- Chief Kevin C. Beach
  301 No. James St.
  Rome, NY 13440
  (315) 339-7705
  beachk@romepd.com
- Utica PD
- Chief Mark Williams
  413 Oriskany St. W.
  Utica, NY 13502
  (315) 735-3301
  mayor@cityofutica.com
- Vernon PD
- Ofcr.-in-Charge Paul Thompson
  8 Ruth St. PO Box 1137
  Vernon, NY 13476
  (315) 829-2550
  vernonpolice@tds.net

Onondaga County

- Onondaga County SO
- Sheriff Kevin E. Walsh
  407 So. State St.
  Syracuse, NY 13202
  (315) 435-3044
  sheriffwalsh@hotmail.com
- Baldwinsville PD
- Chief Michael W. Lefancheck
  16 W. Genesee St.
  Baldwinsville, NY 13027
  (315) 635-3131
  police@baldwinsville.org
- Camillus PD
- Chief Thomas M. Winn
  4600 W. Genesee St.
  Syracuse, NY 13219
  (315) 487-0102
  twinn@townofcamillus.com
- Cicero PD
- Chief Joseph F. Snell
  8236 Brewerton Rd.
  Cicero, NY 13039
  (315) 699-3677, ext. 10
  jsnell@ciceropd.us
- De Witt PD
- Chief Eugene J. Conway
  5400 Butternut Dr.
  De Witt, NY 13214
  (315) 449-3640
  supervisor@townofdewitt.com
- East Syracuse PD
- Chief Donald L. Morris
  204 No. Center St.
  East Syracuse, NY 13057
  (315) 435-2333
  pderby@villageofeastsyracuse.com
- Geddes PD
- Chief Vic Gillette
  1000 Woods Rd.
  Syracuse, NY 13209
  (315) 468-3283
  jalbrigo@townofgeddes.com

- Jordan PD
- Ofcr.-in-Charge Edward *Ed* Healy
  7 Mechanic St. PO Box 561
  Jordan, NY 13080
  (315) 689-7350
  police@villageofjordan.org
- Liverpool PD
- Chief Donald L. Morris
  310 Sycamore St.
  Liverpool, NY 13088
  (315) 457-3441
  chiefofpolice@villageofliverpool.org
- Manlius PD
- Chief Francis R. Marlowe
  1 Arkie Albanese Ave.
  Manlius, NY 13104
  (315) 682-2212
  police@manliuspolice.org
- North Syracuse PD
- Chief Michael Crowell
  608 So. Bay Rd.
  North Syracuse, NY 13212
  (315) 458-5670
  chiefcrowell@northsyracuseny.org
- Solvay PD
- Chief Richard Cox
  507 Charles Ave.
  Solvay, NY 13209
  (315) 468-2510
  website@solvaypd.com
- Syracuse PD
- Chief Frank L. Fowler
  511 So. State St.
  Syracuse, NY 13202
  (315) 442-5250
  CityHall@SyrGov.net

Ontario County

- Ontario County SO
- Sheriff Philip C. Povero
  74 Ontario St.
  Canandaigua, NY 14424
  (585) 394-4560
  sheriff@co.ontario.ny.us
- Canandaigua PD
- Chief Jonathan P. *Jon* Welch
  21 Ontario St.
  Canandaigua, NY 14424
  (716) 396-5030
  Jon.Welch@CanandaiguaNewYork.gov
- Clifton Springs PD
- Chief Scott Upchurch
  1 W. Main St.
  Clifton Springs, NY 14432
  (315) 462-2422
  villcs@fltg.net
- Geneva PD
- Chief Jeffrey E. Trickler
  255 Exchange St.
  Geneva, NY 14456
  (315) 789-1111
  ralcock@geneva.ny.us
- Phelps PD
- Chief John Storer
  8 Banta St.
  Phelps, NY 14532
  (315) 548-8237
  police@phelpsny.com

Orange County

- Chester PD
- Chief Peter J. Graziano, Jr.
  47 Main St.
  Chester, NY 10918
  (845) 469-2388
  mayor@villageofchesterny.com
- Cornwall PD
- Chief Todd Hazard
  183 Main St.
  Cornwall, NY 12518
  (845) 534-8100
  kquigley@cornwallny.gov
- Cornwall-On-Hudson PD
- Chief Steven Dixon
  325 Hudson St.
  Cornwall-On-Hudson, NY 12520
  (845) 534-8100
  mayor@cornwall-on-hudson.org
- Deerpark PD
- Chief William R. Werner
  231 Rt. 209 PO Box 119
  Huguenot, NY 12746
  (845) 858-4529
  deerparkpolice@frontiernet.net
- Florida PD
- Chief James Coleman
  2 Cohen Cir.
  Florida, NY 10921
  (845) 651-7800
  vofmayor@warwick.net

- Greenwood Lake PD
- Chief John Hansen
  16 Church St. PO Box 491
  Greenwood Lake, NY 10925
  (845) 477-9211
  Gwlpol@optonline.net
- Harriman PD
- Chief Randy Heidle
  1 Maple Ave.
  Harriman, NY 10926
  (845) 782-6644
  hpd@frontiernet.net
- Highland Falls PD
- Chief Kenneth Scott
  301 Main St.
  Highland Falls, NY 10928
  (845) 446-4911
  kscott@highlandfallsny.org
- Maybrook PD
- Chief Arnold *Butch* Amthor
  109 Main St.
  Maybrook, NY 12543
  (845) 427-2226
  vjohnson@villageofmaybrook.com
- Middletown PD
- Chief Ramon Bethencourt
  2 James St.
  Middletown, NY 10940
  (845) 343-3151
  rbethencourt@middletownpolice.com
- Monroe PD
- Chief A. Alex Melchiorre
  104 Stage Rd.
  Monroe, NY 10950
  (845) 782-8644
  d.conklin@monroepd.org
- Montgomery PD
- Chief John DiMilia
  65 Bachlor St.
  Montgomery, NY 12549
  (845) 457-3666
  jDiMilia@villageofmontgomery.org
- Mount Hope PD
- Chief Paul J. Rickard
  7 Baker St. PO Box 871
  Otisville, NY 10963
  (845) 386-8886
  chief@mounthopepolice.com
- Town of Newburgh PD
- Chief Michael Clancy
  300 Gardnertown Rd.
  Newburgh, NY 12550
  (845) 564-1100
  mclancy@townofnewburghpd.org
- New Windsor PD
- Chief Michael C. Biasotti
  555 Union Ave.
  New Windsor, NY 12553
  (845) 565-7000
  info@town.new-windsor.ny.us
- Port Jervis PD
- Chief William Worden
  20 Hammond St.
  Port Jervis, NY 12771
  (845) 856-5101
  portjervispolice@yahoo.com
- Walden PD
- Chief Jeffry Holmes
  1 Municipal Sq.
  Walden, NY 12586
  (845) 778-5595
  WaldenPD@hvc.rr.com
- Wallkill PD
- Chief Robert Hertman
  600 Rt. 211 E.
  Middletown, NY 10941
  (845) 692-4166
  chiefofpolice@townofwallkill.com
- Warwick PD
- Chief Thomas McGovern, Jr.
  132 Kings Hwy
  Warwick, NY 10990
  (845) 986-3423
  townhall@townofwarwick.org
- Washingtonville PD
- Chief Stephen J. Bogert
  38 E. Main St.
  Washingtonville, NY 10992
  (845) 496-9123
  wpdchief@hvc.rr.com

Orleans County

- Orleans County SO
- Sheriff Scott D. Hess
  13925 State Rt. 31
  Albion, NY 14411
  (585) 590-4137
  ocsher@orleansny.com

- Albion PD
- Chief Roland Nenni
  106 No. Platt St.
  Albion, NY 14411
  (585) 589-5627
  albionpd@rochester.rr.com
- Medina PD
- Chief Jose L. Avila
  600 Main St.
  Medina, NY 14103
  (585) 798-5602
  Police@villagemedina.org

Oswego County

- Oswego County SO
- Sheriff Reuel A. Todd
  39 Churchill Rd.
  Oswego, NY 13126
  (315) 349-3307
  sheriff@oswegocounty.com
- Oswego PD
- Chief Tory L. DeCaire
  169 W. 2nd St.
  Oswego, NY 13126
  (315) 343-8120
  crimewatch@oswegony.org
- Phoenix PD
- Chief Martin Nerber
  455 Main St.
  Phoenix, NY 13135
  (315) 695-4484
  info@villageofphoenix-ny.gov
- Pulaski PD
- Chief Ellery D. Terpening
  4917 Jefferson St.
  Pulaski, NY 13142
  (315) 298-7525
  chiefterpening@yahoo.com

Otsego County

- Otsego County SO
- Sheriff Richard J. Devlin, Jr.
  172 Co. Hwy 33 W. PO Box 326
  Cooperstown, NY 13326
  (607) 547-4271
  SHERIFF@otsegocounty.com
- Oneonta PD
- Chief Dennis R. Nayor
  79-81 Main St.
  Oneonta, NY 13820
  (607) 432-1113
  dnayor@oneonta.ny.us

Putnam County

- Putnam County SO
- Sheriff Donald B. Smith
  3 County Center
  Carmel, NY 10512
  (845) 225-4300
  putnam.sheriff@putnamcountyny.gov

Queens County

- Queens County SO
- Sheriff Edgar A. Domenech
  Also Sheriff for Bronx, Kings, NY& Richmond counties
  144-06 94th Ave.
  Jamaica, NY 11435
  (718) 298-7500
  fucitoj@finance.nyc.gov

Rensselaer County

- East Greenbush PD
- Chief Christopher P. Lavin
  225 Columbia Turnpike
  Rensselaer, NY 12144
  (518) 479-2525
  info@eastgreenbush.org
- Hoosick Falls PD
- Chief Robert B. Ashe
  24 Main St.
  Hoosick Falls, NY 12090
  (518) 686-7651
  themayorhf@gmail.com
- Nassau Village PD
- Act. Chief Thomas Jones
  40 Malden St.
  PO Box 426
  Nassau, NY 12123
  (518) 766-9293
  jones@nassaupd.com
- North Greenbush PD
- Chief Robert J. Durivage
  133 Blooming Grove Dr.
  North Greenbush, NY 12144
  (518) 283-6006
  info@northgreenbushpolice.com
- Schodack PD
- Chief Bernhard Peter
  1797 Columbia Turnpike
  Castleton, NY 12033
  (518) 477-7973
  Chief@schodackpolice.com

- Troy PD
- Chief John Tedesco
  55 State St.
  Troy, NY 12180
  (518) 270-4421
  MayorsOffice@Troyny.gov

Richmond County

- Richmond County SO
- Sheriff Edgar A. Domenech
  Also Sheriff for Bronx, Kings, NY & Queens counties
  350 Saint Marks Ave.
  Staten Island, NY 10304
  (718) 815-8407
  fucitoj@finance.nyc.gov

Rockland County

- Rockland County SD
- Sheriff Louis Falco III
  55 New Hempstead Rd.
  New City, NY 10956
  (845) 638-5464
  falco@rcpin.net
- Clarkstown PD
- Chief Michael R. Sullivan
  20 Maple Ave.
  New City, NY 10956
  (845) 639-5800
  a.gromack@clarkstown.org
- Town of Haverstraw PD
- Chief Charles Miller
  101 W. Ramapo Rd.
  Garnerville, NY 10923
  (845) 354-1500
  jnugent@haverstrawpolice.org
- Orangetown PD
- Chief Kevin Nulty
  1 Police Plaza
  Orangeburg, NY 10962-1798
  (845) 359-3700
  supervisor@orangetown.com
- Piermont PD
- Chief Michael O'Shea
  478 Piermont Ave.
  Piermont, NY 10968
  (845) 359-0240
  police@piermont-ny.com
- Spring Valley PD
- Chief Paul J. Modica
  200 No. Main St.
  Spring Valley, NY 10977
  (845) 356-7400
  police@villagespringvalley.org
- Stony Point PD
- Chief Brian J. Moore
  79 Rt. 210
  Stony Point, NY 10980
  (845) 786-2422
  supervisor@townofstonypoint.org
- Suffern PD
- Chief Clarke Osborn
  61 Washington Ave.
  Suffern, NY 10901
  (845) 357-2300
  info@suffernpolice.com

St. Lawrence County

- St. Lawrence County SD
- Sheriff Kevin Wells
  48 Court St.
  Canton, NY 13617
  (315) 379-2222
  kwells@stlawco.org
- Canton PD
- Chief Lori McDougal
  60 Main St.
  Canton, NY 13617
  (315) 386-4561
- Chief@cantonny.us
- Massena PD
- Chief Timmy J. Currier
  60 Main St.
  Massena, NY 13662
  (315) 769-3577
  police@village.massena.ny.us
- Ogdensburg PD
- Chief Richard Polniak, Jr.
  800 Park St.
  Ogdensburg, NY 13669
  (315) 393-1551
  rpolniak@ogdensburg.org
- Potsdam PD
- Chief Kevin A. Bates
  38 Main St.
  Potsdam, NY 13676
  (315) 265-2121
  kbates@potsdampolice.com

Saratoga County

- Saratoga County SO
- Sheriff James D. Bowen
  6010 County Farm Rd.
  Ballston Spa, NY 12020
  (518) 885-2450
  jbowen@saratogacountyny.gov
- Corinth PD
- Chief Robert Kane
  260 Main St.
  Corinth, NY 12822
  (518) 654-6832
  vocclerk@adelphia.net
- Mechanicville PD
- Chief Joseph Waldron
  36 No. Main St.
  Mechanicville, NY 12118
  (518) 664-7383
  chief.waldron@mechanicvilleny.gov
- South Glens Falls PD
- Chief Kevin Judd
  46 Saratoga Ave.
  South Glens Falls, NY 12803
  (518) 793-1455
  info@sgfny.com
- Stillwater PD
- Chief Dennis D. Latham
  1 Lansing Rd. PO Box 700
  Stillwater, NY 12170
  (518) 664-4611, ext. 14
  stillwaterpd@stillwaterny.org
- Waterford PD
- Comm. John Tanchak
  65 Broad St.
  Waterford, NY 12188
  (518) 237-3341
  tanchakj@town.waterford.ny.us

Schenectady County

- Schenectady County SO
- Sheriff Dominic Dagastino
  320 Veeder Ave.
  Schenectady, NY 12307
  (518) 388-4300
  contact-us@schenectadycounty.com
- Glenville PD
- Chief Michael D. Ranalli
  18 Glenridge Rd.
  Glenville, NY 12302
  (518) 384-3444
  MRanalli@townofglenville.org
- Niskayuna PD
- Chief John Lubrant
  1 Niskayuna Circle
  Niskayuna, NY 12309
  (518) 386-4585
  jlubrant@niskayuna.org
- Rotterdam PD
- Chief James J. Hamilton
  101 Princetown Rd.
  Rotterdam, NY 12306
  (518) 355-7331
  tculbert@rotterdamny.org
- Schenectady PD
- Chief Brian A. Kilcullen
  531 Liberty St.
  Schenectady, NY 12305
  (518) 382-5201
  bkilcullen@schenectadypd.com
- Scotia PD
- Chief Pete Frisoni, Jr.
  4 No. Ten Broeck St.
  Scotia, NY 12302
  (518) 374-3848
  pfrisoni@villageofscotiany.gov

Schoharie County

- Schoharie County SO
- Sheriff Anthony Desmond
  157 Depot Ln. PO Box 689
  Schoharie, NY 12157
  (518) 295-2266
  philip.r.skowfoe.jr@co.schoharie.ny.us
- Schoharie PD
- Chief *(vacant)*
  PO Box 219
  Schoharie, NY 12157
  (518) 295-8566
  schopd@midtel.net

Schuyler County

- Schuyler County SO
- Sheriff William E. Yessman, Jr.
  106 10th St.
  Watkins Glen, NY 14891
  (607) 535-8222
  wyessman@co.schuyler.ny.us

Seneca County

- Seneca County SO
- Sheriff Jack S. Stenberg
  6150 State Rt. 96
  Romulus, NY 14541
  (315) 220-3200
  jstenberg@co.seneca.ny.us

- Interlaken PD
- Chief Leon Anderson
  Railroad Ave.
  Interlaken, NY 14847
  (607) 532-4466
  landerson@villageofinterlaken.org
- Seneca Falls PD
- Chief Stuart Peenstra
  60 State St.
  Seneca Falls, NY 13148
  (315) 568-4850
  dearle@senecafalls.com
- Waterloo PD
- Chief Doyle L. Marquart
  41 W. Main St.
  Waterloo, NY 13165
  (315) 539-2022
  villageoffice@waterloony.com

Steuben County

- Steuben County SO
- Sheriff David V. Cole
  7007 Rumsey St. Ext.
  Bath, NY 14810
  (607) 622-3901
  coledv@co.steuben.ny.us
- Hammondsport PD
- Act. Chief (*Sgt.*) Ryan Sincerbox
  41 Lake St.
  Hammondsport, NY 14840
  (607) 569-3703
  hammondsportpd@frontiernet.net

Suffolk County

- Suffolk County SO
- Sheriff Vincent F. DeMarco
  100 Center Dr.
  Riverhead, NY 11901
  (631) 852-2200
  Suffolk_Sheriff@suffolkcountyny.gov
- Amityville PD
- Chief Donald Dobby
  21 Ireland Pl.
  Amityville, NY 11701
  (631) 264-0400
  mayor@amityville.com
- Village of East Hampton PD
- Chief Gerald Larsen
  1 Cedar St.
  East Hampton, NY 11937
  (631) 324-0777
  ehvpd@easthamptonvillage.org
- Ocean Beach PD
- Act. Chief (*Sgt.*) George Hesse
  Bay Walk
  Ocean Beach, NY 11770
  (631) 583-5866
  info@villageofoceanbeach.org
- Quogue PD
- Chief Robert B. Coughlan
  115 Jessup Ave.
  Quogue, NY 11959
  (631) 653-4791
  contact@villageofquogue.com
- Riverhead PD
- Chief David J. Hegermiller
  210 Howell Ave.
  Riverhead, NY 11901
  (631) 727-4500, ext. 315
  policechief@townofriverheadny.gov
- Sag Harbor PD
- Chief Thomas Fabiano
  70 Division St.
  PO Box 660
  Sag Harbor, NY 11963
  (631) 725-0247
  clerk@sagharborny.gov
- Shelter Island PD
- Chief James J. Read
  44 No. Ferry Rd. PO Box 1056
  Shelter Island, NY 11964
  (631) 749-0600
  jread@shelterislandtown.us
- Town of Southampton PD
- Chief Robert Pearce
  110 Old Riverhead Rd.
  Hampton Bays, NY 11946
  (631) 702-2220
  rpearce@southamptontownny.gov
- Village of Southampton PD
- Chief Thomas Cummings
  151 Windmill Ln.
  Southampton, NY 11968
  (631) 283-0083
  info@southamptonvillage.org
- Southold PD
- Chief Martin Flatley
  41405 Rt. 25 PO Box 911
  Peconic, NY 11958
  (631) 765-2600
  mflatley@town.southold.ny.us

- Suffolk County PD
- Comm. Edward Webber
  30 Yaphank Ave.
  Yaphank, NY 11980
  (631) 852-6000
  SCPDINFO@suffolkcountyny.gov
- Westhampton Beach PD
- Chief Raymond Dean
  165 Mill Rd.
  Westhampton Beach, NY 11978
  (631) 288-3444
  info@westhamptonbeach.org

Sullivan County

- Sullivan County SO
- Sheriff Michael A. Schiff
  4 Bushnell Ave.
  Monticello, NY 12701
  (845) 794-7100
  michael.schiff@co.sullivan.ny.us
- Fallsburg PD
- Chief Simmie Williams
  19 Railroad Plaza PO Box 568
  South Fallsburg, NY 12779
  (845) 434-4422
  fpd362@fallsburgny.com
- Liberty PD
- Chief Scott Kinne
  159 No. Main St.
  Liberty, NY 12754
  (845) 292-4422
  mhess@libertyvillageny.org
- Monticello PD
- Chief Robert Mir
  2 Pleasant St.
  Monticello, NY 12701
  (845) 794-4422
  info@villageofmonticello.com

Tioga County

- Owego PD
- Chief Karen Vinti
  90 Temple St.
  Owego, NY 13827
  (607) 687-2233
  opdchief@stny.rr.com
- Waverly PD
- Chief Grady Updyke
  32 Ithaca St.
  Waverly, NY 14892
  (607) 565-2836
  GUpdyke@WaverlyBarton.com

Tompkins County

- Tompkins County SO
- Sheriff Kenneth W. *Ken* Lansing
  779 Warren Rd.
  Ithaca, NY 14850
  (607) 257-1345
  klansing@tompkins-co.org
- Cayuga Heights PD
- Chief James M. Steinmetz
  836 Hanshaw Rd.
  Ithaca, NY 14850
  (607) 257-1011
  jsteinmetz@cayuga-heights.ny.us
- Dryden PD
- Chief Margaret E. Ryan
  16 South St.
  PO Box 820
  Dryden, NY 13053
  (607) 844-8118
  chief100@dryden-ny.org
- Groton PD
- Act. Chief (*Lt.*) Tim Williams
  108 E. Cortland St.
  Groton, NY 13073
  (607) 898-3131
  grotonvil@gmail.com
- Ithaca PD
- Chief John R. Barber
  120 E. Clinton St.
  PO Box 6557
  Ithaca, NY 14851
  (607) 272-9973
  jbarber@cityofithaca.org
- Trumansburg PD
- Chief Thomas L Ferretti
  5 Elm St.
  Trumansburg, NY 14886
  (607) 387-6513
  chief@trumansburgpolice.com

Ulster County

- Ulster County SO
- Sheriff Paul J. Van Blarcum
  380 Blvd
  Kingston, NY 12401
  (845) 340-3802
  sheriff@co.ulster.ny.us
- Ellenville PD
- Chief Philip Mattracion
  2 Elting Ct.
  Ellenville, NY 12428
  (845) 647-4422
  pmattracion@villageofellenville.com

- Kingston PD
- Chief Egidio F. Tinti
  1 Garraghan Dr.
  Kingston, NY 12401
  (845) 331-1671
  etinti@kingston-ny.gov
- Lloyd PD
- Chief Daniel Waage
  12 Church St.
  Highland, NY 12528
  (845) 691-2144
  phansut@townoflloyd.com
- New Paltz PD
- Chief Joseph A. Snyder
  83 So. Putt Corners Rd, Ste. 1
  New Paltz, NY 12561
  (845) 255-7112
  chief@newpaltzny.org
- Rosendale PD
- Chief Perry Soule
  520 Lefever Falls
  PO Box 443
  Rosendale, NY 12472
  (845) 658-9000
  police@townofrosendale.com
- Saugerties PD
- Chief Joseph A. Sinagra
  4 High St.
  Saugerties, NY 12477
  (845) 246-9800
  jsinagra@police.saugerties.ny.us
- Shawangunk PD
- Chief Frank Petrone
  13 Bonaventure PO Box 247
  Wallkill, NY 12589
  (845) 895-2317
  jvalkjr@hvc.rr.com
- Ulster PD
- Chief Anthony E. Cruise
  1 Town Hall Dr.
  Lake Katrine, NY 12449
  (845) 382-1111
  aecruise@ulsterpolice.com
- Woodstock PD
- Chief Clayton Keefe
  76 Tinker St.
  Woodstock, NY 12498
  (845) 679-2422
  supervisor@woodstockny.org

Warren County

- Warren County SO
- Sheriff Nathan H. *Bud* York
  1400 State Rt. 9
  Lake George, NY 12845
  (518) 743-2500
  wcso@sheriff.co.warren.ny.us
- Bolton Landing PD
- Chief Jim Neumann
  PO Box 752
  Bolton Landing, NY 12814
  (518) 644-9717
  police@town.bolton.ny.us
- Glens Falls PD
- Chief William F. Valenza
  42 Ridge St.
  Glens Falls, NY 12801
  (518) 761-3840
  wvalenza@glensfallspd.com

Washington County

- Washington County SO
- Sheriff Jeffrey *Jeff* Murphy
  399 Broadway
  Fort Edward, NY 12828-1021
  (518) 746-2475
  sheriffmurphy@co.washington.ny.us
- Cambridge PD
- Chief George G. Bell
  56 No. Park St.
  Cambridge, NY 12816
  (518) 677-2622
  chiefbell@cambridgeny.gov
- Fort Edward PD
- Chief Walter Sandford
  118 Broadway
  Fort Edward, NY 12828
  (518) 747-6365
  chief@fepd.org
- Hudson Falls PD
- Chief Randy Diamond
  218 Main St.
  Hudson Falls, NY 12839
  (518) 747-4011
  hfpdchief@roadrunner.com
- Whitehall PD
- Chief Matthew Dickinson
  8 Montcalm Ave.
  Whitehall, NY 12887
  (518) 499-1316
  chief@whitehallpolice.org

Wayne County

- Wayne County SO
- Sheriff Barry C. Virts
  7368 Rt. 31
  Lyons, NY 14489
  (315) 946-9711
  tip@co.wayne.ny.us
- Clyde PD
- Ofcr.-in-Charge Brian Ritchie
  41 Ford St.
  Clyde, NY 14433
  (315) 923-3121
  policechief@clydeny.com
- Lyons PD
- Chief Richard J. Bogan
  72 William St.
  Lyons, NY 14489
  (315) 946-4151
  bogan@lyonspolice.us
- Macedon PD
- Chief John P. Colella
  1620 Wayneport Rd.
  Macedon, NY 14502
  (315) 986-4121
  macpd@rochester.rrr.com
- Newark PD
- Chief David L. Christler
  100 E. Miller St.
  Newark, NY 14513
  (315) 331-3701
  dchristler@newarkpd.net
- Palmyra PD
- Chief David M. Dalton
  144 E. Main St.
  Palmyra, NY 14522
  (315) 597-9211
  bvdaly@hotmail.com
- Sodus PD
- Chief William Critchfield
  14 Mill St.
  Sodus, NY 14551
  (315) 483-9353
  soduspolice@soduspolice.com
- Sodus Point PD
- Chief Stanley Knutowicz, Jr.
  8356 Bay St.
  Sodus Point, NY 14555
  (315) 483-0480
  TDurham@soduspoint.info
- Wolcott PD
- Comm. Gary J. Baker
  6 New Hartford St.
  Wolcott, NY 14590
  (315) 594-2323
  wolcottpd@rochester.rr.com

Westchester County

- Westchester County DPS
- Sheriff George N. Longworth
  1 Saw Mill River Pkwy
  Hawthorne, NY 10532
  (914) 864-7700
  psef@westchestergov.com
- Ardsley PD
- Chief Emil Califano
  505 Ashford Ave.
  Ardsley, NY 10502
  (914) 693-1700
  mayorporcino@ardsleyvillage.com
- Bedford Town PD
- Chief William Hayes
  307 Bedford Rd.
  Bedford Hills, NY 10507
  (914) 241-3111
  BedfordPolice@BedfordNY.gov
- Briarcliff Manor PD
- Chief Norman Campion
  1111 Pleasantville Rd.
  Briarcliff Manor, NY 10510
  (914) 941-2130
  policedepartment@briarcliffmanor.org
- Buchanan PD
- Chief Brian J. Tubbs
  236 Tate Ave.
  Buchanan, NY 10511
  (914) 739-6776
  SMurray@villageofbuchanan.com
- Croton-On-Hudson PD
- Chief Anthony Tramaglini
  1 Van Wyck St.
  Croton-On-Hudson, NY 10520
  (914) 271-5177
  lwiegman@crotononhudson-ny.gov
- Dobbs Ferry PD
- Chief Betsy Gelardi
  112 Main St.
  Dobbs Ferry, NY 10522
  (914) 231-8517
  bgelardi@dobbsferrypolice.com

- Town of Eastchester PD
- Chief Timothy J. Bonci
  40 Mill Rd.
  Eastchester, NY 10709
  (914) 961-3464
  police@eastchester.org
- Elmsford PD
- Comm. Frank Rescigno
  15 So. Stone Ave.
  Elmsford, NY 10523
  (914) 592-8383
  frescigno@elmsfordpd.com
- Greenburgh PD
- Chief Joseph DeCarlo
  188 Tarrytown Rd.
  White Plains, NY 10607
  (914) 682-5300
  gpdwebmail@greenburghny.com
- Harrison PD
- Chief Anthony Marraccini
  650 North St.
  Harrison, NY 10528
  (914) 813-7425
  rbelmont@harrison-ny.gov
- Hastings-On-Hudson PD
- Chief David Bloomer
  7 Maple Ave.
  Hastings-On-Hudson, NY 10706
  (914) 478-2344
  dbloomer@hastingsgov.org
- Irvington PD
- Chief Michael P. Cerone
  85 Main St.
  Irvington, NY 10533
  (914) 591-8080
  mcerone@irvingtonpolice.com
- Lewisboro PD
- Chief Frank Secret
  11 Main St.
  PO Box 500
  South Salem, NY 10590
  (914) 763-8903
  chieflpd@lewisborogov.com
- Mamaroneck PD
- Chief Richard Rivera
  740 W. Boston Post Rd.
  Mamaroneck, NY 10543
  (914) 381-6100
  policechief@townofmamaroneck.org
- Mount Kisco PD
- Chief Steven J Anderson
  40 Green St.
  Mount Kisco, NY 10549
  (914) 241-1100
  jpalmer@mountkisco.org
- Mount Pleasant PD
- Chief Russell Beckley
  1 Town Hall Plaza
  Valhalla, NY 10595
  (914) 769-1941
  lalagno@mtpleasantny.com
- New Castle PD
- Chief Charles Ferry
  200 So. Greeley Ave.
  Chappaqua, NY 10514
  (914) 238-7292
  cferry@town.new-castle.ny.us
- New Rochelle PD
- Comm. Patrick J. Carroll
  475 North Ave.
  New Rochelle, NY 10801
  (914) 654-2300
  nbramson@newrochelleny.com
- North Castle PD
- Chief William A. Fisher
  15 Bedford Rd.
  Armonk, NY 10504
  (914) 273-9500
  supervisor@northcastleny.com
- North Salem PD
- Chief Thomas Howley
  274 Titicus Rd.
  North Salem, NY 10560
  (914) 669-5540
  thowley@northsalemny.org
- Peekskill PD
- Chief Eric Johansen
  2 Nelson Ave.
  Peekskill, NY 10566
  (914) 737-8000
  ejohansen@peekskillpolice.com
- Pelham PD
- Chief Joseph Benefico
  34 5th Ave.
  Pelham, NY 10803
  (914) 738-2000
  info@pelhamgov.com

- Pelham Manor PD
- Chief Al Mosiello
  4 Penfield Pl.
  Pelham Manor, NY 10803
  (914) 738-1000
  info@pelhammanor.org
- Pleasantville PD
- Chief Richard Love
  80 Wheeler Ave.
  Pleasantville, NY 10570
  (914) 769-1500
  rlove@pleasantville-ny.gov
- Pound Ridge PD
- Chief David M. Ryan
  177 Westchester Ave.
  Pound Ridge, NY 10576
  (914) 764-4206
  dryan@townofpoundridge.com
- Rye PD
- Comm. William R. Connors
  21 Mccullough Pl.
  Rye, NY 10580
  (914) 967-1234
  police@ryepd.ryeny.gov
- Scarsdale PD
- Chief John A. Brogan
  50 Tompkins Rd.
  Scarsdale, NY 10583
  (914) 722-1200
  police@scarsdale.com
- Sleepy Hollow PD
- Chief Gregory Camp
  28 Beekman Ave.
  Sleepy Hollow, NY 10591
  (914) 631-0800
  kwray@villageofsleepyhollow.org
- Somers PD
- Chief Michael Driscoll
  100 Primrose St., 335 Rt. 202
  Somers, NY 10589
  (914) 232-9622
  police@somersny.com
- Tarrytown PD
- Chief Scott W. Brown
  One Depot Plaza
  Tarrytown, NY 10591
  (914) 631-5544
  tarrytownpd@aol.com
- Tuckahoe PD
- Chief John Costanzo
  65 Main St.
  Tuckahoe, NY 10707
  (914) 961-4800
  secklond@tuckahoe-ny.com
- Yorktown PD
- Chief Daniel M. McMahon
  2281 Crompond Rd.
  Yorktown Heights, NY 10598
  (914) 962-4141
  info@yorktownpd.org

Wyoming County

- Wyoming County SO
- Sheriff Farris S. Heimann
  151 No. Main St.
  Warsaw, NY 14569
  (585) 786-8989
  FHeimann@wyomingco.net
- Perry PD
- Chief James A. Case
  46 Main St. No.
  Perry, NY 14530
  (585) 237-5445
  jcase@villageofperry.com

Yates County

- Yates County SO
- Sheriff Ronald G. Spike
  227 Main St.
  Penn Yan, NY 14527
  (315) 536-4438
  sheriff@yatescounty.org
- Penn Yan PD
- Chief Mark Hulse
  1 Basin St.
  Penn Yan, NY 14527
  (315) 536-4426
  pymayor@villageofpennyan.com

State Agencies

- NY State Police-HQ
- Supt. Joseph D'Amico
  1220 Washington Ave., Bldg 22
  Albany, NY 12226-2252
  (518) 474-5331
  nyspmail@troopers.ny.gov
- NY State Assn.
- Aux. Police Pres. Glenn Kearney
  PO Box 351
  Massapequa, NY 11758
  (516) 795-4378
  stateassoc@auxiliary-police.org

- SUNY-Old Westbury PD
- Chief Michael Yanniello
  PO Box 210
  Old Westbury, NY 11568
  (516) 876-3146
  yanniellom@oldwestbury.edu

NORTH CAROLINA

Alamance County

- Alamance County SO
- Sheriff Terry S. Johnson
  109 So. Maple St.
  Graham, NC 27253
  (336) 570-6311
  terry.johnson@alamance-nc.com
- Burlington PD
- Chief Jeffrey Smythe
  267 W. Front St.
  Burlington, NC 27215
  (336) 229-3503
  jsmythe@ci.burlington.nc.us
- Elon PD
- Chief Cliff Parker
  104 So. Williamson Ave.
  Elon, NC 27244
  (336) 584-1301
  cparker@ci.elon.nc.us
- Gibsonville PD
- Chief Mike Woznick
  129 W. Main St.
  Gibsonville, NC 27249
  (336) 449-7926, ext. 132
  (See also Guilford County)
  chief@gibsonville.net
- Graham PD
- Chief Jeff Prichard
  216 So. Maple St.
  Graham, NC 27253
  (336) 570-6711
  jprichard@cityofgraham.com
- Haw River PD
- Chief Neal Dickens
  105 Stone St.
  Haw River, NC 27258
  (336) 578-4141
  ndickens@townofhawriver.com
- Mebane PD
- Chief Terrance *Terry* Caldwell
  103 W. Washington St.
  Mebane, NC 27302
  (919) 563-9031
  tcaldwell@mebanepd.com

Alexander County

- Alexander County SO
- Sheriff Chris Bowman
  29 W. Main Ave.
  Taylorsville, NC 28681
  (828) 632-4658
  cbowman@alexandercountync.gov
- Taylorsville PD
- Chief Tony Jones
  67 Main Ave.
  Taylorsville, NC 28681
  (828) 632-2218
  policechief@taylorsvillenc.com

Alleghany County

- Alleghany County SO
- Sheriff David R. Edwards
  40 Alleghany St. PO Box 53
  Sparta, NC 28675
  (910) 372-4455
  acsdrecords@skybest.com
- Sparta PD
- Chief Bob Lane
  100 Alleghany St. PO Box 1018
  Sparta, NC 28675
  (910) 372-4252
  pchoate@townofsparta.org

Anson County

- Anson County SO
- Sheriff Tommy W. Allen, Jr.
  119 No. Washington St.
  Wadesboro, NC 28170
  (704) 694-4188
  tallen@co.anson.nc.us
- Wadesboro PD
- Chief Thedis L. Spencer
  111 So. Washington St.
  Wadesboro, NC 28170
  (704) 694-2167
  contact@wadesboropolice.com

Ashe County

- Ashe County SO
- Sheriff James Williams
  140 Government Cir.
  Jefferson, NC 28640
  (336) 846-5633
  sheriff@ashecountygov.com
- Jefferson PD
- Chief David Neaves
  213 E. Main St. PO Box 67
  Jefferson, NC 28640
  (336) 846-5529
  jeffersonpd@skybest.com
- West Jefferson PD
- Chief Jeff Rose
  PO Box 490
  West Jefferson, NC 28694
  (336) 246-3551
  police@townofwj.com

Avery County

- Avery County SO
- Sheriff Kevin L. Frye
  300 Schultz Cir.PO Box 426
  Newland, NC 28657
  (828) 733-2071
  kevin.frye@averycountync.gov
- Avery County Publ. Schools PD
- Chief John Millan
  401 High School PO Box 1300
  Newland, NC 28657-1300
  (828) 733-0151
  johnmillan@averyschools.net
- Beech Mountain PD
- Chief Jay Hefner
  403 Beech Mountain Pkwy
  Beech Mountain, NC 28604
  (See also Watauga County)
  (828) 387-2342
  chief@townofbeechmountain.com
- Newland PD
- Chief Jason Brown
  301 Cranberry St.
  Newland, NC 28657
  (828) 733-2023
  newlandpd@yahoo.com
- Seven Devils PD
- Chief Chuck Davis
  1356 Seven Devils Rd.
  Seven Devils, NC 28604
  (See also Watauga County)
  (828) 963-5343
  policechief@sevendevils.net
- Sugar Mountain PD
- Chief David Henson
  251 Dick Trundy Ln.
  Sugar Mountain, NC 28604
  (828) 898-4349
  webmaster@blueridgeparkway.org

Beaufort County

- Beaufort County SO
- Sheriff R. Alan Jordan
  210 No. Market St.
  Washington, NC 27889
  (252) 946-7111
  jordan@sheriff.co.beaufort.nc.us
- Belhaven PD
- Chief F.P. *Fred* Clingenpeel
  137 E. Main St. PO Box 220
  Belhaven, NC 27810
  (252) 943-2242
  policedepartment@belhavennc.us
- Chocowinity PD
- Chief M. Todd Alligood
  3359 Hwy 17S PO Box 145
  Chocowinity, NC 27817
  (252) 946-2882
  townofchoco@suddenlinkmail.com
- Washington PD
- Chief Stacy Drakeford
  201 W. 3rd St.
  Washington, NC 27889
  (252) 975-9378
  sdrakeford@washingtonnc.gov

Bertie County

- Bertie County SO
- Sheriff John Holley
  104 Dundee St. PO Box 157
  Windsor, NC 27983
  (252) 794-5330
  john.holley@bertie.nc.gov

Bladen County

- Bladen County SO
- Sheriff Prentis Bentson
  201 E. King St. PO Box 396
  Elizabethtown, NC 28337
  (910) 862-6960
  pbentson@bladenco.org
- Elizabethtown PD
- Chief Robert L. *Bobby* Kinlaw
  805 W. Broad St. PO Box 1278
  Elizabethtown, NC 28337
  (910) 862-3125
  police@elizabethtownnc.org
- White Lake PD
- Chief Bruce Smith
  1823 Lake Rd. PMB 7250
  White Lake, NC 28337
  (910) 862-4057
  whitelakenc@yahoo.com

Brunswick County

- Brunswick County SO
- Sheriff John W. Ingram V
  70 Stamp Act Dr. PO Box 9
  Bolivia, NC 28422
  (910) 253-2777
  sheriffingram@brunsco.net
- Boiling Springs Lake PD
- Chief Bradford Shirley
  9 E. Boiling Spring Rd.
  Boiling Springs Lake, NC 28461
  (910) 845-2247
  bshirley@cityofbsl.org

- Caswell Beach PD
- Chief George Kassler
  1100 Caswell Beach Rd.
  Caswell Beach, NC 28465
  (910) 278-1555
  police@caswellbeach.org
- Holden Beach PD
- Chief Wallace *Wally* Layne
  110 Rothschild St.
  Holden Beach, NC 28462
  (910) 842-6707
  wallace.layne@hbtownhall.com
- Leland PD
- Chief Mike James
  102 Town Hall Dr.
  Leland, NC 28451
  (910) 371-1100
  info@townofleland.com
- Northwest PD
- Chief Copelen L. Taylor
  4889 Vernon Rd.
  Leland, NC 28451
  (910) 655-3300
  taylor@cityofnorthwest.com
- Navassa PD
- Chief Preston Howell
  334 Main St.
  Navassa, NC 28451
  (910) 371-0155
  chief@townofnavassa.org
- Oak Island PD
- Chief Van Eddinger
  4621 E. Oak Island Dr.
  Oak Island, NC 28465
  (910) 278-5595
  veddinger@ci.oak-island.nc.us
- Ocean Isle Beach PD
- Chief John W. Goodwin
  3 W. 3rd St.
  Ocean Isle Beach, NC 28469
  (910) 579-4221
  john@oibgov.com
- Shallotte PD
- Chief Rodney Gause
  115 Wall St.
  Shallotte, NC 28470
  (910) 754-6008
  sandystrickland@atmc.net
- Southport PD
- Chief Jerry Dove
  201 E. Moore St.
  Southport, NC 28461
  (910) 457-7913
  jdove@southportpd.com
- Sunset Beach PD
- Chief Lisa Massey
  700 Sunset Blvd No.
  Sunset Beach, NC 28468
  (910) 579-2151
  sunsetpolice@atmc.net

Buncombe County

- Buncombe County SD
- Sheriff Van Duncan
  202 Haywood St.
  Asheville, NC 28801
  (828) 250-4503
  van.duncan@buncombecounty.org
- Asheville PD
- Chief William J. Anderson
  100 Court Plaza PO Box 7148
  Asheville, NC 28802
  (828) 252-1110
  wanderson@ashevillenc.gov
- Biltmore Forest PD
- Chief Eric Tinsley
  355 Vanderbilt Rd.
  Biltmore Forest, NC 28803
  (828) 274-0822
  chieftinsley@biltmoreforest.org
- Black Mountain PD
- Chief Steve Padgett
  106 Montreat Rd.
  Black Mountain, NC 28711
  (828) 669-9194
  townboard@townofblackmountain.org
- Woodfin PD
- Chief Brett Holloman
  90 Elk Mountain Rd.
  Woodfin, NC
  (828) 253-4889
  jasonyoung@woodfin-nc.gov

Burke County

- Burke County SO
- Sheriff Steve Whisenant
  150 Government Dr.
  Morganton, NC 28655
  (828) 438-5500
  admins@burkesheriff.org

- Drexel PD
- Chief Mike Swink
  202 Church St. PO Box 188
  Drexel, NC 28619
  (828) 437-7421
  mswink@ci.drexel.nc.us
- Morgantown PD
- Chief Mark Tolbert
  304 So. College St.
  Morgantown, NC 28655
  (828) 437-1211
  pubinfo@ci.morganton.nc.us
- Rhodhiss PD
- Chief Tim Anthony
  PO Box 40
  Rhodhiss, NC 28667
  (See also Caldwell County)
  (828) 396-8401
  rhodhiss1@abts.net
- Valdese PD
- Chief Jack Moss
  121 Faet St.
  Valdese, NC 28690
  (828) 879-2102
  jmoss@ci.valdese.nc.us

Cabarrus County

- Cabarrus County SO
- Sheriff Brad Riley
  30 Corban Ave. SE
  Concord, NC 28025
  (704) 920-3000
  dbriley@cabarruscounty.us
- Concord PD
- Chief Guy Smith
  41 Cabarrus Ave. W.
  Concord, NC 28026
  (704) 920-5007
  smithg@concordnc.gov
- Kannapolis PD
- Chief James W. *Woody* Chavis
  314 So. Main St.
  Kannapolis, NC 28081
  (See also Rowan County)
  (704) 920-4010
  jwchavis@cityofkannapolis.com

Caldwell County

- Caldwell County SO
- Sheriff Alan C. Jones
  2351 Morganton Blvd SW
  Lenoir, NC 28645
  (828) 758-2324
  ajones@caldwellcountync.org
- Granite Falls PD
- Chief Ritch Bolick
  5 Falls Ave.
  Granite Falls, NC 28630
  (828) 396-3358
  rbolick@granitefallspolicenc.us
- Hudson PD
- Chief Andy E. Day
  550 Central St.
  Hudson, NC 28638
  (828) 728-5021
  records@hudsonpolicedepartment.net
- Lenoir PD
- Chief Scott Brown
  1035 West Ave. NW
  Lenoir, NC 28645
  (828) 757-2121
  sbrown@ci.lenoir.nc.us
- Rhodhiss PD
- Chief Tim Anthony
  PO Box 40
  Rhodhiss, NC 28667
  (See also Burke County)
  (828) 396-8401
  rhodhiss1@abts.net

Camden County

- Camden County SO
- Sheriff Tony E. Perry
  117 No. NC 343 PO Box 57
  Camden, NC 27921
  (252) 338-5046
  tperry@camdencountync.gov

Carteret County

- Carteret County SO
- Sheriff Asa B. Buck III
  304 Craven St. PO Drawer 239
  Beaufort, NC 28516
  (252) 504-4800
  asab@carteretcountygov.org
- Atlantic Beach PD
- Chief Allen Smith
  125 W. Ft. Macon PO Box 10
  Atlantic Beach, NC 28512
  (252) 726-2523
  policechief@atlanticbeach-nc.com
- Beaufort PD
- Chief Steven C. *Steve* Lewis
  610 Broad St.
  Beaufort, NC 28516
  (252) 728-4561
  s.lewis@beaufortnc.org

- Cape Carteret PD
- Chief Donald *Don* Miller
  102 Dolphin St.
  Cape Carteret, NC 28584
  (252) 393-2183
  ccpd@eastnc.twcbc.com
- Emerald Isle PD
- Act. Chief Jeff Waters
  7500 Emerald Dr.
  Emerald Isle, NC 28594
  (252) 354-2021
  jwaters@emeraldisle-nc.org
- Morehead City PD
- Chief Wrenn Johnson
  202 So. 8th St.
  Morehead City, NC 28557
  (252) 726-3131
  wrenn@bizec.rr.com
- Newport PD
- Chief Jeff Clark
  255 Howard Blvd PO Box 1869
  Newport, NC 28570
  (252) 223-5410
  newportchief@ec.rr.com

Caswell County

- Caswell County SO
- Sheriff Michael L. Welch
  314 North Ave. PO Box 1177
  Yanceyville, NC 27379
  (336) 694-9311, ext. 234
  mwelch@caswellcountync.gov

Catawba County

- Catawba County SO
- Sheriff Coy Reid
  100 B SW Blvd PO Box 385
  Newton, NC 28658
  (828) 464-5241
  coy@catawbacountync.gov
- Catawba PD
- Chief Mike Nash
  107 So. Main St.
  Catawba, NC 28609
  (828) 241-4888
  catawbapd@embarqmail.com
- Claremont PD
- Chief Gary Bost
  3301 E. Main St. PO Box 446
  Claremont, NC 28610
  (828) 459-9295
  pshook@cityofclaremont.org
- Conover PD
- Chief Steve Brewer
  115 E. 2nd St.
  Conover, NC 28613
  (828) 464-4698
  steve.brewer@conovernc.gov
- Hickory PD
- Chief Tom Adkins
  347 2nd Ave. SW
  Hickory, NC 28602-2844
  (828) 261-2600
  tadkins@hickorync.gov
- Longview PD
- Chief Cecil L. *Buck* Rogers
  2404 1st Ave. SW
  Longview, NC 28602
  (828) 328-2343
  cecil.rogers@mail.ci.longview.nc.us
- Maiden PD
- Chief Tracy Ledford
  201 W. Main St.
  Maiden, NC 28650
  (828) 428-5005
  tledford@mail.ci.maiden.nc.us
- Newton PD
- Chief Donald G. Brown II
  411 No. Main Ave.
  Newton, NC 28658
  (828) 695-4306
  tclark@newtonnc.gov

Chatham County

- Chatham County SO
- Sheriff Richard H. Webster
  295 West St. PO Box 429
  Pittsboro, NC 27312
  (919) 545-8122
  richard.webster@chathamsheriff.com
- Pittsboro PD
- Chief David Collins
  635 East St. PO Box 759
  Pittsboro, NC 27312
  (919) 542-3200, ext. 33
  chiefcollins@pittsboronc.gov
- Siler City PD
- Chief Gary T. Tyson
  311 No. 2nd Ave.
  Siler City, NC 27344
  (919) 742-5626
  gtyson@silercity.org

Cherokee County

- Cherokee County SO
- Sheriff Keith Lovin
  577 Regal St.
  Murphy, NC 28906
  (828) 837-2589, ext. 236
  keith.lovin@cherokeecounty-nc.gov
- Andrews PD
- Chief Josh Litchfield
  1101 Main St.
  Andrews, NC 28901
  (828) 321-4224
  mayor@andrewsnc.com
- Murphy PD
- Chief Justin J. Jacobs
  93 Peachtree St.
  Murphy, NC 28906
  (828) 837-2214
  jjacobs@murphypolice.com

Chowan County

- Chowan County SO
- Sheriff Dwayne L. Goodwin
  305 W. Freemason PO Box 78
  Edenton, NC 27932
  (252) 482-8484
  dwayne.goodwin@chowancounty-nc.org
- Edenton PD
- Chief Jay Fortenbery
  305 W. Freemason St.
  Edenton, NC 27932
  (252) 482-5144
  jay.fortenbery@edenton.nc.gov

Clay County

- Clay County SO
- Sheriff Vic Davis
  295 Courthouse PO Box 720
  Hayesville, NC 28904
  (828) 389-6354
  claycountysheriff@claync.org

Cleveland County

- Cleveland County SO
- Sheriff Alan Norman
  100 Justice Pl. PO Box 1508
  Shelby, NC 28150
  (704) 484-4817
  alan.norman@clevelandcounty.com
- Boiling Springs PD
- Chief Randy Page
  PO Box 1014
  Boiling Springs, NC 28017
  (704) 434-9691
  randy.page@boilingspringsnc.net
- Kings Mountain PD
- Chief Melvin Proctor
  112 So. Piedmont PO Box 7
  Kings Mountain, NC 28086
  (See also Gaston County)
  (704) 734-4585
  melvinp@cityofkm.com
- Shelby PD
- Chief Jeff Ledford
  311 So. Lafayette St.
  Shelby, NC 28150
  (704) 484-6845
  police@cityofshelby.com

Columbus County

- Columbus County SO
- Sheriff Christopher L. Batten
  805 Washington
  PO Box 280
  Whiteville, NC 28472
  (910) 642-6551
  cbatten@columbusco.org
- Chadbourn PD
- Chief Steven Shaw
  602 No. Brown St.
  Chadbourn, NC 28431
  (910) 654-4146
  stevenshaw@bizec.rr.com
- Fair Bluff PD
- Chief Justin Hewett
  PO Box 126
  Fair Bluff, NC 28439
  (910) 649-7323
  fbpdchief@gmail.com
- Tabor City PD
- Chief Don Dowless
  1108 E. 5th St.
  Tabor City, NC 28463
  (910) 653-3149
  tcpd@taborcitypd.net
- Whiteville PD
- Chief Jerry Britt
  117 E. Columbus PO Box 607
  Whiteville, NC 28472
  (910) 642-5111
  jbritt@ci.whiteville.nc.us

Craven County

- Craven County SO
- Sheriff Jerry G. Monette
  1100 Clarks Rd.
  New Bern, NC 28563
  (252) 636-6620
  jmonette@cravencountync.gov

- Bridgeton PD
- Chief Steve Brown
  408 Bridge St. PO Box 130
  Bridgeton, NC 28519
  (252) 637-3697
  swatcop.chris@gmail.com
- Havelock PD
- Chief G. Wayne Cyrus
  PO Box 368
  Havelock, NC 28532
  (252) 447-3212
  WCyrus@HavelockNC.US
- New Bern PD
- Chief Toussaint E. Summers, Jr.
  601 George St.
  New Bern, NC 28560
  (252) 672-4190
  summerst@newbernpd.org
- Riverbend PD
- Chief Ryland E. Matthews, Jr.
  45 Shoreline Dr.
  Riverbend, NC 28562
  (252) 638-1108
  policechief@riverbendnc.org
- Trent Woods PD
- Chief Michael A. Register
  912 Country Club Dr.
  Trentwoods, NC 28562
  (252) 637-3030
  maregister@embarqmail.com
- Vanceboro PD
- Chief James L. Jenkins, Jr.
  7905 Main St. PO Box 306
  Vanceboro, NC 28586
  (252) 244-0440
  jamesj@vanceboronc.com

Cumberland County

- Cumberland County SO
- Sheriff Earl R. Butler
  131 Dick St.
  Fayetteville, NC 28301-5793
  (910) 677-5410
  sheriff@ccsonc.org
- Spring Lake PD
- Chief Troy McDuffie
  PO Box 617
  Spring Lake, NC 28390
  (910) 703-8916, ext. 1406
  tmcduffie@spring-lake.org

Currituck County

- Currituck County SO
- Sheriff Susan D. Johnson
  407 Maple Rd.
  Maple, NC 27956
  (252) 453-8204
  susan.johnson@currituckcountync.gov

Dare County

- Dare County SO
- Sheriff Doug Doughtie
  962 Marshall C. Collins
  Manteo, NC 27954
  (252) 475-5980, ext. 5978
  doug.doughtie@darenc.com
- Duck PD
- Chief Phillip Ferguson
  1259 Duck Rd.
  Duck, NC 27949
  (252) 261-1112
  policeinfo@townofduck.com
- Kill Devil Hills PD
- Chief Gary L. Britt
  102 Town Hall Dr. PO Box 1605
  Kill Devil Hills, NC 27948
  (252) 449-5337
  glbrit@kdhnc.com
- Kitty Hawk PD
- Chief Joel Johnson
  101 Veterans Memorial
  Kitty Hawk, NC 27949
  (252) 261-3895
  jcjohnson@kittyhawktown.net
- Manteo PD
- Chief Vance Haskett
  PO Box 246
  Manteo, NC 27954
  (252) 473-2069
  haskett@townofmanteo.com
- Nags Head PD
- Chief Kevin Brinkley
  5401 So. Croatan Hwy
  Nags Head, NC 27959
  (252) 449-2012, ext. 253
  kevinbrinkley@nagsheadnc.gov
- Southern Shores PD
- Chief David Kole
  6 Skyline Rd.
  Southern Shores, NC 27949
  (252) 261-3331
  sspdchief@southernshores.org

Davidson County

- Davidson County SO
- Sheriff David S. Grice
  110 W. Center St. PO Box 513
  Lexington, NC 27292
  (336) 242-2100
  david.grice@davidsoncountync.gov
- Denton PD
- Chief Mark Hicks
  201 W. Salisbury St.
  Denton, NC 27239
  (336) 859-2164
  TDenton@triad.rr.com
- Lexington PD
- Chief Tad Kepley
  106 No. Main St.
  Lexington, NC 27292
  (336) 243-3302
  TWKepley@LexingtonNC.gov
- Thomasville PD
- Chief Jeffrey *Jeff* Insley
  7 W. Guilford St.
  Thomasville, NC 27360
  (336) 475-4275
  jeff.insley@thomasville-nc.gov

Davie County

- Davie County SO
- Sheriff Andy Stokes
  140 So. Main St.
  Mocksville, NC 27028
  (336) 751-6238
  astokes@dcsonc.com
- Mocksville PD
- Chief Robert Cook
  278 No. Main St.
  Mocksville, NC 27028
  (336) 751-6231
  rcook@mocksvillenc.gov
- Cooleemee PD
- Chief Bobby R. West
  114 Duke St.
  Cooleemee, NC 27014
  (336) 284-4098
  townofcooleemee@cooleemee.org

Duplin County

- Duplin County SO
- Sheriff Blake Wallace
  112 W. Hill St. PO Box 908
  Kenansville, NC 28349
  (910) 296-2150
  blakew@duplincountync.com
- Beulaville PD
- Chief Joey Carter
  111 W. Quinn St.
  Beulaville, NC 28518
  (910) 298-5360
  beulavillepd@intrstar.net
- Kenansville PD
- Chief Rusty Merritt
  141 Routledge Rd. PO Box 370
  Kenansville, NC 28349
  (910) 296-0369
  adunn@embarqmail.com
- Rose Hill PD
- Chief Michael O'Connell
  110 SE Railroad St.
  Rose Hill, NC 28458
  (910) 289-3020
  rhpd@embarqmail.com
- Wallace PD
- Chief Bobby Maready
  316 E. Murray St.
  Wallace, NC 28466
  (910) 285-2126
  bmaready@townofwallace.com
- Warsaw PD
- Chief Mike Webster
  128 W. Bay St.
  Warsaw, NC 28398
  (910) 293-7816
  jmweb.wpd01@yahoo.com

Durham County

- Durham County SO
- Sheriff Worth L. Hill
  201 E. Main St. PO Box 170
  Durham, NC 27702
  (919) 560-0897
  sheriff@shf.co.durham.nc.us
- Durham PD
- Chief Jose L. Lopez, Sr.
  505 W. Chapel Hill St.
  Durham, NC 27701
  (919) 560-4322
  jose.lopez@durhamnc.gov

Edgecombe County

- Edgecombe County SO
- Sheriff James L. Knight
  3005 Anaconda PO Box 219
  Tarboro, NC 27886
  (252) 641-7914
  sheriff.knight@co.edgecombe.nc.us

- Pinetops PD
- Chief Greg Bethea
  101 E. Hamlet St.
  Pinetops, NC 27864
  (252) 827-5014
  gbethea@pinetopsnc.com
- Rocky Mount PD
- Chief James Moore
  330 So. Church St. PO Box 1180
  Rocky Mount, NC 27802-1180
  (See also Nash County)
  (252) 972-1411
  james.moore@rockymountnc.gov
- Sharpsburg PD
- Chief Alvin Coley
  108 Railroad St. PO Box 1759
  Sharpsburg, NC 27878
  (See also Nash & Wilson counties)
  (252) 977-0004
  acoley@sharpsburgnc.com
- Tarboro PD
- Chief Damon Williams
  106 W. Church St.
  Tarboro, NC 27886
  (252) 641- 4239
  damonwilliams@tarboro-nc.com

Forsyth County

- Forsyth County SO
- Sheriff William T. Schatzman
  120 W. 3rd St. PO Box 21089
  Winston Salem, NC 27101
  (336) 717-7001
  schatzwt@fcso.us
- Kernersville PD
- Chief Grady C. *Neal* Stockton
  134 E. Mountain St.
  Kernersville, NC 27285
  (336) 996-2390
  sbowman@toknc.com

Franklin County

- Franklin County SD
- Sheriff Jerry W Jones
  285 T. Kemp Rd.
  Louisburg, NC 27549
  (919) 496-2186
  jjones@franklincountync.us
- Franklinton PD
- Chief John Green
  7 W. Mason
  Franklinton, NC 27525
  (919) 494-2151
  jgreen@franklintonnc.us
- Louisburg PD
- Chief Rick Lassiter
  Johnson St.
  Louisburg, NC 27549
  (919) 496-4175
  lbgpdchf@ncrrbiz.com
- Youngsville PD
- Chief Daren Kirts
  118 No. Cross St.
  Youngsville, NC 27596
  (919) 556-0500
  dakirts@aol.com

Gaston County

- Gaston County SO
- Sheriff Alan Cloninger
  425 No. Marietta PO Box 1578
  Gastonia, NC 28054
  (704) 869-6800
  acloninger@gcps.org
- Belmont PD
- Chief Charlie Franklin
  201 Chronicle St. PO Box 551
  Belmont, NC 28012
  (704) 829-4022
  franklin@belmontpolice.org
- Cherryville PD
- Chief Woodrow *Woody* Burgess
  704 E. Church St.
  Cherryville, NC 28021
  (704) 435-1717
  wburgess@cherryville.com
- Cramerton PD
- Chief Greg Ratchford
  155 No. Main St.
  Cramerton, NC 28032
  (704) 824-7964
  administration@cramertonpd.org
- Dallas PD
- Chief GW *Gary* Buckner
  131 No. Gaston St.
  Dallas, NC 28034
  (704) 922-3131
  gbuckner@dallasnc.net

- Gaston County PD
- Chief James Buie
  420 W. Franklin Blvd
  Gastonia, NC 28053
  (704) 866-3320
  records@gcps.org
- Gastonia PD
- Chief Stacy Conley
  200 E. Long Ave.
  Gastonia, NC 28053
  (704) 866-6890
  police@cityofgastonia.com
- Kings Mountain PD
- Chief Melvin Proctor
  112 So. Piedmont PO Box 7
  Kings Mountain, NC 28086
  (See also Cleveland County)
  704) 734-4585
  melvinp@cityofkm.com
- Lowell PD
- Chief Mark Buchanan
  101 E. 1st St.
  Lowell, NC 28098
  (704) 824-8540
  buchanan@lowellnc.com
- Mount Holly PD
- Chief David Belk
  400 E. Central PO Box 406
  Mount Holly, NC 28120
  (704) 822-2936
  david.belk@mtholly.us

Gates County

- Gates County SO
- Sheriff Edward E. Webb
  202 Court St. PO Box 154
  Gatesville, NC 27938
  (252) 357-0210
  gatescoso@hotmail.com

Graham County

- Graham County SO
- Sheriff Mickey Anderson
  300 Rodney Orr Bypass
  Robbinsville, NC 28771
  (704) 479-3352
  anderson.mickey50@yahoo.com

Granville County

- Granville County SO
- Sheriff Brindell B. Wilkins, Jr.
  143 Williamsboro St.
  Oxford, NC 27565
  (919) 693-3213
  sheriff@granvillecounty.org
- Creedmoor PD
- Chief Dennis Williams
  111 Masonic St.
  Creedmoor, NC 27522
  (919) 528-1515
  dwilliams@cityofcreedmoor.org
- Oxford PD
- Chief John M. Wolford
  204 E. McClanahan St.
  Oxford, NC 27565
  (919) 693-3161
  police@oxfordnc.org

Greene County

- Greene County SD
- Sheriff Lemmie Smith
  301 No. Greene St.
  Snow Hill, NC 28580
  (252) 747-3411, ext. 222
  lsmith@co.greene.nc.us

Guilford County

- Guilford County SO
- Sheriff B.J. Barnes
  400 W. Washington St.
  Greensboro, NC 27401
  (336) 641-3694
  bbarnes@coguilford.nc.us
- Gibsonville PD
- Chief Mike Woznick
  129 W. Main St.
  Gibsonville, NC 27249
  (336) 449-7926, ext. 132
  (See also Alamance County)
  chief@gibsonville.net
- High Point PD
- Chief Marty Sumner
  1009 Leonard Ave.
  High Point, NC 27260
  (336) 841-7970
  marty.sumner@highpointnc.gov

Halifax County

- Halifax County SO
- Sheriff Jeff P. Frazier
  355 Ferrell Ln. PO Box 36
  Halifax, NC 27839
  (252) 583-8201
  frazierj@halifaxnc.com
- Enfield PD
- Chief Willie L. Tillery, Jr.
  115 SE Railroad St.
  Enfield, NC 27823
  (252) 445-5122
  wtillery@enfieldnc.org

- Roanoke Rapids PD
- Chief T.R. Hathaway
  1040 Roanoke Ave.
  Roanoke Rapids, NC 27870
  (252) 533-2810
  thathaway@roanokerapidsnc.com
- Scotland Neck PD
- Chief Joe Williams
  101 E. 11th St.
  Scotland Neck, NC 27874
  (252) 826-4112
  scotneck@embarqmail.com

Harnett County

- Harnett County SO
- Sheriff Larry Rollins
  175 Bain St. PO Box 399
  Lillington, NC 27546
  (910) 893-9111
  lrollins@harnett.org
- Angier PD
- Chief Bobby Hallman
  55 No. Broad St. W.
  Angier, NC 27501
  (919) 639-2699
  bhallman@www.angier.org
- Coats PD
- Chief Matthew Jeremy Hall
  PO Box 675
  Coats, NC 27521
  (910) 897-5183
  mhall@coatsnc.org
- Dunn PD
- Chief J.D. Pope
  401 E. Broad St. PO Box 1065
  Dunn, NC 28335
  (910) 230-3533
  jpope@dunn-nc.org
- Erwin PD
- Chief Warren M. Morrisette
  100 W. F St.
  Erwin, NC 28339
  (910) 897-5122
  wmorrisette@erwin-nc.org

Haywood County

- Haywood County SO
- Sheriff Bobby Suttles
  1612 Brown Ave.
  Waynesville, NC 28786
  (828) 452-6768
  suttles@haywoodnc.net
- Clyde PD
- Chief Gerard Ball
  105 Depot St.
  Clyde, NC 28721
  (828) 627-2940, ext. 16
  gerard.ball@townofclyde.com
- Maggie Valley PD
- Chief Scott Sutton
  3987 Soco Rd.
  Maggie Valley, NC 28751
  (828) 926- 0867, ext. 118
  ssutton@maggiepd.com
- Waynesville PD
- Chief Bill Hollingsed
  9 So. Main St., Ste. 100
  Waynesville, NC 28786
  (828) 456-5363
  wpdchief@waynesvillepd.com

Henderson County

- Henderson County SO
- Sheriff Rick Davis
  201 No. Main St.
  Hendersonville, NC 28792
  (828) 697-4596
  rdavis@hendersoncountync.org
- Fletcher PD
- Chief Erik Summey
  110 Parrish Municipal Dr.
  Fletcher, NC 28732
  (828) 687-7922
  info@fletchernc.org
- Hendersonville PD
- Chief Herbert Blake
  127 6th Ave. E.
  Hendersonville, NC 28793
  (828) 697-3031
  hblake@cityofhendersonville.org
- Laurel Park PD
- Chief Bobbie K. Trotter
  441 White Pine Dr.
  Laurel Park, NC 28739
  (828) 682-9399
  btrotter@laurelpark.org

Hertford County

- Hertford County SO
- Sheriff Juan E. Vaughn, Sr.
  701 No. Taylor St. PO Box 176
  Winton, NC 27986
  (252) 358-7800, ext. 3803
  juan.vaughn@hertfordcountync.gov

- Ahoskie PD
- Chief Troy Fitzhugh
  301 Main St. W. PO Box 767
  Ahoskie, NC 27910
  (252) 332-5011
  911info@ahoskiepd.com
- Murfreesboro PD
- Chief R. Darrell Rowe
  115 E. Broad St.
  Murfreesboro, NC 27855
  (252) 398-4151
  townofmurfreesboro@gate811.net

Hoke County

- Hoke County SO
- Sheriff Hubert A. Peterkin
  429 E. Central PO Drawer 300
  Raeford, NC 28376
  (910) 875-5111
  hpeterkin@hokesheriff.org
- Raeford PD
- Chief Franklin K. Crumpler
  315 No. Main St.
  Raeford, NC 28376
  (910) 875-4251
  chiefcrumpler@raefordnc.org

Hyde County

- Hyde County SO
- Sheriff David T. Mason
  1223 Main St. PO Box 189
  Swan Quarter, NC 27885
  (252) 926-3171
  barbaradeese@yahoo.com

Iredell County

- Iredell County SO
- Sheriff Phillip H. Redmond
  230 No. Tradd St. PO Box 287
  Statesville, NC 28687
  (704) 878-3180
  predmond@co.iredell.nc.us
- Statesville PD
- Chief Thomas A. *Tom* Anderson
  301 So. Center St. PO Box 506
  Statesville, NC 28677
  (704) 878-3583
  tanderson@statesvillenc.net
- Troutman PD
- Chief Matthew A. Selves
  400 Eastway Dr. PO Box 26
  Troutman, NC 28166
  (704) 528-7610
  pdmail@townoftroutman.org

Jackson County

- Jackson County SO
- Sheriff Jimmy Ashe
  399 Grindstaff Cove Rd.
  Sylva, NC 28779
  (828) 586-4355, ext. 305
  sheriffashe@jacksonnc.org
- Cherokee PD
- Chief Ben Reed
  468 Sequoyah Tr.
  PO Box 1330
  Cherokee, NC 28719
  (828) 554-6603
  benreed@nc-cherokee.com
- Sylva PD
- Chief Davis C. Woodard
  83 Allen St.
  Sylva, NC 28779
  (828) 586-2916
  woodard@sylvapolice.org

Johnston County

- Johnston County SO
- Sheriff Steve Bizzell
  120 So. 3rd St. PO Box 1809
  Smithfield, NC 27577
  (919) 989-5010
  sbizzell@jcso.org
- Benson PD
- Chief Kenneth Edwards
  303 E. Church St. PO Box 69
  Benson, NC 27504
  (919) 894-3616
  admin@bensonpd.org
- Clayton PD
- Int. Chief R.W. Bridges
  315 E. 2nd St. PO Box 879
  Clayton, NC 27520
  (919) 553-4611
  contact@claytonpolice.org
- Four Oaks PD
- Chief Danny Toppings
  304 No. Main St. PO Box 610
  Four Oaks, NC 27524
  (919) 963-3112, ext. 34
  town.clerk@embarqmail.com
- Kenly PD
- Chief Joshua P. *Josh* Gibson
  206 W. 2nd St. PO Box 519
  Kenly, NC 27542
  (919) 284-2116
  josh.gibson@townofkenly.com

- Micro PD
- Chief Casey Jones
  101 US 301 So. PO Box 9
  Micro, NC 27555
  (919) 284-2572
  micropolice@gmail.com
- Princeton PD
- Chief Tyrone Sutton
  503 Dr. Donnie H. Jones, Jr. Blvd W.
  Princeton, NC 27569
  (919) 936-8171
  tsutton84@myprincetonnc.com
- Selma PD
- Chief Charles M. Bowen
  1200 So. Pollock St.
  Selma, NC 27576
  (919) 965-8189, ext. 211
  PoliceChief@selma-nc.com
- Smithfield PD
- Chief Michael L. Scott
  110 S. 5th St. PO Box 761
  Smithfield, NC 27577
  (919) 934-2121
  daniel.evans@smithfield-nc.com
- Wilson's Mills PD
- Chief Roy Aycock
  100 Railroad St.PO Box 448
  Wilson's Mills, NC 27593
  (919) 938-3885
  info@wilsonsmillspd.org

Jones County

- Jones County SO
- Sheriff Danny Heath
  101 Market St. PO Box 267
  Trenton, NC 28585
  (252) 448-7091
  sheriff@co.jones.nc.us

Lee County

- Lee County SO
- Sheriff Tracy L. Carter
  1401 Elm St. PO Box 4567
  Sanford, NC 27330
  (919) 718-4560
  sheriff@leecountync.gov
- Broadway PD
- Chief Todd Hinnant
  119 So. Main St. PO Box 130
  Broadway, NC 27505
  (919) 258-9232
  bwaytownhall@windstream.net
- Sanford PD
- Chief Ronnie V. Yarborough
  225 E. Weatherspoon
  Sanford, NC 27330
  (919) 775-8268
  kelly.miller@sanfordnc.net

Lenoir County

- Lenoir County SO
- Sheriff W.E. *Billy* Smith
  130 So. Queen St. PO Box 3289
  Kinston, NC 28502
  (252) 559-6100
  wsmith@co.lenoir.nc.us
- Kinston PD
- Chief Bill Johnson
  205 E. King St.
  Kinston, NC 28502
  (252) 939-3224
  bill.johnson@ci.kinston.nc.us

Lincoln County

- Lincoln County SO
- Sheriff David M. Carpenter
  700 John Howell Memorial Dr.
  Lincolnton, NC 28092
  (704) 732-9050
  sheriffcarpenter@lincolnsheriff.org
- Lincolnton PD
- Chief Rodney Jordan
  627 E. Main St.
  Lincolnton, NC 28093
  (704) 736-8909
  rjordan@lincolntonpolice.com

Macon County

- Macon County SO
- Sheriff Robert L. Holland
  1820 Lakeside Dr.
  Franklin, NC 28734
  (828) 349-2104
  rholland@maconnc.org
- Franklin PD
- Chief David Adams
  188 W. Main St. PO Box 1479
  Franklin, NC 28734
  (828) 524-2864
  jcollins@franklinnc.com
- Highlands PD
- Chief Bill Harrell
  PO Box 460
  Highlands, NC 28741
  (828) 526-1769
  highpol@earthlink.net

Madison County

- Madison County SO
- Sheriff J.E. *Buddy* Harwood
  Lower Bridge St. PO Box 998
  Marshall, NC 28753
  (828) 649-2721
  sheriffharwood@madisoncountysheriff.org
- Marshall PD
- Chief Denny Goforth
  180 So. Main St.
  Marshall, NC 28753
  (828) 649-3031
  info@townofmarshall.org
- Mars Hill PD
- Chief David K. Lewis
  280 No. Main St.
  Mars Hill, NC 28754
  (828) 689-2301
  dlewis@townofmarshill.org

Martin County

- Martin County SO
- Sheriff Dan Gibbs, Jr.
  305 E. Main St. PO Box 308
  Williamston, NC 27892
  (252) 789-4500
  dgibbs@martincountyncgov.com
- Robersonville PD
- Chief Darrell Knox
  119 So. Main St. PO Box 865
  Robersonville, NC 27871
  (252) 508-0312
  pleebee@yahoo.com
- Williamston PD
- Chief Travis Cowan
  106 E. Main St. PO Box 506
  Williamston, NC 27892
  (252) 792-2124
  travis.cowan.wpd@gmail.com

McDowell County

- McDowell County SO
- Sheriff Dudley Greene
  593 Spaulding Rd.
  Marion, NC 28752
  (828) 652-2235, ext. 229
  dgreene@mcdowellsheriff.org
- Old Fort PD
- Chief Melvin Lytle
  35 Peggy Loop
  Old Fort, NC 28762
  (828) 668-4244, ext. 14
  rick@oldfort.org

Mecklenburg County

- Mecklenburg County SO
- Sheriff Daniel E. *Chipp* Bailey, Jr.
  700 E. 4th St.
  Charlotte, NC 28202
  (704) 336-2543
  daniel.bailey@mecklenburgcountync.gov
- Charlotte-Mecklenburg PD
- Chief Rodney Monroe
  601 E. Trade St.
  Charlotte, NC 28202
  (704) 336-2337
  spearsall@cmpd.org
- Cornelius PD
- Chief Bence Hoyle
  PO Box 399
  Cornelius, NC 28031
  (704) 892-1363
  bhoyle@corneliuspd.org
- Davidson PD
- Chief Jeanne A. Miller
  216 So. Main St.
  Davidson, NC 28036
  (704) 892-5131
  jmiller@townofdavidson.org
- Matthews PD
- Chief Rob Hunter
  1201 Crews Rd.
  Matthews, NC 28105
  (704) 847-4069
  rhunter@matthewsnc.gov
- Mint Hill PD
- Chief Tim W. Ledford
  4430 Mint Hill Village Ln.
  Mint Hill, NC 28227
  (704) 545-9726
  police@police.minthill.com

Mitchell County

- Mitchell County SO
- Sheriff Donald Street
  63 Crimson Laurel Cir. Ste. 8
  Bakersville, NC 28705
  (828) 688-3982
  mcsd@mitchellcounty.org
- Spruce Pine PD
- Chief Coy Hollifield
  106 Highland Ave.
  Spruce Pine, NC 28777
  (828) 765-2233
  spclerk@bellsouth.net

Montgomery County

- Montgomery County SO
- Sheriff Dempsey Owens
  111 W. Main St.
  Troy, NC 27371
  (910) 572-1313
  mcsosheriff@montgomerycountync.com
- Biscoe PD
- Int. Chief Brent Tedder
  110 W. Main St. PO Box 1228
  Biscoe, NC 27209
  (910) 428-2978
  biscopd@townofbiscoe.com
- Candor PD
- Chief Randy White
  208 So. Main St. PO Box 220
  Candor, NC 27229
  (910) 974-4777
  townofcandor@embarqmail.com
- Mt. Gilead PD
- Chief Cleve Wiloughby
  112 W. Allenton St.
  Mt Gilead, NC 27306
  (910) 439-6711
  cwilloughby@police.mtgileadnc.com
- Star PD
- Chief Tracy Phillips
  PO Box 97
  Star, NC 27356
  (910) 428-9224
  townofstar@gmail.com
- Troy PD
- Chief Kenneth W. *Kenny* Allan
  610 No. Main St.
  Troy, NC 27371
  (910) 576-8151
  troypd@troy.nc.us

Moore County

- Moore County SD
- Sheriff Lane Carter
  101 Courthouse PO Box 40
  Carthage, NC 28327
  (910) 947-2931
  lweaver@moorecountync.gov
- Aberdeen PD
- Chief Mike Connor
  804 No. Sandhills Blvd
  Aberdeen, NC 28315
  (910) 944-9721
  mikeconnor@aberdeenpolice.com
- Southern Pines PD
- Chief Robert Temme
  450 W. Pennsylvania
  Southern Pines, NC 28388
  (910) 692-2732
  pd@southernpines.net
- Whispering Pines PD
- Chief Dominic Campbell
  14 Hardee Ln.
  Whispering Pines, NC 28327
  (910) 949-9961
  campbell@wppolice.com

Nash County

- Nash County SO
- Sheriff Dick Jenkins
  222 W. Washington
  Nashville, NC 27856
  (252) 459-1556
  dick.jenkins@nashcountync.gov
- Bailey PD
- Chief Gerald Coggins
  6260 Main St. PO Box 40
  Bailey, NC 27807
  (252) 235-3561
  baileypolice@embarqmail.com
- Middlesex PD
- Chief Dennis Murray
  10201 So. Nash St.
  Middlesex, NC 27557
  (252) 235-4077
  Dennis@townofmiddlesexnc.com
- Nashville PD
- Chief Thomas Bashore
  501 So. Barnes PO Drawer 987
  Nashville, NC 27856
  (252) 459-4545
  thomas.bashore@townofnashvillenc.gov
- Rocky Mount PD
- Chief James Moore
  330 So. Church PO Box 1180
  Rocky Mount, NC 27802-1180 *(see also Edgecombe County)*
  (252) 972-1411
  james.moore@rockymountnc.gov
- Sharpsburg PD
- Chief Alvin Coley
  108 Railroad St. PO Box 1759
  Sharpsburg, NC 27878
  (See also Edgecombe & Wilson counties)
  (252) 977-0004
  acoley@sharpsburgnc.com

- Whitakers PD
- Chief Chris Wagstaff
  302 NW Railroad St.
  Whitakers, NC 27891
  (252) 437-8011
  info@townofwhitakers.org

New Hanover County

- New Hanover County SO
- Sheriff Ed McMahon
  3950 Juvenile Center Rd.
  Wilmington, NC 28429
  (910) 341-4200
  emcmahon@nhcgov.com
- Carolina Beach PD
- Chief Kurt Bartley
  1121 No. Lake Park Blvd
  Carolina Beach, NC 28428
  (910) 458-2540
  kurt.bartley@carolinabeach.org
- Kure Beach PD
- Chief R.D. *Dennis* Cooper
  114 7th Ave. No.
  Kure Beach, NC 28449
  (910) 458-7586
  rdcooper01@yahoo.com
- Wilmington PD
- Chief Ralph Evangelous
  615 Bess St.
  Wilmington, NC 28401
  (910) 343-3600
  officeofthechief@wilmingtonnc.gov
- Wrightsville Beach PD
- Chief Daniel House
  321 Causeway PO Box 626
  Wrightsville Beach, NC 28480
  (910) 256-7911
  dhouse@towb.org

Northampton County

- Northampton County SO
- Sheriff Wardie P. Vincent, Sr.
  105 W. Jefferson PO Box 176
  Jackson, NC 27845
  (252) 534-2611, ext. 132
  wardie.vincent@ncmail.net
- Conway PD
- Chief Billy W. Duke
  PO Box 365
  Conway, NC 27820
  (252) 585-1155
  conwaytownhall@mchsi.com
- Jackson PD
- Chief John Young
  100 E. Jefferson PO Box 614
  Jackson, NC 27845
  (252) 534-3811
  jacksontownhall@mchsi.com

Onslow County

- Onslow County SO
- Sheriff Ed Brown
  701 Mill Ave.
  Jacksonville, NC 28540
  (910) 455-3113, ext. 152
  sheriff@co.onslowcountync.gov
- Holly Ridge PD
- Chief John E. Moriano
  212 No. Dyson St. PO Box 145
  Holly Ridge, NC 28445
  (910) 329-4076
  admin@hollyridgepd.net
- Jacksonville PD
- Chief Mike G. Yaniero
  206 Marine Blvd
  Jacksonville, NC 28540
  (910) 455-4000
  pdlocator@ci.jacksonville.nc.us
- North Topsail Beach PD
- Chief Casey J. Fillinger
  2008 Loggerhead Ct.
  North Topsail Beach, NC 28460
  (910) 328-0042
  info@ntbpd.org
- Surf City PD
- Chief Michael Halstead
  305 No. New River PO Box 2515
  Surf City, NC 28445
  (See also Pender County)
  (910) 328-7711
  scpd300@gmail.com
- Swansboro PD
- Int. Chief Dwayne Taylor
  502 Church St.
  Swansboro, NC 28584
  (910) 326-5151
  dtaylor@ci.swansboro.nc.us

Orange County

- Orange County SO
- Sheriff Lindy Pendergrass
  144 E. Margaret Ln.
  Hillsborough, NC 27278
  (919) 644-3050
  twpope@co.orange.nc.us

- Carrboro PD
- Chief Carolyn Hutchison
  100 No. Greensboro St.
  Carrboro, NC 27510
  (919) 918-7412
  CHutchison@townofcarrboro.org
- Chapel Hill PD
- Chief Chris Blue
  828 Martin Luther King Blvd
  Chapel Hill, NC 27514
  (919) 968-2760
  cblue@townofchapelhill.org

Pamlico County

- Pamlico County SO
- Sheriff Bill Sawyer, Jr.
  200 Main St. PO Box 437
  Bayboro, NC 28515
  (252) 745-3101
  sheriffsawyer@coastalnet.com
- Oriental PD
- Chief Dwaine Moore
  507 Church St. PO Box 472
  Oriental, NC 28571
  (252) 249-0369
  chief@townoforiental.com

Pasquotank County

- Pasquotank County SO
- Sheriff Randy Cartwright
  206 E. Colonial Ave.
  Elizabeth City, NC 27907
  (252) 338-2191, ext. 1127
  sheriff@co.pasquotank.nc.us
- Elizabeth City PD
- Chief Eddie M. Buffaloe, Jr.
  302 E. Colonial PO Box 347
  Elizabeth City, NC 27907
  (252) 335-4321
  jandcpeel@aol.com

Pender County

- Pender County SO
- Sheriff Carson H. Smith, Jr.
  605 E Fremont St. PO Box 1449
  Burgaw, NC 28425
  (910) 259-1212
  carson.smith@pendersheriff.com
- Atkinson PD
- Chief Virginia Wilson
  PO Box 160
  Atkinson, NC 28421
  (910) 283-7344
  wilsonatcop@aol.com
- Burgaw PD
- Chief Wilbur D. *Bill* King, Jr.
  109 No. Walker St.
  Burgaw, NC 28425
  (910) 259-4924
  townofburgaw@townofburgaw.com
- Surf City PD
- Chief Michael Halstead
  305 No. New River PO Box 2515
  Surf City, NC 28445
  (See also Onslow County)
  (910) 328-7711
  scpd300@gmail.com
- Topsail Beach PD
- Chief Samuel L. Gervase
  812 So. Anderson Blvd
  Topsail Beach, NC 28445
  (910) 328-4851
  policechief@topsailbeach.org

Perquimans County

- Perquimans County SO
- Sheriff Eric V. Tilley
  110 Church St. PO Box 31
  Hertford, NC 27944
  (252) 426-5615
  etilley@perquimanscountync.gov
- Hertford PD
- Chief Douglas Freeman, Jr.
  114B W. Grubb St. PO Box 275
  Hertford, NC 27944
  (252) 426-5587
  chief1@inteliport.com

Person County

- Person County SO
- Sheriff Dewey E. Jones
  120 Court St. PO Box 1156
  Roxboro, NC 27573
  (336) 597-0500
  djones@personcounty.net
- Roxboro PD
- Chief James Boycher
  PO Box 280
  Roxboro, NC 27573
  (336) 599-8345
  tadams@cityofroxboro.com

Pitt County

- Pitt County SO
- Sheriff Neil Elks
  100 W. 3rd St. PO Box 528
  Greenville, NC 27858
  (252) 902-2800
  rnelks@pittcountync.gov
- Ayden PD
- Chief Barry Stanley
  221 West Ave.
  PO Box 219
  Ayden, NC 28513
  (252) 481-5844
  bstanley@ayden.com
- Bethel PD
- Chief Troy Strickland
  111 Andrews St. PO Box 240
  Bethel, NC 27812
  (252) 825-5481
  chiefstrickland@suddenlinkmail.com
- Farmville PD
- Chief Donnie D. Greene
  3672 No. Main St. PO Box 86
  Farmville, NC 27828
  (252) 753-4111
  dgreene@farmville-nc.com
- Greenville PD
- Chief Hassan Aden
  500 So. Greene St. PO Box 7207
  Greenville, NC 27835
  (252) 329-4324
  haden@greenvillenc.gov
- Grifton PD
- Chief Bryan P. Cauley
  6881 So. Highland Blvd, Ste. #B
  Grifton, NC 28530
  (252) 524-4161
  bcauley@grifton.com
- Winterville PD
- Chief Ryan Willhite
  2571 Railroad St. PO Box 1459
  Winterville, NC 28590
  (252) 756-1105
  ryan.willhite@wintervillenc.com

Polk County

- Polk County SO
- Sheriff Donald Hill
  40 Ward St. PO Box 69
  Columbus, NC 28722
  (828) 894-3001
  dhill@polknc.org
- Columbus PD
- Chief Chris Beddingfield
  117 Walker St.
  Columbus, NC 28722
  (828) 894-5464
  mcb@columbusnc.com
- Tryon PD
- Chief Jeff Arrowood
  291 No. Trade St.
  Tryon, NC 28782
  (828) 859-9195
  jba@tryon-nc.com

Randolph County

- Randolph County SO
- Sheriff Maynard B. Reid, Jr.
  727 McDowell Rd.
  Asheboro, NC 27205
  (336) 318-6699
  sheriff@co.randolph.nc.us
- Archdale PD
- Chief Darrel Gibbs
  305 Balfour Dr.
  Archdale, NC 27263
  (336) 434-3134
  police@archdale-nc.gov
- Liberty PD
- Chief Jerry R. Brown
  451 W. Swannanoa
  Liberty, NC 27298
  (336) 622-9053
  townofliberty@rtelco.net
- Ramseur PD
- Chief Larry Lewallen
  724 Liberty St.
  PO Box 545
  Ramseur, NC 27316
  (336) 824-8663
  PoliceDepartment@townoframseur.org
- Randleman PD
- Chief Steven B. *Steve* Leonard
  100 Hilliary St.
  Randleman, NC 27317
  (336) 495-7510
  sleonard@randlemanpolice.org

Richmond County

- Richmond County SO
- Sheriff James E. Clemmons, Jr.
  #1 Court St.
  Rockingham, NC 28379
  (910) 895-3232
  james.clemmons@richmondnc.com

- Hamlet PD
- Chief Amery Griffin
  201 Main St.
  PO Box 1229
  Hamlet, NC 28345
  (910) 582-2551
  tkirkley@carolina.rr.com
- Rockingham PD
- Chief Billy Kelly
  311 E. Franklin St.
  Rockingham, NC 28379
  (910) 895-2468
  bkelly@gorockinghampd.com

Robeson County

- Robeson County SO
- Sheriff Kenneth Sealey
  120 Legend Rd.
  Lumberton, NC 28358
  (910) 671-3100
  sheriff@robesoncoso.org
- Lumberton PD
- Chief Michael McNeill
  1305 Godwin Ave.
  Lumberton, NC 28358
  (910) 671-3850
  mmcneill@ci.lumberton.nc.us
- Parkton PD
- Chief Tammy Lowery
  28 W. David Parnell St.
  Parkton, NC 28371
  (910) 858-2119
  Parktonpolice@aol.com
- Pembroke PD
- Chief Frank Hernandez
  205 E. 3rd St.
  Pembroke, NC 28372
  (910) 521-4333
  info@pembrokenc.com
- Red Springs PD
- Chief Ronnie Patterson
  217 So. Main St.
  Red Springs, NC 28377
  (910) 843-3454
  chiefronpatterson@yahoo.com
- Rowland PD
- Chief John M. Reaves
  206 W. Main St. PO Box 127
  Rowland, NC 28383
  (910) 422-3311
  contact@townofrowland.com
- St. Paul's PD
- Chief R. Thomas Hagens
  210 W. Blue St. PO Box 364
  St. Paul's, NC 28384
  (910) 865-5155
  sppdnc@yahoo.com

Rockingham County

- Rockingham County SD
- Sheriff Samuel S. Page
  170 NC 65 PO Box 128
  Wentworth, NC 27375
  (336) 634-3239
  spage@co.rockingham.nc.us
- Eden PD
- Chief Reece Prytle
  308 E. Stadium Dr.
  Eden, NC 27288
  (336) 623-9755
  Rpyrtle@edennc.us
- Madison PD
- Chief Perry Webster
  310 Carter St.
  Madison, NC 27025
  (336) 548-6097
  Hawkken209oak@gmail.com
- Mayodan PD
- Chief Charles J. Caruso
  101 No. 3rd Ave.
  Mayodan, NC 27027
  (336) 548-6038
  c_j_caruso@embarqmail.com
- Stoneville PD
- Chief Frank Moore
  101 Smith St.
  Stoneville, NC 27048
  (336) 573-9862
  town@town.stoneville.nc.us

Rowan County

- Rowan County SD
- Sheriff Kevin Auten
  232 No. Main St.
  Salisbury, NC 28144
  (704) 216-8700
  kevin.auten@rowancountync.gov
- China Grove PD
- Chief Eddie M. Kluttz
  205 Swink St.
  China Grove, NC 28023
  (704) 857-7755
  ekluttz@cgpolice.com

- East Spencer PD
- Chief Darren Westmoreland
  105 So. Long St. PO Box 340
  East Spencer, NC 28039
  (704) 636-7111
  espdchief@gmail.com
- Granite Quarry PD
- Chief Mark Cook
  PO Box 351
  Granite Quarry, NC 28072
  (704) 279-2952
  office@granitequarrync.gov
- Kannapolis PD
- Chief James W. *Woody* Chavis
  314 So. Main St.
  Kannapolis, NC 28081
  (See also Cabarrus County)
  (704) 920-4010
  jwchavis@cityofkannapolis.com
- Landis PD
- Chief Brian McCoy
  136 No. Central PO Box 8165
  Landis, NC 28088
  (704) 857-2129
  landispd@townoflandis.com
- Salisbury PD
- Chief Rory B. Collins
  130 E. Liberty St. PO Box 421
  Salisbury, NC 28144
  (704) 638-2133
  rcoll@salisburync.gov
- Spencer PD
- Chief Michael T. James
  600 So. Salisbury PO Box 45
  Spencer, NC 28159
  (704) 633-2231
  policechief@ci.spencer.nc.us

Rutherford County

- Rutherford County SO
- Sheriff Chris Francis
  198 No. Washington St.
  Rutherfordton, NC 28139
  (828) 287-6247
  chris.francis@rutherfordcountync.gov
- Forest City PD
- Chief Jay Jackson
  187 So. Church PO Box 552
  Forest City, NC 28043
  (828) 245-5555
  jayjackson@townofforestcity.com
- Lake Lure PD
- Chief Eric Hester
  2950 Memorial Hwy
  Lake Lure, NC 28746
  (828) 625-4685
  policechief@townoflakelure.com
- Rutherfordton PD
- Chief Kevin Lovelace
  129 No. Main St.
  Rutherfordton, NC 28139
  (828) 287-5062
  klovelace@rutherfordton.net
- Spindale PD
- Chief Robert A. *Chip* McIntosh
  125 Reveley St.
  Spindale, NC 28160
  (828) 286-3464
  emurray@rutherfordeveryday.com

Sampson County

- Sampson County SO
- Sheriff Jimmy Thornton
  112 Fontana St.
  Clinton, NC 28328
  (910) 592-4141
  sheriff@intrstar.net
- Clinton PD
- Chief Jay Tilley
  222 Lisbon St.
  Clinton, NC 28328
  (910) 592-3105
  jtilley@cityofclintonnc.us
- Newton Grove PD
- Chief Frankie Harrell
  PO Box 4
  Newton Grove, NC 28366
  (910) 594-0829
  Chief@newtongrove.net

Scotland County

- Scotland County SO
- Sheriff Shepard Jones
  212 Biggs St. PO Box 607
  Laurinburg, NC 28352
  (910) 276-3385
  sheriff@scotlandsheriff.org

Stanly County

- Stanly County SO
- Sheriff Rick Burris
  223 So. 2nd St.
  Albemarle, NC 28001
  (704) 986-3719
  rjburris@co.stanly.nc.us

- Albemarle PD
- Chief William I. Halliburton
  203 No. 2nd St.
  Albemarle, NC 28001
  (704) 984-9500
  whalliburton@ci.albemarle.nc.us
- Badin PD
- Chief Bryan C. Lambert
  36 Falls Rd. PO Box 707
  Badin, NC 28009
  (704) 422-5386
  bclambert@badin.org
- Misenheimer PD
- Chief Erik S. McGinnis
  43197 Ward Dr. PO Box 100
  Misenheimer, NC 28109
  (704) 463-3001
  chief@fsmail.pfeiffer.edu
- Norwood PD
- Chief Randy Smith
  139 No. Main St PO Box 697
  Norwood, NC 28128
  (704) 474-3716
  norwoodpd@carolina.rr.com
- Oakboro PD
- Chief Joe E. Lowder
  109-A No. Main St.
  Oakboro, NC 28129
  (704) 485-4214
  jlowder@oakboro.com
- Stanfield PD
- Chief James *Jimmy* Schneider
  103 W. Stanly St.
  Stanfield, NC 28163
  (704) 888-8257
  kbarbee@freemanwhite.com

Stokes County

- Stokes County SO
- Sheriff Mike Marshall
  1020 Main St. PO Box 118
  Danbury, NC 27016
  (336) 593-8787, ext. 1355
  sheriff@co.stokes.nc.us
- King PD
- Chief Paula May
  110 W. King St.
  King, NC 27021
  (336) 944-6878
  pmay@ci.king.nc.us
- Walnut Cove PD
- Chief Jimmy Hill
  208 W. 3rd St. PO Box 583
  Walnut Cove, NC 27052
  (336) 591-7121
  townmanagerwc@embarqmail.com

Surry County

- Surry County SO
- Sheriff Graham H. Atkinson
  218 No. Main St. PO Box 827
  Dobson, NC 27017
  (336) 401-8900
  atkinsong@co.surry.nc.us
- Dobson PD
- Chief Shawn W. Myers
  307 No. Main St.
  Dobson, NC 27017
  (336) 386-8161
  customerservice@dobson-nc.com
- Elkin PD
- Chief Monroe Wagoner
  226 No. Bridge St. PO Box 857
  Elkin, NC 28621
  (336) 835-1111
  mwagoner@elkinnc.org
- Mt. Airy PD
- Chief Dale Watson
  150 Rockford St.
  Mt Airy, MC 27030
  (336) 786-3535
  dcochran@mountairy.org
- Pilot Mountain PD
- Chief Daryl Bottoms
  124 W. Main St.
  Pilot Mountain, NC 27041
  (336) 368-4725
  Police@townofpilotmountain.com

Swain County

- Swain County SO
- Sheriff Curtis A. Cochran
  95 Brendle St. PO Box 1398
  Bryson City, NC 28713
  (828) 488-0159
  sheriffcochran@swaincountync.gov
- Bryson City PD
- Chief Rick Tabor
  200 Main St. PO Box 818
  Bryson City, NC 28713
  (828) 488-3050
  brysoncitypd2002@yahoo.com

Transylvania County

- Transylvania County SO
- Sheriff David A. Mahoney
  135 Public Safety Way
  Brevard, NC 28712
  (828) 884-3168
  sheriffmahoney@tcsonc.org
- Brevard PD
- Chief J. Phil Harris
  114 W. Jordan St.
  Brevard, NC 28712
  (828) 883-2212
  steve.woodson@cityofbrevard.com

Tyrrell County

- Tyrrell County SO
- Sheriff Darryl Liverman
  405 Main St. PO Box 178
  Columbia, NC 27925
  (252) 796-2251
  dliverman@tyrrellcso.net

Union County

- Union County SO
- Sheriff Eddie Cathey
  3344 Presson Rd.
  Monroe, NC 28112
  (704) 292-2613
  eddiecathey@co.union.nc.us
- Marshville PD
- Chief Carl Webber
  113 W. Main St.
  Marshville, NC 28103
  (704) 624-6767
  cwebber@marshvillepd.org
- Monroe PD
- Chief Debra C. Duncan
  300 W. Crowell St.
  Monroe, NC 28112
  (704) 282-4500
  dduncan@monroenc.org
- Stallings PD
- Chief M.E. Plyler, Jr.
  315 Stallings Rd.
  Stallings, NC 28104
  (704) 821-0300
  mplyler@police.stallingsnc.org
- Waxhaw PD
- Chief Michael T. *Mike* Eiss
  703 W. So. Main PO Box 305
  Waxhaw, NC 28173
  (704) 843-0353
  police@waxhaw.com
- Wingate PD
- Chief Barry Glass
  4114 Hwy 74 E. PO Box 367
  Wingate, NC 28174
  (704) 233-1697
  BGlass@TownofWingateNC.gov

Vance County

- Vance County SO
- Sheriff Peter White
  156 Church St., Ste. 004
  Henderson, NC 27536
  (252) 738-2200
  pwhite@vancecounty.org
- Henderson PD
- Chief Keith L. Sidwell
  110 Young St.
  Henderson, NC 27536
  (252) 431-6056
  ksidwell@hendersonncpd.org

Wake County

- Wake County SO
- Sheriff Donnie Harrison
  330 So. Salisbury PO Box 550
  Raleigh, NC 27602
  (919) 856-6900
  donnie.harrison@co.wake.nc.us
- Apex PD
- Chief John W. Letteney
  205 Saunders St.
  Apex, NC 27502
  (919) 362-8661
  John.Letteney@apexnc.org
- Cary PD
- Chief Patricia *Pat* Bazemore
  316 No. Academy St.
  Cary, NC 27513
  (919) 469-4023
  pat.bazemore@townofcary.org
- Fuquay-Varina PD
- Chief Larry Smith
  401 Old Honeycutt Rd.
  Fuquay-Varina, NC 27526
  (919) 552-1416
  lsmith@fuquay-varina.org
- Garner PD
- Chief Brandon Zuidema
  900 7th Ave.
  Garner, NC 27529
  (919) 772-8810
  webmail@garnernc.gov

- Holly Springs PD
- Chief John Herring
  110 W. Ballentine PO Box 8
  Holly Springs, NC 27540
  (919) 552-7110
  john.herring@hollyspringsnc.us
- Knightdale PD
- Chief Jason Godwin
  950 Steeple Square Ct.
  Knightdale, NC 27545
  (919) 217-2261
  jason.godwin@knightdalenc.gov
- Morrisville PD
- Chief Ira Jones
  260-C Town Hall PO Box 166
  Morrisville, NC 27560
  (919) 463-1600
  ijones@townofmorrisville.org
- Raleigh PD
- Chief Cassandra Deck-Brown
  6716 Six Forks Rd.
  Raleigh, NC 27601
  (919) 890-3385
  cassandra.deck-brown@raleighnc.gov
- Rolesville PD
- Chief Matthew Anderson
  204 Southtown PO Box 250
  Rolesville, NC 27571
  (919) 556-7226
  matthew.anderson@rolesville.nc.gov
- Wendell PD
- Chief Bill Carter
  9 So. Pine St.
  Wendell, NC 27591
  (919) 365-4444
  bcarter@townofwendell.com
- Zebulon PD
- Chief Timothy P. *Tim* Hayworth
  1001 No. Arendell Ave.
  Zebulon, NC 27597
  (919) 823-1818
  thayworth@townofzebulon.org

Warren County

- Warren County SO
- Sheriff Johnny M. Williams
  132 Rafters Ln. PO Box 678
  Warrenton, NC 27589
  (252) 257-3364
  eagleeye@vance.net
- Warrenton PD
- Chief John Younts
  119 E. Market PO Box 281
  Warrenton, NC 27589
  (252) 257-3123
  w.gardner@warrenton.nc.gov

Washington County

- Washington County SO
- Sheriff James Ross
  120 Adams St. PO Box 969
  Plymouth, NC 27962
  (252) 793-2422, ext. 239
  jross@washconc.org
- Plymouth PD
- Chief Steve O'Neal
  132 E. Water St.
  Plymouth, NC 27962
  (252) 793-4680
  townmanager@visitplymouthnc.com

Watauga County

- Watauga County SO
- Sheriff Len D. Hagaman, Jr.
  184 Hodges Gap Rd.
  Boone, NC 28607
  (828) 264-3761
  Len.Hagaman@watgov.org
- Beech Mountain PD
- Chief Jay Hefner
  403 Beech Mountain Pkwy
  Beech Mountain, NC 28604
  (See also Avery County)
  (828) 387-2342
  chief@townofbeechmountain.com
- Blowing Rock PD
- Chief Eric Brown
  143 Park Ave. PO Box 47
  Blowing Rock, NC 28605
  (828) 295-5212
  ebrown303@bellsouth.net
- Boone PD
- Chief Dana Crawford
  1500 Blowing Rock Rd.
  Boone, NC 28607
  (828) 268-6919
  dana.crawford@townofboone.net

- Seven Devils PD
- Chief Chuck Davis
  1356 Seven Devils Rd.
  Seven Devils, NC 28604
  (See also Avery County)
  (828) 963-5343
  policechief@sevendevils.net
- Watauga Med. Center PD
- Chief Shawn Peele
  336 Deerfield Rd.
  Boone, NC 28607
  (828) 262-4168
  police@wataugamc.org

Wayne County

- Wayne County SO
- Sheriff Carey A. Winders
  207 E. Chestnut PO Box 1877
  Goldsboro, NC 27533
  (919) 731-1481
  carey.winders@waynegov.com
- Fremont PD
- Chief Paul Moats
  120 E. Main
  Fremont, NC 27830
  (919) 242-5151
  townhall@fremontnc.gov
- Mt. Olive PD
- Chief Brian Rhodes
  114 E. James St. PO Box 939
  Mt. Olive, NC 28365
  (919) 658-5031, ext. 102
  brhodes@townofmountolivenc.com
- Walnut Creek PD
- Chief Ken Barrett
  103 Village Dr. PO Box 10911
  Goldsboro, NC 27532
  (919) 778-9991
  darrell.horne@walnutcreeknc.com

Wilkes County

- Wilkes County SO
- Sheriff Chris Shew
  201 Curtis Bridge Rd.
  Wilkesboro, NC 28697
  (336) 903-7600
  cshew@wilkescountysheriff.net
- North Wilkesboro PD
- Chief Joe Rankin
  801 Main St. PO Box 218
  North Wilkesboro, NC 28659
  (336) 838-3158
  info@northwilkesboropd.com
- Wilkesboro PD
- Chief Robert Bowlin
  100 West St.
  Wilkesboro, NC 28697
  (336) 667-7277
  rbowlin@wilkesboropd.com

Wilson County

- Wilson County SO
- Sheriff Calvin L. Woodard, Jr.
  100 E. Green St. PO Box 1666
  Wilson, NC 27894
  (252) 237-2118
  cwoodard@wilson-co.com
- Sharpsburg PD
- Chief Alvin Coley
  108 Railroad St. PO Box 1759
  Sharpsburg, NC 27878
  (See also Edgecombe & Nash counties)
  (252) 977-0004
  acoley@sharpsburgnc.com
- Stantonsburg PD
- Chief John C. Hunt
  114 E. Commercial PO Box 10
  Stantonsburg, NC 27883
  (252) 238-3534
  lot1500@yahoo.com
- Wilson PD
- Chief Thomas Hopkins
  120 No. Goldsboro PO Box 10
  Wilson, NC 27894
  (252) 399-2323
  thopkins@wilsonnc.org

Yadkin County

- Yadkin County SO
- Sheriff William *Ricky* Oliver
  210 E. Hemlock St. PO Box 443
  Yadkinville, NC 27055
  (336) 679-4217
  roliver@yadkincountync.gov
- Jonesville PD
- Chief Roger Reece
  1503 NC Hwy 67
  Jonesville, NC 28642
  (336) 835-5020
  policechief@jonesvillenc.gov
- Yadkinville PD
- Chief Tim Parks
  209 E. Hemlock PO Box 816
  Yadkinville, NC 27055-0816
  (336) 679-2863
  tparks@yadkinvillepd.com

Yancey County

- Yancey County SO
- Sheriff D. Gary Banks
  E. Main St. PO Box 6
  Burnsville, NC 28714
  (828) 682-2124
  gary.banks@yanceycountync.gov
- Burnsville PD
- Chief Brian Buchanan
  2 Town Sq. PO Box 97
  Burnsville, NC 28714
  (828) 682-2420
  brian.buchanan@townofburnsville.org

State Agencies

- NC State Highway Patrol
- Comm. (*Col.*) William J. Grey
  4201 Mail Service Center
  Raleigh, NC 27699-4201
  (919) 733-7952
  william.grey@ncps.gov
- Appalachian State U. PD
- Chief Gunther E. Doerr
  461 Rivers St.
  Boone, NC 28608
  (828) 262-2150
  doerrg@appstate.edu
- Western Carolina U. PD
- Chief Ernie Hudson
  114 E. University Way
  Cullowhee, NC 28723
  (828) 227-7301
  ehudson@wcu.edu

OHIO

Adams County

- Adams County SO
- Sheriff Kim *Kimmy* Rogers
  110 W. Main St.
  West Union, OH 45693
  (937) 544-2314
  acohjail@yahoo.com
- Manchester PD
- Chief Bruce Troutman
  400 Pike St.
  Manchester, OH 45144
  (937) 549-3330
  manchesterpolicedivision@yahoo.com
- Peebles PD
- Chief Robert Music
  74 Vine St.
  Peebles, OH 45660
  (937) 587-3191
  chiefmusic@peeblespolice.com

Allen County

- Allen County SO
- Sheriff Samuel A. Crish
  333 No. Main St. PO Box 1243
  Lima, OH 45801
  (419) 993-1400
  crish@acso-oh.us
- Bluffton PD
- Chief Rick Skilliter
  154 No. Main St.
  Bluffton, OH 45817
  (419) 358-2961, ext. 109
  policechief@bluffton-ohio.com
- Elida PD
- Chief Jeremy Hollis
  200 W. Main St. PO Box 3074
  Elida, OH 45807
  (419) 339-9481
  hollis@midohio.twcbc.com
- Lima PD
- Chief Kevin Martin
  117 E. Market St.
  Lima, OH 45801
  (419) 227-4444
  kevin.martin@cityhall.lima.oh.us
- Shawnee Twp PD
- Chief Michael D. *Mike* Keith
  2530 Fort Amanda Rd.
  Lima, OH 45804
  (419) 227-1115
  policechief@shawneetownship.com
- Spencerville PD
- Chief Darin Cook
  116 So. Broadway St.
  Spencerville, OH 45887
  (419) 647-4141
  dcook@spencervilleoh.com
- St. Rita's PD
- Chief Jeff Ramey
  730 W. Market
  Lima, OH 45801
  (419) 226-9663
  jjramey@health-partners.org

Ashland County

- Ashland County SO
- Sheriff E. Wayne Risner
  1205 E. Main St.
  Ashland, OH 44805
  (419) 289-3911
  sheriff@ashlandcounty.org
- Ashland PD
- Chief David T. Marcelli
  1211 E. Main St.
  Ashland, OH 44805
  (419) 289-3639, ext. 1010
  marcelli.david@ashland-ohio.com

Ashtabula County

- Ashtabula County SO
- Sheriff William *Billy* Johnson
  25 W. Jefferson St.
  Jefferson, OH 44047
  (440) 576-0055
  vrobison@ashtabulacounty.us
- Andover PD
- Chief G. Randy Gentry
  134 Maple St.
  Andover, OH 44003
  (440) 293-4555
  chief@andovervillage.com
- Ashtabula PD
- Chief Robert D. Stell
  110 W. 44th St.
  Ashtabula, OH 44004
  (440) 992-7176
  police@cityofashtabula.com
- Conneaut PD
- Chief Charles Burlingham
  294 Main St.
  Conneaut, OH 44030
  (440) 593-7440
  conneautpd@conneautoh.org

- Geneva PD
- Chief Dan Dudik
  44 No. Forest St.
  Geneva, OH 44041
  (440) 466-1111
  policechief@suite224.net
- Roaming Shores PD
- Chief Randy Rasmussen
  2500 Hayford Rd. PO Box 237
  Roaming Shores, OH 44084
  (440) 563-3135
  rspdchief@roamingshoresOH.gov

Athens County

- Athens County SO
- Sheriff Patrick Kelly
  13 W. Washington St.
  Athens, OH 45701
  (740) 593-6633
  bfick@athenssheriff.com

Auglaize County

- Auglaize County SO
- Sheriff Allen F. Solomon
  1051 Dearbaugh PO Box 26
  Wapakoneta, OH 45895
  (419) 739-6565
  sheriff6@bright.net
- Cridersville PD
- Chief John D. Drake
  110 W. Main St.
  Cridersville, OH 45806
  (419) 645-4111
  police@villageofcridersville.com
- Minster PD
- Chief Randy Houseworth
  126 W. 4th St. PO Box 25
  Minster, OH 45865
  (419) 628-2378
  police@minsteroh.com
- New Bremen PD
- Chief Michael Skinner
  214 No. Washington
  New Bremen, OH 45869
  (419) 629-3371
  nbpolice@nktelco.net
- St. Marys PD
- Chief Timothy F. Eberle
  222 Indiana Ave.
  St. Marys, OH 45885
  (419) 394-2325
  teberle@cityofstmarys.net
- Wapakoneta PD
- Chief Russel L. Hunlock
  701 Parlette Ct.
  Wapakoneta, OH 45895
  (419) 738-2222
  rhunlock@wapakoneta.net

Belmont County

- Belmont County SO
- Sheriff David Lucas
  68137 Hammond Rd.
  St. Clairsville, OH 43950
  (740) 695-7933
  jzusack@belmontsheriff.com
- Powhatan Point PD
- Chief Chet Oldfield
  104 Mellott St.
  Powhatan Point, OH 43942
  (740) 795-5755
  powpd64@hotmail.com
- St. Clairsville PD
- Chief Martin Kendzora
  100 No. Market St.
  St. Clairsville, OH 43950
  (740) 695-0123
  stcpolice@stclairsville.com

Brown County

- Brown County SO
- Sheriff Dwayne L. Wenninger
  750 Mt. Orab Pike
  Georgetown, OH 45121
  (937) 378-4435
  bcsowebmaster@browncountyohiosheriff.us
- Fayetteville PD
- Chief Randy Carson
  81 W. Pike St. PO Box 114
  Fayetteville, OH 45118
  (513) 875-3535
  rwcfpd@tds.net
- Georgetown PD
- Chief Forrest Coburn
  108 E. State St.
  Georgetown, OH 45121
  (937) 378-6400
  georgetownchief@roadrunner.com
- Lake Waynoka Security
- Chief Gordon Ellis
  1 Waynoka Dr.
  Sardinia, OH 45171
  (937) 446-3214
  gordon@lakewaynoka.com

- Mt. Orab PD
- Chief Bryan Mount
  211 So. High St.
  Mt. Orab, OH 45154
  (937) 444-2281
  mountbryan@yahoo.com

Butler County

- Butler County SO
- Sheriff Richard K. Jones
  705 Hanover St.
  Hamilton, OH 45011
  (513) 785-1300
  molivas@butlersheriff.org
- Fairfield PD
- Chief Michael J. Dickey
  5230 Pleasant Ave.
  Fairfield, OH 45014-3555
  (513) 829-8201
  mdickey@fairfield-city.org
- Fairfield Twp PD
- Chief Richard J. St. John
  6485 Vonnie Vale Ct.
  Hamilton, OH 45011
  (513) 887-4406
  rstjohn@fairfieldtwp.org
- Middletown PD
- Chief David VanArsdale
  1 Donham Plaza
  Middletown, OH 45042
  (513) 425-7700
  dept_police@cityofmiddletown.org
- Monroe PD
- Chief Gregory Homer
  233 So. Main St.
  Monroe, OH 45050
  (513) 539-9234
  homerg@monroeohio.org
- Oxford Twp PD
- Chief Michael D. Goins
  925 Collins Run PO Box 712
  Oxford, OH 45056
  (513) 523-7131
  mgoins@oxfordtwpohio.org
- Oxford PD
- Chief Robert *Bob* Holzworth
  101 E. High St.
  Oxford, OH 45056
  (513) 524-5247
  bholzworth@cityofoxford.org
- Trenton PD
- Chief Arthur Scott
  11 E. State St.
  Trenton, OH 45067
  (513) 988-6341
  ascott@ci.trenton.oh.us
- West Chester PD
- Chief Erik Niehaus
  9577 Beckett Rd., Ste. 500
  West Chester, OH 45069
  (513) 759-7250
  eniehaus@westchesteroh.org

Carroll County

- Carroll County SO
- Sheriff Dale Williams
  43 2nd St. SE
  Carrollton, OH 44615
  (330) 627-2141
  dwilliams@carrollcountyohio.us
- Carrollton PD
- Chief Ron Yeager
  135 SW 3rd St.
  Carrollton, OH 44615
  (330) 627-2858
  police@villageofcarrollton.com
- Magnolia PD
- Chief Jeff Hager
  328 No. Main St.
  Magnolia, OH 44643
  (330) 866-9434
  chiefhager@magnoliapolice.com

Champaign County

- Champaign County SO
- Sheriff Matthew R. Melvin
  214 No. Main St.
  Urbana, OH 43078
  (937) 484-6091
  scurnutte@co.champaign.oh.us
- Mechanicsburg PD
- Chief Samuel D. Faulkner
  18 No. Main St.
  Mechanicsburg, OH 43044
  (937) 834-2239
  tips@mechanicsburgpd.org
- St. Paris PD
- Chief James Pence
  135 W. Main St. PO Box 572
  St. Paris, OH 43072
  (937) 663-4468
  james.pence@stparisohio.org

- Urbana PD
- Chief Matt Lingrell
  205 So. Main St.
  Urbana, OH 43078
  (937) 652-4350
  policerecords@ci.urbana.oh.us

Clark County

- Clark County SO
- Sheriff Gene A. Kelly
  120 No. Fountain Ave.
  Springfield, OH 45502
  (937) 521-2050
  sheriff@clarkcountyohio.gov
- South Charleston PD
- Chief Brian Redish
  35 So. Chillicothe PO Box X
  South Charleston, OH 45368
  (937) 462-8822
  chief@villageofsouthcharleston.net
- South Vienna PD
- Chief Patrick E. Sullivan
  149 W. Main St.
  South Vienna, OH 45369
  (937) 568-4311
  svmayorkeller@yahoo.com
- Springfield PD
- Chief Stephen P. Moody
  130 No. Fountain Ave.
  Springfield, OH 45502
  (937) 324-7720
  spd@ci.springfield.oh.us

Clermont County

- Clermont County SO
- Sheriff A. J. *Tim* Rodenberg, Jr.
  4470 State Rt. 222
  Batavia, OH 45103
  (513) 732-7500
  clermontsheriff@clermontcountyohio.gov
- Loveland PD
- Chief Tim Sabransky
  120 W. Loveland Ave.
  Loveland, OH 45140
  (513) 583-3000
  ccaudell@safety-center.org
- Milford PD
- Chief Donald *Jamey* Mills
  745 Center St. #100
  Milford, OH 45150
  (513) 248-5084
  swaldmann@milfordohio.org
- New Richmond PD
- Chief Randy Harvey
  102 Willow St.
  New Richmond, OH 45157
  (513) 553-3121
  mayorcarr@fuse.net
- Owensville PD
- Chief (*Col.*) Mike Freeman
  115 W. Main St.
  Owensville, OH 45103
  (513) 732-1171
  rick.mcevoy@villageofowensville.org
- Union Twp PD
- Chief Terry Zinser
  4312 Gleneste-Withamsville Rd.
  Cincinnati, OH 45245
  (513) 752-1230
  tdonnellon@union-township.oh.us
- Williamsburg PD
- Chief Michael Gregory
  107 W. Main St.
  Williamsburg, OH 45176
  (513) 724-6107
  chiefgregory@williamsburgohio.org

Clinton County

- Clinton County SO
- Sheriff Ralph D. Fizer, Jr.
  1645 Davids Dr.
  Wilmington, OH 45177
  (937) 382-1611
  ccso@clintonsheriff.com
- Sabina PD
- Chief Keynon Young
  99 No. Howard St.
  Sabina, OH 45169
  (937) 584-2441
  kyoung@sabinapd.com
- Wilmington PD
- Chief Duane Weyand
  69 No. South St.
  Wilmington, OH 45177
  (937) 382-3833
  dweyand@wilmingtonps.org

Columbiana County

- Columbiana County SO
- Sheriff Raymond L. Stone
  105 So. Market St.
  Lisbon, OH 44432
  (330) 424-1104
  rstone@ccclerk.org

- Leetonia PD
- Chief John M. Soldano
  300 E. Main St.
  Leetonia, OH 44431
  (330) 427-6711
  police@leetonia.org
- Salem PD
- Chief J.T. Panezott
  231 So. Broadway Ave.
  Salem, OH 44460
  (330) 337-7811, ext. 241
  auditor@cityofsalemohio.org
- Wellsville PD
- Chief Joe Scarabino
  1200 Main St.
  Wellsville, OH 43968
  (330) 532-2524
  wellsvilleohio@wellsvilleohio.net

Coshocton County

- Coshocton County SO
- Sheriff Timothy L. *Tim* Rogers
  328 Chestnut St.
  Coshocton, OH 43812
  (740) 622-2411
  sheriffrogers@coshoctoncounty.net
- West Lafayette PD
- Chief Terry Mardis
  116 No. Kirk St.
  West Lafayette, OH 43845
  (614) 545-6324
  davidrogers@coshoctoncounty.net

Crawford County

- Crawford County SO
- Sheriff Scott Kent
  3613 Stetzer Rd.
  Bucyrus, OH 44820
  (419) 562-7906
  ccso@rrohio.com
- Bucyrus PD
- Chief David Koepke
  500 So. Sandusky Ave.
  Bucyrus, OH 44820
  (419) 562-1006
  bpd@cityofbucyrusoh.us
- Galion PD
- Chief Brian Saterfield
  301 Harding Way E.
  Galion, Oh 44833
  (419) 468-5255
  BrianSaterfield@ci.galion.oh.us

Cuyahoga County

- Cuyahoga County SD
- Sheriff Frank Bova
  1215 W. 3rd St.
  Cleveland, OH 44113
  (216) 443-6000
  jschmotzer@cuyahogacounty.us
- Bay Village PD
- Chief David Wright
  28000 Wolf Rd.
  Bay Village, OH 44140
  (440) 899-3461
  dwright@cityofbayvillage.com
- Beachwood PD
- Chief Mark Sechrist
  2700 Richmond Rd.
  Beachwood, OH 44122
  (216) 464-1234
  police@beachwoodohio.com
- Bedford PD
- Chief Gregory A Duber
  165 Center Rd.
  Bedford, OH 44146
  (440) 735-6551
  chiefofpolice@bedfordoh.gov
- Bedford Heights PD
- Chief Michael Marotta
  65 Columbus St.
  Bedford Heights, OH 44146
  (440) 786-3259
  chiefofpolice@bedfordheights.gov
- Berea PD
- Chief Mark Schultz
  17 Berea Commons
  Berea, OH 44017
  (440) 826-5870
  mschultz@bereapolice.org
- Brecksville PD
- Chief Michael J. Carlin III
  9069 Brecksville Rd.
  Brecksville, OH 44141
  (440) 526-8900
  rmannarino@brecksville.oh.us
- Broadview Heights PD
- Chief Michael L. Vizer
  9543 Broadview Rd.
  Broadview Heights, OH 44147
  (440) 526-5400
  cityhall@broadview-heights.org

- Brook Park PD
- Chief James Foster
  17401 Holland Rd.
  Brook Park, OH 44142
  (216) 433-1239
  jfoster@cityofbrookpark.com
- Brooklyn PD
- Chief Scott Mielke
  7619 Memphis Ave.
  Brooklyn, OH 44144
  (216) 749-1234
  smielke@brooklynohio.gov
- Brooklyn Heights PD
- Chief Daniel Algeri
  345 Tuxedo Ave.
  Brooklyn Heights, OH 44131
  (216) 741-2700
  dalgeri@brooklynhts.org
- Chagrin Falls PD
- Chief James T. Brosius
  21 W. Washington St.
  Chagrin Falls, OH 44022
  (440) 247-7321
  jbrosius@chagrinfallspd.com
- Cleveland PD
- Chief Michael McGrath
  1300 Ontario Ave.
  Cleveland, OH 44113
  (216) 623-5000
  mayorsactioncenter@city.cleveland.oh.us
- Cleveland Heights PD
- Chief Jeffrey E. Robertson
  40 Severance Cir.
  Cleveland, OH 44118
  (216) 321-1234
  myp@clvhts.com
- Euclid PD
- Chief Thomas Brickman
  545 E. 222nd St.
  Euclid, OH 44123
  (216) 289-8474
  info@euclidpd.org
- Fairview Park PD
- Chief Patrick Nealon
  20777 Lorain Rd.
  Fairview Park, OH 44126
  (440) 356-4415
  chiefofpolice@fairviewpark.org
- Garfield Heights PD
- Chief Robert Sackett
  5407 Turney Rd.
  Garfield Heights, OH 44125
  (216) 475-1100
  info@garfieldhts.org
- Gates Mills PD
- Chief Steve C. Szeredy
  1470 Chagrin River Rd.
  Gates Mills, OH 44040
  (440) 423-4456, ext. 112
  policechief@gatesmillsvillage.com
- Glenwillow PD
- Chief Robert F. Hagquist
  29555 Pettibone Rd.
  Glenwillow, OH 44139
  (440) 232-8787
  rhagquist@glenwillow-oh.gov
- Greater Cleveland Trans. PD
- Chief John P. Joyce
  1240 W. 6th St.
  Cleveland, OH 44113-1331
  (216) 566-5163
  eyes@gcrta.org
- Highland Heights PD
- Chief James J. Cook
  5827 Highland Rd.
  Highland Heights, OH 44143
  (440) 442-8825
  hhpolice@highlandhts.com
- Highland Hills PD
- Chief Antonio F. Stitt
  3700 Northfield Rd.
  Highland Hills, OH 44122
  (216) 591-2314
  VillageHall@vhhohio.org
- Independence PD
- Int. Chief Jim Polak
  6800 Brecksville Rd.
  Independence, OH 44131
  (216) 524-1234
  polakj@independenceohio.org
- Lakewood PD
- Chief Timothy J. *Tim* Malley
  12650 Detroit Ave.
  Lakewood, OH 44107
  (216) 521-6773
  tim.malley@lakewoodoh.net

- Lyndhurst PD
- Chief Rick Porrello
  5301 Mayfield Rd.
  Lyndhurst, OH 44124
  (440) 442-1234
  porrellor@lyndhurst-oh.com
- Mayfield Heights PD
- Chief Fred W. Bittner
  6154 Mayfield Rd.
  Mayfield Heights, OH 44124
  (440) 442-2323
  fredbittner@mayfieldheights.org
- Mayfield Village PD
- Chief Richard Edelman
  620 S.O.M. Center Rd.
  Mayfield Village, OH 44143
  (440) 461-1234
  police@mayfieldvillage.com
- Newburgh Heights PD
- Chief Gabe Barone
  4071 E. 49th St.
  Newburgh Heights, OH 44105
  (216) 641-5545
  info@newburghhtsoh.gov
- North Olmsted PD
- Chief Jamie Gallagher
  27243 Lorain Rd.
  North Olmsted, OH 44070
  (440) 777-3535
  gallagherj@north-olmsted.com
- North Royalton PD
- Chief John A. Elek
  14000 Bennett Rd.
  North Royalton, OH 44133
  (440) 237-8686
  police@northroyalton.org
- Oakwood Village PD
- Chief Mark A Garratt
  24800 Broadway Ave.
  Oakwood Village, OH 44146
  (440) 232-9988
  dhammett@oakwoodvillageoh.com
- Olmsted Falls PD
- Chief Dan Gilles
  26100 Bagley Rd.
  Olmsted Falls, OH 44138-1897
  (440) 235-3145
  police@olmstedfalls.org
- Olmsted Twp PD
- Chief John W. Minek
  26900 Cook Rd.
  Olmsted Twp, OH 44138
  (440) 235-3335
  chiefminek@olmstedtownship.org
- Parma Heights PD
- Dir. Brent Collins
  6184 Pearl Rd.
  Parma Heights, OH 44130
  (440) 884-9600, ext. 37
  safety@parmaheightsoh.gov
- Seven Hills PD
- Chief Gary Durkin
  7325 Summitview Dr.
  Cleveland, OH 44131
  (216) 524-4423
  mayor7hills@yahoo.com
- Shaker Heights PD
- Chief D. Scott Lee
  3355 Lee Rd.
  Shaker Heights, OH 44120
  (216) 491-1240
  scott.lee@shakeronline.com
- University Heights PD
- Chief Steven Hammett
  2304 Warrensville Center Rd.
  University Heights, OH 44118
  (216) 932-7800, ext. 252
  shammett@universityheights.com
- Valley View PD
- Chief Matthew March
  6899 Hathaway Rd.
  Valley View, OH 44125
  (216) 524-9687
  mmarch@valleyview.net
- Warrensville Heights PD
- Chief William Jelenic
  4301 Warrensville Center Rd.
  Warrensville Heights, OH 44128
  (216) 581-1234
  info@cityofwarrensville.com
- Westlake PD
- Chief Richard A. Walling
  27300 Hilliard Blvd
  Westlake, OH 44145
  (440) 871-3311
  westlakepolicedepartment@yahoo.com

Darke County

- Darke County SO
- Sheriff Toby L. Spencer
  5185 County Home Rd.
  Greenville, OH 45331
  (937) 548-3399
  tspencer@darkecountysheriff.org
- Ansonia PD
- Chief Frank N. Shapiro
  108 W. Canal St. PO Box 824
  Ansonia, OH 45303
  (937) 337-7191
  admin@ansoniaohio.us
- Arcanum PD
- Chief Dan Light
  104 W. South St.
  Arcanum, OH 45304
  (937) 692-8121
  Mayor@villageofarcanum.com
- Greenville PD
- Chief Dennis Butts
  122 W. Main St.
  Greenville, OH 45331
  (937) 548-1103
  contact@cityofgreenville.org
- Union PD
- Chief Mike Blackwell
  118 No. Main St.
  Union, OH 45322
  (937) 836-0912
  mblackwell@ci.union.oh.us
- Versailles PD
- Chief Mark Humphreys
  6 So. Center St. PO Box 288
  Versailles, OH 45380
  (937) 526-3712, ext. 223
  markhumphries@versaillesohio.cc

Defiance County

- Defiance County SO
- Sheriff David J. Westrick
  113 Biede Ave.
  Defiance, OH 43512
  (419) 784-1155
  dcsowebsite@defiance-county.com
- Defiance PD
- Chief Timothy A. Tobias
  324 Perry St.
  Defiance, OH 43512
  (419) 784-5050
  ttobias@cityofdefiance.com
- Hicksville PD
- Chief Douglas Willis
  510 W. High St.
  Hicksville, OH 43526
  (419) 542-6661
  hicksvillepd@defiance-county.com

Delaware County

- Delaware County SO
- Sheriff Russell L. Martin
  149 No. Sandusky St.
  Delaware, OH 43015
  (740) 833-2810
  sheriffinfo@co.delaware.oh.us
- Ashley PD
- Chief Douglas Patrick
  101 E. High St.
  Ashley, OH 43003
  (740) 747-2960
  ashleyohpd@yahoo.com
- Ostrander PD
- Chief Kenneth C. Jones
  19 So. Main St. PO Box 35
  Ostrander, OH 43061-0035
  (740) 666-8500
  opd@ostranderpolice.com
- Powell PD
- Act. Chief (*Dep. Chief*) Stephen Hrytzik
  47 Hall St.
  Powell, OH 43065
  (614) 885-5005
  shrytzik@cityofpowell.us

Erie County

- Erie County SO
- Sheriff Paul A. Sigsworth
  2800 Columbus Ave.
  Sandusky, OH 44870
  (419) 625-7951
  Sheriff@eriecounty.oh.gov
- Huron PD
- Chief Robert J. Lippert
  417 Main St. PO Box 468
  Huron, OH 44839
  (419) 433-4114
  huronpolice@cityofhuron.org
- Kelleys Island PD
- Chief Ron Ehrbar
  122 Division St. PO Box 469
  Kelleys Island, OH 43438
  (419) 746-2735
  mayor@kelleysisland.us

- Milan PD
- Chief Jim Rose
  11 So. Main St. PO Box 1450
  Milan, OH 44846
  (See also Huron County)
  (419) 499-2001
  milanpd5901@milanohio.com
- Sandusky PD
- Chief John Orzech
  222 Meigs St.
  Sandusky, OH 44870
  (419) 627-5869
  jorzech@ci.sandusky.oh.us
- Vermilion PD
- Chief Chris Hartung
  5791 Liberty Ave.
  Vermilion, OH 44089
  (216) 967-6116
  Mayor@vermilion.net

Fairfield County

- Fairfield County SO
- Sheriff Dave Phalen
  221 E. Main St.
  Lancaster, OH 43130
  (740) 653-5223
  sheriff@sheriff.fairfield.oh.us
- Lancaster PD
- Chief Dave Bailey
  130 So. Broad St.
  Lancaster, OH 43130
  (740) 687-6683
  lpd@ci.lancaster.oh.us
- Pickerington PD
- Chief Mike Taylor
  1311 Refugee Rd.
  Pickerington, OH 43147
  (614) 575-6911
  mayorgray@pickerington.net

Fayette County

- Fayette County SO
- Sheriff Vernon P. Stanforth
  113 E. Market St.
  Washington Court House, OH 43160
  (740) 335-6170
  sheriffstanforth@faycoso.com

Franklin County

- Franklin County SO
- Sheriff Zach Scott
  369 So. High St.
  Columbus, OH 43215
  (614) 462-3360
  ssgriffi@franklincountyohio.gov
- Bexley PD
- Chief Larry Rinehart
  2242 E. Main St.
  Bexley, OH 43209
  (614) 239-8881
  bkessler@bexley.org
- Clinton Twp PD
- Chief Don Mapley
  3820 Cleveland Ave.
  Columbus, OH 43224
  (614) 471-1479
  parmentrout@clintontwp-columbus.org
- Columbus Div. of Police
- Chief Kim Jacobs
  120 Marconi Blvd
  Columbus, OH 43215
  (614) 645-4545
  e-mail@columbuspolice.org
- Gahanna PD
- Chief Dennis Murphy
  460 Rocky Fork Blvd
  Gahanna, OH 43230
  (614) 342-4201
  dennis.murphy@gahanna.gov
- Grandview Heights PD
- Chief David Wood
  1016 Grandview Ave.
  Columbus, OH 43212
  (614) 488-7901
  dwood@grandviewheights.org
- Groveport PD
- Chief Ralph J. Portier
  655 Blacklick St.
  Groveport, OH 43125
  (614) 830-2042
  rportier@groveport.org
- Minerva Park Village PD
- Chief Kim Nuesse
  2829 Minerva Lake Rd.
  Minerva Park, OH 43231
  (614) 882-5743
  chief@minervapark.org

- New Albany PD
- Chief Sloan Spalding
  21 E. Granville St.
  New Albany, OH 43054
  (614) 855-1234
  mayor@newalbanyohio.org
- Obetz PD
- Chief Kenneth *Ken* Hinkle
  4175 Alum Creek Dr.
  Columbus, OH 43207
  (614) 491-1080
  gscott@obetz.oh.us
- Perry Twp PD
- Chief Robert Oppenheimer
  7125 Sawmill Rd.
  Dublin, OH 43016
  (614) 889-9153
  Jroper@perrytwp.org
- Reynoldsburg PD
- Chief Jim O'Neill
  7240 E. Main St.
  Reynoldsburg, OH 43068
  (614) 866-6622
  bmccloud@ci.reynoldsburg.oh.us
- Upper Arlington PD
- Chief Brian Quinn
  3600 Tremont Rd.
  Upper Arlington, OH 43221
  (614) 583-5162
  bquinn@uaoh.net
- Westerville PD
- Chief Joe Morbitzer
  29 So. State St.
  Westerville, OH 43081
  (614) 882-7444
  tipline@westerville.org
- Whitehall PD
- Chief Richard R. Zitzke
  365 So. Yearling Rd.
  Whitehall, OH 43213
  (614) 237-6333
  richard.zitzke@whitehall-oh.us
- Worthington PD
- Chief James R. Mosic
  6555 Worthington Galena Rd.
  Worthington, OH 43085
  (614) 885-4463
  council@ci.worthington.oh.us

Fulton County

- Fulton County SO
- Sheriff Roy E. Miller
  129 Courthouse Plaza
  Wauseon, OH 43567
  (419) 335-4010
  vhall@fultoncountyoh.com
- Delta PD
- Chief Richard Sluder
  401 Main St.
  Delta, OH 43515
  (419) 822-3220
  mayor@villageofdelta.org
- Fayette PD
- Chief Jason Simon
  125 W. Main
  Fayette, OH 43521
  (419) 237-2341
  jsimon@villageoffayette.com
- Swanton PD
- Chief William Talbott
  219 Chestnut St.
  Swanton, OH 43558
  (419) 826-4696
  wtalbott@villageofswantonohio.us

Gallia County

- Gallia County SO
- Sheriff Joseph R. Browning
  18 Locust St.
  Gallipolis, OH 45631
  (740) 446-1221
  lbetz@gallianet.net

Geauga County

- Geauga County SO
- Sheriff Dan McClelland
  12450 Merritt Rd.
  Chardon, OH 44024
  (440) 279-2009
  geaugaso@co.geauga.oh.us
- Burton PD
- Chief Richard Smigelski
  14588 W. Park St. PO Box 24
  Burton, OH 44021
  (440) 834-1234
  rsmigelski@villageofburton.org
- Chardon PD
- Chief Tim McKenna
  108 So. Hambden St.
  Chardon, OH 44024
  (440) 286-6123
  police@chardon.cc

- Chester Twp PD
- Chief Mark Purchase
  12696 Opalocka Dr.
  Chesterland, OH 44026
  (440) 729-1239
  jcaputo@chestertwp.org
- Middlefield PD
- Chief Arnold Stanko
  14860 No. State PO Box 1019
  Middlefield, OH 44062
  (440) 632.3527
  astanko@middlefieldpolice.com
- Russell Twp PD
- Chief Timothy Carroll
  14820 Chillicothe Rd.
  Novelty, OH 44072
  (440) 338-6212
  rpd@russellpolice.com

Greene County

- Greene County SD
- Sheriff Eugene Fischer
  120 E. Main St.
  Xenia, OH 45385
  (937) 562-4800
  rvannuys@co.greene.oh.us
- Beavercreek PD
- Chief Dennis Evers
  1388 Research Park Dr.
  Beavercreek, OH 45432
  (937) 426-1225, ext. 296
  eversd@police.ci.beavercreek.oh.us
- Bellbrook PD
- Chief David Helling
  15 E. Franklin St.
  Bellbrook, OH 45305
  (937) 848-8484
  don.buczek@cityofbellbrook.org
- Fairborn PD
- Chief Terry Barlow
  70 W. Hebble Ave.
  Fairborn, OH 45324
  (937) 754-3067
  terry.barlow@ci.fairborn.oh.us
- Jamestown PD
- Chief Rodger D. Tyree
  84 Seaman Dr.
  Jamestown, OH 45335
  (937) 675-4111
  jamestownmayor@yahoo.com
- Sugarcreek Twp PD
- Chief Michael A. Brown
  4398 Clyo Rd.
  Centerville, OH 45459
  (937) 848-6161
  mbrown@sugarcreektownship.com
- Xenia PD
- Chief Randy Person
  101 No. Detroit St.
  Xenia, OH 45385
  (937) 372-9901
  dperson@ci.xenia.oh.us

Guernsey County

- Guernsey County SO
- Sheriff Michael R. McCauley
  601 Southgate Pkwy
  Cambridge, OH 43725
  (740) 439-4455
  contactus@guernseysheriff.com
- Byesville PD
- Chief Misty Milligan
  211 Watson Ave. PO Box 185
  Byesville, OH 43723
  (740) 685-2121
  dgadd@byesville.us
- Cambridge PD
- Chief: Richard Wayt
  601 Southgate Pkwy
  Cambridge, OH 43725
  (740) 439-4431
  cop@cambridgeoh.com

Hamilton County

- Hamilton County SO
- Sheriff Jim Neil
  1000 Sycamore St., Rm. 110
  Cincinnati, OH 45202
  (513) 946-6400
  Jknapp@sheriff.hamilton-co.org
- Addyston PD
- Chief Thomas Von Luehrte
  235 Main St.
  Addyston, OH 45001
  (513) 941-1313, ext. 11
  TVonLuehrte@addystonohio.org
- Blue Ash PD
- Chief (*Col.*) Paul Hartinger
  4343 Cooper Rd.
  Blue Ash, OH 45242
  (513) 745-8555
  police@blueash.com

- Cheviot PD
- Chief Joseph Lally
  3814 Harrison Ave.
  Cheviot, OH 45211
  (513) 661-2917
  skeller@cheviot.org
- Cincinnati PD
- Chief James E. Craig
  310 Ezzard Charles Dr.
  Cincinnati, OH 45214
  (513) 765-1212
  douglas.wiesman@cincinnati-oh.gov
- Cleves PD
- Chief Bill Renner
  101 No. Miami Ave.
  Cincinnati, OH 45002
  (513) 941-1212
  chief@clevespolice.us
- Colerain Twp PD
- Chief Daniel P. Meloy
  4200 Springdale Rd.
  Cincinnati, OH 45251
  (513) 385-7504
  dmeloy@coleraintwp.org
- Deer Park PD
- Chief Michael Schlie
  4250 Matson Ave.
  Deer Park, OH 45236
  (513) 791-8056
  michaelschlie@deerpark-oh.gov
- Delhi Twp PD
- Chief (*Col.*) Jim Howarth
  934 Neeb Rd.
  Cincinnati, OH 45233
  (513) 922-0060
  jhowarth@delhi.oh.us
- Elmwood Place PD
- Chief William Peskin
  300 Maple St.
  Elmwood Place, OH 45216
  (513) 242-0754
  colpeskin@yahoo.com
- Evendale PD
- Chief Niel Korte
  10500 Reading Rd.
  Evendale, OH 45241
  (513) 563-2249
  chief.nkorte@evendaleohio.org
- Fairfax PD
- Chief Steven M. Kelly
  5903 Hawthorne Ave.
  Fairfax, OH 45227
  (513) 527-6503
  skelly@fairfaxoh.org
- Forest Park PD
- Chief Phil Cannon
  1203 W. Kemper Rd.
  Forest Park, OH 45240
  (513) 595-5220
  police@forestpark.org
- Glendale PD
- Chief Dave Warman
  301 E. Sharon Ave.
  Glendale, OH 45246
  (513) 678-1016
  dwarman@glendaleohio.org
- Golf Manor PD
- Chief Eddie Taylor
  6450 Wiehe Rd.
  Cincinnati, OH 45237
  (513) 531-3108
  gm_mayor@current.net
- Green Twp PD
- Chief Bart West
  6303 Harrison Ave.
  Cincinnati, OH 45247
  (513) 574-0007
  police@greentwp.org
- Greenhills PD
- Act. Chief (*Sgt.*) Robert Dean
  11000 Winton Rd.
  Greenhills, OH 45218
  (513) 825-2101, ext. 324
  r.dean@greenhillspd.org
- Indian Hill PD
- Chief (*Col.*) Chuck W. Schlie
  6525 Drake Rd.
  Indian Hill, OH 45243
  (513) 561-7000
  mtulliswp@ci.indian-hill.oh.us
- Lockland PD
- Chief James L. *Jim* Toles
  101 No. Cooper Ave.
  Lockland, OH 45215
  (513) 761-1699
  jimt@lockland.com

- Loveland PD
- Chief Tim Sabransky
  126 So. Lebanon Rd.
  Loveland, OH 45140
  (513) 583-3000
  tsabransky@safety-center.org
- Madeira PD
- Chief Frank A. Maupin
  7141 Miami Ave.
  Madeira, OH 45243
  (513) 272-4214
  police@madeiracity.com
- Mariemont PD
- Chief Richard D. Hines
  6907 Wooster Pike
  Mariemont, OH 45227
  (513) 271-4089
  rhines@mariemont.org
- Mt. Healthy PD
- Chief Marc Waldeck
  7700 Perry St.
  Mt. Healthy, OH 45231
  (513) 728-3183
  mwaldeck@mthealthy.org
- Newtown PD
- Chief Thomas Synan, Jr.
  3536 Church St.
  Newtown, OH 45244-3002
  (513) 825-2280
  tsynan@villageofnewtown.com
- Norwood Police Div.
- Chief William Kramer
  4701 Montgomery Rd.
  Norwood, OH 45212
  (513) 458-4520
  ssd@norwood-ohio.com
- Reading PD
- Chief Scott E. Snow
  1000 Market St.
  Reading, OH 45215
  (513) 733-4122
  rbemmes@readingohio.org
- St. Bernard PD
- Chief Steve Moeller
  4700 Vine St.
  St. Bernard, OH 45217
  (513) 242-2727
  mail@stbernardpolice.org
- Sharonville PD
- Chief Michael G. Schappa
  10900 Reading Rd.
  Sharonville, OH 45241
  (513) 563-1147
  policeinfo@cityofsharonville.com
- Springdale PD
- Chief Michael H. Mathis
  12105 Lawnview Ave.
  Springdale, OH 45246
  (513) 346-5760
  mmathis@springdale.org
- Terrace Park PD
- Chief (*Col.*) Gerald E Hayhow
  428 Elm Ave.
  Terrace Park, OH 45174
  (513) 831-2137
  hayhow@terracepark.org
- Xavier U. PD
- Chief Michael Couch
  3800 Victory Pkwy
  Cincinnati, OH 45207
  (513) 745-1000
  couch@xavier.edu

Hancock County

- Hancock County SO
- Sheriff Michael E. Heldman
  200 W. Crawford St.
  Findlay, OH 45840
  (419) 424-7232
  mrsmith@co.hancock.oh.us
- Findlay PD
- Chief Gregory R. *Greg* Horne
  Municipal Bldg, Rm. 207
  Findlay, OH 45840
  (419) 424-7194
  chorne@findlayohio.com

Hardin County

- Hardin County SO
- Sheriff Keith A. Everhart
  1025 So. Main St.
  Kenton, OH 43326
  (419) 673-1268
  keverhart@hardinsheriff.com
- Ada PD
- Chief Michael Harnishfeger
  115 W. Buckeye Ave.
  Ada, OH 45810
  (419) 634-0010
  d-retterer@onu.edu

- Kenton PD
- Chief John Vermillion
  111 W. Franklin St.
  Kenton, OH 43326
  (419) 673-0771
  kpdkpd@windstream.net

Harrison County

- Harrison County SO
- Sheriff Ronald J. Myers
  114 Court St.
  Cadiz, OH 43907
  (740) 942-2197
  harrisoncountysheriff@frontier.com
- Cadiz PD
- Chief Bryan Dowdle
  128 Court St.
  Cadiz, OH 43907
  (740) 942-8844, ext. 28
  mayor@villageofcadiz.net

Henry County

- Henry County SO
- Sheriff Michael D. Bodenbender
  123 E. Washington
  Napoleon, OH 43545
  (419) 592-8010
  mbodenbender@henrycountysheriff.com
- Deshler PD
- Chief Ryan Bowersox
  101 E. Main St.
  Deshler, OH 43516
  (419) 278-2955
  deshclerk@embarqmail.com
- Napoleon PD
- Chief R.L. Weitzel
  310 Glenwood Ave.
  Napoleon, OH 43545
  (419) 599-2810
  rweitzel@napoleonohio.com

Highland County

- Highland County SO
- Sheriff Ronald D. Ward
  130 Homestead Ave.
  Hillsboro, OH 45133
  (937) 393-1421
  rward@highlandcoso.com
- Leesburg PD
- Chief Timothy Tyree
  57 So. Fairfield St.
  Leesburg, OH 45135
  (937) 780-6735
  ttyree@leesburgohio.org
- Lynchburg PD
- Chief Tim Heizer
  155 So. Main St.
  Lynchburg, OH 45142
  (937) 364-6659
  theizer@lynchburgpd.com

Hocking County

- Hocking County SO
- Sheriff Lanny E. North
  25 E. 2nd St.
  Logan, OH 43138
  (740) 385-2131
  commissioners@co.hocking.oh.us

Holmes County

- Holmes County SO
- Sheriff Timothy W. *Tim* Zimmerly
  8105 TR 574 PO Box 500
  Holmesville, OH 44633-5000
  (330) 674-1936
  webmaster@holmescountysheriff.org
- Millersburg PD
- Chief S. Thomas Vaughn
  6 No. Washington St.
  Millersburg, OH 44654
  (330) 674-5931
  thomas.vaughn@millersburgohio.com

Huron County

- Huron County SO
- Sheriff Dane A. Howard
  255 Shady Lane Dr.
  Norwalk, OH 44857
  (419) 668-6912
  sheriffhoward@huroncountysheriff.org
- Bellevue PD
- Chief Dennis Brandal
  3000 Seneca Industrial Pkwy
  Bellevue, OH 44811
  (419) 484-8400
  geninfo@cityofbellevue.com
- Greenwich PD
- Chief Steve Dorsey
  47 Main St.
  Greenwich, OH 44837
  (419) 752-2681
  dorsey.s@villageofgreenwich.com
- Milan PD
- Chief Jim Rose
  11 So. Main St. PO Box 1450
  Milan, OH 44846
  (See also Erie County)
  (419) 499-2001
  milanpd5901@milanohio.com

- Monroeville PD
- Chief Gary Lyons
  8 Monroe St.
  Monroeville, OH 44847
  (419) 465-2474, ext. 21
  lyons@monroevillepolice.com
- New London PD
- Chief Michael J. Marko
  115 E. Main
  New London, OH 44851
  (419) 929-3504
  nlmayor@newlondonohio.com
- Norwalk PD
- Chief David W. Light
  37 No. Linwood Ave.
  Norwalk, OH 44857
  (419) 663-6780
  cityofnorwalk@accnorwalk.com
- Plymouth PD
- Chief Charles D. Doan
  25 Sandusky St.
  Plymouth, OH 44865
  (419) 687-4321
  plymouthcops@yahoo.com
- Wakeman PD
- Chief Tim Hunker
  59 Hyde St.
  Wakeman, OH 44889
  (440) 839-2511
  wakemanpolice@yahoo.com
- Willard PD
- Chief Mark Holden
  631 So. Myrtle PO Box 367
  Willard, OH 44890
  (419) 933-2561
  mholden@willard-oh.com

Jackson County

- Jackson County SO
- Sheriff Tedd Frazier
  350 Portsmouth St.
  Jackson, OH 45640
  (740) 286-3616
  cjacksoncounty@midohio.twcbc.com

Jefferson County

- Jefferson County SO
- Sheriff Fred J. Abdalla
  16001 State Rt. 7
  Steubenville, OH 43952
  (740) 283-8600
  Fred_Abdalla@JeffersonCountyOH.com
- Amsterdam PD
- Chief R. Todd Walker
  103 Springfield St. PO Box 115
  Amsterdam, OH 43903
  (740) 543-3797
  amsterdampd24@yahoo.com
- Empire PD
- Chief Matthew Donahue
  151 Nessly St.
  Empire, OH 43926
  (740) 537-1802
  STATION39@HOTMAIL.COM
- Steubenville PD
- Chief William A. McCafferty
  123 So. 3rd St.
  Steubenville, OH 43952
  (740) 283-6000, ext. 2300
  police@cityofsteubenville.us
- Tiltonsville PD
- Chief Jerry C. Davis Jr.
  222 Grandview PO Box 127
  Tiltonsville, OH 43963
  (740) 859-2730
  chiefdavis@tiltonsvillepolice.com

Knox County

- Knox County SO
- Sheriff David Shaffer
  11540 Upper Gilchrist Rd.
  Mt Vernon, OH 43050
  (740) 393-6800
  grohler@rrohio.com
- Danville PD
- Chief Monte L. Vance
  512 So. Market St.
  Danville, OH 43014
  (740) 599-6888
  policechief@danvilleohio.org
- Mt. Vernon PD
- Chief Michael K. Merrilees
  5 No. Gay St.
  Mt. Vernon, OH 43050
  (740) 397-2222
  mvpdchief@ecr.net

Lake County

- Lake County SO
- Sheriff Daniel A. Dunlap
  104 E. Erie St.
  Painesville, OH 44077
  (440) 350-5517
  sheriffwebmaster@lakecountyohio.org

- Eastlake PD
- Chief John R. Ruth
  35150 Lake Shore Blvd
  Eastlake, OH 44095
  (440) 951-1400, ext. 224
  lreik@eastlakepd.org
- Fairport Harbor PD
- Chief Mark Kish
  220 3rd St.
  Fairport Harbor, OH 44077
  (440) 352-3620
  chief_kish@sbcglobal.net
- Grand River PD
- Chief Barry D. Dodd
  205 Singer Ave. PO Box 216
  Grand River, OH 44045
  (440) 352-1287
  Policechief@grandriverohio.com
- Holden Arboretum PD
- Chief David Frank
  9500 Sperry Rd.
  Kirtland, OH 44094
  (440) 256-1110
  police@holdenarb.org
- Kirtland PD
- Chief Wayne C. Baumgart
  9301 Chillicothe Rd.
  Kirtland, OH 44094
  (440) 256-3333
  mhauser@kirtlandohio.com
- Madison PD
- Chicf Dawn Shannon
  126 W. Main St.
  Madison, OH 44057
  (440) 428-3421, ext. 103
  clerk@madisonvillagepolice.org
- Mentor PD
- Chief Kevin Knight
  8500 Civic Center Blvd
  Mentor, OH 44060
  (440) 974-5760
  police@cityofmentor.com
- Mentor-on-the-Lake PD
- Chief John Gielink
  5860 Andrews Rd.
  Mentor-on-the-Lake, OH 44060
  (440) 257-7234
  PoliceChief@CityMOL.org
- Painesville PD
- Chief Troy Hager
  28 Mentor Ave.
  Painesville, OH 44077
  (440) 392-5840
  polchief@painesville.com
- Perry PD
- Chief Michael G. Shank
  3758 Center Rd.
  Perry, OH 44081
  (440) 259-5004
  chief@perryvillage.info
- Waite Hill Village PD
- Chief Keith DeWitt
  7215 Eagle Rd.
  Willoughby, OH 44094
  (440) 942-1612
  WaiteHill@WaiteHillOH.gov
- Wickliffe PD
- Chief Randy E. Ice
  28730 Ridge Rd.
  Wickliffe, OH 44092
  (440) 943-1234
  wmargalis@cityofwickliffe.com
- Willoughby Hills PD
- Chief Christopher J. Collins
  35405 Chardon Rd.
  Willoughby Hills, OH 44094
  (440) 942-9111
  Police@WilloughbyHills-OH.gov
- Willowick PD
- Chief Michael T. Lazor
  30435 Lake Shore Blvd
  Willowick, OH 44095
  (440) 585-1234
  mlazor@cityofwillowick.com

Lawrence County

- Lawrence County SO
- Sheriff Jeff Lawless
  115 So. 5th St.
  Ironton, OH 45638
  (740) 532-3525
  helpthesheriff@lawcoso.com
- South Point PD
- Chief Chris Majher
  408 W. 2nd St.
  South Point, OH 45680
  (614) 377-4011
  southpointpd@yahoo.com

Licking County

- Alexandria PD
- Chief Wayne Howard
  4 W. Main St.
  Alexandria, OH 43001
  (740) 924-2001
  whoward@alexandriaoh.org
- Buckeye Lake PD
- Chief James *Jimmy* Hanzey
  5192 Walnut Rd. PO Box 27
  Buckeye Lake, OH 43008
  (740) 928-0999
  bldevelopment@roadrunner.com
- Granville PD
- Chief Jim Mason
  141 E. Broadway
  Granville, OH 43023
  (740) 587-1234
  jmason@granville.oh.us
- Hartford PD
- Chief James R. Hodge
  2 No. High St. PO Box 228
  Croton, OH 43013-0228
  (740) 893-2099
  police@villageofhartford.org
- Heath PD
- Chief Anthony Shepherd
  1287 Hebron Rd.
  Heath, OH 43056
  (740) 522-2141
  policechief@heathohio.gov
- Hebron PD
- Chief D. James Dean
  934 W. Main St.
  Hebron, OH 43025
  (740) 928-9402
  hebronpd@midohio.twcbc.com
- Johnstown PD
- Chief Don Corbin
  599 So. Main St. PO Box 457
  Johnstown, OH 43031
  (740) 967-9911
  dcorbin@villageofjohnstown.org
- Newark Police Div.
- Chief Steven J. Sarver
  40 W. Main St.
  Newark, OH 43055
  (740) 670-7214
  Steven.Sarver@newarkohio.net
- Pataskala PD
- Chief Bruce Brooks
  430 So. Main St.
  Pataskala, OH 43062
  (740) 927-5701
  sbutcher@ci.pataskala.oh.us

Logan County

- Logan County SO
- Sheriff Andrew J. Smith
  284 CR 32 So.
  Bellefontaine, OH 43311
  (937) 592-5731
  webmaster@co.logan.oh.us
- Bellefontaine PD
- Chief Brandon Standley
  135 No. Detroit St. # 6
  Bellefontaine, OH 43311
  (937) 599-1010
  bstandley@ci.bellefontaine.oh.us
- DeGraff PD
- Chief George K. Piersall
  107 So. Main St. PO Box 309
  DeGraff, OH 43318
  (937) 585-4188
  degraffpolice@centurylink.net
- West Liberty PD
- Chief Shane Oelker
  201 No. Detroit St.
  West Liberty, OH 43357
  (937) 465-2801
  admin-wlp@bizwoh.rr.com

Lorain County

- Lorain County SO
- Sheriff Phil R. Stammitti
  9896 Murray Ridge Rd.
  Elyria, OH 44035
  (440) 329-3702
  jcordes@loraincounty.us
- Amherst PD
- Chief Joseph Kucirek
  911 No. Lake St.
  Amherst, OH 44001
  (440) 988-2625
  amherstpolice@amherstpolice.net
- Elyria PD
- Chief Duane Whitely
  18 West Ave.
  Elyria, OH 44035
  (440) 323-3302
  whitely@cityofelyria.org

- Grafton PD
- Chief Dan Clark
  1009 Chestnut St.
  Grafton, OH 44044
  (440) 926-2661
  dclark@graftonpolice.net
- Lagrange PD
- Chief Daniel Moore
  355 So. Center St. PO Box 597
  Lagrange, OH 44050
  (440) 355-4469
  Village@LaGrangeOhio.net
- Lorain PD
- Chief Cel Rivera
  200 W. Erie Ave.
  Lorain, OH 44052
  (440) 204-2103
  Chief@CityofLorain.org
- North Ridgeville PD
- Chief Mike Freeman
  7307 Avon Belden Rd.
  North Ridgeville, OH 44039
  (440) 327-2191
  kcorcoran@nridgeville.org
- Oberlin PD
- Chief Thomas A. Miller
  85 So. Main St.
  Oberlin, OH 44074
  (440) 774-1061
  police@oberlinpd.com
- Sheffield Lake PD
- Chief Larry Shepherd
  609 Harris Rd.
  Sheffield Lake, OH 44054
  (440) 949-7131
  lshepherd@slpolice.com
- Sheffield Village PD
- Chief Larry Bliss
  4340 Colorado Ave.
  Sheffield, OH 44054
  (440) 949-6155
  policechief@sheffieldvillage.com
- Wellington PD
- Chief Steve Rollins
  117 Willard Memorial Sq.
  Wellington, OH 44090
  (440) 647-2244
  ChiefRollins@villageofwellington.com

Lucas County

- Lucas County SO
- Sheriff John Tharp
  1622 Spielbusch Ave.
  Toledo, OH 43624
  (419) 213-4900
  lljenkins@co.lucas.oh.us
- Holland PD
- Chief Robert Reed
  1245 Clarion Ave.
  Holland, OH 43528
  (419) 865-7105
  police.chief@hollandohio.com
- Maumee PD
- Chief Robert G. Zink
  109 E. Dudley St.
  Maumee, OH 43537
  (419) 897-7040
  babka-kathy@maumee.org

Madison County

- Madison County SO
- Sheriff James P. Sabin
  1 W. High St. PO Box 558
  London, OH 43140
  (740) 852-1332
  sabin@madisonsheriff.org
- London PD
- Chief David Wiseman
  10 E. 1st St.
  London, OH 43140
  (740) 852-1111
  policechief@ci.london.oh.us

Mahoning County

- Mahoning County SO
- Sheriff Jerry Greene
  110 5th Ave.
  Youngstown, OH 44503
  (330) 480-5020
  gkountz@sheriff.mahoning.oh.us
- Austintown Twp PD
- Chief Robert Gavalier
  92 Ohltown Rd.
  Austintown, OH 44515
  (330) 799-9721
  Falcon@Austintowntwp.com
- Beaver Twp PD
- Chief Carl N. Frost
  601 W. So. Range Rd.
  North Lima, OH 44452
  (330) 549-5338
  police@beavertwp-oh.gov

- Boardman PD
- Chief Jack Nichols
  8299 Market St.
  Youngstown, OH 44512
  (330) 729-2028
  jnichols@twp.boardman.oh.us
- Campbell PD
- Chief Gus Sarigianopoulos
  351 Tenney Ave.
  Campbell, OH 44405
  (330) 755-1411
  campbellpd@cboss.com
- Canfield PD
- Chief Charles Colucci
  104 Lisbon St.
  Canfield, OH 44406
  (330) 533-4903
  dblystone@ci.canfield.oh.us
- Goshen Police District
- Chief (*Col.*) Ray Snyder
  13991 W. So. Range Rd.
  Salem, OH 44460
  (330) 332-1235
  ray.snyder@goshen-oh.gov
- Lowellville PD
- Chief William Vance
  140 E. Liberty St.
  Lowellville, OH 44436
  (330) 536-6326
  lowellvillemayor@yahoo.com
- Milton Twp Police District
- Chief Charles J. VanDyke, M.S.
  15992 Milton Ave.
  Lake Milton, OH 44429
  (330) 538-0078
  cvandykempd@gmail.com
- Struthers PD
- Dir. Ed Wildes
  6 Elm St.
  Struthers, OH 44471
  (330) 755-9849
  safety@cityofstruthers.com
- Youngstown PD
- Chief Rod Foley
  116 W. Boardman St.
  Youngstown, OH 44503
  (330)742-8921
  ChiefFoley@CityofYoungstownOH.com

Marion County

- Marion County SO
- Sheriff Tim Bailey
  889 Marion Williamsport Rd.
  Marion, OH 43302
  (740) 382-8244
  drussell@co.marion.oh.us
- Marion PD
- Chief Tom Bell
  233 W. Center St.
  Marion, OH 43302
  (740) 387-2525
  tbell@marionohio.org

Medina County

- Medina County SO
- Sheriff Tom Miller
  555 Independence Dr.
  Medina, OH 44256
  (330) 725-0028
  tpmiller@medinaco.org
- Brunswick PD
- Chief Carl DeForest
  4095 Center Rd.
  Brunswick, OH 44212
  (330) 225-9111
  cdeforest@brunswick.oh.us
- Lodi PD
- Chief Keith Keough
  108 Ainsworth St. PO Box 95
  Lodi, OH 44254
  (330) 948-2040
  info@villageoflodi.com
- Medina PD
- Chief Patrick J. Berarducci
  150 W. Friendship St.
  Medina, OH 44256
  (330) 725-7777
  rstarcher@medinaoh.org
- Medina Twp PD
- Chief David L. Arbogast
  3801 Huffman Rd.
  Medina Twp, OH 44256
  (330) 723-1408
  medinatownship@medinatownship.com
- Montville Twp PD
- Chief Terry P. Grice
  6665 Wadsworth Rd.
  Medina, OH 44256
  (330) 725-8314
  tgrice@montvilletwp.org

Meigs County

- Meigs County SO
- Sheriff Keith Wood
  104 E. 2nd St.
  Pomeroy, OH 45769
  (740) 992-3371
  austin.king@meigssheriff.org
- Middleport PD
- Chief Bruce D. Swift
  659 Pearl St.
  Middleport, OH 45760
  (740) 992-6424
  middleportpd@yahoo.com
- Rutland PD
- Chief Jeff Miller
  337 Main St. PO Box 420
  Rutland, OH 45775
  (740) 742-2121
  rutland@voyager.net
- Syracuse PD
- Chief Garry R. Freed
  3rd St. PO Box 266
  Syracuse, OH 45779
  (740) 992-7777
  syracusepolice@charterinternet.com

Mercer County

- Mercer County SO
- Sheriff Jeff Grey
  4835 State Rt. 29 W.
  Celina, OH 45822
  (419) 586-7724
  commissioners@mercercountyohio.org
- Celina PD
- Chief David *Dave* Slusser
  202 No. Main St.
  Celina, OH 45822
  (419) 586-2345
  dslusser.celinapd@celinaohio.org
- Coldwater PD
- Chief Jason R. Miller
  303 W. Main St.
  Coldwater, OH 45828
  (419) 678-2356
  info@coldwaterpd.com
- Rockford PD
- Chief Paul May III
  142 No. Main St. PO Box 282
  Rockford, OH 45882
  (419) 363-3215
  rockford@bright.net
- St. Henry PD
- Chief Bob Garman
  121 W. Washington
  St. Henry, OH 45883
  (419) 678-4141
  shpd2501@yahoo.com

Miami County

- Miami County SO
- Sheriff Charles A. Cox
  201 W. Main St.
  Troy, OH 45373
  (937) 440-6085
  adminassist@miamicountyso.com
- Fletcher PD
- Chief Jack Thomas
  71 No. Walnut St.
  Fletcher, OH 45326
  (937) 368-2547
  pfletchermunici@woh.rr.com
- Piqua PD
- Chief Bruce Jamison
  100 No. Wayne St.
  Piqua, OH 45356
  (937) 778-2027
  policeservices@piquaoh.org
- Tipp City PD
- Chief Thomas N. Davidson
  260 So. Garber Dr.
  Tipp City, OH 45371
  (937) 667-3112
  tippcitypolice@tippcity.net
- Troy PD
- Chief Charles Phelps
  124 E. Main St.
  Troy, OH 45373
  (937) 339-7525
  joe.long@troyohio.gov

Monroe County

- Monroe County SO
- Sheriff Charles R. Black, Jr.
  108 W. Court St. PO Box 595
  Woodsfield, OH 43793
  (740) 472-1612
  rick.shipp@monroesheriff.com

Montgomery County

- Montgomery County SO
- Sheriff Phil Plummer
  345 W. 2nd St. PO Box 972
  Dayton, OH 45422
  (937) 225-4192
  plummerp@mcohiosheriff.org

- Brookville PD
- Chief Doug Jerome
  301 Sycamore St.
  Brookville, OH 45309
  (937) 833-2001
  jerome@brookvilleohio.com
- Centerville PD
- Chief Bruce P. Robertson
  155 W. Spring Valley Rd.
  Centerville, OH 45458
  (937) 433-7661
  kingseed@coollaw.com
- German Twp PD
- Chief Joseph Andzik
  12102 State Rt. 725 W.
  Germantown, OH 45327
  (937) 855-7215
  german_twp_pd@hotmail.com
- Huber Heights PD
- Chief Robert B. Schommer
  6121 Taylorsville Rd.
  Huber Heights, OH 45424
  (937) 237-5850
  rschommer@hhoh.org
- Kettering PD
- Chief James M. O'Dell
  3600 Shroyer Rd.
  Kettering, OH 45429
  (937) 296-2555
  kettering.police@ketteringoh.org
- Miamisburg PD
- Chief John Sedlak
  10 No. 1st St.
  Miamisburg, OH 45342
  (937) 866-3344
  manager@cityofmiamisburg.org
- Moraine PD
- Chief Thomas Schenck
  4200 Dryden Rd.
  Moraine, OH 45439
  (937) 535-1166
  eallison@moraineoh.org
- Trotwood PD
- Dir. Quincy Pope
  35 No. Olive Rd.
  Trotwood, OH 45426
  (937) 854-7205
  qpope@trotwood.org
- Union PD
- Chief Mike Blackwell
  118 No. Main St.
  Union, OH 45322
  (937) 836-0912
  japplegate@ci.union.oh.us
- Vandalia PD
- Chief Douglas L. Knight
  245 J.E. Bohanan Dr.
  Vandalia, OH 45377
  (937) 415-2260
  dknight@vandaliaohio.org
- West Carrollton PD
- Chief Rick Barnhart
  300 E. Central Ave.
  West Carrollton, OH 45449
  (937) 859-3688
  pddeputychief@westcarrollton.org

Morgan County

- Morgan County SO
- Sheriff Thomas C. Jenkins, Sr.
  37 E. Main St.
  McConnelsville, OH 43756
  (614) 962-4044
  brad.bond@morgancounty-oh.gov
- McConnelsville PD
- Act. Chief Troy Copeland
  9 W. Main St.
  McConnelsville, OH 43756
  (614) 962-3163
  tcopeland@vomcc.com

Morrow County

- Morrow County SO
- Sheriff Steven R. Brenneman
  101 Home Rd.
  Mt. Gilead, OH 43338
  (419) 946-4444
  sbrenneman@morrowcountysheriff.com
- Cardington PD
- Chief John Hinton
  215 Park Ave.
  Cardington, OH 43315
  (419) 864-8888
  hinton@cardington.org
- Edison PD
- Chief John A. Edwards
  101 Broadway St.
  Edison, OH 43320
  (614) 206-2751
  buddah@edisonpolice.net

- Mt. Gilead PD
- Chief Brian Zerman
  72 W. High St.
  Mt. Gilead, OH 43338
  (419) 946-3333
  chief-policemtgilead@myomnicity.com

Muskingum County

- Muskingum County SO
- Sheriff Matthew J. Lutz
  1840 E. Pike
  Zanesville, OH 43701
  (740) 455-7928
  Info@ohiomuskingumsheriff.org
- New Concord PD
- Chief Trevor Hayes
  2 W. Main St.
  New Concord, OH 43762
  (740) 826-7616
  thayes@newconcord-oh.gov

Noble County

- Noble County SO
- Sheriff Steve Hannum
  420 Olive St.
  Caldwell, OH 43724
  (740) 732-5631
  deputyrpickenpaugh@yahoo.com
- Caldwell PD
- Chief Brian M Langley
  215 West St.
  Caldwell, OH 43724
  (740) 732-5892
  caldwellohiopd@yahoo.com

Ottawa County

- Ottawa County SO
- Sheriff Steve Levorchick
  315 Madison St.
  Port Clinton, OH 43452
  (419) 734-4404
  slevorchick@ottawacountysheriff.org
- Clay Twp PD
- Chief Terry Mitchell
  21774 W. Holts E. Rd.
  Genoa, OH 43430
  (419) 855-3444
  Chief@claytownshippolice.org
- Elmore PD
- Chief George Hayes
  344 Rice St. PO Box 306
  Elmore, OH 43416
  (419) 862-3980
  elmorepd@amplex.net
- Genoa PD
- Chief Robert L. Bratton
  102 E. 6th St.
  Genoa, OH 43430
  (419) 855-7717
  rbratton@genoaohio.org
- Oak Harbor PD
- Chief Steven R. Weirich
  146 Church St.
  Oak Harbor, OH 43449
  (419) 898-2055
  stevew@oakharbor.oh.us
- Port Clinton PD
- Chief Robert J. Hickman
  1868 E. Perry St.
  Port Clinton, OH 43452
  (419) 734-3121
  pcmayor@portclinton-oh.gov
- Put-In-Bay PD
- Chief Robert Lampela
  431 Catawba Ave. PO Box 268
  Put-In-Bay, OH 43456
  (419) 285-4121
  info@put-in-baypolice.org
- Rocky Ridge PD
- Chief Michael J Frank
  14571 W. 2nd St.
  Rocky Ridge, OH 43458
  (419) 898-9541
  rockyridgepd@gmail.com

Paulding County

- Paulding County SO
- Sheriff David I. Harrow
  500 E. Perry St.
  Paulding, OH 45879
  (419) 399-3791
  dharrow@pauldingohsheriff.com
- Paulding PD
- Chief Randy Crawford
  116 So. Main St.
  Paulding, OH 45879
  (419) 399-3311
  pldgvil@paulding-net.com
- Payne PD
- Chief Rodney Miller
  PO Box 58
  Payne, OH 45880
  (419) 263-2514
  paynemayor@frontier.com

Perry County

- Perry County SO
- Sheriff William R. Barker
  110 W. Brown St. PO Box 107
  New Lexington, OH 43764
  (740) 342-4123
  pceworkinggroup@gmail.com
- Corning PD
- Chief Kevin Wintermute
  115 So. Corning Ave
  Corning, OH 43730
  (740) 347-4476
  VILLAGEOFCORNING@SBCGLOBAL.NET
- Crooksville PD
- Chief Brent Tysinger
  98 So. Buckeye St.
  Crooksville, OH 43731
  (740) 982-2666
  chief_tysinger@crooksville.com
- New Lexington PD
- Chief Scott Ervin
  215 So. Main St.
  New Lexington, OH 43764
  (740) 342-4111
  nlchief@rrohio.com
- New Straitsville PD
- Chief Kevin Groves
  114 W. Main St. PO Box 238
  New Straitsville, OH 43766
  (740) 394-2522
  police@newstraitsvillepolice.net
- Thornville PD
- Chief Nick Garver
  1 So. Main St.
  Thornville, OH 43076
  (740) 246-5511
  mayor.thornville@gmail.com

Pickaway County

- Pickaway County SD
- Sheriff Robert B. Radcliff
  600 Island Rd. PO Box 100
  Circleville, OH 43113
  (740) 474-2176
  jwippel@pickaway.org
- Ashville PD
- Chief Douglas E. Clark
  91 W. Main St. PO Box 195
  Ashville, OH 43103
  (740) 983-8529
  dclark@ashvilleohio.gov
- Circleville PD
- Chief Wayne Gray
  151 E. Franklin St.
  Circleville, OH 43113
  (740) 474-8888
  cpd@circlevillepolice.com
- South Bloomfield PD
- Chief Kendall G. *Ken* McCoy
  5023 So. Union St.
  South Bloomfield, OH 43103
  (740) 983-9482
  rdauberman@southbloomfieldpolice.com

Pike County

- Pike County SO
- Sheriff Richard N. Henderson
  116 So. Market St.
  Waverly, OH 45690
  (740) 947-2111
  rhenderson@pikecosheriff.com
- Waverly PD
- Chief Larry Roe
  202 So. Market St.
  Waverly, OH 45690
  (740) 947-2179
  lroe@waverlypd.net

Portage County

- Portage County SO
- Sheriff David W. Doak
  8240 Infirmary Rd.
  Ravenna, OH 44266
  (330) 678-7012
  ddoak@portageco.com
- Aurora PD
- Chief Seth Riewaldt
  100 So. Aurora Rd.
  Aurora, OH 44202
  (330) 562-8181
  riewaldts@auroraoh.com
- Brady Lake PD
- Chief David Kinney
  6500 Lakeview Rd.
  Ravenna, OH 44266
  (330) 673-5332
  bradylakepolicedepartment@gmail.com
- Brimfield PD
- Chief David A. Oliver
  1287 Tallmadge Rd.
  Kent, OH 44240
  (330) 673-7716
  doliver@brimfieldpolice.com

- Garrettsville PD
- Chief Anthony F. Milicia
  8123 High St.
  Garrettsville, OH 44231
  (330) 527-4717
  chief@garrettsville.org
- Hiram PD
- Chief Ed Samec
  11617 Garfield Rd.
  Hiram, OH 44234
  (330) 569-7677
  hiram.village.hvoh@gmail.com
- Kent PD
- Chief Michelle Lee
  319 So. Water St.
  Kent, OH 44240
  (330) 673-7732
  Fialaj@kent-ohio.org
- Mantua PD
- Chief H.W. Buchert
  4650 W. High St.
  Mantua, OH 44255
  (330) 274-2251
  MantuaPD@sbcglobal.net
- Ravenna PD
- Chief Tim Adkins
  220 Park Way
  Ravenna, OH 44266
  (330) 296-6486
  tim.adkins@ci.ravenna.oh.us
- Streetsboro PD
- Chief Roy E. Mosley III
  2080 State Rt. 303
  Streetsboro, OH 44241
  (330) 626-4976
  info@streetsboropolice.com
- Windham PD
- Chief Windham PD
  9621 E. Center St.
  Windham, OH 44288
  (330) 326-2211, ext. 225
  chiefofpolice@windhamvillage.com

Preble County

- Preble County SO
- Sheriff Michael L. Simpson
  1139 Preble Dr.
  Eaton, OH 45320
  (937) 456-6301
  info@preblecountysheriff.org
- Eaton PD
- Chief Chad DePew
  328 No. Maple St.
  Eaton, OH 45320
  (937) 456-5531
  cdepew@eatonpolice.org
- Gratis PD
- Chief Clayton R. VanWinkle
  404 Harrison St. PO Box 574
  Gratis, OH 45330
  (937) 787-9095
  gratispolice@woh.rr.com
- Lewisburg PD
- Chief Rick McGee
  100 W. Cumberland St.
  Lewisburg, OH 45338
  (937) 962-4677
  Randy.Creech@lewisburg.net
- West Alexandria PD
- Chief Terry Strawser
  16 No. Main St.
  West Alexandria, OH 45381
  (937) 839-4730
  w.alexpd@yahoo.com

Putnam County

- Putnam County SO
- Sheriff Michael C. Chandler
  1035 Heritage Tr.
  Ottawa, OH 45875
  (419) 523-3208
  putcocomm@bright.net
- Columbus Grove PD
- Chief Nick Gilgenbach
  113 E. Sycamore St.
  Columbus Grove, OH 45830
  (419) 659-2404
  cgadmin@q1.net
- Continental PD
- Chief Arnie Hardy
  100 No. Main St. PO Box 447
  Continental, OH 45831-0447
  (419) 596-3833
  cpd@bright.net

Richland County

- Richland County SO
- Sheriff J. Steve Sheldon
  597 Park Ave. E.
  Mansfield, OH 44905
  (419) 774-5881
  ssheldon@richlandcountyoh.us

- Bellville PD
- Chief Ron L. Willey
  320 Bell St.
  Bellville, OH 44813
  (419) 886-2245, ext. 2
  webinfo@bellvilleohio.net
- Lexington PD
- Chief Brett W. Pauley
  44 W. Main St.
  Lexington, OH 44904
  (419) 884-1032
  council@lexingtonohio.us
- Mansfield PD
- Chief Dino Sgambellone
  30 No. Diamond St.
  Mansfield, OH 44902
  (419) 755-9750
  manspd@ci.mansfield.oh.us
- Ontario PD
- Chief Rodney Smith
  555 No. Stumbo Rd.
  Ontario, OH 44906
  (419) 529-2115
  hthomas@ontarioohiopolice.com
- Plymouth PD
- Chief Charles D. Doan
  25 Sandusky St.
  Plymouth, OH 44865
  (419) 687-4321
  plymouthcops@yahoo.com

Ross County

- Ross County SO
- Sheriff George W. Lavender, Jr.
  28 No. Paint St.
  Chillicothe, OH 45601
  (740) 773-1186
  g.lavender@rosssheriff.com
- Chillicothe PD
- Chief Roger Moore
  28 No. Paint St.
  Chillicothe, OH 45601
  (740) 773-1191
  jack.everson@ci.chillicothe.oh.us

Sandusky County

- Sandusky County SO
- Sheriff Kyle Overmyer
  2323 Countryside Dr.
  Fremont, OH 43420
  (419) 332-2613
  overmyer_kyle@co.sandusky.oh.us
- Clyde PD
- Chief Bruce Gower
  222 No. Main St.
  Clyde, OH 43410
  (419) 547-9555
  BGower@clydeohio.org
- Woodville PD
- Chief Roy Whitehead
  219 W. Main St.
  Woodville, OH 43469
  (419) 849-2211
  wpd8901@woodville.net

Scioto County

- Scioto County SO
- Sheriff Marty V. Donini
  1025 16th St.
  Portsmouth, OH 45662
  (740) 355-8261
  scso@sciotocountysheriff.com
- New Boston PD
- Chief Darrold R. Clark
  3978 Rhodes Ave.
  New Boston, OH 45662
  (740) 456-4109
  nbpd@roadrunner.com

Seneca County

- Seneca County SO
- Sheriff William E. Eckelberry
  3040 So. State Rt. 100
  Tiffin, OH 44883
  (419) 447-3456
  scso@sciotocountysheriff.com
- Attica PD
- Chief Keith Turner
  20 So. Main St.
  Attica, OH 44807
  (419) 426-3621
  voa@bright.net
- Bettsville PD
- Chief Don Mason
  308 Emma St.
  Bettsville, OH 44815
  (419) 986-5748
  villageofbettsville@yahoo.com
- Bloomville PD
- Chief Howard Minzer
  10 Beeghly Ave.
  Bloomville, OH 44818
  (419) 983-2100
  bloomvillepolice@yahoo.com

- Fostoria PD
- Chief John McGuire
  213 So. Main St.
  Fostoria, OH 44830
  (419) 435-8573
  policechief@ci.fostoria.oh.us
- Tiffin PD
- Chief Fredrick W. Stevens
  51 E. Market St.
  Tiffin, OH 44883
  (419) 447-2323
  chiefofpolice@tiffinohio.gov

Shelby County

- Shelby County SO
- Sheriff John R. Lenhart
  555 Gearhart Rd.
  Sidney, OH 45365
  (937) 498-1111
  info@shelbycountysheriff.com
- Anna PD
- Chief Scott Evans
  207 W. Main St. PO Box 140
  Anna, OH 45302
  (937) 394-8381
  police@villageofannaoh.com
- Botkins PD
- Chief Wayne T. Glass, Jr.
  210 So. Mill St.
  Botkins, OH 45306
  (937) 693-4341
  chief.glass@botkinspd.com
- Port Jefferson PD
- Chief John Puckett
  100 Spring St. Box 189
  Port Jefferson, OH 45360
  (937) 492-9652
  portjeffersonpolice@gmail.com
- Sidney PD
- Chief Kevin Gessler
  201 W. Poplar St.
  Sidney, OH 45365
  (937) 498-2351
  kgessler@sidneyoh.com

Stark County

- Stark County SO
- Sheriff George Maier
  4500 Atlantic Blvd NE
  Canton, OH 44705
  (330) 430-3801
  strkshrf@raex.com
- Alliance PD
- Chief Scott C. Griffth
  470 E. Market St.
  Alliance, OH 44601
  (330) 823-5532
  mayor@allianceoh.gov
- Beach City PD
- Chief Jim Wood
  302 No. Church PO Box 251
  Beach City, OH 44608
  (330) 756-2449
  beachcity@adelphia.net
- Brewster PD
- Chief Harry Porter
  145 W. 1st St.
  Brewster, OH 44613
  (330) 767-3191
  brewmayor@sssnet.com
- Canal Fulton PD
- Chief Douglas Swartz
  1165 SE Locust St.
  Canal Fulton, OH 44614
  (330) 854-2926
  citymgr@cityofcanalfulton-oh.gov
- Hartville PD
- Chief Larry Dordea
  202 W. Maple St.
  Hartville, OH 44632-0701
  (330) 877-2500
  office@hartvilleoh.com
- Louisville PD
- Chief Andrew Turowski
  215 So. Mill St.
  Louisville, OH 44641
  (330) 875-2871
  policechief@louisvilleohio.org
- Magnolia PD
- Chief Jeff Hager
  328 No. Main St.
  Magnolia, OH 44643
  (330) 866-9434
  chiefhager@magnoliapolice.com
- Massillon PD
- Int. Chief William *Bill* Peel
  2 James Duncan Plaza
  Massillon, OH 44646
  (330) 830-1762
  wpeel@massillonpd.com

- Navarre PD
- Chief Dennis Albaugh
  27 Canal St. W.
  Navarre, OH 44662
  (330) 879-0342, ext. 306
  policechief@navarreohio.net
- Waynesburg PD
- Chief William Bath
  141 E. Lisbon St. PO Box 764
  Waynesburg, OH 44688
  (330) 866-3537
  tips@waynesburgpd.com

Summit County

- Summit County SO
- Sheriff Steve Barry
  53 University Ave.
  Akron, OH 44308
  (330) 643-2122
  rpaolucci@sheriff.summitoh.net
- Akron PD
- Chief James D. Nice
  217 So. High St.
  Akron, OH 44308
  (330) 375-2552
  Police@AkronOhio.gov
- Barberton PD
- Chief Vince Morber
  576 W. Park Ave.
  Barberton, OH 44203
  (330) 848-6701
  police@cityofbarberton.com
- Bath PD
- Chief Michael B. McNeely
  3864 W. Bath Rd.
  Akron, OH 44333
  (330) 666-3736
  policechief@bathtownship.org
- Boston Heights PD
- Chief Raymond Heatwall
  45 E. Boston Mills Rd.
  Boston Heights, OH 44236
  (330) 653-5911
  heatwall382@windstream.net
- Copley PD
- Chief Michael Mier
  1280 Sunset Dr.
  Copley, OH 44321
  (330) 666-4218
  township@copley.oh.us
- Cuyahoga Falls PD
- Chief Thomas L. Pozza
  2310 2nd St.
  Cuyahoga Falls, OH 44221
  (330) 971-8300
  cops@cityofcf.com
- Fairlawn PD
- Chief Kenneth Walsh
  3487 So. Smith Rd.
  Fairlawn, OH 44333
  (330) 670-4300
  walshk@ci.fairlawn.oh.us
- Hudson PD
- Chief Dave Robbins
  40 So. Oviatt St.
  Hudson, OH 44236
  (330) 342-1836
  drobbins@hudson.oh.us
- Macedonia PD
- Chief Jon Golden
  9683 Valley View Rd.
  Macedonia, OH 44056
  (330) 468-1234
  dkuchta@macedonia.oh.us
- Northfield PD
- Chief Mark C. Wentz
  10455 Northfield Rd.
  Northfield, OH 44067
  (330) 467-7139, ext. 16
  mwentz@northfieldvillage-oh.gov
- Norton PD
- Chief Thad Hete
  4060 Columbia Woods Dr.
  Norton, OH 44203
  (330) 825-2491
  chiefhete@cityofnorton.org
- Richfield PD
- Chief Keith D. Morgan
  4410 W. Streetsboro Rd.
  Richfield, OH 44286
  (330) 659-9500
  Police_Department@Richfieldpd.us
- Silver Lake PD
- Chief John Conley
  2961 Kent Rd.
  Silver Lake, OH 44224
  (330) 928-7573
  jconley@villageofsilverlake.com

- Tallmadge PD
- Chief Donald J. Zesiger
  53 Northeast Ave.
  Tallmadge, OH 44278
  (330) 633-4066
  dzesiger@tallmadge-ohio.org
- Warren PD
- Chief Timothy Bowers
  141 So. St. SE
  Warren, OH 44483
  (330) 841-2659
  tbowers@warren.org
- Warren Twp PD
- Chief Russell W. Leffert
  44 Mountain Blvd
  Leavittsburg, OH 44430
  (330) 753-1146
  rleffert@warrenpolice.com
- Weathersfield Twp PD
- Chief Joseph P. Consiglio
  1451 Prospect St.
  Mineral Ridge, OH 44440
  (330) 652-6326
  jconsiglio@weathersfieldtwp.com

Trumbull County

- Trumbull County SO
- Sheriff Thomas L. Altiere
  150 High St. NW
  Warren, OH 44481
  (330) 675-2540
  commissioners@co.trumbull.oh.us

Tuscarawas County

- Tuscarawas County SO
- Sheriff Walter R. *Walt* Wilson
  2295 Reiser Ave. SE
  New Philadelphia, OH 44663
  (330) 339-2000
  SHERIFF@CO.TUSCARAWAS.OH.US
- Barnhill PD
- Chief David F. Cimperman, Jr
  2237 Barnhill Rd.
  Barnhill, OH 44663
  (330) 308-8254
  BarnhillPD@aol.com
- Bolivar PD
- Chief Randy Haugh
  117 No. Central PO Box 556
  Bolivar, OH 44612
  (330) 874-2113
  policedept@villageofbolivar.com
- Dennison PD
- Chief Robert J. Hunt III
  302 Grant St.
  Dennison, OH 44621
  (740) 922-3131
  dennisonpd@att.net
- Dover PD
- Chief Joseph M. Ball
  110 E. 3rd St.
  Dover, OH 44622
  (330) 364-5533
  mayor.homrighausen@doverohio.com
- Gnadenhutten PD
- Chief David E. *Dave* Birker
  131 So. Walnut PO Box 168
  Gnadenhutten, OH 44629
  (740) 254-4116
  gnadpoli@tusco.net
- Midvale PD
- Chief William Ackerman
  3111 Barnhill Rd.
  Midvale, OH 44653
  (330) 339-6254
  midvalepolice@neohio.twcbc.com
- New Philadelphia PD
- Chief Jeff Urban
  122 2nd St. SE
  New Philadelphia, OH 44663
  (330) 343-4488
  nppd@tusco.net
- Strasburg PD
- Chief William J. *Bill* McCamant IV
  358 5th St. SW
  Strasburg, OH 44680
  (330) 878-7011
  BMcCamant@VillageOfStrasburg.com

Union County

- Union County SO
- Sheriff Malcum J. *Jamie* Patton
  221 W. 5th St.
  Marysville, OH 43040
  (937) 645-4100
  webadmin@co.union.oh.us
- Marysville PD
- Chief Floyd Golden
  1250 W. 5th St.
  Marysville, OH 43040
  (937) 645-7300
  fgolden@marysvilleohio.org

Van Wert County

- Van Wert County SO
- Sheriff Thomas M. Riggenbach
  113 No. Market St.
  Van Wert, OH 45891
  (419) 238-3866
  triggenbach@vanwertcountysheriff.com
- Convoy PD
- Chief Steve Haggerty
  PO Box 310
  Convoy, OH 45832
  (419) 238-3866
  convoypd@bright.net
- Van Wert PD
- Chief Joel Hammond
  PO Box 467
  Van Wert, OH 45891
  (419) 238-1993
  dfarmer@vanwert.org

Vinton County

- Vinton County SO
- Sheriff Shawn Justice
  106 So. Market St.
  McArthur, OH 45651
  (740) 596-5242
  sheriff@vintonco.com
- McArthur PD
- Chief Tony Wood
  124 W. Main St.
  McArthur, OH 45651
  (740) 596-2980
  captainschweikert@policemail.us

Warren County

- Warren County SO
- Sheriff Larry L. Sims
  550 Justice Dr.
  Lebanon, OH 45036
  (513) 695-1280
  lisa.dickerson@wcsooh.org
- Carlisle PD
- Chief Mike Bruck
  474 Fairview Dr.
  Franklin, OH 45005
  (937) 746-0117
  mbruck@carlisleoh.org
- Franklin PD
- Chief Russell Whitman
  41 E. 4th St.
  Franklin, OH 45005
  (513) 746-2882
  rwhitman@franklinohio.org
- Harveysburg PD
- Chief John Heisler
  10542 E. State Rt. 73
  Harveysburg, OH 45032
  (513) 897-9926
  villagepolice@erinet.com
- Lebanon PD
- Chief Jeffrey W. Mitchell
  25 W. Silver St.
  Lebanon, OH 45036
  (513) 932-2010
  jmitchell@lebanonohio.gov
- Maineville PD
- Chief John D. Reynolds
  8188 So. State Rt. 48
  Maineville, OH 45039
  (513) 583-0048
  johnreynolds@mainevilleoh.com
- Mason PD
- Chief Ron Ferrell
  202 W. Main St.
  Mason, OH 45040
  (513) 229-8560, ext. 6001
  rferrell@masonoh.org
- Springboro PD
- Chief Jeffrey Kruithoff
  320 W. Central Ave.
  Springboro, OH 45066
  (513) 748-0611
  jeff@cityofspringboro.com
- Waynesville PD
- Chief Gary Copeland
  1400 Lytle Rd.
  Waynesville, OH 45068
  (513) 897-8010
  dstubbs@waynesville-ohio.org

Washington County

- Washington County SO
- Sheriff Larry R. Mincks, Sr.
  205 Putnam St.
  Marietta, OH 45750
  (740) 373-6623
  sheriff.mincks@wcso84.us
- Belpre PD
- Chief Ernest Clevenger
  715 Park Dr. PO Box 160
  Belpre, OH 45714
  (740) 423-7631
  ChiefClevenger@belprepd.com

- Beverly PD
- Chief Mark Sams
  919 Mitchell Ave.
  Beverly, OH 45715
  (740) 984-2611
  beverlypolicechief@yahoo.com
- Marietta PD
- Chief Brett McKitrick
  301 Putnam St.
  Marietta, OH 45750
  (740) 373-4141
  brettmckitrick@mariettaoh.net

Wayne County

- Wayne County SO
- Sheriff Travis Hutchinson
  201 W. North St.
  Wooster, OH 44691
  (330) 287-5750
  wcso@wcjustice-center.org
- Apple Creek PD
- Chief Jason Woodruff
  63 E Main St PO Box 208
  Apple Creek, Ohio 44606
  (330) 698-5811
  applepolice@sssnet.com
- Creston PD
- Chief Bryon Meshew
  120 Brooklyn St.
  Creston, OH 44217
  (330) 435-6534
  williamarmentrout@yahoo.com
- Doylestown PD
- Chief Brian J. Dressler
  24 So. Portage St.
  Doylestown, OH 44230
  (330) 658-6582
  chief@doylestown.com
- Orrville PD
- Chief Joseph D. Routh
  207 No. Main St.
  Orrville, OH 44667
  (330) 684-5025
  routh@orrville.com
- Rittman PD
- Chief Mike Burg
  33 E. Ohio Ave.
  Rittman, OH 44270
  (330) 925-8040
  mburg@Rittman.com
- Shreve PD
- Chief Ron Kiner
  150 W. McConkey St.
  Shreve, OH 44676
  (330) 567-2600
  shrevemayor@yahoo.com
- Smithville PD
- Chief Warren Caskey
  207 W. Main St.
  Smithville, OH 44677
  (330) 669-3471
  Office@SmithvilleOhio.Org
- Wooster PD
- Chief Matthew Fisher
  201 W. North St.
  Wooster, OH 44691
  (330) 287-5720
  mfisher@woosteroh.com

Williams County

- Williams County SO
- Sheriff Steven M. *Steve* Towns
  218 W. Bryan St.
  Bryan, OH 43506
  (419) 636-3151
  wcso@bright.net
- Bryan PD
- Chief Jeff Arnold
  304 W. High St.
  Bryan, OH 43506
  (419) 633-6053
  jarnold@cityofbryan.com
- Montpelier PD
- Chief Dan McGee
  221 Empire St.
  Montpelier, OH 43543
  (419) 485-3121
  dan.mcgee@montpelieroh.org
- Pioneer PD
- Chief Timothy N. Livengood
  205 So. State St. PO Box 426
  Pioneer, OH 43554
  (419) 737-2493, ext. 2701
  tlivengood.villageofpioneer@gmail.com
- West Unity PD
- Chief J.R. Jones
  118 W. Jackson St.
  West Unity, OH 43570
  (419) 924-2271
  westunitypolice@adelphia.net

Wood County

- Wood County SO
- Sheriff Mark Wasylyshyn
  1960 E. Gypsy Ln.
  Bowling Green, OH 43402
  (419) 354-9137
  commissioners@co.wood.oh.us
- Bowling Green Police Div.
- Chief Bradford M. Conner
  175 W. Wooster St.
  Bowling Green, OH 43402-2897
  (419) 352-8775
  bgpolice@wcnet.org
- North Baltimore PD
- Chief Allan D. Baer
  203 No. Main St.
  North Baltimore, OH 45872
  (419) 257-2181
  abaer@northbaltimore.net
- Northwood PD
- Chief Thomas S. Cairl
  6000 Wales Rd.
  Northwood, OH 43619
  (419) 691-5053
  TCairl@northwoodpolice.com
- Pemberville PD
- Chief Jim Darling
  117 E. Front St.
  Pemberville, OH 43450
  (419) 287-3250
  chief_darling@pembervillepolice.com
- Perrysburg PD
- Chief Daniel O. Paez
  330 Walnut St.
  Perrysburg, OH 43551
  (419) 872-8002
  dpaez@ci.perrysburg.oh.us
- Rossford PD
- Chief Glenn B. Goss, Sr.
  99 Hillsdale Ave.
  Rossford, OH 43460
  (419) 666-7390
  ggoss@rossfordohio.com
- Walbridge PD
- Chief Kenneth P. Frost
  111 No. Main St.
  Walbridge, OH 43465
  (419) 466-7459
  kenneth.p.frost@hotmail.com

Wyandot County

- Wyandot County SO
- Sheriff Michael R. Hetzel
  125 E. Wyandot Ave.
  Upper Sandusky, OH 43351
  (419) 294-2362
  dkramer@co.wyandot.oh.us
- Carey PD
- Chief Daniel A. Walter
  127 No. Vance St.
  Carey, OH 43316
  (419) 396-7678
  vocpd@udata.com
- Upper Sandusky PD
- Chief David M. Olds
  120 No. 7th St.
  Upper Sandusky, OH 43351
  (419) 294-2324
  chiefolds@uppersanduskypolice.org

State Agencies

- OH Highway Patrol-HQ
- Col. John Born
  1970 W. Broad St. PO Box 182074
  Columbus, Ohio 43223
  (614) 752-2792
  wwwohp@dps.state.oh.us
- Cleveland State U. PD
- Chief Paul Denton
  2121 Euclid Ave.
  Cleveland, OH 44115
  (216) 688-3742
  denton.25@osu.edu
- Columbus State U. PD
- Chief Sean Asbury
  550 E. Spring St.
  Columbus, OH 43216
  (614) 287-2525
  information@cscc.edu
- Medical U. of OH PD
- Chief Jeff Newton
  3045 Arlington Ave.
  Toledo, OH 43614
  (419) 383-3770
  utpolice@utoledo.edu
- Miami U. PD
- Chief John M. McCandless
  Miami U. Bonham House
  Oxford, OH 45056
  (513) 529-2222
  police@MiamiOH.edu

- OH State U.-Wooster PD
- Chief Paul Denton
  1680 Madison Ave.
  Wooster, OH 44691
  (614) 688-3742
  denton.25@osu.edu
- Ohio U. PD
- Chief Andrew D. Powers
  135 Scott Quad
  Athens, OH 45701
  (740) 593-1911
  powersa@ohio.edu
- Youngstown State U. PD
- Chief John M. Beshara
  One University Plaza
  Youngstown, OH 44555
  (330) 742-3527
  police@ysu.edu

PENNSYLVANIA

Adams County

- Adams County SO
- Sheriff James Muller
  111-117 Baltimore St., Rm. #4
  Gettysburg, PA 17325
  (717) 337-9828
  jmuller@adamscounty.us
- Gettysburg PD
- Chief Joseph Dougherty
  59 E. High St.
  Gettysburg, PA 17325
  (717) 334-1168
  jdougherty@gettysburg-pa.gov
- Littlestown PD
- Chief Charles Keller
  46 E. King St.
  Littlestown, PA 17340
  (717) 359-4511
  ckellar@littlestownboro.org

Allegheny County

- Avalon PD
- Chief Thomas Kokoski
  640 California Ave.
  Pittsburgh, PA 15202
  (412) 761-0352
  tkokoski@boroughofavalon.org
- Bellevue PD
- Chief Matthew Sentner
  537 Bayne Ave.
  Pittsburgh, PA 15202
  (412) 766-7400
  sentner@bellevueboropolice.com
- Bethel Park PD
- Chief John Mackey
  5100 W. Library Ave.
  Bethel Park, PA 15102
  (412) 833-2000
  police@bethelpark.net
- Carnegie PD
- Chief Darlene Pfeffer
  301 Lindsay Rd.
  Carnegie, PA 15106
  (412) 279-4300
  dpfeffer@carnegiepolice.org
- Castle Shannon PD
- Chief Kenneth Truver
  3310 McRoberts Rd.
  Castle Shannon, PA 15234
  (412) 885-9300
  ktruver@csborough.com
- Churchill PD
- Chief Allen L. Park
  2300 William Penn Hwy
  Pittsburgh, PA 15235
  (412) 241-4466
  apark@churchillborough.com
- Coraopolis PD
- Chief Alan DeRusso
  1012 5th Ave.
  Coraopolis, PA 15108
  (412) 264-3000
  police@coraopolispa.com
- Dormont PD
- Chief Michael Bisignani
  710 Washington Rd.
  Pittsburgh, PA 15216
  (412) 561-8900
  bisignani@burough.dormont.pa.us
- Duquesne PD
- Chief Richard Adams
  12 So. 2nd St.
  Duquesne, PA 15110
  (412) 469-3774
  lachtzehn.duquesne@comcast.net
- East McKeesport PD
- Chief Russell Stroschein
  907 Florence Ave.
  East McKeesport, PA 15035
  (412) 824-0324
  chief@eastmckeesportboro.com
- East Pittsburgh PD
- Chief Lori Payne
  811 Linden Ave.
  East Pittsburgh, PA 15112
  (412) 823-6405
  eppdlpayn@tuppergroup.com
- Elizabeth Borough PD
- Chief John Snelson
  206 3rd Ave.
  Elizabeth, PA 15037
  (412) 384-4041
  elizabethtwppolice@comcast.net
- Etna PD
- Chief Vincent Jones
  437 Butler St.
  Pittsburgh, PA 15223
  (412) 781-6271
  pramage@etnaborough.org

- Forest Hills PD
- Chief Charles Williams
  2071 Ardmore Blvd
  Pittsburgh, PA 15221
  (412) 351-4141
  webmaster@foresthillspa.org
- Indiana PD
- Chief Robert W. Wilson
  941 Rt. 910
  Indianola, PA 15051
  (412) 767-5333
  police@indianatownship.com
- Jefferson PD
- Chief Eugene W. Roach, Jr.
  925 Old Clairton Rd.
  Clairton, PA 15025
  (412) 655-2222
  groach@jeffersonhills.net
- Millvale BPD
- Chief Jim Tunstall, Jr.
  501 Lincoln Ave.
  Millvale, PA 15209
  (412) 821-3401
  info@millvaleboro.com
- Monroeville PD
- Chief Steven Pascarella
  2700 Monroeville Blvd
  Monroeville, PA 15146
  (412) 856-3324
  pascas@monroeville.pa.us
- Moon Twp PD
- Chief Leo McCarthy
  1000 Beaver Grade Rd.
  Moon, PA 15108
  (412) 262-5000
  police@moonpolice.us
- Mt. Oliver PD
- Chief Frank Mosesso
  150 Brownsville Rd.
  Mt. Oliver, PA 15210
  (412) 431-2254
  Police@MountOliver.us
- Munhall PD
- Chief Patrick Campbell
  1900 West St.
  Munhall, PA 15120
  (412) 464-7300
  info@munhallpa.us
- Oakdale PD
- Chief Jim Lauria
  6115 Noblestown Rd.
  Oakdale, PA 15071
  (724) 693-8400
  rohbeck@oakdaleborough.com
- Port Vue PD
- Chief Bryan R. Meyers
  1191 Romine Ave.
  Port Vue, PA 15133
  (412) 672-2255
  pvpd135@hotmail.com
- Rankin PD
- Chief James M. Romano
  320 Hawkins Ave.
  Rankin, PA 15104
  (412) 271-1010
  JRomano@scotttownship.org
- Sharpsburg PD
- Chief Leo Rudski Jr.
  1611 Main St.
  Pittsburgh, PA 15215
  (412) 781-0546
  secretary@sharpsburgborough.com
- South Park PD
- Chief Dennis M. McDonough
  2675 Brownsville Rd.
  Library, PA 15129
  (412) 833-1000
  dcmcdonough@southparktwp.com
- Springdale PD
- Chief Joe Naviglia
  325 School St.
  Springdale, PA 15144
  (724) 274-9022
  springdaleboro@hotmail.com
- Tarentum PD
- Chief William S. Vakulick
  318 E. 2nd Ave.
  Tarentum, PA 15084
  (724) 224-1515
  police@tarentumboro.com
- West Deer PD
- Chief Jonathan Lape
  PO Box 2
  Russellton, PA 15076
  (724) 265-1100
  wdpd@westdeertownship.com

- West Homestead PD
- Chief Christopher Deasy
  456 W. 8th Ave.
  West Homestead, PA 15120
  (412) 462-4150
  christopher.deasy@westhomesteadpa.com
- West Mifflin Borough PD
- Chief Kenneth Davis
  4733 Greensprings Ave.
  West Mifflin, PA 15122
  (412) 461-3125
  dwrobleski@westmifflinborough.com
- Whitehall Borough PD
- Chief Richard M. Danko
  100 Borough Park Dr.
  Pittsburgh, PA 15236
  (412) 884-1100
  wpdadmin@whitehallboro.org
- Wilkins Twp PD
- Chief Ed Krancic
  110 Peffer Rd.
  Turtle Creek, PA 15145
  (412) 824-0032
  ekrancic@wilkinstownship.com
- Wilkinsburg PD
- Chief Ophelia Coleman
  605 Ross Ave.
  Wilkinsburg, PA 15221
  (412) 244-2919
  ocoleman@wilkinsburgpa.gov

Armstrong County

- Armstrong County SO
- Sheriff Larry R. Crawford
  500 E. Market St.
  Kittanning, PA 16201
  (724) 548-3265
  sheriff@co.armstrong.pa.us
- Apollo Borough PD
- Chief David Fisher
  405 No. Pennsylvania Ave.
  Apollo, PA 15613
  (724) 478-3091
  apollopolice@windstream.net
- Parker City PD
- Chief David King
  Cooper Ave. PO Box 350
  Parker, PA 16049
  (724) 399-4388
  police@parkeronline.org

Beaver County

- Beaver County SO
- Sheriff George David
  810 3rd St.
  Beaver, PA 15009
  (724) 728-5700
  Sheriff@beavercountypa.gov
- Aliquippa PD
- Chief Andre Davis
  581 Franklin Ave.
  Aliquippa, PA 15001
  (724) 375-6681
  andre.davis@aliquippapa.gov
- Economy Borough PD
- Chief Thomas C. Harrington
  1000 Kenneth Campbell Way
  Baden, PA 15005
  (724) 869-7877
  kanderson@economyboropd.com
- Monaca PD
- Chief William J. Petures
  928 Pennsylvania Ave.
  Monaca, PA 15061
  (724) 775-9613
  sgtpetures@monacapa.net
- North Sewickley PD
- Chief Bryan Landman
  899 Mercer Rd.
  Beaver Falls, PA 15010
  (724) 843-8118
  nspd15010@zoominternet.net
- Patterson PD
- Chief Richard Cindrich
  1800 Dixon Way
  Beaver Falls, PA 15010
  (724) 846-8400
  police.chief@pattersontwp.com
- Rochester PD
- Chief Frank Mercier
  300 W. Park St.
  Rochester, PA 15074
  (724) 775-1100
  policetips@rboro.org
- Shippingport PD
- Chief Robert Davis
  Box 76
  Shippingport, PA 15077
  (724) 643-1371
  shippingportpd@cji.net

Bedford County

- Bedford County SO
- Sheriff Charwin Reichelderfer
  208A Imlertown Rd. RD #1
  Bedford, PA 15522
  (814) 623-2910
  Creichelderfer@bedfordcountypa.org
- Hopewell PD
- Chief Gene Ungarean
  417 Broad St. PO Box 160
  Hopewell, PA 16650
  (814) 928-0044
  chiefgu@tsil.net

Berks County

- Berks County SO
- Sheriff Eric Weaknecht
  633 Court St.
  Reading, PA 19601
  (610) 478-6240
  EWeaknecht@CountyofBerks.com
- Amity PD
- Chief Kent Shuebrook
  2004 Weavertown Rd.
  Douglassville, PA 19518
  (610) 689-6000
  jsowers@amitytownshippa.com
- Bally PD
- Chief Joseph Viola, Jr.
  425 Chestnut St.
  Bally, PA 19503
  (610) 845-2400
  bally@comcast.net
- Bethel Twp PD
- Chief Aaron Ogden
  91 Klahr Rd.
  Box 24
  Bethel, PA 19507
  (717) 933-4210
  twppolicepa@bethel.berksco.org
- Birdsboro PD
- Chief Theodore R. Roth
  200 E. Main St.
  Birdsboro, PA 19508
  (610) 582-6037
  BirdsboroPD@talon.net
- Brecknock PD
- Chief Richard Leisey
  889 Alleghenyville Rd.
  Mohnton, PA 19540
  (717) 445-0656
  brecknockpd@brecknock.berksco.org
- Douglass PD
- Chief David Franke
  1068 Douglass Dr.
  Boyertown, PA 19512
  (610) 367-9474
  dfranke.dougberks@comcast.net
- Exeter PD
- Chief Christopher Neidert
  4975 DeMoss Rd.
  Reading, PA 19606
  (610) 779-1490
  info@exeterpolice.com
- Fleetwood PD
- Chief Steven Stinsky
  110 W. Arch St.
  Fleetwood, PA 19522
  (610) 944-7011
  administration@fleetwoodboro.com
- Hamburg PD
- Chief Pedro A. Rivera
  61 No. 3rd St.
  Hamburg, PA 19526
  (610) 562-7228
  privera.hpd@hamburgboro.com
- Kutztown PD
- Chief Craig M. Summers
  45 Railroad St.
  Kutztown, PA 19530
  (610) 683-3545
  kutztownpd@kutztownpd.org
- Laureldale PD
- Chief Ronald Fisher, Jr.
  3406 Kutztown Rd.
  Laureldale, PA 19605
  (610) 929-8816
  RFisher@Laureldaleboro.org
- Mohnton PD
- Chief Richard G. Leisey, Sr.
  21 No. O'Neil St.
  Mohnton, PA 19540
  (610) 777-6909
  mohntonboro@verizon.net
- Muhlenberg PD
- Chief Erik P. Grunzig
  5401 Leesport Ave.
  Temple, PA 19560
  (610) 929-5454
  egrunzig@muhlenbergtwp.com

- Shillington PD
- Chief Brett A. Hivner
  2 E. Lancaster Ave.
  Reading, PA 19607
  (610) 777-1338
  info@shillingtonpd.com
- Tulpehocken PD
- Chief Kris Kerschner
  22 Rehrersburg Rd.
  Rehrersburg, PA 19550
  (717) 933-5033
  tulpypolice@tulpehocken.berksco.org
- Wernersville PD
- Chief Richard Sichler
  100 No. Reber St.
  Wernersville, PA 19565
  (610) 678-2835
  rsichler@westreadingborough.org
- Womelsdorf PD
- Chief Brian Thumm
  101 W. High St.
  Womelsdorf, PA 19567
  (610) 589-5559
  womelsdorfpd@womelsdorf.berksco.org

Blair County

- Altoona PD
- Chief Janice Freehling
  PO Box 1805
  Altoona, PA 16603-1805
  (814) 949-2490
  altoonapolice@altoonapa.gov
- Duncansville PD
- Chief P. Richard Books
  1146-3rd Ave.
  Duncansville, PA 16635
  (814) 696-0515
  duncansvillepolice@yahoo.com
- Greenfield PD
- Chief Ronald A. Givler
  Ski Gap and Pine Hollow Rds.
  Claysburg, PA 16625-0122
  (814) 239-5313
  gfieldpd840@hotmail.ocm
- Hollidaysburg PD
- Chief Jeffrey Ketner
  401 Blair St.
  Hollidaysburg, PA 16648
  (814) 695-3711
  Mayor@hollidaysburgpa.org
- Logan PD
- Chief Ron Heller
  800 39th St.
  Altoona, PA 16602-1799
  (814) 940-5999
  ronheller@atlanticbbn.net
- Martinsburg PD
- Chief Kerry L. Hoover
  133 E. Allegheny St.
  Martinsburg, PA 16662
  (814) 793-2838
  chiefhoover@martinsburgpa.org
- Williamsburg PD
- Chief Rowdy C. Kagarise
  305 E. 2nd St.
  Williamsburg, PA 16693
  (814) 832-2022
  williamsburgpd@wmsburgpa.com

Bradford County

- Bradford County SD
- Sheriff Gordon Smith
  301 Main St.
  Towanda, PA 18848
  (570) 265-1701
  Info@BradfordSheriff.org
- Towanda PD
- Chief Randy Epler
  10 Park St.
  Towanda, PA 18848
  (570) 265-2522
  towandaboro@comcast.net
- Troy PD
- Chief Jarvis C. Burlingame
  110 Elmira St.
  Troy, PA 16947
  (570) 297-2423
  tbpd@epix.net

Bucks County

- Bucks County SO
- Sheriff Edward Donnelly
  Main & Court Sts.
  Doylestown, PA 18901
  (215) 348-6138
  jlmcclure@co.bucks.pa.us
- Bristol Twp PD
- Chief George F. Stuckey
  2501 Bath Rd.
  Bristol, PA 19007
  (215) 785-4041
  patrol@btpolice.com

- Buckingham PD
- Chief Steven P. Daniels
  4613 Hughesian Dr.
  Buckingham, PA 18912
  (215) 794-8812
  contact@buckinghampa.org
- Chalfont PD
- Chief Frank Campbell
  40 No. Main St.
  Chalfont, PA 18914
  (215) 822-2606
  info@chalfontborough.com
- Doylestown PD
- Chief Dean Logan
  425 Wells Rd.
  Doylestown, PA 18901
  (215) 348-4201
  police@doylestownpa.org
- Dublin PD
- Chief Terrence Thompson
  119 Maple Ave.
  Dublin, PA 18917
  (215) 249-0272
  tthompson@upperdublin.net
- Falls PD
- Chief William J. Wilcox
  188 Lincoln Hwy
  Fairless Hills, PA 19030
  (215) 945-3100
  wilcoxpd@fallstwp.com
- Hilltown PD
- Chief Chris Engelhart
  13 W. Creamery PO Box 260
  Hilltown, PA 18927
  (215) 453-6000
  cengelhart@hilltown.org
- Ivyland PD
- Chief Nicolas Rosato
  991 Pennsylvania Ave.
  Ivyland, PA 18974
  (215) 672-3215
  cmr1215@verizon.net
- Lower Southampton PD
- Chief William Wiegman
  1500 Desire Ave.
  Feasterville, PA 19053
  (215) 357-1235
  wwiegman@lstwp.org
- Middletown PD
- Chief Kenneth Mullus
  5 Municipal Way
  Langhorne, PA 19047
  (215) 750-3845
  kmellus@mtpd.org
- New Britain Twp PD
- Chief James Donnelly
  207 Park Ave.
  Chalfont, PA 18914
  (215) 822-1910
  jdonnelly@doylestownborough.net
- Newtown Borough PD
- Chief Henry *Rick* Pasqualini
  22 Liberty St.
  Newtown, PA 18940
  (215) 860-7835
  chief@twp.newtown.pa.us
- Northampton PD
- Chief Michael B. Clark
  55 Township Rd.
  Richboro, PA 18954
  (215) 322-6111
  mclark@northamptontownship.com
- Penndel PD
- Chief Joseph Sciscio
  300 Bellevue Ave.
  Penndel, PA 19047
  (215) 757-5152
  bdavis@penndelpolice.com
- Perkasie PD
- Chief Joseph V. Gura, Jr.
  311 So. 9th St.
  Perkasie, PA 18944
  (215) 257-6876
  info@perkasiepd.org
- Quakertown PD
- Chief Scott C. McElree
  35 No. 3rd St.
  Quakertown, PA 18951
  (215) 536-5002
  dbender@quakertown.org
- Springfield Twp PD
- Chief Richard J. Ficco, Sr.
  2320 Township Rd.
  Quakertown, PA 18951
  (610) 346-7600
  richf@richlandtownshippd.org

- Upper Makefield PD
- Chief Mark F. Schmidt
  1076 Eagle Rd.
  Newtown, PA 18940
  (215) 968-3020
  info@uppermakefield.org
- Upper Southampton PD
- Chief Ronald MacPherson
  939 Street Rd.
  Southampton, PA 18966
  (215)364-5000
  rmacpherson@ustwp.org
- Warrington PD
- Chief James J. Miller
  852 Easton Rd.
  Warrington, PA 18976
  (215) 343-3311
  mail@warringtontownship.org

Butler County

- Butler County SO
- Sheriff Michael Slupe
  300 So. Main St. PO Box 1208
  Butler, PA 16003
  (724) 284-5245
  sheriff@butlercounty.com
- Butler County Coll. PD
- Chief Patrick Massaro
  PO Box 1203
  Butler, PA 16003-1203
  (724) 287-8711
  patrick.massaro@bc3.edu
- Butler Twp PD
- Chief John R. Hays
  290 So. Duffy Rd.
  Butler, PA 16001
  (724) 285-9600
  police@butlertwp.org
- Callery Borough PD
- Chief David M. Watts
  199 Railroad St. PO Box 150
  Callery, PA 16024
  (724) 538-3141
  callerypd@zoominternet.net
- Cranberry PD
- Act. Chief (*Lt.*) Kevin Meyer
  2525 Rochester Rd, Ste. 500
  Cranberry, PA 16066
  (724) 776-5180
  kevin.meyer@cranberrytownship.org
- Harrisville PD
- Chief Bill Morris
  So. Main St.
  Harrisville, PA 16038
  (724) 735-2030
  police@cityofharrisville.com
- Middlesex PD
- Act. Chief (*Sgt.*) Randy Ruediger
  133 Brownshill Rd.
  Valencia, PA 16059
  (724) 898-3533
  mpd@zoominternet.net
- Zelienople PD
- Chief James A. Miller
  111 W. New Castle St.
  Zelienople, PA 16063
  (724) 452-3003
  zelienoplepd@zoominternet.net

Cambria County

- Adams PD
- Chief William E. Westerman
  125 Mary Dr. PO Box 112
  Sidman, PA 15955
  (814) 487-4712
  adamstwppolicedept@adamstwp.org
- Carrolltown PD
- Chief David J. Murphy
  132 E. Carroll St.
  Carrolltown, PA 15722
  (814) 344-6400
  carrolltownpolice@yahoo.com
- Cresson PD
- Chief Jeffrey Kopsic
  631 2nd St., Ste. 1004
  Cresson, PA 16630
  (814) 886-8571, ext 204
  cbpd@nb.net
- Croyle PD
- Chief Steven Parks
  1654 Railroad St.
  Summerhill, PA 15958
  (814) 495-5679
  CroyleTwpPD@aol.com
- Ebensburg PD
- Chief Terry Wyland
  300 W. High St.
  Ebensburg, PA 15931
  (814) 472-8930
  police@ebensburgpa.com

- Ferndale PD
- Chief Arthur Boring
  109 Station St.
  Johnstown, PA 15905
  (814) 288-4131
  Police@FerndaleBorough.com
- Gallitzin Borough PD
- Chief Gerald E. Hagen
  411 Convent St., Ste. #10
  Gallitzin, PA 16641
  (814) 886-4014
  GallitzinBPD@cji.net
- Hastings PD
- Chief Ronald John Sharkey, Sr.
  207 5th Ave.
  Hastings, PA 16646
  (814) 247-6663
  hpolice@adelphia.net
- Jackson PD
- Act. Chief Philip Vaught, Jr.
  513 Pike Rd.
  Johnstown, PA 15909
  (814) 749-0051
  police@jacksontwppa.com
- Johnstown PD
- Chief Craig Foust
  401 Washington St.
  Johnstown, PA 15901
  (814) 533-2074
  cops@johnstownpolice.com
- St. Francis U. DPS
- Chief Robert Fatula
  114 Franciscan Way
  Loretto, PA 15940
  (814) 472-3360
  rfatula@francis.edu
- Stonycreek PD
- Chief David A. Dunkleberger
  1610 Bedford St.
  Johnstown, PA 15902
  (814) 266-3112
  chief@stonycreektownship.com

Cameron County

- Cameron County SO
- Sheriff Allen Neyman
  20 E. 5th St.
  Emporium, PA 15834
  (814) 486-3338
  camcosd@cameroncountypa.com

Carbon County

- Carbon County SO
- Sheriff Dwight Nothstein
  Courthouse
  Jim Thorpe, PA 18229
  (570) 325-2821
  jhager@carboncourts.com
- Lehighton PD
- Chief Harry *Jimmy* Yenser
  Constitution Ave.
  Lehighton, PA 18235
  (610) 377-4003
  police@lehightonborough.com
- Mahoning PD
- Chief Robert Blee, Jr.
  2685 Mahoning Dr. E.
  Lehighton, PA 18235
  (570) 386-2241
  mahtwppd@ptd.net

Centre County

- Centre County SO
- Sheriff Denny Naudbnau
  Courthouse, E. High St.
  Bellefonte, PA 16823
  (814) 355-6803
  Naudbnau@centrecountypa.gov
- Ferguson PD
- Chief Diane Conrad
  3147 Research Dr.
  State College, PA 16801
  (814) 237-1172
  police@twp.ferguson.pa.us
- Patton PD
- Chief Vince Leppert
  100 Patton Plaza
  State College, PA 16803
  (814) 234-0271
  vleppert@pattonboro.com
- State College PD
- Chief Thomas R. King
  243 So. Allen St.
  State College, PA 16801
  (814) 234-7150
  police@statecollegepa.us

Chester County

- Chester County SO
- Sheriff Carolyn Welsh
  17 No. Church St., Ste. 126
  West Chester, PA 19380
  (610) 344-6850
  jswab@chesco.org

- Birmingham PD
- Chief Thomas R. Nelling
  1040 W. Street Rd.
  West Chester, PA 19382
  (610) 793-3333
  tnelling@comcast.net
- Coatesville PD
- Chief Jack Laufer III
  One City Hall Plaza
  Coatesville, PA 19320
  (610) 384-2300
  jlaufer@coatesville.org
- Downingtown PD
- Chief James R. McGowan III
  10 W. Lancaster Ave.
  Downingtown, PA 19335
  (610) 269-0263
  info@downingtown.org
- East Fallowfield PD
- Chief Chris Porter
  2264 Strasburg Rd.
  East Fallowfield, PA 19320
  (610) 384-9163
  secretary@eastfallowfield.org
- East Pikeland PD
- Chief James Franciscus
  Box 298
  Kimberton, PA 19442
  (610) 935-0606
  tgalloway@eastpikeland.org
- Honey Brook PD
- Chief Patrick J. Ely
  495 Suplee Rd.
  Honey Brook, PA 19344
  (610) 273-7414
  info@hbboro.net
- Malvern PD
- Chief Lou Marcelli
  1 E. 1st Ave., Ste. 1
  Malvern, PA 19355
  (610) 647-0261
  lmarcelli@malvern.org
- New Garden PD
- Chief Gerald Simpson
  8934 Gap Newport Pike
  Avondale, PA 19311
  (610) 268-2907
  office@newgarden.org
- North Coventry PD
- Chief Robert Schurr
  845 So. Hanover St.
  Pottstown, PA 19465
  (610) 323-8360
  AGery@norcopd.org
- Oxford PD
- Chief John Slauch
  PO Box 380
  Oxford, PA 19363
  (610) 932-2500
  chief@theoxfordpd.com
- Parkesburg PD
- Chief Brian C. Sheller
  329 W. 1st Ave.
  Parkesburg, PA 19365
  (610) 857-3535
  Bsheller@parkesburgpolice.org
- Sadsbury PD
- Chief Jerry Ranck
  PO Box 418
  Sadsburyville, PA 19369
  (610) 857-9536
  sadsburytwppolice@comcast.net
- Schuylkill PD
- Chief James R. Fetterman
  111 Valley Park Rd.
  Phoenixville, PA 19460
  (610) 933-5820
  pdadm@schuylkilltwp.org
- South Coatesville PD
- Chief Jack Laufer III
  134 Modena Rd.
  South Coatesville, PA 19320
  (610) 384-3500
  jlaufer@coatesville.org
- Tredyffrin PD
- Supt. Anthony Giaimo
  1100 DuPortail Rd.
  Berwyn, PA 19312
  (610) 644-3221
  police@tredyffrin.org
- Upper Uwchlan PD
- Chief John DeMarco
  140 Pottstown Pike
  Chester Springs, PA 19425
  (610) 458-5862
  jdemarco@upperuwchlan-pa.gov

- Uwchlan PD
- Chief Joseph Pantarelli
  717 No. Ship Rd.
  Exton, PA 19341
  (610) 363-6947
  jpontarelli@uwchlan.com
- Valley PD
- Chief Joseph Friel
  PO Box 467
  Coatesville, PA 19320
  (610) 384-8133
  Chief@ValleyTownship.org
- West Brandywine PD
- Chief Walt Werner
  199 Lafayette Rd.
  Coatesville, PA 19320
  (610) 380-8201
  wwerner@wbrandywinepd.org
- West Caln PD
- Chief Curt A. Martinez
  PO Box 111
  Wagontown, PA 19376
  (610) 384-3115
  cmartinez@westcalnpolice.org
- West Fallowfield PD
- Chief Charles Wilmont
  PO Box 55
  Cochranville, PA 19330
  (610) 593-2442
  smokewfpd@zoominternet.net
- West Goshen PD
- Chief Joseph J. Gleason
  1025 Paoli Pike
  West Chester, PA 19380
  (610) 696-7400
  trafficsafety@westgoshen.org
- West Pikeland PD
- Chief Shane T. Clark
  1649 Art School Rd.
  Chester Springs, PA 19425
  (610) 827-5007
  chief@westpikeland.com
- West Vincent PD
- Chief Michael Swininger
  729 St. Matthews Rd.
  Chester Springs, PA 19425
  (610) 458-3205
  policedepartment@westvincenttwp.org
- West Whiteland PD
- Chief Stephen J. Meacham
  222 No. Pottstown Pike
  Exton, PA 19341
  (610) 363-0200
  chiefpd@westwhiteland.org

Clarion County

- Clarion County SO
- Sheriff Rex Munsee
  Courthouse, Main St.
  Clarion, PA 16214
  (814) 226-7611
  srenninger@co.clarion.pa.us
- Clarion PD
- Chief Mark Hall
  RR 3
  Box 34A
  Clarion, PA 16214
  (814) 226-9140
  bisler@oes.clarion.pa.us
- East Brady PD
- Chief William F. Foley
  502 Ferry St., Ste. 16
  East Brady, PA 16028
  (724) 526-3167
  ebpolice@zoominternet.net
- Knox PD
- Chief Jeff Prugh
  620 So. Main St.
  Knox, PA 16232
  (814) 797-1100
  kbpd@alltell.net

Clearfield County

- Clearfield PD
- Chief Vincent J. McGinnis
  14 So. Front St.
  Clearfield, PA 16830
  (814) 765-7819
  vmcginnis1@verizon.net
- Curwensville PD
- Chief David R. Johnson
  900 Susquehanna Ave.
  Curwensville, PA 16833
  (814) 236-3858
  cpd@atlanticbb.net
- Morris-Cooper Reg. PD
- Chief Todd Lombardo
  PO Box 186
  Allport, PA 16821
  (814) 342-5621
  mcrpolic@csrlink.net

Clinton County

- Lock Haven PD
- Chief Elwood Hocker
  20 E. Church St.
  Lock Haven, PA 17745
  (570) 893-5911
  ehocker@kcnet.org

Columbia County

- Columbia County SO
- Sheriff Timothy Chamberlain
  35 W. Main St. PO Box 380
  Bloomsburg, PA 17815
  (570) 389-5622
  tchamberlain@columbiapa.org
- Bloomsburg PD
- Chief Leo V. Sokoloski
  301 E. 2nd St.
  Bloomsburg, PA 17815
  (570) 784-4155
  leos@bloompd.com
- Catawissa PD
- Chief Anthony Kopitsky
  118 No. 3rd St.
  Catawissa, PA 17820
  (570) 356-7102
  catpolice@verizon.net
- Conyngham PD
- Chief William Spickler
  PO Box 45
  Locustdale, PA 17945
  (570) 339-3930
  conyngham_twp_police@yahoo.com
- Locust PD
- Chief Michael D. VanDine
  1223A Numidia Dr.
  Catawissa, PA 17820
  (570) 799-5806
  locustpd@verizon.net

Crawford County

- Crawford County SO
- Sheriff Walter Hoke
  903 Diamond Park
  Meadville, PA 16335
  (814) 333-7411
  nhoke@co.crawford.pa.us
- Cambridge Springs PD
- Chief Eric Johnson
  161 Carringer St.
  Cambridge Springs, PA 16403
  (814) 398-4112
  cspd@coaxpa.com
- Cochranton PD
- Chief Mike Phillips
  109 E. Adams St.
  Cochranton, PA 16314
  (814) 425-3039
  chief@cochrantonboro.org
- Conneaut Lake Reg. PD
- Chief Todd Pfeifer
  9878 State Hwy 285
  Conneaut Lake, PA 16316
  (814) 382-4364
  clrpd@zoominternet.net
- Meadville PD
- Chief Dave Stefanucci
  984 Water St.
  Meadville, PA 16335
  (814) 724-6100
  DAcker@cityofmeadville.org
- Titusville PD
- Chief Gary Thomas
  323 No. Franklin St.
  Titusville, PA 16354
  (814) 827-1890
  policechief@titusvillepa.com

Cumberland County

- Cumberland County SO
- Sheriff Ronny R. *Ron* Anderson
  1 Courthouse Sq., Rm. 303
  Carlisle, PA 17013
  (717) 240-6390
  sheriff@ccpa.net
- Camp Hill Borough PD
- Chief Gregory J. Ammons
  2199 Walnut St.
  Camp Hill, PA 17011
  (717) 737-1570
  police@camphillpolice.org
- Carlisle PD
- Chief Steven Margeson
  53 W. South St.
  Carlisle, PA 17013
  (717) 243-5252
  SMargeson@carlislepa.org
- East Pennsboro PD
- Chief Todd M. Bashore
  98 So. Enola Dr.
  Enola, PA 17025
  (717) 732-3633
  sdardick@eastpennsboro.net

- Hampden PD
- Chief Harry Clay
  230 So. Sporting Hill Rd.
  Mechanicsburg, PA 17055
  (717) 761-2609
  hclay@hampdentownship.us
- Mechanicsburg PD
- Chief David J. Spotts
  36 W. Allen St., 2nd Fl.
  Mechanicsburg, PA 17055
  (717) 691-3300
  dspotts@mechanicsburgpolice.org
- New Cumberland PD
- Chief Joseph E. Spadaccino
  1120 Market St.
  New Cumberland, PA 17070
  (717) 774-0400
  spadaccino@newcumberlandpolice.com
- North Middleton PD
- Chief Douglas Reitz
  2051 Spring Rd.
  Carlisle, PA 17013
  (717) 243-7910
  police@northmiddleton-police.org
- Shiremanstown PD
- Chief James E. Stoner
  1 Park Ln.
  Shiremanstown, PA 17011
  (717) 737-4356
  stownpd@comcast.net
- Silver Spring PD
- Supt. Richard Hammon
  6475 Carlisle Pike
  Mechanicsburg, PA 17050
  (717) 697-0607
  rehammon@silverspringtwp-pa.gov
- Upper Allen PD
- Chief Clyde R. King
  100 Gettysburg Pike
  Mechanicsburg, PA 17055
  (717) 795-2445
  lfazekas@upperallentwp.org

Dauphin County

- Highspire PD
- Chief John McHale
  640 Eshelman St.
  Highspire, PA 17034
  (717) 939-9866
  police@highspire.org
- Hummelstown PD
- Chief Charles M. Dowell
  136 So. Hanover St.
  Hummelstown, PA 17036
  (717) 566-2555
  cdowell@hummelstown.net
- Lower Swatara PD
- Chief Richard D. Brandt
  1499 Spring Garden Dr.
  Middletown, PA 17057
  (717) 939-0463
  rbrandt@lowerswatara.org
- Middletown PD
- Chief Steven R. Wheeler
  60 W. Emaus St.
  Middletown, PA 17057
  (717) 948-3000
  tkonek@middletownborough.com
- Millersburg PD
- Chief Kurt Braun
  Market Sq.
  Millersburg, PA 17061
  (717) 692-2323
  mbpd@policeone.com
- Steelton PD
- Chief Scott Spangler
  123 No. Front St.
  Steelton, PA 17113
  (717) 939-9841
  sspangler@steeltonpa.com

Delaware County

- Delaware County SO
- Sheriff Joseph McGinn
  201 W. Front St.
  Media, PA 19063
  (610) 891-4296
  AskTheSheriff@co.delaware.pa.us
- Aldan PD
- Chief Kenneth J. Coppola, Sr.
  1 W. Providence Rd.
  Aldan, PA 19018
  (610) 626-3553
  aldanpolice@comcast.net
- Aston PD
- Chief Daniel Ruggieri
  5021 Pennell Rd.
  Aston, PA 19014
  (610) 497-2633
  jstigale@astontownship.net

- Bethel PD
- Chief Tom Worrilow
  1090 Bethel Rd.
  Boothwyn, PA 19061
  (610) 558-0929
  bethelpolice@comcast.net
- East Lansdowne PD
- Chief John J. Zimath
  155 Lexington Ave.
  East Lansdowne, PA 19050
  (610) 623-7131
  INFO@ELPD.ORG
- Eddystone PD
- Chief William Conner
  1300 E. 12th St.
  Eddystone, PA 19022
  (610) 874-9325
  bconner@eddystonepd.com
- Folcroft PD
- Chief Robert Ruskowski
  PO Box 155
  Folcroft, PA 19032
  (610) 522-1300
  folcroftpolice@comcast.net
- Haverford PD
- Chief Carmen D. Pettine
  1010 Darby Rd.
  Havertown, PA 19083
  (610) 853-1298
  MGlenn@haverfordpolice.org
- Lansdowne PD
- Chief Daniel J.Kortan
  12 E. Baltimore Ave.
  Lansdowne, PA 19050
  (610) 623-0700
  lansdownepd@comcast.net
- Marcus Hook PD
- Chief John Ireland
  10th & Green Sts.
  Marcus Hook, PA 19061
  (610) 485-1611
  chief@marcushookpolice.com
- Media PD
- Chief Martin Wusinich
  307 No. Jackson St.
  Media, PA 19063
  (610) 565-6655
  mwusinich@mediapd.org
- Newtown PD
- Chief Henry *Rick* Pasqualini
  209 Bishop Hollow Rd.
  Newtown Square, PA 19073
  (610) 356-0602
  chief@twp.newtown.pa.us
- Parkside PD
- Chief John Eagan
  22 E. Elbon Rd.
  Chester, PA 19015
  (610) 876-0249
  john.egan@parksidepolice.com
- Prospect Park PD
- Chief Cliff Engel
  720 Maryland Ave.
  Prospect Park, PA 19076
  (610) 534-2222
  cengel@prospectparkpolice.com
- Radnor PD
- Supt. William Colarulo
  301 Iven Ave.
  Wayne, PA 19087
  (610) 688-0500
  wcolarulo@radnor.org
- Ridley Park PD
- Chief Mark F. Bascelli
  105 E. Ward St.
  Ridley Park, PA 19078
  (610) 532-9631
  markbascelli@ridleyparkpolice.org
- Sharon Hill PD
- Chief Robert Tinsley
  1110 Spring St.
  Sharon Hill, PA 19079
  (610) 237-6200
  shrecords6190@comcast.net
- Springfield PD
- Chief Joseph Daly
  50 Powell Rd.
  Springfield, PA 19064
  (610) 544-6900
  Dberger@springfieldmontco.org
- Swarthmore PD
- Chief Brian H. Craig
  121 Park Ave.
  Swarthmore, PA 19081
  (610) 543-0123
  swarthpd1@aol.com

- Tinicum PD
- Chief James Sabath
  629 No. Governor Printz Blvd
  Essington, PA 19029-1732
  (610) 521-3830
  ttpd@epix.net
- Trainer PD
- Chief Francis Priscopo
  824 Main St.
  Trainer, PA 19061
  (610) 494-7399
  chief@trainerpolice.com
- Upland PD
- Chief John R. Easton
  224 Castle Ave.
  Upland, PA 19015
  (610) 872-3040
  jeaston@uplandboro.org
- Upper Chichester PD
- Chief Thomas Bush
  8400 Furey Rd.
  Boothwyn, PA 19061
  (610) 485-8400
  ucpd@comcast.com
- Upper Darby PD
- Chief Michael J. Chitwood
  7236 W. Chester Pike
  Upper Darby, PA 19082
  (610) 352-7050
  Chief@udpd.org
- Upper Providence PD
- Chief David Montella
  935 No. Providence Rd.
  Media, PA 19063
  (610) 566-8445
  glebold@upperprovidence.org

Elk County

- Elk County SO
- Sheriff Jeffrey Krieg
  240 Main St. PO Box 448
  Ridgway, PA 15853
  (814) 776-5353
  jkrieg@countyofelkpa.com
- Ridgway PD
- Chief Ralph Tettis
  108 Main St.
  Ridgway, PA 15853
  (814) 773-5125
  ridboro@windstream.net
- St. Marys PD
- Chief Todd Calatagrone
  319 Erie Ave.
  St. Marys, PA 15857
  (814) 781-1315
  policechief@cityofstmarys.com

Erie County

- Erie County SO
- Sheriff Robert Merski
  140 W. 6th St., 4th Fl.
  Erie, PA 16501
  (814) 451-6254
  jhabursky@eriecountygov.org
- Corry PD
- Chief Richard C. Shopene
  20 E. South St.
  Corry, PA 16407
  (814) 664-2222
  corrypolice@tbscc.com
- Edinboro PD
- Chief Jeffrey Craft
  124 Meadville St., Rm. 214
  Edinboro, PA 16412
  (814) 734-1812
  edinboro@edinboro.net
- Erie PD
- Chief Stephen E. Franklin
  626 State St.
  Erie, PA 16501
  (814) 870-1125
  sfranklin@crie.pa.us
- Millcreek PD
- Chief Thomas Carlotti
  3608 W. 26th St.
  Erie, PA 16506
  (814) 833-7777
  carlotti@millcreektownship.com

Fayette County

- Fayette County SO
- Sheriff Gary Brownfield
  61 E. Main St.
  Uniontown, PA 15401
  (724) 430-1295
  sheriff@fayettepa.org
- Connellsville PD
- Chief James Capitos
  110 No. Arch St.
  Connellsville, PA 15425
  (724) 628-2020
  mayorjudyreed@aol.com

- Masontown PD
- Chief Joseph Ryan
  Two Court Ave.
  Masontown, PA 15461
  (724) 583-7770
  fcmjryan@TupperGroup.com
- Perryopolis PD
- Chief Roger Beadling
  PO Box 304
  Perryopolis, PA 15473
  (724) 736-0700
  perryopolispolice@perryopolispolice.com
- South Connellsville PD
- Chief Charles Matthews
  1503 So. Pittsburgh St.
  South Connellsville, PA 15425
  (724) 628-4860
  mayorjudyreed@aol.com

Forest County

- Forest County SO
- Sheriff Robert Wolfgang
  528 Elm St.
  Tionesta, PA 16353
  (814) 755-3541
  rwolfgang@co.forest.pa.us

Franklin County

- Franklin County SO
- Sheriff Dane Anthony
  157 Lincoln Way E.
  Chambersburg, PA 17201
  (717) 261-3877
  sheriff@co.franklin.pa.us
- Chambersburg PD
- Chief David J. Arnold
  116 So. 2nd St.
  Chambersburg, PA 17201
  (717) 264-4131
  darnold@chambersburgpolice.com
- Mercersburg PD
- Chief Mario Angelini
  113 So. Main St.
  Mercersburg, PA 17236
  (717) 328-3116
  mercerboroughmanager@comcast.net
- Washington PD
- Chief Robert Lemons
  13013 Welty Rd.
  Waynesboro, PA 17268
  (717) 762-1447
  info@washingtonpa.us
- Waynesboro PD
- Chief James Sourbier
  57 E. Main St.
  Waynesboro, PA 17268
  (717) 762-2131
  kgreen@waynesboropolice.com

Fulton County

- Fulton County SO
- Sheriff Keith Stains
  Fulton County Courthouse
  McConnellsburg, PA 17233
  (717) 485-4221
  sheriff@co.fulton.pa.us

Greene County

- Greene County SO
- Sheriff Richard Ketchem
  10 E. High St., Ste. 106
  Waynesburg, PA 15370
  (724) 627-7207
  jmarshall@co.greene.pa.us
- Waynesburg PD
- Chief Timothy M. Hawfield
  90 E. High St.
  Waynesburg, PA 15370
  (724) 627-8113
  Wbgboro@windstream.net

Huntingdon County

- Huntingdon County SO
- Sheriff William Walters
  241 Mifflin St.
  Huntingdon, PA 16652
  (814) 643-0880
  sheriff@huntingdoncounty.net
- Huntingdon PD
- Chief Charles Streightiff
  1001 Moore St.
  Huntingdon, PA 16652
  (814) 643-3960
  cstreightiff@huntingdonboro.com
- Juniata Valley Reg. PD
- Chief David Yocum
  PO Box 237
  Petersburg, PA 16669
  (814) 669-9252
  dcy@uplink.net
- Mount Union PD
- Act. Chief (*Cpl.*) Robert K. Lippmann
  16 So. Division St. PO Box 90
  Mount Union, PA 17066
  (814) 542-8822
  mountunionpolice@adelphia.net

Indiana County

- Indiana County SO
- Sheriff Robert E. Fyock
  825 Philadelphia St.
  Indiana, PA 15701
  (724) 465-3930
  skirkland@countyofindiana.org
- Blairsville PD
- Chief Jill Gaston
  201 E. Market St.
  Blairsville, PA 15717
  (724) 459-7555
  blairsvillepd6@yahoo.com
- Clymer PD
- Chief Joseph Douglas
  115 6th St.
  Clymer, PA 15728
  (724) 254-0714
  clymerone@comcast.net
- Homer City PD
- Chief Louis Sacco
  30 E. Wiley St.
  Homer City, PA 15748
  (724) 479-9190
  chiefsacco@verizon.net
- Indiana PD
- Chief William C. Sutton
  80 No. 8th St.
  Indiana, PA 15701
  (724) 349-2121
  wsutton@indianaboro.com
- Saltsburg PD
- Chief Gary Walker
  320 Point St.
  Saltsburg, PA 15681
  (724) 639-9413
  salt@comcast.net

Jefferson County

- Punxsutawney PD
- Chief Thomas M. Fedigan, Jr.
  301 E. Mahoning St.
  Punxsutawney, PA 15767
  (814) 938-6220
  kbrudnock@punxsutawneyboro.com
- Sykesville PD
- Chief John R. Williams, Jr.
  21 E. Main St.
  Sykesville, PA 15865
  (814) 894-2408
  policeadmin@sykesville.net

Juniata County

- Juniata County SO
- Sheriff Thomas Lyter
  225 Bridge St.
  Mifflintown, PA 17059
  (717) 436-2213
  tlyter@juniataco.org

Lackawanna County

- Lackawanna County SD
- Sheriff John Szymanski
  200 No. Washington Ave.
  Scranton, PA 18503
  (570) 963-6719
  szymanskij@lackawannacounty.org
- Archbald PD
- Chief Tim Trently
  400 Church St.
  Archbald, PA 18403
  (570) 876-0426
  archbaldboro@comcast.net
- Blakely PD
- Chief Guy Salermo
  1439 Main St.
  Peckville, PA 18452
  (570) 383-3346
  blaklybo2@comcast.net
- Clarks Summit PD
- Chief Joe Laguzzi
  304 So. State St.
  Clarks Summit, PA 18411
  (570) 587-3026
  clarksmt@epix.net
- Covington PD
- Chief Bernie Klocko
  435 Daleville Box 6315
  Moscow, PA 18444
  (570) 842-6400
  CovTwpPolice@aol.com
- Jessup PD
- Chief Joseph Walsh
  395 Lane St.
  Jessup, PA 18434
  (570) 489-0411
  jessupborough@comcast.net
- Moscow PD
- Chief Ivy L. Brenzel
  123 Van Brunt St.
  Moscow, PA 18444
  (570) 842-2061
  Police@Moscowboro.com

- Scott PD
- Chief Jared Ganz
  Rd 2 Box 432 D
  Olyphant, PA 18447
  (570) 254-7447
  JGanz@scotttownship.org
- Scranton PD
- Chief Carl Graziano
  340 No. Washington Ave.
  Scranton, PA 18503
  (570) 348-4134
  jloscombe@scrantonpa.gov
- South Abington PD
- Chief Robert A. Gerrity
  104 Shady Lane Rd.
  Chinchilla, PA 18410
  (570) 586-2111
  satpd@epix.net
- Taylor Borough PD
- Chief Leonard J. Mickavicz, Jr.
  122 Union St.
  Taylor, PA 18517
  (570) 562-2210
  dzeleniak@taylorborough.com

Lancaster County

- Lancaster County SO
- Sheriff Mark S. Reese
  50 No. Duke St.
  Lancaster, PA 17608
  (717) 299-8200
  McCueA@co.lancaster.pa.us
- Christiana PD
- Chief Frank D. Finfrock
  10 W. Slokom Ave.
  Christiana, PA 17509
  (610) 593-5199
  RFinfrock@ChristianaPD.com
- Columbia PD
- Chief Jack Broomer
  308 Locust St.
  Columbia, PA 17512
  (717) 684-7735
  columbiaborough@comcast.net
- East Earl PD
- Chief Mark Heister
  4610 Division Hwy
  East Earl, PA 17519
  (717) 354-5593
  eastearladmin@police.co.lancaster.pa.us
- East Hempfield PD
- Chief Stephen A. Skiles
  1700 Nissley Rd.
  Landisville, PA 17538
  (717) 898-3103
  skiless@police.co.lancaster.pa.us
- East Lampeter PD
- Act. Chief (*Capt.*) Steve Zerbe
  2250 Old Philadelphia Pike
  Lancaster, PA 17602
  (717) 291-4676
  eastlampadmin@police.co.lancaster.pa.us
- Elizabethtown PD
- Chief Jack Mentzer
  600 So. Hanover St.
  Elizabethtown, PA 17022
  (717) 367-6540
  elizabethtownadmin@police.co.lancaster.pa.us
- Ephrata Borough PD
- Chief William L. Harvey
  124 So. State
  Ephrata, PA 17522
  (717) 738-9265
  harveyw@police.co.lancaster.pa.us
- Lancaster PD
- Chief John Fiorill
  39 W. Chestnut St.
  Lancaster, PA 17603
  (717) 735-3300
  fiorillj@police.co.lancaster.pa.us
- Lititz PD
- Chief William R. Seace
  7 So. Broad St.
  Lititz, PA 17543
  (717) 626-6393
  seacew@police.co.lancaster.pa.us
- Manheim Borough PD
- Chief Mark E. Stivers
  4 No. Wolf St.
  Manheim, PA 17545
  (717) 665-2481
  adminassistant@manheimboro.org
- Manheim Twp PD
- Chief Neil J. Harkins
  1825 Municipal Dr.
  Lancaster, PA 17601
  (717) 569-6401
  mrimer@manheimtownship.org

- Manor PD
- Chief George Valmassoni
  950 W. Fairway Dr.
  Lancaster, PA 17603
  (717) 299-5231
  g.valmassoni@manorborough.com
- Millersville PD
- Chief Peter Anders
  10 Colonial Ave.
  Millersville, PA 17551
  (717) 872-4657
  millersville@millersvilleborough.org
- Mount Joy PD
- Supt. Joe Ardini
  21 E. Main St.
  Mount Joy, PA 17552
  (717) 653-1650
  mountjoypolice@police.co.lancaster.pa.us
- New Holland PD
- Chief Burnell Imhoff
  436 E. Main St.
  New Holland, PA 17557
  (717) 354-4647
  NewHollandBoroughAdmin@police.co.l
  ancaster.pa.us
- Northwestern Lancaster Reg. PD
- Chief Mark E. Mayberry
  159 Mertz Dr.
  Elizabethtown, PA 17022
  (717) 367-8481
  MayberrM@police.co.lancaster.pa.us
- Quarryville PD
- Chief Kenneth Work
  300 St. Catherine St.
  Quarryville, PA 17566
  (717) 786-3121
  workk@police.co.lancaster.pa.us
- Southern Lancaster Reg. PD
- Chief John Fiorill
  3284 Main St. PO Box 254
  Conestoga, PA 17516
  (717) 872-0352
  fiorillj@police.co.lancaster.pa.us
- Strasburg PD
- Chief F. Steven Echternach
  145 Precision Ave.
  Strasburg, PA 17579
  (717) 687-7128
  echterns@police.co.lancaster.pa.us
- Warwick PD
- Chief David Steffen
  315 Clay Rd.
  Lititz, PA 17543
  (717) 626-3162
  warwickpolice@comcast.net
- West Earl Twp PD
- Chief Brian Brandt
  157 W. Metzler PO Box 787
  Brownstown, PA 17508
  (717) 859-3201
  datadept@westearltwp.org
- West Hempfield PD
- Chief Mark G. Pugliese
  3401 Marietta Ave.
  Lancaster, PA 17601
  (717) 285-5191, ext. 115
  manager@twp.west-hempfield.pa.us

Lawrence County

- Lawrence County SO
- Sheriff Perry L. Quahliero
  430 Court St.
  New Castle, PA 16101
  (724) 656-2190
  pquahliero@co.lawrence.pa.us
- Neshannock PD
- Chief Philip S. Carlo
  3131 Mercer Rd.
  New Castle, PA 16105
  (724) 656-9300
  pcarlo@neshannock.org
- Pulaski PD
- Act. Chief Chad Adams
  1172 State Rt. 208
  Pulaski, PA 16143
  (724) 964-8891
  cadams@pulaskitownship.com
- Shenango PD
- Supt. William Phillips
  1000 Willowbrook Rd.
  New Castle, PA 16101
  (724) 654-2243
  wphillips@shenangotwp.com

Lebanon County

- Lebanon County SO
- Sheriff Michael DeLeo
  400 So. 8th St.
  (717) 228-4410
  sheriff@lebcnty.org

- Annville PD
- Chief Bernard G. Dugan
  36 No. Lancaster St.
  Annville, PA 17003
  (717) 867-2711
  annvillepolice@comcast.net
- Cleona PD
- Chief Raymond J. Barry III
  140 W. Walnut St.
  Cleona, PA 17042
  (717) 272-2510
  cleonapd@comcast.net
- Cornwall PD
- Chief Bruce D. Harris
  Burd Coleman Rd. PO Box 667
  Cornwall, PA 17016
  (717) 274-3436
  bharris@cornwallpd.org
- Heidelberg PD
- Chief Vernon Barkley
  111 Mill Rd.
  Schaefferstown, PA 17088
  (717) 949-3855
  info@HeidelbergBorough.com
- Lebanon PD
- Chief Daniel Wright
  400 So. 8th St., Rm. 116
  Lebanon, PA 17042
  (717) 272-6611
  cityadmin@lebanonpa.org
- Millcreek PD
- Chief Thomas E. Carlotti
  3608 W. 26th St.
  Erie, PA 16506
  (814) 838-9515
  carlotti@millcreektownship.com
- North Lebanon PD
- Chief Harold Easter
  725 Kimmerlings Rd.
  Lebanon, PA 17046
  (717) 273-8141
  police@nlpd.org
- North Londonderry PD
- Chief Kevin Snyder
  655 E. Ridge Rd.
  Palmyra, PA 17078
  (717) 838-5276
  ksnyder@nlondtwp.com
- Palmyra PD
- Chief Stanley J. Jasinski, Jr.
  325 So. Railroad St.
  Palmyra, PA 17078
  (717) 838-8188
  sjjasinski@comcast.net
- Richland PD
- Chief Mike Burgan
  5 Pine St.
  Richland, PA 17087
  (717) 272-2054
  rosemary@richlandtownshippd.org
- South Annville PD
- Chief Ben Sutcliffe
  1000 Clearview PO Box 241
  Lebanon, PA 17042
  (717) 867-1003
  chiefsouthannville@comcast.net
- South Lebanon PD
- Chief Michael E. Lesher
  1800 So. 5th Ave.
  Lebanon, PA 17042
  (717) 274-0481
  sltownship@comcast.net
- South Londonderry PD
- Chief William Reigle II
  20 W. Market St. PO Box 3
  Cambelltown, PA 17010
  (717) 838-1376
  police.slpd@gmail.com

Lehigh County

- Allentown PD
- Chief Roger J. Maclean
  425 Hamilton St.
  Allentown, PA 18101
  (610) 437-7753
  Daniel.Warg@allentownpa.gov
- Catasauqua PD
- Chief Douglas Kish
  118 Bridge St.
  Catasauqua, PA 18032
  (610) 264-0577
  information@catapd.org
- Coopersburg PD
- Chief Daniel Trexler
  5 No. Main St.
  Coopersburg, PA 18036
  (610) 282-1444
  dtrexler@coopersburgpd.org

- Coplay PD
- Chief Vincent Genovese
  98 So. 4th St.
  Coplay, PA 18037
  (610) 262-2288
  coplaypd@ptd.net
- Emmaus PD
- Chief David A. Faust
  400 Jubilee St.
  Emmaus, PA 18049
  (610) 967-3113
  Police@emmauspd.org
- Fountain Hill PD
- Chief Ed Bachert
  941 Long St.
  Fountain Hill, PA 18015
  (610) 691-5512
  office@fhpolice.org
- Macungie PD
- Chief Edward Harry
  21 Locust St.
  Macungie, PA 18062
  (610) 966-2222
  eharry@macungiepd.org
- Salisbury PD
- Chief Allen W. Stiles
  3000 So. Pike Ave.
  Allentown, PA 18103
  (610) 797-4000
  info@salisburytownshippa.org
- Upper Saucon PD
- Chief Robert E. Coyle
  5500 Camp Meeting Rd.
  Center Valley, PA 18034
  (610) 282-3064
  email@uppersaucon.org\

Luzerne County

- Luzerne County SO
- Int. Sheriff Jack Robshaw
  200 No. River St.
  Wilkes-Barre, PA 18711
  (570) 825-1651
  Jack.Robshaw@luzernecounty.org
- Avoca PD
- Chief David M Homschek
  752 Main St.
  Avoca, PA 18641
  (570) 457-4011
  avocapd@luzernecounty.org
- Dallas PD
- Chief Robert G. Jolley
  2919 SR 309 Hwy
  Dallas, PA 18612
  (570) 674-2003
  rjolley@dallastwppd.org
- Dupont PD
- Chief Anthony *Tony* DeMark
  600 Chestnut St.
  Dupont, PA 18641
  (570) 654-9971
  dupontboro@adelphia.net
- Duryea PD
- Chief Nicholas A. Lohman
  315 Main St.
  Duryea, PA 18642
  (570) 457-1721
  info@duryeaborough.com
- Forty Fort PD
- Chief Daniel Hunsinger
  1271 Wyoming Ave.
  Forty Fort, PA 18704
  (570) 287-8586
  chiefhunsinger@fortyfort.org
- Nanticoke PD
- Chief William Shultz
  15 E. Ridge St.
  Nanticoke, PA 18634
  (570) 735-2200
  npddet@yahoo.com
- Pittston Twp PD
- Chief Robert Avvisato
  421 Broad St.
  Pittston Twp PA 18640
  (570) 655-6350
  pitttown@comcast.net
- Salem PD
- Chief Robert Kishbaugh
  38 Bomboy Ln.
  Berwick, PA 18603
  (570) 752-3772
  salemtpd@pa.metrocast.net
- West Hazleton PD
- Chief Brian Buglio
  12 So. 4th St.
  West Hazleton, PA 18201
  (570) 455-3733
  whpd@ptd.net

- Wilkes-Barre PD
- Chief Gerard E. Dessoye
  15 No. Washington St.
  Wilkes-Barre, PA 18701
  (570) 208-4207
  cityhall@wilkes-barre.pa.us
- Wright Twp PD
- Chief Joseph M. *Joe* Jacob
  321 So. Mountain Blvd
  Mountaintop, PA 18707
  (570) 474-9251
  wtpd89@ptd.net

Lycoming County

- Jersey Shore PD
- Chief Martin C. Jeirles
  129 So. Pennsylvania Ave.
  Jersey Shore, PA 17740
  (570) 398-2146
  policejsboro@comcast.net
- Montoursville PD
- Chief Jeff Gyurina
  617 No. Loyalsock Ave.
  Montoursville, PA 17754
  (570) 368-2488
  jgyurina@montourpd.org
- Williamsport PD
- Chief Gregory Foresman
  245 W. 4th St.
  Williamsport, PA 17701
  (570) 327-7540
  police@cityofwilliamsport.org

Mercer County

- Mercer County SO
- Sheriff Gary Hartman
  205 So. Erie St., Rm. 102
  Mercer, PA 16137
  (724) 662-6135
  ghartman@mcc.co.mercer.pa.us
- Greenville-West Salem PD
- Chief Dennis Stephens
  125 Main St.
  Greenville, PA 16125
  (724) 588-4190
  joshua_stephens@hotmail.com
- Hermitage PD
- Chief Brian Blair
  800 No. Hermitage Rd.
  Hermitage, PA 16148
  (724) 983-6780
  bblair@hermitage.net
- Sharon PD
- Chief Michael J. Menster
  155 W. Connelly Blvd
  Sharon, PA 16146
  (724) 983-3210
  mmenster@cityofsharon.net
- Sharpsville PD
- Chief Keith Falasco
  1 So. Walnut St.
  Sharpsville, PA 16150
  (724) 962-7829
  sharpsville@roadrunner.com

Mifflin County

- Mifflin County SO
- Sheriff Christopher S. Shade
  20 No. Wayne St.
  Lewistown, PA 17044
  (717) 242-1105
  sheriff@co.mifflin.pa.us
- Mifflin County Reg. PD
- Chief Scott Mauery
  13225 Ferguson Valley Rd.
  Yeagertown, PA 17099
  (717) 248-1900, ext. 628
  jaurand@mcrpd.org

Monroe County

- Monroe County SO
- Sheriff Todd A. Martin
  610 Monroe St.
  Stroudsburg, PA 18360
  (570) 517-3312
  SheriffMartin@monroecountypa.gov
- Barrett PD
- Chief Steven R. Williams
  RR 2 Box 2337
  Cresco, PA 18326
  (570) 595-3476
  btpd@ptd.net
- Pocono Mountain Reg. PD
- Chief Harry W. Lewis
  HC 89, Rt. 940 Box 200
  Pocono Summit, PA 18346
  (570) 895-2400
  wlaverty@pmrpd.com
- Stroud Area Reg. PD
- Chief William Parrish
  100 Day St.
  East Stroudsburg, PA 18301
  (570) 421-6800, ext. 1001
  wparrish@sarpd.com

Montgomery County

- Montgomery County SO
- Sheriff Eileen Whalen Behr
  Court House, 1st Fl. PO Box 311
  Norristown, PA 19404
  (610) 278-3331
  sheriffoffice@montcopa.org
- Bridgeport PD
- Chief Zenny E. Martyniuk
  4th & Mill Sts.
  Bridgeport, PA 19405
  (610) 272-5660
  police@bridgeportpd.com
- Douglass PD
- Chief Barry L. Templin, Jr.
  1320 E. Philadelphia Ave.
  Gilbertsville, PA 19525
  (215) 367-0466
  police@douglasstownship.org
- East Norriton PD
- Chief Karyl Kates
  2501 Stanbridge St.
  Norritown, PA 19401
  (610) 272-0748
  kkates@eastnorritontwp.org
- Franconia PD
- Chief Joseph Kozeniewski
  671 Allentown Rd.
  Franconia, PA 18924
  (215) 723-6777
  police@franconia-township.org
- Hatfield PD
- Chief Mark Toomey
  2000 School Rd.
  Hatfield, PA 19440
  (215) 855-0903
  hatfield@hatfieldtownship.org
- Horsham PD
- Chief Robert H. Ruxton
  1025 Horsham Rd.
  Horsham, PA 19044
  (215) 643-8284, ext. 301
  police@horsham.org
- Jenkintown PD
- Chief Albert J. DiValentino
  700 Summit Ave.
  Jenkintown, PA 19046
  (215) 884-1202
  adivalentino33C1@hotmail.com
- Limerick PD
- Chief William J. Albany
  646 W. Ridge Pike
  Limerick, PA 19468
  (610) 495-7909
  mlconbeer@limerickpa.org
- Lower Gwynedd PD
- Chief Paul Kenny
  1130 No. Bethlehem
  Spring House, PA 19477
  (215) 646-5300
  pkenny@lowergwynedd.org
- Lower Merion PD
- Supt. Michael J. McGrath
  71 E. Lancaster
  Ardmore, PA 19003
  (610) 645-6270
  staff@lowermerion.org
- Lower Moreland PD
- Chief Peter C. Hasson
  640 Red Lion Rd.
  Huntingdon Valley, PA 19006
  (215) 947-3131
  phasson@lower-moreland.org
- Lower Pottsgrove PD
- Chief Michael Foltz
  2199 Buchert Rd.
  Pottstown, PA 19464
  (610) 326-1508
  mfoltz@lowerpottsgrove.org
- Lower Providence PD
- Chief Francis L. Carroll
  100 Parklane Dr.
  Eagleville, PA 19403
  (610) 539-5901
  police@lowerprovidence.org
- Montgomery PD
- Chief Scott Bendig
  1001 Stump Rd.
  Montgomeryville, PA 18936
  (215) 362-2301
  generalinfo@montgomerytwp.org
- New Hanover PD
- Chief Kevin McKeon
  2943 No. Charlotte St.
  Gilbertsville, PA 19525
  (610) 327-1150
  police@newhanoverpolice.org

- Norristown PD
- Int. Chief Willie G. Richet
  235 E. Airy St.
  Norristown, PA 19401
  (610) 270-0977
  wrichet@norristown.org
- North Wales PD
- Act. Chief Terry Hammerstone
  300 School St.
  North Wales, PA 19454
  (215) 699-9279
  nwpd@northwalesborough.org
- Plymouth PD
- Chief Joseph F. Lawrence
  700 Belvoir Rd.
  Plymouth Meeting, PA 19462
  (610) 279-1901
  JLawrence@plymouthtownship.org
- Pottstown PD
- Chief F. Richard Drumheller
  100 E. High St.
  Pottstown, PA 19464-9525
  (610) 970-6580
  PottstownPolice@Pottstown.org
- Rockledge PD
- Chief Gerald Miller
  1 Park Ave.
  Rockledge, PA 19046
  (215) 379-8801
  gmetzinger@rockledgeborough.org
- Royersford PD
- Act. Chief Thomas Nerlinger
  300 Main St. Box 188
  Royersford, PA 19468
  (610) 948-3305
  tnerlinger@royersfordborough.org
- Upper Dublin PD
- Chief Terrence Thompson
  801 Loch Alsh Ave.
  Fort Washington, PA 19034
  (215) 646-2101
  tthompson@upperdublin.net
- Upper Gwynedd PD
- Chief David Duffy
  Parkside Pl. PO Box 1
  West Point, PA 19486
  (215) 699-5861
  ugpolice@uppergwynedd.org
- Upper Merion PD
- Chief Thomas Nolan
  175 W. Valley Forge Rd.
  King of Prussia, PA 19406
  (610) 265-3232, ext. 259
  hnuskey@umtownship.org
- Upper Pottsgrove PD
- Chief William Moffett
  1420 Heather Pl.
  Pottstown, PA 19464
  (610) 326-8446
  uppdchief@gmail.com
- West Norriton PD
- Chief Dale Mabry
  1630 W. Marshall St.
  Norritown, PA 19403
  (610) 630-1701
  dmabry@wntwp.com
- Whitemarsh PD
- Chief T. Michael Beaty
  616 Germantown Pike
  Lafayette Hill, PA 19444
  (610) 825-6530
  mail@whitemarshtwp.org
- Whitpain PD
- Chief Mark A. Smith
  960 Wentz Rd.
  Blue Bell, PA 19422
  (610) 279-9033
  tips@whitpainpolice.org

Montour County

- Montour County SO
- Sheriff Ray C. Gerringer
  29 Mill St.
  Danville, PA 17821
  (570) 271-3020
  sheriffrcg@montourco.org
- Danville PD
- Chief Eric Gill
  235 Mill St.
  Danville, PA 17821
  (570) 275-2101
  chief@danvillepd.net

Northampton County

- Northampton County SD
- Sheriff Randall Miller
  10 E. Church St.
  Bethlehem, PA 18018
  (610) 865-7150
  miller@northhamptoncounty.org

- Bethlehem Twp PD
- Chief Dan Pancoast
  4225 Easton Ave.
  Bethlehem, PA 18020
  (610) 814-6426
  dpancoast@bethlehemtwp.com
- Bushkill PD
- Chief Stanley J. *Stan* Coopersmith
  1114 Bushkill Center Rd.
  Nazareth, PA 18064
  (610) 759-9588
  police@bushkilltownship.com
- Colonial Regional PD
- Chief Roy D. Seiple
  215 E. Main St.
  Bath, PA 18014
  (610) 837-4557
  chief@colonialregionalpd.org
- East Bangor PD
- Chief Robert J. Mulligan
  17 W. Central Ave.
  East Bangor, PA 18013
  (610) 599-1005
  info@eastbangorborough.org
- Easton PD
- Chief Carl Scalzo
  25 So. 3rd St.
  Easton, PA 18042
  (610) 250-6630
  cscalzo@easton-pa.gov
- Forks PD
- Chief Gregory F. Dorney
  1604 Sullivan Tr.
  Easton, PA 18040
  (610) 252-0785, ext. 131
  gdorney@forkstownship.org
- Freemansburg PD
- Chief George Bruneio
  600 Monroe St.
  Freemansburg, PA 18017
  (610) 866-2220, ext. 105
  execadmin@boroughoffreemansburg.org
- Hellertown PD
- Chief Robert Shupp
  685 Main St.
  Hellertown, PA 18055
  (610) 838-7040
  rshupp@hellertownpd.org
- Lower Saucon PD
- Chief Guy Lesser
  3700 Old Philadelphia Pike
  Bethlehem, PA 18015
  (610) 317-6110
  lstpd@lowersaucontownship.org
- Moore PD
- Chief Gary West
  2491 Community Dr.
  Bath, PA 18014
  (610) 759-5077
  gwest@mooretwppolice.com
- North Catasauqua PD
- Chief Kim Moyer
  1068 4th St.
  North Catasauqua, PA 18032
  (610) 437-5252
  ncboro@rcn.com
- Pen Argyl PD
- Chief David A. Strawn
  11-13 No. Robinson Ave.
  Pen Argyl, PA 18072
  (610) 863-6704
  chief@penargylborough.com
- Plainfield PD
- Chief Dean Ceraul
  6292 Sullivan Tr.
  Nazareth, PA 18064
  (610) 759-8517, ext. 201
  supervisors@twp.plainfield.pa.us

Northumberland County

- Northumberland County SO
- Sheriff Chad A. Reiner
  201 Market St.
  Sunbury, PA 17801
  (570) 988-4157
  creiner@norrycopa.net
- Kulpmont PD
- Chief Richard L. Wilson III
  860 Spruce St.
  Kulpmont, PA 17834
  (570) 373-1522
  kulpmont-pd@hotmail.com
- Mount Carmel Borough PD
- Chief Todd Owens
  121 So. Oak St.
  Mount Carmel, PA 17851
  (570) 339-6020
  mayorjkj@ptd.net

- Point PD
- Chief Joshua E. VanKirk
  759 Ridge Rd.
  Northumberland, PA 17857
  (570) 473-9114
  pointpd@ptd.net
- Ralpho PD
- Chief Stu Appel
  28 So. Market St.
  Elysburg, PA 17824
  (570) 672-9892
  supervisors@ralphotownship.org
- Riverside PD
- Chief Isaac L. Ramer
  301 Dewart St. PO Box 307
  Riverside, PA 17868
  (570) 275-4305
  riversidepd@riversideborough.org
- Shamokin PD
- Chief Edward M. Griffiths
  511 No. Franklin St.
  Shamokin, PA 17872
  (570) 648-5708
  cityclerk@shamokincity.org
- Sunbury PD
- Chief Stephen Mazzeo
  440 Market St.
  Sunbury, PA 17801
  (570) 286-4584
  sunbury1@ptd.net
- Watsontown PD
- Chief Dennis Derr
  318 Main St.
  Watsontown, PA 17777
  (570) 538-2773
  watpd@windstream.net

Perry County

- Perry County SO
- Sheriff Carl Nace
  1 Courthouse Sq.
  New Bloomfield, PA 17068
  (717) 582-2131
  cnace@perryco.org

Philadelphia County

- Philadelphia County SO
- Sheriff Jewell Williams
  100 So. Broad St., 5th Fl.
  Philadelphia, PA 19103
  (215) 686-3530
  paris.washington@phila.gov
- Philadelphia PD
- Comm. Charles H. Ramsey
  750 Race St.
  Philadelphia, PA 19106
  (215) 686-3280
  police.commissioner@phila.gov

Pike County

- Pike County SO
- Sheriff Philip Bueki
  500 Broad St.
  Milford, PA 18337
  (570) 296-6459, ext. 1270
  rcaridi@pikepa.org
- Hemlock Farms Police DPS
- Chief William Hamby
  200 Hemlock Farms Rd.
  Hawley, PA 18428
  (570) 775-4242
  pubsafe@ptd.net

Potter County

- Potter County SO
- Sheriff Kenneth Sauley
  102 E. 2nd St.
  Coudersport, PA 16915
  (814) 274-9350
  pcsheriff@pottercountypa.net
- Austin PD
- Chief Kyle B. Day
  81 Scoville St. PO Box 297
  Austin, PA 16720
  (814) 647-8613
  austinboropd@yahoo.com
- Galeton PD
- Chief Christopher Brackman
  4 Sherman St. PO Box 222
  Galeton, PA 16922
  (814) 435-2600
  galpd4120@yahoo.com
- Sweden PD
- Chief Bryan Phelps
  185 So. Dry Run Rd.
  Coudersport, PA 16915
  (814) 274-1110
  swetwp@zitomedia.net

Schuylkill County

- Schuylkill County SO
- Sheriff Joseph Groody
  401 No. 2nd St.
  Pottsville, PA 17901
  (570) 628-1440
  ghalcovage@co.schuylkill.pa.us

- Auburn PD
- Chief Anthony Kuklinski
  451 Pearson St. Box 322
  Auburn, Pennsylvania 17922
  (570) 754-7207
  a.m.kuklinski@att.net
- Cass-Foster PD
- Chief Anthony M. Kuklinski
  1209 Valley Rd.
  Pottsville, PA 17901
  (570) 544-5631
  cassfosterpd@verizon.net
- Coaldale PD
- Chief Timothy Delaney
  3rd & Howard Ave.
  Coaldale, PA 18218
  (570) 645-3060
  chieftd@ptd.net
- Mahanoy City PD
- Chief Mark Wiekrykas
  239 E. Pine St.
  Mahanoy City, PA 17948
  (570) 773-2310
  mcpolice@ptd.net
- New Philadelphia PD
- Chief Eric Sterner
  15 MacComb St.
  New Philadelphia, PA 17959
  (570) 628-3792
  nppd21@comcast.net
- Orwigsburg PD
- Chief Stanley Brozana
  209 No. Warren PO Box 244
  Orwigsburg, PA 17961
  (570) 366-3102
  orwigsburgpd@orwigsburg.net
- Palo Alto PD
- Chief Joseph Kavanaugh
  142 E. Bacon St.
  Palo Alto, PA 17901
  (570) 622-8666
  paloalto@wtvaccess.com
- Pottsville PD
- Chief Joseph H. Murton
  401 No. Centre St.
  Pottsville, PA 17901
  (570) 622-1234
  policechief@city.pottsville.pa.us
- Schuylkill Haven PD
- Chief Jeffrey Walcott
  220 Parkway
  Schuylkill Haven, PA 17972
  (570) 385-9111
  jwalcott@schuylkillhaven.org
- Tremont PD
- Chief Michael Conway
  139 Clay St., Ste. 2
  Tremont, PA 17981
  (570) 695-2215
  conwaym_@hotmail.com

Snyder County

- Snyder County SO
- Sheriff Joseph Reigle
  12 So. Main St.
  Middleburg, PA 17842
  (570) 837-3311
  Commissioners@SnyderCounty.org
- Selinsgrove PD
- Chief Thomas L. Garlock
  100 W. Pine St.
  Selinsgrove, PA 17870
  (570) 374-8655
  borough@selinsgrove.org
- Shamokin Dam PD
- Chief Timothy E. Bremigen
  144 W. 8th Ave.
  Shamokin Dam, PA 17876
  (570) 743-2671
  tbremigen@shamokindam.net

Somerset County

- Somerset County SD
- Sheriff John Mankey
  111 E. Union St., Ste. 100
  Somerset, PA 15501
  (814) 445-1502
  mankeyj@co.somerset.pa.us
- Conemaugh PD
- Chief Louis Barclay
  1120 Tire Hill Rd.
  Johnstown, PA 15905
  (814) 288-1400, ext. 1
  ctpd@contwpsupers.us
- Meyersdale PD
- Chief Ray Gnagey
  611 2nd St. PO Box 60
  Meyersdale, PA 15552-0060
  (814) 445-1525
  mdlepd@verizon.net

- Somerset PD
- Chief Randy Cox
  340 W. Union St.   PO Box 71
  Somerset, PA 15501
  (814) 445-4596
  Ben@somersetborough.com

Sullivan County

- Sullivan County SO
- Sheriff Bryan S. Brady
  Courthouse, Main & Muncy Sts.
  Laporte, PA 18626
  (717) 946-7361
  sheriff57@sullivancounty-pa.us

Susquehanna County

- Susquehanna County SD
- Sheriff Lance Benedict
  Courthouse, Public Ave.
  Montrose, PA 18801
  (570) 278-4600
  susqcotreas@hotmail.com
- Lanesboro PD
- Chief Jim Smith
  PO Box 97
  Lanesboro, PA 18827
  (570) 853-2911
  Lanesboromayor@echoes.net
- Susquehanna PD
- Chief Dominick Andidora
  284 Erie Blvd
  Susquehanna, PA 18847
  (570) 853-3147
  Susqpol@epix.net

Tioga County

- Tioga County SO
- Sheriff Tom Young
  116 Main St.
  Wellsboro, PA 16901
  (570) 724-3491
  tyoung@tiogacountypa.us
- Osceola PD
- Chief Marty Duffus
  PO Box 146
  Osceola, PA 16942
  (814) 258-5301
  oscadmin@iowatelecom.net
- Wellsboro PD
- Chief Jim Bodine
  28 Crafton St.
  Wellsboro, PA 16901
  (570) 724-3119
  borowell@epix.net

Union County

- Union County SO
- Sheriff Ernest Ritter
  103 So. 2nd St.
  Lewisburg, PA 17837
  (570) 524-8717
  eritter@unionco.org
- Buffalo Valley Reg. PD
- Chief Paul Yost
  2009 W. Market St.
  Lewisburg, PA 17837
  (570) 524-4302
  office@lewisburgborough.org
- New Berlin PD
- Act. Chhief L. Eric Hassenplug
  700 Water St.   PO Box 454
  New Berlin, PA 17855
  (570) 966-1735
  nbpolice@windstream.net

Venango County

- Venango County SO
- Sheriff Eric Foy
  1168 Liberty St.   PO Box 831
  Franklin, PA 16323
  (814) 432-9565
  efoy@co.venango.pa.us
- Oil City PD
- Chief Robert Wenner
  21 Seneca St.
  Oil City, PA 16301
  (814) 678-3080
  ocpd@oilcity.org
- Polk PD
- Chief Edward Sharp
  710 Main St.
  Polk, PA 16342
  (814) 432-3484
  info@dirwebservices.com
- Sugarcreek PD
- Chief Matthew R. Carlson
  212 Fox St.
  Franklin, PA 16323
  (814) 437-3702
  sugarcreekpd@llmwx.net

Warren County

- Warren County SO
- Sheriff Kenneth Klakamp
  407 Market St.
  Warren, PA 16365
  (814) 723-7553
  kklakamp@warren-county.net

- Warren PD
- Chief Raymond F. Zydonik
  318 W. 3rd Ave.
  Warren, PA 16365
  (814) 723-2700
  admin@cityofwarrenpa.gov

Washington County

- Washington County SO
- Sheriff Samuel Romano
  100 W. Beau St., Rm. 101
  Washington, PA 15301
  (724) 228-6840
  romanos@co.washington.pa.us
- Bentleyville PD
- Chief John Korsack
  900 Main St.
  Bentleyville, PA 15314
  (724) 239-2332
  admin@villageofbentleyville.com
- Centerville PD
- Chief Michael Ewedosh
  100 E. End Rd.
  Brownsville, PA 15417
  (724) 632-6655
  office@centervilleboro.org
- Charleroi PD
- Chief Paul Pivovarnik
  338 Fallowfield Ave.
  Charleroi, PA 15022
  (724) 483-8010
  Donn@charleroiboro.org
- Charticrs PD
- Chief James M. Horvath
  2 Buccaneer Dr.
  Houston, PA 15342
  (724) 745-8030
  chartierspd@yahoo.com
- Monongahela City PD
- Chief Brian Tempest
  451 W. Main St.
  Monongahela, PA 15063
  (724) 258-5511
  btempest@cityofmonongahela-pa.gov
- North Franklin PD
- Chief Richard Horner
  620 Franklin Farms Rd.
  Washington, PA 15301
  (724) 228-9610
  police@northfranklintownship.com
- North Strabane PD
- Chief Dan Strimel
  1929 Rt. 519 So.
  Canonsburg, PA 15317
  (724) 746-8474
  nspd@northstrabanepolice.com
- Peters PD
- Chief Harry Fruecht
  200 Municipal Dr.
  McMurray, PA 15317
  (724) 942-5030
  MASilvestri@peterstownship.com
- Washington PD
- Chief Robert Lemons
  56 W. Strawberry Ave.
  Washington, PA 15301
  (724) 223-4226
  info@washingtonpa.us

Wayne County

- Wayne County SO
- Sheriff Mark Steelman
  925 Court St.
  Honesdale, PA 18431
  (570) 253-2641
  webmaster@co.wayne.pa.us
- Hawley PD
- Chief Daniel Drake
  Main Ave.
  Hawley, PA 18428
  (570) 253-5752
  hawleypd@ptd.net
- Honesdale PD
- Chief Joseph Lobasso
  962 Main St.
  Honesdale, PA 18431
  (570) 253-1900
  hdleboro@choiceonemail.com
- Waymart PD
- Supt. Wayne Gavin
  PO Box 321
  Waymart, PA 18472
  (570) 488-7575
  waymartpd@socantel.net

Westmoreland County

- Westmoreland County SO
- Sheriff Jonathan Held
  2 No. Main St.
  Greensburg, PA 15601
  (724) 830-3457
  sheriff@co.westmoreland.pa.us

- Allegheny PD
- Chief Charles Moffatt
  136 Community Bldg Rd.
  Leechburg, PA 15656
  (724) 845-9410
  atpolice@akvalley.us
- Greensburg PD
- Chief Walter J. Lyons
  416 So. Main St.
  Greensburg, PA 15601
  (724) 834-3800
  administration@greensburgpa.org
- Irwin PD
- Chief Michael J Thomas
  424 Main St.
  Irwin, PA 15642
  (724) 864-3103
  irwinmanager@comcast.net
- Jeannette PD
- Chief Justin Scalzo
  110 So. 2nd St.
  Jeannette, PA 15644
  (724) 527-4013
  cddept@cityofjnt.com
- Latrobe PD
- Chief James Bumar
  901 Jefferson St.
  Latrobe, PA 15650
  (724) 537-5526
  JBumar@CityofLatrobe.com
- Ligonier Twp PD
- Chief Robert Amicone
  1 Municipal Park Dr.
  Ligonier, PA 15658
  (724) 238-5105
  tjw@wilkinsservices.com
- Lower Burrell PD
- Chief Tim Weitzel
  2800 Bethel St.
  Lower Burrell, PA 15068
  (724) 339-4287
  tweitzel@lbpolice.org
- Manor PD
- Chief George Valmassoni
  47 Race St.
  Manor, PA 15665
  (724) 863-7553
  g.valmassoni@manorborough.com
- Mt. Pleasant PD
- Supt. Jeff Landy
  Municipal Bldg, Etze Ave.
  Mt. Pleasant, PA 15666
  (724) 547-7210
  JLandy@mtpleasantboro.com
- Murrysville PD
- Chief Thomas P. Seefeld
  4120 Sardis Rd.
  Murrysville, PA 15668
  (724) 327-2111
  cweber@murrysvillegov.org
- North Huntingdon PD
- Supt. John Shepard
  11279 Center Hwy
  Huntingdon, PA 15642
  (724) 863-8800
  jshepherd@nhtpa.us
- Penn PD
- Chief James Laughlin
  PO Box 452
  Harrison City, PA 15636
  (724) 744-2343
  info@pennpolice.com
- Scottdale PD
- Chief Barry E. Pritts
  10 Mt. Pleasant Rd.
  Scottdale, PA 15683
  (724) 887-8220
  scottdale.boro@zoominternet.net
- Southwest Greensburg PD
- Chief Christopher Kent
  564 Stanton St.
  Greensburg, PA 15601
  (724) 834-8730
  swgreensburg@gmail.com
- Trafford PD
- Act. Chief (*Capt.*) Carmen Disso
  430 Brinton Ave.
  Trafford, PA 15085
  (412) 372-6550
  TraffordBorough@comcast.net
- Vandergrift PD
- Chief Joseph Caporali
  151C Lincoln Ave.
  Vandergrift, PA 15690
  (724) 568-5507
  caporali@vandergriftpolice.com

- West Newton PD
- Chief Gary Indolf
  112 So. Water St.
  West Newton, PA 15089
  (724) 872-8610
  dwninc@comcast.net

York County

- York County SO
- Sheriff Richard Keuerleber
  45 No. George St.
  York, PA 17401
  (717) 771-9601
  celindquist@ycdes.org
- Fairview PD
- Act. Chief (*Lt.*) Jason C. Loper
  599 Lewisberry Rd.
  New Cumberland, PA 17070
  (717) 901-5267
  dhaus@verizon.net
- Newberry PD
- Chief John Snyder
  1905 Old Trail Rd.
  Etters, PA 17319
  (717) 938-2608
  police@newberrypd.org
- Northeastern Reg. PD
- Chief Bryan Rizzo
  5570 Board Rd.
  Mt. Wolf, PA 17347-9524
  (717) 266-6195
  info@neregionalpd.us
- Penn PD
- Chief Richard L. Pickles
  20 Wayne Ave.
  Hanover, PA 17331
  (717) 637-8751
  ptpdchief@gmail.com
- Southern Reg. PD
- Chief John Forill
  47 E. High St.
  New Freedom, PA 17349
  (717) 235-3944
  admin@srpd.us
- Southwestern Reg. PD
- Chief Gregory M. Bean
  6115 Thoman Dr.
  Spring Grove, PA 17362
  (717) 225-1333
  Askanofficer@SWRPD.org
- Spring Garden PD
- Chief George J. Swartz
  340 Tri Hill Rd.
  York, PA 17403
  (717) 843-0851
  cdh129@comcast.net
- Springettsbury PD
- Chief Thomas H. Hyers
  1501 Mt. Zion Rd.
  York, PA 17402
  (717) 757-3525
  info@ettsbury.com
- Stewartstown PD
- Supt. Guy Hook
  6 No. Main St., Ste. E.
  Stewartstown, PA 17363
  (717) 993-5308
  police@stewartstown.org
- West Manchester PD
- Chief Arthur D. Smith
  2501 Catherine St.
  York, PA 17404
  (717) 792-9514
  police@westmanchestertownship.com
- West Manheim PD
- Chief Timothy J. Hippensteel
  31 Fairview Dr.
  Hanover, PA 17331
  (717) 632-7059
  westmanheimpd@blazenet.net
- West York PD
- Chief Justin D. Seibel
  1700 W. Philadelphia St.
  York, PA 17404
  (717) 854-1975
  wybpd@netzero.net
- York PD
- Chief Thomas G. Gross
  50 W. King St.
  York, PA 17401
  (717) 846-1234
  admin@yapd.org

State Agencies

- PA Capitol PD
- Supt. Richard Shaffer
  70 E. Capitol, E. Wing
  Harrisburg, PA 17125
  (717) 787-3199
  gs-police@state.pa.us

- PA State Police-HQ
- Comm. Frank Noonan
  1800 Elmerton Ave.
  Harrisburg, Pa 17110
  (717) 783-5599
  pspcommissioner@pa.gov
- Kutztown U. PD
- Chief John Dillon
  Old Main, Rm. # 13
  Kutztown, PA 19530
  (610) 683-4002
  dillon@kutztown.edu
- PA State U. PD
- Chief Tyrone Parham
  20 Eisenhower Parking Deck
  University Park, PA 16802
  (814) 863-2521
  tap3@psu.edu
- PA State Office
- Constable Steven Dershem
  PO Box 41
  Bellefonte, PA 16823
  (814) 355-7085
  constableagency@hotmail.com
- PA State Office
- Constable Richard D. Wright, Jr.
  PO Box 62
  Shamokin, PA 17872
  (570) 556-1023
  constablewright@aol.com
- PA State Office
- Constable James L. Corman
  PO Box 69
  Etters, PA 17319
  (717) 577-1999
  PaConstable974@yahoo.com
- PA State Office
- Constable Michael Solow
  PO Box 1111
  Fort Washington, PA 18034
  (215) 280-0060
  constable-1850@juno.com
- PA State Office
- Constable Theodore Grothe
  PO Box 5175
  Harrisburg, PA 17102
  (717) 648-1431
  Ward12Constable@yahoo.com
- PA State Office
- Constable Jeremiah Hetes
  209 Aspen St.
  Middletown, PA 17057-2104
  (717) 343-6986
  Ward3Constable@yahoo.com
- PA State Office
- Constable Rick Porvaznik
  PO Box 636
  Milesburg, PA 16853
  (814) 353-9443
  constable@adelphia.net
- PA State Office
- Constable John J Crerand
  PO Box 1147
  Milford, PA 18337
  (570) 686-3166
  tacco@ptd.net
- PA State Office
- Constable Oren Dahari
  PO Box 148
  New Hope, PA 18938-0148
  (215) 862-0110
  ConstableOren@gmail.com
- PA State Office
- Constable William Derrickson
  PO Box 10421
  Pittsburgh, PA 15234
  (412) 855-6113
  wpd@paconstables.us
- PA State Oil Creek Twp
- Constable Walt Miller
  16589 So. Main St.
  Pleasantville, PA 16341
  (814) 657-0654
  constablewalterjmiller@yahoo.com
- PA State Office
- Constable Sheldon Simpson
  PO Box 1373
  Plymouth Twp, PA 19422
  (610) 275-3369
  info@constablesimpson.com
- PA State Office
- Constable Grace Marks
  R.R. #4 Box 4195-A
  Saylorsburg, PA 18353
  (570) 992-1072
  grasee@ptd.net

- PA State Office
- Constable Jeffery Kisner
  PO Box 3202
  Shiremanstown, PA 17011
  (717) 329-2843
  ConstableCumb@aol.com
- PA State Office
- Constable Jason Searock
  PO Box 264
  Telford, PA 18969-0264
  (215) 837-8639
  telfordconstable@hotmail.com
- PA State Office
- Constable Ken Klock
  PO Box 286
  Titusville, PA 16354
  (814) 673-6026
  KTRECOVERYINC@AOL.COM
- PA State Office
- Constables Margaret & Louis Scarfo, Jr.
  54 Ashton Way
  West Chester, PA 19380
  (610) 436-5748
  consmaggie@comcast.net

RHODE ISLAND

Bristol County

- Barrington PD
- Chief John M. LaCross
  283 County Rd.
  Barrington, RI 02806
  (401) 247-1900
  JLacross@barrington.ri.gov
- Bristol PD
- Chief Josue D. Canario
  395 Metacom Ave.
  Bristol, RI 02809
  (401) 253-6900
  webmaster@bristolri.us
- Warren PD
- Chief Peter T. Achilli
  1 Joyce St.
  Warren, RI 02885
  (401) 245-1311
  peterachilli@warrenripd.com

Kent County

- Coventry PD
- Chief Bryan J. Volpe
  1075 Main St.
  Coventry, RI 02816
  (401) 826-1100
  BVolpe@coventrypd.org
- East Greenwich PD
- Chief (*Col.*) Thomas E. Coyle III
  176 1st Ave.
  East Greenwich, RI 02818
  (401) 884-2244
  tcoyle@eastgreenwichri.com
- West Greenwich PD
- Chief Richard N. *Rick* Ramsay
  280 Victory Hwy
  West Greenwich, RI 02817
  (401) 397-7191
  rramsay@wgpdri.com
- West Warwick PD
- Chief (*Col.*) Richard G. Silva
  1162 Main St.
  West Warwick, RI 02893
  (401) 821-4323
  APadulajr@westwarwickri.org

Newport County

- Jamestown PD
- Chief Edward A. Mello
  250 Conanicus Ave.
  Jamestown, RI 02835
  (401) 423-1212
  trockijamestowntc@gmail.com
- Little Compton PD
- Chief Sidney M. Wordell
  60 Simmons Rd.
  Little Compton, RI 02837
  (401) 635-2311
  policechief@tlcri.com
- Middletown PD
- Chief Anthony M. Pesare
  123 Valley Rd.
  Middletown, RI 02842
  (401) 846-1144
  apesare@middletownri.com
- Newport PD
- Chief Gary T. Silva
  120 Broadway
  Newport, RI 02840
  (401) 847-1306
  gsilva@cityofnewport.com
- Portsmouth PD
- Chief (*Col.*) Lance E. Hebert
  2270 E. Main Rd.
  Portsmouth, RI 02871
  (401) 683-0300
  jfurtado@portsmouthri.com
- Tiverton PD
- Chief Thomas Blakey
  20 Industrial Way
  Tiverton, RI 02878
  (401) 625-6717
  tblakey@townoftivertonri.com

Providence County

- Central Falls PD
- Chief (*Col.*) James J. Mendonca
  160 Illinois St.
  Central Falls, RI 02863
  (401) 616-2550
  jmendonca@centralfallspolice.com
- Cranston PD
- Chief (*Col.*) Marco Palombo, Jr
  5 Garfield Ave.
  Cranston, RI 02920
  (401) 942-2211
  webmaster@cranstonpolice.com
- Cumberland PD
- Chief John Desmarais
  1380 Diamond Hill Rd.
  Cumberland, RI 02864
  (401) 333-2500, ext. 3410
  jdesmarais@cumberlandpolice.com

- East Providence PD
- Chief Joseph Tavares
  750 Waterman Ave.
  East Providence, RI 02914
  (401) 435-7600
  jtavares@cityofeastprov.com
- Foster PD
- Chief Robert E. Coyne, Jr.
  182 Howard Hill Rd.
  Foster, RI 02825
  (401) 397-3317
  info@fosterpd.com
- Glocester PD
- Chief Joseph DelPrete
  162 Chopmist Hill Rd.
  Chepachet, RI 02814
  (401) 568-2533
  townclerk@GlocesterRI.org
- Johnston PD
- Chief Richard S. Tamburini
  1651 Atwood Ave.
  Johnston, RI 02919
  (401) 231-4210, ext. 3117
  chief@johnstonpd.com
- Lincoln PD
- Chief Brian Sullivan
  100 Old River Rd.
  Lincoln, RI 02865
  (401) 333-1111
  jalmond@lincolnri.org
- North Providence PD
- Chief Paul M. Martellini
  1967 Mineral Spring Ave.
  North Providence, RI 02904
  (401) 233-1433
  mlanni@northprovidenceri.gov
- North Smithfield PD
- Chief Steven E. Reynolds
  575 Smithfield Rd.
  North Smithfield, RI 02895
  (401) 762-1212
  sreynolds@nsmithfieldri.org
- Pawtucket PD
- Chief Paul King
  121 Roosevelt Ave.
  Pawtucket, RI 02860
  (401) 727-9100
  administrator@pawtucketpolice.com
- Providence PD
- Chief (*Col.*) Hugh T. Clements, Jr.
  325 Washington St.
  Providence, RI 02903
  (401) 272-3121
  fcolon@providenceri.com
- Scituate PD
- Chief (*Col.*) David M. Randall
  116 Main St.
  Hope, RI 02831
  (401) 821-5900
  Scituatepolice_crimewatch@yahoo.com
- Smithfield PD
- Chief Richard P. St. Sauveur, Jr.
  215 Pleasant View Ave.
  Smithfield, RI 02917
  (401) 231-2500
  rstsauveur@smithfieldpd.com
- Woonsocket PD
- Chief Thomas S. Carey
  242 Clinton St.
  Woonsocket, RI 02895
  (401) 767-8828
  tcarey@woonsocketri.org

Washington County

- Charlestown PD
- Chief Jeffrey S. Allen
  4901 Old Post Rd.
  Charlestown, RI 02813
  (401) 364-1212
  webmaster@charlestownpolice.org
- Hopkinton PD
- Chief David Palmer
  406 Woodville Rd.
  Hopkinton, RI 02833
  (401) 377-7750
  Chief@HopkintonPolice.Org
- Narragansett PD
- Chief Dean Hoxsie
  40 Caswell St.
  Narragansett, RI 02882
  (401) 789-1091
  dhoxsie@narragansettri.gov
- North Kingstown PD
- Chief Thomas J. Mulligan
  8166 Post Rd.
  North Kingstown, RI 02852
  (401) 294-3316, ext. 8200
  tmulligan@northkingstown.org

- Richmond PD
- Chief Elwood M. Johnson, Jr.
  1168 Main St.
  PO Box 203
  Wyoming, RI 02898
  (401) 539-8289
  chief@richmondpd.org
- South Kingstown PD
- Chief Vincent Vespia, Jr.
  1790 Kingstown Rd.
  Wakefield, RI 02879
  (401) 783-3321
  vvespia@skpd.org
- Westerly PD
- Chief Edward St. Clair
  5 Union St.
  Westerly, RI 02891
  (401) 348-6101
  estclair@westerlypolice.org

State Agencies

- RI Police Chiefs Assn.
- Pres. (*Chief*) John R. Desmarais
  Cumberland PD
  1380 Diamond Hill Rd.
  Cumberland, RI 02864
  (401) 333-2500
  jdesmarais@cumberlandpolice.com
- RI State Police-HQ
- Supt. (*Col.*) Steven G. O'Donnell
  311 Danielson Pike No.
  Scituate, RI 02857
  (401) 444-1000
  CustomerRelations@RIPTA.com
- U. of RI PD
- Maj. Stephen Baker
  85 Briar Ln.
  Kingston, RI 02881
  (401) 874-4980
  majorbaker@uri.edu

SOUTH CAROLINA

Abbeville County

- Abbeville County SO
- Sheriff Ray Watson
  21 Old Calhoun Falls Rd.
  Abbeville, SC 29620
  (864) 446-6000
  rwatson@abbevillecountysc.com
- Abbeville PD
- Chief Mark E. Hall
  106 So. Main St.
  Abbeville, SC 29620
  (864) 459-5832
  sherwood@abbevillecitysc.com

Aiken County

- Aiken County SO
- Sheriff Michael E. Hunt
  420 Hampton Ave. NE
  Aiken, SC 29801
  (803) 642-1761
  sheriff@aikencountysheriff.org
- New Ellenton PD
- Chief Alesia Parks
  200 Main St. No. PO Box 459
  New Ellenton, SC 29809
  (803) 652-7770
  nepdchief@yahoo.com
- Perry PD
- Chief Curtis Ward
  1062 E. Railroad Ave. No.
  Perry, SC 29137
  (803) 564-5756
  top@pbtcomm.net

Allendale County

- Allendale County SO
- Sheriff Tom Carter, Jr.
  168 Law Enforcement Ct.
  Allendale, SC 29810
  (803) 584-2361
  gchaney@allendalecounty.com

Anderson County

- Anderson County SO
- Sheriff John Skipper, Jr.
  305 Camson Rd.
  Anderson, SC 29625
  (864) 260-4400
  jskipper@andersonsheriff.com
- Anderson PD
- Chief James S. *Jim* Stewart
  401 So. Main St.
  Anderson, SC 29624
  (864) 231-2277
  jstewart@cityofandersonsc.com
- Belton PD
- Chief Tommy Clamp
  City Hall
  Belton, SC 29627
  (864) 338-8448
  tclamp@cityofbeltonsc.com
- Honea Path PD
- Chief David B. King
  30 No. Main St.
  Honea Path, SC 29654
  (864) 369-0532
  hppd@charterinternet.com
- Iva PD
- Chief T.E. Miller
  E. Jackson St.
  Iva, SC 29655
  (864) 348-6191
  ivatownclerk@wctel.net

Bamberg County

- Bamberg County SO
- Sheriff J. Edward Darnell
  456 2nd St. PO Box 210
  Bamberg, SC 29003
  (803) 245-3011
  bamcntyso@oburg.net

Barnwell County

- Barnwell County SO
- Sheriff Ed Carroll
  PO Box 384
  Barnwell, SC 29812
  (803) 541-1078
  edcarroll@barnwellcountysheriff.net
- Barnwell PD
- Chief Todd Gantt
  124 Burr St. PO Box 776
  Barnwell, SC 29812
  (803) 259-1838
  chiefgantt@cityofbarnwell.com
- Williston PD
- Chief Roger Kaney
  301 W. Main St.
  Williston, SC 29853
  (803) 266-7013
  roger@williston-sc.com

Beaufort County

- Beaufort County SO
- Sheriff P.J. Tanner
  2001 Duke St. PO Box 1758
  Beaufort, SC 29901
  (843) 255-3191
  njohnston@bcgov.net
- Beaufort PD
- Chief Matthew J. Clancy
  1901 Boundary St. PO Box 898
  Beaufort, SC 29901
  (843) 322-7902
  mclancy@bftpolice.com

Berkeley County

- Goose Creek PD
- Chief Harvey Becker
  519 No. Goose Creek Blvd
  Goose Creek, SC 29445
  (843) 863-5200, ext. 2309
  hbecker@cityofgoosecreek.com
- Hanahan PD
- Chief Michael A. Cochran
  1255 Yeamans Hall Rd.
  Hanahan, SC 29406
  (843) 747-5711
  mcochran@cityofhanahan.com

Calhoun County

- Calhoun County SO
- Sheriff Thomas S. Summers, Jr.
  2811 Old Belleville PO Box 749
  St. Matthews, SC 29135
  (803) 874-2741
  tips@calhounscsheriff.com
- St. Matthews PD
- Chief (*Col.*) Norm Mayer
  316 W. Bridge St.
  St. Matthews, SC 29135
  (803) 874-2131
  mnay@stmatthews.org

Charleston County

- Charleston County SO
- Sheriff J. Al Cannon, Jr.
  3505 Pinehaven Dr.
  Charleston, SC 29405
  (843) 554-4700
  jbrady@charlestoncounty.org
- Charleston PD
- Chief Gregory C. Mullen
  180 Lockwood Blvd
  Charleston, SC 29403
  (843) 720-2426
  ambroseb@charleston-sc.gov
- Folly Beach PD
- Chief Dennis Brown
  21 Center St.
  Folly Beach, SC 29439
  (843) 588-2433
  dbrown@cityoffollybeach.com
- Isle Of Palms PD
- Chief Thomas E. Buckhannon III
  30 J.C. Long Blvd PO Box 508
  Isle Of Palms, SC 29451
  (843) 886-6522
  thomasb@iop.net
- Mt. Pleasant PD
- Chief Carl Ritchie
  100 Ann Edwards Ln.
  Mt. Pleasant, SC 29464
  (843) 884-4176, ext. 3415
  critchie@tompsc.com
- Sullivans Island PD
- Chief Daniel Howard
  1610 Middle St. PO Box 427
  Sullivans Island, SC 29482
  (843) 883-5735
  dhoward@sullivansisland-sc.com

Cherokee County

- Cherokee County SO
- Sheriff Steve Mueller
  312 E. Frederick St.
  Gaffney, SC 29340
  (864) 489-4722
  smueller@cherokeecountysheriff.net
- Blacksburg PD
- Chief Jamie P. Ham
  101 So. Shelby St. PO Box 517
  Blacksburg, SC 29702
  (864) 839-2331
  chief@blacksburgpd.com
- Gaffney PD
- Chief Richard E. Turner
  201 No. Limestone PO Box 2109
  Gaffney, SC 29342
  (864) 489-8115
  rramsey@gaffneypd.org

Chester County

- Chester County SO
- Sheriff Alex *Big A* Underwood
  2740 Dawson Dr. PO Box 727
  Chester, SC 29706
  (803) 581-5131
  chestersheriff@chesterso.com

- Chester PD
- Chief André Williams
  2740 Dawson Dr.
  Chester, SC 29706
  (803) 581-2677
  awilliams@chester.sc.gov
- Great Falls PD
- Chief Mike Revels
  324 Dearborn St.
  Great Falls, SC 29055
  (803) 482-2145
  greatfalls@infoave.net

Chesterfield County

- Chesterfield County SO
- Sheriff Rob Lee
  109 Scotch Rd.
  Chesterfield, SC 29709
  (843) 623-2101
  admin@chesterfieldsheriff.org
- Pageland PD
- Chief Larry Brown
  316 W. McGregor St.
  Pageland, SC 29728
  (843) 672-6437
  dispatch1@shtc.net

Clarendon County

- Clarendon County SO
- Sheriff Randy Garrett
  217 Commerce St. PO Box 1289
  Manning, SC 29102
  (803) 435-4414
  sheriffgarrett@ftc-i.net
- Manning PD
- Chief Blair Shaffer
  42 W. Boyce St.
  Manning, SC 29102
  (803) 435-8859
  bshaffer@sc.rr.com

Colleton County

- Colleton County SO
- Sheriff R.A. *Andy* Strickland
  112 So. Miller St. PO Box 433
  Walterboro, SC 29488
  (843) 549-2211
  rastrickland@colletoncounty.org
- Walterboro PD
- Chief Otis Rhodes
  242 Hampton St.
  Walterboro, SC 29488
  (843) 549-1811
  orhodes@walterborosc.org

Darlington County

- Darlington County SO
- Sheriff J. Wayne Byrd
  1621 Harry Byrd PO Box 783
  Darlington, SC 29532
  (843) 398-4501
  sheriff@darcosc.com
- Hartsville PD
- Chief James Hudson
  135 W. Carolina Ave.
  Hartsville, SC 29551
  (843) 383-3011
  james.hudson@hartsvillesc.gov

Dillon County

- Dillon PD
- Chief Joe Rogers
  401 W. Main St. PO Drawer 431
  Dillon, SC 29536
  (843) 774-0051, ext. 1027
  JLDillon@bellsouth.net

Dorchester County

- Dorchester County SO
- Sheriff Luther Carl *L.C.* Knight
  212 Deming Way
  St. George, SC 29477
  (843) 832-0300
  sboisselle@dorchestercounty.net
- St. George PD
- Chief Anthony L. Britt
  601 So. Parler Ave.
  St. George, SC 29477
  (843) 563-3643
  info@stgeorgepd.org
- Summerville PD
- Chief Bruce Owens
  300 W. 2nd No. St.
  Summerville, SC 29483
  (843) 871-2463
  bowens@summervillesc.gov

Edgefield County

- Edgefield County SO
- Sheriff Adell Dobey
  200 Railroad St.
  Edgefield, SC 29824
  (803) 637-5337
  sheriffdobey@edgefieldcountysheriff.org

Fairfield County

- Fairfield County SO
- Sheriff Herman W. Young
  350 Columbia Rd.   PO Box 387
  Winnsboro, SC 29180
  (803) 635-4141
  tsmith@fairfieldsc.com

Florence County

- Johnsonville PD
- Chief Ron Douglas
  146 E. Broadway St.
  Johnsonville, SC 29555
  (843) 386-3500
  rdouglas@cityofjohnsonville.com

Georgetown County

- Georgetown County SO
- Sheriff A. Lane Cribb
  430 No. Fraser St.   PO Box 1292
  Georgetown, SC 29440
  (843) 546-5102
  gcsopio@gtcounty.org
- Andrews PD
- Chief Jennifer Flowers
  101 No. Morgan Ave.
  Andrews, SC 29510
  (843) 264-5223
  chiefofpolice@townofandrews.org
- Georgetown PD
- Chief Paul Gardner
  2222 Highmarket St.
  Georgetown, SC 29440
  (843) 545-4300
  jscoville@cogsc.com

Greenville County

- Greenville County SO
- Sheriff Steve Loftis
  4 McGee St.
  Greenville, SC 29601
  (864) 271-5210
  BTaylor@greenvillecounty.org
- Fountain Inn PD
- Chief A. Keith Morton
  300 No. Main St.
  Fountain Inn, SC 29644
  (864) 862-4461
  keith.morton@fountaininn.org
- Greenville PD
- Chief Terri Wilfong
  4 McGee St.   PO Box 2207
  Greenville, SC 29601
  (864) 467-5310
  jbragg@greenvillesc.gov
- Greer PD
- Chief Dan Reynolds
  101 W. Poinsett St.
  Greer, SC 29650
  (864) 848-2160
  dreynolds@cityofgreer.org
- Mauldin PD
- Chief M. Bryan Turner
  5 E. Butler Rd.
  Mauldin, SC 29662
  (864) 289-8900
  gryan@mauldinpolice.com
- Simpsonville PD
- Chief Steve A. Moore
  405 E. Curtis St.
  Simpsonville, SC 29681
  (864) 967-9536
  chief@simpsonvillepd.com
- Travelers Rest PD
- Chief Lance G. Crowe
  6711 State Park Rd.
  Travelers Rest, SC 29690
  (864) 834-9029
  info@trpolice.com

Greenwood County

- Greenwood County SO
- Sheriff Tony Davis
  528 Edgefield St.
  Greenwood, SC 29646
  (864) 942-8600
  mallison@greenwoodsc.gov
- Greenwood PD
- Chief Gerald L. Brooks
  520 Monument St.
  Greenwood, SC 29648
  (864) 942-8422
  gerald.brooks@cityofgreenwoodsc.com
- Ninety-Six PD
- Chief Robert Shingler
  100 No. Church St.
  Ninety-Six, SC 29666
  (864) 543-3122
  chief96pd@yahoo.com

Hampton County

- Hampton County SO
- Sheriff Thomas *TC* Smalls
  411 Cemetery Rd.
  Varnville, S.C. 29944
  (803) 914-2200
  tcsmalls@hamptoncountysc.org

- Estill PD
- Chief Jerome White
  323 Martin L. King, Jr. Blvd So.
  Estill, SC 29918
  (803) 625-3699
  jeromew@centurylink.net
- Hampton PD
- Chief Perry McAlhaney
  608 1st St. W.
  Hampton, SC 29924
  (803) 943-2421
  pmcalhaney@hamptonsc.gov
- Yemassee PD
- Chief Jack Hagy
  101 Town Cir.
  Yemassee, SC 29945
  (803) 589-6315
  yemassee@hargray.com

Horry County

- Horry County SO
- Sheriff Phillip E. Thompson
  1301 2nd Ave. PO Box 380
  Conway, SC 29526
  (843) 915-5450
  publicinfo_1@horrycounty.org
- Aynor PD
- Chief David *Bubba* Thompson
  600 So. Main St.
  Aynor, SC 29511
  (843) 358-3900
  aynorpd@sccoast.net
- Briarcliffe Acres PD
- Chief Kyle Lamparter
  PO Box 1250
  No. Myrtle Beach, SC 29598
  (843) 997-9500
  bapd29572@gmail.com
- Conway PD
- Chief Reginald E. Gosnell
  200 Laurel St. PO Drawer 1075
  Conway, SC 29526
  (843) 248-1790
  rgosnell@cityofconway.com
- Horry County PD
- Chief Saundra Rhodes
  2560 Main St., Ste. 7
  Conway, SC 29526
  (843) 915-8341
  rhodesS@horrycounty.org
- Loris PD
- Chief Joseph Vaught
  3951 Walnut St.
  Loris, SC 29569
  (843) 756-4000
  policechief@cityofloris.com
- Myrtle Beach PD
- Chief Warren Gall
  1101 Oak St.
  Myrtle Beach, SC 29577
  (843) 918-1382
  info@cityofmyrtlebeach.com
- Surfside Beach DPS
- Chief Rodney Keziah
  811 No. Pine Dr.
  Surfside Beach, SC 29575
  (843) 913-6351
  rkeziah@surfsidebeach.org

Jasper County

- Jasper County SO
- Sheriff Gregory B. Jenkins
  12008 No. Jacob Smart Blvd
  Ridgeland, SC 29936
  (843) 726-7777
  SheriffJenkins@jaspercountysc.gov
- Ridgeland PD
- Chief R.V. Woods
  One Town Sq. PO Box 1719
  Ridgeland, SC 29936
  (843) 726-7530
  rwoods@ridgelandpd.com

Kershaw County

- Kershaw County SO
- Sheriff Jim Matthews
  821 Ridgeway Rd. PO Box 70
  Lugoff, SC 29078
  (803) 425-1512
  kcso@kershaw.sc.gov

Lancaster County

- Lancaster County SO
- Sheriff Barry S. Faile
  1520 Pageland PO Box 908
  Lancaster, SC 29721
  (803) 283-4186
  SheriffFaile@lacoso.net
- Lancaster PD
- Chief Harlean V. Howard
  405 E. Arch St.
  Lancaster, SC 29720
  (803) 283-1173
  hhoward@lancastercitysc.com

Laurens County

- Laurens County SO
- Sheriff Ricky W. Chastain
  216 W. Main St. PO Box 68
  Laurens, SC 29360
  (864) 984-4967
  wpowell@laurenssheriff.com

Lee County

- Lee County SO
- Sheriff Daniel Simon
  113 Gregg St. PO Box 89
  Bishopville, SC 29010
  (803) 428-7149
  dsimon@leecountysc.org
- Bishopville PD
- Chief Calvin Collins
  112 E. Council St.
  Bishopville, SC 29010
  (803) 484-5309
  ccollins@bishopvillepd.org

Lexington County

- Lexington County SO
- Sheriff James R. Metts
  521 Gibson Rd.
  Lexington, SC 29072
  (803) 785-8230
  jmetts@lcsd.sc.gov
- Batesburg-Leesville PD
- Chief William Wallace Oswald
  660 W. Columbia Ave.
  Batesburg, SC 29006
  (803) 532-4408
  jbtaylor@batesburg-leesville.org
- Cayce PD
- Chief Charles E. McNair
  1800 12th St.
  Cayce, SC 29033
  (803) 794-0456
  info@cityofcayce-sc.gov
- Columbia Airport PD
- Dir. Randy Blackmon
  3030 Aviation Way
  West Columbia, SC 29170
  (803) 822-5025
  r.blackmon@columbiaairport.com
- Gaston PD
- Chief John Regalis
  186 No. Carlisle PO Box 429
  Gaston, SC 29053
  (803) 796-8503
  townofgaston@gmail.com
- Irmo PD
- Chief Brian Buck
  1239 Columbia Ave.
  Irmo, SC 29063
  (803) 781-8088
  irmopdchief@townofirmosc.com
- Lexington PD
- Chief Terrence Green
  111 Maiden Ln.
  Lexington, SC 29072
  (803) 359-6260
  tgreen@lexsc.com
- Springdale PD
- Chief Kevin Cornett
  2915 Platt Springs Rd.
  Springdale, SC 29170
  (803) 796-3160
  kcornett@springdalesc.com
- West Columbia PD
- Chief Dennis Tyndall
  200 No. 12th St.
  West Columbia, SC 29171
  (803) 794-0721
  jowens@westcolumbiasc.gov

Marion County

- Marion County SO
- Sheriff Mark W. Richardson
  2715 E. Hwy 76, Ste. C
  Mullins, SC 29574
  (843) 423-8216
  mrichardson@marionsc.org
- Marion PD
- Chief James W. *Jim* Gray, Jr.
  1024 So. Main St. PO Box 1190
  Marion, SC 29571
  (843) 423-8616
  mpolice@marionsc.gov
- Mullins PD
- Chief Mike Bethea
  157 E. Front St.
  Mullins, SC 29574
  (843) 464-0707
  cityofmullins@mullinssc.us
- Nichols PD
- Chief Robert Bullard
  108 So. Nichols PO Box 32
  Nichols, SC 29581
  (843) 526-2193
  nichols2028@bellsouth.net

Marlboro County

- Marlboro County SO
- Sheriff Fred A. Knight
  PO Box 577
  Bennettsville, SC 29512
  (843) 479-5605
  J.Haynes@marlborocounty.sc.gov
- Bennettsville PD
- Chief Larry McNeil
  501 E. Main St.
  Bennettsville, SC 29512
  (843) 479-3620
  larrymcneil@mecsc.net
- Clio PD
- Chief Pearlie Thomas
  110 No. Main St. PO Box 487
  Clio, SC 29525
  (843) 586-2211
  townofclio@bellsouth.net

McCormick County

- McCormick County SO
- Sheriff George H. Reid
  Hammond St. PO Box 1236
  McCormick, SC 29835
  (864) 465-2520
  mcc4sheriff@wctel.net
- McCormick PD
- Chief J.R. Jones
  119 W. Augusta PO Box 306
  McCormick, SC 29835
  (864) 852-2985
  police@townofmccormicksc.org

Newberry County

- Newberry County SO
- Sheriff James Lee Foster
  520 Wilson Rd.
  Newberry, SC 29108
  (803) 321-2211
  lfoster@ncso.sc.gov

Oconee County

- Oconee County SO
- Sheriff Mike Crenshaw
  208 Booker Dr.
  Walhalla, SC 29691
  (864) 638-4111
  jwatt@oconeelaw.com
- Seneca PD
- Chief John Covington
  205 No. Depot St. PO Box 4773
  Seneca, SC 29679
  (864) 885-2718
  info@senecapd.com

Orangeburg County

- Orangeburg County SO
- Sheriff Leroy Ravenell
  1520 Ellis Ave. PO Drawer 9000
  Orangeburg, SC 29115
  (803) 531-4647
  kkinsey@orangeburgcounty.org
- Elloree PD
- Chief Joseph P. Avinger
  2719 Cleveland St. PO Box 28
  Elloree, SC 29047
  (803) 897-2821
  epdchief@elloreesc.com
- Holly Hill PD
- Chief Robert H. Wunderlich
  8807 Old State Rd. PO Box 1108
  Holly Hill, SC 29059
  (803) 496-3811
  HollyHillPDSC@yahoo.com
- North PD
- Chief Mark P. Fallaw
  9305 North Rd. PO Box 399
  North, SC 29112
  (803) 247-5801
  mfallaw@townofnorth-sc.gov

Pickens County

- Pickens County SO
- Sheriff Rick W. Clark
  216 L.E. C Rd.
  Pickens, SC 29671
  (864) 898-5554
  rclark@co.pickens.sc.us
- Central PD
- Chief Kerry Avery
  1067 W. Main St. PO Box 549
  Central, SC 29630
  (864) 639-4020
  jwells@cityofcentral.org
- Clemson PD
- Chief Jimmy Dixon
  1198 Tiger Blvd PO Box 1566
  Clemson, SC 29631 *(29633)*
  (864) 624-2000
  info@cityofclemson.org

- Easley PD
- Chief William D. Traber
  220 NW Main St.
  Easley, SC 29641
  (864) 859-4025
  dtraber@easleypd.org
- Liberty PD
- Chief Adam C. Gilstrap
  206 Front St. PO Box 716
  Liberty, SC 29657
  (864) 843-3956
  msheriff@libertysc.com
- Pickens PD
- Chief Rodney D. Gregory
  304 Johnson St.
  Pickens, SC 29671
  (864) 878-6366
  triggs@pickenscity.com

Richland County

- Richland County SD
- Sheriff Leon Lott
  5623 Two Notch Rd.
  Columbia, SC 29223
  (803) 576-3000
  sheriff@rcsd.net
- Columbia PD
- Int. Chief Ruben Santiago
  #1 Justice Sq.
  Columbia, SC 29201
  (803) 545-3510
  rrsantiago@columbiasc.net

Saluda County

- Saluda County SO
- Sheriff John C. Perry
  100 Law Enforcement Dr.
  Saluda, SC 29138
  (864) 445-2112
  j.perry@saludacounty.sc.gov
- Saluda PD
- Chief Michael Clancey
  101 So. Jefferson St.
  Saluda, SC 29138
  (864) 445-7336
  saludapd@embarqmail.com

Spartanburg County

- Spartanburg County SO
- Sheriff Chuck Wright
  8045 Howard St.
  Spartanburg, SC 29303
  (864) 503-4500
  tivey@spartanburgcounty.org
- Campobello PD
- Chief William C. McNeill
  208 No. Main St.
  Campobello, SC 29322
  (864) 472-9093
  cmcneill@campobellopd.com
- Inman PD
- Chief Keith Tucker
  20 So. Main St.
  Inman, SC 29349
  (864) 472-6200
  tcinmn1@windstream.net
- Lyman PD
- Chief Terry W. Richards
  81 Groce Rd.
  Lyman, SC 29365
  (864) 485-0232
  trichards@lymansc.gov
- Pacolet PD
- Chief Robert Ivey, Sr.
  110 Sunset Dr. PO Box 700
  Pacolet, SC 29372
  (864) 474-3002
  eharris@townofpacolet.com
- Spartanburg DPS
- Dir. Tony Fisher
  145 W. Broad St.
  Spartanburg, SC 29306
  (864) 596-2376
  tfisher@cityofspartanburg.org
- Woodruff PD
- Chief Darrell Dawkins
  231 E. Hayne St.
  Woodruff, SC 29388
  (864) 476-8131
  ddawkins@cityofwoodruff.com

Sumter County

- Sumter County SO
- Sheriff Anthony Dennis
  107 E. Hampton Ave.
  Sumter, SC 29150
  (803) 436-2700
  adennis@sumtercountysc.org
- Sumter PD
- Chief Russell F. Roark III
  107 E. Hampton Ave.
  Sumter, SC 29150
  (803) 436-2739
  chief@sumterpd.com

Union County

- Union County SO
- Sheriff David H. Taylor
  220 W. Main St. PO Box 971
  Union, SC 29379
  (864) 429-1612
  sherifftaylor@countyofunion.com
- Jonesville PD
- Chief Jimmy Wilkins
  149 Pacolet St. PO Box 785
  Jonesville, SC 29353
  (864) 674-5262
  jonesvilleclk@bellsouth.net

Williamsburg County

- Williamsburg County SO
- Sheriff Michael L. Johnson
  126 So. Jackson St.
  Kingstree, SC 29556
  (843) 355-6381
  public.issues@williamsburgcounty.sc.gov
- Kingstree PD
- Chief E.C. Williams
  401 No. Longstreet St.
  Kingstree, SC 29556
  (843) 355-5435
  ewilliams@kingstree.org

York County

- York County SO
- Sheriff Bruce M. Bryant
  1675-2A York Hwy
  York, SC 29745
  (803) 628-3059
  info@yorkcountysheriff.com
- Clover PD
- Chief Randy Grice
  112 Bethel St. PO Box 1060
  Clover, SC 29710
  (803) 222-9494
  cloverpolice@cloversc.org
- Fort Mill PD
- Chief Jeff Helms
  111 Academy St.
  Fort Mill, SC 29716
  (803) 547-2022
  fmpd@comporium.net
- Rock Hill PD
- Chief Chris Watts
  120 E. Black St.
  Rock Hill, SC 29730
  (803) 329-7281
  cwatts@cityofrockhill.com
- Tega Cay PD
- Chief Rick Evelsizer
  7705 Tega Cay Dr.
  Tega Cay, SC 29708
  (803) 548-0340
  evelsizerr@tegacaypolice.org
- York PD
- Chief C.A. Robinson
  12 No. Roosevelt PO Box 500
  York, SC 29745
  (803) 684-4141
  arobinson@yorkcitysc.com

State Agencies

- SC Highway Patrol-HQ
- Comm. (*Col.*) Michael Oliver
  10311 Wilson Blvd PO Box 1993
  Blythewood, SC 29016
  (803) 896-7920
  ciohelpdesk@cio.sc.gov

TENNESSEE

Anderson County

- Anderson County SD
- Sheriff Paul White
  101 So. Main St., Ste. 400
  Clinton, TN 37716
  (865) 457-6210
  sheriff@tnacso.net
- Clinton PD
- Chief Rick Scarbrough
  125 W. Broad St.
  Clinton, TN 37716
  (865) 457-3112
  jcampbell@clintontn.net
- Lake City PD
- Chief Jim Shetterly
  195 So. Main St. PO Box 66
  Lake City, TN 37769
  (865) 426-2838
  cityoflakecity@bellsouth.net
- Norris PD
- Dir. Danny Humphrey
  9 Norris Sq.
  Norris, TN 37828
  (865) 494-0880
  norriscity@comcast.net
- Oak Ridge PD
- Chief James T. Akagi
  200 So. Tulane PO Box 1
  Oak Ridge, TN 37831
  (865) 425-3504
  tbeehan@oakridgetn.gov

Bedford County

- Bedford County SO
- Sheriff Randall Boyce
  103 Lane Pkwy
  Shelbyville, TN 37160
  (931) 684-3232
  rboyce@bedfordcountyso.net
- Shelbyville PD
- Chief Austin Swing
  109 Lane Pkwy
  Shelbyville, TN 37160
  (615) 684-5811
  austin.swing@shelbyvilletnpolice.org
- Wartrace PD
- Chief Daniel Odeneil
  29 Main St. E. PO Box 158
  Wartrace, TN 37183
  (615) 389-6144
  townofwartrace@att.net

Benton County

- Benton County SD
- Sheriff Tony King
  116 So. Rosemary Ave.
  Camden, TN 38320
  (731) 584-4632
  kingtony03@yahoo.com

Bledsoe County

- Bledsoe County SO
- Sheriff James L. Morris
  130 Frazier St. PO Box 246
  Pikeville, TN 37367
  (423) 447-2197
  BCSD1201@BLEDSOE.NET

Blount County

- Blount County SO
- Sheriff James L. Berrong
  940 E. Lamar Alexander Pkwy
  Maryville, TN 37804
  (865) 273-5000
  JBERRONG@BCSO.COM
- Alcoa PD
- Chief Ken Burge
  2020 No. Wright Rd.
  Alcoa, TN 37701
  (865) 981-4111
  mull@cityofalcoa-tn.gov
- Maryville PD
- Chief (*Maj.*) Greg Cooke
  418 W. Broadway
  Maryville, TN 37801
  (865) 981-1370
  gdcooke@maryville-tn.gov

Bradley County

- Bradley County SO
- Sheriff James R. Ruth
  2290 Blythe Ave. SE
  Cleveland, TN 37311
  (423) 728-7333
  JRUTH@BRADLEYCO.NET
- Cleveland PD
- Chief Wes Snyder
  100 Church St. NE
  Cleveland, TN 37311
  (423) 476-1121
  wsnyder@clevelandtn.gov

Campbell County

- Campbell County SO
- Sheriff Robbie K. Goins
  610 Main St.
  Jacksboro, TN 37757
  (423) 562-7446
  SHERIFFGOINS@CAMPBELLCOUNTYGOV.COM

Cannon County

- Cannon County SO
- Sheriff Darrell Young
  110 Alexander Dr.
  Woodbury, TN 37190
  (615) 563-1000, ext. 224
  sheriffyoung@dtccom.net

Carroll County

- Carroll County SO
- Sheriff Andy Dickson
  126 W Paris St.
  Huntingdon, TN 38344
  (731) 986-8947
  adickson@carroll.tn.org
- McKenzie PD
- Int. Chief Kim Barker
  2470 Cedar St.
  McKenzie, TN 38201
  (731) 352-2265
  kim.barker@cityofmckenzie.com

Carter County

- Carter County SO
- Sheriff Chris W. Mathes
  900 E. Elk Ave.
  Elizabethton, TN 37643
  (423) 542-1846
  cwmvolztn@hotmail.com
- Elizabethton PD
- Chief Greg Workman
  525 E. F St.
  Elizabethton, TN 37643
  (423) 542-4141
  rcurta@charter.net

Cheatham County

- Cheatham County SD
- Sheriff John H. Holder
  200 Court St., Ste. 220
  Ashland City, TN 37015
  (615) 792-2027
  PATSY.ANDREWS@CHEATHAMCOUNTYTN.GOV
- Ashland City PD
- Chief Marc Coulon
  101 Court St.
  Ashland City, TN 37015
  (615) 792-4211
  marc.coulon@ashlandcitytn.gov

Chester County

- Chester County SO
- Sheriff Blair Weaver
  333 Eric Bell Dr., Ste. A
  Henderson, TN 38340
  (731) 989-2449
  CCS102@HOTMAIL.COM
- Henderson PD
- Chief Mickey Miller
  3 Executive Park Dr.
  Henderson, TN 38340
  (615) 822-1111
  mickeymiller@hendersonville-pd.org

Claiborne County

- Claiborne County SD
- Sheriff David Ray
  415 Straight Creek PO Box 245
  Tazewell, TN 37879
  (423) 626-3385
  sheriffdavidray.ccso@netcommander.com
- New Tazewell PD
- Chief Johnny Johnson
  PO Box 609
  New Tazewell, TN 37825
  (423) 626-5242
  ntcityhall1@hotmail.com

Clay County

- Clay County SO
- Sheriff Brandon Boone
  400 W. Lake Ave.
  Celina, TN 38551
  (931) 243-3266
  brandonboone8606@yahoo.com

Cocke County

- Cocke County SD
- Sheriff Armando Fontes
  111 Court Ave.
  Newport, TN 37821
  (423) 623-6004
  SHERIFF@COCKECOUNTYSD.COM
- Newport PD
- Chief J. Maurice Shults
  330 E. Main St. PO Box 128
  Newport, TN 37821
  (423) 623-5556
  policechief@cityofnewport-tn.com

Coffee County

- Coffee County SD
- Sheriff Steve Graves
  300 Hillsboro Hwy
  Manchester, TN 37355
  (931) 728-3591
  STEVEGRAVES@COFFEECOUNTYTN.ORG
- Manchester PD
- Chief Mark Yother
  200 W. Fort St.
  Manchester, TN 37355
  (931) 728-2099
  myother@cityofmanchestertn.com
- Tullahoma PD
- Chief Paul Blackwell
  123 No. Jackson
  Tullahoma, TN 37388
  (931) 455-0530
  pblackwell@tullahomatn.gov

Crockett County

- Crockett County SO
- Sheriff Troy Klyce
  899 So. Cavalier Dr.
  Alamo, TN 38001
  (731) 696-2104
  TKLYCE@ME.COM

Cumberland County

- Cumberland County SO
- Sheriff Eucle *Butch* Burgess
  90 Justice Center Dr.
  Crossville, TN 38555
  (931) 484-6176
  CCSD800@GMAIL.COM
- Crossville PD
- Chief David E. Beaty
  141 Henry Ave.
  Crossville, TN 38555
  (931) 484-7231
  mayorgraham@frontiernet.net

Davidson County

- Davidson County SO
- Sheriff Daron Hall
  PO Box 196383
  Nashville, TN 37201
  (615) 862-8170
  dhall@dcso.nashville.org
- Goodlettsville PD
- Chief Gary Goodwin
  105 So. Main St.
  Goodlettsville, TN 37072
  (615) 851-2220
  ggoodwin@cityofgoodlettsville.org
- Nashville PD
- Chief Steve Anderson
  200 James Robertson Pkwy
  Nashville, TN 37201
  (615) 862-7301
  chiefofpolice@nashville.gov

Decatur County

- Decatur County SO
- Sheriff Roy Wyatt
  138 E. Main St. PO Box 427
  Decaturville, TN 38329
  (731) 852-3703
  rwyatt1@netease.net
- Parsons PD
- Chief Dale King
  66 W. 2nd St.
  Parsons, TN 38363
  (731) 847-6358
  admin@cityofparsons.com
- Scotts Hill PD
- Chief David Alexander
  110 Hwy 114 So.
  Scotts Hill, TN 38374
  (731) 549-3175
  info@cityofscottshill.com

DeKalb County

- DeKalb County SD
- Sheriff Patrick R. Ray
  100 Public Sq.
  Smithville, TN 37166
  (615) 597-4935, ext. 7
  sheriffray@gmail.com

Dickson County

- Dickson County SO
- Sheriff Jeff Bledsoe
  140 County Jail PO Box 177
  Charlotte, TN 37036
  (615) 740-4841
  sheriff@dicksoncounty.net
- Dickson PD
- Dir. Ricky Chandler
  202 So. Main St.
  Dickson, TN 37055
  (615) 446-5403
  rchandler@dicksonpd.org

Dyer County

- Dyer County SO
- Sheriff Jeff Box
  401 E. Cedar St.
  Dyersburg, TN 38025-4705
  (731) 285-2802
  SHERIFF@CO.DYER.TN.US
- Dyersburg PD
- Chief Arthur *Art* Heun
  425 W. Market St.
  Dyersburg, TN 38024
  (731) 285-1212
  aheun@dyersburgtn.gov

Fayette County

- Fayette County SO
- Sheriff Bobby Riles
  705 Justice Dr. PO Box 219
  Somerville, TN 38068
  (901) 465-3456
  briles@fayettecountysheriff.org

Fentress County

- Fentress County SO
- Sheriff Anthony *Tony* Choate
  100 So. Smith St. PO Box 730
  Jamestown, TN 38556
  (931) 879-8142
  FENTRESSCOUNTYSHERIFF@LYCOS.COM

Franklin County

- Franklin County SD
- Sheriff Tim G. Fuller
  420 Wilton Cir.
  Winchester, TN 37398
  (931) 962-0123
  Fuller@fcsheriff.org
- Cowan PD
- Chief Robert Reynolds
  106 No. Cherry St.
  Cowan, TN 37318
  (931) 962-0110
  recordersherman@bellsouth.net
- Estill Springs PD
- Chief Allen Rhodes
  PO Drawer 100
  Estill Springs, TN 37330
  (931) 649-5188
  chiefrhodes@estillspringspd.org
- Huntland PD
- Chief John Oalmann
  100 Cumberland PO Drawer H
  Huntland, TN 37345
  (931) 469-7702
  HuntlandPD@gmail.com
- Winchester PD
- Chief Dennis Young
  401 2nd Ave. SW
  Winchester, TN 37398
  (931) 967-3840
  dennisyoung@winchester-tn.com

Gibson County

- Gibson County SO
- Sheriff Charles W. *Chuck* Arnold
  301 No. College St.
  Trenton, TN 38382
  (731) 855-1121
  sheriffarnold@gibsonsheriff.com
- Dyer PD
- Chief Brad Lindsey
  793 So. Main St.
  Dyer, TN 38330
  (731) 692-2843
  blindsey@cityofdyertn.com
- Medina PD
- Chief Chad Lowery
  201 Hwy 45 E No. PO Box 420
  Medina, TN 38355
  (731) 783-1437
  clowery00@click1.net
- Milan PD
- Chief Tim Wright
  7029 Telecom Dr.
  Milan, TN 38358
  (731) 686-3309
  twright@cityofmilantn.com
- Trenton PD
- Chief William F. Sanders
  309 College St.
  Trenton, TN 38382
  (731) 855-1413
  trentonpd@bellsouth.com

Giles County

- Giles County SD
- Sheriff Kyle Helton
  200 Thomas Gatlin Dr.
  Pulaski, TN 38478
  (931) 363-3505
  sheriff.helton@gilessd.com
- Pulaski PD
- Chief John Reynolds
  203 So. 1st St.
  Pulaski, TN 38478
  (931) 424-4404
  plskpdps@bellsouth.net

Grainger County

- Grainger County SD
- Sheriff Scott Layel
  270 Justice Center Dr., Ste. 105
  Rutledge, TN 37861
  (865) 828-3613
  gcsd601@gmail.com

Greene County

- Greene County SD
- Sheriff Steve Burns
  116 E. Depot St.
  Greeneville, TN 37743
  (423) 798-1800
  GCSD1@COMCAST.NET
- Greeneville PD
- Chief Terry Cannon
  200 No. College St.
  Greeneville, TN 37745
  (423) 639-7111
  info@greenevillepd.org

Grundy County

- Grundy County SD
- Sheriff D. Brent Myers
  62 Spring St.
  Altamont, TN 37301
  (931) 692-3466
  grundysheriff@hotmail.com

Hamblen County

- Hamblen County SO
- Sheriff Esco R. Jarnagin
  510 Allison St.
  Morristown, TN 37814
  (423) 585 2770
  ejarnagin@co.hamblen.tn.us
- Morristown PD
- Chief Roger D. Overholt
  100 W. 1st No. St.
  Morristown, TN 37816
  (423) 585-2710
  dlamb@mymorristown.com

Hamilton County

- Hamilton County SO
- Sheriff James W. *Jim* Hammond III
  600 Market St.
  Chattanooga, TN 37402
  (423) 209-7000
  jhammond@hcsheriff.gov
- Chattanooga PD
- Chief Bobby H. Dodd
  3200 Amnicola Hwy
  Chattanooga, TN 37406
  (423) 698-2525
  mayor@chattanooga.gov
- East Ridge PD
- Chief Eddie Phillips
  4214 Ringgold Rd.
  East Ridge, TN 37412
  (423) 867-7516
  ephillips@eastridgepd.org
- Lookout Mountain PD
- Town Marshal/Chief Randall Bowden
  710 Scenic Hwy
  Lookout Mountain, TN 37350
  (423) 821-3151
  chief@lookoutmountaintn.org
- Signal Mountain PD
- Chief Boyd Veal
  1111 Ridgeway Ave.
  Signal Mountain, TN 37377
  (423) 886-2123
  bveal@signalmountaintn.gov

Hancock County

- Hancock County SO
- Sheriff Leamon Maxey
  265 New Jail St.
  Sneedville, TN 37869
  (423) 733-2250
  hancockcoso@yahoo.com

Hardeman County

- Hardeman County SO
- Sheriff John Kevin Doolen
  315 E. Market St.
  Bolivar, TN 38008
  (731) 658-3971, ext. 26
  doolen2010@yahoo.com
- Whiteville PD
- Chief Steven Stanley
  158 Main St. PO Box 324
  Whiteville, TN 38075
  (731) 254-9450
  stevenstanley@townofwhiteville.com

Hardin County

- Hardin County SO
- Sheriff Sammy Davidson
  525 Water St.
  Savannah, TN 38372
  (901) 925-3377
  elisa4232000@yahoo.com

Hawkins County

- Hawkins County SD
- Sheriff Ronnie Lawson
  117 Justice Center Dr., Ste. 1304
  Rogersville, TN 37857
  (423) 272-4848
  SHERIFF.LAWSON@HAWKINSCOUNTYTN.GOV
- Church Hill PD
- Chief Mark Johnson
  PO Box 366
  Church Hill, TN 37642
  (423) 357-7181
  chpdtips@churchhilltn.gov
- Mt. Carmel PD
- Chief Jeff Jackson
  100 E. Main St.
  Mt. Carmel, TN 37645
  (423) 357-4141
  fop1@chartertn.net

Haywood County

- Haywood County SD
- Sheriff Melvin Bond
  100 So. Dupree Ave.
  Brownsville, TN 38012
  (731) 772-6158
  TNHCSD@YAHOO.COM
- Brownsville PD
- Chief Chris Lea
  118 No. Lafayette PO Box 375
  Brownsville, TN 38012
  (901) 772-1260
  contactus@brownsvilletn.gov

Henderson County

- Henderson County SD
- Sheriff Brian Duke
  170 Justice Dr., Ste. C
  Lexington, TN 38351
  (731) 968-7777
  BDUKE@HCSDTN.COM
- Lexington PD
- Chief Roger Loftin
  88 1st St.
  Lexington, TN 38351
  (731) 968-6666
  roger.loftin@lexingtontn.gov
- Scotts Hill PD
- Chief David Alexander
  110 Hwy 114 So.
  Scotts Hill, TN 38374
  (731) 549-3175
  info@cityofscottshill.com

Henry County

- Henry County SO
- Sheriff Monte Belew
  210 Forrest Heights
  Paris, TN 38242
  (731) 642-1672
  sheriff@henrycountysheriff.org
- Paris PD
- Chief Charles Elizondo
  100 No. Caldwell St.
  Paris, TN 38242
  (731) 642-2424
  celizondo@cityofparistn.gov

Hickman County

- Hickman County SO
- Sheriff Randal Ward
  108 College St.
  Centerville, TN 37033
  (931) 729-6143
  sheriff@hickmanco.com
- 21st Jud. Dist. Drug Task Force
- Dir. Joey D. Kimble
  (Hickman, Lewis, Perry & Williamson counties)
  PO Box 1473
  Franklin, TN 37065-1473
  (615) 790-2691
  21dtf@drugtaskforce.net

Houston County

- Houston County SO
- Sheriff Darrell R. Allison
  3330 Hwy 149
  Erin, TN 37061
  (931) 289-4614
  sheriffhcso@gmail.com

Humphreys County

- Humphreys County SO
- Sheriff Chris Davis
  112 Thompson St.
  Waverly, TN 37185
  (931) 296-2301
  cdavis@humphreyscosheriff.com
- McEwen PD
- Chief John Ethridge
  9586 Hwy 70 E. PO Box 236
  McEwen, TN 37101
  (931 582-6922
  mcewenpd@mcewen.net

- New Johnsonville PD
- Chief Wayne Ellison
  323 Long St.
  New Johnsonville, TN 37134
  (931) 535-2700
  njmayor@tds.net

Jackson County
- Jackson County SD
- Sheriff Brad Stafford
  620 Hospital Dr.
  Gainesboro, TN 38562
  (931) 268-6226
  bstafford_44@yahoo.com

Jefferson County
- Jefferson County SD
- Sheriff G.W. Bud McCoig
  765 Justice Center PO Box 915
  Dandridge, TN 37725
  (865) 397-9411
  gwmccoig@jeffersoncountytn.gov
- Dandridge PD
- Chief Carson Williams
  425 E. Meeting St.
  Dandridge, TN 37725
  (865) 397-8862, ext. 25
  townofdandridge.bmccarter@yahoo.com
- White Pine PD
- Chief Charles Epps
  1824 Maple St.
  White Pine, TN 37890
  (865) 674-2555
  info@whitepinetn.com

Johnson County
- Johnson County SO
- Sheriff William M. Reece
  999 Honeysuckle St.
  Mountain City, TN 37683
  (423) 727-8353
  sheriff@johnsoncountysd.org

Knox County
- Knox County SO
- Sheriff Jimmy *J.J.* Jones
  400 Main Ave.
  Knoxville, TN 37902
  (865) 971-3901
  jj@knowsheriff.org

Lake County
- Lake County SO
- Sheriff Bryan K. Avery
  109 So. Court St.
  Tiptonville, TN 38079
  (731) 253-7791
  LCSOAVERY48@YAHOO.COM

Lauderdale County
- Lauderdale County SO
- Sheriff Steve Sanders
  675 Hwy 51 So . PO Box 30
  Ripley, TN 38063
  (731) 635-1311
  ssanderslcso@yahoo.com
- Halls PD
- Chief Ricky DeSpain
  102 So. Front St.
  Halls, TN 38040
  (731) 836-1016
  halls_pd@bellsouth.net
- Ripley PD
- Chief Jerry Temple
  110 So. Washington St.
  Ripley, TN 38063
  (731) 635-1515
  jtemple@ripleypolice.com

Lawrence County
- Lawrence County SO
- Sheriff Jimmy Brown
  240 W. Gaines
  Lawrenceburg, TN 38464
  (931) 762-3626, ext. 4167
  jbrown@lawcosheriff.com

Lewis County
- Lewis County SO
- Sheriff Dwayne Kilpatrick
  437 Swan Ave.
  Hohenwald, TN 38462
  (615) 796-5096
  lcsd02@hotmail.com
- 21st Jud. Dist. Drug Task Force
- Dir. Joey D. Kimble
  (Hickman, Lewis, Perry & Williamson counties)
  PO Box 1473
  Franklin, TN 37065-1473
  (615) 790-2691
  21dtf@drugtaskforce.net

- Hohenwald PD
- Chief Larry Joe Hinson
  118 W. Linden PO Box 40
  Hohenwald, TN 38462
  (615) 796-2231
  citymayor@hohenwald.com

Lincoln County

- Lincoln County SD
- Sheriff Murray Blackwelder
  4151 Thornton Taylor Pkwy
  Fayetteville, TN 37334
  (931) 433-9821
  lcsd501@yahoo.com
- Fayetteville PD
- Chief Doug Carver
  308 W. Market St.
  Fayetteville, TN 37334
  (931) 438-7771
  dcarver@fayettevilletn.com

Loudon County

- Loudon County SO
- Sheriff Tim W. Guider
  12680 Hwy 11 W., Ste. 1
  Lenoir City, TN 37771
  (865) 986-4823
  tguider@loudoncountysheriff.org
- Lenoir City PD
- Chief Don White
  600 E. Broadway PO Box 445
  Lenoir City, TN 37771
  (865) 986-2005
  jfine@lenoircitygov.com
- Loudon PD
- Chief James C. *Bear* Webb
  100 Cedar St.
  Loudon, TN 37774
  (865) 458-4423
  jameswebb@loudonpd.com

Macon County

- Macon County SO
- Sheriff Mark Gammons
  902 Hwy 52 Bypass E.
  Lafayette, TN 37083
  (615) 666-3325
  MCSOSHERIFF@NCTC.COM

Madison County

- Madison County SO
- Sheriff David L. Woolfork
  546 E. College St.
  Jackson, TN 38301
  (731) 423-6000
  dwoolfrk@bellsouth.net
- Jackson PD
- Chief Gill Kendrick
  234 Institute St.
  Jackson, TN 38301
  (731) 425-8466
  gkendrick@cityofjackson.net

Marion County

- Marion County SD
- Sheriff Ronnie Burnett
  5 No. Oak St.
  Jasper, TN 37347
  (423) 942-2525
  ronnieburnett@marioncosheriff.com
- Kimball PD
- Chief Tommy Jordan
  675 Main St.
  Kimball, TN 37347
  (423) 837-7554
  tjordan@townofkimball.com
- South Pittsburg PD
- Chief Dale Winters
  205 Elm Ave.
  South Pittsburg, TN 37380
  (423) 837-5003
  sppd200@yahoo.com
- Whitwell PD
- Chief Rodney Easterly
  13671 Hwy 28
  Whitwell, TN 37397
  (423) 658-5151
  cityrcd.whitwell@att.net

Marshall County

- Marshall County SO
- Sheriff Norman W. Dalton
  209 1st Ave. No.
  Lewisburg, TN 37091
  (931) 359-6122
  n.dalton@marshalltn.com
- Lewisburg PD
- Chief Chuck Forbis
  101 Water St.
  Lewisburg, TN 37091
  (931) 359-4044
  lpd@cityoflew.com

Maury County

- Maury County SO
- Sheriff Enoch R. George
  1300 Lawson White Dr.
  Columbia, TN 38401
  (931) 375-8601
  lwray@maurycounty-tn.gov

- Columbia PD
- Chief Tim Potts
  800 Westover Dr.
  Columbia, TN 38401
  (931) 388-2727
  dean.dickey@columbiatn.com
- Mt. Pleasant PD
- Chief Tommy G. Goetz
  100 Public Sq.
  Mt. Pleasant, TN 38474
  (615) 379-3201
  tgoetz@mountpleasanttn.org
- Spring Hill PD
- Chief Don Brite
  199 Town Center Pkwy
  Spring Hill, TN 37174
  (See also Williamson County)
  (888) 774-8988, ext. 244
  dmcdaniel@springhilltn.org

McMinn County

- McMinn County SO
- Sheriff Joe Guy
  1319 So. White PO Box 649
  Athens, TN 37303
  (423) 745-5620
  MCMINNCOUNTYSHERIFF@GMAIL.COM
- Athens PD
- Chief Charles T. Ziegler
  815 No. Jackson St.
  Athens, TN 37371
  (423) 745-3687
  cziegler@cityofathenstn.com
- Englewood PD
- Chief Darrell Wright
  103-B So. Niota PO Box 150
  Englewood, TN 37329
  (423) 887-6801
  town@townofenglewood.com
- Etowah PD
- Chief Eric Armstrong
  126 8th St.
  Etowah, TN 37331
  (423) 263-5851
  armstrong@cityofetowahtn.com
- Niota PD
- Chief June Parham
  201 E. Main St.
  Niota, TN 37826
  (423) 568-2584
  loispreece@tds.net

McNairy County

- McNairy County SO
- Sheriff Guy Buck
  300 Industrial Park Dr.
  Selmer, TN 38375
  (731) 645-1004
  SHERIFFGUYBUCK@GMAIL.COM

Meigs County

- Meigs County SO
- Sheriff Jackie Melton
  410 River Rd.
  Decatur, TN 37322
  (423) 334-5268
  JMELTON@MEIGSCOUNTYSHERIFF.COM
- Decatur PD
- Chief Monty Rowland
  116 No. Main St. PO Box 188
  Decatur, TN 37322
  (423) 334-5716
  laurasmith@decaturtn.net

Monroe County

- Monroe County SO
- Sheriff Bill Bivens
  319 Hickory St.
  Madisonville, TN 37354
  (423) 423-442-3911, ext. 11
  bbivens56@yahoo.com
- Sweetwater PD
- Chief Robert E. Byrum
  PO Box 267
  Sweetwater, TN 37874
  (423) 337-6151
  jscruggs@sweetwatertn.net

Montgomery County

- Montgomery County SO
- Sheriff John Fuson
  120 Commerce St.
  Clarksville, TN 37040
  (931) 648-0611, ext. 1101
  JSFUSON@MCGTN.NET
- Clarksville PD
- Chief Al Rivers Ansley
  135 Commerce St.
  Clarksville, TN 37040
  (931) 648-0656
  mmackens@clarksvillepd.org

Moore County

- Moore County SD
- Sheriff Mark Logan
  58 So. Elm St.
  Lynchburg, TN 37352
  (931) 759-7323
  mcsd5590@yahoo.com

Morgan County

- Morgan County SD
- Sheriff Glen Freytag
  414 Main St. PO Box 469
  Wartburg, TN 37887
  (423) 346-6262
  gfreytagmcso@highland.net

Obion County

- Obion County SO
- Sheriff Jerry Vastbinder
  1 Law Ln.
  Union City, TN 38261
  (731) 885-5832
  sheriff@obioncountysheriff.com
- Obion PD
- Chief Royce Aker
  PO Box 547
  Obion, TN 38240
  (731) 536-6242
  dispatch@obionpolice.com
- Troy PD
- Chief James Cleek
  106 Westbrook St.
  Troy, TN 38260
  (901) 536-4342
  mwtfd@troytn.com

Overton County

- Overton County SO
- Sheriff W.B. Melton
  1010 John T. Poindexter Dr.
  Livingston, TN 38570
  (931) 823-5635
  SHERIFFCAR1@HOTMAIL.COM

Perry County

- Perry County SO
- Sheriff Tommy Hickerson
  582 Bethel Rd.
  Linden, TN 37096
  (931) 589-8803
  thickersonpcsd@tds.net
- 21st Jud. Dist. Drug Task Force
- Dir. Joey D. Kimble
  (Hickman, Lewis, Perry & Williamson counties)
  PO Box 1473
  Franklin, TN 37065-1473
  (615) 790-2691
  21dtf@drugtaskforce.net

Pickett County

- Pickett County SO
- Sheriff Dana Dowdy
  1 Courthouse Sq., Ste. 300
  Byrdstown, TN 38549
  (931) 864-3210
  pcsheriff@twlakes.net

Polk County

- Polk County SO
- Sheriff Bill Davis
  164 Industrial Access Cir.
  Benton, TN 37307
  (423) 338-4543
  polkcountysotn@yahoo.com

Putnam County

- Putnam County SD
- Sheriff David Andrews
  421 E. Spring St.
  Cookeville, TN 38501
  (931) 528-8484
  sheriffdkandrews@putnamco.org
- Algood PD
- Chief Jim Eldridge
  110 W. Main St.
  Algood, TN 38506
  (931) 537-6830, ext. 224
  algoodpd@frontiernet.net
- Baxter PD
- Chief Danny Holmes
  200 Main St. PO Box 335
  Baxter, TN 38544
  (931) 858-4111, ext. 2
  baxterpolice@twlakes.net

Rhea County

- Rhea County SD
- Sheriff Mike Neal
  444 2nd Ave.
  Dayton, TN 37321
  (423) 775-7837
  mneal@rheacountytn.gov

- Dayton PD
- Chief Chris Sneed
  1191 So Market St. PO Box 226
  Dayton, TN 37321
  (423) 775-8403
  daytonbm@bellsouth.net
- Graysville PD
- Chief Erik Redden
  136 Harrison Ave.
  Graysville, TN 37338-5044
  (423) 775-0173
  redden.erik@graysvilletn.org
- Spring City PD
- Chief Jason Yuhas
  229 Front St PO Box 369
  Spring City, TN 37381
  (423) 365-6225
  CityManager@townofspringcitytn.org

Roane County

- Roane County SO
- Sheriff Jack Stockton
  300 No. 3rd St. PO Box 623
  Kingston, TN 37763
  (865) 376-5582
  jstockton@roanegov.org
- Harriman PD
- Chief Randy Heidle
  130 Pansy Hill Rd. PO Drawer 433
  Harriman, TN 37748
  (865) 882-3585
  mayormason@comcast.net
- Kingston PD
- Chief Jim Washam
  125 Cumberland
  Kingston, TN 37763
  (865) 376-2081
  troybeets@bellsouth.net
- 9th Judicial District
- DA Russell Johnson
  Drug & Violent Crime Task Force
  1008 Bradford Way, Ste. 300
  Kingston, TN 37763
  (865) 376-3599
  lrjohnson@tndagc.org

Robertson County

- Robertson County SD
- Sheriff Bill Holt
  507 So. Brown St.
  Springfield, TN 37172
  (615) 384-7971
  sheriffholt@robertsonsheriff.com
- Coopertown PD
- Chief Shane Sullivan
  2525 Burgess Gower Rd.
  Springfield, TN 37172
  (615) 382-4470
  coopertownpd@charterinternet.com
- Springfield PD
- Chief David Thompson
  802 Willow St.
  Springfield, TN 37172
  (615) 384-8422
  police@Springfield-tn.org

Rutherford County

- Rutherford County SO
- Sheriff Robert Franklin Arnold
  940 New Salem Rd.
  Murfreesboro, TN 37129
  (615) 898-7770
  RARNOLD@RUTHERFORDCOUNTYTN.GOV
- Murfreesboro PD
- Chief Glenn Chrisman
  302 So. Church St.
  Murfreesboro, TN 37130
  (615) 893-1311
  gchrisman@ci.murfreesboro.tn.us
- Smyrna PD
- Chief Kevin Arnold
  315 So. Lowry St.
  Smyrna, TN 37167
  (615) 459-9742, ext. 2385
  kevin.arnold@townofsmyrna.org

Scott County

- Scott County SO
- Sheriff Michael D. *Mike* Cross
  575 Scott High Dr.
  Huntsville, TN 37756
  (423) 663-3111
  mike.cross@scottcounty.com
- Oneida PD
- Chief Daryl Laxton
  121 Municipal Dr.
  Oneida, TN 37841
  (423) 569-4255
  contact@townofoneida.com

Sequatchie County

- Sequatchie County SO
- Sheriff Ronnie Hitchcock
  351A Fredonia Rd.
  Dunlap, TN 37327
  (423) 949-7750, ext. 103
  RHITCH600@YAHOO.COM

Sevier County

- Sevier County SO
- Sheriff Ronald Seals
  106 W. Bruce St.
  Sevierville, TN 37862
  (865) 453-4668
  RSEALS@SEVIERCOUNTYTN.ORG
- Pigeon Forge PD
- Chief Jack H. Baldwin
  225 Pine Mountain PO Box 1350
  Pigeon Forge, TN 37868
  (865) 453-9063
  pd@cityofpigeonforge.com
- Sevierville PD
- Chief Don Myers
  300 Gary Wade Blvd
  Sevierville, TN 37862
  (865) 453-5506
  donm@seviervilletn.org

Shelby County

- Shelby County SO
- Sheriff Bill Oldham
  201 Poplar Ave., 9th Fl.
  Memphis, TN 38103
  (901) 222-5505
  bill.oldham@shelby-sheriff.org
- Bartlett PD
- Chief Gary Rikard
  3730 Appling Rd.
  Bartlett, TN 38133
  (901) 385- 5529, ext. 324
  grikard@bartlettpolice.org
- Collierville PD
- Chief Larry Goodwin
  156 No. Rowlett St.
  Collierville, TN 38017
  (901) 457-2500
  colliervillepd@ci.collierville.tn.us
- Germantown PD
- Chief Richard L. Hall
  1930 So. Germantown Rd.
  Germantown, TN 38183
  (901) 757-7300
  rhall@germantown-tn.gov
- Memphis PD
- Dir. Toney Armstrong
  201 Poplar Ave., 12th Fl.
  Memphis, TN 38103
  (901) 636-3700
  mpd@memphispolice.org
- Millington PD
- Chief Rita Stanback
  7950 Memphis Ave., Ste. 1
  Millington, TN 38053
  (901) 872.3333
  rstanback@millingtonpolice.org

Smith County

- Smith County SO
- Sheriff Steve Hopper
  322 Justice Dr.
  Carthage, TN 37030
  (615) 735-2626
  SHOPPER17@YAHOO.COM

Stewart County

- Stewart County SO
- Sheriff Deryk O. Wyatt
  117 Donelson PO Box 69
  Dover, TN 37058
  (615) 232-5322
  d.wyatt@mchsi.com

Sullivan County

- Sullivan County SO
- Sheriff Wayne Anderson
  140 Blountville Bypass
  Blountville, TN 37617
  (423) 279-6064
  JWAYNE@SCSOTN.COM
- Bluff City PD
- Chief Greg Depew
  661 Railroad St. PO Box 70
  Bluff City, TN 37618
  (423) 538-3700
  bluffcitycityof@aol.com
- Bristol PD
- Chief Blaine E. Wade
  801 Anderson St.
  Bristol, TN 37620
  (423) 989-5600
  bwade@bristoltn.org
- Kingsport PD
- Chief Gale Osborne
  200 Shelby St.
  Kingsport, TN 37660
  (423) 229-9423
  contact@kingsporttn.gov

Sumner County

- Sumner County SO
- Sheriff Roy *Sonny* Weatherford
  117 W. Smith St.
  Gallatin, TN 37066
  (615) 452-2616
  SWEATHERFORD@SUMNERSHERIFF.COM

- Gallatin PD
- Chief Donald W. Bandy
  130 W. Franklin St.
  Gallatin, TN 37066
  (615) 452-1313
  info@gallatinpd.org
- Hendersonville PD
- Chief Mickey Miller
  3 Executive Park Dr.
  Hendersonville, TN 37075
  (615) 822-1111
  mickeymiller@hendersonville-pd.org
- Millersville PD
- Chief Ronnie Williams
  1246 Louisville Hwy
  Millersville, TN 37072
  (615) 859-2758
  policechief@cityofmillersville.com
- Portland PD
- Chief Richard Smith
  433 No. Broadway
  Portland, TN 37148
  (615) 325-2061
  rsmithppd@cityofportlandtn.gov

Tipton County

- Tipton County SO
- Sheriff J.T. *Pancho* Chumley
  1801 So. College St., Ste. 106
  Covington, TN 38019
  (901) 475-3300
  sheriff@tiptonco.com
- Covington PD
- Chief Bennie Carver
  133 E. Pleasant
  Covington, TN 38019
  (901) 476-0243
  contactus@covingtontn.com
- Munford PD
- Chief Jim Harger
  1397 Munford Ave.
  Munford, TN 38058
  (901) 837-0171
  Jharger@munford.com

Trousdale County

- Trousdale County SO
- Sheriff Ray Russell
  315 E. Main St.
  Hartsville, TN 37074
  (615) 374-2114
  Trousdalesheriff@bellsouth.net

Unicoi County

- Unicoi County SD
- Sheriff Michael Hensley
  102 No. Main PO Box 8
  Erwin, TN 37650
  (423) 743-1890
  sheriff@unicoicountytn.gov
- Erwin PD
- Chief Regan Tilson
  211 No. Main PO Box 59
  Erwin, TN 37650
  (423) 743-1871
  erwintnpdcid@comcast.net

Union County

- Union County SO
- Sheriff Earl Loy, Jr.
  130 Veterans St., Ste. B
  Maynardville, TN 37807
  (865) 992-5212
  CHRISTI@UNIONCOUNTYTN.ORG

Van Buren County

- Van Buren County SO
- Sheriff Barney Evans
  17 Veterans Sq.
  Spencer, TN 38585
  (931) 946-2118
  sheriff@vanburentn-sheriff.com

Warren County

- Warren County SO
- Sheriff Jackie Matheny
  108 Security Cir.
  McMinnville, TN 37110
  (931) 473-7863
  wcso@blomand.net
- McMinnville PD
- Chief Bryan Denton
  204 Red Rd. PO Box 7088
  McMinnville, TN 37110
  (931) 473-3808
  bdenton@mcminnvillepd.com

Washington County

- Washington County SO
- Sheriff Ed Graybeal
  112 W. Jackson Blvd
  Jonesborough, TN 37659
  (423) 788-1479
  sheriffgraybeal@wcso.net

- Johnson City PD
- Chief Mark Sirois
  601 E. Main St.
  Johnson City, TN 37605
  (423) 434-6160
  sstevens@johnsoncitytn.org
- Jonesborough PD
- Chief Matt Hawkins
  123 Boone St.
  Jonesborough, TN 37659
  (423) 753-1053
  terryajb@embarqmail.com

Wayne County

- Wayne County SO
- Sheriff Ric Wilson
  1016 Andrew Jackson Dr., Ste. 101
  Waynesboro, TN 38485
  (931) 722-3615
  SHERIFFWILSON@WAYNETNSO.COM
- Collinwood PD
- Chief David Martin
  108 3rd Ave. No. PO Box 98
  Collinwood, TN 38450
  (931) 724-9227
  martind@cityofcollinwood.org
- Waynesboro PD
- Act. Chief (*Sgt.*) Seth Norris
  PO Box 471
  Waynesboro, TN 38485
  (931) 722-5458
  snorris@cityofwaynesboro.org

Weakley County

- Weakley County SO
- Sheriff Michael A. Wilson
  PO Box 545
  Dresden, TN 38225
  (731) 364-5454
  wilson11@frontiernet.net
- Dresden PD
- Chief Randal Walker
  117 W. Main St.
  Dresden, TN 38225
  (731) 364-2270
  dresdenmayor@frontier.com
- Greenfield PD
- Chief Danny Harris
  222 No. Front St.
  Greenfield, TN 38230
  (731) 235-2330
  cityofgreenfield@charter.net
- Martin PD
- Chief David B. Moore
  101 University St.
  Martin, TN 38237
  (731) 587-5355, ext. 221
  dbmoore@martindps.org

White County

- White County SO
- Sheriff Oddie J. Shoupe
  111 Depot St.
  Sparta, TN 38583
  (931) 836-2700
  WHITECOUNTY5900@HOTMAIL.COM
- Sparta PD
- Chief Jeff Guth
  323 E. Bockman Way
  Sparta, TN 38583
  (615) 836-3734
  spdchief@blomand.net

Williamson County

- Williamson County SO
- Sheriff Jeff Long
  408 Century Ct.
  Franklin, TN 37064
  (615) 790-5560
  jeffl@williamson-tn.org
- 21st Jud. Dist. Drug Task Force
- Dir. Joey D. Kimble
  (Hickman, Lewis, Perry & Williamson counties)
  PO Box 1473
  Franklin, TN 37065-1473
  (615) 790-2691
  21dtf@drugtaskforce.net
- Brentwood PD
- Chief Jeff Hughes
  5211 Maryland Way
  Brentwood, TN 37024
  (615) 371-0160
  hughesj@brentwood-tn.org
- Fairview PD
- Chief Terry Harris
  7100 City Center Way
  Fairview, TN 37062
  (615) 799-2431
  policechief@fairview-tn.org
- Franklin PD
- Chief David Rahinsky
  900 Columbia Ave.
  Franklin, TN 37064
  (615) 791-3246
  david.rahinsky@franklintn.gov

- Spring Hill PD
- Chief Don Brite
  199 Town Center Pkwy
  Spring Hill, TN 37174
  (See also Maury County)
  (888) 774-8988, ext. 244
  dmcdaniel@springhilltn.org

Wilson County

- Wilson County SO
- Sheriff Robert Bryan
  105 E. High St.
  Lebanon, TN 37087
  (615) 444-1412
  robertbryan@wcso95.org
- Lebanon PD
- Chief Scott Bowen
  406 Tennessee Blvd
  Lebanon, TN 37087
  (615) 444-2323
  philipcraighead@lebanontn.org
- Mt. Juliet PD
- Chief James Hambrick, Ph.D.
  2425 No. Mt. Juliet Rd.
  Mt. Juliet, TN 37122
  (615) 754-2552
  jhambrick@cityofmtjuliet.org
- Watertown PD
- Chief Joe Hall
  160A So. Statesville Ave.
  Watertown, TN 37184
  (615) 237-3325
  CHIEF@WatertownTN.com

State Agencies

- TN Highway Patrol-HQ
- Col. Tracy Trott
  1150 Foster Ave.
  Nashville, TN 37243
  (615) 251-5175
  email.safety@tn.gov
- East TN State U. DPS
- Dir. Jack R. Cotrel
  Box 70646
  Johnson City, TN 37614
  (423) 439-6900
  cotrel@etsu.edu
- U. TN-Martin DPS
- Dir. Scott Robbins
  215 Hurt St.
  Martin, TN 38238
  (731) 881-7777
  sdrobbins@utm.edu
- Vanderbilt U. PD
- Chief August J. Washington
  111 28th Ave So.
  Nashville, TN 37212
  (615) 343-9750
  august.j.washington@vanderbilt.edu

VERMONT

Addison County

- Addison County SO
- Sheriff Donald M. Keeler, Jr.
  35 Court St.
  Middlebury, VT 05753
  (802) 388-2981
  info@vtacsd.com
- Bristol PD
- Chief Kevin Gibbs
  1 South St.
  Bristol, VT 05443
  (802) 453-2533
  kgibbs@dps.state.vt.us
- Middlebury PD
- Chief Thomas Hanley
  1 Lucius Shaw Ln.
  Middlebury, VT 05753
  (802) 388-3191
  thanley@middleburypolice.org
- Vergennes PD
- Chief George Merkel
  120 Main St.
  Vergennes, VT 05491
  (802) 877-2201
  gmerkel@dps.state.vt.us

Bennington County

- Bennington County SD
- Sheriff Chad D. Schmidt
  212 Lincoln St. PO Box 4207
  Bennington, VT 05201-4207
  (802) 442-1833
  chad.schmidt@state.vt.us
- Bennington PD
- Chief Paul J. Doucette
  118 South St.
  Bennington, VT 05201
  (802) 442-1030
  tcorcoran@benningtonvt.org
- Manchester PD
- Chief Michael Hall
  6041 Main St.
  Manchester, VT 05255
  (802) 362-2022
  michael.l.hall@state.vt.us

Caledonia County

- Caledonia County SO
- Sheriff Dean R. Shatney
  1126 Main St., Ste. 2
  St Johnsbury, VT 05819
  (802)748-6666
  info@caledoniasheriff.com
- Hardwick-Greensboro PD
- Chief Aaron Cochran
  20 Church St. PO Box 447
  Hardwick, VT 05843
  (802) 472-5475
  hardwickpolice@yahoo.com
- St. Johnsbury PD
- Chief Clement J. Houde
  1187 Main St., Ste. 1
  St. Johnsbury, VT 05819
  (802) 748-2314
  clementhoude@state.vt.us

Chittenden County

- Chittenden County SO
- Sheriff Kevin M. McLaughlin
  70 Ethan Allen Dr. PO Box 1426
  South Burlington, VT 05403
  (802) 863-4341
  rojamvt@aol.com
- Burlington PD
- Chief Michael E. Schirling
  1 North Ave.
  Burlington, VT 05401
  (802) 658-2700
  mschirling@bpdvt.org
- Colchester PD
- Chief Charles *Chuck* Kirker
  PO Box 37
  Colchester, VT 05446
  (802) 264-5540
  ckirker@dps.state.vt.us
- Essex PD
- Chief Brad Larose
  81 Main St.
  Essex Junction, VT 05452
  (802) 878-1335
  blarose@essex.org
- Milton PD
- Chief Brett Van Noordt
  37 Bombardier Rd.
  Milton, VT 05468
  (802) 893-6171
  bvannoordt@town.milton.vt.us
- South Burlington PD
- Chief Trevor Whipple
  37 Bombardier Rd.
  South Burlington, VT 05403
  (802) 846-4155
  twhipple@sbpdvt.org

- Williston PD
- Chief Todd C. Shepard
  7878 Williston Rd.
  Williston, VT 05495
  (802) 764-1152
  Todd.Shepard@State.Vt.Us
- Winooski PD
- Chief Steve McQueen
  27 W. Allen St.
  Winooski, VT 05404
  (802) 655-0221
  smcqueen@winooskipolice.com

Essex County

- Essex County SO
- Sheriff Trevor Colby
  91 Courthouse Dr.
  Guildhall, VT 05905
  (802) 676-3500
  crimestoppers@essexsheriff.com

Franklin County

- Franklin County SO
- Sheriff Robert W. Norris
  387 Lake Rd. PO Box 367
  St. Albans, VT 05478
  (802) 524-2121
  fcsosheriff@gmail.com
- St. Albans PD
- Chief Gary Taylor
  30 Lower Welden St.
  St. Albans, VT 05478
  (802) 524-2167
  gary.taylor@statc.vt.us
- Swanton PD
- Chief Leonard Stell
  120 1st St.
  Swanton, VT 05488
  (802) 868-4100
  leonard.stell@state.vt.us

Grand Isle County

- Grand Isle County SO
- Sheriff Ray Allen
  3677 US Rt. 2 PO Box 168
  North Hero, VT 05474
  (802) 372-4482
  clerk@town.grand-isle.vt.us

Lamoille County

- Lamoille County SD
- Sheriff Roger Marcoux Jr.
  PO Box 96
  Hyde Park, VT 05655
  (802) 888-3502
  david@hydeparkvt.com
- Stowe PD
- Chief Donald B. Hull
  350 So. Main St.
  Stowe, VT 05672
  (802) 253-7126
  donald.hull@state.vt.us

Orange County

- Orange County SD
- Sheriff Bill Bohnyak
  11 VT Rt. 113
  Chelsea, VT 05038
  (802) 685-4875
  sheriff@orangecountysheriff.com
- Randolph PD
- Chief James Krakowiecki
  6 Salisbury St. PO Drawer B
  Randolph, VT 05060
  (802) 728-3737
  manager@municipaloffice.randolph.vt.us
- Thetford PD
- Chief James Lanctot
  3910 Rt. 113 PO Box 126
  Thetford, VT 05075
  (802) 785-2200
  townclerk@thetfordvermont.us

Orleans County

- Orleans County SO
- Sheriff Kirk J. Martin
  5578 US Rt. 5 PO Box 355
  Derby, VT 05855
  (802) 334-3333
  bgs-commissioner@state.vt.us
- Hardwick-Greensboro PD
- Chief Aaron Cochran
  20 Church St. PO Box 447
  Hardwick, VT 05843
  (802) 472-5475
  hardwickpolice@yahoo.com
- Newport PD
- Chief Seth DiSanto
  222 Main St.
  Newport, VT 05855
  (802) 334-6733
  jo_ward@comcast.net

Rutland County

- Rutland County SO
- Sheriff Stephen P. Benard
  88 Grove St. PO Box 303
  Rutland, VT 05701
  (802) 775-8002
  sbenard@dps.state.vt.us

- Brandon PD
- Chief Christopher Brickell
  301 Forestdale Rd.
  Brandon, VT 05733
  (802) 247-0222
  christopher.brickell@state.vt.us
- Fair Haven PD
- Chief William Humphries
  3 No. Park Pl.
  Fair Haven, VT 05743
  (802) 265-3010
  William.Humphries@state.vt.us
- Rutland PD
- Chief James Baker
  108 Wales St.
  Rutland, VT 05701
  (802) 773-1820
  jbaker@dps.state.vt.us

Washington County

- Washington County SO
- Sheriff W. Samuel Hill
  10 Elm St. PO Box 678
  Montpelier, VT 05601
  (802) 223-3001
  bgs-commissioner@state.vt.us
- Barre PD
- Chief Timothy Bombardier
  15 4th St.
  Barre, VT 05641
  (802) 476-6613
  tbombard@dps.state.vt.us
- Montpelier PD
- Chief Anthony Facos
  1 Pitkin Ct.
  Montpelier, VT 05602
  (802) 223-3445
  afacos@montpelier-vt.org
- Northfield PD
- Int. Chief James Dziobek
  110 Wall St.
  Northfield, VT 05663
  (Mailing: 51 So. Main St.)
  (802) 485-9181
  Selectboard@northfield.vt.us
- Waterbury PD
- Chief Joby Feccia
  PO Box 9
  Waterbury, VT 05676
  (802) 244-7567
  joby.feccia@state.vt.us

Windham County

- Windham County SD
- Sheriff Keith Clark
  Rt. 30 PO Box 266
  Newfane, VT 05345
  (802) 365-4949
  kclark@windhamsheriff.com
- Bellows Falls PD
- Chief Ron Lake
  170 Rockingham St.
  Bellows Falls, VT 05101
  (802) 463-1234
  bfpdinfo@gmail.com
- Brattleboro PD
- Chief Eugene Wrinn
  230 Main St.
  Brattleboro, VT 05301
  (802) 257-2302
  bpd@sover.net
- Dover PD
- Chief Robert Edwards
  102 Rt. 100 PO Box 428
  W. Dover, VT 05356
  (802) 464-2020
  doverto@sover.net
- Wilmington PD
- Chief Joseph M. Szarejko
  2 E. Main St.
  Wilmington, VT 05363
  (802) 464-8593
  mail@wilmingtonvermont.us

Windsor County

- Windsor County SD
- Sheriff D. Michael Chamberlain
  62 Pleasant St. PO Box 478
  Woodstock, VT 05091
  (802) 457-5211
  windsor.sheriff@sas.state.vt.us
- Hartford PD
- Chief Leonard J. Roberts
  812 VA Cutoff Rd.
  White River Junction, VT 05001
  (802) 295-9425
  lroberts@hartford-vt.org
- Ludlow PD
- Chief Jeffrey P. Billings
  19 W. Hill
  Ludlow, VT 05149
  (802) 228-4411
  tmanager@ludlow.vt.us

- Norwich PD
- Chief Douglas A. *Doug* Robinson
  10 Hazen St.
  Norwich, VT 05055
  (802) 649-1460
  doug.robinson@state.vt.us
- Springfield PD
- Chief Douglas S. Johnston
  96 Main St.
  Springfield, VT 05156
  (802) 885-2112
  kmorris@lovejoytool.com
- Windsor PD
- Chief Stephen J. Soares
  29 Union St.
  Windsor, VT 05089
  (802) 674-9042
  Stephen.Soares@state.vt.us
- Woodstock PD
- Chief Robbie Blish
  Taftsville Rd.
  Woodstock, VT 05091
  (802) 457-1420
  VillageTrustees@townofwoodstock.org

State Agencies

- VT State Police-HQ
- Comm. Keith W. Flynn
  103 So. Main St.
  Waterbury, VT 05671
  (802) 244-8718
  kflynn@dps.state.vt.us

VIRGINIA

Accomack County**

- Accomack County SO
- Sheriff Todd E. Godwin
  23323 Wise Ct. PO Box 149
  Accomack, VA 23301
  (757) 787-1131
  toddgodwin@verizon.net
- Onancock PD
- Chief Eric Williams
  17 North St.
  Onancock, VA 23417
  (757) 787-8577
  onancock@esva.net

Albemarle County

- Albemarle County SO
- Sheriff J. E. Chip Harding
  411 E. High St., Bldg B
  Charlottesville, VA 22902
  (434) 972-4001
  jharding@albemarle.org
- Albemarle County PD
- Chief (*Col.*) Steve Sellers
  1600 5th St., Ste. D
  Charlottesville, VA 22902
  (434) 296-5807
  hintzc@albemarle.org

Alexandria City

- Alexandria (*City*) SO
- Sheriff Dana A. Lawhorne
  2003 Mill Rd.
  Alexandria, VA 22314
  (703) 838-4114
  dana.lawhorne@ci.alexandria.va.us
- Alexandria PD
- Chief Earl L. Cook
  2003 Mill Rd.
  Alexandria, VA 22314
  (703) 838-4444
  shawn.lasher@alexandriava.gov

Alleghany County

- Alleghany County SD
- Sheriff Kevin W. Hall
  268 W. Main St.
  Covington, VA 24426
  (540) 965-1770
  khallacso@ntelos.net

Amelia County

- Amelia County SO
- Sheriff Ricky L. Walker
  16441 Court St. PO Box 463
  Amelia, VA 23002
  (804) 561-2118
  rlwalker@ameliasheriff.org

Amherst County

- Amherst County SO
- Sheriff L. J. Ayers III
  115 Taylor St. PO Box 410
  Amherst, VA 24521
  (434) 946-9381
  ljayers@amherstsheriff.org

Appomattox County

- Appomattox County SO
- Sheriff Barry E. Letterman
  PO Box 366
  Appomattox, VA 24522
  (804) 352-8241
  barry.letterman@appomattoxcountyva.gov

Arlington County

- Arlington County SO
- Sheriff Beth Arthur
  1425 No. Courthouse Rd. #9100
  Arlington, VA 22201
  (703) 228-4460
  sheriff@arlingtonva.us
- Arlington County PD
- Chief M. Douglas Scott
  1425 No. Courthouse Rd.
  Arlington, VA 22201
  (703) 228-4040
  countymanager@arlingtonva.us

Augusta County

- Augusta County SO
- Sheriff Randall D. Fisher
  6 E. Johnson St. PO Box 860
  Staunton, VA 24401
  (540) 245-5333
  rfisher@co.augusta.va.us
- Craigsville PD
- Chief Kerry Kothbauer
  PO Box 237
  Craigsville, VA 24430
  (540) 997-5935
  craigsvilletowncop@yahoo.com

Bath County

- Bath County SO
- Sheriff Robert W. Plecker
  Courthouse Rd. PO Box 218
  Warm Springs, VA 24484
  (540) 839-2375
  bath.cosheriff@tds.net

Bedford County

- Bedford County SO
- Sheriff Michael J. Brown
  1345 Falling Creek Rd.
  Bedford, VA 24523
  (540) 586-4800
  bcso@co.bedford.va.us
- Bedford PD
- Chief James E. Day
  215 E. Main St.
  Bedford, VA 24523
  (540) 587-6011
  police@bedfordva.gov

Bland County

- Bland County SD
- Sheriff Jerry L. Thompson
  PO Box 449
  Bland, VA 24315
  (276) 688-4311
  jthompson40@embarqmail.com

Botetourt County

- Botetourt County SO
- Sheriff Ronald N. Sprinkle
  5 W. Main St. PO Box 18
  Fincastle, VA 24090
  (540) 473-8230
  rsprinkle@botetourt.org

Bristol City

- Bristol (*City*) SO
- Sheriff Jack Weisenburger
  417 Cumberland St.
  Bristol, VA 24201
  (540) 645-7430
  weisenburger@bvso.net
- Bristol PD
- Chief W.H. Price
  501 Scott St.
  Bristol, VA 24201
  (540) 645-7400
  bvacop@bristolva.org

Brunswick County

- Brunswick County SO
- Sheriff Brian K. Roberts
  PO Box 705
  Lawrenceville, VA 23868
  (804) 848-3133
  broberts@brunswickso.org
- Lawrenceville PD
- Chief Everette L. Gibson
  400 No. Main St.
  Lawrenceville, VA 23868
  (804) 848-2414
  elgibson@lawrencevilleweb.com

Buchanan County

- Buchanan County SO
- Sheriff C. Ray Foster
  PO Box 970
  Grundy, VA 24614
  (276) 935-2567
  sheriffray1@gmail.com

Buckingham County

- Buckingham County SO
- Sheriff W. G. *Billy* Kidd, Jr.
  PO Box 50
  Buckingham, VA 23921
  (434) 969-1772
  bkidd@buckinghamcounty.virginia.gov

Buena Vista City

- Buena Vista (*City*) SO
- Sheriff W. Randolph Hamilton, Jr.
  PO Box 1031
  Buena Vista, VA 24416
  (540) 261-8615
  rhamilton@bvcity.org
- Buena Vista PD
- Chief D.W. Slagle
  306 Park Ave.
  Buena Vista, VA 24416
  (540) 261-6174
  bv11@bvcity.org

Campbell County

- Campbell County SO
- Sheriff Steve A. Hutcherson
  87 Courthouse Ln. PO Box 280
  Rustburg, VA 24588
  (434) 332-9580
  sheriff@co.campbell.va.us

- Altavista PD
- Chief Clay Hamilton
  510 7th St.
  Altavista, VA 24517
  (434) 369-4488
  cwhamilton@ci.altavista.va.us
- Brookneal PD
- Chief Richard W. Baldwin
  215 Main St. PO Box 450
  Brookneal, VA 24528-0450
  (434) 376-2650
  chiefbaldwin@townofbrookneal.com

Caroline County

- Caroline County SO
- Sheriff Anthony A. *Tony* Lippa
  118 Courthouse PO Box 39
  Bowling Green, VA 22427
  (804) 633-1120
  sheriff@carolinesheriff.org

Carroll County

- Carroll County SO
- Sheriff John B. *J.B.* Gardner
  PO Box 575
  Hillsville, VA 24343
  (276) 728-4146
  jbgardner@carrollcountyva.org

Charles City County

- Charles City County SO
- Sheriff Javier J. Smith
  10600 Courthouse Rd. PO Box 87
  Charles City, VA 23030
  (804) 829-9265
  jsmith@co.charles-city.va.us

Charlottesville City

- Charlottesville (*City*) SO
- Sheriff James E. Brown III
  315-E. High St.
  Charlottesville, VA 22902-5118
  (434) 970-3777
  brownja@charlottesville.org
- Charlottesville PD
- Chief Timothy J. Longo, Sr.
  606 E. Market St.
  Charlottesville, VA 22901
  (434) 970-3280
  longo@charlottesville.org

Charlotte County

- Charlotte County SO
- Sheriff Thomas D. Jones
  222 Law Ln. PO Box 390
  Charlotte Courthouse, VA 23923
  (434) 542-5141
  sheriff.t.d.jones@gmail.com

Chesapeake City

- Chesapeake (*City*) SO
- Sheriff Jim O'Sullivan
  PO Box 15125
  Chesapeake, VA 23328
  (757) 382-6159
  josullivan@cityofchesapeake.net
- Chesapeake PD
- Chief (*Col.*) K.L. Wright
  304 Albemarle Dr. PO Box 15225
  Chesapeake, VA 23328-5225
  (757) 382-6404
  CPDOfficeoftheChief@CityofChesapeake.net

Chesterfield County

- Chesterfield County SO
- Sheriff Dennis S. Proffitt
  9500 Courthouse PO Box 7
  Chesterfield, VA 23832
  (804) 748-1261
  proffittd@chesterfield.gov
- Chesterfield County PD
- Chief (*Col.*) Thierry G. Dupuis
  10031 Iron Bridge PO Box 148
  Chesterfield, VA 23832
  (804) 748-1266
  DupuisT@chesterfield.gov

Clarke County

- Clarke County SO
- Sheriff Anthony W. Roper
  100 No. Church PO Box 49
  Berryville, VA 22611
  (540) 955-1234
  ccso@earthlink.net
- Berryville PD
- Chief W. Neal White
  23 E. Main St.
  Berryville, VA 22611
  (540) 955-3863
  policeadmin@berryvilleva.gov

Clifton Forge City

- Clifton Forge PD
- Chief Barry G. Balser
  547 Main St.
  Clifton Forge, VA 24422
  (540) 863-2513
  Barry.Balser@cliftonforgeva.gov

Colonial Heights City

- Colonial Heights (*City*) SO
- Sheriff Todd B. Wilson
  401 Temple Ave.
  Colonial Heights, Virginia 23834
  (804) 520-9352
  sheriff@colonialheightsva.gov
- Colonial Heights PD
- Chief (*Col.*) Jeffrey W. Faries
  100A Highland Ave.
  Colonial Heights, VA 23834
  (804) 520-9311
  fariesj@colonialheightsva.gov

Craig County

- Craig County SO
- Sheriff Clifford A. Davidson
  Court St. PO Box 266
  New Castle, VA 24127
  (540) 864-5127
  crgcoso@tds.net

Culpeper County

- Culpeper County SO
- Sheriff Scott H. Jenkins
  110 W. Cameron PO Box 39
  Culpeper, VA 22701
  (540) 727-7520
  sjenkins@culpepercounty.gov
- Culpeper PD
- Chief Chris Jenkins
  740 Old Brandy Rd.
  Culpeper, VA 22701
  (540) 727-3430
  cjenkins@culpeperva.gov

Cumberland County

- Cumberland County SO
- Sheriff Darrell L. Hodges
  PO Box 71
  Cumberland, VA 23040
  (804) 492-4120
  dhodges@cumberlandcounty.virginia.gov

Danville City

- Danville (*City*) SO
- Sheriff Michael S. *Mike* Mondul
  212 Lynn St. PO Box 3405
  Danville, VA 24543
  (434) 799-5135
  mondums@ci.danville.va.us
- Danville PD
- Chief (*Col.*) Philip A. Broadfoot
  PO Box 3300
  Danville, VA 24543
  (434) 799-6510
  kingjc@ci.danville.va.us

Dickenson County

- Dickenson County SO
- Sheriff Bobby G. Hammons
  PO Box 339
  Clintwood, VA 24228
  (276) 926-1600
  bobby.hammons@sheriff.dc911.org
- Clintwood PD
- Chief Rick Mullins
  PO Box 456
  Clintwood, VA 24228
  (276) 926-8710
  jsteele_townofclintwood@verizon.net

Dinwiddie County

- Dinwiddie County SO
- Sheriff D. T. *Duck* Adams
  14230 Sycamore PO Box 120
  Dinwiddie, VA 23841
  (804) 469-4550
  dadams@dinwiddieva.us

Emporia City

- Emporia (*City*) SO
- Sheriff Sam C. Brown
  201 So. Main St. PO Box 511
  Emporia, VA 23847
  (434) 634-4671
  emporiasheriff@hotmail.com
- Emporia PD
- Chief Don R. Wyatt
  310 Budd St.
  Emporia, VA 23847
  (434) 634-2121
  epd@emporiapolice.org

Essex County

- Essex County SO
- Sheriff Stanley S. Clarke
  304 Prince St. PO Box 955
  Tappahannock, VA 22560
  (804) 443-3346
  sclarke@essex-virginia.org
- Tappahannock PD
- Chief James G Ashworth
  315 Duke St. PO Box 266
  Tappahannock, VA 22560
  (804) 443-3992
  info@tapp-pd.org

Fairfax County

- Fairfax County SO
- Sheriff Stan G. Barry
  4110 Chain Bridge Rd.
  Fairfax, VA 22030
  (703) 246-3227
  laurie.ralph@fairfaxcounty.gov
- Fairfax County PD
- Chief (*Col.*) Edwin C. Roessler, Jr.
  4100 Chain Bridge Rd.
  Fairfax, VA 22030
  (703) 246-2195
  fcpd-pio@fairfaxcounty.gov
- Fairfax PD
- Chief (*Col.*) Rick Rappoport
  3730 Old Lee Hwy
  Fairfax, VA 22030
  (703) 385-7960
  Rick.Rappoport@fairfaxva.gov
- Herndon PD
- Chief (*Col.*) Maggie A. DeBoard
  397 Herndon Pkwy
  Herndon, VA 20170
  (703) 435-6846
  steve.thompson@herndon-va.gov
- Vienna PD
- Chief (*Col.*) James Morris
  215 Center St. So.
  Vienna, VA 22180
  (703) 255-6390
  police@viennava.gov

Falls Church City

- Falls Church (*City*) SO
- Sheriff S. Stephen Bittle
  300 Park Ave.
  Falls Church, VA 22046
  (703) 248-5111
  sbittle@fallschurchva.gov
- Falls Church PD
- Chief (*Col.*) Harry W. Reitze
  300 Park Ave.
  Falls Church, VA 22046
  (703) 241-5053
  police@fallschurchva.gov

Fauquier County

- Fauquier County SO
- Sheriff Charlie Ray Fox, Jr.
  78 W. Lee St., Ste. 200
  Warrenton, VA 20186
  (540) 422-8600
  sheriff.fox@fauquiercounty.gov
- Warrenton PD
- Chief Louis Battle
  333 Carriage House Ln.
  Warrenton, VA 22186
  (540) 347-1107
  lbattle@warrentonva.gov

Floyd County

- Floyd County SO
- Sheriff Shannon B. Zeman
  100 E. Main St., Rm. 206
  Floyd, VA 24091
  (540) 745-9334
  franfcso@swva.net

Fluvanna County

- Fluvanna County SO
- Sheriff Ryant L. Washington
  Court Sq. PO Box 113
  Palmyra, VA 22963
  (434) 589-8211
  rlwashington@fluvannasheriff.com

Franklin County

- Franklin County SO
- Sheriff W.Q. *Bill* Overton, Jr.
  70 E. Court St., Ste. 101
  Rocky Mount, VA 24151
  (540) 483-3000
  billoverton@franklincountyva.org

Frederick County

- Frederick County SO
- Sheriff Robert T. Williamson
  1080 Coverstone Dr.
  Winchester, VA 22601
  (540) 662-6168
  fcso@co.frederick.va.us

- Stephens City PD
- Chief Charles E. Bockey, Jr.
  1033 Locust St. PO Box 610
  Stephens City, VA 22655
  (540) 869-1012
  cbockey@stephenscityva.us

Fredericksburg City

- Fredericksburg (*City*) SO
- Sheriff Paul W. Higgs
  PO Box 448
  Fredericksburg, VA 22404
  (540) 372-1056
  pwhiggs@fredericksburgva.gov

Giles County

- Giles County SO
- Sheriff W. Morgan Millirons
  503 Wenonah Ave.
  Pearisburg, VA 24134
  (540) 921-3842
  mmillirons@gilessheriff.org
- Narrows PD
- Chief Bentley Ratcliffe
  100 Mary St. PO Box 440
  Narrows, VA 24124
  (540) 726-7985
  narrowschief@suddenlinkmail.com
- Pearisburg PD
- Chief Jackie C. Martin
  112 Tazewell St.
  Pearisburg, VA 24134
  (540) 921-0340
  mayor@pearisburg.org

Gloucester County

- Gloucester County SO
- Sheriff Darrell W. Warren, Jr.
  7502 Justice Dr.
  Gloucester, VA 23061
  (804) 693-1371
  dwarren@gloucesterva.info

Goochland County

- Goochland County SO
- Sheriff James L. Agnew
  PO Box 29
  Goochland, VA 23063
  (804) 556-5349
  jlagnew@co.goochland.va.us

Grayson County

- Grayson County SO
- Sheriff Richard A. Vaughan
  PO Box 160
  Independence, VA 24348
  (276) 773-3241
  rvaughan@graysoncountysheriff.com

Greene County

- Greene County SO
- Sheriff Steven S. Smith
  10005 Spotswood Tr.
  Stanardsville, VA 22973
  (434) 985-2222
  ssmith@gcvasheriff.us

Greensville County

- Greensville County SO
- Sheriff James R. Edwards, Jr.
  174 Uriah Branch Way
  Emporia, VA 23847
  (804) 348-4200
  gcso@telpage.net

Halifax County

- Halifax County SO
- Sheriff Fred S. Clark
  PO Box 370
  Halifax, VA 24558
  (434) 476-3339
  hcso@hcso.us.com

Hampton City

- Hampton (*City*) SO
- Sheriff B.J. Roberts
  1928 W. Pembroke Ave.
  Hampton, VA 23669
  (757) 926-2540
  dsmith@hampton.gov
- Hampton PD
- Chief Thomas H. Townsend
  40 Lincoln St.
  Hampton, VA 23669
  (757) 727-6111
  chiefsoffice@hampton.gov

Hanover County

- Hanover County SO
- Sheriff David R. Hines
  PO Box 40
  Hanover, VA 23069
  (804) 537-6110
  drhines@hanovercounty.gov

Henrico County

- Henrico County SO
- Sheriff Michael L. Wade
  PO Box 90775
  Richmond, VA 23273
  (804) 501-4571
  sheriff@co.henrico.va.us
- Henrico County PD
- Chief (*Col.*) Douglas A. Middleton
  7721 E. Parham PO Box 27032
  Richmond, VA 23273
  (804) 501-5000
  police@co.henrico.va.us

Henry County

- Henry County SD
- Sheriff Lane A. Perry
  3250 Kings Mountain Rd.
  Martinsville, VA 24112
  (276) 656-4200
  lperry@co.henry.va.us

Highland County

- Highland County SO
- Sheriff Timothy J. Duff
  PO Box 485
  Monterey, VA 24465
  (540) 468-2210
  hcso@ntelos.net

Hopewell City

- Hopewell (*City*) SO
- Sheriff Greg L. Anderson
  PO Box 1193
  Hopewell, VA 23860
  (804) 541-2300
  ganderson@hopewellva.gov
- Hopewell PD
- Chief John F. Keohane
  300 No. Main St.
  Hopewell, VA 23860
  (804) 541-2275
  info@hopewellva.gov

Isle Of Wight County

- Isle Of Wight County SO
- Sheriff Mark A. Marshall
  PO Box 75
  Isle of Wight, VA 23397
  (757) 357-2151
  mmarshall@isleofwightus.net
- Smithfield PD
- Chief Steven G. Bowman
  913 So. Church St.
  Smithfield, VA 23430
  (804) 357-3247
  sbowman@smithfieldva.gov

James City County

- James City County SO
- Sheriff Robert J. *Bob* Deeds
  5201 Monticello Ave, Ste. 5
  Williamsburg, VA 23187
  (757) 564-2220
  bob.deeds@jamescitycountyva.gov
- James City County PD
- Chief Emmett H. Harmon
  4600 Opportunity Way
  Williamsburg, VA 23185
  (757) 253-1800
  police@jamescitycountyva.gov

King George County

- King George County S
- Sheriff Steve F. Dempsey
  10445 Government Center Blvd
  King George, VA 22485
  (540) 775-2049
  sdempsey@co.kinggeorge.state.va.us

King & Queen County

- King & Queen County SO
- Sheriff John R. Charboneau
  PO Box 38
  King & Queen C.H., VA 23085
  (804) 785-7400
  sheriff@kingandqueenco.net

King William County

- King William County SO
- Sheriff J.S. Walton
  PO Box 98
  King William, VA 23806
  (804) 769-0999
  kwso@kingwilliamcounty.us

Lancaster County

- Lancaster County SO
- Sheriff Ronald D. Crockett
  8293 Mary Ball Rd.
  Lancaster, VA 22503
  (804) 462-5111
  crockett@lancastersheriff.net

- Kilmarnock PD
- Chief Mike Bedell
  514 No. Main St. PO Box 1357
  Kilmarnock, VA 22482
  (804) 435-1552, ext. 29
  ch1ef1@verizon.net

Lee County

- Lee County SO
- Sheriff Gary B. Parsons
  PO Box 177
  Jonesville, VA 24263
  (540) 346-7753
  gparsons@leecountysheriff.net

Lexington City

- Lexington PD
- Chief Al Thomas
  11 Fuller St. PO Box 938
  Lexington, VA 24450
  (540) 462-3705
  lexpolice@lexingtonva.gov

Loudoun County

- Loudoun County SO
- Sheriff Michael L. *Mike* Chapman
  880 Harrison St. SE
  Leesburg, VA 22075
  (703) 777-0407
  mike.chapman@loudoun.gov
- Leesburg PD
- Chief Joseph Price
  25 SW Market St.
  Leesburg, VA 20175
  (703) 771-4500
  policecommunityservices@leesburgva.gov
- Middleburg PD
- Chief A.J. Panebianco
  10 W. Marshall St. PO Box 187
  Middleburg, VA 20118
  (540) 687-6633
  cpearson@townofmiddleburg.org
- Purcellville PD
- Chief Darryl Smith
  125 Hirst Rd., Ste. 7-A
  Purcellville, VA 20132
  (540) 338-7700
  dsmith9@purcellvilleva.gov

Louisa County

- Louisa County SO
- Sheriff Ashland D. Fortune
  PO Box 504
  Louisa, VA 23093
  (540) 967-1234
  gmassey@louisa.org

Lunenburg County

- Lunenburg County SO
- Sheriff Arthur Townsend, Jr.
  160 Courthouse Sq.
  Lunenburg, VA 23952
  (434) 696-4452
  sheriff@lunenburgva.net

Lynchburg City

- Lynchburg (*City*) SO
- Sheriff Ronald L. Gillispie
  PO Box 217
  Lynchburg, VA 24505
  (434) 847-1301
  rgillispie@lynchburgva.gov
- Lynchburg PD
- Chief (*Col.*) Parks H. Snead III
  905 Court St.
  Lynchburg, VA 24505
  (434) 455-6045
  ph.snead@lynchburgva.gov

Madison County

- Madison County SO
- Sheriff Erik J. Weaver
  PO Box 322
  Madison, VA 22727
  (540) 948-5161
  eweaver@madisonco.virginia.gov

Manassas City

- Manassas PD
- Chief Douglas W. Keen
  9518 Fairview Ave.
  Manassas, VA 20110
  (703) 257-8000
  dkeen@ci.manassas.va.us
- Manassas Park PD
- Chief John Evans
  329 Manassas Dr.
  Manassas Park, VA 20111
  (703) 361-1136
  k.barton@manassasparkva.gov

Martinsville City

- Martinsville SO
- Sheriff Steve M. Draper
  PO Box 1326
  Martinsville, VA 24114
  (276) 656-5151
  smdraper@ci.martinsville.va.us

- Martinsville PD
- Chief (*Col.*) Michael E. Rogers
  55 W. Church St.   PO Box 1101
  Martinsville, VA 24112
  (276) 403-5300
  kadkins@ci.martinsville.va.us

Mathews County

- Mathews County SO
- Sheriff L. Mark Barrick
  PO Box 190
  Mathews, VA 23109
  (804) 725-7177
  sheriff@co.mathews.va.us

Mecklenburg County

- Mecklenburg County SO
- Sheriff RW *Bobby* Hawkins, Jr.
  PO Box 390
  Boydton, VA 23917
  (434) 738-6171
  rhawkins@mcsova.us
- Chase City PD
- Chief J.A. Jordan
  219 E. 2nd St.
  Chase City, VA 23924
  (434) 372-5112
  ccpd@kerrlake.com

Middlesex County

- Middlesex County SO
- Sheriff David P. Bushey
  PO Box 207
  Saluda, VA 23149
  (804) 758-2779
  sheriffbushey@co.middlesex.va.us

Montgomery County

- Montgomery County SO
- Sheriff J.T. Whitt
  16 So. Franklin St.
  Christiansburg, VA 24073
  (540) 382-6906
  whittjt@montgomerycountyva.gov
- Blacksburg PD
- Chief Kimberley S. Crannis
  200 Clay St. SW
  Blacksburg, VA 24060
  (540) 961-1152
  police@blacksburg.gov
- Christiansburg PD
- Chief Mark Sisson
  10 E. Main St.
  Christiansburg, VA 24073
  (540) 382-3131
  msisson@christiansburg.org

Nelson County

- Nelson County SO
- Sheriff W. David Brooks
  PO Box 36
  Lovingston, VA 22949
  (434) 263-7050
  dbrooks@nelsoncounty.org

New Kent County

- New Kent County SO
- Sheriff F.W. Howard, Jr.
  PO Box 186
  New Kent, VA 23124
  (804) 966-9500
  fwhsheriff@co.newkent.state.va.us

Newport News City

- Newport News (*City*) SO
- Sheriff Gabe A. Morgan
  224 26th St.   PO Box 57
  Newport News, VA 23607
  (757) 926-8759
  gabemorgan@nngov.com
- Newport News PD
- Chief James D. Fox
  9710 Jefferson Ave.
  Newport News, VA 23607
  (757) 928-4300
  chfoff@nngov.com

Norfolk City

- Norfolk SO
- Sheriff Robert J. McCabe
  811 E. City Hall Ave.
  Norfolk, VA 23510
  (757) 664-4951
  robert.mccabe@norfolk.gov
- Norfolk PD
- Chief Michael Goldsmith
  100 Brooke Ave.
  Norfolk, VA 23510
  (757) 441-5610
  police@norfolk.gov

Northampton County

- Northampton County SO
- Sheriff David L. Doughty, Jr.
  PO Box 68
  Eastville, VA 23347
  (757) 678-0460
  ddoughty@co.northampton.va.us
- Cape Charles PD
- Chief Charles *Sambo* Brown
  2 Plum St.
  Cape Charles, VA 23310
  (757) 331-3096
  chief@capecharles.org
- Exmore PD
- Chief Angelo DiMartino
  3305 Main St.
  PO Box 647
  Exmore, VA 23350
  (757) 710-8544
  mayor@exmore.org

Northumberland County

- Northumberland County SO
- Sheriff Charles A. *Chuck* Wilkins
  PO Box 310
  Heathsville, VA 22473
  (804) 580-5221
  ncso@sylvaninfo.net

Norton City

- Norton (*City*) SO
- Sheriff Carlos J. Noaks
  PO Box 307
  Norton, VA 24273
  (540) 679-5308
  nortonsheriff@notonva.gov
- Norton PD
- Chief James C. Lane
  618 Virginia Ave. NW
  Norton, VA 24273
  (540) 679-1211
  info@nortonpd.org

Nottoway County

- Nottoway County SO
- Sheriff Larry J. Parrish
  PO Box 6
  Nottoway Courthouse, VA 23955
  (804) 645-9044
  ljparrish@nottowaysheriff.org
- Blackstone PD
- Chief Nicholas Kuzmiak
  101 W. Elm St.
  Blackstone, VA 23824
  (804) 292-3322
  chiefnck@blackstonepd.org

Orange County

- Orange County SO
- Sheriff Mark A. Amos
  PO Box 445
  Orange, VA 22960
  (540) 672-9435
  mamos@orangecountyva.gov
- Gordonsville PD
- Chief Clay Corbin
  112 So. Main St. PO Box 276
  Gordonsville, VA 22942
  (540) 832-2234
  ccorbin@gordonsville.org
- Orange PD
- Chief James L. Fenwick
  249 Blue Ridge Dr.
  Orange, VA 22960
  (540) 672-1491
  policechief@townoforangeva.org

Page County

- Page County SO
- Sheriff John B. Thomas
  108 So. Court St.
  Luray, VA 22835
  (540) 743-6571
  sheriff@pagesheriff.com
- Luray PD
- Chief Page D. Campbell, Jr.
  45 E. Main St.
  Luray, VA 22835
  (540) 743-5343
  pcampbell@townofluray.com
- Shenandoah PD
- Chief Paul W. Davis
  411 2nd St.
  Shenandoah, VA 22849
  (540) 652-8193
  info@townofshenandoah.com
- Stanley PD
- Chief Timmy Foster
  276 E. Main St.
  Stanley, VA 22851
  (540) 778-2615
  stanelypolicedept@earthlink.net

Patrick County

- Patrick County SO
- Sheriff Daniel M. Smith
  PO Box 128
  Stuart, VA 24171
  (540) 694-3161
  dmsmith@sheriff.co.patrick.va.us

Petersburg City

- Petersburg (*City*) SO
- Sheriff Vanessa R. Crawford
  8 Courthouse Ave.
  Petersburg, VA 23804
  (804) 733-2369
  sheriffcrawford@petersburg-so.com
- Petersburg PD
- Chief John I. Dixon III
  37 E. Tabb St.
  Petersburg, VA 23803
  (804) 732-4222
  citycouncil@petersburg-va.org

Pittsylvania County

- Pittsylvania County SO
- Sheriff Michael W. *Mike* Taylor
  PO Box 407
  Chatham, VA 24531
  (434) 432-7800
  mike.taylor@pittgov.org
- Chatham PD
- Chief Marvin L. Wright
  16 Court Pl.
  Chatham, VA 24531
  (434) 432-8121
  chathampd@yahoo.com
- Gretna PD
- Chief David Wilkes
  105 So. Shelton PO Box 602
  Gretna, VA 24557
  (434) 656-6123
  gretna.police@townofgretna.org

Portsmouth City

- Portsmouth (*City*) SO
- Sheriff WO *Bill* Watson
  701 Crawford St.
  Portsmouth, VA 23704
  (757) 393-5461
  emtinc@aol.com
- Portsmouth PD
- Chief Edward Hargis
  710 Crawford St.
  Portsmouth, VA 23704
  (757) 393-8536, ext. 7226
  clarkj@portsmouthva.gov

Powhatan County

- Powhatan County SO
- Sheriff Gregory A. Neal
  PO Box 133
  Powhatan, VA 23139
  (804) 598-5655
  ganeal@powhatansheriff.net

Prince Edward County

- Prince Edward County SO
- Sheriff Wesley W. Reed
  PO Box 25
  Farmville, VA 23901
  (434) 392-8101
  Sheriff@co.prince-edward.va.us

Prince George County

- Prince George County SO
- Sheriff Harold E. *Bucky* Allin III
  PO Box 366
  Prince George, VA 23875
  (804) 733-2690
  hallin@princegeorgeva.org

Prince William County

- Prince William County SO
- Sheriff Glendell Hill
  9311 Lee Ave.
  Manassas, VA 20110
  (703) 792-6070
  ghill@pwcgov.org
- Dumfries PD
- Chief Robert E. Forker
  18130 Triangle Shopping Plaza
  Dumfries, VA 22026
  (703) 221-1111
  chiefofpolice@dumfriesva.gov
- Haymarket PD
- Chief James E. Roop
  14710 Washington PO Box 1125
  Haymarket, VA 20169
  (703) 753-2700
  chief@townofhaymarket.org

- Occoquan PD
- Chief (*Sgt.*) Sheldon E. Levi
  314 Mill St.
  Occoquan, VA 22125
  (703) 491-1918
  slevi@occoquanva.gov
- Prince William County PD
- Chief Stephan M. *Steve* Hudson
  1 County Complex Ct.
  Prince William, VA 22192
  (703) 792-6650
  cstewart@pwcgov.org
- Quantico PD
- Chief John Patrick Clair
  405 Broadway St.
  Quantico, VA 22134
  (703) 640-7500
  Mayor@townofquantico.org

Pulaski County

- Pulaski County SO
- Sheriff James A. Davis
  86 E. Main St.
  Pulaski, VA 24301
  (540) 980-7800
  jdavis@sheriffsoffice.org
- Dublin PD
- Chief Jay C. Vest
  101 Dublin Park PO Box 1066
  Dublin, VA 24084
  (540) 674-5167
  dublinpd@pd.org
- Pulaski PD
- Chief Gary Roche
  42 1st St. NW
  Pulaski, VA 24301
  (540) 994-8680
  info@pulaskipd.net

Radford City

- Radford (*City*) SO
- Sheriff Mark R. Armentrout
  619 2nd St, Ste. 8
  Radford, VA 24143
  (540) 731-5501
  marmentrout@radford.va.us
- Radford PD
- Chief Don Goodman
  20 Robertson St.
  Radford, VA 24141
  (540) 731-3624
  info@radford.va.us

Rappahannock County

- Rappahannock County SO
- Sheriff Connie Compton Smith
  PO Box 487
  Washington, VA 22747
  (540) 675-5300
  ccsmith@rappahannockcountyva.gov

Richmond City

- Richmond (*City*) SO
- Sheriff CT Woody, Jr.
  1701 Fairfield Way
  Richmond, VA 23223
  (804) 646-0930
  ct.woody@richmondgov.com
- Richmond PD
- Chief Ray J. Tarasovic
  200 W. Grace St.
  Richmond, VA 23219
  (804) 646-6700
  policemediarelations@richmondgov.com

Richmond County

- Richmond County SO
- Sheriff Douglas A. Bryant
  PO Box 115
  Warsaw, VA 22572
  (804) 333-3611
  bryantdouglas901@yahoo.com
- Warsaw PD
- Int. Chief A.J. Panebianco
  78 Belleville Ln. PO Box 730
  Warsaw, VA 22572
  (804) 333-3737
  warsawpd@town.warsaw.va.us

Roanoke City

- Roanoke (*City*) SO
- Sheriff Octavia L. Johnson
  340 Campbell Ave. SW
  Roanoke, VA 24016
  (540) 853-2941
  sheriffjohnson@roanokeva.gov
- Roanoke PD
- Chief Chris Perkins
  348 Campbell Ave. SW
  Roanoke, VA 24011
  (540) 853-2211
  police@roanokeva.gov

Roanoke County

- Roanoke County SO
- Sheriff Michael G. *Mike* Winston
  PO Box 510
  Salem, VA 24153
  (540) 387-6203
  mwinston@roanokecountyva.gov
- Roanoke County PD
- Chief Howard B. Hall
  5925 Cove Rd.
  Roanoke, VA 24019
  (540) 562-3265
  rkern@roanokecountyva.gov
- Vinton PD
- Chief Ben Cook
  311 So. Pollard St.
  Vinton, VA 24179
  (540) 983-0617, ext. 158
  bcook@vintonva.gov

Rockbridge County

- Rockbridge County SO
- Sheriff Christopher J. Blalock
  258 Greenhouse Rd.
  Lexington, VA 24450
  (540) 463-7328
  cjblalock@rockbridge.net
- Glasgow PD
- Sgt. Aaron Britton (*resigned 10-1-14*)
  420 Catawba St.
  Glasgow, VA 24555
  (540) 258-2732
  jhigginbotham@glasgowvirginia.org

Rockingham County

- Rockingham County SO
- Sheriff Bryan F. Hutcheson
  25 So. Liberty St.
  Harrisonburg, VA 22801
  (540) 564-3800
  bhutcheson@rockinghamcounty.va.gov
- Broadway PD
- Chief Jay P. Lantz
  116 Broadway Ave.
  Broadway, VA 22815
  (540) 896-1174
  jplantz@town.broadway.va.us
- Dayton PD
- Chief Donald L. Conley
  125-A Eastview St.
  Dayton, VA 22821
  (540) 879-2161, ext. 320
  daytonpd@daytonva.us
- Elkton PD
- Chief Kevin Whitfield
  173 W. Spotswood Ave.
  Elkton, VA 22827
  (540) 298-9441
  chiefwhitfield@townofelkton.com
- Grottoes PD
- Chief John E. Painter
  601 Dogwood Ave. PO Box 146
  Grottoes, VA 24441
  (540) 249-9256
  jpainter@ci.grottoes.va.us
- Massanutten PD
- Chief J.S. Gordon, Jr.
  1735 Massanutten Dr.
  McGaheysville, VA 22840
  (540) 289-9466
  police@massanuttenvillage.com
- Timberville PD
- Chief Keith Hand
  392 So. Main St. PO Box 102
  Timberville, VA 22853
  (540) 896-7058
  timbervillepd@msn.com

Russell County

- Russell County SO
- Sheriff Steven L. Dye
  PO Box 338
  Lebanon, VA 24266
  (540) 889-8033
  rcso@russellcountyva.us
- Lebanon PD
- Chief Stephanie Kegley
  244 W. Main St.
  Lebanon, VA 24266
  (540) 889-7227
  lebanonva@policeone.com

Salem City

- Salem (*City*) SO
- Sheriff Eric A. Atkins
  2 E. Calhoun St.
  Salem, VA 24153
  (540) 375-3040
  ratkins@salemva.gov
- Salem PD
- Chief James R. Bryant
  36 E. Calhoun St.
  Salem, VA 24153
  (540) 375-3078
  salempolice@salemva.gov

Scott County

- Scott County SO
- Sheriff W. John Puckett
  267 Willow St, Ste. 102
  Gate City, VA 24251
  (276) 386-7679
  sheriff@scottcountyva.com
- Gate City PD
- Chief Kim Birchfield
  1378 W. Jackson St.
  Gate City, VA 24251
  (276) 386-6363
  kbirchfield@gatecitypolice.com

Shenandoah County

- Shenandoah County SO
- Sheriff Timothy C. Carter
  109 W. Court St.
  Woodstock, VA 22664
  (540) 459-6100
  tccscso@shentel.net
- Mt. Jackson PD
- Chief JD Fadley
  5945 Main St.
  Mt. Jackson, VA 22842
  (540) 477-2242
  townoffice@mountjackson.com
- Strasburg PD
- Chief Tim Sutherly
  174 E. King PO Box 351
  Strasburg, VA 22657
  (540) 465-5230
  tsutherly@strasburgva.com
- Woodstock PD
- Chief Eric L. Reiley
  134 No. Muhlenberg St.
  Woodstock, VA 22664
  (540) 459-2141
  eric.reiley@townofwoodstockva.gov

Smyth County

- Smyth County SO
- Sheriff R. David Bradley
  819 Matson Dr.
  Marion, VA 24354
  (276) 783-7204
  sheriff@smythcounty.org
- Marion PD
- Chief W. Rex Anders
  555 So. Park St.
  Marion, VA 24354
  (276) 783-8145
  randers@marionpd.net

Southampton County

- Southampton County SO
- Sheriff J.B. *Jack* Stutts
  PO Box 70
  Courtland, VA 23837
  (757) 653-2100
  stutts@shso.org

South Boston City

- South Boston (*City*) PD
- Chief (*Col.*) James W. Binner
  640 Hamilton Blvd
  South Boston, VA 24592
  (434) 575-4270
  jjones@southbostonva.us

Spotsylvania County

- Spotsylvania County SO
- Sheriff Roger L. Harris
  PO Box 124
  Spotsylvania, VA 22553
  (540) 582-7115
  RLHarris@spotsylvania.va.us

Stafford County

- Stafford County SO
- Sheriff Charles E. Jett
  PO Box 189
  Stafford, VA 22554
  (540) 658-4450
  cjett@staffordcountyva.gov

Staunton City

- Staunton (*City*) SO
- Sheriff Alex L. Caldwell, Jr.
  PO Box 64
  Staunton, VA 24402
  (540) 332-3880
  caldwellal@ci.staunton.va.us
- Staunton PD
- Chief James E. *Jim* Williams
  116 W. Beverley St.
  Staunton, VA 24401
  (540) 332-3845
  Owensf@ci.staunton.va.us

Suffolk City

- Suffolk (*City*) SO
- Sheriff Raleigh H. Isaacs, Sr.
  150 No. Main St.
  Suffolk, VA 23434-4428
  (757) 514-7840
  risaacs@suffolkva.us

- Suffolk PD
- Chief Thomas E. Bennett
  120 No. Wellons St.
  Suffolk, VA 23434
  (757) 514-7900
  info@suffolkva.us

Surry County

- Surry County SO
- Sheriff Alvin W. Clayton, Sr.
  PO Box 233
  Surry, VA 23883
  (757) 294-5264
  aclayton@surrycountyva.gov

Sussex County

- Sussex County SO
- Sheriff Raymond Bell
  PO Box 1326
  Sussex, VA 23884
  (804) 246-5000
  sussexsheriffdept@erols.com

Tazewell County

- Tazewell County SD
- Sheriff Brian L. Hieatt
  315 School St., Ste. 3
  Tazewell, VA 24651
  (276) 988-5966
  brian.hieatt@tazewellcountysheriff.org
- Tazewell PD
- Chief Dewitt Cooper
  201 No. Central Ave.
  Tazewell, VA 24651
  (276) 988-2503
  tazpolchf@taztown.org

Virginia Beach City

- Virginia Beach (*City*) SO
- Sheriff Kenneth W. *Ken* Stolle
  2501 James Madison Blvd
  Virginia Beach, VA 23456
  (757) 385-4073
  kstolle@vbso.net
- Virginia Beach PD
- Chief James A. *Jim* Cervera
  Municipal Center
  Virginia Beach, VA 23456
  (757) 427-4141
  vbpd@vbgov.com

Warren County

- Warren County SO
- Sheriff Daniel T. McEathron
  200 Skyline Vista Dr.
  Front Royal, VA 22630
  (540) 635-4128
  sheriffmceathron@warrencountysheriff.org
- Front Royal PD
- Chief Norman A. Shiflett
  24 W. Main St.
  Front Royal, VA 22630
  (540) 635-2111
  darr@frontroyalva.com

Washington County

- Washington County SO
- Sheriff Fred P. Newman
  20281 Rustic Ln.
  Abingdon, VA 24210
  (276) 676-6000
  fnewman@washso.org
- Abingdon PD
- Chief Phillip A. *Tony* Sullivan
  425 W. Main St.
  Abingdon, VA 24210
  (276) 628-3111
  psullivan@abingdon-va.gov

Waynesboro City

- Waynesboro (*City*) SO
- Sheriff Joe Harris, Jr.
  PO Box 189
  Waynesboro, VA 22980
  (540) 942-6639
  harrisj@ci.waynesboro.va.us

Westmoreland County

- Westmoreland County SO
- Sheriff CO Balderson
  PO Box 305
  Montross, VA 22520
  (804) 493-8066
  sheriff@westcoso.us

Williamsburg-James City

- Williamsburg (*City*) SO
- Sheriff Robert J. Deeds
  5201 Monticello Ave., Ste. 5
  Williamsburg, VA 23187
  (757) 564-2220
  wjccso@wjccso.hrcoxmail.com

- Williamsburg PD
- Chief Dave Sloggie
  425 Armistead Ave.
  Williamsburg, VA 23185
  (757) 259-7202
  dsloggie@williamsburgva.gov

Winchester City

- Winchester (*City*) SO
- Sheriff Lenny W. Millholland
  5 No. Kent St.
  Winchester, VA 22601
  (540) 667-5770 x457
  wincsheriff@ci.winchester.va.us
- Winchester PD
- Chief Kevin L. Sanzenbacher
  231 E. Piccadilly St., Ste. 310
  Winchester, VA 22601
  (540) 662-4131
  jwillingham@ci.winchester.va.us

Wise County

- Wise County SO
- Sheriff Ronnie Oakes
  PO Box 916
  Wise, VA 24293-0916
  (276) 328-3566
  sheriff@wiseso.net
- Appalachia PD
- Act. Chief (*Capt.*) Brad Gibson
  508 W. Main St. PO Box 112
  Appalachia, VA 24216
  (276) 565-3904
  admin@townofappalachiava.us
- Big Stone Gap PD
- Chief Stephen Hamm
  505 E. 5th St.
  Big Stone Gap, VA 24219
  (276) 523-0117
  info@bigstonegap.org
- Pound PD
- Chief Jeff Rose
  8422 No. River Rd.
  Pound, VA 24279
  (276) 796-5747
  info@poundva.com

Wythe County

- Wythe County SO
- Sheriff Douglas W. King
  PO Box 819
  Wytheville, VA 24382
  (276) 223-6000
  dking@wytheco.org
- Rural Retreat PD
- Chief Scott Mitchell
  247 Edwards Ln. PO Box 130
  Rural Retreat, VA 24368
  (276) 686-4221
  smitchell@townofruralretreat.com
- Wytheville PD
- Chief Rick Arnold
  185 W. Spring St.
  Wytheville, VA 24382
  (276) 223-3310
  rwa0219@wytheville.org

York County-Poquoson

- York County-Poquoson SO
- Sheriff JD Diggs
  PO Box 99
  Yorktown, VA 23690
  (757) 890-3630
  sheriff@yorkcounty.gov

State Agencies

- VA State Police-HQ
- Supt. (*Col.*) W. Steven Flaherty
  7700 Midlothian Turnpike
  (Mailing: PO Box 27472
  North Chesterfield, VA 23235
  Richmond, VA 23261)
  (804) 674-2000
  questions@vsp.virginia.gov
- Old Dominion U. PD
- Chief Rhonda L. Harris
  4516 Monarch Way
  Norfolk, VA 23529
  (757) 683-4003
  rlharris@odu.edu
- Radford U. PD
- Chief Colleen T. Roberts
  801 E. Main St. PO Box 6883
  Radford, VA 24142
  (540) 831-5500
  ctroberts@radford.edu
- VA State U. PD
- Chief Michael C. Wallace
  21012 Service Rd. PO Box 9405
  Petersburg, VA 23806
  (804) 524-5598
  mwallace@vsu.edu

**** Note:** ***VA has independent cities that are not affiliated with any county.***

WEST VIRGINIA

Barbour County

- Barbour County SO
- Sheriff John W. Hawkins
  8 No. Main St.
  Philippi, WV 26416
  (304) 457-2352
  wvdeputy801@hotmail.com

Berkeley County

- Berkeley County SO
- Sheriff Kenneth Lemaster
  802 Emmett Rousch Dr.
  Martinsburg, WV 25401
  (304) 267-7000
  bcs0802@earthlink.net
- Martinsburg PD
- Chief Kevin Miller
  232 No. Queen St.
  Martinsburg, WV 25401
  (304) 264-2100
  k_miller@martinsburgpd.org

Boone County

- Boone County SO
- Sheriff Rodney Miller
  200 State St.
  Madison, WV 25130
  (304) 369-7390
  ramiller@boonecountywv.net

Braxton County

- Braxton County SO
- Sheriff George Keener
  300 Main St. PO Box 546
  Sutton, WV 26601
  (304) 765-2838
  SRT760@citynet.net

Brooke County

- Brooke County SD
- Sheriff Richard Ferguson
  300 Courthouse Sq.
  Wellsburg, WV 26070
  (304) 737-3660
  ferguson@sheriff.state.wv.us
- Follansbee PD
- Chief John Schwertfeger
  1083 Jefferson St.
  Follansbee, WV 26037
  (304) 527-1211
  follansbeecitymgr@comcast.net

Cabell County

- Cabell County SO
- Sheriff Thomas *Tom* McComas
  750 5th Ave., Rm. 101
  Huntington, WV 25701
  (304) 526-8664
  cabellcountysheriff@gmail.com
- Huntington PD
- Chief WH *Skip* Holbrook
  675 10th St.
  Huntington, WV 25701
  (304) 696-4470
  holbrooks@huntingtonwvpolice.com

Calhoun County

- Calhoun County SO
- Sheriff Allen Parsons
  PO Box 340
  Grantsville, WV 26147
  (304) 354-6333
  Sheriff@calhounwvsheriff.com

Clay County

- Clay County SO
- Sheriff Randy Holcomb
  207 Main St. PO Drawer 429
  Clay, WV 25043
  (304) 587-4260
  claywvsheriff05@hotmail.com

Doddridge County

- Doddridge County SO
- Sheriff Michael Headley
  PO Box 219
  West Union, WV 26456
  (304) 873-1944
  shiwi3@aol.com

Fayette County

- Fayette County SD
- Sheriff Steve W. Kessler
  100 Church St. PO Box 509
  Fayetteville, WV 25840
  (304) 574-4259
  skessler@fayettesheriff.net
- Oak Hill PD
- Chief Michael W. Whisman, Jr.
  691 Virginia St. PO Box 1245
  Oak Hill, WV 25901
  (304) 465-0597
  cityohcmo@suddenlinkmail.com

Gilmer County

- Gilmer County SO
- Sheriff Mickey Metz
  10 Howard St.
  Glenville, WV 26351
  (304) 462-7441
  gcsd1@hotmail.com

Grant County

- Grant County SO
- Sheriff Bill Feaster
  5 Highland Ave.
  Petersburg, WV 26847
  (304) 257-1818
  gcsheriffsdept@citlink.net

Greenbrier County

- Greenbrier County SO
- Sheriff James Childers
  PO Box 347
  Lewisburg, WV 24901
  (304) 647-6678
  JamesW.Childers@greenbriercounty.net
- Lewisburg PD
- Chief T.L. Stover
  119 W. Washington St.
  Lewisburg, WV 24901
  (304) 645-1626
  police@lewisburg-wv.com

Hampshire County

- Hampshire County SO
- Sheriff Nathan Sions
  66 No. High St., Rm. 2
  Romney, WV 26757
  (304) 822-3894
  nsions60@yahoo.com
- Romney PD
- Chief Donald E. See
  260 School St.
  Romney, WV 26757
  (304) 822-4060
  mayorofromney@atlanticbbn.com

Hancock County

- Hancock County SO
- Sheriff Mike White
  102 No. Court St.
  New Cumberland, WV 26047
  (304) 564-3911
  whitehouse248@yahoo.com

Hardy County

- Hardy County SO
- Sheriff Robert Bob Ferrell
  Courthouse PO Box 643
  204 Washington St.
  Moorefield, WV 26836
  (304) 530-0222
  bob.ferrell@hardysheriff.com
- Wardensville PD
- Chief Jeffrey A Driskill
  25 Warrior Way PO Box 7
  Wardensville, WV 26851
  (304) 874-3950
  jim@wardensville.net

Harrison County

- Harrison County SO
- Sheriff Albert Marano
  301 W. Main St.
  Clarksburg, WV 26301
  (304) 624-8550
  afmarano@harrco911.org
- Bridgeport PD
- Chief John Walker
  515 W. Main St.
  Bridgeport, WV 26330
  (304) 842-8260
  jwalker@bridgeportwv.com
- Clarksburg PD
- Chief M. Goff
  222 W. Main St.
  Clarksburg, WV 26301
  (304) 624-1610
  MGoff@cityofclarksburgwv.com

Jackson County

- Jackson County SO
- Sheriff Michael *Mike* Bright
  PO Box 106
  Ripley, WV 25271
  (304) 373-2290
  mike.bright@jacksoncountywv.com
- Ravenswood PD
- Chief Lance B. Morrison
  333 Virginia St.
  Ravenswood, WV 26164
  (304) 273-3500
  mike@makrepairs.com

Jefferson County

- Jefferson County SO
- Sheriff Bobby Shirley
  102 Industrial Blvd
  PO Box 9
  Kearneysville, WV 25430
  (304) 728-3205
  rshirley@jcsdwv.com
- Charles Town PD
- Chief Chris Kutcher
  114 W. Liberty St.
  Charles Town, WV 25414
  (304) 725-2714
  ckutcher@charlestownpolice.com
- Harpers Ferry PD
- Chief John D. Brown
  1000 Washington PO Box 217
  Harpers Ferry, WV 25425
  (304) 535-6366
  jbrown@harpersferrywv.us
- Ranson PD
- Chief William Roper
  700 No. Preston St.
  Ranson, WV 25438
  (304) 725-2411
  chief@cityofransonwv.net
- Shepherdstown PD
- Chief David Ransom
  207 So. Princess PO Box 248
  Shepherdstown, WV 25443
  (304) 876-6036
  dransom@shepherdstown.us

Kanawha County

- Kanawha County SD
- Sheriff Mike Rutherford
  409 Virginia St. E. PO Box 75087
  Charleston, WV 25375
  (304) 357-0239
  sheriffrutherford@kcso.us
- Charleston PD
- Chief Brent Webster
  501 Virginia St. E. PO Box 2749
  Charleston, WV 25330
  (304) 348-6460
  brent.webster@charlesonwvpolice.org
- Chesapeake PD
- Chief (*Col.*) K. L. Wright
  12404 MacCorkle Ave.
  Chesapeake, WV 25315
  (304) 949-1496
  webmaster@cityofchesapeake.net
- Clendenin PD
- Chief David Brinckman
  103 1st St. PO Box 694
  Clendenin, WV 25045
  (304) 348-8111
  dbrinckman@clendeninwv.org
- Pratt PD
- Chief Eric L. Eagle
  WV Rt. 61 PO Box 128
  Pratt, WV 25162
  (304) 442-0103
  topmayor.pratt@yahoo.com

Lewis County

- Lewis County SO
- Sheriff Michael Gissy
  110 Center Ave. PO Box 150
  Weston, WV 26452
  (304) 269-8251
  lcsomikegissy@yahoo.com

Lincoln County

- Lincoln County SO
- Sheriff Jerry Bowman
  PO Box 467
  Hamlin, WV 25523
  (304) 824-7999
  jerrybowman@lincolncountywv.org

Logan County

- Logan County SO
- Sheriff Sonya M. Dingiss Porter
  300 Stratton St.
  Logan, WV 25601
  (304) 792-8626
  logancountycommission@yahoo.com

Marion County

- Marion County SO
- Sheriff Joe Carpenter
  PO Box 1348
  Fairmont, WV 26554
  (304) 367-5300
  sheriff@marioncountywv.com

Marshall County

- Marshall County SD
- Sheriff Kevin Cecil
  600 6th St.
  Moundsville, WV 26041
  (304) 843-1500
  sheriff@marshallcountywv.org

- Benwood PD
- Chief Frank Longwell
  430 Main St.
  Benwood, WV 26031
  (304) 232-2121
  ChiefLongwell@comcast.net
- Cameron PD
- Chief Michael Younger
  44 Main St.
  Cameron, WV 26033
  (304) 686-23213
  cameronpolicedept@swave.net

Mason County

- Mason County SO
- Sheriff David L. Anthony II
  200 6th St.
  Point Pleasant, WV 25550
  (304) 675-3838
  mcsodare@yahoo.com
- Point Pleasant PD
- Chief Ernie Watterson
  400 Viane St.
  Point Pleasant, WV 25550
  (304) 675-1104
  ewatterson.pppd@ptpleasantwv.org

McDowell County

- McDowell County SO
- Sheriff Danny Mitchell
  90 Wyoming St., Ste. 117
  Welch, WV 24801
  (304) 436-8541
  dwm102cfd@yahoo.com
- War PD
- Chief RE Harman
  PO Box 280
  War, WV 24892
  (304) 875-2213
  r_e_harman@yahoo.com

Mercer County

- Mercer County SO
- Sheriff Danny Wills
  1501 W. Main St., Ste. 31
  Princeton, WV 24740
  (304) 487-8389
  sheriff@wvmcs.org

Mineral County

- Mineral County SO
- Sheriff Jeremy S. Taylor
  150 Armstrong St.
  Keyser, WV 26726
  (304) 788-0341
  jstaylor@mineralsheriff.com
- Keyser PD
- Chief Karen Shumaker
  111 No. Davis St.
  Keyser, WV 26726
  (304) 788-1311
  mayoramtower@cityofkeyser.com

Mingo County

- Mingo County SD
- Sheriff Lonnie Hannah
  2nd Ave. PO Box 1270
  Williamson, WV 25661
  (304) 235-0300
  rhoda1420@yahoo.com
- Delbarton PD
- Chief David Nunley
  1 Riverside Dr. PO Box 730
  Delbarton, WV 25670
  (304) 475-3359
  policeinfo@delbartonwv.us

Monongalia County

- Monongalia County SD
- Sheriff Kenneth Al Kisner
  155 Chancery Row
  Morgantown, WV 26505
  (304) 291-7260
  akisner@monsheriff.com
- Morgantown PD
- Chief Ed Preston
  300 Spruce St.
  Morgantown, WV 26505
  (304) 284-7496
  epreston@cityofmorgantown.org
- Star City PD
- Chief Vic Propst
  370 Broadway Ave.
  Star City, WV 26505
  (304) 599-3550, ext. 402
  scpolice@comcast.net

Monroe County

- Monroe County SO
- Sheriff Michael Gravely
  PO Box 350
  Union, WV 24983
  (304) 772-3018
  NEbridges39@msn.com

Morgan County

- Morgan County SO
- Sheriff Vince Shambaugh
  1260 Valley Rd.
  Berkeley Springs, WV 25411
  (304) 258-1067
  vince@mcsdwv.com

Nicholas County

- Nicholas County SD
- Sheriff Wetzel Bennett
  700 Main St., Ste. 3
  Summersville, WV 26651
  (304) 872-9611
  wetzelbennett@yahoo.com
- Summersville PD
- Chief John Nowak
  400 No. Broad St.
  Summersville, WV 26651
  (304) 872-1211
  robertshafer@summersvillewv.org

Ohio County

- Ohio County SO
- Sheriff Patrick Butler
  1500 Chapline St. PO Box 188
  Wheeling, WV 26003
  (304) 234-3784
  pbutler@ohcoso.com

Pendleton County

- Pendleton County SO
- Sheriff Kevin Puffenberger
  PO Box 687
  Franklin, WV 26807
  (304) 358-2214
  p12kpuff@yahoo.com

Pleasants County

- Pleasants County SD
- Sheriff Ted Maston
  305 Barkwill St.
  St Marys, WV 26170
  (304) 684-2285
  tmast31@sheriff.state.wv.us
- St. Marys PD
- Chief Bill Stull
  418 2nd St.
  St. Marys, W V 26170
  (304) 684-7011
  smpdwv@frontiernet.net

Pocahontas County

- Pocahontas County SO
- Sheriff David Jonese
  9001/2 10th Ave.
  Marlinton, WV 24954
  (304) 799-4710
  drjonese@sheriff.state.wv.us

Preston County

- Preston County SD
- Sheriff Dallas Wolfe
  103 W. Main St.
  Kingwood, WV 26537
  (304) 329-1611
  DDWolfe@prestonsheriff.net

Putnam County

- Putnam County SD
- Sheriff Mark Smith
  3389 Winfield Rd.
  Winfield, WV 25213
  (304) 586-0256
  msmith@putnamwv.org
- Eleanor PD
- Chief Joe Crawford
  401 Roosevelt PO Box 185
  Eleanor, WV 25070
  (304) 586-2319
  eleanortown@verizon.net
- Hurricane PD
- Chief W.M. *Mike* Mullins
  3255 Teays Valley PO Box 1086
  Hurricane, WV 25526
  (304) 562-9911
  info@hurricanewv.com
- Poca PD
- Chief William Seanze
  100 Main St.
  Poca, WV 25159
  (304) 755-5102
  Seanze1@verizon.net

Raleigh County

- Raleigh County SO
- Sheriff Steve Tanner
  215 Main St.
  Beckley, WV 25801
  (304) 255-9195
  stanner@rcso-wv.com
- Beckley PD
- Chief Timothy P. Deems
  340 Prince St.
  Beckley, WV 25802
  (304) 256-1710
  tdeems@beckleypd.com
- Sophia PD
- Chief Tomi Sue Peck
  PO Box 700
  Sophia, WV 25921
  (304) 683-3331
  SophiaPoliceDepartment@gmail.com

Randolph County

- Randolph County SO
- Sheriff Jack Roy, Jr.
  4 Randolph Ave. PO Box 1338
  Elkins, WV 26241
  (304) 636-2100
  rcsd100@verizon.net
- Elkins PD
- Chief Rob White
  401 Davis Ave.
  Elkins, WV 26241
  (304) 636-0678
  hwhite@cityofelkinswv.com

Ritchie County

- Ritchie County SO
- Sheriff Bryan Backus
  109 North St.
  Harrisville, WV 26362
  (304) 643-2262
  ritchiesheriff@hotmail.com

Roane County

- Roane County SO
- Sheriff Mike Harper
  200 Main St.
  Spencer, WV 25276
  (304) 927-2540
  mharper@sheriff.state.wv.us

Summers County

- Summers County SO
- Sheriff Edward Dolphin
  123 Temple St.
  Hinton, WV 25951
  (304) 466-7111
  creekrun@wildblue.net

Taylor County

- Taylor County SD
- Sheriff Robert Beltner
  216 W. Main St. PO Box 189
  Grafton, WV 26354
  (304) 265-3428
  lawman58@comcast.net
- Grafton PD
- Chief Robert W. Beltner
  1 W. Main St.
  Grafton, WV 26354
  (304) 265-1412, ext. 17
  graftonpolicedept@comcast.net

Tucker County

- Tucker County SO
- Sheriff Thomas Felton
  318 2nd St.
  Parsons, WV 26287
  (304) 478-2321
  sheriffeuell@hotmail.com

Tyler County

- Tyler County SO
- Sheriff Bob Kendle, Jr.
  121 Court St. PO Box 7
  Middlebourne, WV 26149
  (304) 758-4229
  sarge_202@hotmail.com
- Paden City PD
- Chief Michael Kelly
  208 W. Main St.
  Paden City, WV 26159
  (See also Wetzel County)
  (304) 337-2281
  pcpd@suddenlinkmail.com

Upshur County

- Upshur County SO
- Sheriff Virgil Miller
  38 W. Main St., Rm. 101
  Buckhannon, WV 26201
  (304) 472-1185
  vmiller@upshurcounty.org
- Buckhannon PD
- Chief Matthew *Matt* Gregory
  70 E. Main St.
  Buckhannon, WV 26201
  (304) 472-5723
  mattgregory@buckhannonpolice.com

Wayne County

- Wayne County SO
- Sheriff Greg Farley
  PO Box 218
  Wayne, WV 25570
  (304) 272-6378
  sheriff@waynesheriff.net
- Kenova PD
- Chief William *Bud* Lett
  1501 Pine St.
  Kenova, WV 25530
  (304) 453-1281
  mayor@kenovawv.com

Webster County

- Webster County SO
- Sheriff Jerry Hamrick
  2 Court Sq. G3
  Webster Springs, WV 26288
  (304) 847-2006
  jfhamrickwcsd@yahoo.com

Wetzel County

- Wetzel County SO
- Sheriff James Hoskins
  PO Drawer D
  New Martinsville, WV 26155
  (304) 455-2430
  hoskins08@yahoo.com
- Paden City PD
- Chief Michael Kelly
  208 W. Main St.
  Paden City, WV 26159
  (See also Tyler County)
  (304) 337-2281
  pcpd@suddenlinkmail.com

Wirt County

- Wirt County SO
- Sheriff Keith Wilson, Jr.
  PO Box 669
  Elizabeth, WV 26143
  (304) 275-4222
  wirtsheriff@hotmail.com

Wood County

- Wood County SO
- Sheriff Jeff Sandy
  328 2nd St.
  Parkersburg, WV 26101
  (304) 424-1834
  sheriff@woodcountywv.com
- Parkersburg PD
- Chief Joseph Martin
  1 Government Sq.
  Parkersburg, WV 26101
  (304) 485-8501
  kroberts@netassoc.net
- Vienna PD
- Chief George Young
  604 29th St.
  Vienna, WV 26105
  (304) 295-8563
  contactus@viennapolice.com

Wyoming County

- Wyoming County SD
- Sheriff Randall Aliff
  PO Box 529
  Pineville, WV 24874
  (304) 732-8000
  wyomingcountysheriff@verizon.net
- Mullens PD
- Chief Ray Toler
  316 Moran Ave.
  Mullens, WV 25882
  (304) 294-7132
  mullenspolice@aol.com

State Agencies

- WV State Police-HQ
- Supt. (*Col.*) CR *Jay* Smithers
  725 Jefferson Rd.
  South Charleston, WV 25309
  (304) 746-2115
  kcarson@wvsp.state.wv.us

WISCONSIN

Adams County

- Adams County SO
- Sheriff Sam Wollin
  301 Adams St.
  Friendship, WI 53934
  (608) 339-3304
  sam.wollin@co.adams.wi.us

Ashland County

- Ashland County SO
- Sheriff Michael Brennan
  220 E. 6th St.
  Ashland, WI 54806
  (715) 685-7640
  mick.brennan@ashlandcountysheriff.us
- La Pointe PD
- Chief Mike Anderson
  270 Main St.
  La Pointe, WI 54850
  (715) 747-6913
  info@townoflapointewi.gov

Barron County

- Barron County SD
- Sheriff Chris Fitzgerald
  1420 State Hwy 25 No.
  Barron, WI 54812
  (715) 537-3106
  chris.fitzgerald@co.barron.wi.us
- •Barron PD
- Chief Byron Miller
  307 E. Lasalle Ave.
  Barron, WI 54812
  (715) 537-3101
  miller@barronpd.com
- Chetek PD
- Chief Mark R. Peterson
  101 Moore St.
  Chetek, WI 54728
  (715) 924-3686
  mpetersen@chibardun.net
- New Auburn PD
- Dir. Bill James
  130 E. Elm St.
  New Auburn, WI 54757
  (715) 237-3200
  webit@auburnalabama.org
- Rice Lake PD
- Chief Steve Roux
  34 So. Wilson Ave.
  Rice Lake, WI 54868
  (715) 234-2116
  rlpdsgr@ricelakegov.com
- Turtle Lake PD
- Chief Al Gabe
  114 E. Martin Ave. PO Box 11
  Turtle Lake, WI 54889
  (715) 986-2942
  tlpd@chibardun.net

Bayfield County

- Bayfield County SO
- Sheriff Paul G. Susienka
  117 E. 6th St.
  Washburn, WI 54891
  (715) 373-6300
  bkurtz@bayfieldcounty.org
- Bayfield PD
- Chief Ellis Casper
  125 So. 1st St.
  Bayfield, WI 54814
  (715) 779-5097
  citypolice@charter.net

Brown County

- Brown County SO
- Sheriff John R. Gossage
  300 E. Walnut St.
  Green Bay, WI 54301
  (920) 448-4200
  gossage_jr@co.brown.wi.us
- Denmark PD
- Chief Ron K. Towns
  118 E. Main St.
  Denmark, WI 54208
  (920) 863-2126
  ron1@villageofdenmark.com
- Green Bay PD
- Chief Thomas Molitor
  307 So. Adams St.
  Green Bay, WI 54301
  (920) 448-3200
  deborahne@greenbaywi.gov
- Pulaski PD
- Chief Randal S. Dunford
  421 So. St. Augustine
  Pulaski, WI 54162
  (920) 822-5110
  chief@villageofpulaski.org

Buffalo County

- Buffalo County SO
- Sheriff Michael J. Schmidtknecht
  407 So. 2nd St. PO Box 396
  Alma, WI 54610-0396
  (608) 685-4433
  michael.schmidtknecht@buffalocounty.com

Burnett County

- Burnett County SD
- Sheriff Dean W. Roland
  7410 City Rd. K #122
  Siren, WI 54872
  (715) 349-2121
  droland@burnettcounty.org
- Grantsburg PD
- Chief Jeff Schinzing
  416 So. Pine St.
  Grantsburg, WI 54840
  (715) 463-2405
  police@grantsburgwi.com
- Siren PD
- Chief Christopher Sybers
  PO Box 23
  Siren, WI 54872
  (715) 349-7181
  sirenpd@sirentel.net
- St. Croix Tribal PD
- Chief Frank Taylor
  24663 Angeline Ave.
  Webster, WI 54893
  (715) 349-8638
  frankt@stcroixtribalcenter.com
- Webster PD
- Chief Michael J. Spafford
  7505 Main St. W.
  Webster, WI 54893
  (715) 349-2121
  websterwipd@gmail.com

Calumet County

- Brillion PD
- Chief Daniel R. Alloy
  130 Calumet St.
  Brillion, WI 54110
  (920) 756-2221
  brillionchief@ci.brillion.wi.us
- Chilton PD
- Chief Larry Seipel
  42 School St.
  Chilton, WI 53014
  (920) 849-4855
  chiltonchief@chiltonwi.com
- New Holstein PD
- Chief Brian Reedy
  2110 Washington St.
  New Holstein, WI 53061
  (920) 898-4241
  reedy.brian@ci.new-holstein.wi.us

Chippewa County

- Chippewa County SO
- Sheriff James L. Kowalczyk
  32 E. Spruce St.
  Chippewa Falls, WI 54729
  (715) 726-7719
  jkowalczyk@co.chippewa.wi.us
- Bloomer PD
- Chief Jared Zwiefelhofer
  1200 15th Ave.
  Bloomer, WI 54724
  (715) 568-5924
  rsummerfield@ci.bloomer.wi.us
- Cadott PD
- Chief Louis L. Eslinger
  110 Central St. PO Box 40
  Cadott, WI 54727
  (715) 289-4238
  cadottpd201@yahoo.com
- Chippewa Falls PD
- Chief Wendy Stelter
  210 Island St.
  Chippewa Falls, WI 54729
  (715) 723-4424
  policedept@chippewafalls-wi.gov
- Lake Hallie PD
- Chief Wendy Stelter
  13141 30th Ave.
  Chippewa Falls, WI 54729
  (715) 726-2666
  policedept@chippewafalls-wi.gov
- Stanley PD
- Chief Russel Killmansberger
  116 3rd Ave.
  Stanley, WI 54768
  (715) 644-5975
  policechief@stanleywisconsin.us

Clark County

- Clark County SO
- Sheriff Greg Herrick
  517 Court St.
  Neillsville, WI 54456
  (715) 743-3157
  greg.herrick@co.clark.wi.us
- Abbotsford PD
- Chief Ron Gosse
  203 E. Birch St.
  Abbortsford, WI 54405
  (715) 223-2313
  rgosse@charter.net

- Granton PD
- Chief Charles E. Wenten
  210 Maple St.
  Granton, WI 54436
  (715) 238-7481
  cwenten@village.grafton.wi.us
- Loyal PD
- Chief Matthew Kubista
  301 No. Main St.
  Loyal, WI 54446
  (715) 255-8986
  stoufar@loyalwi.com
- Neillsville PD
- Chief Bradley C. Lindner
  118 W. 5th St.
  Neillsville, WI 54456
  (715) 743-3122
  npolice@tds.net

Columbia County

- Columbia County SO
- Sheriff Dennis E. Richards
  723 E. Cook St. PO Box 132
  Portage, WI 53901
  (608) 742-4166
  coso@palacenet.net
- Columbus PD
- Chief Daniel Meister
  105 No. Dickason Blvd
  Columbus, WI 53925
  (920) 623-5919
  dmeister@columbuswi.us
- Fall River PD
- Chief Daniel S. Racine
  641 So. Main St.
  Fall River, WI 53932
  (920) 484-3707
  police@fallriverwi.com
- Lodi PD
- Chief William Laughlin
  113 So. Main St.
  Lodi, WI 53555
  (608) 592-5401
  wlaughlin@wppienergy.org
- Portage PD
- Chief Ken Manthey
  117 W. Pleasant St.
  Portage, WI 53901
  (608) 742-2171
  ken.manthey@ci.portage.wi.us
- Poynette PD
- Chief Donald L. White
  106 So. Main St.
  Poynette, WI 53955
  (608) 635-2588
  dwhite@poynette-wi.gov
- Randolph PD
- Chief Michael J Klavekoske
  136 W. Stroud St.
  Randolph, WI 53956
  (920) 326-4620
  randolphpd@powerweb.net
- Rio PD
- Chief Jeff Becker
  207 Lincoln Ave.
  Rio, WI 53960
  (920) 992-5454
  jbecker@riowi.us
- Wisconsin Dells PD
- Chief Jody J. Ward
  712 Oak St.
  Wisconsin Dells, WI 53965
  (608) 253-1611
  jward@wdpd.com
- Wyocena PD
- Chief Doug Jarzynski
  PO Box 913
  Wyocena, WI 53969
  (608) 429-3263
  wyocenapd@hotmail.com

Crawford County

- Crawford County SO
- Sheriff Dale McCullick
  224 No. Beaumont Rd.
  Prairie Du Chien, WI 53821
  (608) 326-0241
  dmccullick@crawfordcounty.wi.org
- Prairie Du Chien PD
- Chief Chad Abram
  228 No. Beaumont Rd.
  Prairie Du Chien, WI 53821
  (608) 326-2421
  pdcpdchief@mhtc.net

Dane County

- Dane County SO
- Sheriff David J. Mahoney
  115 W. Doty St.
  Madison, WI 53703
  (608) 284-6100
  sheriff.web.contact@co.dane.wi.us

- Belleville PD
- Chief William Eichelkraut
  31 E. Main St.
  Belleville, WI 53508
  (608) 424-3129
  bellevillepolice@villageofbelleville.com
- Blue Mounds PD
- Chief Andrew D. Rose
  11011 Brigham Ave.
  Blue Mounds, WI 53517
  (608) 437-5197
  ngretzinger@bluemoundspolice.com
- Brooklyn PD
- Chief James F. Barger
  102 No. Rutland Ave.
  Brooklyn, WI 53521
  (608) 455-2131
  police@brooklynwi.gov
- DeForest PD
- Chief Robert Henze
  305 E. Holum St.
  DeForest, WI 53532
  (608) 846-6756
  police@vi.deforest.wi.us
- Fitchburg PD
- Chief Thomas A. Blatter
  5520 Lacy Rd.
  Fitchburg, WI 53711
  (608) 270-4351
  thomas.blatter@city.fitchburg.wi.us
- Marshall PD
- Chief Lee Hellenbrand
  130 So. Pardee PO Box 540
  Marshall, WI 53559-0540
  (608) 655-3533, ext. 211
  lhellenbrand@marshall-wi.com
- McFarland PD
- Chief Craig J. Sherven
  5915 Milwaukee PO Box 110
  McFarland, WI 53558
  (608) 838-3151
  police.dept@mcfarland.wi.us
- Middleton PD
- Chief Brad Keil
  7341 Donna Dr.
  Middleton, WI 53562
  (608) 824-7300
  police@ci.middleton.wi.us
- Monona PD
- Chief Walter J. Ostrenga
  5211 Schluter Rd.
  Monona, WI 53716
  (608) 222-0463
  dispatch@ci.monona.wi.us
- Mount Horeb PD
- Chief Jeff Veloff
  222 E. Front St.
  Mt Horeb, WI 53572
  (608) 437-5522
  rrohe@mhpd.org
- Shorewood Hills PD
- Chief Dennis Pine
  810 Shorewood Blvd
  Shorewood Hills, WI 53705
  (608) 267-1110
  dpine@shorewood-hills.org
- Stoughton PD
- Chief Greg Leck
  321 So. 4th St.
  Stoughton, WI 53589
  (608) 873-3374
  gleck@ci.stoughton.wi.us
- Sun Prairie PD
- Chief Patrick J. Anhalt
  300 E. Main St.
  Sun Prairie, WI 53590
  (608) 825.1153
  panhalt@cityofsunprairie.com
- Verona PD
- Chief Bernard Coughlin
  111 Lincoln St.
  Verona, WI 53593
  (608) 845-7623
  Bill.burns@ci.verona.wi.us
- Waunakee PD
- Chief Kevin Plendl
  205 No. Klein Dr.
  Waunakee, WI 53597
  (608) 849-4523
  kplendl@waunakeepd.org

Dodge County

- Dodge County SO
- Sheriff Patrick Ninmann
  141 No. Main St.
  Juneau, WI 53039
  (920) 386-3726
  pninmann@co.dodge.wi.us

- Clyman PD
- Chief Randy Kramer
  713 Morgan St. PO Box 129
  Clyman, WI 53016
  (920) 696-3883
  krisk@voclyman.com
- Hustisford PD
- Chief Daniel Link
  201 So. Lake St.
  Hustisford, WI 53034
  (920) 349-3122
  DLink@Hustisfordpd.com
- Iron Ridge PD
- Chief Charles Young
  205 Park St.
  Iron Ridge, WI 53035
  (920) 387-3300
  villageir@yahoo.com
- Juneau PD
- Chief Dave Beal
  150 Miller St.
  Juneau, WI 53039
  (920) 386-4810
  dbeal@cityofjuneau.net
- Reeseville PD
- Chief Scott Bahr
  214 Firehouse Dr.
  Reeseville, WI 53579
  (920) 927-5272
  reesevillepd@netwurx.net

Door County

- Door County SO
- Sheriff Terry J. Vogel
  1201 So. Duluth Ave.
  Sturgeon Bay, WI 54235
  (920) 746-2400
  sheriff@co.door.wi.us
- Sturgeon Bay PD
- Chief Arleigh R. Porter
  421 Michigan St.
  Sturgeon Bay, WI 54235
  (920) 746-2450
  aporter@sturgeonbaywi.org

Douglas County

- Douglas County SO
- Sheriff Thomas Dalbec
  1316 No. 14th St.
  Superior, WI 54880
  (715) 395-1371
  dalbect@ci.superior.wi.us
- Superior PD
- Chief Charles LaGesse
  1316 No. 14th St., Ste. 150
  Superior, WI 54880
  (715) 395-7234
  policedept@ci.superior.wi.us

Dunn County

- Dunn County SO
- Sheriff Dennis Smith
  615 Stokke Pkwy
  Menomonie, WI 54751
  (715) 232-1348
  dsmith@co.dunn.wi.us
- Colfax PD
- Chief Pete Gehring
  603 Main St.
  Colfax, WI 54730
  (715) 962-3136
  colfax@villageofcolfaxwi.org
- Elk Mound PD
- Chief Michael Tietz
  E206 Menomonie St.
  Elk Mound, WI 54739
  (715) 879-4411
  police@elk-mound.org
- Menomonie PD
- Chief Eric Atkinson
  615 Stokke Pkwy
  Menomonie, WI 54751
  (715) 231-2659
  atkinsone@menomonie-wi.gov

Eau Claire County

- Eau Claire County SO
- Sheriff Ron D. Cramer
  728 2nd Ave.
  Eau Claire, WI 54703
  (715) 839-4709
  john.vogler@co.eau-claire.wi.us
- Altoona PD
- Chief James Small
  1904 Spooner Ave.
  Altoona, WI 54720
  (715) 839-6090
  jamess@ci.altoona.wi.us
- Fall Creek PD
- Chief Chad Dachel
  122 E. Lincoln Ave.
  Fall Creek, WI 54742
  (715) 877-3231
  policedepartment@fallcreekwi.gov

Fond Du Lac County

- Fond Du Lac County SO
- Sheriff Mylan C. Fink, Jr.
  180 So. Macy St.
  Fond Du Lac, WI 54936
  (920) 929-3391
  rick.olig@fdlco.wi.gov
- Brandon PD
- Chief Thomas R Dornbrook
  115 No. Center
  Brandon, WI 53919
  (920) 346-5555
  Chief@bfpolice.org
- Campbellsport PD
- Chief Bret Anderson
  177 E. Main St.
  Campbellsport, WI 53010
  (920) 533-5391
  cpd53010@yahoo.com
- Fond Du Lac PD
- Chief William Lamb
  126 No. Main St.
  Fond Du Lac, WI 54935
  (920) 322-3700
  info@fdlpolice.com
- Oakfield PD
- Chief Renee Schuster
  105 W. White St.
  Oakfield, WI 53065
  (920) 583-3834
  rschuster@villageofoakfield.com
- Ripon PD
- Chief Dave Lukoski
  100 E. Jackson St.
  Ripon, WI 54971
  (920) 748-2888
  dlukoski@cityofripon.com
- Rosendale PD
- Chief Kevin Verdine
  208 No. Main St.
  Rosendale, WI 54974
  (920) 872-5050
  kverdine@villageofrosendale.com
- Waupun PD
- Chief Dale Heeringa
  16 E. Main St.
  Waupun, WI 53963
  (920) 324-7911
  dale@waupunpd.org

Forest County

- Crandon PD
- Chief Dan Packard, Jr.
  103 So. Hazeldell Ave.
  Crandon, WI 54520
  (715) 478-3821
  cpd54520@frontiernet.net

Grant County

- Grant County SD
- Sheriff Nathan Reckman
  1000 No. Adams St.
  Lancaster, WI 53813
  (608) 723-2157
  ndreckman@co.grant.wi.gov
- Dickeyville PD
- Chief Steve Zabel
  100 Short Ave.
  Dickeyville, WI 53808
  (608) 568-7284
  SteveZ@lancasterwisconsin.com
- Hazel Green PD
- Chief Brian Klein
  1610 Fairplay St.
  Hazel Green, WI 53811
  (608) 854-2951
  hgpd@yousq.net
- Muscoda PD
- Chief Bill Schram
  PO Box 192
  Muscoda, WI 53573
  (608) 739-3144
  cljohnsonwp@pienergy.org
- Platteville PD
- Chief Doug McKinley
  5 W. Mineral St.
  Platteville, WI 53818
  (608) 348-2313
  borgend@platteville.org

Green County

- Green County SO
- Sheriff Jeffrey S. Skatrud
  2827 6th St.
  Monroe, WI 53566
  (608) 328-9400
  grso@greensheriff.com
- Albany PD
- Chief Robert J. Levitt
  206 No. Water St.
  Albany, WI 53502
  (608) 862-3255
  villageclerk@albanywi.org

- Brodhead PD
- Chief Thomas D Moczynski
  1004 W. Exchange St.
  Brodhead, WI 53520
  (608) 897-2112
  bhpd@brodheadpolice.com
- Brooklyn PD
- Chief James F. Barger
  102 No. Rutland Ave.
  Brooklyn, WI 53521
  (608) 455-4201
  police@brooklynwi.gov
- Monroe PD
- Chief Frederick A. Kelley
  1811 12th St.
  Monroe, WI 53566
  (608) 325-4122
  monroepd@pdmonroe.com
- New Glarus PD
- Chief Burt Boldebuck
  319 2nd St.
  New Glarus, WI 53574
  (608) 527-2145
  chief.ngpd@newglarusvillage.com

Green Lake County

- Green Lake County SO
- Sheriff Mark A. Podoll
  571 County Road A
  Green Lake, WI 54941
  (920) 294-4000
  mpodoll@co.green-lake.wi.us
- Berlin PD
- Chief Joseph Rieder
  108 No. Capron St.
  Berlin, WI 54923
  (920) 361-2121
  godec@nbpolice.org
- Green Lake PD
- Chief Michael Ratter
  534 Mill St.
  Green Lake, WI 54941
  (920) 294-6333
  police@cityofgreenlake.com
- Princeton PD
- Chief Matt Bargenquast
  531 So. Fulton St.
  Princeton, WI 54968
  (920) 295-6250
  jweidl@cityofprincetonwi.com

Iowa County

- Iowa County SO
- Sheriff Steven Michek
  1205 No. Bequette St.
  Dodgeville, WI 53533
  (608) 935-3314
  steve.michek@iowacounty.org
- Arena PD
- Chief Lonnie Drinkall
  345 West St.
  Arena, WI 53503
  (608) 753-2297
  arenapd@charterinternet.net
- Barneveld PD
- Chief Jeremy Oyen
  403 E. Business
  Barneveld, WI 53507
  (608) 924-6861
  barneveldpd@mhtc.net
- Dodgeville PD
- Chief David Kieffer
  111 W. Merrimac St.
  Dodgeville, WI 53533
  (608) 935-3238
  dk50@cityofdodgeville.com
- Highland PD
- Chief Peter Hojnicki
  PO Box 284
  Highland, WI 53543
  (608) 929-4848
  phojnicki@highland.in.gov

Jackson County

- Jackson County SO
- Sheriff Duane M. Waldera
  30 No. 3rd St.
  Black River Falls, WI 54615
  (715) 284-9009
  sheriff@co.jackson.wi.us
- Melrose PD
- Chief Cal D. Smokowicz
  112 No. Washington
  Melrose, WI 54642
  (608) 488-3191
  police@melrosewi.com
- Merrillan PD
- Village Marshall Kelly Bakken
  101 So. Main St.
  Merrillan, WI 54754
  (715) 333-2332
  merrillanpolice@centurytel.net

Jefferson County

- Jefferson County SO
- Sheriff Paul Milbrath
  411 So. Center Ave.
  Jefferson, WI 53549
  (920) 674-7310
  sheriff@jeffersoncountywi.gov
- Fort Atkinson PD
- Chief Anthony J. *Tony* Brus
  101 So. Water St. W.
  Fort Atkinson, WI 53538
  (920) 563-7777
  tbrus@fortpd.com
- Johnson Creek PD
- Chief Gary Bleecker
  125 Depot St.
  Johnson Creek, WI 53038
  (920) 699-2111
  garyb@johnsoncreekwi.org
- Lake Mills PD
- Chief Patrick Matuszewski
  200A Water St.
  Lake Mills, WI 53551
  (920) 648-2354
  pmatuszewski@ci.lake-mills.wi.us
- Waterloo PD
- Chief Timothy Thomas
  136 No. Monroe St.
  Waterloo, WI 53594
  (920) 478-2343
  police@waterloowi.us

Juneau County

- Juneau County SO
- Sheriff Brent Oleson
  200 Oak St.
  Mauston, WI 53948
  (608) 847-5649
  sheriff1@co.juneau.wi.us
- Lyndon Station PD
- Chief Greg Jessen
  116 No. Lemonwein
  Lyndon Station, WI 53944
  (608) 666-2500
  clerk@lyndonstation-wi.com
- Mauston PD
- Chief Mark Messer
  303 Mansion St.
  Mauston, WI 53948
  (608) 847-6363
  mspolice@mauston.com
- Necedah PD
- Chief Seth S. Tully
  PO Box 38
  Necedah, WI 54646
  (608) 565-2405
  necedahpolice@necedah.us
- New Lisbon PD
- Chief Brent Granger
  218 E. Bridge St.
  New Lisbon, WI 53950
  (608) 562-3333
  nlpd@mwt.net

Kenosha County

- Kenosha County SO
- Sheriff David B. *Bill* Beth
  1000 55th St.
  Kenosha, WI 53140
  (262) 605-5100
  bill.beth@kenoshacounty.org
- Kenosha PD
- Chief John W. Morrissey
  1000 55th St.
  Kenosha, WI 53140
  (262) 605-5202
  jwm309@kenoshapolice.com
- Pleasant Prairie PD
- Chief David Smetana
  8600 Green Bay Rd.
  Pleasant Prairie, WI 53158
  (262) 694-7353
  dsmetana@plprairie.com
- Silver Lake PD
- Chief Dan Kingsley
  113 So. 1st St.
  Silver Lake, WI 53170
  (262) 889-4100
  slpolice@bizwi.rr.com
- Twin Lakes PD
- Chief Dale R. Racer
  920 Lance Dr.
  Twin Lakes, WI 53181
  (262) 877-9056
  racer@twinlakespolice.org

Kewaunee County

- Kewaunee County SD
- Sheriff Matthew J. Joski
  620 Juneau St.
  Kewaunee, WI 54216
  (920) 388-3100
  joskim@kewauneeco.org

- Kewaunee PD
- Chief Frank Salentine
  77 Ellis St.
  Kewaunee, WI 54216
  (920) 388-5010
  paralfarms@yahoo.com

La Crosse County

- La Crosse County SO
- Sheriff Steven J. Helgeson
  333 Vine St.
  La Crosse, WI 54601
  (608) 785-5942
  Helgeson.Steve@co.la-crosse.wi.us
- Bangor PD
- Chief Scott Alo
  100 17th Ave. No.
  Bangor, WI 54614
  (608) 486-4276
  Smiller@villageofbangor.com
- Campbell PD
- Chief Ronald Tischer
  2219 Bainbridge St.
  La Crosse, WI 54603
  (608) 785-5942
  tischerr@cityoflacrosse.org
- Holmen PD
- Chief Mike McHugh
  421 So. Main
  Holmen, WI 54636
  (608) 526-4212
  mchugh@holmenwi.com
- Onalaska PD
- Chief Jeffrey S. Trotnic
  230 Main St.
  Onalaska, WI 54650
  (608) 781-9550
  jtrotnic@cityofonalaska.com
- West Salem PD
- Chief Charles E. Ashbeck
  175 So. Leonard St.
  West Salem, WI 54669
  (608) 786-0407
  cashbeck@westsalempolice.org

Lafayette County

- Lafayette County SO
- Sheriff Scott E. Pedley
  626 No. Main St.
  Darlington, WI 53530
  (608) 776-4870
  scott.pedley@lafayettecountywi.org
- Belmont PD
- Chief Daniel J. DeSmidt
  222 Mound Ave.
  Belmont, WI 53510
  (608) 762-5326
  police@belmont.gov
- Blanchardville PD
- Chief Thomas M. Marson
  208 Mason St.
  Blanchardville, WI 53516
  (608) 523-4320
  blanchardvillepd@tds.net
- Darlington PD
- Chief Jason King
  627 Main St.
  Darlington, WI 53530
  (608) 776-4980
  jason.king@cityofdarlingtonwi.org
- Shullsburg PD
- Chief Richard Moyer
  125 So. Kennedy St.
  Shullsburg, WI 53586
  (608) 965-4436
  moyer@cityofshullsburg.org

Langlade County

- Langlade County SO
- Sheriff William *Bill* Greening
  840 Clermont St.
  Antigo, WI 54409
  (715) 627-6411
  bgreening@co.langlade.wi.us
- Antigo PD
- Chief Eric J. Roller
  840 Clermont St.
  Antigo, WI 54409
  (715) 623-4111
  ANPD@antigo-city.org

Lincoln County

- Lincoln County SO
- Sheriff Jeffrey W. Jaeger
  1104 E. 1st St.
  Merrill, WI 54452
  (715) 536-6272
  jjaeger@co.lincoln.wi.us
- Merrill PD
- Chief Ken Neff
  1004 E. 1st St.
  Merrill, WI 54452
  (715) 536-2311
  Police@ci.merrill.wi.us

- Tomahawk PD
- Chief Al Alvins
  219 W. Soma Ave.
  Tomahawk, WI 54487
  (715) 453-2121
  policedepartment@cityoftomahawk.com

Manitowoc County

- Manitowoc County SO
- Sheriff Robert C. Hermann
  1025 So. 9th St.
  Manitowoc, WI 54220
  (920) 683-4200
  countyclerk@co.manitowoc.wi.us
- Cleveland PD
- Chief Tim Barber
  1202 W. Washington
  Cleveland, WI 53015
  (920) 693-3442
  Police@Clevelandwi.gov
- Kiel PD
- Chief Dave Funkhouser
  621 6th St.
  Kiel, WI 53042
  (920) 894-2211
  dfunkhouser@kielpolice.com
- Manitowoc PD
- Chief Oscar *Tony* Dick
  910 Jay St.
  Manitowoc, WI 54220
  (920) 686-6573
  odick@manitowoc.org
- Valders PD
- Chief William Riesterer
  207 So. Liberty St.
  Valders, WI 54245
  (920) 775-4522
  valderspolice@tds.net

Marathon County

- Marathon County SD
- Sheriff Scott Parks
  500 Forest St.
  Wausau, WI 54403
  (715) 261-1200
  sheriff@mail.co.marathon.wi.us
- Athens PD
- Chief Aaron Stencil
  221 Caroline St.
  Athens, WI 54411
  (715) 257-7611
  athenspolice@villageofathens.com
- Edgar PD
- Chief Andrew Deininger
  224 So. 3rd Ave.
  Edgar, WI 54426
  (715) 352-2891
  edgarpd@dwave.net
- Everest Metro PD
- Chief Wally Sparks
  5303 Mesker St.
  Weston, WI 54476
  (715) 359-4202
  empd@everestmetropolice.org
- Kronenwetter PD
- Chief Ken Muelling
  1582 Kronenwetter Dr.
  Mosinee, WI 54455
  (715) 693-4215
  policechief@mosinee.wi.us
- Marathon PD
- Chief Kory Gertschen
  311 Walnut St.
  Marathon, WI 54448
  (715) 443-2470
  mcpd@marathoncity.org
- Rothschild PD
- Chief Jeremy P. Hunt
  211 Grand Ave.
  Rothschild, WI 54474
  (715) 359-3879
  info@rothschildwi.com
- Spencer PD
- Chief Shawn Bauer
  105 So. Park St.
  Spencer, WI 54479
  (715) 659-5453
  spencerpd@vil.spencer.wi.us
- Stratford PD
- Chief Korey Schillinger
  265 3rd St.
  Stratford, WI 54484
  (715) 687-3131
  Stratfordpolice@stratfordwi.com

Marinette County

- Coleman PD
- Chief Ida Soletske
  107 W. Main St.
  Coleman, WI 54112
  (414) 897-4400
  clerk@villageofcoleman.com

- Crivitz PD
- Chief Michael G. Frievalt
  PO Box 402
  Crivitz, WI 54114
  (715) 854-7667
  mfrievalt@cpd2.com
- Marinette PD
- Chief John Mabry
  1905 Hall Ave.
  Marinette, WI 54143
  (715) 732-5200
  smonahan@marinette.wi.us

Marquette County

- Marquette County SO
- Sheriff Kim V. Gaffney
  67 Park St.
  Montello, WI 53949
  (608) 297-2115
  kgaffney@co.marquette.wi.us
- Oxford PD
- Chief John Slauch
  129 So. Franklin PO Box 122
  Oxford, WI 53952
  (608) 586-4428
  chief@theoxfordpd.com
- Westfield PD
- Chief Louis Rudolph
  109 E. 3rd St.
  Westfield, WI 53964
  (608) 297-2115
  vilwestpolicechief@frontier.com

Milwaukee County

- Milwaukee County SO
- Sheriff David A. Clarke, Jr.
  821 W. State St., Rm. 107
  Milwaukee, WI 53233
  (414) 278-4726
  sheriff@milncnty.com
- Brown Deer PD
- Chief Edward A. Flynn
  4800 W. Green Brook Dr.
  Milwaukee, WI 53223
  (414) 371-2900
  webhelp@milwaukee.gov
- Fox Point PD
- Chief Tom Czaja
  7300 No. Santa Monica Blvd
  Fox Point, WI 53217
  (414) 351-8911
  tczaja@vil.fox-point.wi.us
- Greendale PD
- Chief Robert Malasuk
  5911 W. Grange Ave.
  Greendale, WI 53129
  (414) 423-2121
  greendalepd@greendalepolice.org
- Greenfield PD
- Chief Brad Wentlandt
  5300 W. Layton Ave.
  Greenfield, WI 53220
  (414) 761-5300
  brad.wentlandt@gfpd.org
- Milwaukee PD
- Chief Edward Flynn
  749 W. State St.
  Milwaukee, WI 53233
  (414) 933-4444
  webhelp@milwaukee.gov
- Oak Creek PD
- Chief John Edwards
  7625 So. Howell Ave.
  Oak Creek, WI 53154
  (414) 762-8200
  jedwards@oakcreekwi.org
- St. Francis PD
- Chief Brian Kaebisch
  4235 So. Nicholson Ave.
  St. Francis, WI 53235
  (414) 481-2232
  policechief@stfranwi.org
- Shorewood PD
- Chief David Banaszynski
  3936 No. Murray Ave.
  Shorewood, WI 53211
  (414) 847-2610
  police@villageofshorewood.org
- South Milwaukee PD
- Chief Ann M. Wellens
  2424 15th Ave.
  South Milwaukee, WI 53172
  (414) 768-8060
  wellens@smwi.org
- Whitefish Bay PD
- Chief Michael Young
  5300 No. Marlborough Dr.
  Whitefish Bay, WI 53217
  (414) 962-3830
  m.young@wfbvillage.org

Monroe County

- Monroe County SD
- Sheriff Peter Quirin
  210 W. Oak St.
  Sparta, WI 54656-2185
  (608) 269-2117
  sheriff.reports@co.monroe.wi.us
- Tomah PD
- Chief Wes Revels
  819 Superior Ave.
  Tomah, WI 54660
  (608) 374-7400
  tomahpd@tomahpolice.com

Oconto County

- Gillett PD
- Chief William A. Pecha
  150 No. Mckenzie St.
  Gillett, WI 54124
  (920) 855-2125
  webmaster@ci.gillett.wi.us
- Lena PD
- Chief Jessie Keplinger
  117 E. Main St. PO Box 176
  Lena, WI 54139
  (920) 829-5950
  lenapd@villageoflena.net
- Oconto PD
- Chief Mike Roberts
  1210 Main St.
  Oconto, WI 54153
  (920) 834-7700
  miker@ci.ocontofalls.wi.us
- Suring PD
- Chief Nick School
  604 E. Main St.
  Suring, WI 54174
  (920) 842-2125
  suringpolice@ci.suring.wi.us

Oneida County

- Oneida County SD
- Sheriff Grady Hartman
  2000 E. Winnebago St.
  Rhinelander, WI 54501
  (715) 361-5100
  ghartman@co.oneida.wi.us
- Minocqua PD
- Chief David J. Jaeger
  418 Chicago Ave. PO Box 346
  Minocqua, WI 54548
  (715) 356-3234
  djaeger@minocquapd.com
- Rhinelander PD
- Chief Michael Steffes
  201 No. Brown St.
  Rhinelander, WI 54501
  (715) 365-5300
  msteffes@rhinelanderpd.com
- Three Lakes PD
- Chief Scott E. Lea
  PO Box 5
  Three Lakes, WI 54562
  (715) 546-2211
  slea@mail.co.oneida.wi.us

Outagamie County

- Outagamie County SO
- Sheriff Bradley G. Gehring
  410 So. Walnut St.
  Appleton, WI 54911
  (920) 832-5605
  donna.leski@outagamie.org
- Combined Locks PD
- Chief Erick Misselt
  405 Wallace St.
  Combined Locks, WI 54113
  (920) 731-6321
  erik.misselt@fvmpd.org
- Fox Valley Metro PD
- Chief Erick Misselt
  200 W. McKinley Ave.
  Little Chute, WI 54140
  (920) 788-1511
  paula.stanislawski@fvmpd.org
- Kaukauna PD
- Chief John Manion
  201 W. 2nd St.
  Kaukauna, WI 54130
  (920) 766-6333
  manionjn@kaukauna-wi.org
- Seymour PD
- Chief Richard A. Buntrock
  306 No. Main St.
  Seymour, WI 54165
  (920) 833-2366
  rbuntrock@seymour-pd.com
- Shiocton PD
- Chief Kristin Brownson
  N5605 State Rt. 76
  Shiocton, WI 54170
  (920) 986-3294
  kbrownson@shiocton.us

Ozaukee County

- Ozaukee County SO
- Sheriff Maury Straub
  1201 So. Spring St.
  Port Washington, WI 53074
  (262) 284-7172
  ctyclerk@co.ozaukee.wi.us
- Cedarburg PD
- Chief Thomas J. Frank
  W75 N444 Wauwatosa Rd.
  Cedarburg, WI 53012
  (262) 375-7620
  cpd@ci.cedarburg.wi.us
- Grafton PD
- Chief Charles E. Wenten
  1981 Washington St.
  Grafton, WI 53024
  (262) 375-5320
  cwenten@village.grafton.wi.us
- Mequon PD
- Chief Steven D. Graff
  11300 No. Buntrock Ave.
  Mequon, WI 53092
  (262) 242-3500
  sgraff@ci.mequon.wi.us
- Port Washington PD
- Chief Kevin Hingiss
  365 No. Wisconsin St.
  Port Washington, WI 53074
  (262) 284-2611
  khingiss@pwpd.org
- Saukville PD
- Chief William Meloy
  639 E. Green Bay Ave.
  Saukville, WI 53080
  (262) 284-0444
  bmeloy@village.saukville.wi.us
- Thiensville PD
- Chief Scott H. Nicholson
  250 Elm St.
  Thiensville, WI 53092
  (262) 242-2100
  snicholson@village.thiensville.wi.us

Pepin County

- Pepin County SO
- Sheriff John Andrews
  740 7th Ave. W.
  Durand, WI 54736
  (715) 672-5945
  jandrews@co.pepin.wi.us
- Durand PD
- Chief Stan Ridgeway
  740 7th Ave. W.
  Durand, WI 54736-0039
  (715) 672-5948
  police@cityofdurand.com

Pierce County

- Pierce County SO
- Sheriff Nancy Hove
  432 W. Main St.
  Ellsworth, WI 54011
  (715) 273-5051
  mercordrobert@comcast.net
- Ellsworth PD
- Chief Darrin Foss
  130 No. Chestnut
  Ellsworth, WI 54011
  (715) 273-3275
  chief@ellsworthpolice.org
- Prescott PD
- Chief Bill Dravis
  1601 Pine St.
  Prescott, WI 54021
  (715) 262-5512
  bdravis@prescottcity.org
- River Falls PD
- Chief Roger E. Leque
  111 No. 2nd St.
  River Falls, WI 54022
  (715) 425-0909
  rleque@rfcity.org
- Spring Valley PD
- Chief Dennis Sorenson
  E. 121 So. 2nd St.
  Spring Valley, WI 54767
  (715) 778-5678
  chief@svpolice.org

Polk County

- Polk County SO
- Sheriff Peter M. Johnson
  1005 W. Main St.
  Balsam Lake, WI 54810
  (715) 485-8300
  peterj@co.polk.wi.us
- Amery PD
- Chief Thomas M. *Tom* Marson
  120 Center St.
  Amery, WI 54001
  (715) 268-7411
  tom.marson@amerypd.org

- Balsam Lake PD
- Chief Thomas Thompson
  404 Main St. PO Box 506
  Balsam Lake, WI 54810
  (715) 485-3544
  balsamlakepd@lakeland.ws
- Frederic PD
- Chief Dale Johnson
  PO Box 567
  Frederic, WI 54837
  (715) 327-8851
  police@fredericwi.com
- Osceola PD
- Chief Tim Lauridsen
  310 Chieftain St. PO Box 217
  Osceola, WI 54020
  (715) 294-3628
  chflauridsen@vil.osceola.wi.us

Portage County

- Portage County SD
- Sheriff John E. Charewicz
  1500 Strongs Ave.
  Stevens Point, WI 54481
  (715) 346-1400
  sheriff@co.portage.wi.us
- Plover PD
- Chief Dwayne D. Wierzba
  2420 Post Rd. PO Box 37
  Plover, WI 54467
  (715) 345-5255
  dwierzba@ploverwi.gov
- Stevens Point PD
- Chief David A. Sonntag
  1515 Strongs Ave.
  Stevens Point, WI 54481
  (715) 346-1500
  phillipspd@pctcnet.net

Price County

- Price County SO
- Sheriff Brian S. Schmidt
  164 Cherry St.
  Phillips, WI 54555
  (715) 339-3011
  sheriff@co.price.wi.us
- Park Falls PD
- Chief Scott Straetz
  400 4th Ave. So. PO Box 146
  Park Falls, WI 54552
  (715) 762-2446
  mayor@cityofparkfalls.com

Racine County

- Racine County SO
- Sheriff Christopher Schmaling
  717 Wisconsin Ave.
  Racine, WI 53403
  (262) 636-3211
  RCSheriff@goracine.org
- Burlington PD
- Chief Peter A. Nimmer
  224 E. Jefferson St.
  Burlington, WI 53105
  (262) 342-1100
  pnimmer@burlington-wi.gov
- Caledonia PD
- Chief E. Toby Schey
  6900 Nicholson Rd.
  Caledonia, WI 53108
  (262) 835-4423
  eschey@caledoniawipd.com
- Norway PD
- Chief John Hanrahan
  6419 Heg Park Rd.
  Wind Lake, WI 53185
  (262) 895-2195
  norwaypd@wi.rr.com
- Racine PD
- Chief Arthell Art Howell
  730 Center St.
  Racine, WI 53403
  (262) 635-7710
  Arthel.Howell@cityofracine.org
- Waterford PD
- Chief Tom Ditscheit
  122 No. 2nd St.
  Waterford, WI 53185
  (262) 534-3911
  tditscheit@waterfordpd.com

Richland County

- Richland County SO
- Sheriff Darrell Berglin
  181 W. Seminary St.
  Richland Center, WI 53581
  (608) 647-2106
  berglinda@co.richland.wi.us
- Richland Center PD
- Chief John Annear
  470 So. Main St.
  Richland Center, WI 53581
  (608) 647-2103
  rcpd@rcpolice.net

Rock County

- Clinton PD
- Chief James R. Korth
  301 Cross St.
  Clinton, WI 53525
  (608) 676-5140
  clnpd@aol.com
- Evansville PD
- Chief Scott McElroy
  535 E. Madison St.
  Evansville, WI 53536
  (608) 882-2292
  s.mcelroy@ci.evansville.wi.gov
- Janesville PD
- Chief David J. Moore
  18 No. Jackson St.
  Janesville, WI 53545
  (608) 755-3100
  aagaardc@ci.janesville.wi.us
- Milton PD
- Chief Dan Layber
  120 Parkview Dr.
  Milton, WI 53563
  (608) 868-6910
  miltonpd@milton-wi.gov
- Orfordville PD
- Chief Dave Wickstrum
  106 No. Center St.
  Orfordville, WI 53576
  (608) 879-9212
  Police@Orfordville.org

Rusk County

- Rusk County SO
- Sheriff David Kaminski
  311 E. Miner Ave., Ste. L100
  Ladysmith, WI 54848
  (715) 532-2189
  dk101@ruskcountywi.us
- Ladysmith PD
- Chief Allen S. Lobermeier
  311 Miner Ave. E.
  Ladysmith, WI 54848
  (715) 532-2186
  ladysmithpd@ruskcountywi.us

St. Croix County

- St. Croix County SO
- Sheriff John Shilts
  1101 Carmichael Rd.
  Hudson, WI 54016
  (715) 381-4320
  john.shilts@co.saint-croix.wi.us
- Baldwin PD
- Chief Jim Widiker
  1090 10th Ave.
  Baldwin, WI 54002
  (715) 684-3856
  tracy@villageofbaldwin.com
- Glenwood City PD
- Chief Robert John Darwin
  412 2nd St.
  Glenwood City, WI 54013
  (715) 265-4227
  chiefdarwin@glenwoodcitypd.com
- Hammond PD
- Chief Rick Coltrain
  455 Davis St. PO Box 299
  Hammond, WI 54015
  (715) 796-2345
  vohpolice@centurytel.net
- Star Prairie PD
- Chief Steven Lewis
  310 Hill Ave.
  Star Prairie, WI 54026
  (715) 248-7720
  starpv@frontiernet.net
- Woodville PD
- Chief Lori Hetfeld
  102 So. Main St.
  Woodville, WI 54028
  (715) 698-2169
  jan@villageofwoodville.org

Sauk County

- Sauk County SO
- Sheriff Chip Meister
  1300 Lange Ct.
  Baraboo, WI 53913
  (608) 356-4895
  mkrueger@co.sauk.wi.us
- Baraboo PD
- Chief Mark Schauf
  135 4th St.
  Baraboo, WI 53913
  (608) 355-2720
  mschauf@cityofbaraboo.com
- Lake Delton PD
- Chief Thomas D. Dorner
  PO Box 510
  Lake Delton, WI 53940
  (608) 254-7571
  lakedeltonpd@lakedelton.org

- Spring Green PD
- Chief Kevin J. Wilkins
  112 W. Monroe St.
  Spring Green, WI 53588
  (608) 588-2125
  springgreendepclerk@charter.net

Sawyer County

- Hayward PD
- Chief Joel Clapero
  120 E. 1st St.
  Hayward, WI 54843
  (715) 634-8961
  jclapero@haywardpolice.org

Shawano County

- Bonduel PD
- Chief Todd Chaney
  117 W. Green Bay St.
  Bonduel, WI 54107
  (715) 526-3111
  bonduelpd@villageofbonduel.com
- Shawano PD
- Chief John Gutho
  125 So. Sawyer St.
  Shawano, WI 54166
  (715) 524-4545
  swpd@co.shawano.wi.us

Sheboygan County

- Sheboygan County SD
- Sheriff Todd W. Priebe
  525 No. 6th St.
  Sheboygan, WI 53081
  (920) 459-3112
  Dave.Adams@SheboyganCounty.com
- Cascade PD
- Chief Cory Roeseler
  301 1st St.
  Cascade, WI 53011
  (920) 459-3112
  cascade@wi.rr.com
- Elkhart Lake PD
- Chief Michael Meeusen
  40 Pine St.
  Elkhart Lake, WI 53020
  (920) 876-2244
  mmeeusen@elkhartlakewi.gov
- Kohler PD
- Chief William J. Rutten
  319 Highland Dr.
  Kohler, WI 53044
  (920) 459-3877
  wrutten@kohlerpolice.com
- Sheboygan PD
- Chief Christopher Domagalski
  828 Center Ave.
  Sheboygan, WI 53081
  (920) 459-3333
  christopher.domagalski@ci.sheboygan.wi.us

Taylor County

- Taylor County SD
- Sheriff Bruce Daniels
  224 So. 2nd St.
  Medford, WI 54451
  (715) 748-2200
  ewancr@tds.net
- Gilman PD
- Chief Thomas Tallier
  115 Davlin St.
  Gilman, WI 54433
  (715) 447-5700
  gilmanpd@centurytel.net
- Medford PD
- Chief Ken Coyer
  224 So. 2nd St.
  Medford, WI 54451
  (715) 748-1447
  elk.river@live.com

Trempealeau County

- Trempealeau County SO
- Sheriff Richard Anderson
  36245 Main St. PO Box 67
  Whitehall, WI 54773
  (715) 538-4509
  tcsheriff@tremplocounty.com
- Galesville PD
- Chief Paul Evanson
  16773 So. Main St.
  Galesville, WI 54630
  (608) 582-4013
  cityofgalesville@tcc.coop
- Osseo PD
- Chief Tim Wilson
  13712 8th St.
  Osseo, WI 54758
  (715) 597-2481
  tawilson@cityofosseo.us
- Trempealeau PD
- Chief Rick Niedfeldt
  24455 E. 3rd St.
  Trempealeau, WI 54661
  (608) 534-6875
  tremplopolice@centurytel.net

Vernon County

- Vernon County SO
- Sheriff John Spears
  400 Courthouse Sq.
  Viroqua, WI 54665
  (608) 637-2124
  jspears@vernoncounty.org
- Hillsboro PD
- Chief Thomas Richardson
  836 Prairie Ave.
  Hillsboro, WI 54634
  (608) 489-2800
  chiefr@hillsborowi.com
- La Farge PD
- Chief Benjamin Bakken
  Main St.
  La Farge, WI 54639
  (608) 625-4500
  lafpd@mwt.net
- Viroqua PD
- Chief Daron Jefson
  702 E. Broadway St.
  Viroqua, WI 54665
  (608) 637-2121
  vpd@mwt.net

Vilas County

- Boulder Junction PD
- Chief James Hanson
  PO Box 534
  Boulder Junction, WI 54512
  (800) 472-7290
  clerk@townofboulderjunction.org
- Eagle River PD
- Chief Mark Vander Bloomen
  525 Maple St.
  Eagle River, WI 54521
  (715) 479-4343
  mavand@co.vilas.wi.us

Walworth County

- Walworth County SO
- Sheriff David A. Graves
  W4054 City Rd. NN
  Elkhorn, WI 53121
  (262) 741-4400
  walcosh@co.walworth.wi.us
- Bloomfield PD
- Chief Dennis Linn
  N1100 Townhall
  PO Box 47
  Pell Lake, WI 53157
  (262) 279-3454
  chief@townofbloomfield.com
- Delavan PD
- Chief Timothy S. O'Neill
  5621 Town Hall Rd.
  Delavan, WI 53115
  (262) 728-9777
  tdpd@pensys.com
- Elkhorn PD
- Chief Joel Christensen
  404 No. Washington St.
  Elkhorn, WI 53121
  (262) 723-2210
  info@elkhornpd.org
- Fontana PD
- Chief Steve Olson
  185 Douglas Ave. PO Box 325
  Fontana, WI 53125
  (262) 275-2275
  police.department@villageoffontana.com
- Genoa City PD
- Chief Joseph Balog
  PO Box 428
  Genoa City, WI 53128
  (262) 279-6252
  balog@genoacitypolice.org
- Lake Geneva PD
- Chief Michael Rasmussen
  626 Geneva St.
  Lake Geneva, WI 53147
  (262) 248-4455
  lgpd@genevaonline.com
- Sharon PD
- Chief Brad Buchholz
  125 Plain St.
  Sharon, WI 53585
  (262) 736-4617
  Bbuchholz@sharonwipolice.com
- Whitewater PD
- Chief Lisa Otterbacher
  312 W. Whitewater St.
  Whitewater, WI 53190
  (262) 473-0555
  lotterbacher@whitewater-wi.gov

- Williams Bay PD
- Chief Robert Pruessing
  250 Williams St.
  Williams Bay, WI 53191
  (262) 245-2710
  wbpd@williamsbaypolice.us

Washburn County

- Washburn County SO
- Sheriff Terry Dryden
  421 Hwy 63 PO Box 429
  Shell Lake, WI 54871
  (715) 468-4700
  lawenfor@co.washburn.wi.us
- Shell Lake PD
- Chief David Wilson
  501 1st
  Shell Lake, WI 54871
  (715) 468-7679
  slpdchief@shelllake.org
- Spooner PD
- Chief Robert Andrea
  305 Elm St.
  Spooner, WI 54801
  (715) 635-3527
  spoonerpd@centurytel.net

Washington County

- Washington County SO
- Sheriff Dale K. Schmidt
  500 No. Schmidt Rd.
  West Bend, WI 53095
  (262) 335-4378
  inquiry@washingtoncountysheriffwi.org
- Germantown PD
- Chief Peter G. Hoell
  N112W16877 Mequon Rd.
  Germantown, WI 53022
  (262) 253-7780
  gtpd@germantownpolice.org
- Hartford PD
- Chief David A Groves
  110 No. Johnson St.
  Hartford, WI 53027
  (262) 673-8273
  mbenton@ci.hartford.wi.us
- Jackson PD
- Chief Jed M. Dolnick
  N168W20733 Main St.
  Jackson, WI 53037
  (262) 677-4949
  chiefdolnick@jacksonwipd.com
- Kewaskum PD
- Chief Thomas F. Bishop
  204 1st St. Box 38
  Kewaskum, WI 53040
  (262) 626-2323
  policeinfo@village.kewaskum.wi.us
- Trenton PD
- Chief Joseph Gabrish
  1071 Hwy 33E
  Trenton, WI 53095
  (262) 689-0661
  trentonpolice@charterinternet.com
- West Bend PD
- Chief Kenneth Meuler
  1115 So. Main St.
  West Bend, WI 53095
  (262) 335-5000
  dispatch@ci.west-bend.wi.us

Waukesha County

- Waukesha County SO
- Sheriff Daniel J. Trawicki
  515 W. Moreland Blvd
  Waukesha, WI 53188
  (262) 548-7117
  sheriff@waukeshacounty.gov
- Delafield PD
- Chief Scott Taubel
  500 No. Genesee St.
  Delafield, WI 53018
  (262) 646-6240
  staubel@ci.delafield.wi.us
- Hartland PD
- Chief Robert J. Rosch
  210 Cottonwood Ave.
  Hartland, WI 53029
  (262) 367-2323
  police@villageofhartland.com
- Lannon PD
- Chief Mark A. Flessert
  20399 W. Main St.
  Lannon, WI 53046
  (262) 251-4930
  police@villageoflannon.com
- Menomonee Falls PD
- Chief Anna Ruzinski
  W156 N8480 Pilgrim Rd.
  Menomonee Falls, WI 53051
  (262) 532-8700
  aruzinski@menomonee-falls.org

- Mukwonago PD
- Chief Kevin B. Schmidt
  627 So. Rochester St.
  Mukwonago, WI 53149
  (262) 363-6434
  kschmidt@mkpd.org
- Muskego PD
- Chief Craig A. Moser
  S76 W17858 Janesville Rd.
  Muskego, WI 53150
  (262) 679-4130
  cmoser@cityofmuskego.org
- Nashotah PD
- Chief Ken Donovan
  N44 W32950 Watertown Plank Rd.
  Nashotah, WI 53058
  (262) 367-8440
  nashotahclerk@sbcglobal.net
- New Berlin PD
- Chief Joseph Rieder
  16300 W. National Ave.
  New Berlin, WI 53151
  (262) 782-6640
  godec@nbpolice.org
- North Prairie PD
- Chief Sal Tamez
  130 No. Harrison St.
  North Prairie, WI 53153
  (262) 392-2229
  police@northprairie.net
- Oconomowoc PD
- Chief David Beguhn
  174 E. Wisconsin Ave.
  Oconomowoc, WI 53066
  (262) 567-4401
  monstad@oconomowoc-wi.gov
- Pewaukee PD
- Chief Timothy J. Otto
  W240 N3065 Pewaukee Rd.
  Pewaukee, WI 53072
  (262) 691-0921
  totto@villageofpewaukee.com
- Waukesha PD
- Chief Russell Jack
  1901 Delafield St.
  Waukesha, WI 53188
  (262) 524-3820
  rjack@ci.waukesha.wi.us

Waupaca County

- Waupaca County SO
- Sheriff Brad Hardel
  1402 E. Royalton St.
  Waupaca, WI 54981
  (715) 258-4466
  waupaca.sheriff@co.waupaca.wi.us
- Clintonville PD
- Chief Terry Lorge
  50 A 10th St.
  Clintonville, WI 54929
  (715) 823-3117
  clintonvillepd@frontiernet.net
- Fremont PD
- Int. Chief Richard Lucero
  317 Wolf River Dr.
  Fremont, WI 54940
  (920) 446-2299
  fremontpolice167@centurytel.net
- Manawa PD
- Chief David Walker
  500 So. Bridge St. PO Box 248
  Manawa, WI 54949
  (920) 596-3390
  manawapd@wolfnet.net
- New London PD
- Chief Jeffery Schlueter
  700 Shiocton St.
  New London, WI 54961
  (920) 982-8505
  nl19tla@newlondonwi.org
- Ogdensburg PD
- Chief Robert Karsk
  540 Main St. PO Box 80
  Ogdensburg, WI 54962
  (920) 244-7000
  ogpd@wolfnet.net
- Waupaca PD
- Chief Timothy Goke
  124 So. Washington St.
  Waupaca, WI 54981
  (715) 258-4400
  tgoke@cityofwaupaca.org
- Weyauwega PD
- Chief Jerry Poltrock
  109 E. Main St.
  Weyauwega, WI 54983
  (920) 867-4141
  gpoltrock@cityofweyauwega-wi.gov

Waushara County

- Waushara County SD
- Sheriff Dave Peterson
  430 E. Division St.
  Wautoma, WI 54982
  (920) 787-3321
  sheriffweb.sheriff@co.waushara.wi.us
- Wild Rose PD
- Chief Russell Saunder
  500 Main St.
  Wild Rose, WI 54984
  (920) 622-4148
  villageofwildrose@centurytel.net

Winnebago County

- Winnebago County SO
- Sheriff John F. Matz
  4311 Jackson St.
  Oshkosh, WI 54901
  (920) 236-7300
  jmatz@co.winnebago.wi.us
- Neenah PD
- Chief Kevin E. Wilkinson
  2111 Marathon Ave.
  Neenah, WI 54956
  (920) 751-4677
  police@ci.neenah.wi.us
- Omro PD
- Chief James Reed
  205 So. Webster Ave.
  Omro, WI 54963
  (920) 685-7007
  jreed@omro-wi.com
- Oshkosh PD
- Chief Scott Greuel
  420 Jackson St.
  Oshkosh, WI 54901
  (920) 236-5700
  sgreuel@ci.oshkosh.wi.us
- Winneconne PD
- Chief Harold Minch
  30 So. 1st St. PO Box 650
  Winneconne, WI 54986
  (920) 582-9944
  prunning@winneconnewi.gov

Wood County

- Wood County SO
- Sheriff Thomas Reichert
  400 Market St.
  Wisconsin Rapids, WI 54495
  (715) 421-8715
  treichert@co.wood.wi.us
- Marshfield PD
- Chief Gary Jepsen
  110 W. 1st St.
  Marshfield, WI 54449
  (715) 384-3113
  Gary.Jepsen@ci.marshfield.wi.us
- Nekoosa PD
- Chief Shawn Woods
  951 Market St.
  Nekoosa, WI 54457
  (715) 886-7890
  policechief@nekoosawi.com
- Port Edwards PD
- Chief Joe Zurfluh
  201 Market Ave.
  Port Edwards, WI 54469
  (715) 887-3030
  chief.zurfluh@port-edwards.org

State Agencies

- WI State Patrol-HQ
- Supt. Stephen Fitzgerald
  4802 Sheboygan Ave., Rm. 551
  Madison, WI 53707-7912
  (608) 266-3212
  opa.exec@dot.wi.gov
- U. of WI-Milwaukee PD
- Chief Scott Rohde
  3410 No. Maryland Ave.
  Milwaukee, WI 53211
  (414) 229-4627
  Fax: (414) 229-4918
  srohde@uwlax.edu

MEET THE AUTHORS

Mary Gonzales Brhel is a longtime, former educator, who served many years as Field Representative for the California State Assembly. Her legislative forte, among other topics, includes conducting identity theft seminars for constituents. Her co-author enjoyed watching her utilize the expertise of some of the same cops he relied on, in court, in order to educate and protect her community.

Mary is also an inventor, i.e., a new product designer, and has amazing culinary skills. She's also a skilled photographer, posting many of her pictures at www.fineartamerica.com. And, her arts and crafts knack is second to none. Some folks are talented. Few are so multi-talented.

Marty is a retired prosecutor who was also a criminal defense attorney, and a Staff Counsel, in charge of the DMV Los Angeles legal office. His post-DA-retirement civil rights practice, kept him busy in both state and federal courts. Also a Judge Pro Tem in two contiguous counties, beginning several decades ago, he commenced a two-year term in January 2015, on the City of Laguna Niguel's Traffic & Transportation Commission.

He started writing books in the 1980's, creating his own **Copper Bible Book Company** to publish his Courtroom Survival books, primarily for police officers. His first three books, written during 1988-90, are *Catch 55: Courtroom Survival for Traffic Officers*, *Catch 56: Courtroom Survival for DUI Cops*, and *Courtroom Survival for Small Claims Court Litigants*.

Brhel also created *Hey Doc Copper!*, a monthly practical advice column for cops, formerly available by subscription, as a regular feature in several national law enforcement publications, and as a free public service to the cops in his own county, where he served as a DA, until retirement. His prosecutorial duties, standing alone, were more than enough to get in the way of his writing.

His creation of a pair of non-profits, **Crime Control Education Foundation**, a tax exempt think tank, and politically active **Crime Control Foundation of America,** consumed every free second he formerly had available, relegating his writing to stand-by status, until his so-called retirement commenced. So-called, because Mary insists Marty *keeps failing retirement*.

HDC! is available again, but exclusively at www.CourtroomSurvival.com, his own website, as is his conservative political commentary, *Taking the First*, which focuses mostly on public safety issues. At present, his books, available in both print and Kindle, are in several genres.

They include: *Deadly Duty*, first novel in his *Joshua Travers, DA Adventure Series*, biography/expose *America's Two Toughest Sheriffs* (subtitle: *President #44 On the Run?*), and *Courtroom Survival for Traffic Officers*. Many more are planned.

Readers can easily locate any of Marty's books. Just type **Martin Brhel** into the search bar at Amazon.com. Click on any cover? Thanks to Amazon, you can read a free excerpt. And, the author encourages anyone who does this to please take the time to write a review.

Brhel remains licensed to practice law up to, and including, the U.S. Supreme Court. He and Mary met more than twenty years ago, fell in love, and got married at the Palm Springs Botanical Gardens.

ELUCIDATIONS

As you peruse *NLED*, you will find many words in *italics*. Many are either nicknames of formal first names, or initials listed by Chiefs and Sheriffs. Others signify departmental rank. For example, let's say you find a listed rank, other than Chief, in parentheses; to its left, you find the designation: *Act. Chief.* That is short for *Acting Chief.*

We did this to identify such individuals as their agency's top cop. They handle the same basic duties they would handle, if they actually held the rank, *Chief of Police*. Others may be listed as Int. (*Interim*) Chief by their own department. Interim and acting are the equivalent of saying *six*, verses *half a dozen*. Same basic duties. Same responsibilities.

Let's talk about monikers for a moment. Many Sheriffs and Chiefs herein have nicknames. We won't list them all on this page. But, you will discover them yourself, as you turn *NLED's* many pages. Like us, we suspect each one is accompanied by an interesting tale concerning its origin. If you're in law enforcement, you know the many ways cop nicknames occur.

Twp is the abbreviation for township. Please see Luke Henry's provided link for additional details. Or, simply go online for added help. What else? *No*? Short for north. *So* is south. *PO* is Post Office. *PMB* is private mail box.

You will find many Chiefs and at least one Sheriff, also described as *Colonels*. That requires further explanation. Some ranking officers earn that title at their respective departments. For others, it is bestowed by elected government officials, such as their own state's Governor or Secretary of State.

According to Wikipedia, verbatim: "Kentucky colonel is the highest title of honor bestowed by the Commonwealth of Kentucky. Commissions for Kentucky colonels are given by the Governor and the Secretary of State to individuals in recognition of noteworthy accomplishments and outstanding service to a community, state or the nation. The sitting governor of the Commonwealth of Kentucky bestows the honor of a colonel's Commission, by issuance of letters patent."

Copious attention to detail goes into any book that totals this many pages. You may also call this the expenditure of blood, sweat and tears. I do. That is especially so, for this one. In short, our exhaustive research has found no contemporary competitor. It appears no one else has taken the time to provide thousands upon thousands of E-mail addresses, accompanied by the names of agencies, and their heads. Obtaining such information requires many hours, entailing numerous phone calls, seemingly endless visits to an ongoing shopping list of websites, as well as even more time online, just digging for facts and figures.

We intend every detail herein be 100% accurate. But, things happen that prevent the planned completion of law enforcement careers. Peace officers resign. They retire. Some are terminated. New folks join the team. Others are no longer employed as sworn personnel, due to work-related injuries and deaths; sad events we had to deal with, even as we assembled *NLED*.

Additionally, a number of agencies simply do not exist anymore. The common story Mary got, during her many phone calls, was the lack of needed public monies, resulting in agency disbandment, being melded into other municipal agencies, or being taken over by their own county's Sheriff.

Just because something was a fact when *NLED* went to press doesn't mean the status quo will be maintained, by the time you read this, including any E-mail addresses we so meticulously compiled. We encourage every law enforcement agency to have your own E-mail address, even if it's just a general one for your entire department. The community you protect and serve deserves being able to reach you, for non-emergency reasons, any time of the day or night. E-mail is consummately convenient. And, your community appreciates such attention to detail.

Final aside, due to this book's original length, it was necessary to break the information down into two books, this one and its brethren, *National Law Enforcement Directory, Western USA*. Now, having said all this, please enjoy the exclusive contents of *NLED, Eastern USA*.

Printed in Dunstable, United Kingdom

91223529R00275